VOLUME XV

The Works
of John Dryden

Plays

ALBION AND ALBANIUS
DON SEBASTIAN
AMPHITRYON

D1541009

University of California Press
Berkeley   Los Angeles   London
1976

UNIVERSITY OF CALIFORNIA PRESS
Berkeley and Los Angeles, California

UNIVERSITY OF CALIFORNIA PRESS, LTD.
London, England

The copy texts of this edition have been drawn in the
main from the Dryden Collection of the
William Andrews Clark Memorial Library

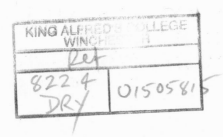

The Works of John Dryden

General Editor

H. T. SWEDENBERG, JR.

Associate General Editors

GEORGE R. GUFFEY

ALAN ROPER

Textual Editor

VINTON A. DEARING

VOLUME FIFTEEN

EDITOR

Earl Miner

TEXTUAL EDITOR

George R. Guffey

ASSOCIATE EDITOR

Franklin B. Zimmerman

Dom Sebastião, King of Portugal
By Cristóvão De Morais
Courtesy of the Museu Nacional de Arte Antiga, Lisbon

In Gratitude for Their Support
of the California Edition of Dryden
the Editors Dedicate This Volume to
David S. Saxon, President,
University of California,
and to
Charles E. Young, Chancellor,
Franklin P. Rolfe, Dean Emeritus of Letters and Science,
Philip Levine, Dean of Humanities,
U C L A

Preface

After the performance of The Duke of Guise *late in 1682, Dryden seems to have intended to retire from playwriting. He was
brought back to the theater almost unawares, first to do an
operatic prologue for a play not his own, a new venture that
must have aroused his curiosity. Event followed event, however,
and before he was through Dryden had written the libretto for
one of the earliest English operas,* Albion and Albanius, *composed by the French musician, Louis Grabu. It was performed
in June 1685. In many matters extrinsic to poetry, the opera
possesses great interest; its perhaps uniquely full stage directions, for example, are a treasure-house of information for the
historian of the theater. But Dryden worked in subordination to
the composer, and his poetry shows it. In his preface to the
opera, Dryden makes clear that he has learned never again to
be subservient to a composer; on reflection he must have been
acutely aware of the poor quality of his verse, which is altogether lacking in that intellectual force and harmonious language that characteristically mark his style. But Dryden apparently learned other lessons as well from working with the
composer, for his later composition for music includes some of
his most seasoned writing:* A Song for St. Cecilia's Day, *set by*
Giovanni Baptista Draghi; *the* Ode, on the Death of Mr. Henry
Purcell, *set by* John Blow; *and* Alexander's Feast, *set by Jeremiah Clarke. Dryden also made amends for the deficiencies of*
Albion and Albanius *in his other opera,* King Arthur, *set by*
Henry Purcell, *and in* The Secular Masque, *set by Daniel Purcell and performed with* The Pilgrim. Albion and Albanius,
*then, was an experiment whose benefits were great but de-
layed.*

*Dryden did not return to writing plays until after the Revolu-
tion of 1688, when his dismissal from public posts required that
he do so to eke out a living. The immediate results of his return to the theater were two of his greatest plays,* Don Sebastian *(late in 1689), and* Amphitryon *(1690), the chief works in
this volume. In addition to the opera and the masque which he
wrote in the last decade of his life, he was to write only two*

more plays, the tragedy, Cleomenes, *and the tragicomedy,* Love
Triumphant. *It has been the verdict of many that* Don Sebastian *is Dryden's greatest tragedy, although some prefer* All for
Love. Amphitryon *is one of the most effective of Dryden's
comedies. Both* Don Sebastian *and* Amphitryon *might well be
classified as tragicomedies, given the prominence of the comic
subplot in the former and the seeming danger and very serious
questions raised in the latter. In any event, given the probing
and harsher style of* Don Sebastian, *and the very bleak ending
of* Amphitryon, *it is clear that during the early years of the reign
of William and Mary, Dryden's thoughts about the nature of
man and his world turned darker than they had ever been.*

*The textual approach to this volume follows with few excep-
tions that of previously published volumes. Vinton A. Dearing,
Textual Editor of the edition, has written a computer program,
however, which now makes possible the comparison of prose
texts as well as poetic texts, and the program was put into operation for the first time in this volume. The commentary also
follows a pattern that will be familiar to readers of previous
volumes in this edition. The special nature of* Albion and
Albanius, *however, has led to a greater emphasis upon its
theatrical features—which are indeed its primary interest—
than upon its literary character. The stage directions of Thomas
Betterton make possible a detailed account of the production,
with its numerous machines from above, behind, and below.
And we owe to Franklin B. Zimmerman the commentary on the
music of the opera. No literary scholar and but few musicolo-
gists possess his knowledge of the operatic music of England in
the late seventeenth century. Readers who find in the libretto
itself a curious falling-off in Dryden's powers may now discover
some possible explanations in the account of the staging and
music. Because of the extraordinary length of* Don Sebastian
*as well as its extended use of Moorish detail, the commentary
for it is the fullest. But for all three plays in this volume we
have made a particular point of emphasizing Dryden's language. In a letter to his second cousin, Mrs. Elizabeth Stewart,
in November, 1699, Dryden wrote not only of his adhering to*

his Catholic faith but also of his wishing the government to "consider me as a Man, who have done my best to improve the Language, and Especially the Poetry" of the nation. In spite of this fervent testimony to the aims of his life, no adequate study of Dryden's English has yet appeared. The annotations in this volume are no substitute for such an examination. We have, however, glossed words and phrases as extensively as possible, especially with the aid of the Oxford English Dictionary. We believe that these glosses will assist readers to appreciate better the vigor and special character of Dryden's language. Often he is cited as the first or the last user of a word, or as one of the few, or as adapter into a figurative usage. Sometimes indeed the OED furnishes no example at all of his usage. Language and poetry, of course, consist of more than single words, and we have therefore offered some brief characterizations of his prose and verse styles in the two principal works of this volume, along with elucidation of the ideas and values of those plays.

These efforts have been generously assisted by the knowledge and cooperative endeavors of others. C. P. Vernier has contributed greatly, by supplying unpublished material on the prologue to Don Sebastian—some of it having derived from Dr. Williams' Library—as well as by his comments. We express our thanks not only to him, but also to Harold F. Brooks for his further comments, and to the Reverend Kenneth Twinn, Librarian of Dr. Williams' Library, for permission to quote from manuscript material. Very useful help was given us by two UCLA colleagues who died as the commentary was nearing completion: Hugh G. Dick, who once more—as in so many earlier volumes of this edition—assisted us on astrological and scientific details; and Gustav von Grunebaum, whose knowledge of the Near East was of immense help. The Spanish elements in Don Sebastian, the lore about that "hidden king," and the many retellings of his story proved to be an enormously complex subject, and we are grateful to Hispanists for assistance: in particular, to A. A. Parker, Mary Elizabeth Brooks, and Enrique Cortes. To these we must add John Loftis, whose qualifications in matters relating Restoration drama to Spain require *no elaboration in this edition. In classical matters and details of translation, we have enjoyed the assistance of Philip Levine and Norman Austin once again, and also of Michael J. B. Allen and Patrick McCloskey. We are also thankful for assistance on particular points to Charles E. Ward, Louis A. Landa, Alan Roper, Maximillian E. Novak, and R. W. Dent.*

The first work on the commentary was done in the Bodleian Library in the spring and summer of 1967, and was continued thereafter in the William Andrews Clark Memorial Library, UCLA. The Editor is grateful to the staff of both of these libraries for their kind assistance, and to the Oriental Institute at Oxford and to St. Antony's College as well, for their helpfulness. The Editor also acknowledges the assistance in 1966–1967 of a Fulbright Lectureship to Oxford, and of the generous support of the Committee on Research at UCLA, both then and through 1972. It is a great honor to be able to acknowledge another debt to UCLA, the Clark Library Committee's appointment of the Editor as the third Clark Library Professor, in 1971–1972. The appointment made possible completion of the commentary for this volume. The Rare Books Department of the Firestone Library at Princeton has greatly assisted in obtaining photographs and in setting other last details for the volume. We wish to thank the Ministério da Educação e Cultura for permission to reproduce the portrait of Don Sebastian which is in the collection of the Museu Nacional de Arte Antiga in Lisbon.

The persons thanked belong to many universities, but it will be clear that our central obligation is to the people and institutions at UCLA, where the Editor spent seventeen very happy years. The dedication of this volume is to four colleagues who have effectively supported the California Dryden. They will appreciate that the dedication is intended as a representative thanks to UCLA itself, to the people, the place, and the culture.

It gives particular pleasure to thank the editorial staff concerned with this volume of the edition. The Textual Editor of this volume, George R. Guffey, has raised numerous helpful questions and suggestions about the commentary, and should be thought of as participating in it. H. T. Swedenberg, General Editor of the edition, should be included as primus inter pares *in both the previous paragraph and here. It would be impossible to imagine a more harmonious working relationship than that which we have enjoyed with him. And once again it is a pleasure to acknowledge the encouragement, the perspicacity, and the devotion of the Editorial Assistant of the edition, Mrs. Geneva Phillips. She and we have enjoyed the help of the following people during their careers as graduate students at UCLA: Jane Abelson, Laurence Behrens, Patricia Brereton, Linda Boose, Ted Diaconoff, Diane Eliel, Cyndia Goodman, Sherron Knopp, Janette Lewis, Sharon McMurray, Sidney Orr, Melanie Richter-Bernburg, and especially Sandra Fischer.*

E. M.

Contents

Illustrations

ALBION AND ALBANIUS

ALBION

AND

ALBANIUS:

AN

OPERA.

Perform'd at the QUEENS Theatre,
in *Dorfet* Garden.

Written by *Mr.* Dryden.

Difcite juftitiam, moniti & non temnere Divos. Virg.

LONDON,

Printed for *Jacob Tonfon*, at the *Judge's Head* in
Chancery-lane, near *Fleet-ftreet.* 1685.

THE PREFACE.

IF Wit has truly been defin'd a propriety of Thoughts and Words, then that Definition will extend to all sorts of Poetry; and amongst the rest, to this present entertainment of an *Opera*. Propriety of thought is that Fancy which arises naturally from the Subject, or which the Poet adapts to it. Propriety of Words, is the cloathing of those thoughts with such Expressions, as are naturally proper to them: and from both these, if they are judiciously perform'd, the delight of Poetry results. An *Opera* is a poetical Tale or Fiction, repre-
10 sented by Vocal and Instrumental Musick, adorn'd with Scenes, Machines and Dancing. The suppos'd Persons of this musical Drama, are generally supernatural, as Gods and Goddesses, and *Heroes,* which at least are descended from them, and are in due time, to be adopted into their Number. The Subject therefore being extended beyond the Limits of Humane Nature, admits of that sort of marvellous and surprizing conduct, which is rejected in other Plays. Humane Impossibilities, are to be receiv'd, as they are in Faith; because where Gods are introduc'd, a Supreme Power is to be understood; and second Causes
20 are out of doors. Yet propriety is to be observ'd even here. The Gods are all to manage their peculiar Provinces: and what was attributed by the Heathens to one Power, ought not to be perform'd by any other. *Phœbus* must foretel, *Mercury* must charm with his *Caduceus,* and *Juno* must reconcile the Quarrels of the Marriage-bed. To conclude, they must all act according to their distinct and peculiar Characters. If the Persons represented were to speak upon the Stage, it wou'd follow of necessity, That the Expressions should be lofty, figurative and majestical: but the nature of an *Opera* denies the frequent use
30 of those poetical Ornaments: for Vocal Musick, though it often

13 *Heroes*] Heroes F1, Q, F3, D; *omitted from F2 (Grabu's dedication replaced Dryden's preface).* [These sigla are identified in the Textual Notes, where also fluctuations in the texts cited are explained.]
26 Characters.] Q, F3, D; ~∧ F1; *omitted from F2.*

admits a loftiness of sound: yet always exacts an harmonious
sweetness; or to distinguish yet more justly, The recitative part
of the *Opera* requires a more masculine Beauty of expression
and sound: the other, which (for want of a proper *English*
Word) I must call *The Songish Part,* must abound in the softness and variety of Numbers: its principal Intention, being to
please the Hearing, rather than to gratify the understanding.
It appears indeed Preposterous at first sight, That Rhyme, on
any consideration, shou'd take place of Reason. But in order to
10 resolve the Probleme, this fundamental proposition must be
settled, That the first Inventors of any Art or Science, provided
they have brought it to perfection, are, in reason, to give Laws
to it; and according to their Model all after Undertakers are to
build. Thus in Epique Poetry, no Man ought to dispute the
Authority of *Homer,* who gave the first being to that Master-
piece of Art, and endued it with that form of Perfection in all
its Parts, that nothing was wanting to its excellency. *Virgil*
therefore, and those very few who have succeeded him, endeavour'd not to introduce or innovate any thing in a Design
20 already perfected, but imitated the plan of the Inventor: and
are only so far true Heroique Poets, as they have built on the
Foundations of *Homer.* Thus *Pindar,* the Author of those Odes,
(which are so admirably restor'd by Mr. *Cowley* in our Language,) ought for ever to be the Standard of them; and we are
bound according to the practice of *Horace* and Mr. *Cowley,* to
Copy him. Now, to apply this Axiom, to our present purpose,
whosoever undertakes the writing of an *Opera,* (which is a
modern Invention, though built indeed, on the foundations of
Ethnique Worship,) is oblig'd to imitate the Design of the

---

4   other,] Q, F3, D; ~∧ F1; *omitted from F2.*
4   *English*] English F1, Q, F3, D; *omitted from F2.*
5   call] Q, F3, D; ~ , F1; *omitted from F2.*
6   Numbers] F1 *(some copies),* Q, F3, D; Numb rs F1 *(some copies); omitted
from F2.*
8   indeed] Q, F3, D; ~ , F1; *omitted from F2.*
9   consideration,] D; ~∧ F1, Q, F3; *omitted from F2.*
22 Author] F1 *(some copies),* Q, F3, D; Au hor F1 *(some copies); omitted
from F2.*
29 Worship] Q, F3, D; Worsh p F1; *omitted from F2.*

Italians, who have not only invented, but brought to perfection, this sort of Dramatique Musical Entertainment. I have not been able by any search, to get any light either of the time, when it began, or of the first Author. But I have probable Reasons, which induce me to believe, that some *Italians* having curiously observ'd the gallantries of the *Spanish Moores* at their *Zambra's,* or Royal Feasts, where Musick, Songs and Dancing were in perfection; together with their Machines, which are usual at their *Sortiia's,* or running at the Ring, and other Solemnities,
10 may possibly have refin'd upon those *Moresque* Divertisements, and produc'd this delightful Entertainment, by leaving out the warlike Part of the Carousels, and forming a poetical Design for the use of the Machines, the Songs and Dances. But however it began, (for this is only conjectural,) we know that for some Centuries, the knowledge of Musick has flourish'd principally in *Italy,* the Mother of Learning and of Arts; that Poetry and Painting have been there restor'd, and so cultivated by *Italian* Masters, That all *Europe* has been enrich'd out of their Treasury: and the other Parts of it in relation to those delightful
20 Arts, are still as much provincial to *Italy,* as they were in the time of the *Roman* Empire. Their first *Opera's* seem to have been intended for the Celebration of the Marriages of their Princes, or for the magnificence of some general time of Joy. Accordingly the Expences of them were from the Purse of the Soveraign, or of the Republick, as they are still practis'd at *Venice, Rome,* and other Places at their Carnivals. *Savoy* and *Florence* have often us'd them in their Courts, at the Weddings of their Dukes: And at *Turin* particularly, was perform'd the *Pastor Fido,* written by the famous *Guarini,* which is a Pastoral
30 *Opera* made to solemnize the Marriage of a Duke of *Savoy.* The Prologue of it, has given the Design to all the *French,* which is a Complement to the Soveraign Power by some God or Goddess: so that it looks no less than a kind of Embassy from Heaven to Earth. I said, in the beginning of this Preface, that the

6 *Moores*] Q, F3, D; Moores F1; *omitted from F2.*
6–7 *Zambra's*] Q, F3, D; Zambra's F1; *omitted from F2.*
10 *Moresque*] Moresque F1, Q, F3, D; *omitted from F2.*
32 Goddess] F3; Goddesses F1, Q, D; *omitted from F2.*

Persons represented in *Opera's,* are generally Gods, Goddesses
and *Heroes* descended from them, who are suppos'd to be their
peculiar care: which hinders not, but that meaner Persons, may
sometimes gracefully be introduc'd, especially if they have relation to those first times, which Poets call the *Golden Age:*
wherein by reason of their Innocence, those happy Mortals, were
suppos'd to have had a more familiar intercourse with Superiour
Beings: and therefore Shepherds might reasonably be admitted,
as of all Callings, the most innocent, the most happy, and who
10 by reason of the spare time they had, in their almost idle Employment, had most leisure to make Verses, and to be in Love;
without somewhat of which Passion, no *Opera* can possibly
subsist.

'Tis almost needless to speak any thing of that noble Language, in which this Musical *Drama,* was first invented and perform'd. All, who are conversant in the *Italian,* cannot but observe, that it is the softest, the sweetest, the most harmonious,
not only of any modern Tongue, but even beyond any of the
Learned. It seems indeed to have been invented for the sake of
20 Poetry and Musick: the Vowels are so abounding in all Words,
especially in the Terminations of them, that excepting some
few Monosyllables, the whole Language ends in them. Then
the Pronunciation is so manly and so sonorous, that their very
speaking has more of Musick in it, than *Dutch* Poetry and Song.
It has withal deriv'd so much Copiousness and Eloquence from
the *Greek* and *Latin* in the composition of Words, and the
formation of them, that (if after all, we must call it barbarous)
'tis the most beautiful and most learned of any Barbarism in
Modern Tongues. And we may, at least, as justly praise it, as
30 *Pyrrhus* did the *Roman* Discipline, and Martial Order, that it
was of *Barbarians,* (for so the *Greeks* call'd all other Nations)
but had nothing in it of barbarity. This Language has in a
manner been refin'd and purified from the *Gothick,* ever since
the time of *Dantè,* which is above four hundred Years ago; and

1   generally] Q, F3, D; ~ , F1; *omitted from F2.*
2   *Heroes*] Heroes F1, Q, F3, D; *omitted from F2.*
24   *Dutch*] Q, F3, D; ~ , F1; *omitted from F2.*
26   *Greek . . . Latin*] Q, F3, D; Greek . . . Latin F1; *omitted from F2.*

the *French,* who now cast a longing Eye to their Country, are
not less ambitious to possess their Elegance in Poetry and Musick: in both which they labour at Impossibilities. 'Tis true indeed, they have reform'd their Tongue, and brought both their
Prose and Poetry to a Standard: the Sweetness as well as the
Purity is much improv'd, by throwing off the unnecessary Consonants, which made their Spelling tedious, and their pronunciation harsh: But after all, as nothing can be improv'd beyond
its own Species, or farther than its original Nature will allow
10 (as an ill Voice, though never so thoroughly instructed in the
Rules of Musick, can never be brought to sing harmoniously,
nor many an honest Critick, ever arrive to be a good Poet), so
neither can the natural harshness of the *French,* or their perpetual ill Accent, be ever refin'd into perfect Harmony like the
Italian. The *English* has yet more natural disadvantages than
the *French;* our original *Teutonique* consisting most in Monosyllables, and those incumber'd with Consonants, cannot possibly
be freed from those Inconveniences. The rest of our Words,
which are deriv'd from the *Latin* chiefly, and the *French,* with
20 some small sprinklings of *Greek, Italian* and *Spanish,* are some
relief in Poetry; and help us to soften our uncouth Numbers,
which together with our *English* Genius, incomparably beyond
the triffling of the *French,* in all the nobler Parts of Verse, will
justly give us the Preheminence. But, on the other hand, the
Effeminacy of our pronunciation, (a defect common to us, and
to the *Danes*) and our scarcity of female Rhymes, have left the
advantage of musical composition for Songs, though not for
recitative, to our neighbors.

Through these Difficulties, I have made a shift to struggle, in
30 my part of the performance of this *Opera;* which, as mean as it
is, deserves at least a Pardon, because it has attempted a discovery beyond any former Undertaker of our Nation: only re-

---

9–12 allow (as . . . Poet),] ~ : ~ . . . ~ , F1; ~ ; ~ . . . ~ ; Q, F3, D;
omitted from F2.
15 *English*] Q, F3, D; English F1; *omitted from F2.*
15 disadvantages] Q, F3, D; disadvantage F1; *omitted from F2.*
16 *Teutonique*] Q, F3, D; Teutonique F1; *omitted from F2.*
17 Consonants,] Q, F3, D; ~∧ F1; *omitted from F2.*

member, that if there be no North-East Passage to be found, the fault is in Nature, and not in me. Or as *Ben. Johnson* tells us in the *Alchymist*, when Projection had fail'd, and the Glasses were all broken, there was enough however in the Bottoms of them to cure the Itch; so I may thus far be positive, That if I have not succeeded, as I desire, yet there is somewhat still remaining, to satisfy the Curiosity or Itch of Sight and Hearing. Yet I have no great reason to despair; for I may without vanity, own some Advantages, which are not common to every Writer; 10 such as are the knowledge of the *Italian* and *French* Language, and the being conversant with some of their best Performances in this kind; which have furnish'd me with such variety of measures, as have given the composer Monsieur *Grabu* what occasions he cou'd wish, to show his extraordinary Tallent, in diversifying the Recitative, the Lyrical part, and the Chorus: In all which, (not to attribute any thing to my own Opinion) the best Judges, and those too of the best Quality, who have honor'd his Rehersals with their Presence, have no less commended the happiness of his Genius than his Skill. And let me 20 have the liberty to add one thing; that he has so exactly express'd my Sence, in all places, where I intended to move the Passions, that he seems to have enter'd into my thoughts, and to have been the Poet as well as the Composer. This I say, not to flatter him, but to do him right; because amongst some *English* Musicians, and their Scholars, (who are sure to judge after them,) the imputation of being a *French-man,* is enough to make a Party, who maliciously endeavour to decry him. But the knowledge of *Latin* and *Italian* Poets, both which he possesses, besides his skill in Musick, and his being acquainted 30 with all the performances of the *French Opera's,* adding to these the good Sence to which he is Born, have rais'd him to a degree above any Man, who shall pretend to be his Rival on our Stage. When any of our Country-men excel him, I shall be glad, for the sake of old *England,* to be shown my error: in the

---

3   *Alchymist*] Q, F3, D; Alchymist F1; *omitted from F2.*
13   *Grabu*] Grabut F1, Q, F3, D; *omitted from F2.*
34   glad,] Q, F3, D; ~∧ F1; *omitted from F2.*

mean time, let Vertue be commended, though in the Person of
a Stranger.

If I thought it convenient, I cou'd here discover some Rules
which I have given to my self in the Writing of an *Opera* in
general; and of this *Opera* in Particular: But I consider, that the
effect would only be, to have my own performance measur'd
by the Laws I gave; and consequently to set up some little
Judges, who not understanding throughly, wou'd be sure to fall
upon the faults, and not to acknowledge any of the Beauties:
10 (an hard measure which I have often found from false Cri-
tiques.) Here therefore, if they will Criticise, they shall do it out
of their own *Fond;* But let them be first assur'd, that their eares
are nice; for there is neither writing nor judging on this Subject, without that good quality. 'Tis no easy matter in our Language to make words so smooth, and numbers so harmonious,
that they shall almost set themselves, and yet there are rules for
this in nature: and as great a certainty of quantity in our Syllables, as either in the *Greek* or *Latin:* But let Poets and Judges
understand those first, and then let them begin to study *English.*
20 When they have chaw'd awhile upon these preliminaries, it
may be they will scarce adventure to tax me with want of
Thought, and elevation of Fancy in this Work; for they will
soon be satisfy'd, That those are not of the nature of this sort of
Writing: The necessity of double Rhymes, and ordering of the
Words and Numbers for the sweetness of the Voice, are the
main hinges, on which an *Opera* must move; and both of these
are without the compass of any Art to teach another to perform;
unless Nature in the first place has done her part, by enduing
the Poet with that nicety of hearing, that the discord of sounds
30 in Words shall as much offend him, as a Seventh in Musick
wou'd a good Composer. I have therefore no need to make excuses for meanness of thought in many places: The *Italians,*
with all the advantages of their Language, are continually
forc'd upon it; or rather they affect it. The chief secret is in the
choice of Words; and by this choice I do not here mean Elegancy
of expression, but propriety of sound to be varyed according to
the Nature of the Subject. Perhaps a time may come, when I

may treat of this more largely, out of some Observations which
I have made from *Homer* and *Virgil,* who amongst all the Poets,
only understood the Art of Numbers, and of that which was
properly call'd *Rhythmus* by the Ancients.

   The same reasons which depress thought in an *Opera,* have
a Stronger effect upon the Words; especially in our Language:
for there is no maintaining the Purity of *English* in short measures, where the Rhyme returns so quick, and is so often Female, or double Rhyme, which is not natural to our Tongue,
10 because it consists too much of Monosyllables, and those too,
most commonly clogg'd with Consonants: for which reason I
am often forc'd to Coyn new Words, revive some that are Antiquated, and botch others: as if I had not serv'd out my time
in Poetry, but was bound 'Prentice to some doggrel Rhymer,
who makes Songs to Tunes, and sings them for a lively-hood.
'Tis true, I have not been often put to this drudgery; but where
I have, the Words will sufficiently show, that I was then a Slave
to the composition, which I will never be again: 'Tis my part to
Invent, and the Musicians to Humour that Invention. I may be
20 counsell'd, and will always follow my Friends advice, where I
find it reasonable; but will never part with the Power of the
Militia.

   I am now to acquaint my Reader with somewhat more particular concerning this *Opera,* after having begg'd his pardon for
so long a Preface to so short a work. It was Originally intended
only for a Prologue to a Play, Of the Nature of the *Tempest;*
which is, a Tragedy mix'd with *Opera;* or a *Drama* Written in
blank Verse, adorn'd with Scenes, Machines, Songs and Dances:
So that the Fable of it is all spoken and acted by the best of the
30 Comedians; the other part of the entertainment to be perform'd
by the same Singers and Dancers who are introduc'd in this
present *Opera.* It cannot properly be call'd a Play, because the
action of it, is suppos'd to be conducted sometimes by supernatural means, or Magick; nor an *Opera* because the Story of
it is not sung. But more of this at its proper time: But some
intervening accidents having hitherto deferr'd the performance

---

26 *Tempest*] Q, F3, D; Tempest F1; *omitted from F2.*

of the main design, I propos'd to the Actors, to turn the intended Prologue into an Entertainment by it self, as you now
see it, by adding two acts more to what I had already Written.
The Subject of it is wholly Allegorical; and the Allegory it self
so very obvious, that it will no sooner be read than understood.
'Tis divided according to the plain and Natural method of
every action, into Three parts. For even *Aristotle* himself is
contented to say simply, That in all actions there is a beginning,
a middle, and an end; after which Model, all the *Spanish* Plays
10 are built.

The descriptions of the Scenes, and other decorations of the
Stage, I had from Mr. *Betterton*, who has spar'd neither for
industry, nor cost, to make this Entertainment perfect, nor for
Invention of the Ornaments to beautify it.

To conclude, tho' the Enemies of the Composer are not few,
and that there is a Party form'd against him, of his own Profes-
sion, I hope, and am perswaded, that this prejudice, will turn
in the end to his advantage. For the greatest part of an Audience is always uninteress'd, though seldom knowing; and if the
20 Musick be well compos'd, and well perform'd, they who find
themselves pleas'd, will be so Wise as not to be impos'd upon,
and fool'd out of their satisfaction. The newness of the undertaking is all the hazard: When *Opera's* were first set up in
France, they were not follow'd over eagerly; but they gain'd
daily upon their Hearers, till they grew to that heigth of Reputation, which they now enjoy. The *English* I confess, are not
altogether so Musical as the *French,* and yet they have been
pleas'd already, with the *Tempest,* and some pieces that follow'd, which were neither much better Written, nor so well
30 Compos'd as this. If it finds encouragement, I dare promise my
self to mend my hand, by making a more pleasing Fable: In the
mean time, every Loyal *English-man,* cannot but be satisfy'd
with the Moral of this, which so plainly represents the double
restoration of his Sacred Majesty.

28 *Tempest*] Q, F3, D; Tempest F1; *omitted from F2.*

POSTSCRIPT.

This Preface being wholly Written before the Death of my late Royal Master, (quem semper acerbum, semper honoratum, sic Dii voluistis, habebo,) *I have now, lately, review'd it, as supposing I shou'd find many notions in it, that wou'd require correction on cooler thoughts. After four Months lying by me, I look'd on it as no longer mine, because I had wholly forgotten it; but, I confess, with some satisfaction, and perhaps a little vanity, that I found my self entertain'd by it; my own Judgment was new to me, and pleas'd me when I look'd on it, as another*
10 *Man's. I see no Opinion that I wou'd retract or alter, unless it be, that possibly the* Italians *went not so far as* Spain, *for the Invention of their* Opera's. *They might have it in their own Country; and that by gathering up the Shipwrecks of the* Athenian *and* Roman *Theaters; which we know were adorn'd with Scenes, Musick, Dances and Machines, especially the* Grecian. *But of this the Learned Monsieur* Vossius, *who has made our Nation his second Country, is the best, and perhaps the only Judge now living: As for the* Opera *it self, it was all compos'd, and was just ready to have been perform'd when he, in Honor*
20 *of whom it was principally made, was taken from us.*

He had been pleas'd twice or thrice to command, that it shou'd be practis'd, before him, especially the first and third Acts of it; and publickly declar'd more than once, That the composition and Chorus's, were more Just, and more Beautiful, than any he had heard in England. *How nice an Ear he had in Musick is sufficiently known; his praise therefore has establish'd the Reputation of it, above censure, and made it in a manner Sacred. 'Tis therefore humbly and Religiously dedicated to his Memory.*
30 *It might reasonably have been expected, that his Death must have chang'd the whole Fabrick of the* Opera; *or at least a great part of it. But the design of it Originally, was so happy, that it needed no alteration, properly so call'd: for the addition of*

twenty or thirty lines, in the Apotheosis of Albion, *has made it entirely of a Piece. This was the only way which cou'd have been invented, to save it from a botch'd ending; and it fell luckily into my imagination. As if there were a kind of fatality, even in the most trivial things concerning the Succession; a change was made, and not for the worse, without the least confusion or disturbance: And those very causes which seem'd to threaten us with troubles, conspir'd to produce our lasting Happiness.*

PROLOGUE
To the OPERA.

Full *twenty years and more, our lab'ring Stage*
Has lost, on this incorrigible age:
Our Poets, the John Ketches *of the Nation,*
Have seem'd to lash yee, ev'n to excoriation:
But still no sign remains; which plainly notes,
You bore like Hero's, *or you brib'd like* Oates.
What can we do, when mimicking a Fop,
Like beating Nut-trees, makes a larger Crop?
Faith, we'll e'en spare our pains: and to content you,
10 *Will fairly leave you what your Maker meant you.*
Satyre was once your Physick, Wit your Food;
One nourisht not, and t' other drew no Blood.
Wee now prescribe, like Doctors in despair,
The Diet your weak appetites can bear.
Since hearty Beef and Mutton will not do,
Here's Julep dance, Ptisan of Song and show:
Give you strong Sense, the Liquor is too heady;
You're come to farce, that's Asses milk, already.
Some hopeful Youths there are, of callow Wit,
20 *Who one Day may be Men, if Heav'n think fit;*
Sound may serve such, ere they to Sense are grown;
Like leading strings, till they can walk alone:
But yet to keep our Friends in count'nance, know,
The Wise Italians *first invented show;*
Thence, into France *the Noble Pageant past;*
'Tis England's *Credit to be cozn'd last.*

OPERA] OPERA. *By Mr.* Dryden F1 (*some copies*), Q, F3; *omitted from some copies of F1 and from all copies of F2, D.*
1–6 *twenty* . . . [*to*] . . . *like*] *italics and romans reversed in F1; omitted from F2 (entire prologue omitted).*
6–26 *or* . . . [*to*] . . . *last*] *italics and romans reversed in F1; omitted from F2.*
9 *Faith,*] ~_∧_ F1, Q, F3, D (Faith F1; *'Faith* D); *omitted from F2.*

Freedom *and* Zeal *have chous'd you o'er and o'er;*
Pray give us leave to bubble you once more;
You never were so cheaply fool'd before.

30 *Wee bring you change, to humour your Disease;*
Change for the worse has ever us'd to please:
Then 'tis the mode of France, *without whose Rules,*
None must presume to set up here for Fools:
In France, *the oldest Man is always young,*
Sees Opera's *daily, learns the Tunes so long,*
Till Foot, Hand, Head, keep time with ev'ry Song.
Each sings his part, echoing from Pit and Box,
With his hoarse Voice, half Harmony, half Pox.
Le plus grand Roy du Monde *is always ringing;*
40 *They show themselves good Subjects by their singing.*
On that condition, set up every Throat;
You Whiggs *may sing, for you have chang'd your Note.*
Cits and Citesses, raise a joyful strain,
'Tis a good Omen to begin a Reign:
Voices may help your Charter to restoring;
And get by singing, what you lost by roaring.

27–42 *and . . . have . . .* [to] *. . . You*] italics and romans reversed in *F1;*
omitted from *F2.*
28 *Pray*] D; *'Pray' F1,* Q ('Pray' F1); *'Pray' F3; omitted from F2.*
39 Monde] ~ , F1, Q, F3, D (*Monde* F1); *omitted from F2.*
42–46 *may . . .* [italics] *. . . roaring*] in romans in *F1; omitted from F2.*

Names of the Persons Represented; in the same Order
as they appear first upon the Stage.

Mercury.

Augusta. London.

Thamesis.

Democracy.

Zelota. Feign'd Zeal.

Archon. The General.

Juno.

Iris.

Albion.

Albanius.

Pluto.

Alecto.

Apollo.

Neptune.

Nereids.

Acacia. Innocence.

Tyranny.

Asebia. Atheism or *Ungodliness.*

Proteus.

Venus.

Fame.

A Chorus of *Cities.*

A Chorus of *Rivers.*

A Chorus of *the People.*

A Chorus of *Furies.*

A Chorus of *Nereids* and *Tritons.*

A Grand Chorus of *Hero's, Loves*
   and *Graces.*

Stage] D; STAGE F1, Q; STAGE F3; *omitted from F2.*
Loves and] *Loves and* F1, Q, F3, D (*Loves,* Q, D); *omitted from F2 (entire list of*
persons omitted).

THE FRONTISPIECE.

THE *Curtain rises, and a new Frontispiece is seen, joyn'd to the great Pylasters, which are on each side of the Stage: On the flat of each Basis is a Shield, adorn'd with Gold: In the middle of the Shield on one side, are two Hearts, a small Scrowl of Gold over 'em, and an Imperial Crown over the Scrowl; on the other, in the Shield are two Quivers full of Arrows Saltyre,* &c. *Upon each Basis stands a Figure bigger than the life; one represents* Peace, *with a Palm in one, and an Olive Branch in the other Hand; t' other* Plenty, *holding a Cornu-*
10 *copia, and resting on a Pillar. Behind these Figures are large Columns of the* Corinthian *Order adorn'd with Fruit and Flowers: over one of the Figures on the Trees is the King's Cypher; over the other the Queens: over the Capitals, on the Cornice sits a Figure on each side; one presents* Poetry *crown'd with Lawrel, holding a Scrowl in one Hand, the other with a Pen in it, and resting on a Book; the other,* Painting, *with a Pallat and Pencils,* &c. *On the sweep of the Arch lies one of the* Muses, *playing on a Base Voyal; another of the* Muses, *on the other side, holding a Trumpet in one Hand, and the other on a*
20 *Harp. Between these Figures, in the middle of the Sweep of the Arch, is a very large Pannel in a frame of Gold; in this Pannel is painted on one side a Woman representing the City of* Lon-*don, leaning her Head on her Hand in a dejected Posture (shewing her Sorrow and Penitence for her Offences;) the other Hand holds the Arms of the City, and a Mace lying under it: on the other side, is a Figure of the* Thames *with his Legs shakl'd, and leaning on an empty Urn: behind these are two*

THE FRONTISPIECE] F3; The FRONTISPIECE F1, Q, D; *omitted from F2.*
8 Peace] D; *Peace* F1, Q, F3; *omitted from F2 (entire description of frontis-piece omitted).*
9 Plenty] D; *Plenty* F1, Q, F3; *omitted from F2.*
14 Poetry] Q, F3, D; *Poetry* F1; *omitted from F2.*
15 *Hand,*] Q, F3, D; ~∧ F1; *omitted from F2.*
16 *other,* Painting,] Q, F3, D; *other painting* F1; *omitted from F2.*
18 Muses . . . Muses] *Muses . . . Muses* F1, Q, F3, D; *omitted from F2.*
27 *shakl'd,*] Q, F3, D; *shakle'd*∧ F1; *omitted from F2.*

*Imperial Figures; one representing his present Majesty; the
other the Queen; by the King stands* Pallas (*or Wisdom, and
Valor,*) *holding a Charter for the City, the King extending his
Hand, as raising her drooping Head, and restoring her to her
ancient Honor and Glory: over the City are the envious de-
vouring* Harpyes *flying from the face of Majesty: by the Queen
stand the three* Graces *holding Garlands of Flowers, and at her
feet* Cupids *bound, with their Bows and Arrows broken, the
Queen pointing with her Scepter to the River, and command-*
10 *ing the* Graces *to take off his Fetters: over the King in a Scrowl,
is this Verse of* Virgil,

Discite justitiam, moniti, & non temnere Divos.

Over the Queen, this of the same Author,

Non ignara mali, miseris succurrere disco.

6 Harpyes] Q, F3, D; *Harpyes* F1; *omitted from F2.*
7, 10 Graces] Q, F3, D; *Graces* F1; *omitted from F2.*
14 succurrere] Q, F3, D; succurere F1; *omitted from F2.*

ALBION,

AND

ALBANIUS;

AN OPERA.

Decorations of the Stage in the First Act.

THE *Curtain rises, and there appears on either side of the Stage, next to the Frontispiece, a Statue on Horse-back, of Gold, on Pedestal's of Marble, enrich'd with Gold, and bearing the Imperial Armes of* England: *one of these Statues is taken from that of the late King, at* Charing-Cross; *the other, from that Figure of his present Majesty (done by that noble Artist Mr.* Gibbons) *at* Windsor.

The Scene, is a Street of Palaces, which lead to the Front of the Royal Exchange; *the great Arch is open, and the view is continued through the open part of the* Exchange, *to the Arch on the other side, and thence to as much of the Street beyond, as could properly be taken.*

Mercury *descends in a Chariot drawn by Ravens.*

He comes to Augusta, *and* Thamesis. *They lye on Couches, at a distance from each other, in dejected postures; She attended by Cities, He by Rivers.*

On the side of Augusta's *Couch are painted Towers falling,*

could] Q, F3, D; ~ , F1; *omitted from F2.*
Mercury] *Mercury* F1, Q, F3; MERCURY D; *omitted from F2.*
descends . . . [to] . . . Ravens] *in romans in F1, Q, F3, D; omitted from F2.*
painted] *Painted* F1, Q, F3, D; *omitted from F2.*

*a Scarlet Gown, and Gold Chaine, a Cap of Maintenance thrown
down, and a Sword in a Velvet Scabbard thrust through it, the
City Arms, a Mace with an old useless Charter, and all in disorder. Before* Thamesis *are broken Reeds, Bull-rushes, Sedge,
&c. with his Urn Reverst.*

ACT I. SCENE I.

Mercury *descends.*

Merc. Thou glorious Fabrick! stand for ever, stand:
Well Worthy Thou to entertain
The God of Traffique, and of Gain!
To draw the Concourse of the Land,
And Wealth of all the Main.
But where the shoales of Merchants meeting?
Welcome to their Friends repeating,
Busie Bargaines deafer sound?
Tongues Confus'd of every Nation?
10 Nothing here but Desolation,
Mournful silence reignes around.
 Aug. O *Hermes!* pity me!
I was, while Heav'n did smile,
The Queen of all this Isle,
Europes Pride,
And *Albions* Bride;
But gone my Plighted Lord! ah, gone is Hee!
O *Hermes!* pity mee!
 Tham. And I the Noble Flood, whose tributary Tide
20 Does on her Silver Margent smoothly glide;
But Heav'n grew jealous of our happy state,

Thamesis *are*] Q, F3, D; ∼ , ∼ F1; *omitted from F2.*
ACT I. SCENE I.] ACT I. F1–3, Q, D.
s.d. descends] F3; *Descends* F1, Q, D; *s.d. omitted from F2.*
8 sound?] ∼ ! F1, Q, F3, D; ∼ , F2. 12 *Hermes*] F2–3, Q, D; Hermes F1
15–16 *Europes . . . Albions*] F2–3, Q, D; Europes . . . Albions F1.
21 state,] F2; ∼ : F1, Q, F3, D.

And bid revolving Fate,
Our Doom decree:
No more the King of Floods am I,   ⎤   *These two Lines are sung*
No more the Queen of *Albion,* She! ⎦   *by Reprises, betwixt*
                                       Augusta *and* Thamesis.

    Aug. O *Hermes!* pity me!   ⎤ *Sung by* Augusta *and* Thamesis
    Tham. O *Hermes!* pity me! ⎦   *together.*
    Aug. Behold!
    Tham. Behold!
30   *Aug.* My Turrets on the ground
That once my Temples crown'd!
    Tham. The Sedgy Honours of my Brow's disperst!
My Urn reverst!
    Merc. Rise, rise, *Augusta,* rise!
And wipe thy weeping Eyes:
Augusta! for I call thee so!
'Tis lawful for the Gods to know
Thy Future Name,
And growing Fame.
40 Rise, rise, *Augusta,* rise.
    Aug. O never, never will I rise!
Never will I cease my mourning,
Never wipe my Weeping Eyes,
Till my plighted Lord's returning!
Never, never will I rise!
    Merc. What brought Thee, Wretch, to this despair?
The Cause of thy Misfortune show.
    Aug. It seems the Gods take little Care
Of Humane things below,
50 When even our Suff'rings here they do not know!
    Merc. Not unknowing came I down,
Disloyal Town!
Speak! did'st not Thou
Forsake thy Faith, and break thy Nuptial Vow?

24–25 *s.d. sung*] Q, F3, D; *Sung* F1; *s.d. omitted from* F2.
24–25 *s.d.* Thamesis] F3; Thamisis F1; Tham. Q, D; *s.d. omitted from* F2.
40 Rise,] F2–3, Q, D; ~∧ F1.   45 Never,] F2–3, Q, D; ~∧ F1.

Aug. Ah 'tis too true! too true!
But what cou'd I, unthinking City, do?
Faction sway'd me,
Zeal allur'd me,
Both assur'd me,
60 Both betray'd me!
    Merc. Suppose me sent
Thy *Albion* to restore,
Can'st thou repent?
    Aug. My falshood I deplore!
    Tham. Thou seest her mourn; and I
With all my Waters, will her Tears supply.
    Merc. Then by some loyal Deed regain
Thy long lost Reputation,
To wash away the stain
70 That blots a Noble Nation!
And free thy famous Town again
From force of Usurpation!
    Chor. of all. We'll wash away the stain
That blots a noble Nation,
And free this famous Town again
From force of Usurpation.   [*Dance of the followers of* Mercury.
    Aug. Behold *Democracy* and *Zeal* appear,
She that allur'd my Heart away,
And He that after made a prey.
80   *Merc.* Resist, and do not fear!
    Chor. of all. Resist, & do not fear!

Enter Democracy *and* Zeal *attended by* Archon.

Democ. Nymph of the City! bring thy Treasures,
Bring me more
To waste in Pleasures.
    Aug. Thou hast exhausted all my Store,

---

81   *Chor. of all.*] D; ~. ~ ~.] F1; Chorus. F2; *Chorus* ~ ~.] Q, F3.
81–81+ *s.d.* fear! / *Enter*] F3, D; ~! [~ F1, Q (*s.d. at right margin*); *s.d. omitted from* F2.

And I can give no more.
  Zeal. Thou Horny Flood, for *Zeal* provide
A new Supply; And swell thy Moony tide,
That on thy buxom Back the floating Gold may glide.
90   *Tham.* Not all the Gold the Southern Sun produces,
Or Treasures of the fam'd *Levant,*
Suffice for Pious uses,
To feed the sacred hunger of a Saint!
  Democ. Woe to the Vanquisht, woe!
Slave as thou art,
Thy Wealth impart,
And me thy Victor know!
  Zeal. And me thy Victor know,
Resistless Arms are in my hand,
100 Thy Barrs shall burst at my Command,
Thy Towry Head lye low.
Woe to the Vanquish'd, woe!
  Aug. Were I not bound by fate
For ever, ever here,
My Walls I would translate
To some more happy Sphere,
Remov'd from servile fear.
  Tham. Remov'd from servile fear,
Wou'd I could disappear
110 And sink below the Mayn;
For Commonwealth's a Load
My old Imperial Flood
Shall never, never, never bear again.

A Commonwealth's a Load   ⎤ *Thamesis and* Augusta
Our old Imperial Flood   ⎬   *together.*
Shall never, never, never bear again. ⎦

  Dem. Pull down her Gates, Expose her bare;
I must enjoy the proud, disdainful fair.
Haste, *Archon,* Haste

---

87   Flood,] F2–3, Q, D; ~ₐ F1.   102   *line indented in F1, Q, D.*
113   Shall never,] F2–3; ~ ~ₐ F1, Q, D.
116   never, never, never] F3; ~ₐ ~ₐ ~ F1, Q, D; ~ , ~ F2.
117   Gates,] F2–3, Q, D; ~ₐ F1.

120 To lay her waste!
    Zel. I'll hold her fast
To be embrac'd!
    Dem. And she shall see
A Thousand Tyrants are in thee,
A Thousand thousand more in mee!
    Archon to Aug. From the *Caledonian* Shore
Hither am I come to save thee,
Not to force or to enslave thee,
But thy *Albion* to restore:
130 Hark! the peales the People ring,
Peace, and freedom and a King.
    Chor. Hark! the Peales the People ring,
Peace and freedom and a King.
    Aug. Tham. To Armes! to Armes!
    Archon. I lead the way!
    Merc. Cease your Alarmes!
And stay, brave *Archon,* stay!
'Tis Doom'd by Fates Decree!
'Tis Doom'd that *Albion*'s dwelling,
140 All other Isles excelling,
By Peace shall Happy be!
    Archon. What then remaines for me?
    Merc. Take my *Caduceus!* take this aweful Wand,
With this th' Infernal Ghosts I can command,
And strike a Terror thro the *Stygian* Land.
Common-wealth will want pretences,
Sleep will Creep on all his Senses;
Zeal that lent him her assistance,
                [Archon *touches* Democracy *with a Wand.*
Stand amaz'd without resistance.
150   *Dem.* I feel a lazy slumber layes me down!

---

126 *Archon to Aug.*] *Archon* to *Aug.* F1, Q, F3, D; *Archon.* F2.
126 *Caledonian*] F2–3, Q, D; *Caledonion* F1.
132 *Chor.*] F2, D; ∼ .] F1, Q, F3.   132 ring,] F2–3, Q, D; ∼ . F1.
146 pretences,] F2–3, Q, D; ∼∧ F1.

Let *Albion!* let him take the Crown!
Happy let him reign,
Till I wake again!   *[Falls asleep.*
   Zel. In vain I rage, In vain
I rouze my Powers;
But I shall wake again;
I shall to better Houres.
Ev'n in slumber
I will vex him;
160 Still perplex him,
Still incumber:
Know you that have ador'd him,
And Soveraign power afford him,
Wee'll reap the gains
Of all your paines
And seem to have restor'd him!   *[Zel. falls asleep.*
   Aug. and Tham. A stupyfying sadness
Leaves Her without motion;
But sleep will cure her madness,
170 And coole her to Devotion.
    A double Pedestal rises: On the Front of it is painted, in
    Stone colour, two Women; one holding a double-fac'd
    Vizor; the other a Book, representing Hypocricy *and*
    Phanaticism. *When* Archon *has charmed* Democracy *and*
    Zeal *with the* Caduceus *of* Mercury, *they fall asleep on*
    the Pedestal, and it sinks with them.
   Merc. Cease, *Augusta!* Cease thy mourning,
Happy dayes appeare,
Godlike *Albion* is returning

---

153 *s.d. Falls]* F3, D; *falls* F1, Q; *s.d. omitted from F2.*
154–155 vain / I] F3, D; ∼ , / ∼ F1, Q; ∼ ∼ F2.
158–159 Ev'n . . . slumber / I . . . him] ∼ . . . ∼ ∼ . . . ∼ F1–3, Q, D.
167 *Aug. and]* Aug. and F1, Q, F3, D; *Augusta.* F2.
170+ *s.d. double-fac'd]* Q, F3, D; *double Fac'd* F1; *s.d. omitted from F2.*
170+ *s.d.* Hypocricy] F1 (*errata*); Hypocracy F1; Hypocrisie Q, F3, D; *s.d. omitted from F2.*
170+ *s.d.* Phanaticism. *When]* F3; ∼ ; *when* F1, Q, D; *s.d. omitted from F2.*
170+ *s.d. asleep]* Q, F3, D; *a sleep* F1; *s.d. omitted from F2.*

Loyal Hearts to Cheere!
Every Grace his youth Adorning,
Glorious as the Star of Morning,
Or the Planet of the Year.
    Chor. Godlike *Albion* is returning, *&c.*
    Merc. to Arch. Hast away, Loyal chief, hast away.
180 No delay, but obey:
To receive thy lov'd Lord! hast away.   [*Ex.* Arch.
    Tham. Medway and *Isis,* you that augment me,
Tides that encrease my watry store,
And you that are Friends to Peace and Plenty,
Send my merry Boyes all ashore;
Sea Men Skipping,
Mariners Leaping,
Shouting, Tripping,
Send my merry Boyes all ashore!

A Dance of Watermen in the King's and Duke's Liveries.

The Clouds divide, and Juno *appears in a Machine
drawn by Peacocks; while a Symphony is playing, it
moves gently forward, and as it descends, it opens and
discovers the Tail of the Peacock, which is so Large,
that it almost fills the opening of the Stage between
Scene and Scene.*

190   *Merc.* The Clouds divide, what Wonders,
What Wonders do I see!
The Wife of *Jove,* 'Tis shee,
That Thunders, More than thundring Hee!
    Juno. No, *Hermes,* No;
'Tis Peace above
As 'tis below:
For *Jove* has left his wandring Love.

179 *Merc. to Arch.*] *Merc. to Arch.* F1, Q, F3, D; *Hermes.* F2.
189+ *s.d. Symphony*] F1 (*corrected form*), Q, F3, D; *Sympohny* F1 (*uncorrected
form*); *s.d. omitted from* F2.
194 *Hermes*] F2–3, Q, D; Hermes F1.

Tham. Great Queen of gathering Clouds,
Whose Moisture fills our Floods,
200 See, we fall before Thee,
Prostrate wee adore Thee!
  Aug. Great Queen of Nuptial Rites,
Whose pow'r the Souls Unites,
And fills the Genial Bed with chast Delights,
See, we fall before Thee,
Prostrate we adore Thee!
  Juno. 'Tis ratifi'd above by every God,
And *Jove* has firm'd it with an Awfull Nod;
That *Albion* shall his love renew:
210 But oh, ungrateful Fair,
Repeated Crimes beware,
And to his Bed be true!

> Iris *appears on a very large Machine. This was really
> seen the* 18th *of* March 1684. *by Capt.* Christopher
> Gunman, *on Board his R. H. Yacht, then in* Calais
> Pierre: *He drew it as it then appear'd, and gave a
> draught of it to us. We have only added the Cloud
> where the Person of* Iris *sits.*

Juno. Speak *Iris,* from *Batavia,* speak the Newes!
Has she perform'd my dread Command,
Returning *Albion* to his longing Land,
Or dares the Nymph refuse?
  Iris. Albion, by the Nymph attended,
Was to *Neptune* recommended,
Peace and plenty spread the Sails:
220 *Venus* in her shell before him,
From the Sands in safety bore him,
And supply'd *Etesian* gales.   [*Retornella.*
Archon on the Shore Commanding,

---

198 Clouds,] F2, D; ~ ; F1, Q, F3.   200 See,] F2–3; ~ ; F1, Q, D.
205 See,] F2–3; ~ ; F1, Q, D.   205 Thee,] F2–3, Q, D; ~∧ F1.
222 *s.d. Retornella.*] F2–3, Q, D; ~∧ F1.

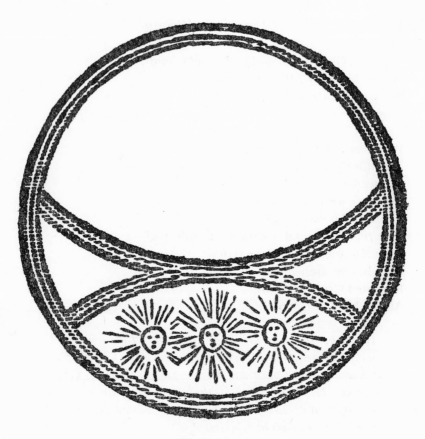

THE CELESTIAL PHENOMENON SEEN AT CALAIS
BY CAPTAIN CHRISTOPHER GUNMAN WHICH FORMED THE
BASIS OF THE MACHINE ON WHICH IRIS APPEARED IN
Albion and Albanius. SEE I, i, 212+ *s.d. and n.*
TAKEN FROM GUNMAN'S SKETCH AS REPRODUCED IN
SCOTT, *Works of Dryden,* I, 301.

Lowly met him at his Landing,
Crowd's of People swarm'd around;
Welcome rang like Peals of Thunder;
Welcome rent the Skies assunder;
Welcome Heav'n and Earth resound.
   Juno. Why stay we then on Earth
230 When Mortals laugh and love?
Tis time to mount above
And send *Astræa* down,
The Ruler of his Birth,
And Guardian of his Crown.
'Tis time to mount above,
And send *Astræa* down.
   Mer. Ju. Ir. 'Tis time to mount above,
And send *Astræa* down.   [*Mer. Ju. and* Iris *ascend.*
   Aug. and Tham. The Royal Squadron Marches,
240 Erect Tryumphal Arches,
For *Albion* and *Albanius:*
Rejoyce at their returning,
The passages adorning:
The Royal Squadron marches,
Erect Triumphal Arches
For *Albion* and *Albanius.*
   Part of the Scene disappears, and the 4 *Triumphal Arches
erected at his Majesties Coronation are seen.*

   Albion *appears,* Albanius *by his side, preceded by* Archon,
followed by a Train, &c.

   Full Chor. Hail, Royal *Albion*, Hail.
   Aug. Hail, Royal *Albion*, Hail to thee,
Thy longing Peoples expectation!
250   *Tham.* Sent from the Gods to set us free

226 *Welcome*] Welcome F1, Q, F3, D; *omitted from F2.*
227 *Welcome*] Welcome, F1, Q, F3, D; *omitted from F2.*
228 *Welcome*] Welcome, F1, Q, F3, D; *omitted from F2.*
239 *Aug. and Tham.*] *Aug.* and *Tham.* F1, Q, F3, D; *Augusta. Thamesis.* F2.
248 Hail,] D; ~∧ F1–3, Q.   249 expectation!] ~ : F1, Q, F3, D; ~ ; F2.
250 free] Q, F3, D; ~ . F1; ~ , F2.

From Bondage and from Usurpation!

Aug. To pardon and to pity me,
And to forgive a guilty Nation!

Tham. Behold the differing Climes agree,
Rejoycing in thy Restauration.

Entry; *Representing the Four parts of the World, rejoycing at
the Restauration of* Albion.

[*Exeunt.*

ACT II.   SCENE I.

*The Scene is a Poetical Hell. The Change is Total, the
Upper part of the House, as well as the Side Scenes.
There is the Figure of* Prometheus *chain'd to a Rock,
the Vulture gnawing his Liver;* Sisiphus *rowling the
Stone, the* Belides, &c. *Beyond, abundance of Figures
in various Torments. Then a great Arch of Fire. Behind this, Three Pyramids of Flames in perpetual
agitation. Beyond this, glowing Fire which terminates
the Prospect.*

Enter Pluto, *the Furies, with* Alecto, Democracy *and* Zelota.

Plut. Infernal Offspring of the Night,
Debarr'd of Heav'n your Native right,
And from the glorious Fields of Light,
Condemn'd in shades to dragg the Chain,

---

254   agree,] F2–3, Q, D; ∼ . F1.   255   thy] F1 (*errata*), F2–3, Q, D; the F1.
255+   *s.d.* [*Exeunt.*] *omitted from F1–3, Q, D.*
ACT II. SCENE I.] F2; ACT II. F1, Q, D; ACT. II. F3.
The Change is Total, the] The Change is Total. *The* F1, Q, F3, D; *omitted
from F2.*
Liver;] ∼ . F1, Q, F3, D; *omitted from F2.*
&c.] F3; *&c.* F1, Q, D; *omitted from F2.*
Beyond] D; *beyond* F1, Q, F3; *omitted from F2.*
Behind this,] ∼ ∼∧ F1, Q, F3, D; *omitted from F2.*
s.d. Enter Pluto] Pluto F1, Q, F3, D; *omitted from F2.*

And fill with groans the gloomy Plain;
Since Pleasures here are none below,
Be ill our good, our joy be Woe;
Our Work t' embroil the Worlds above,
Disturb their Union, disunite their Love,
10 And blast the Beautious frame of our Victorious Foe.
    Democ. and Zelot. together. Oh thou for whom those Worlds
      are made,
Thou Sire of all things and their end,
From hence they spring, and when they fade
In Shuffled Heaps they hither tend;
Here Humane Souls receive their Breath,
And wait for Bodies after Death.
    Democ. Hear our Complaint and grant our Pray'r.
    Pluto. Speak what you are,
And whence you fell.
20   *Democ.* I am thy first begotten care,
Conceiv'd in Heav'n; but born in Hell,
When Thou didst bravely undertake in fight
Yon Arbitrary Pow'r,
That rules by Soveraign might,
To set thy Heav'n-born fellows free
And leave no difference in Degree:
In that Auspicious Hour
Was I begot by Thee.
    Zelota. One Mother bore us at a Birth,
30 Her Name was *Zeal* before she fell;
No fairer Nymph in Heav'n or Earth
Till Saintship taught her to rebel:
But loosing Fame
And changing Name
She's now the *Good Old Cause* in Hell.
    Plut. Dear Pledges of a Flame not yet forgot,
Say, what on Earth has been your lot?

11   *and*] and F1, Q, F3, D; *omitted from F2.*   19   fell.] ∼ ? F1–3, Q, D.
23   Yon] F1 *(errata and corrected form),* F2–3, Q, D; You F1 *(uncorrected form).*
26   Degree:] F2; ∼ , F1, Q, F3, D.

Dem. and Zel. The Wealth of *Albion's* Isle was ours,
Augusta stoopt with all her stately Tow'rs!
40   *Dem. Democracy* kept Nobles under.
     Zel. Zeal from the Pulpit roar'd like Thunder.
     Dem. I trampled on the State.
     Zel. I lorded o're the Gown.
     Dem. and Zel. We both in Triumph sate
Usurpers of the Crown.
But oh Prodigious turn of Fate!
Heaven controuling, sent us rowling, rowling, down.
     Plut. I wonder'd how of late our *Acherontique* shore
Grew thin, and Hell unpeopl'd of her Store;
50 *Charon* for want of Use forgot his Oar.
The Souls of Bodies Dead flew all Sublime,
And hither none return'd to purge a Crime:
But now I see since *Albion* is restor'd,
Death has no Bus'ness, nor the vengeful Sword.
'Tis too, too much that here I ly
From glorious Empire hurl'd;
By *Jove* excluded from the Sky,
By *Albion* from the World.
     Dem. Were Common-Wealth restor'd again,
60 Thou should'st have Millions of the slain
To fill thy dark abode.
     Zel. For He a Race of Rebels sends,
And *Zeal* the Path of Heav'n pretends;
But still mistakes the rode.
     Pluto. My lab'ring thought
At length hath wrought

---

38   *and*] and F1, Q, F3, D; *omitted from F2.*
39   Tow'rs] F2–3, Q; Towr's F1, D.
44   *and*] and F1, Q, F3, D; *omitted from F2.*
47   Heaven controuling, sent . . . down.] F2 (*F2 not lined*); $\sim \sim$, / Sent . . .
   $\sim$. F1, Q, F3, D.
48   *Acherontique*] F2; Acherontique F1, Q, F3, D.
49   unpeopl'd] Q, F3, D; unpeople'd F1; unpeopled F2.
55–58   'Tis . . . [*to*] . . . World.] *lines indented in F1, Q, F3, D.*
55   too, too] $\sim_\wedge\sim$ F1, Q, F3, D; too much, too F2.
61   *line indented in F1, Q.*

A bravely bold design,
In which you both shall joyn;
In borrow'd shapes to Earth return;
70   Thou *Common-wealth,* a Patriot seem,
Thou *Zeal,* like true Religion burn,
To gain the giddy Crowds Esteem.
Alecto, thou to fair *Augusta* go,
And all thy Snakes into her Bosom throw.
     Dem. Spare some to fling
Where they may sting
The Breast of *Albion*'s King.
     Zel. Let Jealousies so well be mixt,
That great *Albanius* be unfixt!
80   *Pluto.* Forbear your vain Attempts, forbear;
Hell can have no admittance there:
The Peoples fear will serve as well,
Make him suspected, them Rebel.
     Zel. Y' have all forgot
To forge a Plot
In seeming Care of *Albion*'s Life;
Inspire the Crowd
With Clamours loud
T' involve his Brother and his Wife.
90   *Alecto.* Take of a Thousand Souls at thy Command,
The basest, blackest of the *Stygian* band:
One that will Swear to all they can invent,
So throughly Damn'd that he can n'er repent:
One often sent to Earth,
And still at every Birth
He took a deeper stain:
One that in *Adam*'s time was *Cain:*
One that was burnt in *Sodom*'s flame,
For Crimes ev'n here too black to name:
100   One, who through every form of ill has run:
One who in *Naboth*'s days was *Belial*'s Son:

---

91   *Stygian*] F2, D; Stygian F1, Q, F3.

One who has gain'd a Body fit for Sin;
Where all his Crimes
Of former Times
Lie Crowded in a Skin.
 Pluto. Take him;
Make him
What you please;
For He
110 Can be
A Rogue with ease.
One for mighty Mischief Born:
He can Swear and be Forsworn.
 Pluto and Alecto take him, &c. Take him, make him what
  you please;
For He can be a Rogue with ease.
 Pluto. Let us laugh, let us laugh, let us laugh at our Woes,
The Wretch that is damn'd has nothing to lose.
Yee Furies advance
With the *Ghosts* in a Dance,
120 'Tis a Jubilee here when the World is in trouble:
When People rebel
Wee frolick in Hell;
But when the King falls, the pleasure is double.
 [*A single Entry of a Devil follow'd by an Entry of* 12 *Devils.*
 Chorus. Let us laugh, let us laugh, let us laugh at our Woes,
The Wretch that is damn'd hath nothing to lose.
              [*Exeunt.*

SCENE II.

The Scene changes to a Prospect taken from the mid-
dle of the Thames; *one side of it begins at* York-Stairs,

114 *and . . . take him*] and . . . take him F1, Q, F3; & . . . D; *omitted from*
F2.
123 double.] F2; ∼ : F1, Q, F3, D.
125+ *s.d.* [*Exeunt.*] *omitted from F1–3, Q, D.*
SCENE II.] PRELUDE. F2; *omitted from F1, Q, F3, D.*
Thames] Q, F3, D; *Thames* F1; *omitted from F2.*

thence to White-Hall, *and the* Mill-Bank, &c. *The
other from the* Saw-Mill, *thence to the* Bishop's *Palace,
and on as far as can be seen in a clear Day.*

Enter Augusta; *She has a Snake in her Bosom, hanging down.*

Aug. O Jealousy, Thou raging ill,
Why hast thou found a Room in Lovers Hearts,
Afflicting what thou can'st not kill,
And Poysoning Love himself, with his own Darts?
I find my *Albion's* Heart is gone,
My first offences yet remain,
Nor can repentance Love regain;
One writ in Sand, alas, in Marble one.
I rave, I rave, my Spirits boyl
10　Like flames encreas'd and mounting high with pouring Oyl:
Disdain and Love succeed by turns;
One freezes me, and t' other burns; It burns.
Away soft Love, Thou Foe to rest,
Give Hate the full possession of my Breast.
Hate is the nobler passion far
When Love is ill repay'd;
For at one blow it ends the War,
And Cures the Love-sick Maid.

Enter Democracy *and* Zelota: *one represents
a* Patriot; *the other,* Religion.

Dem. Let not thy generous passion wast its rage,
20　But once again restore our golden Age;
Still to weep and to complain,
Does but more provoke disdain.
Let publick good,

&c.] F3; *&c.* F1, Q, D; *omitted from F2.*
10　pouring] F2–3, Q, D; pou'ring F1.
18+　*s.d.* Zelota: . . . Patriot;] ~ ; . . . ~ , F1, Q, F3, D; *omitted from F2*
18+　*s.d. other,*] D; ~∧ F1, Q, F3; *omitted from F2.*

Inflame thy Blood:
With Crowds of Warlike People thou art stor'd,
And heaps of Gold;
Reject thy old,
And to thy Bed receive another Lord.
 Zel. Religion shall thy Bonds release,
80 For Heav'n can loose, as well as tie all;
And when 'tis for the Nations peace
A King is but a King on Tryal;
When Love is lost, let Marriage end,
And leave a Husband for a Friend.
 Dem. With Jealousy swarming
The People are Arming
And frights of oppression invade 'em.
 Zelot. If they fall to relenting,
For fear of repenting,
40 Religion shall help to perswade 'em.
 Aug. No more, no more Temptations use
To bend my Will;
How hard a task 'tis to refuse
A pleasing ill!
 Dem. Maintain the seeming duty of a Wife,
A modest show will jealous Eyes deceive,
Affect a fear for hated *Albion's* Life,
And for imaginary Dangers grieve.
 Zelot. His Foes already stand protected,
50 His Friends by publick Fame suspected,
Albanius must forsake his Isle:
A Plot Contriv'd in happy hour
Bereaves him of his Royal Pow'r,
For Heav'n to mourn and Hell to smile.

The former Scene continues.

Enter Albion *and* Albanius *with a Train.*

---

44 ill!] F2; $\sim$? F1, Q, F3, D.
54+ *s.d. Enter . . . Train. / Albion.* Then] D; *Enter . . . Train.* Then F1, Q
(*s.d. set as speech tag*); *Albion.* Then F2; *Enter . . . Train. /* Then F3.

Albion. Then Zeal and Common-wealth infest
    My Land again;
    The fumes of madness that possest
    The Peoples giddy Brain,
    Once more disturb the Nations rest,
60   And dye Rebellion in a deeper Stain.

          2.
    Will they at length awake the sleeping Sword,
    And force revenge from their offended Lord?
    How long, yee Gods, how long
    Can Royal patience bear
    Th' Insults and wrong
    Of Mad-mens jealousies, and causeless fear?

          3.
    I thought their love by mildness might be gain'd,
    By Peace I was restor'd, in Peace I Reign'd:
    But Tumults, Seditions,
70   And haughty Petitions,
    Are all the effects of a merciful Nature;
    Forgiving and granting,
    E're Mortals are wanting,
    But leads to Rebelling against their Creator.

        Mercury *descends.*

Merc. With Pity *Jove* beholds thy State,
But *Jove* is circumscrib'd by Fate;
Th' o'erwhelming Tide rowls on so fast,
It gains upon this Islands wast:
And is oppos'd too late! too late!
80   *Albion.* What then must helpless *Albion* do?
    Merc. Delude the fury of the Foe,
And to preserve *Albanius,* let him go;

---

75 Pity] F1 (*errata*), F2, D; pity F1, Q, F3.
75 thy State] F1 (*corrected form*), F2–3, Q, D; thyate F1 (*uncorrected form*).

For 'tis decreed,
Thy Land must bleed,
For Crimes not thine, by wrathful *Jove;*
A Sacred Flood
Of Royal Blood,
Cries *Vengeance, Vengeance* lowd above.

Mercury *ascends.*

    Albion. Shall I, t' asswage
90 Their Brutal rage,
The Regal stem destroy;
Or must I lose,
(To please my Foes,)
My sole remaining joy?
Yee God's what worse,
What greater Curse,
Can all your Wrath employ?
    Alban. Oh *Albion!* hear the Gods and me!
Well am I lost in saving Thee.
100 Not exile or danger can fright a brave Spirit
With Innocence guarded,
With Vertue rewarded;
I make of my sufferings a Merit.
    Albion. Since then the Gods, and Thou wilt have it so;
Go: (can I live once more to bid Thee?) go,
Where thy Misfortunes call Thee and thy Fate:
Go, guiltless Victim of a guilty State,
In War my Champion to defend,
In peaceful Hours, when Souls unbend,
110 My Brother, and what's more, my Friend!
Born where the Foamy Billows roar,
On Seas less Dang'rous than the Shoar:
Go, where the Gods thy Refuge have assign'd:
Go from my sight; but never from my Mind.
    Alban. Whatever Hospitable ground
Shall be for me, unhappy Exile, found,

---

87 Of] Q, F3, D; of F1–2.
88 *Vengeance, Vengeance*] Vengeance, Vengeance F1–3, Q, D.
99 Well] D; ∼ , F1, Q, F3; ∼ ! F2.   110 more,] D; ∼ₐ F1–3, Q.
116 Shall] Q, F3, D; shall F1–2.

Till Heav'n vouchsafe to smile;
What Land so e're,
Tho' none so dear,
120 As this ungrateful Isle;
O think! O think! no distance can remove
My vow'd Allegiance, and my Loyal Love.
  Albion and Alban. The Rosy-finger'd Morn appears,
And from her Mantle shakes her Tears,
In promise of a glorious Day:
The Sun, returning, Mortals chears,
And drives the Rising Mists away,
In promise of a glorious Day.   [*Ritornelle.*

*The farther part of the Heaven opens and discovers a
Machine; as it moves forwards the Clouds which are
before it divide, and shew the Person of Apollo, hold-
ing the Reins in his hand. As they fall lower, the
Horses appear with the Rays and a great glory about
Apollo.*

  Apoll. All Hail yee Royal pair!
130   The Gods peculiar care:
           Fear not the malice of your Foes;
           Their Dark designing
           And Combining,
           Time and truth shall once expose:
           Fear not the malice of your Foes.

                    2.
           My sacred Oracles assure,
           The Tempest shall not long indure;
           But when the Nations Crimes are purg'd away,
           Then shall you both in glory shine;
140   Propitious both, and both Divine:

123 *Albion and*] *Albion.* and F1, Q, F3 (*Albion*∧ F3); *Albion.* F2; *Albi.* & D.
123 Rosy-finger'd] D; Rosy finger'd F1–3, Q.
124 from her] F1 (*errata*), F2–3, Q, D; from andher F1.
130 Gods] F2–3, D; God's F1, Q.

In Lustre equal to the God of Day.
[Apollo *goes forward out of sight.*

Neptune *rises out of the Water, and a Train of Rivers,*
Tritons, *and Sea Nymphs attend him.*

Thames. Old Father *Ocean* calls my Tyde:
Come away, come away;
The Barks upon the Billows ride,
The Master will not stay;
The merry Boson from his side,
His Whistle takes to check and chide
The lingring Lads delay,
And all the Crew alowd has Cry'd,
150   *Come away, come away.*

See the God of Seas attends Thee,
Nymphs Divine, a Beauteous Train:
All the calmer gales befriend Thee
In thy passage o're the Main:
Every Maid her Locks is binding,
Every *Triton's* Horn is winding,
Welcome to the watry Plain.

Chacon.

Two Nymphs and Triton *Sing.*

Yee Nymphs, the Charge is Royal,
Which you must convey;
160   Your Hearts and Hands employ all,
Hasten to obey;
When Earth is grown disloyal,
Shew there's Honour in the Sea.

---

142   *Thames.*] F2, Q, F3, D; ∼ , F1.   142   *Ocean*] F2; Ocean F1, Q, F3, D.
150   *Come* . . . [*to*] . . . *away.*] *in romans in F1–3, Q, D.*

The Chacon *continues.*

The Chorus of Nymphs and Tritons *repeat the same Verses.*

The Chacon *continues.*

Two Nymphs and Triton *Sing.*

Sports and Pleasures shall attend you
Through all the Watry Plains,
Where *Neptune* Reigns:
Venus ready to defend you,
And her Nymphs to ease your Pains.
No storm shall offend you,
170   Passing the Main;
Nor Billow threat in vain,
So Sacred a Train,
Till the Gods that defend you,
Restore you again.

The Chacon *continues.*

The Chorus repeat the same Verses, Sports and Pleasure, &c.

The Chacon *continues.*

The two Nymphs and Triton *Sing.*

See at your blest returning
Rage disappears;
The Widow'd Isle in Mourning
Dries up her Tears,
With Flowers the Meads adorning,
180   Pleasure appears,
And love dispels the Nations causeless fears.

163+ *s.d.* Triton *Sing*] Tritons F1, Q, F3, D; *omitted from* F2 (*but lines 164–174 sung by three voices*).
174+ *s.d.* Pleasure,] Q, F3, D; ~ . F1; *s.d. omitted from* F2.

The Chacon *continues.*

The Chorus of Nymphs and Tritons *repeat the same Verses,*
See at your blest returning, *&c.*

The Chacon *continues.*

Then the Chorus repeat, See the God of Seas, *&c.*
And this Chorus concludes the Act.

[*Exeunt.*

ACT III.   SCENE I.

The Scene is a view of Dover, *taken from the Sea: a
row of Cliffs fill up each side of the Stage, and the Sea
the middle of it, which runs into the* Peer: *beyond the*
Peer, *is the Town of* Dover: *on each side of the Town,
is seen a very high Hill; on one of which is the Castle
of* Dover; *on the other, the great Stone which they call
the* Devils-Drop. *Behind the Town several Hills are
seen at a great distance which finish the view.*

Enter Albion *bareheaded:* Acacia *or* Innocence *with
him.*

Albion. Behold yee Pow'rs! from Whom I own
A Birth immortal, and a Throne:
See a Sacred King uncrown'd,
See your Offspring, *Albion,* bound:
The gifts you gave with lavish hand,
Are all bestow'd in vain:
Extended Empire on the Land,

181+   *s.d.* Tritons] Triton F1, Q, F3, D; *s.d. omitted from* F2 (*but lines repeated by four voices*).
181+   *s.d.* [*Exeunt.*] *omitted from* F1-3, Q, D.
ACT III. SCENE I.] F2; ACT. III. F1, Q; ACT III. F3, D.
Devils-Drop] D; Devils drop F1, Q, F3; *omitted from* F2.

Unbounded o'er the Main.
   Acacia. Empire o'er the Land and Main,
10 Heav'n that gave can take again;
But a mind that's truly brave,
Stands despising,
Storms arising,
And can ne'er be made a Slave.
   Albion. Unhelpt I am, who pity'd the distress'd,
And none oppressing, am by all oppress'd;
Betray'd, forsaken, and of hope bereft.
   Acacia. Yet still the Gods and Innocence are left.
   Albion. Ah! what canst thou avail,
20 Against Rebellion arm'd with zeal,
And fac'd with publick good?
O Monarch's, see
Your Fate in me!
To rule by Love,
To shed no Blood,
May be extol'd above;
But here below,
Let Princes know
'Tis fatal to be good.
30   *Chorus of both*. To rule by Love, *&c.*
   Albion. But see! what prodigies are these?
   Acacia. Your Father *Neptune* from the Seas,
Has *Nereids* and blew *Triton's* sent,
To charm your discontent.

     Nereids *rise out of the Sea and Sing,* Tritons *dance.*

     From the low Palace of old Father *Ocean,*
     Come we in pity your cares to deplore:

---

9 *Acacia*. Empire] F2–3, D; ~ . / ~ F1, Q.
17 bereft.] F2, D; ~ : F1, Q, F3.
22 Monarch's,] ~ᴧ F1, Q, F3, D; ~ ! F2.
30 Love,] F2–3, Q, D; ~ᴧ F1.
35 *Ocean*] F2; Ocean F1, Q, F3, D.
36 Come] F3, D; come F1–2, Q.

Sea-raceing Dolphins are train'd for our Motion,
Moony Tides swelling to rowl us a-shore.

2.

Ev'ry Nymph of the flood, her Tresses rending,
40 Throws off her Armlet of Pearl in the Main;
Neptune in anguish his Charge unattending,
Vessels are foundring, and Vows are in vain.

Enter Tyranny, Democracy, *represented by Men,
attended by* Asebia, Zelota, *Women.*

Tyran. Ha, ha, 'tis what so long I wish'd and vow'd,
Our Plots and delusions,
Have wrought such confusions,
That the Monarch's a Slave to the Crowd.
Democ. A Design we fomented,———
Tyr. By Hell it was new!
Dem. A false Plot invented,———
50 *Tyr.* To cover a true.
Democ. First with promis'd faith we flatter'd,———
Tyr. Then jealousies and fears we scatter'd.
Asebia. We never valu'd right and wrong,
But as they serv'd our cause;———
Zelot. Our Business was to please the throng,
And Court their wild applause:———
Asebia. For this we brib'd the Lawyers Tongue,
And then destroy'd the Law's.
Chor. For this, &c.

---

37 Sea-raceing] F1 (*errata*), Q, F3, D; Sea-spouting F1; Sea-sporting F2.
37 train'd] F1 (*errata*), Q, F3, D; tam'd F1–2.
37 Motion] F1 (*errata*), Q, F3, D; motion F1–2.
38 a-shore.] F2–3, Q, D; ~ , F1.   40 off] Q, F3, D; of F1; *omitted from F2.*
41 unattending] F1 (*errata*), Q, F3, D; unattended F1; *omitted from F2.*
47 fomented,———] ~ ,∧ F1–3, Q, D.
49 invented,———] ~ ,∧ F1–3, Q, D.
51 flatter'd,———] ~ ,∧ F1, Q, F3, D; ~ ;∧ F2.
54 cause;———] ~ ;∧ F1–3, Q; ~ .∧ D.
56 applause:———] ~ :∧ F1–3, Q, D.

60   *Tyran.* To make him safe, we made his Friends our Prey; ⎤
                                                              ⎟
──────   ⎟
      Dem. To make him great we scorn'd his Royal sway,──── ⎬
      Tyran. And to confirm his Crown, we took his Heir away.⎟
      Dem. T' encrease his store,   ⎦
      We kept him poor.
        Tyran. And when to wants we had betray'd him,
      To keep him low,
      Pronounc'd a Foe,
      Who e're presum'd to aid him.
        Asebia. But you forget the noblest part, ⎤
70   And Masterpiece of all your Art,   ⎬
      You told him he was sick at Heart.   ⎦
        Zelot. And when you could not work belief
      In *Albion* of th' imagin'd grief,
      Your perjur'd vouchers in a Breath,
      Made Oath that he was sick to Death;
      And then five hundred Quacks of skill
      Resolv'd 'twas fit he should be ill.
        Asebia. Now heigh for a Common-wealth,
      Wee merrily Drink and Sing,
80   'Tis to the Nations Health,
      For every Man's a King.
        Zelot. Then let the Masque begin,
      The Saints advance,
      To fill the Dance,
      And the Property Boys come in.

        The Boys in White begin a Fantastick Dance.

        Chor. Let the Saints ascend the Throne.
        Dem. Saints have Wives, and Wives have Preachers,
      Guifted men, and able Teachers;
      These to get, and those to own.

60 Prey;────] ~ ;ᴧ F1–3, Q, D.   61 sway,────] ~ ,ᴧ F1–3, Q, D.
64 poor.] ~ : F1, Q, F3, D; ~ ; F2.   73 grief,] F2; ~ ; F1, Q, F3, D.
77 'twas] F2–3, Q, D; t'was F1.   83 Saints] F2; *Saints* F1, Q, F3, D.
89 own.] ~ ; F1, Q, F3, D; ~ : F2.

90   *Chor.* Let the Saints ascend the Throne.
   Asebia. Freedom is a bait alluring;
Them betraying, us securing,
While to Sovereign pow'r we soar.
   Zelota. Old delusions new repeated,
Shews 'em born but to be cheated,
As their Fathers were before.

> *Six Sectaries begin a formal affected Dance, the two*
> *gravest whisper the other Four, and draw 'em into the*
> *Plot: They pull out and deliver Libels to 'em, which*
> *they receive.*

   Democr. See Friendless *Albion* there alone,
Without Defence
But Innocence;
100 *Albanius* now is gone.
   Tyran. Say then, What must be done?
   Dem. The Gods have put him in our hand.
   Zelota. He must be slain!
   Tyran. But who shall then Command?
   Dem. The People: for the right returns to those,
Who did the trust impose.
   Tyran. 'Tis fit another Sun shou'd rise,
To cheer the World, and light the Skyes.
   Dem. But when the Sun,
110 His race has run,
And neither cheers the World, nor lights the Skies;
'Tis fit a Common-wealth of Stars shou'd rise.
   Asebia. Each noble vice,
Shall bear a Price,
And Vertue shall a drug become:
An empty Name
Was all her Fame,
But now she shall be **Dumb.**
   Zelota. If open Vice be what you drive at,
120 A Name so broad we'll ne'er connive at.

Saints love Vice, but more refin'dly,
Keep her close, and use her kindly.
  Tyran. Fall on.
  Dem. Fall on: Ere *Albion's* death we'll try,
If one or many shall his room supply.

*The White Boys dance about the Saints: The Saints
draw out the Association, and offer it to 'em: They
refuse it and quarrel about it: Then the White Boys
and Saints fall into a confus'd Dance, imitating fighting: The White Boys at the end of the Dance, being
driven out by the Sectaries with Protestant Flails.*

  Albion. See the Gods my cause defending,
When all humane help was past!
  Acacia. Factions mutually contending,
By each other fall at last.
30   *Albion.* But is not yonder *Proteus* Cave,
Below that steep,
Which rising Billows brave?
  Acacia. It is: And in it lies the God asleep:
And snorting by,
We may descry,
The Monsters of the deep.
  Albion. He knows the past,
An can resolve the future too.
  Acacia. 'Tis true!
40 But hold him fast,
For he can change his hew.

The Cave of Proteus *rises out of the Sea, it consists of
several Arches of Rock work, adorn'd with mother of
Pearl, Coral, and abundance of Shells of various kinds:
Thro' the Arches is seen the Sea, and parts of* Dover

125+ *s.d. White . . . White . . . White] white . . . white . . . white* F1, Q, F3,
D; *omitted from F2.*

Peer: *In the middle of the Cave is* Proteus *asleep on a Rock adorn'd with Shells,* &c. *like the Cave.* Albion *and* Acacia *seize on him, and while a Symphony is playing, he sinks as they are bringing him forward, and changes himself into a Lyon, a Crocodile, a Dragon, and then to his own shape again: He comes toward the front of the Stage, and Sings.*

Symphony.

Proteus. Albion, lov'd of Gods and Men,
Prince of Peace too mildly Reigning,
Cease thy sorrow and complaining;
Thou shalt be restor'd agen:
Albion, lov'd of Gods and Men.

2.

Still thou art the care of Heav'n,
In thy Youth to Exile driv'n:
Heav'n thy ruin then prevented,
150   Till the guilty Land repented:
In thy Age, when none could aid Thee,
Foes conspir'd, and Friends betray'd Thee;
To the brink of danger driv'n,
Still thou art the Care of Heav'n.

Albion. To whom shall I my preservation owe?
Proteus. Ask me no more! for 'tis by *Neptune*'s Foe.
                                        Proteus *descends.*

Democracy *and* Zelota *return with their Faction.*

Democ. Our seeming Friends, who joyn'd alone,
To pull down one, and build another Throne,

141+   *s.d.* Peer] F3, D; *Peer* F1, Q; *omitted from F2.*
141+   *s.d.* asleep] Q, F3, D; *a sleep* F1; *omitted from F2.*
141+   *s.d.* like] F3, D; *Like* F1, Q; *omitted from F2.*
156+   *s.d.* Proteus *descends*] F3; *Proteus* descends F1, Q, D; PRELUDE F2.

Are all disperst and gone:
160 We brave republick Souls remain.
    Zelot. And 'tis by us that *Albion* must be Slain:
Say, whom shall wee employ
The Tyrant to destroy?
    Democ. That Archer is by Fate design'd,
With one Eye clear, and t' other blind.
    Zelota. He seems inspir'd to do't.
    Omnes. Shoot, Holy *Cyclop,* shoot.

The one-Ey'd Archer advances, the rest follow:
A fire arises betwixt them and Albion.

                                 [*Ritornel.*
    Democ. Lo! Heav'n and Earth combine,
To blast our bold design.
170 What Miracles are shown?
Nature's alarm'd,
And Fires are arm'd,
To guard the Sacred Throne.
    Zelota. What help, when jarring Elements conspire
To punish our audacious Crimes?
Retreat betimes,
To shun th' avenging Fire.
    Chor. To shun th' avenging Fire.   [*Ritor.*
    As they are going back a Fire arises from behind: They all
      sink together.
    Albion. Let our tuneful accents upwards move,
80 Till they reach the vaulted Arch of those above;
Let us adore 'em;
Let us fall before 'em.
    Acacia. Kings they made, and Kings they love.
When they protect a rightful Monarch's Reign,
The Gods in Heav'n, the Gods on Earth maintain.

---

167   Shoot,] F2; ～ₐ F1, Q, F3, D.
167+ *s.d. one-Ey'd*] D; *one Ey'd* F1, Q, F3; *omitted from* F2.
175   Crimes?] F3; ～ . F1, Q, D; ～ , F2.
178   th' avenging] F2, D; the avenging F1, Q, F3.
182   'em.] F2; ～ : F1, Q, F3, D.

Both. When they protect, &c.

Albion. But see what glories guild the main.

Acacia. Bright *Venus* brings *Albanius* back again,
With all the *Loves* and *Graces* in her train.

> *A Machine rises out of the Sea: It opens and discovers*
> Venus *and* Albanius *sitting in a great Scallop-shell,*
> *richly adorn'd:* Venus *is attended by the* Loves *and*
> Graces, Albanius *by* Hero's: *The Shell is drawn by*
> *Dolphins: It moves forward, while a Simphony of*
> *Fluts-Doux,* &c. *is playing, till it Lands 'em on the*
> *Stage, and then it closes and sinks.*

Venus *Sings.*

190   *Albion,* Hail; The Gods present Thee,
All the richest of their Treasures,
Peace and Pleasures,
To content Thee,
Dancing their eternal measures.
           [Graces *and* Loves *Dance an Entry.*

Venus. But above all humane blessing,
Take a Warlike Loyal Brother;
Never Prince had such another:
Conduct, Courage, truth expressing,
All Heroick worth possessing.
           [*Here the* Heros *Dance is perform'd.*

200   *Chor. of all.* But above all, &c.   [*Ritor.*

---

189 *Loves* . . . *Graces*] loves . . . graces F1; Loves . . . Graces F2–3, Q, D.
189+ s.d. Venus *and*] Q, F3, D; ~ , ~ F1; *omitted from F2.*
189+ s.d. Loves . . . Graces] *Loves* . . . *Graces* F1, Q, F3, D; *omitted from F2.*
189+ s.d. *playing,*] F3; ~∧ F1, Q, D; *omitted from F2.*
189+ s.d. Venus *Sings*] Q, F3, D; *Venus* Sings F1; *Venus* F2.
194+ s.d. Graces *and* Loves *Dance an Entry*] *Graces and Loves, Dance an Entry*
F1, Q, F3, D (*Loves*∧ F3, D); AYRE for the Graces and Loves F2.
195 blessing,] F2; ~ ; F1, Q, F3, D.   196 Brother;] D; ~ , F1–3, Q.
199+ s.d. Heros] *Hero's* F1–2; *Heroes* Q, F3, D.

*Whilst a Simphony is playing; a very large, and a very
glorious Machine descends: The figure of it Oval, all
the Clouds shining with Gold, abundance of Angels
and Cherubins flying about 'em, and playing in 'em;
in the midst of it sits* Apollo *on a Throne of Gold: he
comes from the Machine to* Albion.

Phœb. From *Jove's* Imperial Court,
Where all the Gods resort;
In awful Council met,
Surprizing news I bear:
Albion the Great,
Must change his Seat,
For Hee's adopted there.
 Ven. What Stars above shall we displace?
Where shall he fill a Room Divine?
210 *Nept.* Descended from the Sea Gods Race,
Let him by my *Orion* shine.
 Phœb. No, Not by that tempestuous sign:
Betwixt the *Balance* and the *Maid,*
The Just,
August,
And peaceful shade,
Shall shine in Heav'n with Beams display'd,
While great *Albanius* is on Earth obey'd.
 Ven. Albanius Lord of Land and Main,
220 Shall with fraternal vertues Reign;
And add his own,
To fill the Throne;
Ador'd and fear'd, and lov'd no less:
In War Victorious, mild in Peace,
The joy of men, and *Jove's* increase.
 Acacia. O Thou! Who mount'st th' Æthereal Throne,
Be kind and happy to thy own.
Now *Albion* is come,

The People of the Sky,
230 Run gazing and Cry,
Make Room, make Room,
Make room for our new Deity.
>   *Here* Albion *mounts the Machine, which moves upward*
>   *slowly.*

A full Chorus of all that Acacia *sung.*

Ven. Behold what Triumphs are prepar'd to grace ⎤
Thy glorious Race,   ⎟
Where Love and Honour claim an equal place;   ⎬
Already are they fixt by Fate,   ⎦
And only ripening Ages wait.

>   [*Exeunt.*

SCENE II.

The Scene changes to a walk of very high Trees: At the
end of the Walk is a view of that part of Windsor,
which faces Eaton: *In the midst of it is a row of small*
Trees, which lead to the Castle-hill: In the first Scene,
part of the Town and part of the Hill: In the next the
Terrace Walk, the King's Lodgings, and the upper
part of St. George's *Chappel, then the Keep; and lastly,*
that part of the Castle, beyond the Keep.

In the Air is a Vision of the Honors of the Garter,
the Knights in Procession, and the King under a
Canopy: Beyond this, the upper end of St. George's
Hall.

Fame *rises out of the middle of the Stage, standing*
on a Globe; on which is the Arms of England: *The*

231–232   *in romans in F1–3, Q, D.*
237+   s.d. *[Exeunt.] omitted from F1–3, Q, D.*
SCENE II.] PRELUDE. F2; *omitted from F1, Q, F3, D.*
Garter,] ∼ ; F1, Q, F3, D; *omitted from F2.*

Globe rests on a Pedestal: On the Front of the Pedes-
tal is drawn a Man with a long, lean, pale Face, with
Fiends Wings, and Snakes twisted round his Body: He
is incompast by several Phanatical Rebellious Heads,
who suck poyson from him, which runs out of a Tap
in his Side.

Fame. Renown, assume thy Trumpet!
From Pole to Pole resounding
Great *Albion*'s Name;
Great *Albion*'s Name shall be
The Theme of Fame, shall be great *Albion*'s Name,
Great *Albion*'s Name, Great *Albion*'s Name.
Record the Garters glory:
A Badge for *Hero's,* and for Kings to bear:
For Kings to bear!
10 And swell th' Immortal Story,
With Songs of Gods, and fit for Gods to hear;
And swell th' Immortal Story,
With Songs of Gods, and fit for Gods to hear;
For Gods to hear.

A full Chorus of all the Voices and Instruments:
Trumpets and Ho-Boys make Returnello's of all
Fame *sings; and Twenty four Dancers joyn all the*
time in a Chorus, and Dance to the end of the Opera.
                                        [*Exeunt.*

---

1   *Renown*] F2; Renown F1, Q, F3, D.   2   resounding] F2; ∼ : F1, Q, F3, D.
8   *Hero's*] Hero's F1, Q, F3, D; *omitted from F2.*
14+   *s.d.* Opera.] F3, D; Opera. / *FINIS.* F1, Q (FINIS Q); *FINIS.* F2.
14+   *s.d.* [*Exeunt.*] *omitted from F1–3, Q, D.*

EPILOGUE
To the OPERA.

AFTER *our Æsop's Fable shown to day,*
I come to give the Moral of the Play.
Feign'd Zeal, you saw, set out the speedier pace;
But, *the last heat,* Plain Dealing *won the Race:*
Plain Dealing *for a Jewel has been known;*
But ne'er till now the Jewel of a Crown.
When Heav'n made Man, to show the work Divine,
Truth was his Image, stampt upon the Coin:
And, when a King is to a God refin'd,
10   *On all he says and does, he stamps his Mind:*
This proves a Soul without allay, and pure;
Kings, like their Gold, should every touch endure.
To dare in Fields is Valour; but how few
Dare be so throughly Valiant to be true!
The Name of Great, *let other Kings affect:*
He's Great indeed, the Prince that is direct.
His Subjects know him now, and trust him more,
Than all their Kings, and all their Laws before.
What safety could their publick Acts afford?
20   *Those he can break; but cannot break his Word.*
So great a Trust to him alone was due;
Well have they trusted whom so well they knew.
The Saint, who walk'd on Waves, securely trod,
While he believ'd the beckning of his God;
But, when his Faith no longer bore him out,

OPERA] OPERA. *By Mr.* Dryden F1 *(some copies),* Q, F3; *omitted from some copies of F1 and from all copies of F2, D.*
1–2   *our . . .* [to] *. . . Play.*] *italics and romans reversed in F1; omitted from F2.*
3–15   *you . . .* [to] *. . . of*] *italics and romans reversed in F1; omitted from F2.*
14   *true!*] ~ ? F1, Q, F3, D (true F1); *omitted from F2.*
15–34   *let . . .* [to] *. . . made*] *italics and romans reversed in F1; omitted from F2.*

Began to sink, as he began to doubt.
Let us our native Character maintain,
'Tis of our growth, to be sincerely plain.
T' excel in Truth, we Loyally may strive;
30 *Set Privilege against Prerogative:*
He Plights his Faith; and we believe him just;
His Honour is to Promise, ours to Trust.
Thus Britain's *Basis on a Word is laid,*
As by a Word the World it self was made.

FINIS.

DON SEBASTIAN,
KING OF PORTUGAL

DON
SEBASTIAN,
King of Portugal :
A
TRAGEDY
Acted at the
Theatre Royal.

Written by Mr. *DRYDEN*

———*Nec tarda Senectus*
Debilitat vires animi, mutatque vigorem. Virgil.

LONDON:

Printed for *Jo. Hindmarsh*, at the *Golden Ball* in
Cornhil. M DC XC.

TITLE PAGE OF THE FIRST EDITION (MACDONALD 89A)

TO THE Right Honourable
Philip, Earl of *Leycester,* &c.

F AR be it from me, (My most Noble Lord) to think, that any thing which my meanness can produce, shou'd be worthy to be offer'd to your Patronage; or that ought which I can say of you shou'd recommend you farther, to the esteem of good men in this present Age, or to the veneration which will certainly be paid you by Posterity. On the other side, I must acknowledg it a great presumption in me, to make you this Address; and so much the greater, because by the common suffrage even of contrary parties, you have been always regarded,
10 as one of the first Persons of the Age, and yet no one Writer has dar'd to tell you so: Whether we have been all conscious to our selves that it was a needless labour to give this notice to Mankind, as all men are asham'd to tell stale news, or that we were justly diffident of our own performances, as even *Cicero* is observ'd to be in awe when he writes to *Atticus;* where knowing himself overmatch'd in good sense, and truth of knowledg, he drops the gawdy train of words, and is no longer the vainglorious Orator. From whatever reason it may be, I am the first bold offender of this kind: I have broken down the fence,
20 and ventur'd into the Holy Grove; how I may be punish'd for my profane attempt, I know not; but I wish it may not be of ill Omen to your Lordship, and that a crowd of bad Writers, do not rush into the quiet of your recesses after me. Every man in all changes of Government, which have been, or may possibly arrive, will agree, that I cou'd not have offer'd my Incense, where it cou'd be so well deserv'd. For you, My Lord, are secure in your own merit; and all Parties, as they rise uppermost, are sure to court you in their turns; 'tis a tribute which has ever been paid your vertue: The leading men still bring their bul-
30 lion to your mint, to receive the stamp of their intrinsick value,

---

Caption: *Philip,*] D; ~∧ Q1-2, F. [These sigla are identified in the textual notes, where also fluctuations in the texts cited are explained.]
22 Lordship,] ~ ; Q1-2, F, D.

that they may afterwards hope to pass with human kind. They rise and fall in the variety of Revolutions; and are sometimes great, and therefore wise in mens opinions, who must court them for their interest: But the reputation of their parts most commonly follows their success; few of 'em are wise, but as they are in power: Because indeed, they have no sphere of their own, but like the Moon in the *Copernican* Systeme of the World, are whirl'd about by the motion of a greater Planet. This it is to be ever busie; neither to give rest to their Fellow creatures, nor,
10 which is more wretchedly ridiculous, to themselves: Tho truly, the latter is a kind of justice, and giving Mankind a due revenge, that they will not permit their own hearts to be at quiet, who disturb the repose of all beside them. Ambitious Meteors! how willing they are to set themselves upon the Wing; and taking every occasion of drawing upward to the Sun: Not considering that they have no more time allow'd them for their mounting, than the short revolution of a day: and that when the light goes from them, they are of necessity to fall. How much happier is he, (and who he is I need not say,
20 for there is but one Phœnix in an Age,) who centring on himself, remains immovable, and smiles at the madness of the dance about him. He possesses the midst, which is the portion of safety and content: He will not be higher, because he needs it not; but by the prudence of that choice, he puts it out of Fortunes power to throw him down. 'Tis confest, that if he had not so been born, he might have been too high for happiness; but not endeavoring to ascend, he secures the native height of his station from envy; and cannot descend from what he is, because he depends not on another. What a glorious Character
30 was this once in *Rome;* I shou'd say in *Athens,* when in the disturbances of a State as mad as ours, the wise *Pomponius* transported all the remaining wisdom and vertue of his Country, into the Sanctuary of Peace and Learning. But, I wou'd ask the World, (for you, My Lord, are too nearly concern'd to judge this Cause) whether there may not yet be found,

---

7 *Copernican*] D; Copernican Q1-2, F.

a Character of a Noble *Englishman,* equally shining with that
illustrious *Roman?* Whether I need to name a second *Atticus;*
or whether the World has not already prevented me, and fix'd
it there without my naming? Not a second with a *longo sed
proximus intervallo;* not a Young *Marcellus,* flatter'd by a Poet,
into a resemblance of the first, with a *frons læta parum, &
dejecto lumina vultu,* and the rest that follows, *si qua fata
aspera rumpas Tu Marcellus eris:* But a Person of the same
stamp and magnitude; who owes nothing to the former, besides
10 the Word *Roman,* and the Superstition of reverence, devolving
on him by the precedency of eighteen hundred years: One who
walks by him with equal paces, and shares the eyes of beholders
with him: One, who had been first, had he first liv'd; and in
spight of doating veneration is still his equal: Both of them
born of Noble Families in unhappy Ages, of change and tumult; both of them retiring from Affairs of State: Yet, not
leaving the Common-wealth, till it had left it self; but never
returning to publick business, when they had once quitted it;
tho courted by the Heads of either Party. But who wou'd trust
20 the quiet of their lives, with the extravagancies of their Countrymen, when they were just in the giddiness of their turning;
when the ground was tottering under them at every moment;
and none cou'd guess whether the next heave of the Earthquake, wou'd settle them on the first Foundation, or swallow it?
Both of them knew Mankind exactly well; for both of them
began that study in themselves; and there they found the best
part of humane composition: the worst they learn'd by long
experience of the folly, ignorance, and immorality of most
beside them. Their Philosophy on both sides, was not wholly
30 speculative, for that is barren, and produces nothing but vain
Ideas of things which cannot possibly be known; or if they
cou'd, yet wou'd only terminate in the understanding; but it
was a noble, vigorous, and practical Philosophy, which exerted
it self in all the offices of pity, to those who were unfortunate,

1 *Englishman*] Englishman Q1-2, F; *English* Man D.
4 naming?] ~ . Q1-2, F, D. 5 *intervallo;*] F; ~ , Q1-2, D.
11 years:] ~ . Q1-2, F, D. 14 equal:] F; ~ . Q1, D; ~ , Q2.
27 composition:] ~ , Q1-2, F, D.

and deserv'd not so to be. The Friend was always more consider'd by them than the cause: And an *Octavius,* or an *Anthony* in distress, were reliev'd by them, as well as a *Brutus* or a *Cassius;* For the lowermost party, to a noble mind, is ever the fittest object of good will. The eldest of them, I will suppose for his honour, to have been of the Academick Sect, neither Dogmatist nor Stoick; if he were not, I am sure he ought in common justice, to yield the precedency to his younger Brother. For stiffness of Opinion is the effect of Pride, and not of Philosophy: 'Tis a
10 miserable Presumption of that knowledg which humane Nature is too narrow to contain. And the ruggedness of a Stoick is only a silly affectation of being a God: To wind himself up by Pulleys, to an insensibility of suffering; and at the same time to give the lye to his own Experience, by saying he suffers not what he knows he feels. True Philosophy is certainly of a more pliant Nature, and more accommodated to human use; *Homo sum, humani à me nihil alienum puto.* A wise man will never attempt an impossibility; and such it is to strain himself beyond the nature of his Being; either to become a Deity, by being
20 above suffering, or to debase himself into a Stock or Stone, by pretending not to feel it. To find in our selves the Weaknesses and Imperfections of our wretched Kind, is surely the most reasonable step we can make towards the Compassion of our fellow Creatures. I cou'd give Examples of this kind in the second *Atticus.* In every turn of State, without meddling on either side, he has always been favorable and assisting to opprest Merit. The Praises which were given by a great Poet to the late Queen Mother on her rebuilding *Somerset Palace,* one part of which was fronting to the mean Houses on the other side
30 of the Water, are as justly his:

> *For, the distrest, and the afflicted lye*
> *Most in his Thoughts, and always in his Eye.*

Neither has he so far forgotten a poor Inhabitant of his Suburbs, whose best prospect is on the Garden of *Leicester-House;*

---

3 *Cassius;*] F; ~ . Q1-2, D.   4 party,] D; ~∧ Q1-2, F.
14 not] F; ~ , Q1-2, D.   15 True] D; ~ , Q1-2, F.

but that more than once he has been offering him his Patronage, to reconcile him to a World, of which his Misfortunes have
made him weary. There is another *Sidney* still remaining, tho
there can never be another *Spencer* to deserve the Favor. But
one *Sidney* gave his Patronage to the applications of a Poet; the
other offer'd it unask'd. Thus, whether as a second *Atticus,*
or a second Sir *Philip Sidney,* the latter, in all respects, will not
have the worse of the comparison; and if he will take up with
the second place, the World will not so far flatter his Modesty,
10 as to seat him there, unless it be out of a deference of Manners,
that he may place himself where he pleases at his own Table.

I may therefore safely conclude, that he, who by the consent of all men, bears so eminent a Character, will out of his
inborn Nobleness, forgive the Presumption of this Address.
'Tis an unfinish'd Picture, I confess, but the Lines and Features
are so like, that it cannot be mistaken for any other; and without writing any name under it, every beholder must cry out,
at the first sight, *this was design'd for Atticus; but the bad Artist, has cast too much of him into shades.* But I have this Ex-
20 cuse, that even the greater Masters commonly fall short of the
best Faces. They may flatter an indifferent Beauty; but the
excellencies of Nature, can have no right done to them: For
there both the Pencil and the Pen are overcome by the Dignity
of the Subject; as our admirable *Waller* has express'd it,

The Hero's Race transcends the Poet's Thought.

There are few in any Age who can bear the load of a Dedication; for where Praise is undeserv'd, 'tis Satyr: Tho Satyr on
Folly is now no longer a Scandal to any one Person, where a
whole Age is dipt together; yet I had rather undertake a Multi-
30 tude one way, than a single *Atticus* the other; for 'tis easier to
descend, than 'tis to climb. I shou'd have gone asham'd out of
the World, if I had not at least attempted this Address, which I
have long thought owing: And if I had never attempted, I

18–19 *this . . . [to] . . . shades] except for "Atticus", in romans in Q1-2, F, D.*
24 *it,] ∼ ; Q1-2; ∼ : F; ∼ . D.*   30 *Atticus] Q2, F, D; Aiticus Q1.*

might have been vain enough to think I might have succeeded in it: now I have made the Experiment, and have fail'd, through my Unworthiness, I may rest satisfi'd, that either the Adventure is not to be atchiev'd, or that it is reserv'd for some other hand.

Be pleas'd therefore, since the Family of the *Attici* is and ought to be above the common Forms of concluding Letters, that I may take my leave in the Words of *Cicero* to the first of them: *Me, O Pomponi, valdè pœnitet vivere: tantùm te oro, ut* 10 *quoniam me ipse semper amâsti, ut eodem amore sis; ego nimirum, idem sum. Inimici mei mea mihi non meipsum ademerunt. Cura, Attice, ut valeas.*

Dabam Cal.
Jan. 1690.

---

3 Unworthiness,] F, D; ~ . Q1-2.

THE PREFACE.

WHETHER *it happen'd through a long disuse of Writing,
that I forgot the usual compass of a Play; or that by
crowding it, with Characters and Incidents, I put a
necessity upon my self of lengthning the main Action, I know
not; but the first days Audience sufficiently convinc'd me of my
error; and that the Poem was insupportably too long. 'Tis an ill
ambition of us Poets, to please an Audience with more than
they can bear: And, supposing that we wrote as well, as vainly
we imagin our selves to write; yet we ought to consider, that no*
10 *man can bear to be long tickled. There is a nauseousness in a
City feast when we are to sit four hours after we are cloy'd. I
am, therefore, in the first place, to acknowledg with all manner
of gratitude, their civility; who were pleas'd to endure it with
so much patience, to be weary with so much good nature and
silence, and not to explode an entertainment, which was
design'd to please them; or discourage an Author, whose misfortunes have once more brought him against his will, upon the
Stage. While I continue in these bad circumstances, (and truly
I see very little probability of coming out:) I must be oblig'd to*
20 *write, and if I may still hope for the same kind usage, I shall
the less repent of that hard necessity. I write not this out of any
expectation to be pityed, for I have Enemies enow to wish me
yet in a worse condition; but give me leave to say, that if I can
please by writing, as I shall endeavour it, the Town may be
somewhat oblig'd to my misfortunes, for a part of their diversion. Having been longer acquainted with the Stage, than any
Poet now living, and having observ'd how difficult it was to
please, that the humours of Comedy were almost spent, that
Love and Honour (the mistaken Topicks of Tragedy) were*
30 *quite worn out, that the Theaters cou'd not support their
charges, that the Audience forsook them, that young men with-*

---

4 *lengthning*] D; *lenghthning* Q1-2; *lengthening* F.
22 *pityed,*] ~ ; Q1-2, F, D.   28 *please,*] ~ ; Q1-2, F, D.

out Learning set up for Judges, and that they talk'd loudest,
who understood the least: all these discouragements had not
only wean'd me from the Stage, but had also given me a loathing
of it. But enough of this: the difficulties continue; they increase,
and I am still condemn'd to dig in those exhausted Mines.
Whatever fault I next commit, rest assur'd it shall not be that
of too much length: Above twelve hunder'd lines have been cut
off from this Tragedy, since it was first deliver'd to the Actors.
They were indeed so judiciously lopt by Mr. Betterton, *to*
10 *whose care and excellent action, I am equally oblig'd, that the*
connexion of the story was not lost; but on the other side, it was
impossible to prevent some part of the action from being pre-
cipitated, and coming on without that due preparation, which
is requir'd to all great events: as in particular, that of raising
the Mobile, in the beginning of the Fourth Act; which a Man
of Benducar's *cool Character, cou'd not naturally attempt, with-*
out taking all those precautions, which he foresaw wou'd be
necessary to render his design successful. On this consideration,
I have replac'd those lines, through the whole Poem; and
20 *thereby restor'd it, to that clearness of conception, and (if I may*
dare to say it) that lustre, and masculine vigour, in which it was
first written. 'Tis obvious to every understanding Reader, that
the most poetical parts, which are Descriptions, Images, Simili-
tudes, and Moral Sentences; are those, which of necessity were
to be par'd away, when the body was swoln into too large a
bulk for the representation of the Stage. But there is a vast
difference betwixt a publick entertainment on the Theatre, and
a private reading in the Closet: In the first we are confin'd to
time, and though we talk not by the hour-glass, yet the Watch
30 *often drawn out of the pocket, warns the Actors, that their Audi-*
ence is weary; in the last, every Reader is judge of his own con-
venience; he can take up the book, and lay it down at his
pleasure; and find out those beauties of propriety, in thought
and writing, which escap'd him in the tumult and hurry of
representing. And I dare boldly promise for this Play, that in
the roughness of the numbers and cadences, (which I assure
was not casual, but so design'd) you will see somewhat more

masterly arising to your view, than in most, if not any of my former Tragedies. There is a more noble daring in the Figures and more suitable to the loftiness of the Subject; and besides this some newnesses of English, *translated from the Beauties of Modern Tongues, as well as from the elegancies of the* Latin; *and here and there some old words are sprinkled, which for their significance and sound, deserv'd not to be antiquated; such as we often find in* Salust *amongst the* Roman *Authors, and in* Milton's Paradise *amongst ours; though perhaps the* 10 *latter instead of sprinkling, has dealt them with too free a hand, even sometimes to the obscuring of his sense.*

As for the story or plot of the Tragedy, 'tis purely fiction; for I take it up where the History has laid it down. We are assur'd by all Writers of those times, that Sebastian, *a young Prince of great courage and expectation, undertook that War partly upon a religious account, partly at the sollicitation of* Muley-Mahumet, *who had been driven out of his Dominions, by* Abdelmelech, *or as others call him,* Muley-Moluch, *his nigh Kinsman, who descended from the same Family of the* Xeriff's; *whose Fathers* 20 Hamet *and* Mahomet *had conquer'd that Empire with joint Forces; and shar'd it betwixt them after their victory: That the body of Don* Sebastian *was never found in the Field of Battel; which gave occasion for many to believe, that he was not slain: that some years after, when the* Spaniards *with a pretended title, by force of Arms had Usurp'd the Crown of* Portugal, *from the House of* Braganza, *a certain Person who call'd himself Don* Sebastian, *and had all the marks of his body and features of his face, appear'd at* Venice, *where he was own'd by some of his Country-men; but being seiz'd by the* Spaniards *was first Im-* 30 *prison'd, then sent to the Gallies, and at last put to Death in private. 'Tis most certain, that the* Portugueses *expected his*

---

5 Latin] D; *Latin* Q1–2, F.
8 Salust] D; *Salust* Q1–2, F.   8 Roman] F, D; *Roman* Q1–2.
9 Paradise] *Paradise* Q1–2, F, D.   14 Sebastian,] F; ~∧ Q1–2, D.
18 *him,*] D; ~∧ Q1–2, F.
18 Muley-Moluch,] Muley-Moluch∧ Q1–2, F, D.
22 *Don*] Don Q1–2, F, D.   23 *slain:*] ~ ; Q1–2, F, D.
26 *Don*] Don Q1–2, F, D.

*return for almost an Age together after that Battel; which is at
least a proof of their extream love to his Memory; and the usage
which they had from their new Conquerors, might possibly
make them so extravagant in their hopes and wishes for their
old Master.*

   *This ground-work the History afforded me, and I desire no
better to build a Play upon it: For where the event of a great
action is left doubtful, there the Poet is left Master: He may
raise what he pleases on that foundation, provided he makes it*
10 *of a piece, and according to the rule of probability. From hence
I was only oblig'd, that* Sebastian *shou'd return to* Portugal *no
more; but at the same time I had him at my own disposal,
whether to bestow him in* Affrick, *or in any other corner of the
World, or to have clos'd the Tragedy with his death; and the
last of these was certainly the most easie, but for the same
reason, the least artful; because as I have somewhere said, the
poyson and the dagger are still at hand, to butcher a Heroe,
when a Poet wants the brains to save him. It being therefore
only necessary according to the Laws of the* Drama, *that*
20 Sebastian *shou'd no more be seen upon the Throne, I leave it
for the World to judge, whether or no I have disposed of him
according to art, or have bungled up the conclusion of his
adventure. In the drawing of his character I forgot not piety,
which any one may observe to be one principal ingredient of it;
even so far as to be a habit in him; though I show him once
to be transported from it by the violence of a sudden passion, to
endeavor a self-murther. This being presuppos'd, that he was
Religious, the horror of his incest, tho innocently committed,
was the best reason which the Stage cou'd give for hind'ring his*
30 *return. 'Tis true I have no right to blast his Memory, with such
a crime: but declaring it to be fiction, I desire my Audience to
think it no longer true, than while they are seeing it represented: For that once ended, he may be a Saint for ought I
know; and we have reason to presume he is. On this supposition, it was unreasonable to have kill'd him; for the Learned*

---

6 *ground-work*] F, D; *ground work* Q1–2.
27 *self-murther*] F, D; *self murther* Q1–2.

Mr. Rymer *has well observ'd, that in all punishments we are to regulate our selves by Poetical justice; and according to those measures an involuntary sin deserves not death; from whence it follows, that to divorce himself from the beloved object, to retire into a desart, and deprive himself of a Throne, was the utmost punishment, which a Poet cou'd inflict, as it was also the utmost reparation, which* Sebastian *cou'd make. For what relates to* Almeyda, *her part is wholly fictitious: I know it is the surname of a noble Family in* Portugal, *which was very instru-* mental in the Restoration of Don John de Braganza, *Father to the most Illustrious and most Pious Princess, our Queen* Dowager. *The* French *Author of a Novel, call'd* Don Sebastian, *has given that name to an* Affrican *Lady of his own invention, and makes her Sister to* Muley-Mahumet. *But I have wholly chang'd the accidents, and borrow'd nothing but the supposition, that she was belov'd by the King of* Portugal. *Tho, if I had taken the whole story, and wrought it up into a Play, I might have done it exactly according to the practice of almost all the Ancients; who were never accus'd of being Plagiaries, for build-* ing their Tragedies on known Fables. Thus *Augustus* Cæsar *wrote an* Ajax, *which was not the less his own, because* Euripides *had written a Play before him on that Subject. Thus of late years* Corneille *writ an* Oedipus *after* Sophocles; *and I have design'd one after him, which I wrote with Mr.* Lee, *yet neither the* French *Poet stole from the* Greek, *nor we from the* Frenchman. *'Tis the contrivance, the new turn, and new characters, which alter the property and make it ours. The* Materia Poetica *is as common to all Writers, as the* Materia Medica *to all Physicians. Thus in our* Chronicles, Daniels *History is still* his own, though *Matthew Paris, Stow and Hollingshed writ before him; otherwise we must have been content with their dull relations, if a better Pen had not been allow'd to come after them, and write his own account after a new and better manner.*

I must farther declare freely, that I have not exactly kept to

---

the three Mechanick rules of unity: I knew them and had
them in my eye, but follow'd them only at a distance; for the
Genius of the English *cannot bear too regular a Play; we are*
given to variety, even to a debauchery of Pleasure. My Scenes
are therefore sometimes broken, because my Under-plot re-
quir'd them so to be; though the General Scene remains of the
same Castle; and I have taken the time of two days, because the
variety of accidents, which are here represented, cou'd not
naturally be suppos'd to arrive in one: But to gain a greater
10 *Beauty, 'tis lawful for a Poet to supersede a less.*

   I must likewise own, that I have somewhat deviated from the
known History, in the death of Muley-Moluch, *who, by all*
relations dyed of a feaver in the Battel, before his Army had
wholly won the Field; but if I have allow'd him another day of
life, it was because I stood in need of so shining a Character of
brutality, as I have given him; which is indeed the same, with
that of the present Emperor Muley-Ishmael, *as some of our*
English *Officers, who have been in his Court, have credibly*
inform'd me.

20   *I have been listning what objections had been made, against*
the conduct of the Play, but found them all so trivial, that if I
shou'd name them, a true critick wou'd imagin that I play'd
booty, and only rais'd up fantoms for my self to conquer. Some
are pleas'd to say the Writing is dull; but ætatem habet de se
loquatur: *Others that the double poyson is unnatural; let the*
common received opinion, and Ausonius *his famous Epigram*
answer that. Lastly a more ignorant sort of Creatures than either
of the former, maintain that the Character of Dorax, *is not only*
unnatural, but inconsistent with it self; let them read the Play
30 *and think again, and if yet they are not satisfied, cast their eyes*
on that Chapter of the Wise Montaigne, *which is intituled* de
l'Inconstance des actions humaines. *A longer reply, is what*
those Cavillers deserve not; but I will give them and their
fellows to understand, that the Earl of Dorset, *was pleas'd to*
read the Tragedy twice over before it was Acted; and did me

17   Muley-Ishmael] Q2, F, D; Muley Ishmael Q1.
25   loquatur:] ∼ . Q1–2, F, D.

the favour to send me word, that I had written beyond any of my former Plays; and that he was displeas'd any thing shou'd be cut away. If I have not reason to prefer his single judgment to a whole Faction, let the World be judge; for the opposition is the same with that of Lucan's *Heroe against an* Army; concurrere bellum, atque virum. *I think I may modestly conclude, that whatever errors there may be, either in the design, or writing of this Play, they are not those which have been objected to it. I think also, that I am not yet arriv'd to the Age* 10 *of doating; and that I have given so much application to this Poem, that I cou'd not probably let it run into many gross absurdities; which may caution my Enemies from too rash a censure; and may also encourage my friends, who are many more than I cou'd reasonably have expected, to believe their kindness has not been very undeservedly bestowed on me. This is not a Play that was huddled up in hast; and to shew it was not, I will own, that beside the general Moral of it, which is given in the four last lines, there is also another Moral, couch'd under every one of the principal Parts and Characters, which a* 20 *judicious Critick will observe, though I point not to it in this Preface. And there may be also some secret Beauties in the decorum of parts, and uniformity of design, which my puny judges will not easily find out; let them consider in the last Scene of the fourth Act, whether I have not preserv'd the rule of decency, in giving all the advantage to the Royal Character; and in making* Dorax *first submit: Perhaps too they may have thought, that it was through indigence of Characters, that I have given the same to* Sebastian *and* Almeyda; *and consequently made them alike in all things but their Sex. But let* 30 *them look a little deeper into the matter, and they will find that this identity of Character in the greatness of their Souls was intended for a preparation of the final discovery, and that the likeness of their nature, was a fair hint to the proximity of their blood.*

To avoid the imputation of too much vanity (for all Writers, and especially Poets, will have some) I will give but one other

---

31   *Souls*] ∼ ; Q1–2, F; ∼ , D.   36   *Poets,*] F; ∼∧ Q1–2, D.

instance, in relation to the Uniformity of the design. I have observ'd, that the English *will not bear a thorough Tragedy; but are pleas'd, that it shou'd be lightned with underparts of mirth. It had been easie for me to have given my Audience a better course of Comedy, I mean a more diverting, than that of* Antonio *and* Morayma. *But I dare appeal even to my Enemies, if I or any man cou'd have invented one, which had been more of a piece, and more depending, on the serious part of the design: for what cou'd be more uniform, than to draw from*
10 *out of the members of a Captive Court, the Subject of a Comical entertainment? To prepare this Episode, you see* Dorax *giving the Character of* Antonio, *in the beginning of the Play, upon his first sight of him at the Lottery; and to make the dependence,* Antonio *is ingag'd in the Fourth Act, for the deliverance of* Almeyda; *which is also prepar'd, by his being first made a Slave to the Captain of the Rabble.*

I shou'd beg pardon for these instances; but perhaps they may be of use to future Poets, in the conduct of their Plays: At least if I appear too positive; I am growing old, and thereby,
20 *in possession of some experience, which men in years will always assume for a right of talking. Certainly, if a Man can ever have reason to set a value on himself, 'tis when his ungenerous Enemies are taking the advantage of the Times upon him, to ruin him in his reputation. And therefore for once, I will make bold to take the Counsel of my Old Master* Virgil.

Tu, ne cede malis; sed, contrà, audentior ito.

---

9 *design:*] F; ∼ . Q1–2, D.   9 *for*] *For* Q1–2, F, D.

PROLOGUE TO *Don Sebastian, King of Portugal.*

Spoken by a Woman.

THE *Judge remov'd, tho he's no more My Lord,*
 May plead at Bar, or at the Council-Board:
 So may cast Poets write; there's no Pretension,
To argue loss of Wit from loss of Pension.
Your looks are cheerful; and in all this place
I see not one, that wears a damning face.
The British *Nation, is too brave to show,*
Ignoble vengeance, on a vanquish'd foe.
At least be civil to the Wretch imploring;
10 *And lay your Paws upon him, without roaring:*
Suppose our Poet was your foe before;
Yet now, the bus'ness of the Field is o'er;
'Tis time to let your Civil Wars alone,
When Troops are into Winter-quarters gone.
Jove *was alike to* Latian *and to* Phrygian;
And you well know, a Play's of no Religion.
Take good advice, and please your selves this day;
No matter from what hands you have the Play.
Among good Fellows ev'ry health will pass,
20 *That serves to carry round another glass:*
When, with full bowls of Burgundy *you dine,* ⎫
Tho at the Mighty Monarch you repine, ⎬
You grant him still most Christian, in his Wine. ⎭
 Thus far the Poet, but his brains grow Addle;
And all the rest is purely from this Noddle.
You've seen young Ladies at the Senate door,
Prefer Petitions, and your grace implore;
However grave the Legislators were,

Caption: *Don Sebastian, King of*] F (SEBASTIAN_∧); DON SEBASTIAN_∧ King of Q1–2; *omitted from* D.
8   *foe.*] D; ~ , Q1–2; ~ ; F.   22   *Monarch*] Q2, F, D; Monarch Q1.
28   *However*] Q2, F, D; *How ever* Q1.   28   *were,*] F, D; ~ . Q1–2.

Their Cause went ne'er the worse for being fair.
30   *Reasons as weak as theirs, perhaps I bring;*
But I cou'd bribe you, with as good a thing.
I heard him make advances of good Nature;
That he for once, wou'd sheath his cutting Satyr:
Sign but his Peace, he vows he'll ne'er again
The sacred Names of Fops and Beaus profane.
Strike up the Bargain quickly; for I swear,
As Times go now, he offers very fair.
Be not too hard on him, with Statutes neither;   ⎫
Be kind; and do not set your Teeth together,   ⎬
40   *To stretch the Laws, as Coblers do their Leather.* ⎭
Horses, by Papists are not to be ridden;
But sure the Muses Horse was ne'er forbidden:
For in no Rate-Book, it was ever found
That Pegasus *was valued at Five-pound:*
Fine him to daily Drudging and Inditing;
And let him pay his Taxes out, in Writing.

---

29   *fair.*] F, D; ∼ , Q1–2.
38   *neither;*] ∼ , Q1–2, F, D.   42   *Muses*] Q2, F, D; Muses Q1.
42   *forbidden:*] ∼ . Q1–2, F, D.

PROLOGUE,

*Sent to the Authour by an unknown hand,
and propos'd to be spoken
By Mrs.* Montfort *drest like an Officer.*

BRIGHT *Beauties who in awfull Circle sit,
And you grave Synod of the dreadfull Pit,
And you the Upper-tire of pop-gun wit,*

*Pray ease me of my wonder if you may:
Is all this Crowd barely to see the play,
Or is't the Poets Execution day?*

*His breath is in your hands I will presume,
But I advise you to deferr his doom,
Till you have got a better in his room;*

10 *And don't maliciously combine together,
As if in spight and spleen you were come hither,
For he has kept the Pen tho' lost the feather.*

*And on my Honour, Ladies, I avow,
This Play was writ in Charity to you:
For such a dearth of Wit who ever knew?*

*Sure 'tis a Judgment on this Sinfull Nation
For the abuse of so great Dispensation:
And therefore I resolv'd to change Vocation.*

Caption: PROLOGUE,] D; ~ . Q1-2; *entire prologue omitted from F.*
Caption: Montfort] Monford Q1; Montford Q2, D.
3 *wit,*] D; ~ . Q1-2.   4 *may:*] D; ~∧ Q1-2.
7 *presume,*] D; ~∧ Q1-2.
8 *doom,*] D; ~ : Q1-2.   9 *room;*] D; ~ . Q1-2.
13 *Honour, Ladies,*] D; ~∧ ~∧ Q1-2.
14 *you:*] D; ~ , Q1-2.
15 *who ever*] D; *whoever* Q1-2.

For want of Petty-coat I've put on buff,
20 To try what may be got by lying rough:
How think you Sirs, is it not well enough?

Of Bully Criticks I a Troup wou'd lead;
But one reply'd, thank you there's no such need,
I at Groom-Porters, Sir, can safer bleed.

Another who the name of danger loaths,
Vow'd he would go, and swore me Forty Oaths,
But that his Horses were in body-cloaths.

A third cry'd, Dam my bloud, I'd be content
To push my Fortune, if the Parliament
30 Would but recall Claret from Banishment.

A Fourth (and I have done) made this excuse,
I'd draw my Sword in Ireland, Sir, to chuse:
Had not their Women gouty leggs and wore no shoes.

Well, I may march, thought I, and fight and trudge,
But of these blades, the Devill a man will budge;
They there would fight e'n just as here they judge.

Here they will pay for leave to find a fault,
But when their Honour calls they can't be bought;
Honour in danger, bloud, and wounds is sought.

23–24 thank . . . [*romans*] . . . at] *thank . . . [italics] . . . at* Q1–2, D.
24 Groom-Porters, Sir,] *Groom-Porters*₍ₐ₎ *Sir*₍ₐ₎ Q1–2; *Groom-Porter's, Sir,* D.
24 can safer bleed] *can safer bleed* Q1–2, D.
28 Dam my bloud, I'd] *Dammy bloud, I'de* Q1; *Dam my bloud, I'd* Q2, D.
28–30 be . . . [*romans*] . . . Banishment] *be . . . [italics] . . . Banishment* Q1–2, D.
31 *excuse,*] D; ~₍ₐ₎ Q1–2.
32 I'd . . . [*romans*] . . . in] *I'de . . . [italics] . . . in* Q1–2, D (*I'd* D).
32 Ireland,] D; ~₍ₐ₎ Q1–2.
32–33 Sir, . . . [*romans*] . . . shoes.] *Sir*₍ₐ₎ . . . *[italics] . . . shoes?* Q1–2, D (*Sir*, D; *shoes:* Q2; *shoes.* D).
34 *march, . . . I,*] D; ~₍ₐ₎ . . . ~₍ₐ₎ Q1–2.   35 *blades,*] ~₍ₐ₎ Q1–2, D.
35 *budge;*] D; ~ , Q1–2.   38 *bought;*] D; ~ , Q1–2.
39 *bloud,*] ~₍ₐ₎ Q1–2, D.

40   *Lost Virtue whither fled, or where's thy dwelling,*
Who can reveal? at least 'tis past my telling,
Unless thou art Embarkt for Iniskelling.

On Carrion tits those Sparks denounce their rage,
In boot of wisp and Leinster *freese ingage:*
What would you do in such an Equipage?

The Siege of Derry *does you Gallants threaten:*
Not out of Errant shame of being beaten,
As fear of wanting meat or being eaten.

Were Wit, like honour, to be won by fighting,
50   *How few just Judges would there be of writing!*
Then you would leave this Villanous back-biting.

Your Talents lye how to express your spight,
But where is he knows how to praise aright?
You praise like Cowards but like Criticks fight.

Ladies be wise, and wean these yearling Calves
Who in your Service too are meer faux-braves,
They Judge and write and fight, and⸺⸺Love by halves.

---

40   whither] D; *whether* Q1–2.   41   *reveal?*] D; ~ , Q1–2.
43   *rage,*] D; ~∧ Q1–2.   44   Leinster] D; *Leinster* Q1–2.
44   *ingage:*] D; ~ , Q1–2.
49   *Wit, . . . honour, . . . fighting,*] D (*Wit*∧); ~∧ . . . ~∧ . . . ~∧ Q1–2.
50   *writing!*] ~ , Q1–2, D.   53   *aright?*] D; ~ , Q1–2.

Don Sebastian, King of Portugal.
A Tragedy.

Persons Represented.

1 Don *Sebastian*, King of *Portugal*,————By Mr. *Williams.*
2 *Muley-Moluch*, Emperor of *Barbary*,——Mr. *Kynaston.*
3 *Dorax*, a Noble *Portuguese*, now a Renegade, formerly
   Don *Alonzo de Sylvera*, Alcalde, or Governor of *Alcazar*,
   ————————————————————————————Mr. *Betterton.*
4 *Benducar*, Chief Minister and Favourite to the Emperor,
   ————————————————————————————Mr. *Sandford.*
5 The *Mufti, Abdalla*,————————————Mr. *Underhill.*
6 *Muley-Zeydan*, Brother to the Emperor,—Mr. *Powell*, Jun.
7 Don *Antonio*, a young, noble, amorous *Portuguese*, now
   a Slave,————————————————————Mr. *Montfort.*
8 Don *Alvarez*, an old Counsellor to Don *Sebastian*, now a
   Slave also,————————————————Mr. *Boweman.*
9 *Mustapha*, Captain of the Rabble,————Mr. *Leigh.*
10 *Almeyda*, a Captive Queen of *Barbary*,————Mrs. *Barry.*
11 *Morayma*, Daughter to the *Mufti*,————Mrs. *Montfort.*
12 *Johayma*, Chief Wife to the *Mufti*,————Mrs. *Leigh.*
   Two Merchants.
   Rabble.
   A Servant to *Benducar.*
   A Servant to the *Mufti.*

Sebastian,] ∼∧ Q1–2; *omitted from* F, D.
Sebastian,] D; Sebastian∧ Q1–2, F (Sebastian Q2).
Portugal] D; Portugal Q1–2, F.
Muley-Moluch,] D; Muley-Moluch∧ Q1–2; Muley-Moluch, F.
Barbary] D; Barbary Q1–2, F.   *Dorax*] D; Dorax Q1–2, F.
Portuguese,] D; Portuguese∧ Q1–2; Portuguese, F.
Alonzo de Sylvera,] D; Alonzo de Sylvera∧ Q1–2, F.
Alcazar] D; Alcazar Q1–2, F.   *Benducar*] D; Benducar Q1–2, F.
Mufti,] Mufti∧ Q1–2, F, D.   *Abdalla*] D; Abdalla Q1–2, F.
Muley-Zeydan,] D; Muley-Zeydan∧ Q1–2; Muley-Zeydan, F.
Antonio] D; Antonio Q1–2, F.   young, noble,] D; Young∧ Noble∧ Q1–2, F.
Portuguese] D; Portuguese Q1–2, F.
Montfort] Betterton Q1; Montford Q2, F, D.
Alvarez] D; Alvarez Q1–2, F.   *Sebastian*] D; Sebastian Q1–2, F.
Mustapha,] D; Mustapha∧ Q1–2; Mustapha, F.   Rabble,] Q2, F; ∼ . Q1, D.
Almeyda,] D; Almeyda∧ Q1–2; Almeyda, F.   *Barbary*] D; Barbary Q1–2, F.

Scene in the Castle of *Alcazar.*

Morayma] D; Morayma Q1–2, F.
Johayma] D; Johayma Q1–2, F.
Benducar] D; Benducar Q1–2, F.
Alcazar] D; Alcazar Q1–2, F.

Mufti] D; Mufti Q1–2, F.
Mufti] D; Mufti Q1–2, F.
Mufti] D; Mufti Q1–2, F.

DON SEBASTIAN,
KING OF PORTUGAL.

ACT I. SCENE I.

The Scene at Alcazar, *representing a Market-Place
under the Castle.*

Enter Muley-Zeydan, Benducar.

Muly-Zeyd. Now *Affrica*'s long Wars are at an end,
And our parch'd earth is drench'd in Christian Blood,
My conquering Brother will have Slaves enow,
To pay his cruel Vows for Victory.
What hear you of *Sebastian,* King of *Portugal?*
    Benducar. He fell among a heap of slaughter'd *Moors;*
Though yet his mangled Carcase is not found.
The Rival of our threatned Empire, *Mahumet,*
Was hot pursued; and in the general rout,
10 Mistook a swelling Current for a Foord;
And in *Mucazer's* Flood was seen to rise;
Thrice was he seen; at length his Courser plung'd,
And threw him off; the Waves whelm'd over him,
And helpless in his heavy arms he drownd.
    Mul. Zeyd. Thus, then, a doubtful Title is extinguish'd:
Thus, *Moluch,* still the Favorite of Fate,
Swims in a sanguine torrent to the Throne;

ACT I. SCENE I.] Q2, F, D; Aᴄᴛ I. Sᴄᴇɴᴇ I. Q1.
s.d. Enter Muley-Zeydan, Benducar] D; *Muley-Zeydan, Benducar* Q1-2, F.
1 end,] D; ∼ ; Q1-2, F.   6 *Moors*] D; Moors Q1-2, F.
17 Throne;] ∼ . Q1-2, F; ∼ : D.

As if our Prophet only work'd for him:
The Heavens and all the Stars are his hir'd Servants,
20 As *Muley-Zeydan* were not worth their care,
And younger Brothers but the draff of Nature.
    Bend. Be still, and learn the soothing Arts of Court;
Adore his fortune, mix with flattering Crowds,
And when they praise him most, be you the loudest;
Your Brother is luxurious, close, and cruel,
Generous by fits, but permanent in mischief.
The shadow of a discontent wou'd ruin us;
We must be safe before we can be great:
These things observ'd, leave me to shape the rest.
30   *Mul. Zeyd.* You have the Key, he opens inward to you.
    Bend. So often try'd, and ever found so true,
Has given me trust, and trust has given me means
Once to be false for all. I trust not him:
For now his ends are serv'd, and he grown absolute,
How am I sure to stand who serv'd those ends?
I know your nature open, mild, and grateful;
In such a Prince the People may be blest,
And I be safe.
    Mul. Zeyd. My Father!   *[Embracing him.*
40   *Bend.* My future King! (auspicious *Muley-Zeydan:*)
Shall I adore you? No, the place is publick;
I worship you within; the outward act
Shall be reserv'd till Nations follow me,
And Heaven shall envy you the kneeling World.
You know th' Alcalde of *Alcazar, Dorax?*
    Mul. Zeyd. The gallant Renegade you mean?
    Bend.   The same:
That gloomy outside, like a rusty Chest,
Contains the shining Treasure of a Soul,
Resolv'd and brave; he has the Souldiers hearts,
50 And time shall make him ours.
    Mul. Zeyd.   He's just upon us.

---

19 Servants,] D; ∼ . Q1-2, F.   45 Alcalde] Alcald Q1; Alcade Q2, F, D.
50 *Mul. Zeyd.*] D; *Mul.* Q1-2, F.

Bend. I know him from a far, by the long stride
And by the sullen port: retire my Lord.
Wait on your Brothers Triumph, yours is next,
His growth is but a wild and fruitless Plant,
I'll cut his barren branches to the stock,
And graft you on to bear.
    Mul. Zeyd.   My Oracle!   [*Exit* Muley-Zeyd.
    Bend. Yes, to delude your hopes, poor credulous Fool,
To think that I wou'd give away the Fruit
Of so much toil, such guilt, and such damnation;
60 If I am damn'd, it shall be for my self:
This easie Fool must be my Stale, set up
To catch the Peoples eyes; he's tame and merciful,
Him I can manage, till I make him odious
By some unpopular act, and then dethrone him.

Enter Dorax.

Now *Dorax!*
    Dorax.   Well, *Benducar!*
    Bend.   Bare *Benducar!*
    Dor. Thou wouldst have Titles, take 'em then, Chief Minister,
First Hangman of the State.
    Bend.   Some call me Favourite.
    Dorax. What's that, his Minion?
Thou art too old to be a Catamite!
70 Now prithee tell me, and abate thy pride,
Is not *Benducar* Bare, a better Name
In a Friend's mouth, than all those gawdy Titles,
Which I disdain to give the Man I love?
    Bend. But always out of humor,———

51–52   *Bend.* I . . . far, by . . . stride   /   And . . . port: retire . . . Lord.]
Bend. I . . . far, / By . . . stride and . . . port: / Retire . . . Lord. Q1–2, F, D.
64+   *s.d.* Enter Dorax] D; Enter *Dorax* Q1–2, F (*s.d. at right margin*).
65   *Dorax.*] F, D (*Dor.* D); ∼ , Q1–2.
65   Well,] ∼ ∧ Q1–2, F, D.
65   *Benducar . . . Benducar*] *Bemboucar . . . Bemboucar* Q1–2, F, D.
68   *Dorax.*] F, D; ∼ , Q1–2.

Dorax.   I have cause:
Tho all mankind is cause enough for Satyr.
  Bend. Why then thou hast reveng'd thee on mankind;
They say in fight, thou hadst a thirsty Sword,
And well 'twas glutted there.
  Dorax. I spitted Frogs, I crush'd a heap of Emmets,
80 A hundred of 'em to a single Soul,
And that but scanty weight too: the great Devil
Scarce thank'd me for my pains; he swallows Vulgar
Like whip'd Cream, feels 'em not in going down.
  Bend. Brave Renegade! cou'dst thou not meet *Sebastian?*
Thy Master had been worthy of thy Sword.
  Dorax. My Master? By what title,
Because I happen'd to be born where he
Happen'd to be a King? And yet I serv'd him,
Nay, I was fool enough to love him too.
90 You know my story, how I was rewarded,
For Fifteen hard Campaigns, still hoop'd in Iron,
And why I turn'd Mahometan: I'm grateful,
But whosoever dares to injure me,
Let that man know, I dare to be reveng'd.
  Bend. Still you run off from biass; say, what moves
Your present spleen?
  Dorax.   You mark'd not what I told you:
I kill'd not one that was his Makers Image;
I met with none but vulgar two-leg'd Brutes.
Sebastian was my aim; he was a Man:
100 Nay, though he hated me, and I hate him,
Yet I must do him right; he was a Man,
Above man's height, ev'n towring to *Divinity.*
Brave, pious, generous, great, and liberal:
Just as the Scales of Heaven that weigh the Seasons,
He lov'd his People, him they idoliz'd:
And thence proceeds my mortal hatred to him,

That thus unblameable to all besides
He err'd to me alone:
His goodness was diffus'd to human kind,
110 And all his cruelty confin'd to me.
        Bend. You cou'd not meet him then?
        Dorax.   No, though I sought
Where ranks fell thickest; 'twas indeed the place
To seek *Sebastian:* through a track of Death
I follow'd him, by Groans of dying Foes,
But still I came too late, for he was flown
Like Lightning, swift before me to new Slaughters.
I mow'd across, and made irregular Harvest,
Defac'd the pomp of Battel, but in vain,
For he was still supplying Death elsewhere:
120 This mads me that perhaps ignoble hands
Have overlaid him, for they cou'd not conquer:
Murder'd by Multitudes, whom I alone
Had right to slay; I too wou'd have been slain,
That catching hold upon his flitting Ghost
I might have robb'd him of his opening Heav'n;
And drag'd him down with me, spight of Predestination.
        Bend. 'Tis of as much import as *Affrick's* worth
To know what came of him, and of *Almeyda*
The Sister of the Vanquish'd *Mahumet,*
130 Whose fatal Beauty to her Brother drew
The Lands third part, as *Lucifer* did Heav'ns.
        Dor. I hope she dy'd in her own Female calling,
Choak'd up with Man, and gorg'd with Circumcision.
As for *Sebastian* we must search the Field,
And where we see a Mountain of the Slain,
Send one to climb, and looking down below,
There he shall find him at his Manly length
With his face up to Heav'n, in the red Monument,

---

111 *Dorax.*] Q2, F, D *(Dor.);* ∼ , Q1.   115 still] Q2, F, D; st ll Q1.
116 Lightning] Q2, F, D; Ligtning Q1.   116 Slaughters.] D; ∼ , Q1–2, F.
127 *Affrick's*] *Affric's* Q1; *Affrica's* Q2; *Africa's* F, D.
136 below,] F, D; ∼∧ Q1–2.

Which his true Sword has digg'd.
140   *Bend.* Yet we may possibly hear farther news;
For while our *Affricans* pursu'd the Chase,
The Captain of the Rabble issued out,
With a black shirt-less train to spoil the dead,
And seize the living.
       Dor.   Each of 'em an Hoast,
A Million strong of Vermine ev'ry Villain:
No part of Government, but Lords of Anarchy,
Chaos of Power, and priviledg'd destruction.
       Bend. Yet I must tell you Friend, the Great must use 'em,
Sometimes as necessary tools of tumult.
150   *Dor.* I wou'd use 'em
Like Dogs in times of Plague, out-laws of Nature,
Fit to be shot and brain'd, without a process,
To stop infection, that's their proper death.
       Bend. No more,
Behold the Emperor coming to survey
The Slaves, in order to perform his Vow.

Enter Muley-Moluch *the Emperor, with Attendants,*
the Mufti, *and* Muley-Zeydan.

       Moluch. Our Armours now may rust, our idle scymitars
Hang by our sides, for Ornament not use:
Children shall beat our Atabals and Drums,
160 And all the noisie trades of War, no more
Shall wake the peaceful morn: the *Xeriff's* blood
No longer in divided Channels runs,
The younger House took end in *Mahumet.*
Nor shall *Sebastian's* formidable Name,
Be longer us'd to lull the crying babe!
       Mufti. For this Victorious day our Mighty Prophet
Expects your gratitude, the Sacrifice

---

148   Friend,] Q2, F, D; ~ᴧ Q1.   152   brain'd,] F; ~ ; Q1; ~ : Q2, D.
156+   *s.d. Attendants,*] ~ . Q1-2, F, D.   156+   *s.d. the*] *The* Q1-2, F, D.
156+   *s.d.* Mufti] F, D; Mufty Q1-2.   166   *Mufti*] *Mufty* Q1-2; *Muf.* F, D.

Of Christian Slaves, devoted, if you won.

Mol. The purple present shall be richly paid:
170 That Vow perform'd, fasting shall be abolish'd:
None ever serv'd Heav'n well with a starv'd face:
Preach Abstinence no more; I tell thee *Mufti*
Good feasting is devout: and thou our Head,
Hast a Religious, ruddy Countenance:
We will have learned Luxury: our lean Faith
Gives scandal to the Christians; they feed high:
Then look for shoals of Converts, when thou hast
Reform'd us into feasting.

Muf. Fasting is but the Letter of the Law:
180 Yet it shows well to Preach it to the Vulgar.
Wine is against our Law, that's literal too,
But not deny'd to Kings and to their Guides,
Wine is a Holy Liquor, for the Great.

Dorax aside. This *Mufti* in my conscience is some *English* Renegade, he talks so savourly of toping.

Mol. Bring forth th' unhappy Relicks of the War.

Enter Mustapha, *Captain of the Rabble, with his followers
of the Black Guard,* &c. *and other* Moors: *with them a
Company of* Portuguese *Slaves, without any
of the chief Persons.*

M. Mol. These are not fit to pay an Emperors Vow;
Our Bulls and Rams had been more noble Victims;
These are but garbidge not a Sacrifice.
190 *Muf.* The Prophet must not pick and choose his Offrings;
Now he has giv'n the Day, 'tis past recalling:
And he must be content with such as these.

---

172 *Mufti*] F; *Mufty* Q1–2, D.
174 Countenance] Q2, F, D; Countenancc Q1.
181 that's] Q2, F, D; thar's Q1.
183–184 Great. / *Dorax aside.* This] Great. [*Dorax aside.* / This Q1–2, F (*line
184 indented*); Great. / Dor. [*aside.*] This D.
184–185 *set as verse in* Q1–2, F, D (. . . / Renegade).
186+ *s.d.* Mustapha, . . . *Rabble,*] ~_∧_ . . . ~_∧_ Q1–2, F, D (*Rabble,* F, D).
186+ *s.d.* Moors] D; *Moors* Q1–2, F.   186+ *s.d. Slaves,*] D; ~_∧_ Q1–2, F.

M. Mol. But are these all? Speak you who are their Masters.

Musta. All, upon my Honour: If you'll take 'em as their Fathers got 'em, so. If not, you must stay till they get a better generation: These Christians are mere bunglers; they procreate nothing but out of their own Wives; And these have all the looks of Eldest Sons.

M. Mol. Pain of your lives let none conceal a Slave.

200   *Must.* Let every Man look to his own Conscience, I am sure mine shall never hang me.

Bend. Thou speak'st as thou wert privy to concealments: Then thou art an Accomplice.

Must. Nay if Accomplices must suffer, it may go hard with me; but here's the Devil on't, there's a Great Man, and a Holy Man too, concern'd with me. Now if I confess, he'll be sure to scape between his Greatness and his Holiness, and I shall be murder'd, because of my Poverty and Rascality.

Mufti winking at him. Then if thy silence save the Great and
        Holy,

210 'Tis sure thou shalt go straight to Paradise.

Must. 'Tis a fine place they say; but Doctor I am not worthy on't: I am contented with this homely World, 'tis good enough for such a poor rascally Musulman as I am: Besides I have learnt so much good manners, Doctor, as to let my Betters be serv'd before me.

M. Mol. Thou talk'st as if the *Mufti* were concern'd.

Must. Your Majesty may lay your Soul on't: but for my part, though I am a plain Fellow, yet I scorn to be trick'd into Paradice, I wou'd he shou'd know it. The troth on't is, an't like you,

220 His reverence bought of me the flower of all the Market; these————these are but Dogs meat to 'em, and a round price he pay'd me too I'll say that for him; but not enough for me to venture my neck for: If I get Paradice when my time comes

---

194   All,] ∼ₐ Q1–2, F, D.   205   Man,] F, D; ∼ₐ Q1–2.
209   *Mufti . . . him.* Then] Mufti . . . *him.* / Then Q1–2, F; *Mufty.* [. . .
him.] Then D.   210   Paradise.] Q2, F; ∼ₐ Q1; ∼ , D.
216   *Mufti*] F, D; *Mufty* Q1–2.   216   concern'd.] F, D; ∼ : Q1–2.
219   is,] F, D; ∼ₐ Q1–2.

I can't help my self; but I'll venture nothing before-hand, upon
a blind Bargain.

M. Mol. Where are those Slaves? produce 'em.

Muf. They are not what he says.

M. Mol.   No more excuses.

                               [*One goes out to fetch them.*

Know thou may'st better dally

With a dead Prophet, than a living King.

230   *Muf.* I but reserv'd 'em to present thy Greatness

An Off'ring worthy thee.

Must. By the same token there was a dainty Virgin, (*Virgin*
said I! but I won't be too positive of that neither) with a
roguish leering eye! he paid me down for her upon the nail a
thousand golden *Sultanins;* or he had never had her I can tell
him that: Now is it very likely he would pay so dear for such
a delicious Morsel, and give it away out of his own mouth;
when it had such a farewel with it too?

>   *Enter* Sebastian *conducted in mean habit, with* Alvarez,
>   Antonio, *and* Almeyda: *her face veil'd with a* Barnus.

M. Mol. Ay; These look like the Workmanship of Heav'n:
240 This is the porcelain clay of human kind,

And therefore cast into these noble moulds.

Dorax aside while the Emperor whispers Benducar. By all my
    wrongs

'Tis he; damnation seize me but 'tis he!

My heart heaves up and swells; he's poyson to me;

My injur'd honour, and my ravish'd love,

Bleed at their Murderers sight.

Bend. to Dor. aside. The Emperor wou'd learn these Pris'ners
    names;

You know 'em.

---

232   *Virgin*] Virgin Q1–2, F, D.
242   *Dorax . . . Benducar.* By] Dorax . . . Benducar. / By Q1–2, F, D ("By"
indented).
247   *Bend. to Dor. aside.* The] [Bend. *to* Dor. *aside.* / The Q1–2, F (*speech tag
at right margin;* "The" *indented*); Benducar *to* Dorax *aside.* The D.

Dor. Tell him, no,
250 And trouble me no more.————I will not know 'em.   [*Aside.*
Shall I trust Heav'n, that Heav'n which I renounc'd,
With my revenge? then, where's my satisfaction?
No, it must be my own; I scorn a Proxy.
    M. Mol. 'Tis decreed,
These of a better aspect, with the rest
Shall share one common Doom, and Lots decide it.
For ev'ry number'd Captive put a ball
Into an Urn; three only black be there,
The rest, all white, are safe.
260   *Muf.* Hold Sir, the Woman must not draw.
    M. Mol.   O *Mufti,*
We know your reason, let her share the danger.
    Muf. Our Law says plainly Women have no Souls.   ,
    M. Mol. 'Tis true; their Souls are mortal, set her by:
Yet were *Almeyda* here, though Fame reports her
The fairest of her Sex, so much unseen,
I hate the Sister of our Rival House,
Ten thousand such dry Notions of our Alcoran
Shou'd not protect her life; if not Immortal:
Dye as she cou'd, all of a piece, the better
270 That none of her remain.

*Here an Urn is brought in: the Pris'ners approach with great
concernment; and among the rest Sebastian, Alvarez and
Antonio; who come more chearfully.*

Dor. Poor abject Creatures, how they fear to dye!   [*Aside.*
These never knew one happy hour in life,
Yet shake to lay it down: is load so pleasant?
Or has Heav'n hid the happiness of Death

249 no,] D; ~ . Q1-2, F.
250-251 *s.d.* 'em. [*Aside.* / Shall . . . renounc'd,] 'em. / Shall . . . renounc'd,
[*Aside.* Q1-2, F, D.
260 *Mufti,*] D; ~ . Q1-2; ~ ! F.   262 Souls.] F, D; ~ : Q1-2.
267 Alcoran] *Alcoran* Q1-2, F, D.   269 better] ~ , Q1-2, F, D.
271 Creatures,] D; ~∧ Q1-2, F.

That Men may bear to live?————Now for our Heroes.

                             The three approach.

O, these come up with Spirits more resolv'd!

Old venerable *Alvarez,* well I know him,

The Fav'rite once of this *Sebastian's* Father;

Now Minister, (too honest for his Trade,)

280 Religion bears him out, a thing taught young,

In Age ill practis'd, yet his prop in Death.

O, he has drawn a black; and smiles upon't,

As who shou'd say *my Faith and Soul are white*

Tho my Lot swarthy: Now if there be hereafter

He's blest; if not, well cheated, and dyes pleas'd.

    Anton. holding his Lot in his clench'd hand. Here I have

      thee,

Be what thou wilt: I will not look too soon.

Thou hast a colour; if thou prov'st not right,

I have a minute good ere I behold thee.

290 Now, Let me rowl, and grubble thee,

Blind Men say white feels smooth, and black feels rough;

Thou hast a rugged skin; I do not like thee.

    Dor. There's th' Amorous airy spark, *Antonio;*

The wittiest Womans toy in *Portugal.*

Lord what a loss of Treats and Serenades!

The whole She Nation will b' in mourning for him.

    Antonio. I've a moist sweaty palm; the more's my Sin;

If it be black, yet only dy'd, not odious

Damn'd Natural Ebony, there's hope in rubbing

300 To wash this *Ethiope* white.————(*Looks.*) Pox of the Proverb!

As black as Hell: another lucky saying!

I think the Devil's in me:————good again,

I cannot speak one syllable, but tends

To Death or to Damnation.   [*Holds up his ball.*

---

279 Minister, . . . Trade,] ~ ; . . . ~ₐ Q1-2, F, D.

283-284 *my* . . . [*to*] . . . *swarthy*] in *romans in* Q1-2, F, D.

286 Anton. . . . hand. Here] D; Anton. . . . hand. / Here Q1-2, F (*speech tag in middle of page; "Here" indented*).

300 *Ethiope*] D; Ethiope Q1-2, F.   300 s.d. Looks.] Looksₐ Q1-2, F, D.

302 Devil's] F, D; Devils Q1-2.

Dor. He looks uneasie at his future Journey: [*Aside.*
And wishes his Boots off again; for fear
Of a bad Road, and a worse Inn at night.
Go to bed fool, and take secure repose
For thou shalt wake no more.
                    (Sebastian *comes up to draw.*)
310 *M. Mol. to Ben.* Mark him who now approaches to the
          Lott'ry,
He looks secure of Death, superior greatness,
Like *Jove* when he made Fate, and said *thou art*
The Slave of my Creation; I admire him.
     Bend. He looks as Man was made, with face erect,
That scorns his brittle Corps, and seems asham'd
He's not all spirit, his eyes with a dumb Pride,
Accusing Fortune that he fell not warm:
Yet now disdains to live.   (Sebast. *draws a black.*)
     M. Mol.   He has his wish;
And I have fail'd of mine!
320 *Dor.* Robb'd of my Vengeance, by a trivial chance!   [*Aside.*
Fine work above, that their anointed care
Shou'd dye such little Death: or did his Genius
Know mine the stronger *Demon,* fear'd the grapple,
And looking round him, found this nook of fate
To skulk behind my Sword? shall I discover him?
Still he wou'd dye not mine: no thanks to my
Revenge: reserv'd but to more royal shambles.
'Twere base too; and below those Vulgar Souls,
That shar'd his danger, yet not one disclos'd him:
330 But struck with Rev'rence kept an awful silence.
I'll see no more of this: Dog of a Prophet!   [*Exit* Dorax.
     Mul. Mol. One of these Three is a whole Hecatomb;
And therefore only one of 'em shall dye.
The Rest are but mute Cattle; and when Death
Comes, like a rushing Lion, couch like Spaniels,

---

310 *to*] to Q1–2, F, D.
312–313 *thou . . . [to] . . . Creation*] in romans in Q1–2, F, D.
325 Sword?] D; ~ ; Q1–2; ~ : F.

With lolling tongues, and tremble at the paw:
Let Lots again decide it.
        (*The Three draw again: and the Lot falls on* Sebastian.)
    Sebast. Then there's no more to manage! if I fall
It shall be like my self; a setting Sun
340 Shou'd leave a track of Glory in the Skies.
Behold *Sebastian* King of *Portugal.*
    M. Mol. Sebastian! ha! it must be he; no other
Cou'd represent such suff'ring Majesty:
I saw him, as he terms himself, a Sun
Strugling in dark Eclipse, and shooting day
On either side of the black Orb that veil'd him.
    Sebast. Not less ev'n in this despicable now,
Than when my Name fill'd *Affrick* with affrights,
And froze your hearts beneath your torrid Zone.
350   *Bend. to M. Mol.* Extravagantly brave! ev'n to an Impudence
Of Greatness.
    Sebast.   Here satiate all your fury;
Let fortune empty her whole Quiver on me,
I have a Soul, that like an ample Shield
Can take in all; and verge enough for more.
I wou'd have conquer'd you; and ventur'd only
A narrow neck of Land for a third World;
To give my loosen'd Subjects room to play.
Fate was not mine,
Nor am I Fate's: Now I have pleas'd my longing,
360 And trod the ground which I beheld from far,
I beg no pity for this mouldring Clay:
For if you give it burial, there it takes
Possession of your Earth:
If burnt and scatter'd in the air, the Winds
That strow my dust diffuse my royalty,
And spread me o'er your Clime: for where one Atome
Of mine shall light; know there *Sebastian* Reigns.

---

336 paw:] ~ , Q1-2, F, D.   348 *Affrick*] F, D; Affrick Q1-2.
350 *to*] to Q1-2, F, D.   362 burial,] D; ~∧ Q1-2, F.
364-365 air, . . . dust] ~ : . . . ~ , Q1-2, F, D (air; F).

M. Mol. What shall I do to conquer thee?

Seb.   Impossible!

Souls know no Conquerors.

370   *M. Mol.* I'll show thee for a Monster through my *Affrick.*

Seb. No thou canst only show me for a Man:

Affrick is stor'd with Monsters; Man's a Prodigy,

Thy Subjects have not seen.

Mul. M.   Thou talk'st as if

Still at the head of Battel.

Seb.   Thou mistak'st,

For then I would not talk.

Bend.   Sure he wou'd sleep.

Sebast. Till Dooms-day; when the Trumpet sounds to rise;

For that's a Soldiers call.

M. Mol.   Thou'rt brave too late:

Thou shou'dst have dy'd in battel, like a Soldier.

Seb. I fought and fell like one, but Death deceiv'd me,

380   I wanted weight of feeble *Moors* upon me,

To crush my Soul out.

M. Mol.   Still untameable!

In what a ruine has thy head-strong Pride,

And boundless thirst of Empire plung'd thy People.

Sebast. What say'st thou? ha! No more of that.

M. Mol.   Behold,

What Carcases of thine thy Crimes have strew'd,

And left our *Affrick* Vultures to devour.

Bend. Those Souls were those thy God intrusted with thee,

To cherish not destroy.

Sebast.   Witness, O Heaven, how much

This sight concerns me! Wou'd I had a Soul

390   For each of these: How gladly wou'd I pay

The Ransom down: But since I have but one,

'Tis a King's life, and freely 'tis bestow'd.

Not your false Prophet, but eternal Justice

370, 372   *Affrick*] F, D; Affrick Q1–2.   377   call.] F, D; ~ , Q1–2.
378   Soldier.] F, D; ~ , Q1–2.   380   *Moors*] D; Moors Q1–2, F.
384   thou?] D; ~ , Q1, F; ~_∧ Q2.   385   have] F; has Q1–2, D.
386   *Affrick*] Affric Q1; Affrick Q2; *Africk* F, D.

Has destin'd me the Lot, to dye for these:
'Tis fit a Sovereign so shou'd pay such Subjects;
For Subjects such as they are seldom seen,
Who not forsook me at my greatest need;
Nor for base lucre sold their Loyalty,
But shar'd my dangers to the last event,
400 And fenc'd 'em with their own. These thanks I pay you:
                                        [*Wipes his Eyes.*
And know, that when *Sebastian* weeps, his Tears
Come harder than his Blood.
      M. Mol.   They plead too strongly
To be withstood: My Clouds are gath'ring too,
In kindly mixture with this Royal showr:
Be safe, and owe thy Life, not to my gift,
But to the greatness of thy mind, *Sebastian:*
Thy Subjects too shall live; a due reward
For their untainted Faith, in thy concealment.
      Mufti. Remember, Sir, your Vow.   [*A general shout.*
      Mul. M.   Do thou remember
410 Thy Function, Mercy, and provoke not blood.
      Mul. Zeyd. One of his generous Fits, too strong to last.
                                        [*Aside to* Benducar.
      Bend. The *Mufti* reddens, mark that holy Cheek.   [*To him.*
He frets within, froths Treason at his mouth,
And churns it through his teeth; leave me to work him.
      Sebast. A mercy unexpected, undesir'd,
Surprizes more: You've learnt the art to vanquish:
You cou'd not (give me leave to tell you Sir)
Have giv'n me life but in my Subjects safety:
Kings, who are Fathers, live but in their People.
420   *M. Mol.* Still great, and grateful, that's thy character.
Unveil the Woman; I wou'd view the Face
That warm'd our *Mufti's* Zeal:
These pious Parrots peck the fairest Fruit:
Such Tasters are for Kings.

---

400   own.] ~ : Q1–2, F, D.   409   *Mufti.*] Q2, F, D; ~ , Q1.
412   reddens] F, D; *reddens* Q1–2.

[*Officers go to* Almeyda *to unveil her.*
Almeyda. Stand off ye Slaves, I will not be unveil'd.
M. Mol. Slave is thy Title. Force her.
Seb.   On your lives,
Approach her not.
M. Mol.   How's this!
Seb.   Sir pardon me,
And hear me speak.———
Almeyda.   Hear me; I will be heard:
I am no Slave; the noblest blood of *Affrick*
430 Runs in my Veins; a purer stream than thine;
For, though deriv'd from the same Source, thy Current
Is puddl'd, and defil'd with Tyranny.
        M. Mol. What Female Fury have we here!
Almeyda.   I shou'd be one,
Because of kin to thee: Wou'dst thou be touch'd
By the presuming hands of sawcy Grooms?
The same respect, nay more, is due to me:
More for my Sex; the same for my descent.
These hands are only fit to draw the Curtain.
Now, if thou dar'st, behold *Almeydas* face.   [*Unveils her self.*
440 *Bend.* Wou'd I had never seen it!   [*Aside.*
Almeyda. She whom thy *Mufti* tax'd to have no Soul;
Let *Affrick* now be judg;
Perhaps thou think'st I meanly hope to 'scape,
As did *Sebastian* when he own'd his greatness.
But to remove that scruple, know, base Man,
My murther'd Father, and my Brother's Ghost
Still haunt this Brest, and prompt it to revenge.
Think not I cou'd forgive nor dare thou pardon.
        M. Mol. Woud'st thou revenge thee, Trait'ress, hadst thou
            pow'r?
450 *Alm.* Traitor, I wou'd; the Name's more justly thine:

----
425 *Almeyda.*] Q2, F, D; ~ , Q1.   426 Title.] ~ : Q1–2, F, D.
428 *Almeyda.*] Q2, F, D; ~ , Q1.   429 *Affrick*] *Affric* Q1–2; *Africk* F, D.
433 *Almeyda.*] Q2, F, D; ~ , Q1.   439 dar'st,] D; ~$_\wedge$ Q1–2, F.
440 *s.d. Aside*] F, D; *aside* Q1–2.   441 *Almeyda.*] Q2, F, D; ~ , Q1.
442 *Affrick*] *Affric* Q1–2; *Africk* F, D.   445 scruple,] F, D; ~$_\wedge$ Q1–2.

Thy Father was not more than mine, the Heir
Of this large Empire; but with arms united
They fought their way, and seiz'd the Crown by force:
And equal as their danger was their share:
For where was Eldership, where none had right,
But that which Conquest gave? 'Twas thy ambition
Pull'd from my peaceful Father what his Sword
Help'd thine to gain: Surpriz'd him and his Kingdom,
No provocation given, no War declar'd.
460   *M. Mol.* I'll hear no more.
       Alm. This is the living Coal that burning in me
Wou'd flame to vengeance, cou'd it find a vent:
My Brother too, that lies yet scarcely cold
In his deep watry bed: My wandring Mother,
Who in exile died:
O that I had the fruitful Heads of *Hydra,*
That one might bourgeon where another fell!
Still wou'd I give thee work; still, still, thou Tyrant,
And hiss thee with the last.
470   *M. Mol.* Something, I know not what, comes over me:
Whether the Toyls of Battel, unrepaird
With due repose, or other sudden qualm.
Benducar do the rest.   [*Goes off, the Court follows him.*
       Bend. Strange; in full health! This pang is of the Soul;
The Body's unconcern'd: I'll think hereafter.
Conduct these Royal Captives to the Castle;
Bid *Dorax* use 'em well, till farther order.   [*Going off, stops.*
The inferior Captives their first owners take,
To sell, or to dispose.————You, *Mustapha,*
480 Set ope the Market for the sale of Slaves.   [*Exit* Benducar.

       The Masters and Slaves come forward, and Buyers of several
       Qualities come in and chaffer about the several Owners,
                  who make their Slaves do Tricks.

---

462   vent:] F, D; ∼ . Q1; ∼∧ Q2.   465   died:] ∼ . Q1-2, F, D.
480   Slaves.] F, D; ∼∧ Q1-2.

Mustapha. My Chattels are come into my hands again, and my Conscience will serve me to sell 'em twice over; any price now, before the *Mufti* comes to claim 'em.

First Merchant to Mustapha. What do'st hold that old Fellow at? [*Pointing to* Alvarez.] He's tough, and has no service in his limbs.

Must. I confess he's somewhat tough; but I suppose you wou'd not boyl him. I ask for him a thousand Crowns.

1st. Mer. Thou mean'st a thousand *Marvedi's.*

490   *Must.* Prithee Friend, give me leave to know my own meaning.

1st. Mer. What virtues has he to deserve that price?

Must. Marry come up Sir! Virtues quoth a! I took him in the King's Company; he's of a great Family, and rich; What other Virtues wou'dst thou have in a Noble-man?

1st. Mer. I buy him with another man's Purse, that's my comfort. My Lord *Dorax,* the Governor, will have him at any rate: ———There's Handsel. Come, old Fellow, to the Castle.

Alvar. To what is miserable Age reserv'd!   [*Aside.*
500 But oh the King! And oh the fatal Secret!
Which I have kept thus long, to time it better,
And now I wou'd disclose, 'tis past my pow'r.

[*Exit with his Master.*

Must. Something of a Secret, and of the King I heard him mutter: A Pimp I warrant him, for I am sure he is an old Courtier. Now to put off t' other remnant of my Merchandize.———Stir up, Sirrah!   [*To* Antonio.

Anton. Dog, what wou'dst thou have?

Must. Learn better manners, or I shall serve you a Dog-trick;

---

481   *Mustapha.*] F, D; ~ , Q1–2.
484   *First . . . Mustapha.* What] *First . . .* Mustapha. / What Q1–2, F; *First . . .* Must.] What D.
485   at? [*Pointing . . .* Alvarez.] He's] ~ ? [~ . . . ~ . / ~ Q1–2, F, D.
489   *1st.*] 1st. Q1–2, D; *First* F.   489   *Marvedi's*] Marvedi's Q1–2, F, D.
492   *1st.*] 1st. Q1–2, D; *First* F.   493   a] D; ah Q1–2, F.
494   rich;] D; ~ , Q1–2, F.   496   *1st.*] D; 1st. Q1–2; *First* F.
505–506   Merchandize.] F; ~ , Q1–2, D.   506   Sirrah!] ~∧ Q1–2; ~ . F, D.
506   *s.d. To*] F, D; *to* Q1–2.   507   have?] D; ~ ! Q1–2, F.

come, down upon all four immediately; I'll make you know
510 your Rider.

Ant. Thou wilt not make a Horse of me?

Must. Horse or Ass, that's as thy Mother made thee:————
But take earnest in the first place for thy Sawcyness. [*Lashes him
with his Whip.*] Be advis'd Friend, and buckle to thy Geers: Behold my Ensign of Royalty display'd over thee.

Ant. I hope one day to use thee worse in *Portugal*.

Must. Ay, and good reason, Friend, if thou catchest me a conquering on thy side of the water, lay me on lustily, I'll take it
as kindly as thou dost this.————

[*Holds up his Whip.*

520 　　*Antonio lying down.* Hold, my dear Thrum-cap: I obey thee
chearfully, I see the Doctrine of Non-Resistance is never practis'd thoroughly but when a Man can't help himself.

Enter a Second Merchant.

2d. Merchant. You, Friend, I wou'd see that Fellow do his
Postures.

Mustapha bridling Antonio. Now Sirrah follow, for you have
rope enough: To your paces, Villain, amble, trot, and gallop:
————Quick, about there.————Yeap, the more Money's bid-
den for you, the more your credit.

　　Antonio *follows at the end of the Bridle on his hands and
feet, and does all his Postures.*

2d. Merch. He's well chin'd, and has a tolerable good back;
530 that's half in half.————[*To* Mustapha.] I wou'd see him strip,
has he no Diseases about him?

Must. He's the best piece of Man's flesh in the Market, not an

513–514　Sawcyness. [*Lashes* . . . *Whip.*] Be] ~ . / [~ . . . ~ . / ~ Q1–2, F, D.
520　*Antonio* . . . *down.* Hold,] D (Hold∧); Antonio . . . *down.* / Hold∧ Q1–
2, F.
523　2d.] 2d. Q–2, D; Second F.
525　*Mustapha* . . . *Antonio.* Now] D (Ant.); Mustapha . . . Antonio. / Now
Q1–2, F (*speech tag centered;* "Now" *indented*).
526　paces,] F, D; ~∧ Q1–2.　　　　529　2d.] 2d. Q1–2, D; *Second* F.
530　half. ————] ~ .∧ Q1–2, F, D.

Eye-sore in his whole body: Feel his Legs, Master, neither
Splint, Spavin, nor Wind-gall.   [*Claps him on the shoulder.*
Merchant feeling about him, and then putting his hand to his
side. Out upon him, how his flank heaves! The Whorson's
broken-winded.

    Must. Thick-breath'd a little: Nothing but a sorry cold with
lying out a nights in Trenches;————but sound Wind and
540 Limb, I warrant him. Try him at a loose trot a little.

               Puts the Bridle into his hand, he strokes him.

    Anton. For Heaven's sake Owner spare me; you know I am
but new broken.

    2d. Merch. 'Tis but a washy Jade, I see: What do you ask for
this Bauble?

    Must. Bauble do you call him? he's a substantial true-bred
Beast; bravely forehanded; mark but the cleanness of his shapes
too; his Dam may be a Spanish Gennet, but a true Barb by the
Sire, or I have no skill in Horse-flesh.————Marry I ask Six
Hundred *Xeriffs* for him.

Enter Mufti.

550   *Mufti.* What's that you are asking, Sirrah?

    Must. Marry, I ask your Reverence Six Hundred Pardons; I
was doing you a small piece of service here, putting off your
Chattel for you.

    Mufti. And putting the Mony into your own Pocket.

    Must. Upon vulgar reputation, no my Lord, it was for your
profit and emolument. What, wrong the Head of my Religion?
I was sensible you wou'd have damn'd me, or any man that
shou'd have injur'd you in a single Farthing; for I knew that
was Sacrifice.

560   *Mufti.* Sacriledge you mean, Sirrah,————and damning shall

535–536 *Merchant . . . side.* Out] Merchant . . . *side.* / Out Q1–2, F, D ("Out"
indented).
538   Thick-breath'd] F; Thick breath'd Q1–2, D.
543   2d.] 2d. Q1–2, D; *Second* F.
545   him?] D; ~ ; Q1–2, F.   549 *Xeriffs*] Xeriffs Q1–2, F, D.
550, 554, 560 *Mufti.*] Q2, F, D; ~ , Q1.

be the least part of your punishment; I have taken you in the
manner, and will have the Law upon you.

Must. Good my Lord, take pity upon a poor man in this
World, and damn me in the next.

Mufti. No Sirrah, so you may repent, and scape punishment:
Did not you sell this very Slave amongst the rest to me, and take
Mony for him?

Must. Right my Lord.

Mufti. And selling him again? Take Mony twice for the same
570 Commodity? Oh, Villain! But did you not know him to be my
Slave, Sirrah?

Must. Why shou'd I lye to your Honor, I did know him; and
thereupon, seeing him wander about, I took him up for a stray,
and impounded him, with intention to restore him to the right
Owner.

Mufti. And yet at the same time was selling him to another:
How rarely the Story hangs together.

Must. Patience, my Lord. I took him up, as your Heriot, with
intention to have made the best of him, and then have brought
580 the whole product of him in a Purse to you; for I know you
wou'd have spent half of it upon your pious Pleasures, have
hoarded up the other half, and given the remainder in Charities
to the Poor.

Mufti. And what's become of my other Slave? Thou hast sold
him too I have a villainous suspicion.

Must. I know you have, my Lord; but while I was managing
this young robustous Fellow, that old Spark who was nothing
but Skin and Bone, and by consequence, very nimble, slipt
through my fingers like an Eel, for there was no hold fast of
590 him, and ran away to buy himself a new Master.

Mufti to Antonio. Follow me home, Sirrah.————[*To* Must.]

---

565 *Mufti.*] F, D; ~ , Q1; ~∧ Q2.   567 him?] D; ~ . Q1–2, F.
569 *Mufti.*] Q2, F, D; ~ , Q1.   573 about,] D; ~ ; Q1–2, F.
574 restore] Q2, F, D; restote Q1.   576, 584 *Mufti.*] Q2, F, D; ~ , Q1.
591 *Mufti to Antonio.* Follow] F, D (Mufti F; Antonio F; Ant. D); Mufti *to*
Antonio. / Follow Q1–2 (*speech tag centered in* Q1–2; "Follow" *indented in*
Q1–2).
591 Sirrah. ————[*To*] ~ :∧ [*to* Q1–2, F, D (*To* F).

I shall remember you some other time.

[*Exit* Mufti *with* Antonio.

Must. I never doubted your Lordships memory, for an ill
turn: And I shall remember him too in the next rising of the
Mobile, for this act of Resumption; and more especially for the
Ghostly Counsel he gave me before the Emperor, to have hang'd
my self in silence, to have sav'd his Reverence. The best on't is,
I am beforehand with him, for selling one of his Slaves twice
over.————And if he had not come just in the nick, I might
600 have pocketed up t' other: For what should a poor Man do, that
gets his living by hard labor, but pray for bad times when he
may get it easily? O, for some incomparable Tumult! Then
shou'd I naturally wish, that the beaten Party might prevail,
because we have plundered t' other side already, and there's
nothing more to get of 'em.

Both rich and poor for their own interest pray,
'Tis ours to make our Fortunes while we may;
For Kingdoms are not conquer'd every day.

[*Exit* Mustaph.

ACT II.   SCENE I.

*Suppos'd to be a terrace Walk, on the side of
the Castle of Alcazar.*

Enter Emperor, Benducar.

Emper. And think'st thou not it was discover'd?
Bend.   No:
The thoughts of Kings are like religious Groves,
The Walks of muffled Gods: Sacred retreat,
Where none but whom they please t' admit, approach.
  Emp. Did not my conscious Eyes flash out a Flame

---

602 easily?] D; ∼ . Q1-2, F.
ACT II. SCENE I. / *Suppos'd*] Q2, F, D; Act II. / Scene 1. *Suppos'd* Q1.
s.d. Enter Emperor,] Emperor. Q1-2; *Enter* Emperor, F, D (Emperor *and* D).
1 think'st . . . discover'd] Q2, F, D (thinkst Q2, D); thinkest . . . discovered
Q1.

To lighten those brown horrors, and disclose
The secret path I trod?
   Bend. I cou'd not find it, 'till you lent a Clue
To that close Labarynth; how then shou'd they?
10   *Emp.* I wou'd be loth they shou'd: it breeds contempt
For Herds to listen, or presume to pry,
When the hurt Lion groans within his Den:
But is't not strange?
   Bend. To love? not more than 'tis to live; a Tax
Impos'd on all by Nature, paid in kind,
Familiar as our being.
   Emp.   Still 'tis strange
To me: I know my Soul as wild as winds,
That sweep the Desarts of our moving Plains;
Love might as well be sow'd upon our Sands,
20 As in a brest so barren:
To love an Enemy, the only One
Remaining too, whom yester Sun beheld,
Must'ring her charms, and rolling as she past
By every Squadron her alluring eyes,
To edge her Champions Swords, and urge my ruin.
The shouts of Soldiers, and the burst of Cannon,
Maintain ev'n still a deaf and murm'ring noise;
Nor is Heav'n yet recover'd of the sound
Her Battel rows'd: Yet spight of me I love.
30   *Bend.* What then controuls you?
Her Person is as prostrate as her Party.
   Emp. A thousand things controul this Conqueror,
My native pride to own th' unworthy passion,
Hazard of Int'rest, and my Peoples love:
To what a Storm of Fate am I expos'd!
What if I had her murder'd? 'tis but what
My Subjects all expect, and she deserves.
Wou'd not th' impossibility
Of ever, ever seeing, or possessing,

---

40 Calm all this rage, this Hurrican of Soul?
    Bend. That *ever, ever,*
(I mark'd the double,) shows extream reluctance
To part with her for ever.
    Emp.   Right, thou hast me,
I wou'd, but cannot kill: I must enjoy her:
I must, and what I must, be sure I will.
What's Royalty but pow'r to please my self?
And if I dare not, then am I the Slave,
And my own Slaves the Sovereigns,————'tis resolv'd,
Weak Princes flatter when they want the pow'r
50 To curb their People; tender Plants must bend,
But when a Government is grown to strength,
Like some old Oak, rough with its armed Bark,
It yields not to the tug, but only nods,
And turns to sullen State.
    Bend.   Then you resolve
T' implore her pity, and to beg relief?
    Emp. Death, must I beg the pity of my Slave?
Must a King beg? Yes, Love's a greater King;
A Tyrant, nay a Devil that possesses me:
He tunes the Organs of my voice, and speaks
60 Unknown to me within me; pushes me,
And drives me on by force.————
Say I shou'd wed her, wou'd not my wise Subjects
Take check, and think it strange? perhaps revolt?
    Bend. I hope they wou'd not.
    Emp.   Then thou doubt'st they wou'd?
    Bend. To whom?
    Emp. To her
Perhaps, or to my Brother, or to Thee.
    Bend. in disorder. To me! me did you mention? how I trem-
        ble!

---

41 *ever, ever*] ever, ever Q1–2, F, D.
42 (I . . . double,)] ∧~ . . . ~ ,∧ Q1–2, F, D.
43 Right,] F, D; ~∧ Q1–2.   45 must, be] D; ~∧~ Q1–2, F.
68 *Bend. in disorder.* To] F, D; [*Bend. in disorder.* / To Q1–2 ("To" *indented*).

The name of Treason shakes my honest Soul.
70 If I am doubted, Sir,
Secure your self this moment, take my life.
    Emp. No more: if I suspected thee———I wou'd.
    Bend. I thank your kindness: Guilt had almost lost me!
                                     [Aside.
    Emp. But clear my doubts: think'st thou they may rebel?
    Bend. aside. This goes as I wou'd wish.———(*To th' Emp.*)
'Tis possible.
A secret Party still remains, that lurks
Like Embers rak'd in ashes———wanting but
A breath to blow aside th' involving dust,
And then they blaze abroad.
    Emp.   They must be trampled out.
80   *Bend.* But first be known.
    Emp.   Torture shall force it from 'em.
    Bend. You wou'd not put a Nation to the rack?
    Emp. Yes, the whole World; so I be safe, I care not.
    Bend. Our Limbs and Lives
Are yours, but mixing Friends with Foes is hard.
    Emp. All may be foes; or how to be distinguish'd,
If some be friends?
    Bend.   They may with ease be winnow'd:
Suppose some one, who has deserv'd your trust,
Some one who knows Mankind, shou'd be employ'd
To mix among 'em, seem a Malcontent,
90 And dive into their breasts, to try how far
They dare oppose your love?
    Emp. I like this well: 'Tis wholesom wickedness.
    Bend. Whomever he suspects, he fastens there,
And leaves no cranny of his Soul unsearch'd:
Then, like a Bee bag'd with his honey'd venome,
He brings it to your Hive: if such a Man
So able, and so honest, may be found;

---

74   rebel?] D; ～. Q1–2, F.
75   *Bend. aside.* This] F, D; [*Bend. aside.* / This Q1–2 ("This" *indented in Q1*).
75   wish.] ～ : Q1–2, F, D.   75 *s.d. To*] F; *to* Q1–2, D.

If not, my project dyes.————
    Emp. By all my hopes thou hast describ'd thy self:————
100 Thou, thou alone art fit to play that Engine,
Thou only coudst contrive.
    Bend.   Sure I cou'd serve you:
I think I cou'd:————but here's the difficulty;
I'm so entirely yours,
That I shou'd scurvily dissemble hate;
The cheat wou'd be too gross.
    Emp.   Art thou a Statesman
And canst not be a Hypocrite? Impossible:
Do not distrust thy Vertues.
    Bend. If I must personate this seeming Villain,
Remember 'tis to serve you.
    Emp.   No more words:
110 Love goads me to *Almeyda*, all affairs
Are troublesom but that; and yet that most.   [*Going.*
Bid *Dorax* treat *Sebastian* like a King;
I had forgot him;————but this Love marrs all,
And takes up my whole brest.   [*Exit Emperor.*
    Bend. to the Emp.   Be sure I'll tell him————
With all the aggravating Circumstances   [*Alone.*
I can, to make him swell at that Command.
The Tyrant first suspected me:
Then, with a sudden gust, he whirld about,
And trusted me too far: Madness of Pow'r!
120 Now, by his own consent, I ruin him.
For, shou'd some feeble Soul, for fear or gain
Bolt out t' accuse me, ev'n the King is cozen'd,
And thinks he's in the secret.
How sweet is Treason when the Traytor's safe!

    (*Sees the* Mufti *and* Dorax *entring and seeming to confer.*)

----

102 difficulty;] ∼ , Q1–2, F, D.
114 *to the Emp.*] (to the *Emp.*) Q1–2, F; [*to the Emp.*] D.
114 him] ∼ . Q1–2, F, D.
116 Command.] D; ∼ , Q1–2, F.

The *Mufti,* and with him my sullen *Dorax;*
That first is mine already.
'Twas easie work to gain a cov'tous mind,
Whom rage to loose his Pris'ners had prepar'd:
Now, caught himself,
130 He wou'd seduce another; I must help him:
For Church-men, though they itch to govern all,
Are silly, woful, awkard Politicians;
They make lame mischief, though they mean it well:
Their Int'rest is not finely drawn, and hid,
But seams are coarsly bungled up, and seen.
    Muf. He'll tell you more.
    Dor.   I've heard enough already
To make me loath thy Morals.
    Bend. to Dor.   You seem warm:
The good Man's zeal, perhaps has gon too far.
    Dor. Not very far; not farther than zeal goes
140 Of course; a small days journey short of Treason.
    Muf. By all that's Holy, Treason was not nam'd:
I spar'd the Emperors broken Vows to save
The Slaves from Death, though it was cheating Heav'n;
But I forgave him that.
    Dor.   And slighted o'er   *[Scornfully.*
The wrongs himself sustain'd in property:
When his bought Slaves were seiz'd by force, no loss
Of his consider'd, and no cost repaid.
    Mufti. Not wholly slighted o'er, not absolutely:
Some modest hints of private wrongs I urg'd.
150   *Dorax.* Two thirds of all he said: there he began;
To shew the fulness of his heart, there ended:
Some short excursions of a broken Vow,
He made indeed, but flat insipid stuff:
But when he made his loss the Theme, he flourish'd,
Reliev'd his fainting Rhetorick with new Figures,

---

125   *Dorax;*] ∼ , Q1-2, F; ∼ . D.   137 *to*] to Q1-2, F, D.
143   Death, . . . Heav'n;] ∼ ; . . . ∼ , Q1-2, F, D.
144   *s.d. Scornfully*] D; *scornfully* Q1-2, F.   148 *Mufti.*] F, D (*Muf.*); ∼ , Q1-2.
150   *Dorax.*] Q2, F, D (*Dor.* F, D); ∼ , Q1.

And thunder'd at oppressing Tyranny.
    Mufti. Why not, when Sacrilegious Pow'r wou'd seize
My Property? 'tis an affront to Heav'n,
Whose Person, though unworthy, I sustain.
160   *Dorax.* You've made such strong Alliances above,
That 'twere Profaneness in us Laiety
To offer earthly Aid.
I tell thee, *Mufti,* if the World were wise,
They wou'd not wag one finger in your quarrels.
Your Heav'n you promise, but our Earth you covet;
The *Phaethons* of mankind, who fire that World,
Which you were sent by Preaching but to warm.
    Bend. This goes beyond the mark.
    Mufti.   No, let him rail;
His Prophet works within him;
170 He's a rare Convert.
    Dorax.   Now his Zeal yearns,
To see me burnt; he damns me from his Church,
Because I wou'd restrain him to his Duty;
Is not the care of Souls a load sufficient?
Are not your holy stipends pay'd for this?
Were you not bred apart from worldly noise,
To study Souls, their Cures and their Diseases?
If this be so, we ask you but our own:
Give us your whole Employment, all your care:
The Province of the Soul is large enough
180 To fill up every Cranny of your time,
And leave you much to answer, if one Wretch
Be damn'd by your neglect.
    Bend. to the Mufti.   He speaks but reason.
    Dorax. Why then these forein thoughts of State-Employ-
    ments,
Abhorrent to your Function and your Breeding?

---

157   *Mufti.*] F, D (*Muf.*); ∼ , Q1–2.   158   Property?] ∼ , Q1–2, F, D.
165   covet;] ∼ . Q1–2, F, D.   166 *Phaethons*] D; Phaethons Q1–2, F.
168   *Mufti.*] F, D (*Muf.*); ∼ , Q1–2.
170   *Dorax.*] F, D (*Dor.*); ∼ , Q1–2.   174 not] Q2, F, D; nor Q1.
182   *to the*] to the Q1–2, F, D.   183 *Dorax.*] Q2, F, D (*Dor.* F, D); ∼ , Q1.

Poor droaning Truants of unpractis'd Cells,
Bred in the Fellowship of bearded Boys,
What wonder is it if you know not Men?
Yet there, you live demure, with down-cast Eyes,
And humble as your Discipline requires:
190 But, when let loose from thence to live at large,
Your little tincture of Devotion dies:
Then Luxury succeeds, and set agog
With a new Scene of yet untasted Joys,
You fall with greedy hunger to the Feast.
Of all your College Vertues, nothing now
But your Original Ignorance remains:
Bloated with Pride, Ambition, Avarice,
You swell, to counsel Kings and govern Kingdoms.
    Mufti. He prates as if Kings had not Consciences,
200 And none requir'd Directors but the Crowd.
    Dorax. As private men they want you, not as Kings;
Nor wou'd you care t' inspect their publick Conscience,
But that it draws dependencies of Pow'r,
And Earthly Interest which you long to sway.
Content you with monopolizing Heav'n,
And let this little hanging Ball alone;
For give you but a foot of Conscience there,
And you, like *Archimedes,* toss the Globe.
We know your thoughts of us, that Laymen are
210 Lag Souls, and rubbish of remaining Clay,
Which Heav'n, grown weary of more perfect work,
Set upright with a little puff of breath,
And bid us pass for Men.
    Mufti.   I will not answer,
Base foul mouth'd Renegade; but I'll pray for thee,
To shew my Charity.   *Exit* Mufti.
    Dorax. Do; but forget not him who needs it most:
Allow thy self some share. He's gone too soon;

201 *Dorax.*] Q2, F, D (*Dor.*); ~ , Q1.   209 us,] F; ~∧ Q1–2, D.
214 thee,] D; ~∧ Q1–2, F.   216 *Dorax.*] Q2, F, D (*Dor.*); ~ , Q1.
217 share.] ~ : Q1–2, F, D.

I had to tell him of his holy jugglings;
Things that wou'd startle Faith, and make us deem
220 Not this or that, but all Religions false.
    Bend. Our Holy Oratour has lost the Cause: [*Aside.*
But I shall yet redeem it.————(*To* Dorax.) Let him go;
For I have secret Orders from the Emperour,
Which none but you must hear: I must confess
I cou'd have wish'd some other hand had brought 'em.
When did you see your Pris'ner Great *Sebastian?*
    Dorax. You might as well have ask'd me when I saw
A crested Dragon, or a Basilisk;
Both are less Poison to my Eyes and Nature.
230 He knows not I am I; nor shall he see me
Till time has perfected a lab'ring thought,
That rouls within my brest.
    Bend.   'Twas my mistake:
I guess'd indeed that time, and his misfortunes,
And your returning duty had effac'd
The mem'ry of past wrongs; they wou'd in me;
And I judg'd you as tame and as forgiving.
    Dorax. Forgive him! no, I left my foolish Faith
Because it wou'd oblige me to forgiveness.
    Bend. I can but grieve to find you obstinate:
240 For you must see him; 'tis our Emp'rours will,
And strict Command.
    Dorax.   I laugh at that Command.
    Bend. You must do more than see; serve, and respect him.
    Dorax. See, serve him, and respect, and after all
My yet uncancell'd wrongs, I must do this!
But I forget my self.
    Bend.   Indeed you do.
    Dorax. The Emp'rour is a stranger to my wrongs;
I need but tell my story, to revoke
This hard Commission.

---

222   *s.d. To* Dorax.] D (*Dorax*); to *Dorax*_∧ Q1-2, F.
222   Let] D; let Q1-2, F.
227, 237, 241, 243, 246   *Dorax.*] Q2, F, D (*Dor.*); ∼ , Q1.

  Bend.   Can you call me Friend,
  And think I cou'd neglect to speak, at full,
250 Th' Affronts you had from your ungrateful Master?
  Dorax. And yet enjoyn'd my Service, and Attendance?
  Bend. And yet enjoyn'd 'em both: wou'd that were all;
  He scru'd his Face into a harden'd smile,
  And said, *Sebastian* knew to govern Slaves.
  Dorax. Slaves are the growth of *Affrick,* not of *Europe:*
  By Heav'n I will not lay down my Commission;
  Not at his foot, I will not stoop so low;
  But if there be a part in all his Face
  More sacred than the rest, I'll throw it there.
260 *Bend.* You may; but then you lose all future means
  Of Vengeance on *Sebastian,* when no more
  Alcalde of this Fort.
  Dorax.   That thought escap'd me.
  Bend. Keep your Command; and be reveng'd on both:
  Nor sooth your self; you have no pow'r t' affront him;
  The Emp'rours love protects him from insults.
  And he, who spoke that proud ill-natur'd word,
  Following the bent of his impetuous temper,
  May force your reconcilement to *Sebastian:*
  Nay bid you kneel, and kiss th' offending foot,
270 That kick'd you from his Presence.
  But think not to divide their punishment;
  You cannot touch a hair of loath'd *Sebastian,*
  While *Muley-Moluch* lives.
  Dorax.   What means this Riddle?
  Bend. 'Tis out: there needs no *Oedipus* to solve it.
  Our Emp'rour is a Tyrant, fear'd and hated;
  I scarce remember in his Reign, one day
  Pass guiltless o'er his execrable head.
  He thinks the Sun is lost that sees not bloud:
  When none is shed we count it Holiday.

---

249 full,] D; ~ᴧ Q1-2, F.   251, 255 *Dorax.*] Q2, F, D (*Dor.*); ~ , Q1.
255 *Affrick*] Q2; *Africk* Q1, F, D.   262 *Dorax.*] Q2, F, D (*Dor.*); ~ , Q1.
265 insults.] Q2, F, D; ~ . . Q1.   273 *Dorax.*] Q2, F, D (*Dor.*); ~ , Q1.
275 and] Q2, F, D; aud Q1.

280 We, who are most in favour, cannot call
This hour our own:————you know the younger Brother,
Mild *Muley-Zeydan;*————
  Dorax.   Hold and let me think.
  Bend. The Soldiers Idolize you,
He trusts you with the Castle,
The Key of all his Kingdom.
  Dorax. Well; and he trusts you too.
  Bend.   Else I were mad,
To hazard such a daring Enterprize.
  Dorax. He trusts us both; mark that, shall we betray him?
A Master who reposes Life and Empire
290 On our fidelity: I grant he is a Tyrant,
That hated name my nature most abhors;
More, as you say, has loaded me with scorn:
Ev'n with the last contempt, to serve *Sebastian.*
Yet more, I know he vacates my revenge;
Which, but by this revolt I cannot compass:
But, while he trusts me, 'twere so base a part
To fawn and yet betray, I shou'd be hiss'd
And whoop'd in Hell for that Ingratitude.
  Bend. Consider well what I have done for you.
300   *Dorax.* Consider thou what thou woud'st have me do.
  Bend. You've too much honour for a Renegade.
  Dorax. And thou too little faith to be a Fav'rite.
Is not the bread thou eat'st, the Robe thou wear'st,
Thy Wealth, and Honours, all the pure indulgence
Of him thou wou'dst destroy?
And wou'd his Creature, nay his Friend betray him?
Why then no Bond is left on human kind:
Distrusts, debates, immortal strifes ensue;
Children may murder Parents, Wives their Husbands;
310 All must be Rapine, Wars, and Desolation,

281   own:] F, D; ∼ ? Q1-2.   281   Brother,] D; ∼∧ Q1-2, F.
282   *Muley-Zeydan*] F, D; *Muley Zeydan* Q1-2.
282, 286, 288   *Dorax.*] Q2, F, D (*Dor.*); ∼ , Q1.   294   more,] ∼∧ Q1-2, F, D.
300, 302, 315, 326, 328   *Dorax.*] Q2, F, D (*Dor.*); ∼ , Q1.

When trust and gratitude no longer bind.
    Bend. Well have you argued in your own defence:
You, who have burst asunder all those bonds,
And turn'd a Rebel to your Native Prince.
    Dorax. True, I rebell'd: but when did I betray?
Indignities, which Man cou'd not support,
Provok'd my vengeance to this noble Crime.
But he had strip'd me first of my Command,
Dismiss'd my Service, and absolv'd my Faith;
320 And, with disdainful Language, dar'd my worst.
I but accepted War, which he denounc'd.
Else had you seen, not *Dorax,* but *Alonzo,*
With his couch'd Lance against your foremost *Moors:*
Perhaps too turn'd the fortune of the day;
Made *Affrick* mourn, and *Portugal* triumph.
    Bend. Let me embrace thee.
    Dorax.   Stand off Sycophant,
And keep Infection distant.
    Bend.   Brave and honest.
    Dorax. In spight of thy Temptations.
    Bend.   Call 'em Trials:
They were no more: thy faith was held in Balance,
330 And nicely weigh'd by jealousie of Pow'r;
Vast was the trust of such a Royal Charge;
And our wise Emperour, might justly fear
Sebastian might be freed and reconcil'd,
By new Obligements to thy former love.
    Dorax. I doubt thee still; thy reasons were too strong,
And driv'n too near the head, to be but Artifice.
And after all, I know thou art a Statesman,
Where truth is rarely found.
    Bend.   Behold the Emperour;

(*Enter Emp.* Seb. *and* Almeyda.)

---

332   our] Q2, F, D; onr Q1.
335   *Dorax.*] Q2, F, D (*Dor.*); ~ , Q1.
338+   *s.d. Emp.*] Emp. Q1-2, F, D.

Ask him, I beg thee, to be justify'd,
340 If he employ'd me not to foord thy Soul,
And try the footing whether false or firm.
    Dorax. Death to my Eyes, I see *Sebastian* with him!
Must he be serv'd? avoid him; if we meet,
It must be like the crush of Heav'n and Earth,
T' involve us both in ruin.   (*Exit* Dorax.
    Bend. 'Twas a bare saving game I made with *Dorax*,
But better so than lost; he cannot hurt me,
That I precaution'd: I must ruin him.
But now this Love; Ay, there's the gath'ring storm!
350 The Tyrant must not wed *Almeyda;* no,
That ruins all the Fabrick I am raising.
Yet seeming to approve it gave me time,
And gaining time gains all.
    (Benducar *goes and waits behind the Emperour. The Em-*
    perour, Sebastian *and* Almeyda *advance to the front of*
    the Stage: Guards and Attendants.
    Emp. to Seb. I bad 'em serve you, and if they obey not,
I keep my Lions keen within their Dens,
To stop their maws with disobedient Slaves.
    Seb. If I had Conquer'd,
They cou'd not have with more observance waited:
Their eyes, hands, feet,
360 Are all so quick they seem t' have but one motion,
To catch my flying words. Onely the Alcalde
Shuns me, and with a grim Civility,
Bows, and declines my Walks.
    Emp.   A Renegade:
I know not more of him: but that he's brave,
And hates your Christian Sect. If you can frame

---

339   thee,] F, D; ∼∧ Q1–2.   341 firm.] Q2, F, D; ∼ , Q1.
342 *Dorax.*] Q2, F, D (*Dor.*); ∼ , Q1.
343 serv'd? . . . him;] ∼ ! . . . ∼ , Q1–2, F, D.
352 it] Q2, F, D; ∼ , Q1.
353+ *s.d. Emperour.*] Emperour.) Q1–2, F, D (Emperor.∧ D).
353+ *s.d. The*] D; (∼ Q1–2, F.   353+ *s.d. Emperour,*] F, D; ∼ ; Q1–2.
353+ *s.d. Stage:*] D; ∼ .) Q1–2, F.   354 *to*] to Q1–2, F, D.
361 Alcalde] *Alcayde* Q1; *Alcade* Q2, F, D.

A farther wish, give wing to your desires,
And name the thing you want.
 Sebast.   My Liberty:
For were ev'n Paradise it self my Prison,
Still I shou'd long to leap the Chrystal walls.
370 *Emp.* Sure our two Souls have somewhere been acquainted
In former beings; or, struck out together,
One spark to *Affrick* flew, and one to *Portugal.*
Expect a quick deliverance.————(*Turning to* Alm.) Here's a
  third,
Of kindred Soul to both: pity our Stars
Have made us Foes! I shou'd not wish her death.
 Almeyda. I ask no pity; if I thought my Soul
Of kin to thine, soon wou'd I rend my heart-strings,
And tear out that Alliance: but thou, Viper,
Hast cancell'd kindred, made a rent in Nature,
380 And through her holy bowels gnaw'd thy way,
Through thy own Bloud to Empire.
 Emper.   This again:————
And yet she lives; and only lives t' upbraid me.
 Sebast. What honour is there in a Womans death!
Wrong'd as she says, but helpless to revenge;
Strong in her Passion, impotent of Reason,
Too weak to hurt, too fair to be destroy'd.
Mark her Majestick Fabrick; She's a Temple
Sacred by birth, and built by Hands Divine;
Her Soul's the Deity, that lodges there:
390 Nor is the Pile unworthy of the God.
 Emp. She's all that thou canst say or I can think.
But the perversness of her clam'rous Tongue
Strikes Pity deaf.
 Seb.   Then onely hear her Eyes;

---

370 acquainted] D; ∼ : Q1–2; ∼ , F.   372 *Affrick*] Q2; *Africk* Q1, F, D.
373 deliverance.————] ∼ :∧ Q1–2, D; ∼ ;∧ F.
373 *s.d. Turning to* Alm.] turning to *Alm:* Q1–2, F (*Alm.* Q2, F); *turning to*
Almeyda. D.
373 Here's] D; here's Q1–2, F.
376 *Almeyda.*] Q2, F, D (*Alm.* F, D); ∼ , Q1.
378 thou, Viper,] ∼∧ ∼∧ Q1–2, F, D.

Though they are mute they plead; nay more, command;
For beauteous Eyes have Arbitrary Power.
All Females have prerogative of Sex,
The Shes ev'n of the salvage herd are safe;
And when they snarl or bite, have no return
But Courtship from the Male.
400   *Emp.* Were She not She, and I not *Muley-Moluch,*
She's Mistress of unevitable Charms,
For all but me; nor am I so exempt,
But that—I know not what I was to say—
But I am too obnoxious to my Friends;
And sway'd by your Advice.
         Sebast.   Sir, I advis'd not.
By Heav'n, I never counsell'd Love but Pity.
         Emp. By Heav'n thou didst: deny it not, thou didst:
For what was all that Prodigality
Of praise, but to enflame me?————
         Sebast.   Sir,————
         Emp.   No more:
410 Thou hast convinc'd me, that she's worth my Love.
         Seb. Was ever Man so ruin'd by himself!   *(Aside.*
         Almeyda. Thy Love; that odious Mouth was never fram'd
To speak a word so soft:
Name Death again, for that thou canst pronounce
With horrid grace, becoming of a Tyrant.
Love is for human hearts, and not for thine,
Where the brute Beast extinguishes the Man.
         Emper. Such if I were, yet rugged Lions love,
And grapple, and compel their savage Dames.————
420 Mark, my *Sebastian,* how that sullen frown,   [*She frowns.*
Like flashing Lightning, opens angry Heaven;
And while it kills, delights. But yet, insult not
Too soon, proud Beauty, I confess no love.
         Seb. No Sir, I said so, and I witness for you:

---

412 *Almeyda.*] Q2, F, D (*Alm.*); ∼ , Q1.   420 Mark,] F; ∼∧ Q1-2, D.
422 kills,] D; ∼∧ Q1-2, F.
424 you:] D; ∼ , Q1-2, F.

Not love, but noble pity mov'd your mind:
Int'rest might urge you too to save her life;
For those who wish her party lost, might murmur
At shedding Royal Blood.
  Emp.   Right, thou instruct'st me;
Int'rest of State requires not Death, but Marriage;
430 T' unite the jarring Titles of our Line.
  Seb. Let me be dumb for ever, all I plead,   [*Aside.*
Like Wild-fire thrown against the Wind, returns
With double force to burn me.
  Emp. Cou'd I but bend to make my beauteous Foe
The Partner of my Throne, and of my Bed———
  Almeyda. Still thou dissemblest, but I read thy heart,
And know the power of my own Charms; thou lov'st,
And I am pleas'd for my revenge thou dost.
  Emp. And thou hast cause.
440 *Alm.* I have; for I have pow'r to make thee wretched.
Be sure I will, and yet despair of freedom.
  Emp. Well then, I love,———
And 'tis below my greatness to disown it:
Love thee implacably, yet hate thee too;
Wou'd hunt thee bare-foot, in the mid-day Sun,
Through the parch'd Desarts, and the scorching Sands,
T' enjoy thy Love, and once enjoy'd, to kill thee.
  Alm. 'Tis a false Courage, when thou threat'nest me;
Thou canst not stir a hand to touch my Life:
450 Do not I see thee tremble while thou speak'st?
Lay by the Lions Hide, vain Conqueror,
And take the Distaff; for thy Soul's my Slave.
  Emp. Confusion! How thou viewest my very Heart!
I cou'd as soon,
Stop a Spring-tide, blown in, with my bare hand,
As this impetuous Love:———Yes, I will wed thee;
In spight of thee, and of my self, I will.

---

425 love,] F, D; ~ ; Q1–2.   435 Bed] ~ . Q1–2, F, D.
436 *Almeyda.*] Q2, F, D (*Alm.*); ~ , Q1.
447 enjoy'd,] D; ~∧ Q1–2, F.

Alm. For what? To people *Affrick* with new Monsters,
Which that unnatural mixture must produce?
460 No, were we joyn'd, ev'n tho it were in death,
Our Bodies burning in one Funeral Pile,
The Prodigy of *Thebes* wou'd be renew'd,
And my divided flame shou'd break from thine.
    Emp. Serpent, I will engender Poyson with thee;
Joyn Hate with Hate, add Venom to the birth;
Our Off-spring, like the seed of Dragons Teeth,
Shall issue arm'd, and fight themselves to death.
    Alm. I'm calm again; thou canst not marry me.
    Emp. As gleams of Sun-shine soften storms to show'rs,
470 So, if you smile, the loudness of my rage
In gentle Whispers shall return but this,————
That nothing can divert my Love, but Death.
    Alm. See how thou art deceiv'd, I am a Christian;
'Tis true, unpractis'd in my new Belief,
Wrongs I resent, nor pardon yet with ease:
Those Fruits come late, and are of slow increase
In haughty Hearts, like mine: Now, tell thy self
If this one word destroy not thy designs:
Thy Law permits thee not to marry me.
480   *Emp.* 'Tis but a specious Tale, to blast my hopes,
And baffle my pretensions. Speak, *Sebastian,*
And, as a King, speak true.
    Sebast.   Then, thus adjur'd,
On a King's word 'tis truth, but truth ill tim'd;
For her dear Life is now expos'd anew;
Unless you wholly can put on Divinity,
And graciously forgive.
    Alm.   Now learn by this,
The little value I have left for life,
And trouble me no more.
    Emp.   I thank thee, Woman;

---

458 *Affrick*] Q2; *Affric* Q1; *Africk* F; *Africa* D.
460 ev'n] F, D; e'vn Q1; e'ven Q2.
471 return] ~ , Q1–2, F, D.   488 thee,] F, D; ~∧ Q1–2.

Thou hast restor'd me to my native Rage;
490 And I will seize my happiness by force.
    Sebast. Know *Muley-Moluch* when thou dar'st attempt——
    Emp. Beware, I wou'd not be provok'd to use
A Conqueror's right, and therefore charge thy silence.
If thou wou'dst merit to be thought my Friend,
I leave thee to perswade her to compliance:
If not, there's a new gust in Ravishment,
Which I have never try'd.
    Bend.   They must be watch'd;   *[Aside.*
For something I observ'd creates a doubt.
                    [Exeunt Emperour and Benducar.
    Seb. I've been too tame, have basely born my Wrongs,
500 And not exerted all the King within me;
I heard him, O sweet Heavens, he threat'ned Rape;
Nay insolently urg'd me to perswade thee,
Ev'n thee, thou Idol of my Soul and Eyes;
For whom I suffer Life, and drag this being.
    Alm. You turn my Prison to a Paradise;
But I have turn'd your Empire to a Prison:
In all your Wars good fortune flew before you;
Sublime you sate in Triumph on her Wheel,
Till in my fatal Cause your Sword was drawn;
510 The weight of my misfortunes drag'd you down.
    Seb. And is't not strange, that Heav'n shou'd bless my Arms
In common Causes, and desert the best?
Now in your greatest, last extremity,
When I wou'd ayd you most, and most desire it,
I bring but Sighs, the succors of a Slave.
    Alm. Leave then the luggage of your fate behind,
To make your flight more easie, leave *Almeyda.*
Nor think me left a base ignoble Prey,
Expos'd to this inhuman Tyrant's lust;

---

491   attempt——] ~ .—— Q1, D; ~ . Q2, F.
497   *s.d. Aside*] F, D; *aside* Q1-2.
498+   *s.d. Emperour*] Emperour Q1-2, F, D.   500   King] Q2, F, D; ~ , Q1.
508   Wheel,] ~ ; Q1-2, F, D.   514   wou'd] Q2, F, D; ~ , Q1.

520 My Virtue is a guard beyond my strength,
And Death, my last defence, within my call.
    Seb. Death may be call'd in vain, and cannot come;
Tyrants can tye him up from your relief:
Nor has a Christian privilege to dye.
Alas thou art too young in thy new Faith;
Brutus and *Cato* might discharge their Souls,
And give 'em Furlo's for another World:
But we, like Centry's, are oblig'd to stand
In starless Nights, and wait the 'pointed hour.
530   *Alm.* If shunning ill be good, then Death is good
To those who cannot shun it but by Death:
Divines but peep on undiscover'd Worlds,
And draw the distant Landshape as they please:
But who has e'er return'd from those bright Regions,
To tell their Manners, and relate their Laws?
I'll venture landing on that happy shoar
With an unsully'd Body, and white Mind;
If I have err'd, some kind Inhabitant
Will pity a stray'd Soul, and take me home.
540   *Seb.* Beware of Death, thou canst not dye unperjur'd,
And leave an unaccomplish'd Love behind:
Thy Vows are mine; nor will I quit my claim:
The tye of Minds are but imperfect Bonds,
Unless the Bodies joyn to seal the Contract.
    Alm. What Joys can you possess or can I give,
Where groans of Death succeed the sighs of Love?
Our Hymen has not on his Saffron Robe;
But muffled up in Mourning, downward holds
His dropping Torch, extinguish'd with his Tears.
550   *Seb.* The God of Love stands ready to revive it
With his etherial breath.
    Alm. 'Tis late to joyn, when we must part so soon.
    Seb. Nay rather let us haste it, ere we part:
Our Souls, for want of that acquaintance here,

---

529 'pointed] pointed Q1-2, F; appointed D.
545-546 give, . . . Love?] ~ ? . . . ~ . Q1-2, F, D.

May wander in the starry Walks above,
And, forc'd on worse Companions, miss our selves.
    Alm. The Tyrant will not long be absent hence;
And soon I shall be ravish'd from your arms.
    Seb. Wilt thou thy self become the greater Tyrant,
560 And give not Love, while thou hast Love to give?
In dang'rous days, when Riches are a Crime,
The wise betimes make over their Estates:
Make o'er thy Honour, by a deed of trust,
And give me seizure of the mighty wealth.
    Alm. What shall I do! O teach me to refuse!
I wou'd; and yet I tremble at the grant.
For dire presages fright my Soul by day,
And boding Visions haunt my Nightly Dreams:
Sometimes, methinks, I hear the groans of Ghosts;
570 Thin, hollow sounds, and lamentable screams;
Then, like a dying Eccho, from afar,
My Mothers Voice, that cries, *Wed not, Almeyda!*
Forewarn'd, Almeyda, Marriage is thy Crime.
    Seb. Some envious *Demon,* to delude our joys;
Love is not Sin, but where 'tis sinful Love.
    Alm. Mine is a flame so holy, and so clear,
That the white taper leaves no soot behind;
No smoak of Lust; but chast as Sisters love,
When coldly they return a Brothers kiss,
580 Without the zeal that meets at lovers mouths.
    Seb. Laugh then at fond presages; I had some;
Fam'd *Nostradamus,* when he took my Horoscope,
Foretold my Father I shou'd wed with Incest:
Ere this unhappy War my Mother dy'd;
And Sisters I had none; vain Augury!
A long Religious Life, a Holy Age,
My Stars assign'd me too; impossible.

---

563 o'er] Q2, F, D; oer Q1.   572 *Wed not,*] Wed not Q1–2, F, D (not, D).
573 *Forewarn'd,*] Forewarn'd_∧ Q1–2, F, D.
573 *Marriage . . . [to] . . . Crime*] *in romans in Q1–2, F, D.*
578 Sisters] Q2, F, D; Sister's Q1.

For how can Incest suit with Holiness,
Or Priestly Orders with a Princely State?
590   *Alm.* Old venerable *Alvarez!*———   (*Sighing.*)
       Seb. But why that sigh in naming that good Man?
       Alm. Your Fathers Counsellor and Confident———
       Seb. He was; and, if he lives, my second Father.
       Alm. Mark'd our farewel, when, going to the fight,
You gave *Almeyda* for the word of Battel;
'Twas in that fatal Moment, he discover'd
The Love that long we labour'd to conceal.
I know it; though my eyes stood full of tears,
Yet through the mist, I saw him stedfast gaze:
600 Then knock'd his Aged breast, and inward groan'd;
Like some sad Prophet, that foresaw the doom
Of those whom best he lov'd, and cou'd not save.
       Seb. It startles me! and brings to my remembrance,
That, when the shock of Battel was begun,
He wou'd have much complain'd (but had not time)
Of our hid passion; then, with lifted hands,
He beg'd me by my Fathers Sacred Soul,
Not to espouse you, if he dy'd in fight:
For if he liv'd, and we were Conquerors,
610 He had such things to urge against our Marriage,
As, now declar'd, wou'd blunt my sword in Battel;
And dastardize my Courage.
       Alm.   My blood cruddles;
And cakes about my heart.
       Seb. I'll breath a sigh, so warm into thy bosom,
Shall make it flow again. My Love, he knows not
Thou art a Christian; that produc'd his fear:
Lest thou shoud'st sooth my Soul with charms so strong,
That Heav'n might prove too weak.
       Alm.   There must be more:
This cou'd not blunt your Sword.
620   *Seb.* Yes, if I drew it, with a curst intent,

---

590   *s.d. Sighing*] D; sighing Q1–2, F.   593   Father.] F, D; ~ : Q1–2.
594   when,] ~∧ Q1–2, F, D.   599   Yet] Q2, F, D; ~ , Q1.

To take a Misbeliever to my Bed;
It must be so.
   Alm.   Yet———
   Seb.   No, thou shalt not plead
With that fair mouth, against the Cause of Love.
Within this Castle is a Captive Priest,
My Holy Confessor, whose free access
Not ev'n the barb'rous Victors have refus'd;
This happy hour his hands shall make us one.
   Alm. I go; with Love and Fortune, two blind Guides,
To lead my way: half loth and half consenting.
630 If, as my Soul fore-bodes, some dire event
Pursue this Union, or some Crime unknown,
   Forgive me Heav'n; and all ye Blest above,
   Excuse the frailty of unbounded Love.

                            Exeunt Ambo.

SCENE II.

Suppos'd a Garden; with Lodging Rooms
behind it; or on the sides.

Enter Mufti; Antonio *as a Slave; and* Johayma
the Mufti's *Wife.*

Mufti. And how do you like him? look upon him well; he's a personable Fellow of a Christian Dog. Now I think you are fitted, for a Gardiner: Ha what say'st thou *Johayma?*
   Johayma. He may make a shift to sow lettice, raise Melons, and water a Garden-plat: But otherwise a very filthy Fellow; how odiously he smells of his Country garlike! fugh, how he stinks of *Spain.*
   Mufti. Why honey-bird, I bought him a purpose for thee; didst not thou say thou long'dst for a Christian Slave?

SCENE II. / *Suppos'd*] Q2, F; Scene 2. *Suppos'd* Q1; SCENE II. *Suppos'd* D.
1 him?] ~ , Q1–2, F, D.   5 Garden-plat:] Garden-plat. Q1–2, F, D.
8 honey-bird,] D; ~∧ Q1–2, F.

10   *Joh.* Ah, but the sight of that loathsom creature has almost cur'd me; And how can I tell that he's a Christian? and he were well search'd he may prove a *Jew* for ought I know. And besides I have always long'd for an Eunuch; for they say that's a Civil Creature, and almost as harmless as your self, Husband. Speak fellow, are not you such a kind of peaceable thing?

    Ant. I was never taken for one in my own Country; and not very peaceable neither, when I am well provok'd.

    Mufti. To your Occupation Dog; bind up the Jessamines in yond Arbor, and handle your pruning knife with dexterity; 20 tightly I say, go tightly to your business; you have cost me much; and must earn it in your work; here's plentiful provision for you, rascal, sallating in the Garden, and water in the tanck, and on Holydays the licking of a platter of Rice, when you deserve it.

    Joh. What have you been bred up to Sirrah, and what can you perform to recommend you to my service?

    Antonio making legs. Why Madam, I can perform as much as any Man, in a fair Ladies Service. I can play upon the Flute, and Sing; I can carry your Umbrella, and fan your Ladyship, 30 and cool you when you are too hot: in fine, no Service either by day or by night shall come amiss to me; and besides am of so quick an apprehension, that you need but wink upon me at any time, to make me understand my duty.   [*She winks at him.*

    Anton. Very fine, she has tipt the wink already.———— [*Aside.*

    Joh. The Whelp may come to something in time, when I have enter'd him into his business.

    Muf. A very malapert Cur, I can tell him that; I do not like his fawning, you must be taught your distance Sirrah.

                            (*Strikes him.*)

    Joh. Hold, hold.————He has deserv'd it I confess; but for 40 once let his ignorance plead his pardon; we must not discourage a beginner. Your Reverence has taught us Charity ev'n to Birds

---

14   self,] F, D; ∼ₐ Q1-2.
14-15   Husband. Speak] Husband: speak Q1-2, F, D (Speak F, D).
27   *Antonio . . . legs.* Why] D; [Antonio *. . . legs. /* Why Q1-2, F (ₐAntonio F; "Why" *indented*).
39   has] Q2, F, D; ha's Q1.

and Beasts. Here you filthy brute you:————take this little
Alms, to buy you plaisters.   (*Gives him a piece of money.*)
    Ant. Money and a Love-pinch in the inside of my palm into
the bargain.   [*Aside.*

Enter a Servant.

    Serv. Sir, my Lord *Benducar* is coming to wait on you, and is
already at the Palace Gate.
    Muf. Come in *Johayma*, regulate the rest of my Wives and
Concubines, and leave the Fellow to his work.
50   *Joh.* Look how stupidly he stares about him, like a Calf new
come into the World. I shall teach you Sirrah to know your
business, a little better.————This way you awkard rascal, here
lyes the Arbour, must I be showing you eternally?
                                          (*Turning him about.*)
    Muf. Come away Minion; you shall show him nothing.
    Joh. I'll but bring him into the Arbor, where a Rose-tree and
a Myrtle are just falling for want of a prop; if they were bound
together they wou'd help to keep up one another.————He's a
raw Gardiner, and 'tis but Charity to teach him.
    Muf. No more deeds of Charity to day; come in, or I shall
60 think you a little better dispos'd than I cou'd wish you.
    Joh. Well, go before, I will follow my Pastor.
    Muf. So you may cast a sheeps eye behind you: In before me.
And you, sawciness, mind your pruning knife; or I may chance
to use it for you.
                              Exeunt Mufti *and* Johayma.
    Ant. alone. Thank you for that; but I am in no such hast to
be made a Musulman. For his Wedlock, with all her haughti-
ness, I find her coming. How far a Christian shou'd resist, I
partly know; but how far a lewd young Christian can resist is

42 Beasts. Here] ∼ : here Q1–2, F, D (Beasts; F).
43 s.d. Gives] F, D; gives Q1–2.
43 s.d. money.] Q2, F, D; ∼∧ Q1.   45+   s.d. Enter] Q2, F, D; (∼ Q1.
46 Serv. Sir] F, D; Sir Q1–2 ("Sir" indented).   51   World.] ∼ : Q1–2, F, D.
52 This] F; this Q1–2, D.   53+   s.d. Turning] F, D; turning Q1–2.
57 another.] F; ∼ : Q1–2, D.   64+   s.d. Johayma] Q2, F, D; Johayma Q1.

another question. She's tolerable, and I am a poor Stranger, far
70 from better Friends, and in a bodily necessity: Now have I a
strange temptation to try what other Females are belonging to
this Family: I am not far from the Womens apartment I am
sure; and if these Birds are within distance, here's that will
chuckle 'em together. (*Pulls out his Flute.*) If there be variety of
Moors flesh in this Holy Market 'twere madness to lay out all
my money upon the first bargain.   [*He plays.*

A Grate opens and Morayma *the* Mufti's *Daughter appears at it.*

Anton. Ay there's an Apparition! This is a Morsel worthy of
a *Mufti;* this is the relishing bit in secret; this is the Mystery of
his Alcoran, that must be reserv'd from the knowledg of the
80 profane Vulgar. This is his Holyday Devotion; see, she beckons
too.————

                                        (*She beckons to him.*)
Morayma. Come a little nearer and speak softly.
Ant. I come, I come I warrant thee; the least twinckle had
brought me to thee; such another kind syllable or two, wou'd
turn me to a Meteor and draw me up to thee.
Mor. I dare not speak, for fear of being over-heard; but if
you think my Person worth your hazard, and can deserve my
love————the rest this Note shall tell you.————(*Throws down
a handkerchief.*) No more, my heart goes with you.
                                        Exit from the Grate.
90 *Antonio.* O thou pretty little heart; art thou flown hither? I'll
keep it warm I warrant it, and brood upon it in the new nest:
but now for my Treasure trove, that's wrapt up in the handkerchief: No peeping here, though I long to be spelling her *Arabick* scrawls and pot-hooks. But I must carry off my prize, as
Robbers do; and not think of sharing the booty, before I am

---

74 *s.d. Pulls*] F; *pulls* Q1–2, D.   74 *s.d. Flute.*] F; ~ˌ Q1–2, D.
75 *Moors*] Moors Q1–2, F, D.   88 you.] ~ˌ Q1–2, F, D.
88–89 *s.d. Throws down a handkerchief*] F, D (*throws*); throws down a handkerchief Q1–2.
90 hither?] F, D; ~ , Q1–2.   93–94 *Arabick*] F; Arabick Q1–2, D.

free from danger, and out of eye-shot from the other Windows.
If her wit be as poynant as her Eyes, I am a double Slave. Our
Northern Beauties are meer dough to these: Insipid white
Earth, meer Tobaccopipe-clay; With no more Soul and Motion
100 in 'em, than a Fly in Winter.

Here the warm Planet ripens, and sublimes
The well-bak'd Beauties of the Southern Climes;
Our *Cupid*'s but a bungler in his Trade;
His keenest Arrows are in *Affrick* made.

[*Exit* Antonio.

ACT III. SCENE I.

*A Terrace-walk; or some other publick place
in the Castle of Alcazar.*

Enter Emperor Muley-Moluch; Benducar.

Emper. Marry'd! I'll not believe it; 'tis imposture;
Improbable they shou'd presume t' attempt,
Impossible they shou'd effect their wish.
   Bend. Have patience till I clear it.
   Emp.   I have none:
Go bid our moving Plains of Sand lye still,
And stir not, when the stormy South blows high:
From top to bottom thou hast toss'd my Soul,
And now 'tis in the madness of the Whirl,
Requir'st a sudden stop? unsay thy lye,
10 That may in time do somewhat.
   Bend.   I have done:
For, since it pleases you it shou'd be forg'd,

102–104 *not indented in Q1.*   102 well-bak'd] F, D; well bak'd Q1–2.
103 *Cupid's*] D; Cupid's Q1–2, F.   104 *Affrick*] F, D; Affrick Q1–2.
ACT III. SCENE I. / A] Q2, F, D (ACT. Q2); ACT. III. / Scene 1. A Q1.
s.d. Enter Emperor Muley-Moluch; Benducar] F, D; *Emperor Muley-Moluch;
Benducar* Q1–2.

'Tis fit it shou'd: far be it from your Slave,
To raise disturbance in your Sacred brest.
    Emp. Sebastian is my Slave as well as thou;
Nor durst offend my love by that presumption.
    Bend. Most sure he ought not.
    Emp.   Then all means were wanting;
No Priest, no Ceremonies of their Sect;
Or, grant we these defects cou'd be supply'd,
How cou'd our Prophet do an Act so base,
20 So to resume his gifts, and curse my Conquests
By making me unhappy! No, the Slave
That told thee so absurd a story, ly'd.
    Bend. Yet, till this moment I have found him faithful:
He said he saw it too.
    Emp.   Dispatch; what saw he?
    Bend. Truth is, considering with what earnestness
Sebastian pleaded for *Almeyda's* life,
Inhanc'd her beauty, dwelt upon her praise,———
    Emp. O stupid, and unthinking as I was!
I might have mark'd it too: 'twas gross and palpable!
30   *Bend.* Methought I trac'd a Lover ill disguis'd;
And sent my spy, a sharp observing Slave,
T' inform me better, if I guess'd aright.
He told me, that he saw *Sebastians* Page
Run cross the Marble Square; who soon return'd,
And after him there lag'd a puffing Fryar;
Close wrap'd he bore some secret Instrument
Of Christian Superstition in his hand:
My servant follow'd fast, and through a chink,
Perceiv'd the Royal Captives hand in hand:
40 And heard the hooded Father mumbling charms,
That make those Misbelievers Man and Wife.
Which done, the Spouses kiss'd with such a fervour,
And gave such furious earnest of their flames,
That their eyes sparkled, and their mantling blood
Flew flushing o'er their faces.

---

25 earnestness] D; ∼ , Q1–2, F.

Emp.   Hell confound 'em!
Bend. The Reverend Father, with a Holy leer,
Saw he might well be spar'd, and soon withdrew:
This forc'd my Servant to a quick retreat,
For fear to be discover'd; guess the rest.
50   *Emp.* I do. My fancy is too exquisite,
And tortures me with their imagin'd bliss.
Some Earthquake shou'd have ris'n, and rent the ground,
Have swallow'd him, and left the longing Bride
In Agony of unaccomplish'd Love.   (*Walks disorderly.*)

Enter the Mufti.

Bend. In an unlucky hour   [*Aside.*
That Fool intrudes, raw in this great affair,
And uninstructed how to stem the tide.
The Emp'ror must not marry, nor enjoy;
                    [*Coming up to the* Mufti (*aside*).
Keep to that point; stand firm, for all's at stake.
60   *Emperor, seeing him.* You, Druggerman of Heaven, must I
          attend
Your droaning Prayers? Why came you not before?
Do'st thou not know the Captive King has dar'd
To wed *Almeyda?* Cancel me that Marriage,
And make her mine; about the business, quick,
Expound thy *Mahomet;* make him speak my sense,
Or he's no Prophet here, and thou no *Mufti,*
Unless thou know'st the trick of thy vocation,
To wrest and rend the Law to please thy Prince.
     Mufti. Why, verily the Law is monstrous plain:
70 There's not one doubtful Text in all the Alchoran,
Which can be wrench'd in favor to your Project.

---

53   Bride] D; ∼ , Q1–2, F.   54   *s.d. disorderly.*] F, D; ∼ₐ Q1–2.
58–58+   *s.d.* The . . . enjoy; / [*Coming* . . . Mufti (*aside*).] *Coming* . . . Mufti
aside. / The . . . enjoy; Q1–2, F (*s.d. centered;* "The" *indented in Q1–2*); [*Coming* . . . Mufti *aside.* / The . . . enjoy; D ("The" *indented*).
60   *Emperor,*] ∼ₐ Q1–2; *Emp.* F, D.   65   *Mahomet*] F, D; Mahomet Q1–2.
69   *Mufti.*] Q2, F, D (*Muf.*); ∼ , Q1.

Emp. Forge one, and foist it into some by-place,
Of some old rotten Roll; do't, I command thee:
Must I teach thee thy Trade?
　　Mufti.　　　　　　　　　It cannot be.
For Matrimony being the dearest point
Of Law, the People have it all by heart:
A Cheat on Procreation will not pass.
Besides th' offence is so exorbitant,　　　　　　[*In a higher tone.*
To mingle with a misbelieving Race,
80　That speedy Vengeance wou'd pursue your Crime,
And holy *Mahomet* launch himself from Heav'n,
Before th' unready Thunderbolt were form'd.
　　　*Emperor taking him by the Throat with one hand, snatches
　　　　out his Sword with the other, and points it to his Brest.*
　　Emp. Slave, have I rais'd thee to this pomp and pow'r,
To preach against my Will? Know I am Law;
And thou, not *Mahomet's* Messenger, but mine:
Make it, I charge thee, make my pleasure lawful:
Or first I strip thee of thy ghostly greatness,
Then send thee post, to tell thy Tale above;
And bring thy vain Memorials to thy Prophet
90　Of Justice done below for Disobedience.
　　Mufti. For Heaven's sake hold, the respite of a moment,

To think for you.
　　Emp.　　　　　　　And for thy self.————
　　Mufti.　　　　　　　　　　　　For both.
　　Bend. Disgrace, and Death, and Avarice have lost him! [*Aside.*
　　Mufti. 'Tis true, our Law forbids to wed a Christian;
But it forbids you not to ravish her.
You have a Conqueror's right upon your Slave;
And then, the more despight you do a Christian,
You serve the Prophet more who loaths that Sect.
　　Emp. Oh now it mends; and you talk reason, *Mufti.*

100 But stay! I promis'd freedom to *Sebastian:*
Now shou'd I grant it, his revengeful Soul
Wou'd ne'er forgive his violated Bed.
    Mufti. Kill him, for then you give him liberty:
His Soul is from his earthly Prison freed.
    Emp. How happy is the Prince who has a Churchman
So learn'd and pliant to expound his Laws!
    Bend. Two things I humbly offer to your prudence.
    Emp. Be brief; but let not either thwart my love.
    Bend. First, since our holy Man has made Rape lawful,
110 Fright her with that: proceed not yet to force:
Why shou'd you pluck the green distastful Fruit
From the unwilling Bough,
When it may ripen of it self and fall?
    Emp. Grant her a day; tho that's too much to give
Out of a Life which I devote to Love.
    Bend. Then next, to bar
All future hopes of her desir'd *Sebastian,*
Let *Dorax* be enjoyn'd to bring his head.
    Emperor to the Mufti. Go *Mufti,* call him to receive his
        Orders.   [*Exit* Mufti.
120 I taste thy Counsel, her desires new rowz'd,
And yet unslak'd, will kindle in her fancy,
And make her eager to renew the Feast.
    Bend. aside. Dorax, I know before, will disobey:
There's a Foe's Head well cropt.————
But this hot love precipitates my Plot;
And brings it to projection ere its time.

    Enter Sebastian *and* Almeyda *hand in hand; upon sight of the
        Emperor, they separate and seem disturb'd.*

    Almeyda. He breaks, at unawares, upon our Walks,
And like a mid-night Wolf invades the Fold:

---

106 Laws!] D; ~ . Q1-2, F.
119 *Emperor . . . Mufti.* Go] F, D (Mufti D); Emperor . . . Mufti. / Go Q1-2
(Emperour Q2; *speech tag centered;* "Go" *indented*).
127, 174 *Almeyda.*] Q2, F, D (*Alm.* F); ~ , Q1.

Make speedy preparation of your Soul,
130 And bid it arm apace: He comes for answer,
And brutal mischief sits upon his brow.
　　Sebast. Not the last sounding, cou'd surprize me more,
That summons drowzy Mortals to their doom,
When call'd in haste, they fumble for their Limbs,
And tremble unprovided for their charge:
My sense has been so deeply plung'd in Joys,
The Soul out-slept her hour; and, scarce awake,
Wou'd think too late, and cannot! But brave Minds
At worst can dare their Fate.————
　　　　　　　　　　　　Emperor coming up to them.
　　Emp.　　　　　　　　　Have you perform'd
140 Your Embassy, and treated with success?
　　Sebast. I had not time.
　　Emp.　　　　　　No, not for my Affairs,
But for your own too much.
　　Sebast. You talk in Clouds, explain your meaning, Sir.
　　Emp. Explain yours first: What meant you hand in hand,
And when you saw me, with a guilty start,
You loos'd your hold, affrighted at my presence?
　　Seb. Affrighted?
　　Emp.　　　　　Yes, astonish'd, and confounded.
　　Seb. What mak'st thou of thy self, and what of me?
Art thou some Ghost, some Demon, or some God?
150 That I shou'd stand astonish'd at thy sight?
If thou cou'dst deem so meanly of my Courage,
Why didst thou not engage me man for man,
And try the virtue of that *Gorgon* Face,
To stare me into statue?
　　Emp. Oh, thou art now recover'd, but by Heav'n,
Thou wert amaz'd at first, as if surpriz'd
At unexpected baseness brought to light.
For know, ungrateful man, that Kings, like Gods,
Are every where; walk in th' abyss of minds,
160 And view the dark recesses of the Soul.
　　Seb. Base and ungrateful never was I thought;

Nor till this turn of fate, durst thou have call'd me;
But, since thou boast'st th' omniscience of a God,
Say, in what cranny of *Sebastian's* Soul,
Unknown to me, so loath'd a Crime is lodg'd?
    Emp. Thou hast not broke my trust repos'd in thee?
    Seb. Impos'd, but not receiv'd: Take back that falsehood.
    Emp. Thou art not marry'd to *Almeyda?*
    Seb.   Yes.
    Emp. And own'st the usurpation of my Love?
170   *Seb.* I own it in the face of Heav'n and thee
No Usurpation; but a lawful claim,
Of which I stand possest.
    Emp.   Sh' has chosen well,
Betwixt a Captive and a Conqueror.
    Almeyda. Betwixt a Monster and the best of Men.
He was the envy of his neighb'ring Kings;
For him their sighing Queens despis'd their Lords,
And Virgin Daughters blush'd when he was nam'd.
To share his noble Chains is more to me,
Than all the salvage greatness of thy Throne.
180   *Seb.* Were I to choose again, and knew my fate,
For such a night I wou'd be what I am.
The Joys I have possest are ever mine;
Out of thy reach behind Eternity,
Hid in the sacred treasure of the past;
But bless'd remembrance brings 'em hourly back.
    Emp. Hourly indeed, who hast but hours to live:
O mighty purchase of a boasted bliss!
To dream of what thou hadst one fugitive night,
And never shalt have more.
190   *Seb.* Barbarian, thou canst part us but a moment;———
We shall be one again in thy despight:
Life is but air,
That yields a passage to the whistling Sword,
And closes when 'tis gone.
    Alm. How can we better dye than close embrac'd,

---

185 brings] Q2, F, D; bring's Q1.

Sucking each others Souls while we expire?
Which so transfus'd, and mounting both at once,
The Saints deceiv'd, shall by a sweet mistake,
Hand up thy Soul for mine, and mine for thine.
200   *Emp.* No, I'll untwist you:
I have occasion for your stay on earth:
Let him mount first, and beat upon the Wing,
And wait an Age for what I here detain,
Or sicken at immortal Joys above,
And languish for the Heav'n he left below.
    Alm. Thou wilt not dare to break what Heav'n has joyn'd?
    Emp. Not break the Chain, but change a rotten link,
And rivet one to last.
Think'st thou I come to argue right and wrong?
210 Why lingers *Dorax* thus? Where are my Guards,
                 [Benducar *goes out for the Guards, and returns.*
To drag that Slave to death? [*Pointing to* Sebast.] Now storm
    and rage;
Call vainly on thy Prophet, then defie him
For wanting power to save thee.
    Seb. That were to gratifie thy Pride: I'll shew thee
How a Man shou'd, and how a King dare dye:
So even, that my Soul shall walk with ease
Out of its flesh, and shut out Life as calmly
As it does words; without a Sigh, to note
One struggle in the smooth dissolving frame.
220   *Almeyda to the Emperor.* Expect revenge from Heav'n, in-
    human Wretch;
Nor hope t' ascend *Sebastian's* holy Bed.
Flames, Daggers, Poysons, guard the sacred steps:
Those are the promis'd Pleasures of my love.
    Emp. And these might fright another, but not me.
Or me, if I design'd to give you pleasure;
I seek my own, and while that lasts, you live.

203   detain,] D; ~ . Q1–2, F.
211   Sebast.] Now . . . rage;] ~ . / ~ . . . ~ , Q1–2, F, D.
220   *Almeyda . . . Emperor.* Expect] D; Almeyda . . . ~ . / ~ Q1–2, F (*speech tag centered;* "Expect" *indented*).

Enter two of the Guards.

Go, bear the Captive to a speedy death,
And set my Soul at ease.
   Alm. I charge you hold, ye Ministers of death.
230 Speak my *Sebastian;*
Plead for thy life: Oh ask it of the Tyrant;
'Tis no dishonor, trust me, Love, 'tis none:
I wou'd die for thee, but I cannot plead;
My haughty heart disdains it, ev'n for thee.
Still silent! Will the King of *Portugal*
Go to his death, like a dumb Sacrifice?
Beg him to save my life in saving thine.
   Seb. Farewel, my life's not worth another word.
   Emp. to the Guards. Perform your Orders.
   Alm.   Stay, take my fare-
wel too!
240 Farewel the greatness of *Almeyda*'s Soul!
Look, Tyrant, what excess of love can do,
It pulls me down thus low, as to thy feet;   [*Kneels to him.*
Nay to embrace thy Knees with loathing hands,
Which blister when they touch thee: Yet ev'n thus,
Thus far I can to save *Sebastian*'s life.
   Emp. A secret pleasure trickles through my Veins:
It works about the inlets of my Soul,
To feel thy touch; and pity tempts the pass;
But the tough metal of my heart resists;
250 'Tis warm'd with the soft fire, not melted down.
   Alm. A flood of scalding Tears will make it run,
Spare him, Oh spare; can you pretend to love,
And have no pity? Love and that are Twins.
Here will I grow;
Thus compass you with these supplanting Cords,
And pull so long till the proud Fabrick falls.
   Emp. Still kneel, and still embrace; 'tis double pleasure
So to be hugg'd, and see *Sebastian* dye.

---

229 death.] F; ~ , Q1–2, D.   239 too!] ~ : Q1–2, F, D.

Alm. Look Tyrant, when thou nam'st *Sebastian's* death,
260 Thy very Executioners turn pale;
Rough as they are, and harden'd in the trade
Of Death, they start at an anointed Head,
And tremble to approach.————He hears me not;
Nor minds th' impression of a God on Kings;
Because no stamp of Heav'n was on his Soul:
But the resisting Mass drove back the Seal.
Say, though thy heart be rock of Adamant,
Yet Rocks are not impregnable to Bribes:
Instruct me how to bribe thee: Name thy price;
270 Lo, I resign my Title to the Crown;
Send me to exile with the Man I love,
And banishment is Empire.
    Emp.   Here's my claim;
                  [*Clapping his hand to his Sword.*
And this extinguish'd thine; thou giv'st me nothing.
    Alm. My Father's, Mothers, Brothers death I pardon:
That's somewhat sure; a mighty Sum of Murther,
Of innocent and kindred blood strook off.
My Prayers and Penance shall discount for these,
And beg of Heav'n to charge the Bill on me:
Behold what price I offer, and how dear,
280 To buy *Sebastian's* life.
    Emp. Let after-reck'nings trouble fearful fools;
I'll stand the tryal of those trivial Crimes:
But, since thou beg'st me to prescribe my terms,
The only I can offer are thy love;
And this one day of respite to resolve.
Grant or deny, for thy next word is Fate;
And Fate is deaf to Pray'r.
    Alm.   May Heav'n be so   [*Rising up.*
At thy last breath to thine: I curse thee not,
For who can better curse the Plague or Devil,

260   pale;] ~ , Q1–2, F, D.   263   approach.] ~ : Q1–2, F, D.
279   dear,] ~∧ Q1–2, F, D.
281   after-reck'nings] D; after reck'nings Q1–2, F.

290 Than to be what they are? That Curse be thine.
Now, do not speak *Sebastian,* for you need not,
But dye, for I resign your Life. Look Heav'n,
Almeyda dooms her dear *Sebastian*'s death!
But is there Heav'n? for I begin to doubt;
The Skyes are hush'd; no grumbling Thunders roul.
Now take your swing, ye impious; Sin unpunish'd;
Eternal providence seems overwatch'd,
And with a slumb'ring Nod assents to Murther.

Enter Dorax *attended by three Soldiers.*

Emp. Thou mov'st a Tortoise pace to my relief.
300 Take hence that, once a King; that sullen pride
That swells to dumbness; lay him in the Dungeon,
And sink him deep with Irons; that when he wou'd,
He shall not groan to hearing; when I send,
The next Commands are death.
　　　Alm. Then Prayers are vain as Curses.
　　　Emp. 　　　　　　　　　　　Much at one
In a Slaves mouth, against a Monarch's Pow'r.
This day thou hast to think;
At night, if thou wilt curse, thou shalt curse kindly;
Then I'll provoke thy lips, lay siege so close,
310 That all thy sallying breath shall turn to Blessings.
Make haste, seize, force her, bear her hence.
　　　Alm. Farewel, my last *Sebastian!*
I do not beg, I challenge Justice now.
O Pow'rs, if Kings be your peculiar care,
Why plays this Wretch with your Prerogative?
Now flash him dead, now crumble him to ashes;
Or henceforth live confin'd in your own Palace;
And look not idely out upon a World

292　Life.] ~ : Q1-2, F, D.　　294　Heav'n?] D; ~ , Q1-2, F.
295　roul.] ~ : Q1-2, F, D.　　303　hearing;] ~ , Q1-2, F, D.
303　send,] ~∧ Q1-2, F, D.　　309　lips,] F; ~ ; Q1-2, D.
313　now.] ~ ; Q1-2, F, D.

That is no longer yours.
>   *She is carried off strugling, Emperour and* Benducar *follow.*
>   Sebastian *struggles in his Guards Arms, and shakes off*
>   *one of them, but two others come in, and hold him; he*
>   *speaks not all the while.*

320   *Dor.* I find I'm but a half-strain'd Villain yet;   [*Aside.*
But mungril-mischievous; for my Blood boyl'd,
To view this brutal act; and my stern Soul
Tug'd at my arm to draw in her defence.
Down thou rebelling Christian in my heart;
Redeem thy fame on this *Sebastian* first;
Then think on others wrongs, when thine are righted.
>   [*Walks a turn.*
But how to right 'em? on a Slave disarm'd,
Defenceless, and submitted to my rage?
A base revenge is vengeance on my self.   [*Walks again.*
330 I have it; and I thank thee, honest head,
Thus present to me at my great necessity.————
>   [*Comes up to* Sebastian.
You know me not?
      Sebast.   I hear Men call thee *Dorax.*
      Dor. 'Tis well, you know enough for once: you speak too;
You were struck mute before.
      Sebast. Silence became me then.
      Dor.   Yet we may talk hereafter.
      Seb. Hereafter is not mine:————
Dispatch thy work, good Executioner.
      Dor. None of my blood were hangmen; add that falshood
To a long Bill that yet remains unreckon'd.
340   *Seb.* A King and thou can never have a reck'ning.
      Dor. A greater summ perhaps than you can pay.
Mean time I shall make bold t' increase your debt,
>   (*Gives him his Sword.*)
Take this, and use it at your greatest need.

319+   s.d. *Emperour*] Emperour Q1–2, F, D.
329   self.] ∼ ? Q1; ∼ ; Q2, F, D.
329   s.d. *Walks*] F, D; *walks* Q1–2.   331   necessity.] ∼ : Q1–2, F, D.
342+   s.d. *Gives . . . Sword.*] F, D; *gives . . . ∼*∧ Q1–2 (*Sword.* Q2).

Seb. This hand and this, have been acquainted well;
(*Looks on it.*)
It shou'd have come before into my grasp,
To kill the Ravisher.
    Dor. Thou heardst the Tyrants orders; Guard thy life
When 'tis attack'd, and guard it like a Man.
    Seb. I'm still without thy meaning but I thank thee.
350   *Dor.* Thank me when I ask thanks; thank me with that.
    Seb. Such surly kindness did I never see!
    Dorax to the Captain of his Guards. Muza, draw out a file,
      pick man by man,
Such who dare dye, and dear will sell their death.
Guard him to th' utmost; now conduct him hence,
And treat him as my Person.
    Seb.   Something like
That voice methinks I shou'd have somewhere heard:
But floods of woes have hurry'd it far off;
Beyond my kenn of Soul.
Exit Sebastian *with the Soldiers.*
    Dor. But I shall bring him back, ungrateful Man!   [*Solus.*
360 I shall, and set him full before thy sight,
When I shall front thee, like some staring Ghost,
With all my wrongs about me.————What, so soon
Return'd? This hast is boding.

Enter to him Emperor, Benducar, Mufti.

    Emp. She's still inexorable, still Imperious;
And loud, as if like *Bacchus* born in thunder.
Be quick, ye false Physicians of my mind,
Bring speedy Death or Cure.

---

352 *Dorax to . . . Guards. Muza*] D ([*to . . . Guards*∧]); (Dorax *to . . .*
Guards.) | *Muza* Q1–2, F (*speech tag centered;* "*Muza*" *indented*).
355 And] *as in* Q2, F, D; *indented in* Q1.
359 back,] F, D; ~∧ Q1–2.   359 Man!] ~ , Q1–2, F, D.
362 What,] ~∧ Q1–2, F, D.
363+ *s.d. Emperor*] Emperor Q1–2, F, D.
365 *Bacchus*] F, D; Bacchus Q1–2.

Bend. What can be counsell'd while *Sebastian* lives?
The Vine will cling, while the tall poplar stands:
370 But that cut down creeps to the next support,
And twines as closely there.
    Emp. That's done with ease, I speak him dead: proceed.
    Muf. Proclaim your Marriage with *Almeyda* next,
That Civil Wars may cease; this gains the Crowd;
Then you may safely force her to your will:
For People side with violence and injustice,
When done for publick good.
    Emp.   Preach thou that doctrine.
    Bend. Th' unreasonable fool has broach'd a truth   [*Aside.*
That blasts my hopes; but since 'tis gone so far,
380 He shall divulge *Almeyda* is a Christian:
If that produce no tumult, I despair.
    Emp. Why speaks not *Dorax?*
    Dor. Because my Soul abhors to mix with him.
Sir, let me bluntly say, you went too far,
To trust the Preaching pow'r on State Affairs,
To him or any Heavenly Demagogue.
'Tis a limb lopt from your Prerogative,
And so much of Heav'ns Image blotted from you.
    Muf. Sure thou hast never heard of Holy Men
390 (So Christians call 'em) fam'd in State Affairs;
Such as in *Spain, Ximenes, Albornoz,*
In *England, Woolsey;* match me these with Laymen.
    Dorax. How you triumph in one or two of these,
Born to be Statesmen, hap'ning to be Church-men:
Thou call'st 'em holy; so their function was;
But tell me, *Mufti,* which of 'em were Saints?
Next, Sir, to you; the summ of all is this;
Since he claims pow'r from Heav'n, and not from Kings,
When 'tis his int'rest, he can int'rest Heav'n
400 To preach you down; and Ages oft depend

---

381 tumult,] D; ~ᴀ Q1–2, F.   384 far,] F, D; ~ᴀ Q1–2.
391 *Spain,*] F, D; ~ᴀ Q1–2.   392 *England,*] F; ~ᴀ Q1–2, D.
395 call'st] Q2, F, D; call st Q1.

On hours, uninterrupted, in the Chair.
   Emp. I'll trust his Preaching while I rule his pay.
And I dare trust my *Affricans,* to hear
Whatever he dare Preach.
   Dor.   You know 'em not.
The genius of your *Moors* is mutiny;
They scarcely want a Guide to move their madness:
Prompt to rebel on every weak pretence,
Blustring when courted, crouching when opprest;
Wise to themselves, and fools to all the World;
410   Restless in change, and perjur'd to a Proverb.
They love Religion sweeten'd to the sense;
A good, luxurious, palatable faith.
Thus Vice and Godliness, prepost'rous pair,
Ride cheek by joul; but Churchmen hold the Reins.
And, when ere Kings wou'd lower Clergy greatness,
They learn too late what pow'r the Preachers have,
And whose the Subjects are; the *Mufti* knows it;
Nor dares deny what pass'd betwixt us two.
   Emp. No more; what ere he said was by Command.
420   *Dor.* Why then no more, since you will hear no more;
Some Kings are resolute to their own ruin.
   Emp. Without your medling where you are not ask'd,
Obey your Orders, and dispatch *Sebastian.*
   Dor. Trust my revenge; be sure I wish him dead.
   Emp. What mean'st thou! what's thy wishing to my will?
Dispatch him, rid me of the Man I loath.
   Dor. I hear you Sir, I'll take my time and do't————
   Emp. Thy time! what's all thy time, what's thy whole life
To my one hour of ease? no more replies,
430   But see thou do'st it; Or————
   Dor. Choak in that threat: I can say *Or,* as loud.
   Emp. 'Tis well, I see my words have no effect,

---

405 *Moors*] D; Moors Q1–2, F.
408–409 opprest; . . . World;] D; ∼. . . . . ∼. Q1–2, F.
411 sweeten'd] F; sweetn'd Q1–2, D.   425 will?] D; ∼ ; Q1; ∼. Q2, F.
426 loath.] F; ∼, Q1–2, D.   428 time!] ∼? Q1–2, F, D.
431 *Or*] Or Q1–2, F, D.

But I may send a Message to dispose you.
                                                        [*Is going off.*
   Dor. Expect an answer worthy of that Message.
   Muf. The Prophet ow'd him this: [*Aside.*
And thank'd be Heav'n, he has it.
   Bend. By Holy Alha, I conjure you stay,
And judge not rashly of so brave a Man.
                    (*Draws the Emperor aside and whispers him.*)
I'll give you reasons why he cannot execute
440 Your Orders now, and why he will hereafter.
   Muf. Benducar is a fool to bring him off,   [*Aside.*
I'll work my own revenge, and speedily.
   Bend. The Fort is his, the Soldiers hearts are his;
A thousand Christian Slaves are in the Castle,
Which he can free to reinforce his pow'r;
Your Troops far off, beleaguering *Larache,*
Yet in the Christians hands.
   Emp.   I grant all this;
But grant me he must dye.
   Bend.   He shall; by poyson:
'Tis here, the deadly drug prepar'd in powder,
450 Hot as Hell-fire:———then, to prevent his Soldiers
From rising to revenge their Gen'rals death,
While he is struggling with his Mortal pangs,
The Rabble on the sudden may be rais'd
To seize the Castle.
   Emp.   Do't; 'tis left to thee.
   Bend. Yet more; but clear your brow; for he observes.
                                        (*They whisper again.*)
   Dor. What, will the Fav'rite prop my falling fortunes?
O Prodigie of Court!   [*Aside.*
                    Emperor and Benducar *return to* Dorax.
   Emp. Your Friend has fully clear'd your Innocence;

438+   *s.d. Emperor*] Emperor Q1-2, F, D.
450   Hell-fire] Q2, F; Hell fire Q1, D.
454   To] Q2, F, D; to Q1.   456   What,] F, D; ~ ∧ Q1-2.
456   fortunes?] D; ~ , Q1-2, F.
457+   *s.d. Emperor and*] Emperor and Q1-2, F, D (*and* Q2, F, D).

I was too hasty to condemn unheard,
460 And you perhaps too prompt in your replies.
As far as fits the Majesty of Kings,
I ask excuse.
  Dor. I'm sure I meant it well.
  Emp. I know you did:————this to our love renew'd.————
               [*Emperor drinks.*
Benducar, fill to *Dorax.*
       [Benducar *turns and mixes a powder in it.*
  Dor. Let it go round, for all of us have need
To quench our heats; 'tis the Kings health *Benducar,*————
                [*He drinks.*
And I wou'd pledge it though I knew 'twere poyson.
  Bend. Another Bowl, for what the King has touch'd,
        [*Drinks out of another Bowl.*
And you have pledg'd, is sacred to your loves.————
470 *Muf.* Since Charity becomes my calling, thus
Let me provoke your friendship: and heav'n bless it,
As I intend it well.————
   Drinks; and turning aside pours some drops out of a little
   Vial into the Bowl; then presents it to Dorax.
  Dor.   Heav'n make thee honest,
On that condition we shall soon be friends.———— [*Drinks.*
  Muf. Yes, at our meeting in another World; [*Aside.*
For thou hast drunk thy passport out of this.
Not the *Nonacrian* fount, nor *Lethe's* Lake,
Cou'd sooner numb thy nimble faculties
Than this, to sleep eternal.
  Emp. Now farewel *Dorax;* this was our first quarrel,
480 And I dare prophesie will prove our last.
      Exit Emperor with Benducar *and the* Mufti.
  Dor. It may be so: I'm strangely discompos'd;
Quick shootings through my limbs, and pricking pains,

463+ *s.d. Emperor*] Emperor Q1–2, F, D.   464 *Benducar,*] D; ~ₐ Q1–2, F.
465 round,] F, D; ~ₐ Q1–2.   466 *Benducar,*] ~ . Q1–2, F, D.
471 it,] D; ~ₐ Q1–2, F.
476 *Nonacrian* . . . *Lethe's*] F, D; Nonacrian . . . Lethe's Q1–2.
480+ *s.d. Emperor*] Emperor Q1–2, F, D.

The Habit of the Women in Constantinople

A Turkish Woman with "Barnus"
From Paul Rycaut, *The History of the Present State
of the Ottoman Empire,* 5th ed., 1682

Qualms at my heart, Convulsions in my nerves,
Shiv'rings of cold, and burnings of my entrails
Within my little World make medley War,
Lose and regain, beat and are beaten back;
As momentary Victors quit their ground.
Can it be poyson! poyson's of one tenour,
Or hot or cold; this neither, and yet both.
490 Some deadly Draught, some enemy of life
Boils in my bowels, and works out my Soul.
Ingratitude's the growth of ev'ry Clime;
Affrick, the Scene remov'd, is *Portugal.*
    Of all Court-service learn the common lot;
    To day 'tis done, to morrow 'tis forgot.
    Oh were that all! my honest Corps must lye
    Expos'd to scorn, and publick Infamy:
    My shameful Death will be divulg'd alone;
    The worth and honour of my Soul unknown.

                                                    [*Exit.*

SCENE II.

A Night Scene of the Mufti's *Garden where
an Arbour is discover'd.*

Enter Antonio.

Ant. She names her self *Morayma;* the *Mufti's* only Daughter,
and a Virgin! This is the time and place that she appointed in
her letter, yet she comes not. Why, thou sweet delicious Creature, why to torture me with thy delay! dar'st thou be false to
thy Assignation? What, in the cool and silence of the night, and
to a new Lover? Pox on the Hypocrite, thy Father, for instructing thee so little in the sweetest point of his Religion. Hark, I

---

493 *Affrick . . . Portugal*] F, D; Affrick . . . Portugal Q1–2.
SCENE II. / *A*] Scene 2. *Is a* Q1–2, F (SCENE II. Q2, F); SCENE II. *A* D.
3   Why,] ~∧ Q1–2, F, D.

hear the rustling of her Silk Mantle. Now she comes; now she
comes; no, hang't, that was but the whistling of the wind
10 through the Orange Trees. Now again, I hear the pit-a-pat of a
pretty foot through the dark Alley: No, 'tis the Son of a Mare
that's broken loose and munching upon the Melons:————Oh
the misery of an expecting Lover! Well I'll e'en despair, go into
my Arbour, and try to sleep; in a dream I shall enjoy her in
despight of her.   [*Goes into the Arbour and lyes down.*

Enter Johayma *wrapt up in a* Moorish *Mantle.*

Joh. Thus far my love has carry'd me, almost without my
knowledg whither I was going: Shall I go on, shall I discover my
self?————What an injury am I doing to my old Husband!
————Yet what injury, since he's old, and has three Wives and
20 six Concubines besides me! 'Tis but stealing my own Tythe
from him.
                    [*She comes a little nearer the Arbour.*
     Antonio raising himself a little and looking. At last 'tis she:
this is no illusion I am sure; 'tis a true She-devil of Flesh and
Blood; and she cou'd never have taken a fitter time to tempt
me.————
     Joh. He's young and handsome————
     Ant. Yes, well enough, I thank nature.   [*Aside.*
     Joh. And I am yet neither old nor ugly: sure he will not re-
fuse me.
30   *Ant.* No, thou mayst pawn thy Maiden-head upon't he won-
not.   [*Aside.*
     Joh. The *Mufti* wou'd feast himself upon other Women, and
keep me fasting.
     Ant. O, the holy Curmudgeon!   [*Aside.*
     Joh. Wou'd Preach abstinence, and practice luxury! but I

---

10   Orange] D; *Orange* Q1-2, F.   10   pit-a-pat] F; pit a pat Q1-2, D.
15+   s.d. Moorish] D; *Moorish* Q1-2, F.   18   self?] ~ ! Q1-2, F, D.
22   *Antonio . . . looking.* At] Antonio . . . *looking.* / At Q1-2, F (*speech tag
centered;* "At" *indented*); Ant. . . . *looking.*] At D.
26   handsome] ~ . Q1-2, F, D.
27   enough,] F; ~ᴀ Q1-2, D.

thank my Stars, I have edify'd more by his example than his precept.

Anton. aside. Most divinely argu'd; she's the best Casuist in all *Affrick.*————[*He rushes out and embraces her.*] I can hold
40 no longer from embracing thee my dear *Morayma:* the old un-conscionable Whorson thy Father, cou'd he expect cold chastity from a Child of his begetting?

Joh. What nonsense do you talk? do you take me for the *Mufti's* Daughter?

Ant. Why, are you not, Madam?

                                        [*Throwing off her Barnus.*
Joh. I find you had an appointment with *Morayma.*

Ant. By all that's good, the nauseous Wife.   [*Aside.*
Joh. What, you are confounded and stand mute?

Ant. Somewhat nonplust I confess; to hear you deny your
50 name so positively; why, are not you *Morayma* the *Mufti's* Daughter? Did not I see you with him, did not he present me to you? Were you not so charitable as to give me Money? Ay and to tread upon my foot, and squeeze my hand too, if I may be so bold to remember you of past favours.

Joh. And you see I am come to make 'em good, but I am nei-ther *Morayma* nor the *Mufti's* Daughter.

Ant. Nay, I know not that: but I am sure he is old enough to be your Father: and either Father, or Reverend Father, I heard you call him.

60 *Johayma.* Once again, how came you to name *Morayma?*

Ant. Another damn'd mistake of mine: For, asking one of my fellow Slaves, who were the chief Ladies about the house; he answer'd me *Morayma* and *Johayma;* but she it seems is his Daughter, with a Pox to her, and you are his beloved Wife.

Joh. Say your beloved Mistris, if you please; for that's the Title I desire. This Moon-shine grows offensive to my Eyes,

---

38–39 *Anton. aside.* . . . *Affrick.*————[*He* . . . *her.*] I] *Anton.* . . . *Affrick.* [*Aside. | He* . . . *her. |* I Q1–2, F, D.   45 Why,] F, D; ~∧ Q1–2.
45 not,] F, D; ~∧ Q1–2.   45+ *s.d. Throwing*] F, D; *throwing* Q1–2.
48 What,] F, D; ~∧ Q1–2.   50 why,] D; ~∧ Q1–2, F.
60 *Johayma.*] Q2, F, D (*Joh.*); ~ , Q1.

come, shall we walk into the Arbor? There we may rectifie all
mistakes.

Ant. That's close and dark.

70   *Joh.* And are those faults to Lovers?

Ant. But there I cannot please my self, with the sight of your
beauty.

Joh. Perhaps you may do better.

Ant. But there's not a breath of air stirring.

Joh. The breath of Lovers is the sweetest air; but you are
fearful.

Ant. I am considering, indeed, that if I am taken with
you———

Joh. The best way to avoid it, is to retire, where we may not
80 be discover'd.

Ant. Where lodges your Husband?

Joh. Just against the face of this open Walk.

Ant. Then he has seen us already, for ought I know.

Joh. You make so many Difficulties, I fear I am displeasing
to you.

Ant. aside. If *Morayma* comes and takes me in the Arbor with
her, I have made a fine exchange of that Diamond for this
Pebble.

Joh. You are much fall'n off, let me tell you, from the fury
90 of your first embrace.

Ant. I confess, I was somewhat too furious at first, but you
will forgive the transport of my passion; now I have consider'd
it better, I have a qualm of Conscience.

Joh. Of Conscience! Why, what has Conscience to do with
two young Lovers that have opportunity?

Ant. Why truly Conscience is something to blame for interposing in our matters: But how can I help it, if I have a Scruple
to betray my Master?

Joh. There must be something more in it; for your Con-
100 science was very quiet when you took me for *Morayma.*

Ant. I grant you, Madam, when I took you for his Daughter:

---

78 you] ∼ . Q1–2, F, D.

For then I might have made you an honorable amends by Marriage.

Joh. You Christians are such peeking Sinners, you tremble at
a Shadow in the Moon-shine.

Ant. And you *Affricans* are such Termagants, you stop at
nothing. I must be plain with you, you are married, and to a
Holy Man, the Head of your Religion: Go back to your Chamber, go back, I say, and consider of it for this night; as I will
110 do on my part: I will be true to you, and invent all the Argu-
ments I can to comply with you; and who knows, but at our
next meeting, the sweet Devil may have more power over me: I
am true flesh and blood, I can tell you that for your comfort.

Joh. Flesh without blood I think thou art; or if any, 'tis as
cold as that of Fishes. But I'll teach thee, to thy cost, what Vengeance is in store for refusing a Lady, who has offer'd thee her
Love.———Help, Help, there! will no body come to my assistance?

Ant. What do you mean, Madam? for Heaven's sake peace;
120 your Husband will hear you; think of your own danger, if you
will not think of mine.

Joh. Ingrateful Wretch, thou deserv'st no pity. Help, Help,
Husband, or I shall be ravish'd! The Villain will be too strong
for me! Help, help, for pity of a poor distressed Creature!

Ant. Then I have nothing but impudence to assist me: I must
drown her clamor what e'er comes on't.

  He takes out his Flute, and plays as loud as he can possibly,
  and she continues crying out.

  Enter the Mufti *in his Night-gown, and two Servants.*

Mufti. O thou Villain, what horrible impiety art thou committing? What, ravishing the Wife of my Bosom? Take him

---

106 *Affricans*] F, D; Affricans Q1-2. 117 Love.] ∼ : Q1-2, F; ∼∧ D.
117 there!] ∼ ; Q1-2, F, D. 119 Madam?] D; ∼ , Q1-2, F.
122 pity.] F; ∼ : Q1-2, D.
123-124 ravish'd! . . . me! . . . Creature!] ∼ : . . . ∼ . . . . ∼ . Q1-2, F, D
(ravish'd; F).
127 *Mufti.*] F, D (*Muf.*); ∼ , Q1-2.
128 What,] D; ∼∧ Q1-2, F.

away, ganch him, impale him, rid the World of such a Monster.

[*Servants seize him.*

130 *Ant.* Mercy, dear Master, Mercy: Hear me first, and after, if I have deserved hanging, spare me not: What have you seen to provoke you to this cruelty?

Mufti. I have heard the out-crys of my Wife; the bleatings of the poor innocent Lamb: Seen nothing, say'st thou? If I see the Lamb lye bleeding, and the Butcher by her with his Knife drawn and bloody, is not that evidence sufficient of the Murther? I come too late, and the Execution is already done.

Ant. Pray think in reason, Sir, is a Man to be put to death for a similitude? No Violence has been committed; none in-
140 tended: The Lamb's alive; and if I durst tell you so, no more a Lamb than I am a Butcher.

Joh. How's that, Villain, dar'st thou accuse me?

Ant. Be patient Madam, and speak but truth, and I'll do any thing to serve you: I say again, and swear it too, I'll do any thing to serve you.

Joh. aside. I understand him; but I fear, 'tis now too late to save him.———Pray hear him speak, Husband; perhaps he may say something for himself; I know not.

Mufti. Speak thou, has he not violated my Bed and thy
150 Honor?

Joh. I forgive him freely; for he has done nothing: What he will do hereafter, to make me satisfaction, himself best knows.

Ant. Any thing, any thing, sweet Madam: I shall refuse no drudgery.

Muf. But, did he mean no mischief? Was he endeavouring nothing?

Joh. In my Conscience, I begin to doubt he did not.

Muf. 'Tis impossible: Then what meant all those out-crys?

Joh. I heard Musick in the Garden, and at an unseasonable
160 time of night; and I stole softly out of my Bed, as imagining it might be he.

---

133 *Mufti.*] Q2, F, D (*Muf.*); ∼ , Q1.   147 him.] ∼ : Q1–2, F, D.
149 *Mufti.*] Q2, F, D (*Muf.*); ∼ , Q1.

Muf. How's that *Johayma?* Imagining it was he, and yet you went?

Joh. Why not, my Lord? Am not I the Mistris of the Family? And is it not my place to see good Orders kept in it? I thought he might have allur'd some of the Shee-slaves to him; and was resolv'd to prevent what might have been betwixt him and them; when on the sudden he rush'd out upon me, caught me in his arms, with such a fury——

170 *Muf.* I have heard enough, away with him.——

Joh. Mistaking me, no doubt, for one of his fellow Slaves: With that, affrighted as I was, I discover'd my self, and cry'd aloud: But as soon as ever he knew me, the Villain let me go, and I must needs say, he started back, as if I were some Serpent; and was more afraid of me than I of him.

Muf. O thou corrupter of my Family, that's cause enough of death; once again, away with him.

Joh. What, for an intended Trespass? No harm has been done, whatever may be. He cost you five hundred Crowns I take

180 it.——

Muf. Thou say'st true, a very considerable Sum: He shall not dye, tho he had committed folly with a Slave; 'tis too much to lose by him.

Ant. My only fault has ever been to love playing in the dark, and the more she cry'd, the more I play'd; that it might be seen I intended nothing to her.

Muf. To your Kennel, Sirrah, mortifie your flesh, and consider in whose Family you are.

Joh. And one thing more; remember from henceforth to obey

190 better.

Muf. aside. For all her smoothness, I am not quite cur'd of my Jealousie; but I have thought of a way that will clear my doubts. [*Exit* Mufti *with* Johayma *and Servants.*

Ant. I am mortify'd sufficiently already, without the help of his ghostly Counsel. Fear of Death has gone farther with me in two Minutes, than my Conscience wou'd have gone in two Months. I find my self in a very dejected condition, all over me;

_____
169 fury] ∼ . Q1-2, F, D.

poor Sin lyes dormant, Concupiscence is retir'd to his winter
quarters; and if *Morayma* shou'd now appear, I say no more,
200 but alas for her and me!

(Morayma *comes out of the Arbour; she steals behind him,
and claps him on the back.*)

Morayma. And if *Morayma* shou'd appear, as she does appear,
alas, you say, for her and you!

Antonio. Art thou there, my sweet temptation! my Eyes, my
Life, my Soul, my all!

Morayma. A mighty Complement, when all these, by your
own Confession, are just nothing.

Ant. Nothing, till thou cam'st to new create me; thou dost
not know the power of thy own Charms: let me embrace thee,
and thou shalt see how quickly I can turn wicked.

210 *Morayma stepping back.* Nay, if you are so dangerous, 'tis
best keeping you at a distance; I have no mind to warm a frozen
Snake in my bosom; he may chance to recover, and sting me for
my pains.

Ant. Consider what I have suffer'd for thy sake already; and
make me some amends: two disappointments in a night, O cruel
Creature!

Mor. And you may thank your self for both: I came eagerly to
the Charge, before my time, through the back walk behind the
Arbour; and you, like a fresh-water Soldier, stood guarding the
220 Pass before: if you miss'd the Enemy, you may thank your own
dulness.

Anton. Nay, if you will be using stratagems, you shall give me
leave to make use of my advantages, now I have you in my
power: we are fairly met; I'll try it out, and give no quarter.

Mor. By your favour, Sir, we meet upon treaty now, and not
upon defiance.

---

201 *Morayma.*] F, D (*Mor.*); ∼ , Q1-2.
202 alas, . . . say,] ∼∧ . . . ∼∧ Q1-2, F, D.
203 *Antonio.*] F, D (*Ant.*); ∼ , Q1-2.
205 *Morayma.*] Q2, F, D (*Mor.*); ∼ , Q1.

Ant. If that be all, you shall have *Carte blanche* immediately;
for I long to be ratifying.

Mor. No, now I think on't, you are already enter'd into Arti-
230 cles with my Enemy *Johayma: Any thing to serve you Madam;
I shall refuse no drudgery:* whose words were those, Gentleman?
was that like a Cavalier of honour?

Anton. Not very heroick; but self preservation is a point
above Honour and Religion too.————*Antonio* was a Rogue I
must confess; but you must give me leave to love him.

Mor. To beg your life so basely; and to present your Sword
to your Enemy; Oh Recreant!

Ant. If I had died honourably, my fame indeed wou'd have
sounded loud, but I shou'd never have heard the blast: Come,
240 don't make your self worse natur'd than you are: to save my life,
you wou'd be content I shou'd promise any thing.

Mor. Yes, if I were sure you wou'd perform nothing.

Ant. Can you suspect I wou'd leave you for *Johayma?*

Mor. No; but I can expect you wou'd have both of us: Love is
covetous, I must have all of you; heart for heart is an equal
truck. In short, I am younger; I think handsomer; and am sure
I love you better: she has been my step-mother these fifteen
years: you think that's her face you see, but 'tis only a dawb'd
Vizard: she wears an Armour of proof upon't: an inch thick of
250 Paint, besides the Wash: her Face is so fortifi'd that you can
make no approaches to it, without a Shovel. But for her constancy, I can tell you for your comfort, she will love till death,
I mean till yours: for when she has worn you out, she will certainly dispatch you to another world, for fear of telling tales; as
she has already serv'd three Slaves, your Predecessors, of happy
memory, in her favours. She has made my pious Father a three-
pil'd Cuckold to my knowledg: and now she wou'd be robbing
me of my single Sheep too.

230–231 *Any* . . . [*to*] . . . *drudgery:*] in romans in Q1–2, F, D.
231 those,] F, D; ∼∧ Q1–2.   234 too.] Q2, F, D; ∼∧ Q1.
247 better:] D; ∼ , Q1–2; ∼ ; F.
255–256 Predecessors, . . . memory,] ∼∧ . . . ∼∧ Q1–2, F, D.
256–257 three-pil'd] F; three pil'd Q1–2, D.

Ant. Prithee prevent her then; and at least take the shearing
260 of me first.

Mor. No; I'll have a Butchers Pen'worth of you; first secure
the Carcass, and then take the fleece into the bargain.

Ant. Why sure, you did not put your self and me to all this
trouble, for a dry come-off: by this hand――― *(Taking it.)*

Mor. Which you shall never touch; but upon better assur-
ances than you imagine. *(Pulling her hand away.)*

Ant. I'll marry thee, and make a Christian of thee, thou
pretty damn'd Infidel.

Mor. I mean you shall: but no earnest, till the bargain be
270 made before witness: there's love enough to be had, and as
much as you can turn you to; never doubt it, but all upon
honourable terms.

Ant. I vow and swear by Love; and he's a Deity in all Religions.

Mor. But never to be trusted in any: he has another name
too, of a worse sound. Shall I trust an Oath, when I see your
Eyes languishing, your Cheeks flushing, and can hear your heart
throbbing? no, I'll not come near you: He's a foolish Physitian
who will feel the pulse of a Patient, that has the Plague-spots
280 upon him.

Ant. Did one ever hear a little Moppet argue so perversly
against so good a Cause! Come, prithee, let me anticipate a little
of my Revenue.

Mor. You wou'd feign be fingring your Rents before-hand;
but that makes a man an ill Husband ever after. Consider, Marriage is a painful Vocation, as you shall prove it; manage your
Incomes as thriftily as you can, you shall find a hard task on't,
to make even at the years end, and yet to live decently.

Ant. I came with a Christian intention, to revenge my self
290 upon thy Father; for being the head of a false Religion.

Mor. And so you shall; I offer you his Daughter for your Sec-

---

264   come-off] F; come off Q1–2, D.
264   s.d. *Taking it.*] F, D; taking it: Q1–2.
267   thee, thou] F, D; ~ ∧ ~ Q1–2.   281   Moppet] F; ~ , Q1–2, D.
286   it;] ~ , Q1–2, F, D.

ond: but since you are so pressing, meet me under my Window,
to morrow night, body for body, about this hour; I'll slip down
out of my Lodging, and bring my Father in my hand.

Ant. How, thy Father!

Mor. I mean, all that's good of him; his Pearls, and Jewels,
his whole contents, his heart, and Soul; as much as ever I can
carry. I'll leave him his Alchoran; that's revenue enough for
him: every page of it is Gold and Diamonds. He has the turn of
300 an Eye, a demure Smile, and a godly Cant, that are worth Millions to him. I forgot to tell you, that I will have a Slave prepar'd at the Postern gate, with two Horses ready sadled: no
more, for I fear, I may be miss'd; and think I hear 'em calling
for me.————If you have constancy and Courage————

Ant. Never doubt it: and love in abundance, to wander with
thee all the World over.

Mor. The value of twelve hundred thousand Crowns in a
Casket!————

Ant. A heavy burden, Heaven knows! but we must pray for
310 patience to support it.

Mor. Besides a willing Titt that will venture her Corps with
you:————Come, I know you long to have a parting blow with
me; and therefore to shew I am in Charity————

                                        (*He kisses her.*)

Ant. Once more, for pity; that I may keep the flavour upon
my lips till we meet again.

Mor. No; frequent Charities make bold Beggars: and besides
I have learnt of a Falconer, never to feed up a Hawk when I
wou'd have him fly: that's enough————but if you will be nib-
ling, here's a hand to stay your stomach.   (*Kissing her hand.*)
320   *Anton.* Thus Conquer'd Infidels, that Wars may cease,
            Are forc'd to give their hands, and sign the Peace.
         Mor. Thus Christians are outwitted by the Foe;
            You had her in your Pow'r, and let her go.

---

296   mean,] ~ₐ Q1-2, F, D.
304   me.————If] ~ ,————if Q1-2, F, D (meₐ————D).
304   Courage] D; ~ . Q1-2, F.
305   love . . . abundance,] D; ~ , . . . ~ₐ Q1-2, F (abundance, F).
309   burden,] F, D; ~ₐ Q1-2.

If you release my hand, the fault's not mine;
You shou'd have made me seal, as well as sign.
She runs off, he follows her to the door; then comes back
again, and goes out at the other.

ACT IV.   SCENE I.

Benducar'*s Pallace in the Castle of* Alcazar.

Enter Benducar.

    Bend. My future Fate, the colour of my life,   (*Solus.*
My all depends on this important hour:
This hour my Lott is weighing in the Scales,
And Heav'n, perhaps, is doubting what to do.
Almeyda and a Crown, have push'd me forward;
'Tis fix'd, the Tyrant must not ravish her:
He and *Sebastian* stand betwixt my hopes;
He most, and therefore first to be dispatch'd.
These and a thousand things are to be done
10 In the short compass of this rowling Night,
And nothing yet perform'd,
None of my Emissaries yet return'd.

Enter Haly—*First Servant.*

Oh *Haly,* thou hast held me long in pain.
What hast thou learnt of *Dorax?* is he dead?
    Haly. Two hours I warily have watch'd his Palace;
All doors are shut, no Servant peeps abroad;
Some Officers with striding hast pass'd in,
While others outward went on quick dispatch;

ACT IV. SCENE I. / Benducar's] Q2, F, D; ACT IV. / Scene 1. Benducar's Q1.
s.d. Enter Benducar.] *omitted from Q1–2, F, D.*
8   most,] F; ∼ ; Q1–2, D.   10   Night,] Q2, F, D; ∼ . Q1.
12+   *s.d.* Haly] F, D; *Haly* Q1–2.   15   *Haly.*] Q2, F, D; ∼ , Q1.

Sometimes hush'd silence seem'd to reign within;
20 Then Cries confus'd, and a joint clamour follow'd;
Then Lights went gliding by, from room to room,
And shot like thwarting Meteors cross the house:
Not daring farther to enquire, I came
With speed, to bring you this imperfect news.
     Bend. Hence I conclude him either dead or dying:
His mournful Friends, summon'd to take their leaves,
Are throng'd about his Couch, and sit in Council.
What those Caballing Captains may design,
I must prevent, by being first in Action.
30 To *Muley-Zeydan* fly with speed, desire him
To take my last instructions; tell th' importance,
And hast his presence here.   (*Exit* Haly.
How has this Poison lost its wonted way?
It shou'd have burnt its passage, not have linger'd
In the blind Labyrinths and crooked turnings
Of human Composition; now it moves
Like a slow Fire that works against the Wind,
As if his stronger Stars had interpos'd.

Enter Hamet.

Well *Hamet,* are our Friends the Rabble rais'd?
40 From *Mustapha,* what Message?
     Hamet.   What you wish:
The streets are thicker in this noon of Night,
Than at the Mid-day Sun: a drowzy horrour
Sits on their Eyes, like fear not well awake;
All crowd in heaps, as at a Night Alarm;
The Bees drive out upon each others backs,

---

23 enquire,] ∼ : Q1–2, F, D.   27 Council.] F, D; ∼ , Q1–2.
29 I . . . prevent, by . . . Action.] D; ∼ . . . ∼ , / By . . . ∼ . Q1–2, F.
30 *Muley-Zeydan*] Q2, F, D; *Muley Zeydan* Q1.
31 importance,] D; ∼∧ Q1–2, F.   40 *Mustapha*] Q2, F, D; *Mustafa* Q1.
40 *Hamet.*] Q2, F, D (*Ham.* D); ∼ , Q1.   41 Night,] D; ∼ : Q1–2, F.
43 awake;] ∼ , Q1–2, F, D.   44 *as in* Q2, F, D; *line indented in Q1.*
44 Alarm;] ∼∧ Q1–2, F, D.

T' imboss their Hives in clusters; all ask news:
Their busie Captain runs the weary round
To whisper Orders; and, commanding silence,
Makes not noise cease, but deafens it to murmurs.
50   *Bend.* Night wasts apace: when, when will he appear?
Hamet. He only waits your Summons.
Bend.   Hast their coming.
Let secrecy and silence be enjoin'd
In their close march: what news from the Lieutenant?
Hamet. I left him at the Gate, firm to your Interest,
T' admit the Townsmen at their first appearance.
Bend. Thus far 'tis well: go hasten *Mustapha.*

                                              (*Exit* Ham.

Enter Orchan—*the Third Servant.*

O, *Orchan,* did I think thy diligence
Wou'd lag behind the rest? what from the *Mufti?*
Orchan. I sought him round his Palace; made enquiry
60 Of all the Slaves: in short, I us'd your name
And urg'd th' importance home; but had for answer
That since the shut of Evening none had seen him.
Bend. O the curst fate of all Conspiracies!
They move on many Springs, if one but fail
The restiff *Machine* stops.————In an ill hour he's absent;
'Tis the first time, and sure will be the last
That e'er a *Mufti* was not in the way,
When Tumult and Rebellion shou'd be broach'd.
Stay by me; thou art resolute and faithful;
70 I have Employment worthy of thy Arm.   (*Walks.*

Enter Muley-Zeydan.

48–49 and, . . . silence, . . . cease,] ∼∧ . . . ∼∧ . . . ∼ ; Q1–2, F, D.
51, 54 Hamet.] Q2, F, D (*Ham.* D); ∼ , Q1.
56 *Mustapha*] Q2, F, D; *Mustafa* Q1.
56+ s.d. Orchan—] F; ∼∧ Q1–2; ∼ , D.
59 Orchan.] D (*Orc.*); ∼ , Q1–2, F.   70 s.d. Walks.] Q2, F, D; ∼ , Q1 (?).
70+ s.d. Muley-Zeydan] Q2, F, D; Muley Zeydan Q1.

Muley-Zeyd. You see me come impatient of my hopes,
And eager as the Courser for the Race:
Is all in readiness?
 Bend.   All but the *Mufti.*
 Mul. Zeyd. We must go on without him.
 Bend.   True we must;
For 'tis ill stopping in the full Career,
How e'er the leap be dangerous and wide.
 Orchan looking out. I see the blaze of Torches from afar;
And hear the trampling of thick beating feet;
This way they move.
 Bend.   No doubt the Emperour.
80 We must not be surpriz'd in Conference.
Trust to my management the Tyrants death;
And hast your self to join with *Mustapha.*
The Officer who guards the Gate is yours;
When you have gain'd that Pass, divide your Force;
Your self in Person head one chosen half,
And march t' oppress the Faction in Consult
With dying *Dorax:* Fate has driv'n 'em all
Into the Net: you must be bold and sudden:
Spare none, and if you find him strugling yet
90 With pangs of Death, trust not his rowling Eyes
And heaving gasps; for Poison may be false:
The home-thrust of a friendly Sword is sure.
 Mul. Zeyd. Doubt not my Conduct: they shall be surpriz'd;
Mercy may wait without the Gate one Night,
At Morn I'll take her in.————
 Bend.   Here lies your way,
You meet your Brother there.
 Mul. Zeyd.   May we ne'er meet:
For, like the Twins of *Leda,* when I mount
He gallops down the Skies.————

          Exit Muley-Zeyd.

---

71 *Muley-Zeyd.*] F, D; *Muley Zeyd.* Q1–2.
82 *Mustapha*] F, D; *Mustafa* Q1–2.   91   false:] ∼ , Q1–2, F, D.
98 *s.d.* Muley-Zeyd.] F, D; Muley Zeyd. Q1–2.

Bend.   He comes: now Heart
Be rib'd with Iron for this one attempt:
100 Set ope thy Sluces, send the vigorous bloud
Through every active Limb for my relief:
Then, take thy rest within thy quiet Cell,
For thou shalt drum no more.

Enter Muley-Moluch *and* Guards *attending him.*

Mul. Mol. What news of our Affairs, and what of *Dorax?*
Is he no more? say that, and make me happy.
Bend. May all your Enemies be like that Dog,
Whose parting Soul is lab'ring at the Lips.
Mul. Mol. The People, are they rais'd?
Bend.   And Marshall'd too;
Just ready for the March.
Mul. Mol.   Then I'm at ease.
110 *Bend.* The Night is yours, the glitt'ring Hoast of Heav'n
Shines but for you; but most the Star of Love,
That twinckles you to fair *Almeyda*'s Bed.
Oh there's a joy, to melt in her embrace,
Dissolve in pleasures;
And make the gods curse Immortality,
That so they cou'd not dye.
But haste, and make 'em yours.
Mul. Mol.   I will; and yet
A kind of weight hangs heavy at my Heart;
My flagging Soul flyes under her own pitch,
120 Like Fowl in air too damp, and lugs along,
As if she were a body in a body,
And not a mounting substance made of Fire.
My Senses too are dull and stupifi'd,
Their edge rebated; sure some ill approaches,
And some kind Spirit knocks softly at my Soul,
To tell me Fate's at hand.

103+ *s.d.* Muley-Moluch] D; Muley Moluch Q1-2, F.
119 pitch,] ~ ; Q1-2, F, D.

Bend.   Mere Fancies all.
Your Soul has been beforehand with your Body,
And drunk so deep a Draught of promis'd bliss,
She slumbers o'er the Cup; no danger's near,
130 But of a Surfeit at too full a Feast.
Mul. Mol. It may be so; it looks so like the Dream
That overtook me at my waking hour
This Morn; and Dreams they say are then divine,
When all the balmy Vapors are exhal'd,
And some o'er-pow'ring God continues sleep.
'Twas then methought *Almeyda,* smiling, came
Attended with a Train of all her Race,
Whom in the rage of Empire I had murther'd.
But now, no longer Foes, they gave me Joy
140 Of my new Conquest, and with helping hands
Heav'd me into our Holy Prophet's arms,
Who bore me in a purple Cloud to Heav'n.
Bend. Good Omen, Sir; I wish you in that Heaven
Your Dream portends you,————[*Aside.*] Which presages
    death.————
Mul. Mol. Thou too wert there;
And thou methought didst push me from below,
With thy full force to Paradise.
Bend.   Yet better.
Mul. Mol. Ha! What's that grizly Fellow that attends thee?
Bend. Why ask you Sir?
Mul. Mol.   For he was in my Dream;
150 And help'd to heave me up.
Bend.   With Pray'rs and Wishes;
For I dare swear him honest.
Mul. Mol.   That may be;
But yet he looks Damnation.
Bend.   You forget
The Face wou'd please you better: Do you love,

143   Sir;] D; ∼ , Q1–2, F.
144   you,————[*Aside.*] Which . . . death.————] you. / Which . . . death.
————[*Aside.* Q1–2, F, D.
152   forget] F, D; ∼ , Q1–2.

And can you thus forbear?
    Mul Mol.   I'll head my People;
Then think of dalliance, when the danger's o'er.
My warlike Spirits work now another way;
And my Soul's tun'd to Trumpets.
    Bend.   You debase your self,
To think of mixing with th' ignoble Herd.
Let such perform the servile Work of War,
160 Such who have no *Almeyda* to enjoy.
What, shall the People know their God-like Prince
Skulk'd in a nightly Skirmish? Stole a Conquest,
Headed a Rabble, and profan'd his Person,
Shoulder'd with Filth, born in a tide of Ordure,
And stifled with their rank offensive Sweat?
    Mul. Mol. I am off again: I will not prostitute
The Regal Dignity so far, to head 'em.
    Bend. There spoke a King.
Dismiss your Guards to be employ'd elsewhere
170 In ruder Combats: You will want no Seconds
In those Alarms you seek.
    Mul. Mol.   Go joyn the Crowd.   [*To the Guards.*
Benducar, thou shalt lead 'em, in my place.   [*Exeunt Guards.*
The God of Love once more has shot his Fires
Into my Soul; and my whole Heart receives him.
Almeyda now returns with all her Charms;
I feel her as she glides along my Veins,
And dances in my Blood: So when our Prophet
Had long been ham'ring in his lonely Cell,
Some dull, insipid, tedious Paradise,
180 A brisk *Arabian* Girl came tripping by;
Passing she cast at him a side-long glance,
And look'd behind in hopes to be pursu'd:
He took the hint, embrac'd the flying Fair;
And having found his Heav'n, he fix'd it there. [*Exit* Mul. Mol.

---

161 What,] D; ~ Q1-2, F.   171 Crowd.] ~ ; Q1-2, F, D.
171 s.d. To] F, D; *to* Q1-2.
180 *Arabian*] F, D; Arabian Q1-2.

Bend. That Paradise thou never shalt possess.
His death is easie now, his Guards are gone;
And I can sin but once to seize the Throne.
All after Acts are sanctify'd by pow'r.
   Orchan. Command my Sword and Life.
   Bend.   I thank thee *Orchan,*
190 And shall reward thy Faith: This Master Key
Frees every Lock, and leads us to his Person;
And shou'd we miss our blow, as Heav'n forbid,
Secures retreat: Leave open all behind us;
And first set wide the *Mufti*'s Garden Gate,
Which is his private passage to the Palace:
For there our Mutineers appoint to meet,
And thence we may have aid. Now sleep ye Stars
That silently o'erwatch the fate of Kings;
   Be all propitious Influences barr'd,
200 And none but murd'rous Planets mount the Guard.
                              [*Exit with* Orchan.

SCENE II.

A Night Scene of the Mufti's *Garden.*

Enter the Mufti *alone, in a Slave's habit, like that of* Antonio.

Mufti. This 'tis to have a sound Head-piece; by this I have
got to be chief of my Religion; that is, honestly speaking, to
teach others what I neither know nor believe my self. For what's
Mahomet to me, but that I get by him? Now for my Policy of
this night: I have mew'd up my suspected Spouse in her Chamber. No more Embassies to that lusty young Stallion of a Gardiner. Next my habit of a Slave; I have made my self as like him
as I can, all but his youth and vigor; which when I had, I pass'd

---

191   Person;] ~ : Q1–2, F, D.
199–200   *lines not indented in Q1–2, F, D.*
SCENE II.] *omitted from Q1–2, F, D.*
1   *Mufti.*] Q2, F, D (*Muft.* Q2, D; *Muf.* F); ~ , Q1.

my time as well as any of my Holy Predecessors. Now walking
10 under the Windows of my Seraglio, if *Johayma* look out, she
will certainly take me for *Antonio,* and call to me; and by that
I shall know what Concupiscence is working in her: she cannot
come down to commit Iniquity, there's my safety; but if she
peep, if she put her Nose abroad, there's demonstration of her
pious Will: And I'll not make the first precedent for a Church-
man to forgive Injuries.

Enter Morayma *running to him with a Casket in her hand,
and embracing him.*

Mor. Now I can embrace you with a good Conscience; here
are the Pearls and Jewels, here's my Father.

Muf. I am indeed thy Father; but how the Devil didst thou
20 know me in this disguise? And what Pearls and Jewels dost thou
mean?

Mor. going back. What have I done, and what will now become of me!

Muf. Art thou mad, *Morayma?*

Mor. I think you'll make me so.

Muf. Why, what have I done to thee? Recollect thy self, and
speak sense to me.

Mor. Then give me leave to tell you, you are the worst of
Fathers.

30 *Muf.* Did I think I had begotten such a Monster? Proceed
my dutiful Child, proceed, proceed.

Mor. You have been raking together a mass of Wealth, by
indirect and wicked means; the Spoils of Orphans are in these
Jewels, and the Tears of Widows in these Pearls.

Muf. Thou amazest me!

Mor. I wou'd do so. This Casket is loaded with your Sins; 'tis
the Cargo of Rapines, Simony, and Extortions; the Iniquity of
thirty Years *Muftiship,* converted into Diamonds.

Muf. Wou'd some rich rayling Rogue would say as much to
40 me, that I might squeeze his Purse for scandal.

---

12 her:] ∼ ; Q1–2, F, D.   22 *back.*] Q2, F; ∼ , Q1; ∼ʌ D.
22 What] F;———What Q1–2, D.   38 *Muftiship*] Muftiship Q1–2, F, D.

Mor. No Sir, you get more by pious Fools than Raylers, when you insinuate into their Families, manage their Fortunes while they live, and beggar their Heirs by getting Legacies when they dye. And do you think I'll be the receiver of your Theft? I discharge my Conscience of it: Here take again your filthy Mammon, and restore it, you had best, to the true Owners.

Muf. I am finely documented by my own Daughter.

Mor. And a great credit for me to be so: Do but think how decent a Habit you have on, and how becoming your Function
50 to be disguis'd like a Slave, and eves-dropping under the Womens Windows, to be saluted, as you deserve it richly, with a Piss-pot: If I had not known you casually by your shambling gate, and a certain reverend awkardness that is natural to all of your Function, here you had been expos'd to the laughter of your own Servants; who have been in search of you through your whole Seraglio, peeping under every Petticoat to find you.

Muf. Prithee Child, reproach me no more of human Failings; they are but a little of the pitch and spots of the World that are still sticking on me; but I hope to scour 'em out in
60 time: I am better at bottom than thou think'st; I am not the Man thou tak'st me for.

Mor. No, to my sorrow Sir, you are not.

Muf. It was a very odd beginning, tho, methought, to see thee come running in upon me with such a warm embrace; prithee what was the meaning of that violent hot Hug?

Mor. I am sure I meant nothing by it, but the zeal and affection which I bear to the Man of the World, whom I may love lawfully.

Muf. But thou wilt not teach me at this age the nature of a
70 close Embrace?

Mor. No indeed; for my Mother in Law complains, that you are past teaching: But if you mistook my innocent Embrace for Sin, I wish heartily it had been given where it wou'd have been more acceptable.

---

46   it, . . . best,] F, D; ~∧ . . . ~∧ Q1–2.   57   Child,] ~∧ Q1–2, F, D.
62   Sir,] F, D; ~∧ Q1–2.   63   tho,] F; ~∧ Q1–2, D.

Muf. Why, this is as it shou'd be now: Take the Treasure again, it can never be put into better hands.

Mor. Yes, to my knowledg but it might. I have confess'd my Soul to you, if you can understand me rightly; I never disobey'd you till this night, and now since through the violence of my 80 Passion, I have been so unfortunate, I humbly beg your pardon, your blessing, and your leave, that upon the first opportunity I may go for ever from your sight; for Heaven knows, I never desire to see you more.

Muf. wiping his Eyes. Thou mak'st me weep at thy unkindness; indeed dear Daughter we will not part.

Mor. Indeed dear Daddy but we will.

Muf. Why if I have been a little pilfering, or so, I take it bitterly of thee to tell me of it; since it was to make thee rich; and I hope a Man may make bold with his own Soul, without 90 offence to his own Child: Here take the jewels again, take 'em I charge thee upon thy Obedience.

Mor. Well then, in vertue of Obedience I will take 'em; but on my Soul, I had rather they were in a better hand.

Muf. Meaning mine, I know it.

Mor. Meaning his whom I love better than my life.

Muf. That's me again.

Mor. I wou'd have you think so.

Muf. How thy good nature works upon me; well, I can do no less than venture damning for thee, and I may put fair for it, if 100 the Rabble be order'd to rise to Night.

Enter Antonio *in an* Affrican *rich habit.*

Ant. What do you mean my Dear, to stand talking in this suspicious place, just underneath *Johayma's* Window?————(*To the* Mufti.) You are well met Comerade, I know you are the friend of our flight; are the horses ready at the postern gate?

Muf. Antonio, and in disguise! now I begin to smell a rat.

84   *wiping*] *Wiping* Q1–2, F, D.   98   well,] D; ∼∧ Q1–2, F.
102–103   ————(*To the* Mufti.)] (to the *Mufti*∧) Q1–2; (*To the* Mufti∧) F; [*To the* Mufti.] D.
104   flight;] D; ∼ ? Q1–2, F.

Ant. And I another, that out-stinks it; false *Morayma,* hast thou thus betray'd me to thy Father!

Mor. Alas, I was betray'd my self: He came disguis'd like you, and I poor Innocent ran into his hands.

110 *Muf.* In good time you did so; I laid a trap for a Bitch Fox, and a worse Vermine has caught himself in it: you wou'd fain break loose now, though you left a limb behind you; but I am yet in my own Territories and in call of Company, that's my comfort.

Antonio, taking him by the throat. No; I have a trick left to put thee past thy squeeking: I have giv'n thee the quinzey; that ungracious tongue shall Preach no more false Doctrin.

Mor. What do you mean? you will not throttle him? consider he's my Father.

120 *Ant.* Prithee let us provide first for our own safety; if I do not consider him, he will consider us with a vengeance afterwards.

Mor. You may threaten him for crying out, but for my sake give him back a little cranny of his Wind-pipe, and some part of Speech.

Ant. Not so much as one single Interjection. Come away, Father-in-Law, this is no place for Dialogues; when you are in the Mosque you talk by hours, and there no Man must interrupt you; this is but like for like, good Father-in-Law; now I

130 am in the Pulpit 'tis your turn to hold your tongue. [*He struggles.*] Nay if you will be hanging back, I shall take care you shall hang forward.

(*Pulls him along the Stage, with his Sword at his reins.*)

Mor. T' other way to the Arbour with him; and make hast before we are discover'd.

Ant. If I only bind and gag him there, he may commend me

---

115 *Antonio . . . throat.* No] F, D; [Antonio . . . throat. | No Q1-2 (*speech tag flush right; "No" indented*).
126 Interjection.] ~ : Q1-2, F, D.
126 away,] F; ~∧ Q1-2, D.
127 Dialogues;] D; ~ , Q1-2, F.
130-131 tongue. [*He struggles.*] Nay] F, D (*struggles.*∧ F); tongue. | [*He struggles.* | Nay Q1-2.
132+ *s.d. Stage,*] ~ ; Q1; ~∧ Q2, F, D.

hereafter for civil usage; he deserves not so much favour by
any action of his life.

Mor. Yes, pray bate him one, for begetting your Mistress.

Ant. I wou'd, if he had not thought more of thy Mother than
140 of thee; once more come along in silence, my *Pythagorean*
Father-in-Law.

Joh. at the Balcony. A Bird in a Cage may peep at least;
though she must not fly. What bustle's there beneath my Window? *Antonio* by all my hopes, I know him by his habit; but
what makes that Woman with him, and a Friend, a Sword
drawn, and hasting hence? this is no time for silence. Who's
within? call there, where are the Servants? why *Omar, Abedin,
Hassan* and the rest, make hast and run into the Garden; there
are Thieves and Villains; arm all the Family, and stop 'em.

150 *Antonio turning back.* O that Schriech Owl at the Window!
we shall be pursu'd immediatly; which way shall we take?

Morayma giving him the Casket. 'Tis impossible to escape
them; for the way to our Horses lyes back again by the House;
and then we shall meet 'em full in the teeth; here take these
Jewels; thou may'st leap the Walls and get away.

Ant. And what will become of thee then, poor kind Soul?

Mor. I must take my fortune; when you are got safe into
your own Country, I hope you will bestow a sigh on the memory of her who lov'd you!

160 *Ant.* It makes me mad, to think how many a good night will
be lost betwixt us! take back thy Jewels; 'tis an empty Casket
without thee; besides I shou'd never leap well with the weight
of all thy Fathers sins about me, thou and they had been a
bargain.

---

140 *Pythagorean*] F; Pythagorean Q1-2, D.
142 *at the Balcony*] F, D (*At*); At the Balcony Q1-2.
142 A] F;———A Q1-2, D.　　　143 fly. What] ~ ; what Q1-2, F, D (What F).
146 silence.] ~ : Q1-2, F, D.　　　147 within?] ~ , Q1, F, D; ~∧ Q2.
147 Servants?] F, D; ~ , Q1-2.
150 *Antonio . . . back.* O] F, D; [Antonio . . . back. / O Q1-2 (*speech tag
flush right;* "O" *indented*).
152 *Morayma . . . Casket.* 'Tis] F, D (*Casket.*) F; *Casket.*] D); (Morayma . . .
Casket.) / 'Tis Q1-2 ([Morayma . . . *Casket.*] Q2; *speech tag centered;* " 'Tis"
indented).
156 then,] F, D; ~∧ Q1-2.

Mor. Prithee take 'em, 'twill help me to be reveng'd on him.

Ant. No; they'll serve to make thy peace with him.

Mor. I hear 'em coming; shift for your self at least; remember I am yours for ever.

(*Servants crying* This way, this way, *behind the Scenes.*)

Ant. And I but the empty shadow of my self without thee! 170 Farewel Father-in-Law, that shou'd have been, if I had not been curst in my Mothers belly.————Now which way fortune?————

(*Runs amazedly backwards and forwards.*)

Servants within. Follow, follow, yonder are the Villains.

Ant. O here's a gate open; but it leads into the Castle; yet I must venture it. [*Going out.*

(*A shout behind the Scenes where* Antonio *is going out.*)

Ant. There's the Rabble in a Mutiny; what, is the Devil up at Midnight!————however 'tis good herding in a Crowd.

[*Runs out.* Mufti *runs to* Morayma *and lays hold on her, then snatches away the Casket.*

Muf. Now, to do things in order, first I seize upon the Bag, and then upon the Baggage: for thou art but my flesh and blood, but these are my Life and Soul.

180 *Mor.* Then let me follow my flesh and blood, and keep to your self your Life and Soul.

Muf. Both or none; come away to durance.

Mor. Well, if it must be so, agreed; for I have another trick to play you; and thank your self for what shall follow.

Enter Servants.

168+ *s.d.* This way, this way] *this way, this way* Q1-2, F, D (*This way, this* D).
170   Farewel] F, D; farewel Q1-2.
171   belly.] ~∧ Q1-2, F, D.
171   fortune?] ~ . Q1-2, D; ~∧ F.
172   Follow . . . [*romans*] . . . Villains] F; *Follow* . . . [*italics*] . . . *Villains* Q1-2, D.
174+ *s.d. A shout behind the Scenes where* Antonio *is going out.*] F, D (*s.d. centered in* F); A shout behind the Scenes where *Antonio* is going out∧ Q1-2 (*s.d. flush left in* Q1, *centered in* Q2).
175   what,] ~∧ Q1-2, F, D.
176+ *s.d. out.* Mufti . . . *Casket.*] ~ . / (~ . . . ~ .) Q1; ~ . / ~ . . . ~ .] Q2; ~ . / ~ . . . ~ . F; ~ . / [~ . . . ~ . D.
184+ *s.d. Enter*] F, D; [~ Q1-2 (*at right*).

Joh. from above. One of them took through the private way
into the Castle; follow him be sure, for these are yours already.

Mor. Help here quickly *Omar, Abedin;* I have hold on the
Villain that stole my jewels; but 'tis a lusty Rogue, and he will
prove too strong for me; what, help I say, do you not know
190 your Masters Daughter?

Muf. Now if I cry out they will know my voice; and then I
am disgrac'd for ever: O thou art a venomous Cockatrice!

Mor. Of your own begetting.   [*The Servants seize him.*

First Servant. What a glorious deliverance have you had,
Madam, from this bloody-minded Christian!

Mor. Give me back my Jewels, and carry this notorious Male-
factor to be punish'd by my Father. I'll hunt the other dry-foot.
          (*Takes the Jewels and runs out after* Antonio *at the same
          Passage.*)

First Servant. I long to be handselling his hide, before we
bring him to my Master.

200   *Second Servant.* Hang him, for an old Covetous Hypocrite: he
deserves a worse punishment himself for keeping us so hardly.

First Servant. Ay, wou'd he were in this Villains place; thus I
wou'd lay him on, and thus.   [*Beats him.*

Second Servant. And thus wou'd I revenge my self of my last
beating.————————————————————————
          (*He beats him too, and then the rest.*)

Muf. Oh, oh, oh!

First Servant. Now supposing you were the *Mufti,* Sir,————
                    [*Beats him again.*

Muf. The Devil's in that supposing Rascal. I can bear no
more; and I am the *Mufti:* Now suppose your selves my Ser-
210 vants, and hold your hands; an anointed halter take you all.

First Servant. My Master! you will pardon the excess of
our zeal for you, Sir; indeed we all took you for a Villain, and
so we us'd you.

Mufti. Ay so I feel you did; my back and sides are abundant

185   *from above*] Q2, F, D (*From* Q2, F); From above Q1.
187   *Omar,*] D; ~ˌ Q1–2, F.   194–195   had, Madam,] F, D; ~ˌ ~ˌ Q1–2.
205   beating.] Q2, F, D; ~ , Q1.   208   Rascal.] ~ ; Q1–2, F, D.
212   Sir;] ~ , Q1–2, F, D.

testimonies of your zeal. Run Rogues, and bring me back my
Jewels, and my Fugitive Daughter: run I say.

(*They run to the Gate and the first Servant runs back again.*)

First Servant. Sir, the Castle is in a most terrible combustion;
you may hear 'em hither.

Muf. 'Tis a laudable commotion: The voice of the Mobile
220 is the voice of Heaven. I must retire a little, to strip me of the
Slave, and to assume the *Mufti;* and then I will return: for the
piety of the People must be encouraged; that they may help
me to recover my Jewels, and my Daughter.

Exit Mufti *and Servants.*

SCENE III.

The Scene changes to the Castle-yard, and discovers Antonio,
Mustapha, *and the Rabble shouting: they come forward.*

Ant. And so at length, as I inform'd you, I escap'd out of his
covetous clutches; and now fly to your illustrious feet for my
protection.

Must. Thou shalt have it, and now defie the *Mufti.* 'Tis the
first Petition that has been made to me since my exaltation to
Tumult; in this second Night of the Month *Abib,* and in the
year of the *Hegyra;*————the Lord knows what year; but 'tis no
matter; for when I am settled, the Learned are bound to find
it out for me: for I am resolv'd to date my Authority over the
10 Rabble, like other Monarchs.

Ant. I have always had a longing to be yours again; though
I cou'd not compass it before, and had design'd you a Casket of
my Masters jewels too; for I knew the Custom, and wou'd not
have appear'd before a Great Person, as you are, without a
present: But he has defrauded my good intentions, and basely

————

SCENE III.] *omitted from Q1–2, F, D.*   *s.d. The Scene*] Q2, F, D; *Scene* Q1.
s.d. Antonio,] F, D; ~∧ Q1–2.   *s.d.* Mustapha] Q2, F, D; Mustafa Q1.
s.d. shouting:] D; ~ , Q1–2, F.
7   *Hegyra;*————] D; ~ ;∧ Q1–2, F.

robb'd you of 'em: 'tis a prize worth a Million of Crowns, and
you carry your Letters of mark about you.

    Must. I shall make bold with his Treasure, for the support
of my New Government. [*The People gather about him.*] What
20 do these vile Ragga-muffins so near our Person? Your savour
is offensive to us; bear back there, and make room for honest
Men to approach us. These fools and knaves are always impu-
dently crowding next to Princes, and keeping off the more deserving. Bear back I say. [*They make a wider Circle.*] That's
dutifully done; now shout to show your Loyalty. (*A great shout.*)
Hear'st thou that, Slave *Antonio?* these obstreperous Villains
shout, and know not for what they make a noise. You shall see
me manage 'em, that you may judge what ignorant Beasts they
are. For whom do you shout now? who's to Live and Reign? tell
30 me that, the wisest of you.

    First Rabble. Even who you please, Captain.

    Must. La you there; I told you so.

    Second Rabble. We are not bound to know who is to Live
and Reign; our business is only to rise upon command, and
plunder.

    Third Rabble. Ay, the Richest of both Parties; for they are
our Enemies.

    Must. This last Fellow is a little more sensible than the rest;
he has enter'd somewhat into the merits of the Cause.

40   *First Rabble.* If a poor Man may speak his mind, I think,
Captain, that your self are the fittest to Live and Reign; I mean
not over, but next and immediatly under the People; and thereupon I say, *A Mustapha, A Mustapha!*

    All cry. A *Mustapha,* A *Mustapha!*

16 'em:] D; ∼ , Q1–2, F.   19 *s.d. him.*]] ∼ ·ʌ Q1–2, F, D.
20 Your] F; your Q1–2, D.   22 us. These] ∼ ; these Q1–2, F, D.
23–24 deserving. Bear] ∼ , bear Q1–2; ∼ ; bear F, D.
24 say. [*They . . . Circle.*] That's] ∼ . / [∼ . . . ∼ ·ʌ / ∼ Q1–2, F, D (say.
[They F, D).
30 that,] F; ∼ʌ Q1–2, D.   31 please,] F, D; ∼ʌ Q1–2.
41 Reign;] ∼ , Q1–2, F, D.
43 *Mustapha,* A *Mustapha!*] F, D (A *Mustapha.* F); *Mustafa,* A *Mustafa.*] Q1–2.
44 *All cry.*] (*All Cry*ʌ) Q1–2; (*All Cry,* F; [*All cry,* D.
44 A *Mustapha,* A *Mustapha!*] A *Mustafa,* A *Mustafa.* Q1–2; A *Mustapha,* A
Mustapha. F; *A Mustapha, A Mustapha!* D.

Must. I must confess the sound is pleasing, and tickles the ears of my Ambition; but alas good People, it must not be: I am contented to be a poor simple Vice-Roy; but Prince *Muley-Zeydan* is to be the Man: I shall take care to instruct him in the arts of Government; and in his duty to us all: and therefore
50 mark my Cry: *A Muley-Zeydan, A Muley-Zeydan!*
    All cry. A *Muley-Zeydan,* A *Muley-Zeydan!*
    Must. You see, Slave *Antonio,* what I might have been.
    Antonio. I observe your Modesty.
    Must. But for a foolish promise I made once to my Lord *Benducar,* to set up any one he pleas'd.

(*Re-enter the* Mufti *with his Servants.*)

Ant. Here's the Old Hypocrite again; now stand your ground, and bate him not an inch. Remember the Jewels, the Rich and Glorious Jewels; they are destin'd to be yours, by virtue of Prerogative.
60   *Must.* Let me alone to pick a quarrel, I have an old grudge to him upon thy account.
    Mufti, making up to the Mobile. Good People, here you are met together.
    First Rabble. Ay, we know that without your telling, but why are we met together, Doctor? for that's it which no body here can tell.
    Second Rabble. Why to see one another in the Dark; and to make Holy-day at Midnight.
    Muf. You are met, as becomes good Musulmen; to settle the
70 Nation; for I must tell you, that though your Tyrant is a lawful Emperor, yet your lawful Emperor is but a Tyrant.
    Ant. What stuff he talks!

---

50 *Muley-Zeydan!*] D; *Muley Zeydan.* Q1–2, F (*Muley-Zeydan* Q2, F).
51 *All cry.*] (*All Cry*ʌ) Q1–2; *All Cry,* F; [*All cry,* D.
51 A *Muley-Zeydan,* A *Muley-Zeydan!*] A *Muley-Zeydan,* A *Muley-Zeydan.* Q1–2, F; A *Muley-Zeydan,* A *Muley-Zeydan!* D.
52 see,] F, D; ~ʌ Q1–2.
62 *Mufti, . . . Mobile.* Good] F, D (*Mobile.*) F; *Mobile*ʌ] D); (Mufti, . . . *Mobile.*) / Good Q1–2 (*speech tag centered;* "Good" *indented*).

Must. 'Tis excellent fine matter indeed, Slave *Antonio;* he
has a rare tongue; Oh, he wou'd move a Rock of Elephant!

Ant. aside. What a Block have I to work upon!————[*To
him.*] But still remember the Jewels, Sir, the Jewels.

Must. Nay that's true on t' other side: the Jewels must be
mine; but he has a pure fine way of talking; my Conscience
goes along with him, but the Jewels have set my heart against
80 him.

Muf. That your Emperor is a Tyrant is most manifest; for
you were born to be *Turks,* but he has play'd the *Turk* with
you; and is taking your Religion away.

Second Rabble. We find that in our decay of Trade; I have
seen for these hunder'd years, that Religion and Trade always
go together.

Mufti. He is now upon the point of Marrying himself, without your Sovereign consent; and what are the effects of Marriage?

90   *Third Rabble.* A scoulding, domineering Wife, if she prove
honest; and if a Whore, a fine gawdy Minx, that robs our
Counters every Night, and then goes out, and spends it upon
our Cuckold-makers.

Mufti. No, the natural effects of Marriage are Children: Now
on whom wou'd he beget these Children? Even upon a Christian! Oh horrible; how can you believe me, though I am ready
to swear it upon the Alcoran! Yes, true Believers, you may believe me, that he is going to beget a Race of Misbelievers.

Must. That's fine, in earnest; I cannot forbear hearkening to
100 his enchanting Tongue.

Ant. But yet remember————

Must. Ay, Ay, the Jewels! Now again I hate him; but yet my
Conscience makes me listen to him.

Mufti. Therefore to conclude all, Believers, pluck up your
Hearts, and pluck down the Tyrant: Remember the Courage

75   *aside*] *Aside* Q1–2, F, D.   75   upon!] D; ~ , Q1–2; ~ . F.
75–76   *s.d.* ————[*To him.*] But . . . Jewels.] [*To him.* But . . . Jewels. Q1–2,
F (((*To him.*) F); But . . . Jewels. [*To him.* D.
97   Alcoran] D; *Alcoran* Q1–2, F.   101   remember] ~ . Q1–2, F, D.
104   *Mufti.*] Q2, F, D (*Muf.* F, D); ~ , Q1.

of your Ancestors; remember the Majesty of the People; remember your selves, your Wives and Children; and lastly, above all, remember your Religion, and our holy *Mahomet;* all these require your timous assistance;—shall I say, they beg it? No, they
110 claim it of you, by all the nearest and dearest Tyes of these three P's, Self-Preservation, our Property, and our Prophet. Now answer me with an unanimous chearful Cry, and follow me, who am your Leader, to a glorious Deliverance.

    (*All cry,* A Mufti, A Mufti, *and are following him off the Stage.*)

    Ant. Now you see what comes of your foolish Qualms of Conscience: The Jewels are lost, and they are all leaving you.

    Must. What, am I forsaken of my Subjects? Wou'd the Rogue purloin my liege People from me! I charge you in my own Name, come back ye Deserters; and hear me speak.

    1st. Rabble. What, will he come with his Balderdash, after the
120 *Mufti's* eloquent Oration?

    2d. Rabble. He's our Captain, lawfully pick'd up, and elected upon a Stall; we will hear him.

    Omnes. Speak, Captain, for we will hear you.

    Must. Do you remember the glorious Rapines and Robberies you have committed? Your breaking open and gutting of Houses, your rummaging of Cellars, your demolishing of Christian Temples, and bearing off in triumph the superstitious Plate and Pictures, the Ornaments of their wicked Altars, when all rich Moveables were sentenc'd for idolatrous, and all that was
130 idolatrous was seiz'd? Answer first for your remembrance, of all these sweetnesses of Mutiny; for upon those Grounds I shall proceed.

    Omnes. Yes we do remember, we do remember.

    Must. Then make much of your retentive Faculties. And who

109   assistance;— . . . say,] $\sim$;$_\wedge$ . . . $\sim_\wedge$ Q1–2, F, D.
111   P's,] D; $\sim_\wedge$ Q1–2, F.   113   Leader,] F; $\sim_\wedge$ Q1–2, D.
113+   *s.d.* A . . . A] *A . . . A* Q1–2, F, D.   116   What,] F, D; $\sim_\wedge$ Q1–2.
118   Name,] F; $\sim_\wedge$ Q1–2, D.   119   *1st.*] 1st. Q1–2, D; *First* F.
119   *Rabble.*] Q2, F, D; $\sim$, Q1.   119   What,] F, D; $\sim_\wedge$ Q1–2.
121   *2d.*] 2d. Q1–2, D; *Second* F.   121   *Rabble.*] Q2, F, D; $\sim$, Q1.
123   *Omnes.*] Q2, F, D; $\sim$, Q1.   123   Speak,] D; $\sim_\wedge$ Q1–2, F.
133   *Omnes.*] Q2, F, D; $\sim$, Q1.

led you to those Hony-Combs? Your *Mufti?* No, Believers, he
only preach'd you up to it; but durst not lead you; he was but
your Counsellor, but I was your Captain; he only loo'd you, but
'twas I that led you.

Omnes. That's true, that's true.

140   *Ant.* There you were with him for his Figures.

Must. I think I was, Slave *Antonio.* Alas I was ignorant of
my own Talent.————Say then, Believers, will you have a Captain for your *Mufti?* Or a *Mufti* for your Captain? And further
to instruct you how to Cry, Will you have *A Mufti,* or *No
Mufti?*

Omnes. No *Mufti,* no *Mufti!*

Must. That I laid in for 'em, Slave *Antonio.*————Do I then
spet upon your Faces? Do I discourage Rebellion, Mutiny,
Rapine, and Plundering? You may think I do, Believers, but

150 Heaven forbid: No, I encourage you to all these laudable Un-
dertakings; you shall plunder, you shall pull down the Government; but you shall do this upon my Authority, and not by his
wicked Instigation.

3d. Rabble. Nay, when his turn is serv'd, he may preach up
Loyalty again, and Restitution, that he might have another
Snack among us.

1st. Rabble. He may indeed; for 'tis but his saying 'tis Sin,
and then we must restore; and therefore I wou'd have a new
Religion, where half the Commandments shou'd be taken away,

160 the rest mollifi'd, and there shou'd be little or no Sin remaining.

Omnes. Another Religion, a new Religion, another Religion!

Must. And that may easily be done, with the help of a little
Inspiration: For I must tell you, I have a Pigeon at home, of
Mahomet's own breed; and when I have learnt her to pick
Pease out of my Ear, rest satisfi'd 'till then, and you shall have

---

137 loo'd] F, D; lood Q1-2.   139 *Omnes.*] Q2, F, D; ~ , Q1.
144-145 *A . . . No Mufti*] a . . . no Mufti Q1-2, F, D (*Mufti* Q2, F, D).
146 *Omnes.*] Q2, F; ~ , Q1; ~∧ D.   146 no *Mufti!*] ~~ . Q1-2, F, D.
154 *3d.*] 3d. Q1-2, D; *Third* F.   154 *Rabble.*] F, D; ~ , Q1; ~∧ Q2.
157 *1st.*] 1st. Q1-2, D; *First* F.   157 *Rabble.*] Q2, F, D; ~ , Q1.
162 *Omnes.*] F, D; ~ , Q1-2.   162 Religion!] ~ . Q1-2, F, D.

another. But now I think on't, I am inspir'd already, that 'tis no
Sin to depose the *Mufti*.

Ant. And good reason; for when Kings and Queens are to be
170 discarded, what shou'd Knaves do any longer in the pack?

Omnes. He is depos'd, he is depos'd, he is depos'd!

Must. Nay, if he and his Clergy will needs be preaching up
Rebellion, and giving us their Blessing, 'tis but justice they
shou'd have the first fruits of it.————Slave *Antonio,* take him
into custody; and dost thou hear, Boy? be sure to secure the
little transitory Box of Jewels: If he be obstinate, put a civil
Question to him upon the Rack, and he squeaks, I warrant him.

Ant. seizing the Mufti. Come my *quondam* Master, you and
I must change Qualities.

180   *Mufti.* I hope you will not be so barbarous to torture me; we
may preach Suffering to others, but alas, holy Flesh is too well
pamper'd to endure Martyrdom.

Must. Now, late *Mufti,* not forgetting my first Quarrel to
you, we will enter our selves with the Plunder of your Palace:
'tis good to sanctifie a Work, and begin a God's name.

1st. Rabble. Our Prophet let the Devil alone with the last
Mob.

Mob. But he takes care of this himself.

As they are going out enter Benducar *leading* Almeyda: *He
with a Sword in one hand;* Benducar's *Slave follows
with* Muley-Moluch's *Head upon a Spear.*

Must. Not so much hast Masters; come back again: you are so
190 bent upon mischief, that you take a man upon the first word of
Plunder. Here's a sight for you: the Emperour is come upon
his head to visit you. [*Bowing.*] Most Noble Emperour, now

168   *Mufti*] Q2, F, D; Mufti Q1.   171   *Omnes.*] Q2, F, D; ∼ , Q1.
171   depos'd!] ∼ . Q1–2, F, D.   175   Boy?] ∼ , Q1–2, F, D.
177   squeaks,] ∼∧ Q1–2, F, D.   180   *Mufti.*] Q2, F, D (*Muf.* F, D); ∼ , Q1.
180   me;] D; ∼ , Q1–2, F.   186   *1st.*] 1st. Q1–2, D; *First* F.
186   *Rabble.*] Q2, F, D; ∼ , Q1.   187   Mob] D; *Mob* Q1–2, F.
188+   s.d. Muley-Moluch's] F, D; Muly-Moluch's Q1–2.
189   *Must.* Not] Q2, F, D; Not Q1 (*but c.w. are* "Must. Not").
192   s.d. Bowing.] ∼∧ Q1–2, F, D.

I hope you will not hit us in the teeth, that we have pull'd you
down, for we can tell you to your face, that we have exalted you.
                                                    [*They all shout.*]
    Benducar to Almeyda apart. Think what I am, and what your
      self may be,
In being mine: refuse not proffer'd Love
That brings a Crown.
    Almeyda to him. I have resolv'd,
And these shall know my thoughts.
    Bend. to her.   On that I build.————
                  (*He comes up to the Rabble.*)
200 Joy to the People for the Tyrants Death!
Oppression, Rapine, Banishment and Bloud
Are now no more; but speechless as that tongue
That lyes for ever still.
How is my grief divided with my joy,
When I must own I kill'd him! bid me speak,
For not to bid me, is to disallow
What for your sakes is done.
    Mustapha. In the name of the People we command you speak:
But that pretty Lady shall speak first; for we have taken some-
210 what of a likeing to her Person. Be not afraid Lady to speak to
these rude Ragga-muffians: there's nothing shall offend you,
unless it be their stink, and please you.   [*Making a Legg.*
    Almeyda. Why shou'd I fear to speak, who am your Queen?
My peacefull Father sway'd the Scepter long;
And you enjoy'd the Blessings of his Reign,
While you deserv'd the name of *Affricans.*
Then not commanded, but commanding you,
Fearless I speak: know me for what I am.

---

195 *Benducar to Almeyda*] Benducar *to* / Almeyda Q1-2; *Bend.* (to *Alm.* F;
Bend. [*to* Almeyda D.
197 That] Q2, F, D; that Q1.
198 *Almeyda to him.*] [Almeyda *to* / [*him.* Q1-2; *Alm.* (to *him.*) F; *Alm.* [*to
him.*] D.
199 *Bend.*] F, D; *Bend.* Q1-2 (Bend Q2).
208 *Mustapha*] *Mustafa* Q1-2; *Must.* F, D.
210 Person. Be] D; ~ , be Q1-2, F.   213 speak,] F, D; ~∧ Q1-2.

Bend. How she assumes! I like not this beginning.   [*Aside.*
220 *Almeyda.* I was not born so base, to flatter Crowds,
And move your pitty by a whining tale:
Your Tyrant would have forc'd me to his Bed;
But in th' attempt of that foul brutal Act,
These Loyall Slaves secur'd me by his Death.   [*Pointing to* Ben.
    Bend. Makes she no more of me then of a Slave?   [*Aside.*
Madam, I thought I had instructed you   [*To* Alm.
To frame a Speech more suiting to the times:
The Circumstances of that dire design,
Your own despair, my unexpected ayd,
230 My Life endanger'd by his bold defence,
And after all, his Death, and your Deliv'rance,
Were themes that ought not to be slighted o're.
    Mustapha. She might have pass'd over all your petty busi-
nesses and no great matter: But the Raising of my Rabble is an
Exploit of consequence; and not to be mumbled up in silence,
for all her pertness.
    Almeyda. When force invades the gift of Nature, Life,
The eldest Law of nature bids defend:
And if in that defence, a Tyrant fall,
240 His Death's his Crime not ours:
Suffice it that he's Dead: all wrongs dye with him;
When he can wrong no more I pardon him:
Thus I absolve my self; and him excuse,
Who sav'd my life, and honour; but praise neither.
    Benducar. 'Tis cheap to pardon, whom you would not pay;
But what speak I of payment and reward?
Ungratefull Woman, you are yet no Queen;
Nor more than a proud haughty Christian slave:
As such I seize my right.   [*Going to lay hold on her.*

---

219   s.d. *Aside.*] F, D; *aside*ᴧ Q1; *aside.* Q2.
225   s.d. *Aside*] F, D; *aside* Q1–2.   226   s.d. *To*] F, D; *to* Q1–2.
230   My] Q2, F, D; my Q1.   233   *Mustapha.*] *Mustafa.* Q1–2; *Must.* F, D.
235   silence,] F, D; ~ᴧ Q1–2.
239–240 fall, / His . . . ours:] D; fall, his . . . ours: Q1–2, F.
248   Christian] F, D; *Christian* Q1–2.
249   s.d. *Going*] F, D; *going* Q1–2.

250 *Almeyda drawing a Dagger.* Dare not to approach me. Now
       Affricans,
     He shows himself to you; to me he stood
     Confest before, and own'd his Insolence
     T' espouse my person, and assume the Crown,
     Claym'd in my Right: for this he slew your Tyrant;
     Oh no, he only chang'd him for a worse,
     Imbas'd your Slavery by his own vileness,
     And loaded you with more ignoble bonds:
     Then think me not ungratefull, not to share,
     Th' Imperial Crown with a presuming Traytor.
260 He says I am a Christian; true, I am,
     But yet no Slave: If Christians can be thought,
     Unfit to govern those of other Faith,
     'Tis left for you to judge.
         Benducar. I have not patience; she consumes the time
     In Idle talk, and owns her false Belief:
     Seize her by force, and bear her hence unheard.
         Almeyda to the People. No, let me rather dye your sacrifice
     Than live his Tryumph;
     I throw my self into my Peoples armes;
270 As you are Men, compassionate my wrongs,
     And as good men, Protect me.
         Antonio aside. Something must be done to save her.———
     [*To* Mustapha.] This is all address'd to you Sir: She singled you
     out with her eye, as Commander in chief of the Mobility.
         Mustapha. Think'st thou so Slave *Antonio?*
         Antonio. Most certainly Sir; and you cannot in honour but
     protect her. Now look to your hits, and make your fortune.

---

250 *Almeyda . . . a*] F, D; [Almyda . . . / [*a* Q1–2 (Almeyda Q2).
250 me. Now *Affricans,*] me; / Now *Affricans,* Q1–2, F, D (Now Q1).
260 Christian] F, D; *Christian* Q1–2.   260 true,] F; ∼∧ Q1–2, D.
261 Christians] F, D; *Christians* Q1–2.
267 *Almeyda . . . People*] F, D; [Almeyda . . . / [*People* Q1–2.
270–271 Men, . . . men,] D; ∼∧ . . . ∼∧ Q1–2, F.
272 *Antonio aside.*] F; [Antonio *aside*∧ Q1–2; *Ant.* D.
272 her.———] ∼ .∧ Q1–2, F, D.
273 *s.d.* Mustapha.]] Mustafa. Q1–2; Must.) F; Must.] D.
275 *Mustapha.*] *Mustafa.* Q1–2; *Must.* F, D.   277 her.] ∼ ; D; ∼ , Q1–2, F.

Mustapha. Methought indeed she cast a kind leer towards
me: Our Prophet was but just such another Scoundrell as I am,
280 till he rais'd himself to power, and consequently to Holyness, by
marrying his masters Widow: I am resolved I'le put forward for
my self: for why should I be my Lord *Benducars* Fool and Slave,
when I may be my own fool and his Master?

Benducar. Take her into possession, *Mustapha.*

Mustapha. That's better Counsell than you meant it: Yes I
do take her into possession, and into protection too. What say
you, Masters, will you stand by me?

Omnes. One and all; One and all.

Benducar. Hast thou betray'd me Traytor?
290 *Mufti* speak & mind 'em of Religion.   [Mufti *shakes his head.*

Mustapha. Alas the poor Gentleman has gotten a cold, with
a Sermon of two hours long, and a prayer of four: and besides,
if he durst speak, mankind is grown wiser at this time of day,
than to cut one anothers throats about Religion. Our *Mufti's* is
a Green coat, and the Christian's is a black coat; and we must
wisely go together by the ears, whether green or black shall
sweep our spoils.   [*Drums within and shouts.*

Benducar. Now we shall see whose numbers will prevail:
The Conquering Troups of *Muley-Zeydan* come
300 To crush Rebellion, and espouse my Cause.

Mustapha. We will have a fair Tryall of Skill for't, I can tell
him that. When we have dispatch'd with *Muley-Zeydan,* your
Lordship shall march in equall proportions of your body, to the
four gates of the City; and every Tower shall have a Quarter
of you.

[Antonio *draws them up and takes* Almeyda *by the hand.*
[*Shouts again and Drums.*

278 *Mustapha*] *Mustafa* Q1–2; *Must.* F, D.
284 *Mustapha*] F, D; *Mustafa* Q1–2.
285 *Mustapha*] *Mustafa* Q1–2; *Must.* F, D.
286 too. What] ~ : what Q1–2, F, D (What F, D).
291 *Mustapha.*] *Mustafa.* Q1–2; *Must.* F, D.   294 *Mufti's*] D; *Mufti* Q1–2, F.
295 Christian's] D; *Christians* Q1–2; Christian F.
299 *Muley-Zeydan*] D; ~∧~ , Q1; ~ - ~ , Q2, F.
301 *Mustapha.*] *Mustafa.* Q1–2 (*Mustaafa* Q2); *Must.* F, D.
302 *Muley-Zeydan*] F, D; *Muley Zeydan* Q1–2.
305 you.] F, D; ~ , Q1–2.   305+ *s.d. hand.*] F, D; ~∧ Q1–2.

Enter Dorax *and* Sebastian *attended by* Affrican *Soldiers
and* Portugueses. Almeyda *and* Sebastian *run into
each others armes and both speak together.*

Seb. and Alm. My *Sebastian!* My *Almeyda!*
Alm. Do you then live?
Seb. And live to love thee ever.
Bend. How! *Dorax* and *Sebastian* still alive!
The *Moors* and Christians joyn'd! I thank thee Prophet.
310   *Dorax.* The Citadell is ours; and *Muley-Zeydan*
Safe under Guard, but as becomes a Prince.
Lay down your armes: such base Plebeian bloud
Would only stain the brightness of my Sword,
And blunt it for some nobler work behind.
   Must. I suppose you may put it up without offence to any
man here present. For my part, I have been Loyall to my Sov-
eraign Lady: though that Villain *Benducar,* and that Hypocrite
the *Mufti,* would have corrupted me; but if those two scape
publick Justice, then I and all my late honest Subjects here,
320 deserve hanging.
   Benducar to Dorax. I'm sure I did my part to poyson thee,
What Saint soe're has Sodder'd thee again.
A Dose less hot had burst through ribs of Iron.
   Muf. Not knowing that, I poyson'd him once more,
And drench'd him with a draught so deadly cold
That, had'st not thou prevented, had congeal'd
The channell of his bloud, and froze him dry.
   Bend. Thou interposing Fool, to mangle mischief,
And think to mend the perfect work of Hell.
330   *Dorax.* Thus, when Heaven pleases, double poysons cure.
I will not tax thee of Ingratitude
To me thy Friend, who hast betray'd thy Prince:

305+ *s.d.* Portugueses] F, D; *Portugueses* Q1–2.
305+ *s.d.* Almeyda] D; (∼ Q1–2, F.
306 and] and Q1–2, F, D.   309 *Moors*] Moors Q1–2, F, D.
310 *Muley-Zeydan*] F, D; *Muley Zeydan* Q1–2.
316 present.] D; ∼ ? Q1–2, F.
321 *Benducar to Dorax.*] D; [Benducar / *to* Dorax.] Q1; [*Benducar* / *to Dorax.*]
Q2; *Bend. (to* Dorax∧) F.

Death he deserv'd indeed, but not from thee.
But fate it seems reserv'd the worst of men
To end the worst of Tyrants.
Go bear him to his fate,
And send him to attend his Masters Ghost.
Let some secure my other poys'ning Friend,
Whose double dilligence preserv'd my life.

340   *Ant.* You are fall'n into good hands, Father in law; your
sparkling Jewells, and *Morayma's* eyes may prove a better bail
than you deserve.

Muf. The best that can come of me, in this condition, is to
have my life begg'd first, and then to be begg'd for a Fool afterwards. [*Exit* Antonio *with the* Mufti, *and at the same time*
                Benducar *is carry'd off.*

Dorax to Mustapha. You and your hungry herd depart un-
        touch'd;
For Justice cannot stoop so low, to reach
The groveling sin of Crowds: but curst be they
Who trust revenge with such mad Instruments,
350 Whose blindfold bus'ness is but to destroy:
And like the fire Commission'd by the Winds,
Begins on sheds, but rouling in a round,
On Pallaces returns. Away ye skum,
That still rise upmost when the Nation boyls:
Ye mungrill work of Heaven, with humane shapes,
Not to be damn'd, or sav'd, but breath, and perish,
That have but just enough of sence, to know
The masters voice, when rated, to depart.
                    [*Exeunt* Mustapha *and Rabble.*
    Almeyda kneeling to him. With gratitude as low, as knees can
        pay

336   fate,] D; ~ . Q1–2; ~ ; F.   341   *Morayma's*] Q2, F, D; Morayma's Q1.
346   *Dorax to Mustapha.*] [Dorax *to* / Mustafa.] Q1; (Dorax *to* / Mustapha.)
Q2; *Dor. (to* Must.) F; *Dor.* [*to* Must.] D.
358+   *s.d.* Mustapha] F, D; Mustafa Q1–2.
358+   *s.d. Rabble*] D; Rabble Q1–2, F.
359   *Almeyda kneeling* . . . *him.* With . . . pay] [Almeyda *kneeling* . . . *him.* /
With . . . pay Q1–2, F ((Almeyda Q2, F; "With" *indented in Q1–2*); *Alm.* With
. . . pay / [*Kneeling* . . . *him.* D.

360 To those blest holy Fires, our Guardian Angells,
Receive these thanks; till Altars can be rais'd.
    Dorax raising her up. Arise fair Excellence, and pay no
        thanks,
Till time discover what I have deserv'd.
    Seb. More then reward can answer.
If *Portugal* and *Spain* were joyn'd to *Affrica,*
And the main Ocean crusted into Land,
If Universall Monarchy were mine,
Here should the gift be plac'd.
    Dorax. And from some hands I shou'd refuse that gift:
370 Be not too prodigall of Promises;
But stint your bounty to one only grant,
Which I can ask with honour.
    Seb.   What I am
Is but thy gift, make what thou canst of me,
Secure of no Repulse.
    Dorax to Sebastian. Dismiss your Train.
[*To* Almeyda.] You, Madam, please one moment to retire.
        [Sebastian *signes to the* Portugueses *to go off.* Almeyda
            bowing to him, goes off also: The Affricans *follow her.*
    Dorax to the Captain of his Guard. With you one word in
        private.
                    [*Goes out with the Captain.*
    Sebastian solus. Reserv'd behaviour, open Nobleness,
A long misterious Track of a stern bounty:
But now the hand of Fate is on the Curtain,
380 And draws the Scene to sight.

---

362 *Dorax raising . . . up.* Arise . . . thanks,] [Dorax *raising . . . up*ₐ / Arise
. . . thanks, Q1-2, F ((Dorax Q2, F; *up.* F; "Arise" *indented in* Q1-2); Dor.
Arise . . . Thanks, / [*Raising . . . up.* D.
365 *Portugal*] Q2, F, D; *Portugall* Q1.
365 *Affrica*] Affrique Q1; *Affrique* Q2; *Afrique* F; *Africa* D.
373 me,] D; ∼ . Q1-2, F.   374 *to*] D; to Q1-2, F.
374 *Sebastian.*] D (*Seb.*); ∼ : Q1-2, F.
375 *s.d.* Almeyda.]] D; ∼ .ₐ Q1-2 (*line indented in* Q1); ∼ .) F.
375+ *s.d.* Portugueses] D; *Portugueses* Q1-2, F.
376 *to*] F; *To* Q1-2, D.   376 *Guard.* With] D; ∼ . / ∼ Q1-2, F.
377 *solus*] D; *Solus* Q1-2, F.   378 bounty:] ∼ . Q1-2, F, D.

Re-enter Dorax, *having taken off his Turbant and put on a Peruque, Hat and Crevat.*

Dorax.   Now do you know me?
Seb. Thou shouldst be *Alonzo.*
Dorax.   So you shou'd be *Sebastian:*
But when *Sebastian* ceas'd to be himself,
I ceas'd to be *Alonzo.*
Seb.   As in a Dream
I see thee here, and scarce believe mine eyes.
Dorax. Is it so strange to find me, where my wrongs,
And your Inhumane Tyranny have sent me?
Think not you dream: or, if you did, my Injuries
Shall call so loud, that Lethargy should wake;
And Death should give you back to answer me.
390 A Thousand Nights have brush'd their balmy wings
Over these eyes, but ever when they clos'd,
Your Tyrant Image forc'd 'em ope again,
And dry'd the dewes they brought.
The long expected hour is come at length,
By manly Vengence to redeem my fame;
And that once clear'd, eternall sleep is welcome.
Sebast. I have not yet forgot I am a King;
Whose Royall Office is redress of Wrongs:
If I have wrong'd thee, charge me face to face;
400 I have not yet forgot I am a Soldier.
Dorax. 'Tis the first Justice thou hast ever done me.
Then, though I loath this Womans War of tongues,
Yet shall my Cause of Vengeance first be clear:
And, Honour, be thou Judge.
Sebast.   Honour befriend us both.
Beware, I warn thee yet, to tell thy griefs
In terms becoming Majesty to hear:
I warn thee thus, because I know thy temper
Is Insolent and haughty to Superiours:

---

380 *s.d. Peruque,*] F, D; ~∧ Q1–2.
385 *Dorax.*] Q2, F, D *(Dor.)*; *Dorax*∧ Q1.

How often hast thou brav'd my peacefull Court,
410 Fill'd it with noisy brawls, and windy boasts;
And, with past service, nauseously repeated,
Reproach'd ev'n me thy Prince!
  Dorax. And well I might, when you forgot reward,
The part of Heav'n in Kings: for punishment
Is Hangmans work, and drudgery for Devils.
I must and will reproach thee with my service,
Tyrant: it irks me, so to call my Prince;
But just resentment and hard usage coyn'd
Th' unwilling word; and grating as it is,
420 Take it, for 'tis thy due.
  Sebast.   How, Tyrant?
  Dorax.   Tyrant.
  Sebast. Traytour! that name thou canst not Eccho back:
That Robe of Infamy, that Circumcision
Ill hid beneath that Robe, proclaim thee Traytor:
And, if a Name
More foul than Traytor be, 'tis Renegade.
  Dorax. If I'm a Traytor, think, and blush, thou Tyrant,
Whose Injuries betray'd me into treason,
Effac'd my Loyalty, unhing'd my Faith,
And hurryed me from hopes of Heaven to Hell.
430 All these, and all my yet unfinish'd Crimes,
When I shall rise to plead before the Saints,
I charge on thee, to make thy damning sure.
  Sebast. Thy old presumptuous Arrogance again,
That bred my first dislike, and then my loathing.
Once more be warn'd, and know me for thy King.
  Dorax. Too well I know thee; but for King no more:
This is not *Lisbonne,* nor the Circle this,
Where, like a Statue, thou hast stood besieg'd,

---

412 Prince!] ~ ? Q1–2, F, D.   417 Tyrant:] ~ , Q1–2, F, D (*T*yrant Q1).
417 it] (~ Q1–2, F, D.   417 me,] ~∧ Q1–2, F, D.
417 Prince;] ~ .) Q1–2, D; ~ ,) F.   419 is,] D; ~∧ Q1–2, F.
420 How,] D; ~∧ Q1–2, F.   420 *Dorax.*] Q2, F, D (*Dor.*); ~∧ Q1.
421 Traytour!] ~ ? Q1; ~ ; Q2, F, D.   426 think,] Q2, F, D; ~∧ Q1.
427 treason,] D; ~ . Q1–2, F.

By Sycophants and Fools, the growth of Courts;
440 Where thy gull'd eyes, in all the gawdy round,
Met nothing but a lye in every face,
And the gross flattery of a gaping Crowd,
Envious who first should catch, and first applaud
The Stuff of Royall Nonsence: when I spoke,
My honest homely words were carp'd, and censur'd,
For want of Courtly Stile: related Actions,
Though modestly reported, pass'd for boasts:
Secure of Merit if I ask'd reward,
Thy hungry Minions thought their rights invaded,
450 And the bread snatch'd from Pimps and Parasits.
Enriquez answer'd, with a ready lye
To save his King's, the boon was begg'd before.
        Sebast. What sayst thou of *Enriquez?* now, by Heaven,
Thou mov'st me more by barely naming him,
Than all thy foul unmanner'd scurril taunts.
        Dorax. And therefore 'twas to gaul thee, that I nam'd him:
That thing, that nothing, but a cringe and smile;
That Woman, but more dawb'd; or if a man,
Corrupted to a Woman: thy Man Mistress.
460   *Sebast.* All false as Hell or thou.
        Dorax.   Yes; full as false
As that I serv'd thee fifteen hard Campaignes,
And pitch'd thy Standard in these Forreign Fields:
By me thy greatness grew; thy years grew with it,
But thy Ingratitude outgrew 'em both.
        Sebast. I see to what thou tend'st, but tell me first
If those great Acts were done alone for me;
If love produc'd not some, and pride the rest?
        Dorax. Why Love does all that's noble here below;
But all th' advantage of that love was thine.
470 For, coming fraughted back, in either hand
With Palm and Olive, Victory and Peace,

439 Courts;] ~ : Q1–2, F, D.   441 face,] ~ ; Q1–2, F, D.
451 lye] ~ , Q1–2, F, D.
453 now, . . . Heaven,] ~ʌ . . . ~ʌ Q1–2, F, D.

I was indeed prepar'd to ask my own:
(For *Violante's* vows were mine before:)
Thy malice had prevention, ere I spoke;
And ask'd me *Violante* for *Enriquez.*
 Seb. I meant thee a reward of greater worth.
 Dor. Where justice wanted, could reward be hop'd?
Could the robb'd Passenger expect a bounty,
From those rapacious hands who stript him first?
480 *Seb.* He had my promise, e're I knew thy love.
 Dor. My Services deserv'd thou should'st revoke it.
 Seb. Thy Insolence had cancell'd all thy Service:
To violate my Laws, even in my Court,
Sacred to peace, and safe from all affronts;
Ev'n to my face, as done in my despight,
Under the wing of awfull Majesty
To strike the man I lov'd!
 Dor. Even in the face of Heaven, a place more Sacred,
Would I have struck the man, who, propt by power,
490 Would Seize my right, and rob me of my Love:
But, for a blow provok'd by thy Injustice,
The hasty product of a just despair,
When he refus'd to meet me in the field,
That thou shoud'st make a Cowards Cause thy own!
 Seb. He durst; nay more, desir'd and begg'd with tears,
To meet thy Challenge fairly: 'twas thy fault
To make it publique; but my duty, then,
To interpose, on pain of my displeasure,
Betwixt your Swords.
 Dor.   On pain of Infamy
500 He should have disobey'd.
 Seb. Th' Indignity thou didst, was ment to me;
Thy gloomy eyes were cast on me, with scorn,

---

476 worth.] F, D; ~ : Q1-2.   480 love.] F, D; ~ , Q1-2.
485 Ev'n] D; E'ven Q1-2; Even F.   489 who,] D; ~∧ Q1-2, F.
493 refus'd] Q2 (?), F, D; resus'd Q1 (?).   495 more,] D; ~∧ Q1-2, F.
497 To] Q2, F, D; o Q1.   498 interpose,] ~ ; Q1-2, F, D.
499 Swords.] F, D; ~ , Q1-2.

As who should say, *the blow was there intended;*
But that thou didst not dare to lift thy hands
Against Annointed power: so was I forc'd
To do a Soveraign justice to my self;
And spurn thee from my presence.
    Dor.   Thou hast dar'd
To tell me, what I durst not tell my self:
I durst not think that I was spurn'd, and live;
510 And live to hear it boasted to my face.
All my long Avarice of honour lost,
Heap'd up in Youth, and hoarded up for Age;
Has honours Fountain then suck'd back the stream?
He has; and hooting Boys, may dry-shod pass,
And gather pebbles from the naked Foord.
Give me my Love, my Honour; give 'em back:———
Give me revenge; while I have breath to ask it.———
    Seb. Now, by this honour'd Order which I wear,
More gladly would I give, than thou dar'st ask it:
520 Nor shall the Sacred Character of King
Be urg'd, to shield me from thy bold appeal.
If I have injur'd thee, that makes us equall:
The wrong, if done, debas'd me down to thee.
But thou hast charg'd me with Ingratitude:
Hast thou not charg'd me? speak!
    Dor.   Thou know'st I have:
If thou disown'st that Imputation, draw,
And prove my Charge a lye.
    Seb. No; to disprove that lye, I must not draw:
Be conscious to thy worth, and tell thy Soul
530 What thou hast done this day in my defence:
To fight thee, after this, what were it else,
Than owning that Ingratitude thou urgest?
That Isthmus stands betwixt two rushing Seas;
Which, mounting, view each other from afar;
And strive in vain to meet.

503   say,] D; ~∧ Q1-2, F.
503   the . . . [to] . . . intended] *in romans in Q1-2, F, D.*
525   me? speak!] ~ ; ~ ? Q1-2, F, D.   533, 535 Isthmus] *Isthmus* Q1-2, F, D.

Dor.   I'le cut that Isthmus.
Thou know'st I meant not to preserve thy Life,
But to reprieve it, for my own revenge.
I sav'd thee out of honourable malice:
Now draw; I should be loath to think thou dar'st not:
540 Beware of such another vile excuse.
    Seb. O patience Heaven!
    Dor.   Beware of Patience too;
That's a Suspicious word: it had been proper
Before thy foot had spurn'd me; now 'tis base:
Yet, to disarm thee of thy last defence,
I have thy Oath for my security:
The only boon I begg'd was this fair Combat:
Fight or be Perjur'd now; that's all thy choice.
    Sebas. drawing. Now I can thank thee as thou wouldst be
        thank'd:
Never was vow of honour better pay'd,
550 If my true Sword but hold, than this shall be.
The sprightly Bridegroom, on his Wedding Night,
More gladly enters not the lists of Love.
Why 'tis enjoyment to be summon'd thus.
Go: bear my Message to *Enriquez* Ghost;
And say his Master and his Friend reveng'd him.
    Dor. His Ghost! then is my hated Rivall dead?
    Seb. The question is beside our present purpose;
Thou seest me ready; we delay too long.
    Dor. A minute is not much in eithers Life,
560 When there's but one betwixt us; throw it in,
And give it him of us, who is to fall.
    Sebast. He's dead: make hast, and thou mayst yet o're take
        him.
    Dor. When I was hasty, thou delay'st me longer.
I prethee let me hedge one moment more
Into thy promise; for thy life preserv'd,

---

548 *Sebas. drawing.* Now . . . thank'd:] [Sebas. *drawing:*] Now . . . thank'd:
Q1-2, F (*Seb.* F); *Seb.* Now . . . thank'd: / [*Drawing.* D.
554 Go] Q2, F, D; Go Q1.   554 *Enriquez*] *Henriquez* Q1-2, F, D.
560 there's] Q2, F, D; their's Q1.   565 preserv'd,] D; ∼ : Q1-2, F.

Be kind; and tell me how that Rivall dy'd,
Whose Death next thine I wish'd.
    Seb. If it would please thee, thou should'st never know:
But thou, like Jealousy, enquir'st a truth,
570 Which, found, will torture thee: He dy'd in Fight:
Fought next my person; as in Consort fought:
Kept pace for pace, and blow for every blow;
Save when he heav'd his Shield in my defence;
And on his naked side receiv'd my wound.
Then, when he could no more, he fell at once:
But rowl'd his falling body cross their way;
And made a Bulwark of it for his Prince.
    Dor. I never can forgive him such a death!
    Seb. I prophecy'd thy proud Soul could not bear it.
580 Now, judge thy self, who best deserv'd my Love.
I knew you both; (and durst I say) as Heaven
Foreknew among the shining Angell host
Who would stand firm, who fall.
    Dor. Had he been tempted so, so had he fall'n;
And so, had I been favour'd, had I stood.
    Seb. What had been, is unknown; what is, appears:
Confess he justly was preferr'd to thee.
    Dor. Had I been born with his indulgent Stars,
My fortune had been his, and his been mine.
590 O, worse than Hell! what Glory have I lost,
And what has he acquir'd, by such a death!
I should have fallen by *Sebastians* side;
My Corps had been the Bulwark of my King.
His glorious end was a patch'd work of fate,
Ill sorted with a soft effeminate life:
It suited better with my life than his
So to have dy'd: mine had been of a peice,
Spent in your service, dying at your feet.
    Seb. The more effeminate and soft his life,
600 The more his fame, to struggle to the field,
And meet his glorious fate: Confess, proud Spirit,

---

568 thee,] D; ~∧ Q1–2, F.   586 been, . . . is,] D; ~∧ . . . ~∧ Q1–2, F.

(For I will have it from thy very mouth)
That better he deserv'd my love than thou.
   Dor. O, whither would you drive me! I must grant,
Yes I must grant, but with a swelling Soul,
Enriquez had your Love with more desert:
For you he fought, and dy'd; I fought against you;
Through all the mazes of the bloudy field,
Hunted your Sacred life; which that I miss'd
610 Was the propitious errour of my fate,
Not of my Soul; my Soul's a Regicide.
   Seb. Thou might'st have given it a more gentle name:

                              [*More calmly.*

Thou meant'st to kill a Tyrant, not a King:
Speak, didst thou not, *Alonzo?*
   Dor.   Can I speak!
Alas, I cannot answer to *Alonzo:*
No, *Dorax* cannot answer to *Alonzo:*
Alonzo was too kind a name for me.
Then, when I fought and conquer'd with your Armes,
In that blest Age I was the man you nam'd:
620 Till rage and pride debas'd me into *Dorax;*
And lost like *Lucifer,* my name above.
   Seb. Yet, twice this day I ow'd my life to *Dorax.*
   Dor. I sav'd you but to kill you; there's my grief.
   Seb. Nay, if thou can'st be griev'd, thou can'st repent:
Thou coud'st not be a Villain, though thou woud'st:
Thou own'st too much, in owning thou hast err'd;
And I too little, who provok'd thy Crime.
   Dor. O stop this headlong Torrent of your goodness:
It comes too fast upon a feeble Soul,
630 Half drown'd in tears, before; spare my confusion:

---

604   whither] F, D; whether Q1–2.   606 *Enriquez*] *Henriquez* Q1–2, F, D.
612–613 name: / [*More calmly.* / Thou . . . King:] name: / [*more calmly.*]
Thou . . . King: Q1–2, F; name: / Thou . . . King: [*More calmly.* D.
614 Speak,] F, D; ~ˬ Q1–2.   616, 620, 622 *Dorax*] Q2, F, D; *Dorax* Q1.

For pitty spare, and say not, first, you err'd.
For yet I have not dar'd, through guilt and shame,
To throw my self beneath your Royall feet.   [*Falls at his feet.*
Now spurn this Rebell, this proud Renegade:
'Tis just you should, nor will I more complain.
     Seb. Indeed thou shoud'st not ask forgiveness first,
But thou preventst me still, in all that's noble.   [*Taking him up.*
Yet I will raise thee up with better news:
Thy *Violante's* heart was ever thine;
640 Compell'd to wed, because she was my Ward,
Her Soul was absent when she gave her hand:
Nor could my threats, or his pursuing Courtship,
Effect the Consummation of his Love:
So, still indulging tears, she pines for thee,
A Widdow and a Maid.
     Dor. Have I been cursing Heav'n while Heav'n blest me!
I shall run mad with extasy of joy:
What, in one moment, to be reconcil'd
To Heaven, and to my King, and to my Love!
650 But pitty is my Friend, and stops me short,
For my unhappy Rivall: poor *Enriquez!*
     Seb. Art thou so generous too, to Pitty him?
Nay, then I was unjust to love him better.
Here let me ever hold thee in my arms: [*Embracing him.*
And all our quarrells be but such as these,
Who shall love best, and closest shall embrace:
Be what *Enriquez* was; be my *Alonzo.*
     Dor. What, *my Alonzo* sayd you? *my Alonzo!*
Let my tears thank you; for I cannot speak:
660 And if I cou'd,

633–634 To . . . feet. [*Falls at his feet.* / Now] D (Feet. / [*Falls*); [*Falls at his
To . . . feet. / feet*ʌ] Now Q1–2, F (*feet.* Q2, F).
637 *s.d.* But . . . noble. [*Taking him up.*] D (Noble. / [*Taking*); [*taking him
up.* But . . . noble. Q1–2, F.
651 *Enriquez*] *Henriquez* Q1–2, F, D (*Henriquez* Q1).
654–655 Here . . . arms: [*Embracing him.* / And] D; *Embrac-* Here . . . arms:
/ *ing him.* And Q1–2, F.
658 *my . . . my*] my . . . my Q1–2, F, D.

Words were not made to vent such thoughts as mine.
   Seb. Thou canst not speak, and I can ne're be silent.
Some Strange reverse of Fate must sure attend
This vast profusion, this extravagance
Of Heaven, to bless me thus. 'Tis Gold so pure
   It cannot bear the Stamp, without allay.
   Be kind, ye Powers, and take but half away:
   With ease the gifts of Fortune I resign:
   But, let my Love, and Friend, be ever mine.

                                    Exeunt.

ACT V.   SCENE I.

The Scene is a Room of State.

Enter Dorax *and* Antonio.

   Dor. Joy is on every face, without a Cloud:
As, in the Scene of opening Paradice,
The whole Creation danc'd at their new being:
Pleas'd to be what they were; pleas'd with each other.
Such Joy have I, both in my self, and Friends:
And double Joy, that I have made 'em happy.
   Antonio. Pleasure has been the bus'ness of my life;
And every change of Fortune easy to me,
Because I still was easy to my self.
10 The loss of her I lov'd would touch me nearest;
Yet, if I found her, I might love too much;
And that's uneasy Pleasure.
   Dor.   If she be fated
To be your Wife, your fate will find her for you:
Predestinated ills are never lost.

663 must] F, D; ~ , Q1–2.   666–669 *lines not indented in Q1–2, F, D.*
669+ *s.d. Exeunt.*] Q2, F, D; ~∧ Q1.
ACT V. SCENE I. / *The*] D; ACT V. *The* Q1–2, F.
7 *Antonio.*] Q2, F, D (*Ant.*); ~ , Q1.

Anton. I had forgot
T' Enquire before, but long to be inform'd,
How, poison'd and betray'd, and round beset,
You could unwind your self from all these dangers;
And move so speedily to our relief!
20   *Dor.* The double poisons, after a short Combat,
Expell'd each other in their Civill War,
By natures benefit: and rows'd my thoughts
To Guard that life which now I found Attack'd.
I summon'd all my Officers in hast,
On whose experienc'd Faith I might rely:
All came; resolv'd to dye in my defence,
Save that one Villain who betray'd the Gate.
Our diligence prevented the surprize
We justly fear'd: so, *Muley-Zeydan* found us
30 Drawn-up in Battle, to receive the charge.
     Ant. But how the *Moors* and Christian slaves were joyn'd,
You have not yet unfolded.
     Dor.   That remains.
We knew their Int'rest was the same with ours:
And though I hated more than Death, *Sebastian;*
I could not see him dye by Vulgar hands:
But prompted by my Angell, or by his,
Freed all the Slaves, and plac'd him next my self,
Because I would not have his Person known.
I need not tell the rest, th' event declares it.
40   *Ant.* Your Conquest came of course; their men were raw,
And yours were disciplin'd: one doubt remains,
Why you industriously conceal'd the King,
Who, known, had added Courage to his Men?
     Dor. I would not hazard civill broils, betwixt
His Friends and mine; which might prevent our Combat:
Yet, had he fall'n, I had dismiss'd his Troops;
Or, if Victorious, order'd his escape.
But I forgot a new increase of Joy,

---

31   Christian] *Christian* Q1–2, F, D.   45   mine;] ∼ : Q1–2, F, D.

To feast him with surprize; I must about it:
50 Expect my swift return.   [*Exit* Dorax.

Enter a Servant to Antonio.

Serv. Here's a Lady at the door, that bids me tell you, she is
come to make an end of the game, that was broken off betwixt
you.

Ant. What manner of Woman is she? Does she not want two
of the four Elements? has she any thing about her but ayr and
fire?

Servant. Truly, she flys about the room, as if she had wings
instead of legs; I believe she's just turning into a bird: a house-
bird I warrant her: and so hasty to fly to you, that, rather than
60 fail of entrance, she wou'd come tumbling down the Chimney,
like a Swallow.

Enter Morayma.

Antonio running to her and Embracing her. Look if she be
not here already: what, no deniall it seems will serve your turn?
why! thou little dun, is thy debt so pressing?

Mor. Little Devill if you please: your lease is out, good Mr.
Conjurer; and I am come to fetch you Soul and Body; not an
hour of lewdness longer in this world for you.

Ant. Where the Devill hast thou been? and how the Devill
didst thou find me here?

70   *Mor.* I follow'd you into the Castle-yard: but there was nothing but Tumult, and Confusion: and I was bodily afraid of
being pick'd up by some of the Rabble; considering I had a
double charge about me,————my Jewells & my Mayden-head.

Ant. Both of 'em intended for my Worships sole use and
Property.

50+   *s.d.* Antonio.] Q2, F, D; ∼ , Q1.
57   *Servant.*] Q2; *Servaut.* Q1; *Serv.* F, D.
62   *Antonio . . . her.* Look] D; [*Antonio . . . her.* / Look Q1–2, F ("Look"
indented).
72   Rabble;] ∼ : Q1–2, F, D.

Mor. And what was poor little I among 'em all?

Ant. Not a mouthfull a piece: 'twas too much odds, in Conscience.

Mor. So, seeking for shelter, I naturally ran to the old place
80 of Assignation, the Garden-house: where for want of instinct,
you did not follow me.

Ant. Well, for thy Comfort, I have secur'd thy Father; and
I hope thou hast secur'd his effects for us.

Mor. Yes truly I had the prudent foresight to consider that
when we grow old, and weary of Solacing one another, we
might have, at least, wherewithall to make merry with the
World; and take up with a worse pleasure of eating and drinking, when we were disabled for a better.

Ant. Thy fortune will be e'en too good for thee: for thou art
90 going into the Country of Serenades, and Gallantries; where thy
street will be haunted every Night, with thy foolish Lovers, and
my Rivals; who will be sighing, and singing under thy inexorable windows, lamentable ditties, and call thee Cruell, & Goddess, & Moon, and Stars, and all the Poeticall names of wicked
rhyme: while thou and I, are minding our bus'ness, and jogging
on, and laughing at 'em; at leisure-minuts, which will be very
few: take that by way of threatning.

Mor. I am afraid you are not very valiant, that you huff so
much before hand: but, they say, your Churches are fine places
100 for Love-devotion: many a she-Saint is there worship'd.

Ant. Temples are there, as they are in all other Countries,
good conveniences for dumb enterviews: I hear the Protestants
an't much reform'd in that point neither; for their Sectaries
call their Churches by the naturall name of Meeting-houses.
Therefore I warn thee in good time, not more of devotion than
needs must, good future Spowse; and allways in a veile; for
those eyes of thine are damn'd enemies to mortification.

Mor. The best thing I have heard of Christendom, is that we
women are allow'd the priviledge of having Souls; and I assure

---

77 odds,] ∼ₐ Q1–2, F, D.   79 So,] ∼ₐ Q1–2, F, D.
82 Well,] D; ∼ₐ Q1–2, F.   90 into] Q2, F, D; iuto Q1.
97 few:] ∼ , Q1–2, F, D.   105 Therefore] Q2, F, D; therefore Q1.

110 you, I shall make bold to bestow mine, upon some Lover, when
ever you begin to go astray, and, if I find no Convenience in a
Church, a private Chamber will serve the turn.

Ant. When that day comes, I must take my revenge and turn
Gardener again: for I find I am much given to Planting.

Mor. But take heed, in the mean time, that some young
Antonio does not spring up in your own Family; as false as his
Father, though of another mans planting.

Re-enter Dorax *with* Sebastian *and* Almeyda. Sebastian *enters
speaking to* Dorax, *while in the mean time* Antonio
presents Morayma *to* Almeyda.

Seb. How fares our Royall Pris'ner, *Muley-Zeydan?*
Dor. Dispos'd to grant whatever I desire,
120 To gain a Crown, and Freedom: well I know him,
Of easy temper, naturally good,
And faithfull to his word.
Seb.   Yet one thing wants,
To fill the measure of my happiness;
I'm still in pain for poor *Alvarez's* life.
Dor. Release that fear; the good old man is safe:
I pay'd his ransome
And have already order'd his Attendance.
Seb. O bid him enter for I long to see him.

Enter Alvarez *with a Servant, who departs when*
Alvarez *is enter'd.*

Alvarez falling down and embracing the Kings knees. Now
by my Soul, and by these hoary hairs,
130 I'm so ore-whelm'd with pleasure, that I feel
A latter spring within my with'ring limbs,

117+ s.d. *Re-enter*] F, D; *Reenter* Q1–2.
118 *Muley-Zeydan*] D; *Muley Zeydan* Q1–2, F.
123 happiness;] D; ∼ Q1–2, F.   126 ransome] F; ∼ : Q1; ∼ . Q2; ∼ ; D.
129 *Alvarez falling . . . knees.* Now . . . hairs,] [∼∼ . . . ∼ .] / ∼ . . . ∼ ,
Q1–2, F; *Alv.* Now . . . Hairs, / [*Falling . . . Knees.* D.

That Shoots me out again.
    Sebastian, raising him. Thou good old Man!
Thou hast deceiv'd me into more, more joys;
Who stood brim-full before.
    Alv.   O my dear Child!
I love thee so, I cannot call thee King,
Whom I so oft have dandled in these arms!
What, when I gave thee lost, to find thee living!
'Tis like a Father, who himself had scap'd
A falling house, and after anxious search,
140 Hears from afar, his only Son within:
And digs through rubbish, till he drags him out
To see the friendly light.
Such is my hast, so trembling is my joy,
To draw thee forth from underneath thy Fate.
    Seb. The Tempest is ore-blown; the Skys are clear,
And the Sea, charm'd into a Calm so still,
That not a wrinkle ruffles her smooth face.
    Alv. Just such she shows before a rising storm:
And therefore am I come, with timely speed,
150 To warn you into Port.
    Almeyda.   My Soul fore-bodes   [*Aside.*
Some dire event involv'd in those dark words;
And just disclosing, in a birth of fate.
    Alv. Is there not yet an Heir of this vast Empire,
Who still Survives, of *Muley-Moluchs* branch?
    Dor. Yes such a one there is, a Captive here,
And Brother to the Dead.
    Alv.   The Pow'rs above
Be prais'd for that: My prayers for my good Master
I hope are heard.
    Seb.   Thou hast a right in Heav'n,

---

132 *Sebastian, raising him.* Thou . . . Man!] *Sebastian, raising him*ʌ] / **Thou**
. . . Man! Q1-2, F (*him*. Q2, F); *Seb.* Thou . . . Man! [*Raising him.* D.
137 lost,] D; ~ʌ Q1-2, F.
143 hast, . . . joy,] F; ~ʌ . . . ~ʌ Q1-2, D (Haste, D).
150 s.d. *Aside*] D; *aside* Q1-2, F.   155 a one] Q2, F, D; an one Q1.
156 Pow'rs] Q2, F, D; Power's Q1.

But why these prayers for me?
160   *Alv.* A door is open yet for your deliv'rance.
Now you my Country-men, and you *Almeyda,*
Now all of us, and you (my all in one)
May yet be happy in that Captives life.
   Seb. We have him here an honourable Hostage
For terms of peace: what more he can Contribute
To make me blest, I know not.
   Alv.   Vastly more:
Almeyda may be settled in the Throne;
And you review your Native Clime with fame:
A firm Alliance, and eternall Peace,
170 (The glorious Crown of honourable War,)
Are all included in that Princes life:
Let this fair Queen be giv'n to *Muley-Zeydan;*
And make her love the Sanction of your League.
   Seb. No more of that: his life's in my dispose;
And Pris'ners are not to insist on terms.
Or if they were, yet he demands not these.
   Alv. You shou'd exact 'em.
   Alm.   Better may be made;
These cannot: I abhor the Tyrants race;
My Parents Murtherers, my Throne's Usurpers.
180 But, at one blow to cut off all dispute,
Know this, thou busy, old, officious Man,
I am a Christian; now be wise no more;
Or if thou woud'st be still thought wise, be silent.
   Alv. O! I perceive you think your Int'rest touch'd:
'Tis what before the Battail I observ'd:
But I must speak, and will.
   Seb.   I prethee peace;
Perhaps she thinks they are too near of bloud.
   Alv. I wish she may not wed to bloud more near.
   Seb. What if I make her mine?
   Alv.   Now Heav'n forbid!

---

160   deliv'rance.] ∼ , Q1–2, F, D.
189, 190   Heav'n] Q2, F, D; Hea'vn Q1.

190   *Seb.* Wish rather Heav'n may grant;
      For, if I cou'd deserve, I have deserv'd her:
      My toyls, my hazards, and my Subjects lives,
      (Provided she consent) may claim her love:
      And, that once granted, I appeal to these,
      If better, I cou'd chuse a beauteous Bride.
          Ant. The fairest of her Sex.
          Mor.   The pride of Nature.
          Dor. He only merits her; she only him:
      So payr'd, so suited in their minds and Persons,
      That they were fram'd the Tallyes for each other.
200   If any Alien love had interpos'd
      It must have been an eyesore to beholders,
      And to themselves a Curse.
          Alv.   And to themselves
      The greatest Curse that can be, were to joyn.
          Seb. Did I not love thee, past a change to hate,
      That word had been thy ruine; but no more,
      I charge thee on thy life, perverse old man.
          Alv. Know, Sir, I wou'd be silent if I durst:
      But, if on Shipbord, I shou'd see my Friend,
      Grown frantique in a raging Calenture,
210   And he, imagining vain flowry fields,
      Wou'd headlong plunge himself into the deep,
      Shou'd I not hold him from that mad attempt,
      Till his sick fancy were by reason cur'd?
          Seb. I pardon thee th' effects of doting Age,
      Vain doubts, and idle cares, and over-caution;
      The second Non-age of a Soul, more wise,
      But now decay'd, and sunk into the Socket,
      Peeping by fits and giving feeble light.
          Alv. Have you forgot?
          Seb.   Thou mean'st my Fathers Will,
220   In bar of Marriage to *Almeyda*'s bed:

---

190 grant;] ∼ . Q1–2, F, D.   197 him:] ∼ . Q1–2, F, D.
208 Shipbord,] Q2, F, D; ∼ ,, Q1.   214 Age,] ∼ ; Q1–2, F, D.
216 wise,] ∼ ; Q1–2, F, D.

Thou seest my faculties are still entire,
Though thine are much impair'd. I weigh'd that Will,
And found 'twas grounded on our diff'rent Faiths;
But, had he liv'd to see her happy change,
He wou'd have cancell'd that harsh Interdict,
And joyn'd our hands himself.
    Alv.   Still had he liv'd
And seen this change, he still had been the Same.
    Seb. I have a dark remembrance of my Father;
His reas'nings and his Actions both were just;
230 And, granting that, he must have chang'd his measures.
    Alv. Yes, he was just, and therefore cou'd not change.
    Seb. 'Tis a base wrong thou offer'st to the Dead.
    Alv. Now Heav'n forbid,
That I shou'd blast his pious Memory:
No, I am tender of his holy Fame:
For, dying he bequeath'd it to my charge.
Believe, I am; and seek to know no more,
But pay a blind obedience to his will:
For to preserve his Fame I wou'd be silent.
240   *Seb.* Craz'd fool, who woud'st be thought an Oracle,
Come down from off thy Tripos, and speak plain;
My Father shall be justify'd, he shall:
'Tis a Son's part to rise in his defence;
And to confound thy malice, or thy dotage.
    Alv. It does not grieve me that you hold me craz'd;
But, to be clear'd at my dead Masters cost,
O there's the wound! but let me first adjure you,
By all you owe that dear departed Soul,
No more to think of Marriage with *Almeyda.*
250   *Seb.* Not Heav'n and Earth combin'd, can hinder it.
    Alv. Then, witness Heav'n and Earth, how loath I am

---

222 impair'd.] D; ~ , Q1–2, F.
226–227 liv'd / And . . . change, he . . . Same.] liv'd and . . . change, / He
. . . Same. Q1–2, F, D.
233 Heav'n] F, D; Hea'vn Q1–2.   237 Believe,] Q2, F, D; ~∧ Q1.
238 will:] ~ . Q1–2, F, D.   240 Oracle,] D; ~ . Q1–2, F.
243 'Tis] Q2, F, D; 'Tis Q1.   250, 251 Heav'n] F, D; Hea'vn Q1–2.

To say, you must not, nay you cannot wed.
And since not only a dead Fathers fame,
But more, a Ladies honour, must be touch'd,
Which nice as Ermines will not bear a Soil;
Let all retire; that you alone may hear
What ev'n in whispers I wou'd tell your ear.

                            [*All are going out.*

    Alm. Not one of you depart; I charge you stay!
And, were my voice a Trumpet loud as Fame,
260 To reach the round of Heav'n, and Earth, and Sea,
All Nations shou'd be Summon'd to this place.
So little do I fear that Fellows charge:
So shou'd my honour like a rising Swan,
Brush with her wings, the falling drops away,
And proudly plough the waves.

    Seb. This noble Pride becomes thy Innocence:
And I dare trust my Fathers memory,
To stand the charge of that foul forging tongue.

    Alv. It will be soon discover'd if I forge:
270 Have you not heard your Father in his youth,
When newly marry'd, travel'd into *Spain,*
And made a long abode in *Phillips* Court?

    Seb. Why so remote a question? which thy self
Can answer to thy self, for thou wert with him,
His Fav'rite, as I oft have heard thee boast:
And nearest to his Soul.

    Alv. Too near indeed, forgive me Gracious Heaven
That ever I should boast I was so near,
The Confident of all his young Amours.
280 And have not you, unhappy beauty, heard,   [*To* Almeyda.
Have you not often heard, your Exil'd Parents
Were refug'd in that Court, and at that time?

254   more, . . . honour,] ∼ᴧ . . . ∼ᴧ Q1–2, F, D (more, D).
258   stay!] ∼ . Q1–2, F, D.
260   Heav'n] F, D; Hea'vn Q1–2.
278   near,] ∼ . Q1–2, F, D.
280   And . . . heard, [*To* Almeyda.] D; [*To* Almeydaᴧ] And . . . heard, Q1–2,
F.

    Alm. 'Tis true: and often since, my Mother own'd
How kind that Prince was, to espouse her cause;
She Counsell'd, nay, Enjoyn'd me on her blessing
To seek the Sanctuary of your Court:
Which gave me first encouragement to come,
And, with my Brother, beg *Sebastians* aid.
    Sebast. to Alme. Thou help'st me well, to justify my War:
290 My dying Father swore me, then a Boy;
And made me kiss the Cross upon his Sword,
Never to sheath it, till that exil'd Queen
Were by my Arms restor'd.
    Alv.   And can you finde
No mistery, couch'd in this excess of kindness?
Were Kings e're known, in this degenerate Age,
So passionately fond of noble Acts,
Where Interest shar'd not more than half with honour?
    Seb. Base groveling Soul, who know'st not honours worth;
But weigh'st it out in mercenary Scales;
300 The Secret pleasure of a generous Act,
Is the great minds great bribe.
    Alv. Show me that King, and I'le believe the Phœnix.
But knock at your own breast, and ask your Soul
If those fair fatall eyes, edg'd not your Sword,
More than your Fathers charge, and all your vows?
If so, and so your silence grants it is,
Know King, your Father had, like you, a Soul;
And Love is your Inheritance from him.
Almeyda's Mother too had eyes, like her,
310 And not less charming, and were charm'd no less
Than your's are now with her, and her's with you.
    Alm. Thou ly'st Impostor, Perjur'd Fiend thou ly'st.
    Seb. Was't not enough to brand my Father's fame,
But thou must load a Ladies memory?

289–290 *Sebast. to Alme.* Thou . . . War: / My] Sebast. Thou . . . War: / *to*
Alme.] My Q1–2; *Seb.*] Thou . . . War: / *to Alm.*] My F; *Sebast.* Thou . . .
War: / [*To* Alm.] My D.
305 Fathers] Q2, F, D; Fashers Q1.
306 so,] D; ∼ ; Q1–2, F.   313 Was't] D; Wa'st Q1–2, F.

O Infamous, O base, beyond repair:
And, to what end this ill-concerted lye,
Which, palpable and gross, yet granted true,
It barrs not my Inviolable vows.
 Alv. Take heed and double not your Fathers crimes;
320 To his Adult'ry, do not add your Incest.
Know, she is the product of unlawfull Love:
And 'tis your Carnall Sister you wou'd wed.
 Seb. Thou shalt not say thou wert Condemn'd unheard;
Else, by my Soul, this moment were thy last.
 Alm. But think not Oaths shall justify thy charge;
Nor Imprecations on thy cursed head:
For who dares lye to Heaven, thinks Heaven a Jest.
Thou hast confess'd thy self the Conscious Pandar
Of that pretended passion:
330 A Single Witness, infamously known,
Against two Persons of unquestion'd fame.
 Alv. What Int'rest can I have, or what delight
To blaze their shame, or to divulge my own?
If prov'd, you hate me; if unprov'd, Condemn.
Not Racks or Tortures could have forc'd this secret,
But too much care, to save you from a Crime,
Which would have sunk you both. For let me say,
Almeyda's beauty well deserves your love.
 Alm. Out, base Impostor, I abhor thy praise.
340 *Dorax.* It looks not like Imposture: but a truth,
On utmost need reveal'd.
 Sebast. Did I expect from *Dorax,* this return?
Is this the love renew'd?
 Dorax.   Sir, I am silent;
Pray Heav'n my fears prove false.
 Sebast. Away; you all combine to make me wretched.

---

315 Infamous, O] D (o); Infamous∧ Q1–2, F.   315 repair:] F; ∼ . Q1–2, D.
316 ill-concerted] D; ill concerted Q1–2, F.   323 shalt] Q2, F, D; shallt Q1.
323 unheard;] ∼ . Q1–2, F, D.   326 head:] F; ∼ , Q1–2; ∼ . D.
331 fame.] F; ∼ ; Q1–2; ∼ : D.   334 prov'd,] D; ∼∧ Q1–2, F.
334 me;] ∼ , Q1–2, F, D.   334 unprov'd,] D; ∼∧ Q1–2, F.
334 Condemn.] D; ∼ ? Q1–2, F.   338 love.] F, D; ∼ : Q1–2.

    Alv. But hear the story of that fatall Love;
Where every Circumstance shall prove another;
And truth so shine, by her own native light,
That if a Lye were mixt, it must be seen.
350   *Sebast.* No; all may still be forg'd, and of a piece.
No; I can credit nothing thou can'st say.
    Alv. One proof remains, and that's your Fathers hand,
Firm'd with his Signet; both so fully known,
That plainer Evidence can hardly be,
Unless his Soul wou'd want her Heav'n a while,
And come on Earth to swear.
    Seb.   Produce that Writing.
    Alvar. to Dorax. Alonzo has it in his Custody.
The same, which when his nobleness redeem'd me,
And in a friendly visit own'd himself
360 For what he is, I then deposited:
And had his Faith to give it to the King.
    Dorax giving a seal'd Paper to the King. Untouch'd, and
        Seal'd as when intrusted with me,
Such I restore it, with a trembling hand,
Lest ought within disturb your peace of Soul.
    Sebast. tearing open the Seals. Draw near *Almeyda:* thou art
        most concern'd;
For I am most in Thee.
Alonzo, mark the Characters:
Thou know'st my Fathers hand, observe it well:
And if th' Impostors Pen, have made one slip,
370 That shows it Counterfeit, mark that and save me.

---

351   say.] F, D; ~ : Q1–2.
352   remains, . . . hand,] ~ ; . . . ~ : Q1–2, F, D.
355   Heav'n] F, D; Hea'vn Q1–2.
357   *Alvar. to Dorax.*] [*Alvar. to Dorax*ʌ] Q1–2, F; *Alv.* [*to Dorax*ʌ] D.
359   himself] D; ~ , Q1–2, F.
362   *Dorax . . . King.* Untouch'd, . . . me,] Dorax . . . ~ . / ~ , . . . ~ ,
Q1–2, F (*speech tag centered*); *Dor.* Untouch'd, . . . me, / [*giving . . . King.* D.
365   *Sebast. . . . Seals.* Draw . . . concern'd;] Sebast. . . . ~ . / ~ . . . ~ .
Q1–2, F (*speech tag centered*); *Seb*ʌ Draw . . . concern'd: / [*tearing . . . Seals.*
D.
368   hand,] F, D; ~ʌ Q1–2.

Dorax. It looks, indeed, too like my Masters hand:
So does the Signet; more I cannot say;
But wish 'twere not so like.
    Sebast.   Methinks it owns
The black Adult'ry, and *Almeyda's* birth;
But such a mist of grief comes o're my eyes,
I cannot, or I wou'd not, read it plain.
    Alm. Heav'n cannot be more true, than this is false.
    Sebast. O Coud'st thou prove it, with the same assurance!
Speak, hast thou ever seen my Fathers hand?
380   *Alm.* No; but my Mothers honour has been read
By me, and by the world, in all her Acts;
In Characters more plain, and legible
Then this dumb Evidence, this blotted lye.
Oh that I were a man, as my Soul's one,
To prove thee, Traytor, an Assassinate
Of her fair fame: thus wou'd I tear thee, thus:————
                              (*Tearing the Paper.*)
And scatter, o're the field, thy Coward limbs,
Like this foul offspring of thy forging brain.
                            (*Scatt'ring the Paper.*)
    Alv. Just so, shalt thou be torn from all thy hopes:
390   For know proud Woman, know in thy despight,
The most Authentique proof is still behind.
Thou wear'st it on thy finger: 'tis that Ring,
Which match'd with that on his, shall clear the doubt.
'Tis no dumb forgery: for that shall speak;
And sound a rattling peal to eithers Conscience.
    Seb. This Ring indeed, my Father, with a cold
And shaking hand, just in the pangs of Death,
Put on my finger; with a parting sigh,
And wou'd have spoke; but falter'd in his speech,

---

376 not,] F; ~∧ Q1–2, D.   377 Heav'n] Q2, F; Hea'vn Q1; Heaven D.
386 thus:————] Q2, D; ~ ————: Q1; ~∧————F.
386+ s.d. (*Tearing . . . Paper.*] [(~ . . . ~∧ Q1; [~ . . . ~ : Q2, F, D (*Paper.* F, D).
388+ s.d. *Paper.*] F, D; ~∧ Q1–2.   389 hopes:] ~ . Q1–2, F, D.
395 Conscience.] D; ~ : Q1–2, F.

400 With undistinguish'd sounds.
  Alv.   I know it well:
For I was present. Now, *Almeyda,* speak:
And, truly tell us, how you come by yours.
  Alm. My Mother, when I parted from her sight,
To go to *Portugal,* bequeath'd it to me,
Presaging she shou'd never see me more:
She pull'd it from her finger, shed some tears,
Kiss'd it, and told me 'twas a pledge of Love;
And hid a Mistery of great Importance
Relating to my Fortunes.
  Alv.   Mark me now,
410 While I disclose that fatall Mistery.
Those rings, when you were born, and thought anothers,
Your Parents, glowing yet in sinfull love,
Bid me bespeak: a Curious Artist wrought 'em,
With joynts so close, as not to be perceiv'd;
Yet are they both each others Counterpart.
Her part had *Juan* inscrib'd, and his had *Zayda:*
(You know those names are theirs:) and in the midst,
A heart divided in two halves was plac'd.
Now if the rivets of those Rings, inclos'd,
420 Fit not each other, I have forg'd this lye:
But if they joyn, you must for ever part.
    [Seb. *pulling off his Ring,* Alm. *does the same, and gives*
     it to Alv. *who unscrues both the Rings & fits one half*
     to the other.
  Seb. Now life, or death.
  Alm.   And either thine, or ours.————

---

401 present.] ~ : Q1–2, F, D.   402 yours.] D; ~ ? Q1–2, F.
404 *Portugal,*] D; *Portugall*ᴧ Q1–2, F (*Portugal* F).
411–412 Those . . . Your] Q2, F, D; Yhose . . . Tour Q1.
413 'em,] ~ : Q1–2, F, D.   416 *Zayda:*] ~ . Q1–2, F, D.
417 (You] Q2, F, D;) ~ Q1.   421 part.] F, D; ~ , Q1–2.
421+ s.d. [Seb. . . . *other.*] D; *set in position of speech tag for lines 422 and*
423 in Q1–2, F (other.]).
421+ s.d. *Ring,*] D; ~ . Q1; ~ᴧ Q2, F.
422 *Seb.*] Q2, F, D; ~ , Q1.
422 ours.————] ~ ·ᴧ Q1–2, F, D.

DON SEBASTIAN PREVENTED FROM COMMITTING SUICIDE,
ACT V, SCENE 1. FROM THE FRONTISPIECE
TO *Don Sebastian*, 1735

I'm lost for ever.———— (*Swoons. The Women and* Morayma
                                    take her up and carry her off. Seb.
                                    here stands amaz'd without motion,
                                    his eyes fixt upward.

Seb. Look to the Queen my Wife; For I am past
All Pow'r of Aid, to her or to my self.

Alv. His Wife, said he, his Wife! O fatall sound!
For, had I known it, this unwelcome news
Had never reach'd their ears.
So they had still been blest in Ignorance,
430 And I alone unhappy.

    Dor. I knew it, but too late: and durst not speak.

    Seb. starting out of his amazement. I will not live: no not a
    moment more;
I will not add one moment more to Incest.
I'le cut it off, and end a wretched being:
For, should I live, my Soul's so little mine,
And so much hers, that I should still enjoy.
Ye Cruell Powers,
Take me as you have made me, miserable;
You cannot make me guilty; 'twas my fate,
440 And you made that, not I.   [*Draws his Sword.*

    Antonio *and* Alv. *lay hold on him, and* Dorax *wrests the*
    Sword out of his hand.

    An. For Heav'ns sake hold, and recollect your mind.

    Alvarez. Consider whom you punish, and for what;
Your self? unjustly: You have charg'd the fault
On Heav'n, that best may bear it.
Though Incest is indeed a deadly Crime,
You are not guilty, since, unknown 'twas done,
And, known, had been abhorr'd.

―――――――
423 I'm] D; *Alm.* I'm Q1–2, F.
423 s.d. (*Swoons. The* . . . Morayma . . . *off.* Seb. . . . *upward.*] (*swoons*ᴧ) /
(*The* . . . Morayma, . . . *off.*) / [Seb. . . . *upward.*] Q1–2, F (Morayma ᴧ Q2;
*off.*ᴧ F); [*Swoons.* / [*The* . . . Morayma . . . *off.* / [*Sebastian* . . . *upward.* D.
432 *Seb.*] D; [Seb. Q1–2, F.   434 being:] ∼ . Q1–2, F, D.
437 Powers,] F; ∼ᴧ Q1–2, D.
439 fate,] D; ∼ᴧ Q1–2, F.
443, 444 fault . . . Heav'n,] D; ∼ , . . . ∼ᴧ Q1–2, F.

Seb. By Heaven y're Traytours, all, that hold my hands.
If death be but cessation of our thought,
450 Then let me dye for I would think no more.
I'le boast my Innocence above;
And let 'em see a Soul they cou'd not sully:
I shall be there before my Fathers Ghost;
That yet must languish long, in frosts and fires,
For making me unhappy by his Crime.
Stand off and let me take my fill of death;   [*Struggling again.*
For I can hold my breath in your despight,
And swell my heaving Soul out, when I please.
    Alv. Heav'n comfort you!
    Seb.   What, art thou giving comfort!
460 Wou'dst thou give comfort, who hast giv'n despair?
Thou seest *Alonzo* silent; he's a man.
He knows, that men abandon'd of their hopes
Shou'd ask no leave, nor stay for sueing out
A tedious Writ of ease, from lingring Heaven,
But help themselves, as timely as they cou'd,
And teach the fates their duty.
    Dorax to Alv. and Anto.   Let him go:
He is our King; and he shall be obey'd.
    Alv. What, to destroy himself, O Parricide!
    Dor. Be not Injurious in your foolish zeal,
470 But leave him free; or by my sword I swear,
To hew that Arm away, that stops the passage
To his Eternal rest.
    Anto. letting go his hold. Let him be Guilty of his own death
if he pleases: for I'le not be guilty of mine; by holding him.

---

448 hands.] Q2, F, D; ~ , Q1.   455 Crime.] ~ : Q1–2, F, D.
456–457 *s.d.* Stand . . . death; [*Struggling again.* / For] [*struggling* Stand
. . . death; / *again.*] For Q1–2, F; [*Struggling again.* / Stand . . . death; /
For D.
459 What,] F, D; ~ₐ Q1–2.
459 giving] Q2, F, D; given Q1.
466 *Dorax to Alv. and Anto.*] [Dorax to Alv. and Anto.] Q1–2, F; *Dor.* [*to* Alv.
and Ant.] D.
467 obey'd.] D; ~ : Q1–2; ~ , F.
468 What,] D; ~ₐ Q1–2, F.
473 *Anto. . . . hold.*] [Anto. . . . *hold.*] Q1–2, F; *Ant.* [. . . *hold.*] D.

The King shakes off Alvarez.

Alvarez, to Dorax. Infernal Fiend, is this a Subjects part?

Dor. 'Tis a Friends Office.

He has convinc'd me that he ought to dye,

And, rather than he should not, here's my sword

To help him on his Journey.

480   *Seb.* My last, my only Friend, how kind art thou

And how Inhuman these!

     Dor. To make the trifle death, a thing of moment!

     Seb. And not to weigh th' Important cause I had,

To rid my self of life?

     Dor.   True; for a Crime

So horrid in the face of Men and Angells,

As wilfull Incest is!

     Seb.   Not wilfull neither.

     Dor. Yes, if you liv'd and with repeated Acts,

Refresh'd your Sin, and loaded crimes with crimes,

To swell your scores of Guilt.

     Seb.   True; if I liv'd.

490   *Dor.* I said so, if you liv'd.

     Seb. For hitherto was fatall ignorance:

And no intended crime.

     Dor.   That you best know:

But the Malicious World will judge the worst.

     Alv. O what a Sophister has Hell procur'd,

To argue for Damnation!

     Dor.   Peace, old Dotard.

Mankind that always judge of Kings with malice,

Will think he knew this Incest, and pursu'd it.

His only way to rectify mistakes,

And to redeem her honour, is to dye.

474+   *s.d.* Alvarez.] Q2, F, D (Alv. D); ∼ʌ Q1.

475   *Dorax*] D; Dorax Q1–2, F.

475   Fiend, is . . . part?] ∼ , / Is . . . ∼ ? Q1–2, F, D ("Is" *indented in* Q1–2).

477   dye,] F; ∼ . Q1–2, D.   484   Crime] F, D; ∼ . Q1–2.

489   Guilt] Q2, F, D; Guilt Q1.   491   was] Q2, F, D; 'was Q1.

492   *Dor.*] Q2, F, D; *Dor,* Q1.   492   know:] ∼ . Q1–2, F, D.

500   *Seb*. Thou hast it right, my dear, my best *Alonzo!*
And that, but petty reparation too;
But all I have to give.
          Dor.   Your pardon, Sir;
You may do more, and ought.
          Seb.   What, more than death?
          Dor. Death? Why that's Childrens sport: a Stage-Play, Death.
We Act it every Night we go to bed.
Death to a Man in misery is sleep.
Wou'd you, who perpetrated such a Crime
As frighten'd nature, made the Saints above
Shake Heav'ns Eternal pavement with their trembling,
510   To view that act, wou'd you but barely dye?
But stretch your limbs, and turn on t' other side,
To lengthen out a black voluptuous slumber,
And dream you had your Sister in your arms?
          Seb. To expiate this, can I do more then dye?
          Dor. O yes: you must do more; you must be damn'd:
You must be damn'd to all Eternity.
And, sure, self-Murder is the readiest way.
          Seb. How, damn'd?
          Dor.   Why, is that News?
          Alvar.   O, horrour! horrour!
          Dor. What, thou a Statesman,
520   And make a bus'ness of Damnation
In such a World as this! why 'tis a trade;
The Scriv'ner, Usurer, Lawyer, Shop keeper,
And Soldier, cannot live, but by damnation.
The Polititian does it by advance:
And gives all gone before-hand.
          Seb. O thou hast giv'n me such a glimse of Hell,
So push'd me forward, even to the brink,
Of that irremeable burning Gulph,

---

507 Crime] ~ , Q1, F, D; ~ . Q2.   513 arms?] D; ~ . Q1–2, F.
515 *Dor*.] Q2, F, D; *Dor:* Q1.   518 Why,] F, D; ~∧ Q1–2.
520 Damnation] D; ~ ? Q1–2; ~ , F.   521 this!] F, D; ~ , Q1–2.
521 trade;] F; ~ . Q1; ~ , Q2, D.

That looking in th' Abyss, I dare not leap.
530 And now I see what good thou meanst my Soul,
And thank thy pious fraud: Thou hast indeed,
Appear'd a Devill, but didst an Angells work.
    Dor. 'Twas the last Remedy, to give you leisure;
For, if you cou'd but think, I knew you safe.
    Seb. I thank thee, my *Alonzo:* I will live:
But never more to *Portugal* return:
For, to go back and reign, that were to show
Triumphant Incest, and pollute the Throne.
    Alv. Since Ignorance———
    Seb.   O, palliate not my wound:
540 When you have argu'd all you can, 'tis Incest:
No, 'tis resolv'd, I charge you plead no more;
I cannot live without *Almeyda's* sight,
Nor can I see *Almeyda* but I sin.
Heav'n has inspir'd me with a Sacred thought,
To live alone to Heav'n: and dye to her.
    Dorax. Mean you to turn an Anchoret?
    Seb.   What else?
The world was once too narrow for my mind,
But one poor little nook will serve me now;
To hide me from the rest of humane kinde.
550 *Affrick* has desarts wide enough to hold
Millions of Monsters, and I am, sure, the greatest.
    Alv. You may repent, and wish your Crown too late.
    Seb. O never, never: I am past a Boy,
A Scepter's but a play-thing, and a Globe
A bigger bounding Stone. He who can leave
Almeyda, may renounce the rest with ease.
    Dorax. O Truly great!
A Soul fix'd high, and capable of Heav'n:

---

529 Abyss,] D; *Abyss;* Q1–2; *Abyss,* F.   533 leisure;] F; ∼ . Q1; ∼ , Q2, D.
536 *Portugal*] F, D; *Portugall* Q1–2.   544, 545 Heav'n] Q2, F, D; Hea'vn Q1.
550 *Affrick*] Affrique Q1–2; *Africk* F, D.
554 play-thing] F, D; play thing Q1–2.
558 Heav'n:] Hea'vn. Q1; Heav'n. Q2, F, D.

Old as he is, your Uncle Cardinall
560 Is not so far enamour'd of a Cloyster,
But he will thank you, for the Crown you leave him.
   Seb. To please him more, let him believe me dead:
That he may never dream I may return.
Alonzo, I am now no more thy King,
But still thy Friend, and by that holy Name,
Adjure thee, to perform my last request.
Make our Conditions with yon Captive King,
Secure me but my Solitary Cell;
'Tis all I ask him for a Crown restor'd.
570   *Dor.* I will do more:
But fear not *Muley-Zeydan;* his soft mettall
Melts down with easy warmth; runs in the mould,
And needs no farther forge.

Exit Dorax.

Re-enter Almeyda, *led by* Morayma, *and followd
by her Attendants.*

   Seb. See where she comes again.
By Heav'n, when I behold those beauteous eyes,
Repentance laggs and Sin comes hurrying on.
   Alm. This is too cruell!
   Seb. Speak'st thou of Love, of Fortune, or of Death,
Or double Death? for we must part *Almeyda.*
580   *Alm.* I speak of all,
For all things that belong to us are cruell.
But what's most cruell, we must love no more.
O 'tis too much that I must never see you,
But not to love you is impossible:
No, I must love you: Heav'n may bate me that,
And charge that Sinfull Sympathy of Souls

---

559 is,] D; ~ₐ Q1-2, F.   559 Cardinall] D; ~ , Q1-2, F.
562 *Seb.*] Q2, F, D; *Seb,* Q1.   575 Heav'n,] D; Hea'vnₐ Q1; ~ₐ Q2, F.
579 Death?] ~ , Q1-2, F, D.   580 all,] ~ . Q1-2, F, D.
585 Heav'n] Q2, F, D; Hea'vn Q1.   586 Souls] D; ~ ; Q1-2, F.

Upon our Parents, when they lov'd too well.

   Seb. Good Heav'n, thou speakst my thoughts, and I speak
    thine!

Nay then there's Incest in our very Souls,

590 For we were form'd too like.

   Alm.   Too like indeed,

And yet not for each other.

Sure when we part (for I resolv'd it too

Tho' you propos'd it first,) however distant,

We shall be ever thinking of each other,

And, the same moment, for each other pray.

   Seb. But if a wish shou'd come athwart our prayers!

   Alm. It wou'd do well to curb it: if we cou'd.

   Seb. We cannot look upon each others face,

But, when we read our love, we read our guilt,

600 And yet methinks I cannot chuse but love.

   Alm. I wou'd have ask'd you, if I durst for shame,

If still you lov'd. You gave it Air before me.

Ah why were we not born both of a Sex;

For then we might have lov'd, without a Crime!

Why was not I your Brother? though that wish

Involv'd our Parents guilt, we had not parted;

We had been Friends, and Friendship is not Incest.

   Seb. Alas, I know not by what name to call thee!

Sister and Wife are the two dearest Names;

610 And I wou'd call thee both; and both are Sin.

Unhappy we! that still we must confound

The dearest Names, into a common Curse.

   Alm. To love, and be belov'd, and yet be wretched!

   Seb. To have but one poor night of all our lives;

It was indeed a glorious, guilty night:

So happy, that, forgive me Heav'n, I wish

---

588 Heav'n] Q2, F, D; Hea'vn Q1.   588 thine!] ~ . Q1–2, F, D.
589 Souls,] ~ . Q1–2, F, D.   594 other,] ~ . Q1–2, F, D.
596 athwart] Q2, F, D; a thwart Q1.   600 love.] F, D; ~ ; Q1–2.
601 *Alm.*] Q2, F, D; *Alm,* Q1.   602 lov'd. You] ~ ? you Q1–2, F, D (You F).
615 glorious,] F, D; ~ ; Q1–2.
616 Heav'n] Q2, F, D; Hea'vn Q1.

With all its guilt, it were to come again.
Why did we know so soon, or why at all,
That Sin cou'd be conceal'd in such a blisse?
620   *Alm.* Men have a larger priviledge of words,
Else I shou'd speak: but we must part, *Sebastian.*
That's all the name that I have left to call thee.
I must not call thee by the name I wou'd;
But when I say *Sebastian, dear Sebastian,*
I kiss the name I speak.
         Seb. We must make hast, or we shall never part.
I wou'd say something that's as dear as this;
Nay, wou'd do more than say: one moment longer,
And I shou'd break through Laws Divine, and Humane;
630 And think 'em Cobwebs, spred for little man,
Which all the bulky herd of nature breaks.
The vigorous young world was ignorant
Of these restrictions, 'tis decrepit now;
Not more devout, but more decay'd, and cold.
All this is impious; therefore we must part:
For, gazing thus, I kindle at thy sight,
And, once burnt down to tinder, light again
Much sooner then before.

                  Re-enter Dorax.

         Alm. Here comes the sad denouncer of my fate,
640 To toul the mournfull knell of Seperation:
While I, as on my Death-bed, hear the sound,
That warns me hence for ever.
         Sebastian to Dorax.   Now be brief,
And I will try to listen,
And share the minute that remains, betwixt
The care I owe my Subjects and my Love.

---

621 *Sebastian.*] ∼ , Q1–2, F, D.   632 world] Q2, F, D; ∼ , Q1.
638+ *s.d. Re-enter*] Q2, F, D; *Reenter* Q1.
642 *Sebastian to Dorax.*] [Sebastian *to* Dorax. Q1–2 (Dorax.] Q2); [*Sebast.* to
Dor.] F; *Seb.* [*to* Dor.] D.
643 listen,] ∼ . Q1–2, F; ∼ ; D.

Dorax. Your fate has gratify'd you all she can;
Gives easy misery, and makes Exile pleasing.
I trusted *Muley-Zeydan,* as a friend,
But swore him first to Secresy: he wept
650 Your fortune, and with tears, not squeez'd by Art,
But shed from nature, like a kindly shower:
In short, he proffer'd more than I demanded;
A safe retreat, a gentle Solitude,
Unvex'd with noise, and undisturb'd with fears:
I chose you one———
   Alm.   O do not tell me where:
For if I knew the place of his abode,
I shou'd be tempted to pursue his steps,
And then we both were lost.
   Seb.   Ev'n past redemption;
For, if I knew thou wert on that design,
660 (As I must know, because our Souls are one,)
I shou'd not wander but by sure Instinct,
Shou'd meet thee just half-way, in pilgrimage,
And close for ever: for I know my love
More strong than thine, and I more frail than thou.
   Alm. Tell me not that: for I must boast my Crime,
And cannot bear that thou shoud'st better love.
   Dorax. I may inform you both: for you must go,
Where Seas, and winds, and Desarts will divide you.
Under the ledge of *Atlas,* lyes a Cave,
670 Cut in the living Rock, by Natures hands:
The Venerable Seat of holy Hermites,
Who there, secure in separated Cells,
Sacred ev'n to the *Moors,* enjoy Devotion:
And from the purling Streams and savage fruits,
Have wholesome bev'rage, and unbloudy feasts.
   Seb. 'Tis pennance too Voluptuous, for my Crime.

———

648 *Muley-Zeydan*] Q2, F, D; *Muley Zeydan* Q1.   655 one] F; ∼. Q1–2, D.
658 Ev'n] D; E'vn Q1; E'ven Q2; E'en F.   658 redemption;] ∼. Q1–2, F, D.
662 pilgrimage,] D; ∼ᴧ Q1–2, F.   671 Hermites,] ∼. Q1–2, F, D.
673 *Moors*] D; Moors Q1–2, F.

Dor. Your Subjects, conscious of your life, are few:
But all desirous to partake your Exile,
And to do office to your Sacred Person.
680 The rest who think you dead, shall be dismiss'd,
Under safe Convoy till they reach your Fleet.
  Alm. But how am wretched I to be dispos'd?
A vain Enquiry, since I leave my Lord:
For all the world beside is Banishment!
  Dor. I have a Sister, Abbesse in *Tercera,*
Who lost her Lover on her Bridall day.————
  Alm. There, fate provided me a fellow-Turtle;
To mingle sighs with sighs, and tears with tears.
  Dor. Last, for my self, if I have well fullfill'd
690 My sad Commission, let me beg the boon,
To share the sorrows of your last recess:
And mourn the Common losses of our loves.
  Alv. And what becomes of me? must I be left,
(As Age and time had worn me out of use?)
These Sinews are not yet so much unstrung,
To fail me when my Master shou'd be serv'd:
And when they are, then will I steal to death,
Silent, and unobserv'd, to save his tears.
  Seb. I've heard you both. *Alvarez* have thy wish.
700 But thine *Alonzo,* thine, is too unjust.
I charge thee with my last Commands, return,
And bless thy *Violante* with thy vows.
Antonio, be thou happy too, in thine.
Last, let me swear you all to Secresy;
And to conceal my shame conceal my life.
  Dor. Ant. Mor. We swear to keep it secret.
  Alm. Now I wou'd speak the last farewell, I cannot.
It wou'd be still farewell, a thousand times:
And, multiply'd in Eccho's, still farewell.
710 I will not speak; but think a thousand thousand.

677 life,] D; ~‸ Q1-2, F. 678 Exile,] D; ~ : Q1-2; ~ ; F.
685 *Tercera*] S-S; *Tercera's* Q1-2, F, D. 697 death,] D; ~ : Q1-2, F.
699 both.] ~ : Q1; ~ ; Q2, F, D. 706 *Ant.*] Q2, F, D; *Ant,* Q1.
710 thousand.] ~ ; Q1-2, F, D.

And be thou silent too, my last *Sebastian;*
So let us part in the dumb pomp of grief.
My heart's too great; or I wou'd dye this moment:
But Death, I thank him, in an hour, has made
A mighty journey, and I hast to meet him.

                    (*She staggers and her Women hold her up.*)

    Seb. Help to support this feeble, drooping flower,
This tender Sweet, so shaken by the storm:
For these fond arms must, thus be stretch'd in vain,
And never, never must embrace her more.

720   Tis past:————my Soul goes in that word;————farewell.

       Alvarez *goes with* Sebastian *to one end of the Stage;*
       Women *with* Almeyda *to the other:* Dorax *coming up*
       to Antonio *and* Morayma, *who stand on the Middle of*
       the Stage.

    Dor. Hast to attend *Almeyda:* for your sake
Your Father is forgiven: but to *Antonio*
He forfeits half his Wealth: be happy both:
    And let *Sebastian* and *Almeyda*'s Fate,
    This dreadfull Sentence to the World relate,
    That unrepented Crimes of Parents dead,
    Are justly punish'd on their Childrens head.

                           Exeunt.

---

714   Death,] D; ~ₐ Q1-2, F.   715+   *s.d. up.*] D; ~ₐ Q1-2, F.
716   flower,] ~ : Q1-2, F, D.   717   This] Q2, F, D; 'This Q1.
717   storm:] ~ . Q1-2, F, D.   720   Soul] Q2, F, D; Souls Q1.
720+   *s.d. Stage;*] ~ . Q1-2, D; ~ₐ F.
720+   *s.d. other:* Dorax] other. / Dorax, Q1-2, F, D (Doraxₐ Q2, F; Dor. D).
724-727   *lines not indented in Q1-2, F, D.*
727+   *s.d. Exeunt.*] omitted from Q1-2, F, D.
727+   *Q1 and F append* "FINIS."; *Q2 appends* "FINIS.".

EPILOGUE TO *Don Sebastian, King of Portugal.*

Spoken betwixt Antonio *and* Morayma.

MOR. *I quak'd at heart for fear the Royal Fashion*
 Shou'd have seduc'd Us two to Separation:
 To be drawn in, against our own desire,
Poor I to be a Nun, poor You a Fryar.
 Ant. *I trembled when the Old Mans hand was in,*
He would have prov'd we were too near of kin:
Discovering old Intrigues of Love, like t' other,
Betwixt my Father and thy sinfull Mother;
To make Us Sister Turk *and Christian Brother.*
10 Mor. *Excuse me there; that League shou'd have been rather*
Betwixt your Mother and my Mufti-*Father;*
'Tis for my own and my Relations Credit
Your Friends shou'd bear the Bastard, mine shou'd get it.
 Ant. *Suppose us two* Almeyda *and* Sebastian———
With Incest prov'd upon us:———
 Mor.   *Without question*
Their Conscience was too queazy of digestion.
 Ant. *Thou woud'st have kept the Councell of thy Brother*
And sinn'd till we repented of each other.
 Mor. *Beast as you are, on Natures Laws to trample;*
20 *'Twere fitter that we follow'd their Example.*
And since all Marriage in Repentance ends,
'Tis good for us to part while we are Friends.
To save a Maids remorses and Confusions,
E'en leave me now before We try Conclusions.
 Ant. *To copy their Example, first make certain*

Caption: EPILOGUE] ~ . Q1–2, F, D.
Caption: Don Sebastian, King of Portugal.] Don Sebastian, King of Portugall.
Q1–2; *Don* SEBASTIAN *King of* Portugal. F; *omitted from D.*
1 quak'd] D; *Quak'd* Q1–2, F. 9 Turk] D; *Turk* Q1–2, F.
19 are,] D; ~ᴧ Q1–2, F. 20 *Example.*] D; ~ᴧ Q1–2; ~ : F.
23 *Confusions,*] F, D; ~ᴧ Q1–2. 25 *Example,*] D; ~ᴧ Q1–2, F.

Of one good hour like theirs before our parting;
Make a debauch o're Night of Love and Madness;
And marry when we wake in sober sadness.
   Mor. *I'le follow no new Sects of your inventing,*
30 *One Night might cost me nine long months repenting:*
First wed, and if you find that life a fetter,
Dye when you please, the sooner Sir the better:
My wealth wou'd get me love e're I cou'd ask it:
Oh there's a strange Temptation in the Casket:
All these Young Sharpers wou'd my grace importune,
And make me thundring Votes of lives and fortune.

FINIS.

36+   *FINIS.*] *omitted from* Q1–2, F, D.

AMPHITRYON;

OR,

THE TWO SOSIA'S

AMPHITRYON;

OR,

The Two Socia's.

A COMEDY.

As it is Acted at the

Theatre Royal.

Egregiam verò laudem, & spolia ampla refertis;
Una, dolo, Divûm, si Fœmina victa duorum est. Virg.

Written by Mr. *DRYDEN*.

To which is added,

The MUSICK of the SONGS.

Compos'd by Mr. *Henry Purcel*.

Printed for *J. Tonson*, at the *Judges Head* in *Chancery lane*
near *Fleet-street*; and *M. Tonson* at *Gray's-Inn-Gate* in
Gray's-Inn-Lane. 1690.

TITLE PAGE OF THE FIRST EDITION (MACDONALD 90AI)

To the Honourable
Sir *WILLIAM LEVISON GOWER,* Bar.

THERE is one kind of Vertue, which is inborn in the Nobility, and indeed in most of the Ancient Families of this
Nation; they are not apt to insult on the Misfortunes
of their Countrymen. But you, Sir, I may tell it you without
Flattery, have grafted on this natural Commisseration, and
rais'd it to a Nobler Vertue: As you have been pleas'd to honour
me, for a long time, with some part of your Esteem and your
good Will; so in particular, since the late Revolution, you have
increas'd the Proofs of your kindness to me; and not suffer'd the
10 difference of Opinions, which produce such Hatred and Enmity
in the brutal Part of Human kind, to remove you from the
settled Basis of your good Nature and good Sence. This Nobleness of yours, had it been exercis'd on an Enemy, had certainly been a Point of Honour, and as such I might have justly
recommended it to the World: But that of constancy to your
former Choice, and the pursuance of your first Favours, are
Vertues not overcommon amongst *English* Men. All things of
Honour have, at best, somewhat of Ostentation in them, and
Self-love; there is a Pride of doing more than is expected from
20 us, and more than others would have done. But to proceed in
the same Tract of Goodness, Favour, and Protection, is to shew
that a Man is acted by a thorough Principle: It carries somewhat of Tenderness in it, which is Humanity in a Heroical Degree; 'tis a kind of unmoveable good Nature; a word which is
commonly Despis'd, because it is so seldom Practis'd. But after
all, 'tis the most generous Vertue, oppos'd to the most degenerate Vice, which is that of Ruggedness and Harshness to our
Fellow Creatures.

'Tis upon this knowledge of you, Sir, that I have chosen you,
30 with your permission, to be the Patron of this Poem. And, as
since this wonderful Revolution, I have begun with the best

Pattern of Humanity, the Earl of *Leicester;* I shall continue to
follow the same Method, in all, to whom I shall Address; and
endeavour to pitch on such only, as have been pleas'd to own
me in this Ruin of my small Fortune; who, though they are of
a contrary Opinion themselves, yet blame not me for adhering
to a lost Cause; and judging for my self, what I cannot chuse
but judge; so long as I am a patient Sufferer, and no disturber
of the Government. Which, if it be a severe Penance, as a great
Wit has told the World, 'tis at least enjoyn'd me by my self:
10 And *Sancho Panca,* as much a Fool as I, was observ'd to discipline his Body, no farther than he found he could endure the
smart.

You see, Sir, I am not entertaining you, like *Ovid,* with a Lamentable Epistle from *Pontus;* I suffer no more, than I can
easily undergo; and so long as I enjoy my Liberty, which is the
Birth-right of an *English* Man, the rest shall never go near my
Heart. The Merry Philosopher, is more to my Humour than the
Melancholick; and I find no disposition in my self to Cry, while
the mad World is daily supplying me with such Occasions of
20 Laughter. The more reasonable sort of my Countrymen, have
shewn so much favour to this Piece, that they give me no doubt
of their Protection for the future.

As you, Sir, have been pleas'd to follow the Example of their
Goodness, in favouring me: So give me leave to say, that I follow yours in this Dedication, to a Person of a different Perswa-
sion. Though I must confess withal, that I have had a former
Encouragement from you for this Address; and the warm Remembrance of your noble Hospitality to me at *Trentham,* when
some years ago I visited my Friends and Relations in your
30 Country, has ever since given me a violent Temptation to this
boldness.

'Tis true, were this Comedy wholly mine, I should call it a
Trifle, and perhaps not think it worth your Patronage; but
when the Names of *Plautus* and *Moliere* are joyn'd in it; that
is, the two greatest Names of Ancient and Modern Comedy, I
must not presume so far on their Reputation, to think their best

29 ago] Q2, F, D; a go Q1. [These and other sigla are identified in the
textual notes, where also fluctuations in the texts cited are explained.]

and most unquestion'd Productions can be term'd Little. I will
not give you the trouble, of acquainting you what I have added,
or alter'd in either of them, so much it may be for the worse;
but only that the difference of our Stage from the *Roman* and
the *French* did so require it. But I am affraid, for my own Interest, the World will too easily discover, that more than half
of it is mine; and that the rest is rather a lame Imitation of their
Excellencies, than a just Translation. 'Tis enough, that the
Reader know by you, that I neither deserve nor desire any
10 Applause from it: If I have perform'd any thing, 'tis the Genius
of my Authors that inspir'd me; and if it has pleas'd in Representation, let the Actors share the Praise amongst themselves. As
for *Plautus* and *Moliere,* they are dangerous People; and I am
too weak a Gamester to put my self into their Form of Play. But
what has been wanting on my Part, has been abundantly sup-
plyed by the Excellent Composition of Mr. *Purcell;* in whose
Person we have at length found an *English-man,* equal with the
best abroad. At least my Opinion of him has been such, since
his happy and judicious Performances in the late *Opera;* and
20 the Experience I have had of him, in the setting my Three
Songs for this *Amphitryon:* To all which, and particularly to the
Composition of the *Pastoral Dialogue,* the numerous Quire of
Fair Ladies gave so just an Applause on the Third Day. I am
only sorry, for my own sake, that there was one Star wanting, as
Beautiful as any in our Hemisphere, that young *Berenice,* who
is misimploying all her Charms on stupid Country Souls, that
can never know the Value of them; and losing the Triumphs,
which are ready prepar'd for her in the Court and Town. And
yet I know not whether I am so much a loser by her absence; for
30 I have Reason to apprehend the sharpness of her Judgment, if
it were not allay'd with the sweetness of her Nature; and after
all, I fear she may come time enough, to discover a Thousand
Imperfections in my Play, which might have pass'd on Vulgar
Understandings. Be pleas'd to use the Authority of a Father
over her, on my behalf; enjoyn her to keep her own Thoughts
of *Amphitryon* to her self; or at least not to compare him too
strictly with *Moliere's.* 'Tis true, I have an Interest in this Par-

---

tiality of hers; but withal, I plead some sort of Merit for it, in being so Particularly as I am,

SIR,

Your most obedient, humble Servant,

October 24.
1690.

JOHN DRYDEN.

PROLOGUE TO *Amphitryon; or, The Two Sosia's.*

Spoken by Mrs. *Bracegirdle.*

THE *lab'ring Bee, when his sharp Sting is gone,*
   Forgets his Golden Work, and turns a Drone:
   Such is a Satyr, when you take away
That Rage, in which his Noble Vigour lay.
What gain you, by not suffering him to teize ye?
He neither can offend you, now, nor please ye.
The Honey-bag, and Venome, lay so near,
That both, together, you resolv'd to tear;
And lost your Pleasure, to secure your Fear.
How can he show his Manhood, if you bind him
To box, like Boys, with one Hand ty'd behind him?
This is plain levelling of Wit; in which
The Poor has all th' advantage, not the Rich.
The Blockhead stands excus'd, for wanting Sense;
And Wits turn Blockheads in their own defence.
Yet, though the Stages Traffick is undone,
Still Julian's *interloping Trade goes on:*
Though Satyr on the Theatre you smother,
Yet in Lampoons, you Libel one another.
The first produces still, a second Jig;
You whip 'em out, like School-boys, till they gig:
And, with the same success, we Readers guess;
For, ev'ry one still dwindles to a less.
And much good Malice, is so meanly drest,
That we wou'd laugh, but cannot find the Jest.
If no advice your Rhiming Rage can stay,
Let not the Ladies suffer in the Fray.
Their tender Sex, is priviledg'd from War;

Caption: Sosia's] Socia's Q1 (*uncorrected form [first state*]); Sosia's Q1 (*corrected form [second and third states*]); Socia's Q2; Sosia's F; *omitted from* D.
23 *one*] F, D; ∼ , Q1-2.

'Tis not like Knights, to draw upon the Fair.
30 *What Fame expect you from so mean a Prize?*
We wear no murd'ring Weapons, but our Eyes.
Our Sex, you know, was after yours design'd;
The last Perfection of the Makers mind:
Heav'n drew out all the Gold for us, and left your Dross
   behind.

Beauty, for Valours best Reward, He chose;
Peace, after War; and after Toil, Repose.
Hence ye Prophane, excluded from our sights;
And charm'd by Day, with Honour's vain delights,
Go, make your best of solitary Nights.
40 *Recant betimes, 'tis prudence to submit:*
Our Sex, is still your Overmatch, in Wit:
We never fail, with new, successful Arts,
To make fine Fools of you, and all your Parts.

---

37 *Prophane,*] F; ∼ ; Q1-2, D.   43 *you,*] F; ∼ ; Q1-2, D.

DRAMATIS PERSONÆ.

JUPITER,	Mr. *Betterton.*
MERCURY,	Mr. *Lee.*
PHŒBUS,	Mr. *Bowman.*
AMPHITRYON,	Mr. *Williams.*
SOSIA,	Mr. *Nokes.*
GRIPUS,	Mr. *Sandford.*
POLIDAS,	Mr. *Bright.*
TRANIO,	Mr. *Bowen.*
ALCMENA,	Mrs. *Barry.*
PHÆDRA,	Mrs. *Mountfort.*
BROMIA,	Mrs. *Corey.*
NIGHT,	Mrs. *Butler.*

PHŒBUS] F, D; PHOEBUS Q1–2.
AMPHITRYON] Q2, F, D; AMPITRYON Q1.
Mountfort] *Mountford* Q1–2, F, D.

AMPHITRION

FRONTISPIECE TO MOLIÈRE'S *Amphitryon,*
FROM *Oeuvres,* 1682

AMPHITRYON;

OR,

THE TWO SOSIA'S.

The Scene *THEBES*.

ACT I. SCENE I.

Mercury and Phœbus *descend in several Machines.*

Phœb. Know you the Reason of this present Summons?
'Tis neither Council-day, nor is this Heav'n;
What Business has our *Jupiter* on Earth?
Why more at *Thebes* than any other Place?
And why we two of all the Herd of Gods
Are chosen out to meet him in Consult?
They call me God of Wisdom,
But *Mars* and *Vulcan,* the two Fools of Heav'n,
Whose Wit lyes in their Anvil and their Sword,
10 Know full as much as I.
　　Merc. And *Venus* may know more than both of us,
For 'tis some Petticoat Affair I guess.

　　I have discharg'd my Duty; which was to summon you, *Phœbus:* we shall know more anon, when the Thunderer comes down. 'Tis our Part to obey our Father; for, to confess the Truth, we two are little better than Sons of Harlots: and if *Jupiter* had not been pleas'd to take a little pains with our Mothers, instead of being Gods, we might have been a couple of Linck-Boys.

Title: OR,] Q2, F, D; Or$_\Lambda$ Q1.　　　　*Title:* SOSIA'S] F, D; SOCIA'S Q1–2.
ACT I. SCENE I.] D; *omitted from* Q1–2, F.　　　12　guess.] F, D; ～ , Q1–2.

20   *Phœb.* But know you nothing farther, *Hermes?* What news
in Court?

Merc. There has been a devillish Quarrel, I can tell you,
betwixt *Jupiter* and *Juno:* She threaten'd to sue him in the
Spiritual Court, for some Matrimonial Omissions; and he stood
upon his Prerogative. Then she hit him on the Teeth of all
his Bastards; and your Name and mine were us'd with less
reverence than became our Godships. They were both in their
Cups; and at the last the matter grew so high, that they were
ready to have thrown Stars at one anothers Heads.

30   *Phœb.* 'Twas happy for me that I was at my Vocation, driving Day-light about the World; but I had rather stand my
Fathers Thunderbolts, than my Step-mothers Railing.

Merc. When the Tongue-battle was over, and the Cham-
pioness had harness'd her Peacocks, to go for *Samos,* and hear
the Prayers that were made to her————

Phœb. By the way, her Worshippers had a bad time on't; she
was in a damnable Humour for receiving Petitions————

Merc. Jupiter immediately beckons me aside; and charges
me, that as soon as ever you had set up your Horses, you and I
40   shou'd meet him here at *Thebes:* now, putting the Premises
together, as dark as it is, methinks I begin to see Day-light.

Phœb. As plain as one of my own Beams; she has made him
uneasie at home, and he is going to seek his diversion abroad: I
see Heav'n it self is no priviledg'd Place for happiness, if a Man
must carry his Wife along with him.

Merc. 'Tis neither better nor worse, upon my Conscience: he
is weary of hunting in the spacious Forest of a Wife, and is
following his Game *incognito,* in some little Purliew here at
Thebes; that's many an honest Mans Case on Earth too, *Jove*
50   help 'em; as indeed he does to make 'em Cuckolds.

Phœb. But if so *Mercury,* then I, who am a Poet, must indite
his Love-letter; and you, who are by Trade a Porter, must convey it.

Merc. No more, he's coming down sowse upon us, and hears

as far as he can see too; he's plaguy hot upon the business, I
know it by his hard driving.

Jupiter *descends.*

Jupiter. What, you are descanting upon my Actions?
Much good may do you with your Politicks:
All Subjects will be censuring their Kings.
60 Well, I confess I am in love; what then?
    Phœb. Some Mortal, we presume, of *Cadmus* Blood:
Some *Theban* Beauty; some new *Semele,*
Or some *Europa.*
    Merc. I'll say that for my Father, he's constant to an handsom
Family: He knows when they have a good smack with 'em; and
snuffs up Incense so savourly, when 'tis offer'd him by a fair
Hand.
    Jup. Well, my familiar Sons, this sawcy Carriage
I have deserv'd; for he who trusts a Secret
70 Makes his own Man his Master.
    I read your Thoughts;
Therefore you may as safely speak as think.
    Merc. Mine was a very homely Thought; I was considering
into what form your Almighty-ship would be pleas'd to trans-
form your self to night. Whether you wou'd fornicate in the
Shape of a Bull, or a Ram, or an Eagle, or a Swan: What Bird
or Beast you wou'd please to honour, by transgressing your own
Laws, in his likeness; or in short, whether you wou'd recreate
your self in Feathers, or in Leather?
80 *Phœb.* Any disguise to hide the King of Gods.
    Jup. I know your Malice, *Phœbus,* you wou'd say
That when a Monarch sins it shou'd be secret,
To keep exterior show of Sanctity,
Maintain Respect, and cover bad Example:

56+ *s.d.* Jupiter] [*Jupiter* Q1; [Jupiter Q2, F, D.
61   *Cadmus*] F; *Cadmu's* Q1–2; *Cadmus'* D.
82–83 secret, . . . Sanctity,] F; ∼ ; . . . ∼ ; Q1–2, D.

For Kings and Priests are in a manner bound,
For Reverence sake, to be close Hypocrites.
    Phœb. But what necessitates you to this Love,
Which you confess a Crime, and yet commit?
For to be secret makes not sin the less:
90 'Tis only hidden from the vulgar view:
Maintains, indeed, the Reverence due to Princes,
But not absolves the Conscience from the Crime.
    Jup. I Love, because 'twas in the Fates I shou'd.
    Phœb. With reverence be it spoke, a bad excuse:
Thus every wicked Act in Heav'n or Earth,
May make the same defence; but what is Fate?
Is it a blind contingence of Events?
Or sure necessity of Causes linck'd,
That must produce Effects? or is't a Pow'r
100 That orders all things by superior Will,
Foresees his Work, and works in that foresight?
    Jup. Fate is, what I
By vertue of Omnipotence have made it:
And pow'r Omnipotent can do no wrong:
Not to my self, because I will'd it so:
Nor yet to Men, for what they are is mine.
This night I will enjoy *Amphitryon*'s Wife:
For, when I made her, I decreed her such
As I shou'd please to love. I wrong not him
110 Whose Wife she is; for I reserv'd my Right,
To have her while she pleas'd me; that once past,
She shall be his again.
    Merc. Here's Omnipotence with a Vengeance, to make a Man
a Cuckold, and yet not to do him wrong. Then I find, Father
Jupiter, that when you made Fate, you had the wit to contrive
a Holy-day for your self now and then. For you Kings never
Enact a Law, but you have a kind of an Eye to your own Pre-
rogative.
    Phœb. If there be no such thing as right and wrong,

---

85   bound,] ~ₐ Q1–2, F, D.

120 Of an Eternal Being, I have done———
      But if there be———
      Jup.   Peace, thou disputing Fool:
      Learn this; if thou could'st comprehend my ways,
      Then thou wert *Jove,* not I: yet, thus far know,
      That, for the good of Human-kind, this Night
      I shall beget a future *Hercules;*
      Who shall redress the Wrongs of injur'd Mortals,
      Shall conquer Monsters, and reform the World.
      Merc. Ay, Brother *Phœbus;* and our Father made all those
      Monsters for *Hercules* to Conquer, and contriv'd all those Vices
130 on purpose for him to reform too, there's the Jeast on't.
      Phœb. Since Arbitrary Pow'r will hear no Reason, 'tis Wis-
      dom to be silent.———
      Merc. Why that's the Point; this same Arbitrary Power is a
      knock-down Argument; 'tis but a Word and a Blow; now me-
      thinks our Father speaks out like an honest bare-fac'd God, as
      he is; he lays the stress in the right Place, upon absolute Do-
      minion: I confess if he had been a Man, he might have been a
      Tyrant, if his Subjects durst have call'd him to account: But
      you Brother *Phœbus,* are but a meer Country Gentleman, that
140 never comes to Court; that are abroad all day on Horse-back,
      making Visits about the World; are drinking all Night, and in
      your Cups are still rayling at the Government: O these Patriots,
      these bumpkin Patriots, are a very silly sort of Animal.
      Jup. My present Purpose and Design you heard;
      T' enjoy *Amphitryon*'s Wife, the fair *Alcmena:*
      You two must be subservient to my Love.
      Merc. to Phœb. No more of your Grumbletonian Morals,
      Brother; there's Preferment coming, be advis'd and Pimp duti-
      fully.
150 *Jup. Amphitryon,* the brave *Theban* General,
      Has overcome his Countreys Foes in Fight;
      And in a single Duel slain their King:
      His Conquering Troops are eager on their march

---

121 be] Q2, F, D; ~ . Q1.   139 *Phœbus*] Q2, F, D; *Pœbus* Q1.
147 *to*] to Q1–2, F, D.   147 Morals,] Q2, F, D; ~∧ Q1.

Returning home; while their young General
More eager to review his beauteous Wife,
Posts on before, wing'd with impetuous Love,
And, by to morrows dawn, will reach this Town.

 Merc. That's but short warning, Father *Jupiter:* having made
no former advances of Courtship to her, you have need of your
160 Omnipotence, and all your Godship, if you mean to be before
hand with him.

 Phœb. Then how are we to be employ'd this Evening?
Time's precious, and these Summer Nights are short;
I must be early up to light the World.

 Jup. You shall not rise; there shall be no to morrow.

 Merc. Then the World's to be at an end, I find.

 Phœb. Or else a Gap in Nature, of a Day.

 Jup. A day will well be lost to busie Man:
Night shall continue sleep, and care shall cease.
170 So, many Men shall live, and live in peace,
Whom Sun-shine had betray'd to envious Sight,
And Sight to sudden Rage, and Rage to Death.
Now, I will have a night for love and me;
A long luxurious Night, fit for a God
To quench and empty his immortal Heat.

 Merc. I'll lay on the Womans side for all that; that she shall
love longest to night, in spight of your Omnipotence.

 Phœb. I shall be curs'd by all the lab'ring Trades,
That early rise, but you must be obey'd.
180 *Jup.* No matter for the cheating part of Man;
They have a day's sin less to answer for.

 Phœb. When wou'd you have me wake?

 Jup. Why, when *Jove* goes to sleep: when I have finish'd,
Your Brother *Mercury* shall bring you word.

        [*Exit* Phœbus *on his Chariot.*

 Jup. to Merc. Now, *Hermes,* I must take *Amphitryon*'s form,
T' enjoy his Wife;

---

162 Evening?] D; ~ ; Q1–2, F.   165 morrow.] Q2, F, D; ~ ; Q1.
168 day] D; ~ , Q1–2, F.
185 *Jup. to Merc.*] To *Merc.* Q1–2, F; [To *Merc.*] D.

Thou must be *Sosia,* this *Amphitryon*'s slave;
Who, all this Night, is travelling to *Thebes,*
To tell *Alcmena* of her Lords approach;
190 And bring her joyful news of Victory.
    Merc. But why must I be *Sosia?*
    Jup. Dull God of Wit, thou Statue of thy self!
Thou must be *Sosia,* to keep out *Sosia:*
Who, by his entrance, might discover *Jove,*
Disturb my Pleasures, raise unruly Noise,
And so distract *Alcmena*'s tender Soul,
She wou'd not meet my warmth, when I dissolve
Into her Lap, nor give down half her Love.
    Mer. Let me alone; I'll cudgel him away:
200 But I abhor so Villanous a shape.
    Jup. Take it; I charge thee on thy Duty, take it:
Nor dare to lay it down, till I command.
I cannot bear a moments loss of Joy.

            Night appears above in her Chariot.

Look up, the *Night* is in her silent Chariot;
And rouling just o're *Thebes:* bid her drive slowly,
Or make a double turn about the World;
While I drop *Jove,* and take *Amphitryon*'s Dress,
To be the greater, while I seem the less.   [*Exit* Jupiter.
    Merc. to Night. Madam *Night,* a good Even to you: fair and
210 softly, I beseech you Madam: I have a word or two to you, from
no less a God than *Jupiter.*
    Night. O, my nimble finger'd God of Theft, what make you
here on Earth, at this unseasonable hour? what Bankers Shop
is to be broken open to Night? or what Clippers, and Coiners,
and Conspirators, have been invoking your Deity for their assistance?
    Merc. Faith, none of those Enormities; and yet I am still in
my Vocation: for you know I am a kind of Jack of all Trades:

203+   s.d. Night] D; [Night Q1–2, F.   209   *to*] to Q1–2, F, D.
215–216   assistance?] D; ~ . Q1–2, F.   217   Faith,] ~∧ Q1–2, F, D.

at a word, *Jupiter* is indulging his Genius to night, with a cer-
220 tain noble sort of Recreation, call'd Wenching: The truth on't
is, Adultery is its proper name.

Night. *Jupiter* wou'd do well to stick to his Wife *Juno.*

Merc. He has been marry'd to her above these hundred years;
and that's long enough in conscience to stick to one Woman.

Night. She's his Sister too, as well as his Wife; that's a double
tye of affection to her.

Merc. Nay, if he made bold with his own Flesh and Blood,
'tis likely he will not spare his Neighbours.

Night. If I were his Wife, I would raise a Rebellion against
230 him, for the violation of my Bed.

Merc. Thou art mistaken, *Old Night:* his Wife cou'd raise
no faction: all the Deities in Heaven wou'd take the part of the
Cuckold-making God; for they are all given to the Flesh most
damnably. Nay the very Goddesses wou'd stickle in the cause of
Love; 'tis the way to be Popular, to Whore and Love. For what
dost thou think old *Saturn* was depos'd, but that he was cold
and impotent; and made no court to the fair Ladies. *Pallas* and
Juno themselves, as chaste as they are, cry'd shame on him. I
say unto thee, *Old Night,* Wo be to the Monarch that has not
240 the Women on his side.

Night. Then by your rule, *Mercury,* A King who wou'd live
happily, must debauch his whole Nation of Women.

Merc. As far as his ready Money will go, I mean; for *Jupiter*
himself can't please all of 'em. But this is beside my present
Commission; He has sent me to will and require you to make a
swinging long Night for him: for he hates to be stinted in his
Pleasures.

Night. Tell him plainly, I'll rather lay down my Commission:
What, wou'd he make a Bawd of me?

250 *Merc.* Poor Ignorant! why he meant thee for a Bawd when he
first made thee. What art thou good for, but to be a Bawd? Is
not Day-light better for Mankind, I mean as to any other use,
but only for Love and Fornication? Thou hast been a Bawd too,

---

a Reverend, Primitive, Original Bawd, from the first hour of
thy Creation! and all the laudable actions of Love, have been
committed under thy Mantle. Prithee for what dost thou think
that thou art worshipp'd?

Night. Why for my Stars and Moonshine.

Merc. That is, for holding a Candle to iniquity: but if they
260 were put out, thou wou'dst be double worshipt, by the willing
bashful Virgins.

Night. Then for my quiet, and the sweetness of my sleep.

Merc. No, for thy sweet waking all the Night: for sleep comes
not upon Lovers till thou art vanish'd.

Night. But it will be against Nature, to make a long Winters
Night at Midsummer.

Merc. Trouble not your self for that: *Phœbus* is order'd to
make a short Summers Day to morrow: so in four and twenty
Hours all will be at rights again.

270 *Night.* Well, I am edified by your discourse; and my comfort
is, that whatever work is made, I see nothing.

Merc. About your business then: put a Spoke into your Chariot Wheels, and order the Seven Stars to halt, while I put my
self into the habit of a Serving-man; and dress up a false *Sosia,*
to wait upon a false *Amphitryon.* Good night, *Night.*

Night. My service to *Jupiter.* Farewell *Mercury.*

[Night *goes backward. Exit* Mercury.

SCENE II.

Amphitryon's *Pallace.*

Enter Alcmena *alone.*

Alcm. Why was I marri'd to the Man I love!
For, had he been indifferent to my choice,
Or had been hated, absence had been pleasure:
But now I fear for my *Amphitryon's* life:

276+   *s.d. Exit*] F, D; ~ . Q1-2.   SCENE] Q2, F, D; Scene Q1.

At home, in private, and secure from War,
I am amidst an Hoast of armed foes,
Sustaining all his Cares, pierc'd with his Wounds,
And if he falls (which O ye Gods avert)
Am, in *Amphitryon* slain! wou'd I were there,
10 And he were here; so might we change our Fates;
That he might grieve for me, and I might die for him!

Enter Phædra, *running.*

Phæd. Good news, good news, Madam, O such admirable
news, that if I kept it in a moment, I shou'd burst with it!

Alc. Is it from the Army?

Phæd. No matter.

Alc. From *Amphitryon?*

Phæd. No matter, neither.

Alc. Answer me, I charge thee, if thy good news be any thing
relating to my Lord: if it be, assure thy self of a Reward.

20 *Phæd.* Ay, Madam, now you say something to the matter:
you know the business of a poor Waiting-woman, here upon
Earth, is to be scraping up something against a rainy Day,
call'd the Day of Marriage: every one in our own Vocation: but
what matter is it to me if my Lord has routed the Enemies, if I
get nothing of their spoils?

Alc. Say, is my Lord victorious?

Phæd. Why he is victorious; indeed I pray'd devoutly to
Jupiter for a Victory; by the same token, that you shou'd give
me ten pieces of Gold, if I brought you news of it.

30 *Alc.* They are thine; supposing he be safe too.

Phæd. Nay that's a new bargain; for I vow'd to *Jupiter,* that
then you shou'd give me ten Pieces more: but I do undertake
for my Lord's safety; if you will please to discharge his Godship
Jupiter of the debt, and take it upon you to pay.

Alc. When he returns in safety, *Jupiter* and I will pay your
Vow.

---

6 foes,] ∼ : Q1–2, F, D.   8 avert] Q2, F, D; aver. Q1.
33 safety;] ∼ : Q1–2, F, D.

Phæd. And I am sure I articled with *Jupiter,* that if I brought you news, that my Lord was upon return, you shou'd grant me one small favour more, that will cost you nothing.

40   *Alc.* Make haste, thou Torturer; is my *Amphitryon* upon return?

Phæd. Promise me that I shall be your bedfellow to Night, as I have been ever since my Lord's absence,————unless I shall be pleas'd to release you of your word.

Alc. That's a small request, 'tis granted.

Phæd. But swear by *Jupiter.*

Alc. But why by *Jupiter?*

Phæd. Because he's the greatest: I hate to deal with one of your little baffling Gods that can do nothing, but by permis-50 sion: but *Jupiter* can swinge you off; if you swear by him, and are forsworn.

Alc. I swear by *Jupiter.*

Phæd. Then I believe he is Victorious, and I know he is safe: for I look'd through the Key-hole, and saw him knocking at the Gate; and I had the Conscience to let him cool his Heels there.

Alc. And wou'dst thou not open to him! Oh thou Traitress!

Phæd. No, I was a little wiser: I left *Sosia's* Wife to let him in: for I was resolv'd to bring the news, and make my penny-worths out of him; as time shall show.

Enter Jupiter, *in the shape of* Amphitryon, *with* Sosia's *Wife,* Bromia. *He kisses and embraces* Alcmena.

60   *Jup.* O let me live for ever on those Lips!————
The Nectar of the Gods, to these is tasteless.
I swear, that were I *Jupiter,* this Night
I wou'd renounce my Heav'n, to be *Amphitryon.*

     Alc. Then, not to swear beneath *Amphitryon's* Oath,
(Forgive me *Juno* if I am profane)
I swear, I wou'd be what I am this Night;
And be *Alcmena,* rather than be *Juno.*

Brom. Good my Lord, what's become of my poor Bedfellow,
your Man *Sosia?* you keep such a billing and colling here, to
70 set ones Mouth a watring: what, I say, though I am a poor
Woman, I have a Husband as well as my Lady; and shou'd be
as glad as she, of a little honest Recreation.

Phæd. And what have you done with your old Friend, and
my old Sweetheart, Judge *Gripus?* has he brought me home a
cramd Purse that swels with Bribes? if he be rich, I'll make him
welcome, like an honourable Magistrate: but if he has not had
the wit to sell Justice, he judges no Causes in my Court, I warrant him.

Alc. My Lord you tell me nothing of the Battel?
80 Is *Thebes* Victorious, are our Foes destroy'd?
For now I find you safe, I shou'd be glad
To hear you were in danger.

Jup. aside. A Man had need be a God, to stand the fury of
three talking Women! I think, in my Conscience, I made their
Tongues of Thunder.

Bromia pulling him on one side. I ask'd the first question:
answer me, my Lord.

Phædra pulling him on t' other side. Peace, mine's a Lover,
and yours is but a Husband: and my Judge is my Lord too; the
90 Title shall take place, and I will be answer'd.

Jup. Sosia is safe: *Gripus* is rich: both coming:
I rode before 'em, with a Lovers haste.————
Was e're poor God so worri'd! but for my Love,   [*Aside.*
I wish I were in Heav'n again with *Juno.*

Alc. Then I, it seems, am last to be regarded?

Jup. Not so, my Love, but these obstreperous Tongues
Have snatch'd their answers first: they will be heard;
And surely *Jove* wou'd never answer Pray'r

---

69 *Sosia?*] D; ~ : Q1–2, F.
75 Bribes?] Q2, F; ~ : Q1, D.   82 danger.] D; ~ ? Q1–2, F.
84 think, . . . Conscience,] ~∧ . . . ~∧ Q1–2, F, D.
86 *Bromia*] D; Bromia Q1–2, F.
87 me,] Q2, F, D; ~∧ Q1.   88 *Phædra*] D; Phædra Q1–2, F.
88 t' other] Q2, F, D; to'ther Q1.
92–93 haste.———— / Was . . . Love, [*Aside.*] haste.———— [*Aside.* / Was . . .
Love, Q1–2, F, D.

That Women made, but only to be freed
100 From their Eternal Noise: make haste to Bed:
There let me tell my Story, in thy Arms;
There in the gentle pauses of our Love,
Betwixt our dyings, e're we live again,
Thou shalt be told the Battel, and success:
Which I shall oft begin, and then break off;
For Love will often interrupt my Tale,
And make so sweet confusion in our talk,
That thou shalt ask, and I shall answer things,
That are not of a piece: but, patch'd with Kisses,
110 And Sighs, and Murmurs, and imperfect Speech;
And Nonsence shall be Eloquent, in Love.

Brom. to Phædra. My Lord is very hot upon't: this absence is
a great Friend to us poor neglected Wives; it makes us new
again.

Alc. I am the Fool of Love; and find within me
The fondness of a Bride, without the fear.
My whole Desires and Wishes are in you.

Phæd. aside. My Ladies Eyes are pinking to Bedward too;
Now is She to look very sleepy, counterfeiting yauning, but She
120 shall ask me leave first.

Alc. Great *Juno,* thou whose holy care presides
Over the Nuptial Bed, pour all thy Blessings
On this Auspicious Night.

Jup. Juno may grudge: for she may fear a Rival,
In those bright Eyes; but *Jupiter* will grant,
And doubly bless this Night.

Phæd. aside. But *Jupiter* shou'd ask my leave first, were he
here in Person.

Alc. Bromia, prepare the Bed:
130 The tedious journey has dispos'd my Lord,
To seek his needful rest.   [*Exit* Bromia.

Phæd. 'Tis very true, Madam; the poor Gentleman must
needs be weary; and therefore, 'twas not ill contriv'd that he
must lie alone to Night, to recruit himself with sleep, and lay

---

112 *to*] to Q1-2, F, D.

in enough for to morrow Night, when you may keep him
waking.

Alc. to Jupiter. I must confess I made a kind of promise.————

Phædra, almost crying. A kind of promise, do you call it? I
140 see you wou'd fain be coming off: I am sure you swore to me,
by *Jupiter,* that I shou'd be your Bedfellow, and I'll accuse you
to him too, the first Prayers I make: And I'll pray a purpose too,
that I will, though I have not pray'd to him this seven Years.

Jup. O, the malicious Hilding!

Alc. I did swear indeed, my Lord.

Jup. Forswear thy self; for *Jupiter* but laughs
At Lovers Perjuries.

Phæd. The more shame for him if he does: there wou'd be
a fine God indeed for us Women to worship, if he laughs when
150 our Sweet-hearts cheat us of our Maiden-heads: No, no, *Jupiter*
is an honester Gentleman than you make of him.

Jup. I'm all on fire; and wou'd not loose this Night,
To be the Master of the Universe.

Phæd. Ay, my Lord, I see you are on fire: but the Devil a
Bucket shall be brought to quench it, without my leave. You
may go to Bed, Madam; but you shall see how Heav'n will bless
your Nights work, if you forswear your self.———— Some Fool,
some meer Elder-Brother, or some blockheadly Hero, *Jove,* I
beseech thee, send her.

160   *Jup. aside.* Now I cou'd call my Thunder to revenge me,
But that were to confess my self a God,
And then I lost my Love!————*Alcmena,* come,
By Heav'n, I have a Bridegrooms fervour for thee,
As I had ne'er enjoy'd.

Alc. sighing.   She has my Oath;
And sure she may release it if she please.————

Phæd. Why truly Madam, I am not cruel in my nature, to
poor distressed Lovers; for it may be my own case another day:

137 *to*] D; Q1-2, F.   139 *Phædra*] D; Phædra Q1-2, F.
155 leave. You] ~ : you Q1-2, F, D (You F).   157 self.] ~ : Q1-2, F, D.
163 Heav'n,] ~∧ Q1-2, F, D.

And therefore, if my Lord pleases to consider me———

 Jup. Any thing, any thing, but name thy wish, and have
170 it.———

 Phæd. Ay, now you say *any thing, any thing;* but you wou'd
tell me another story to morrow Morning. Look you my Lord,
here's a Hand open to receive; you know the meaning of it:
I am for nothing but the Ready———

 Jup. Thou shalt have all the Treasury of Heav'n.

 Phæd. Yes when you are *Jupiter,* to dispose of it.

 Jup. aside. I had forgot, and show'd my self a God;
This Love can make a Fool of *Jupiter.*

 Phæd. You have got some part of the Enemies Spoil I war-
180 rant you; I see a little trifling Diamond upon your Finger; and
I am proud enough to think it wou'd become mine too.

 Jupiter, taking a Ring off his Finger and giving it. Here, take
  it; this is a very Woman:
Her Sex is Avarice, and she, in One,
Is all her Sex.

 Phæd. Ay, ay, 'tis no matter what you say of us. What, wou'd
you have your Mony out of the Treasury, without paying the
Officers their Fees? Go, get you together, you naughty Couple,
till you are both weary of worrying one another, and then to
morrow morning, I shall have another Fee for parting you.

    [Phædra *goes out before* Alcmena *with a Light.*
190 *Jupiter solus.* Why now I am, indeed, the Lord of all:
For what's to be a God, but to enjoy?
Let human-kind their Sovereign's leisure waite;
Love is, this Night, my great Affair of State:
Let this one Night, of Providence be void:
All *Jove,* for once, is on himself employ'd.
Let unregarded Altars smoke in vain;
And let my Subjects praise me, or complain.

———

168 me———] Q2, F; me.——— Q1, D.
171 say *any thing, any thing*] say, any thing, any thing Q1–2, F, D.
182 *Jupiter*] D; Jupiter Q1–2, F.
182 it; this . . . Woman:] it; / This . . . Woman: Q1–2, F, D.
185 What,] ∼∧ Q1–2, F, D.
190 *Jupiter solus.* Why] *Jupiter solus.* / Why Q1–2, F; *Jup.* Why D.

Yet, if betwixt my Intervals of bliss,
Some am'rous Youth his Oraisons address,
200 His Pray'r is in a happy hour preferr'd:
And when *Jove* loves, a Lover shall be heard. [*Exit.*

ACT II. SCENE I.

Night-Scene of a Pallace.

Enter Sosia *with a Dark-Lanthorn:* Mercury, *in* Sosia's *shape,
with a Dark-Lanthorn also.*

Sosia. Was not the Devil in my Master, to send me out in this dreadful dark Night, to bring the news of his Victory to my Lady? and was not I possess'd with ten Devils, for going on his errand, without a Convoy for the safeguard of my Person? Lord, how am I melted into Sweat with fear! I am diminish'd of my natural weight, above two Stone: I shall not bring half my self home again, to my poor Wife and Family: I have been in an Ague fit, ever since shut of Evening; what with the fright of Trees by the High-way, which look'd maliciously like Thieves,
10 by Moon-shine: and what with Bulrushes by the River-side, that shak'd like Spears, and Lances at me. Well! the greatest Plague of a Serving-man, is to be hir'd to some great Lord! They care not what drudgery they put upon us, while they lie lolling at their Ease a Bed, and stretch their lazy Limbs, in expectation of the Whore which we are fetching for them.

Mer. aside. He is but a poor Mortal, that suffers this! but I, who am a God, am degraded to a foot Pimp; a Waiter without Doors; a very civil employment for a Deity!

Sos. The better sort of 'em will say *Upon my Honour,* at
20 every word: yet ask 'em for our Wages, and they plead the Priviledge of their Honour, and will not pay us; nor let us

201 *s.d.* heard. [*Exit.*] heard. Q1–2, F, D.
ACT II. SCENE I.] D; Act II. Q1; ACT II. Q2, F.
s.d. Enter Sosia] Sosia Q1–2, F, D.   16 but I] Q2, F, D; bur I Q1.
19 say *Upon my Honour*] say, Upon my Honour Q1–2, F, D.

take our Priviledge of the Law upon them. These are a very
hopeful sort of Patriots, to stand up as they do for Liberty and
Property of the Subject: there's Conscience for you!

Mer. aside. This Fellow has something of the Republican
Spirit in him.

Sosia looking about him. Stay; this methinks shou'd be our
House: and I shou'd thank the Gods, now, for bringing me
safe home: but I think I had as good let my Devotions alone,
30 till I have got the reward for my good news, and then thank
'em once for all: for if I praise 'em, before I am safe within
Doors, some damn'd Mastiff Dog may come out, and worry me;
and then my thanks are thrown away upon 'em.

Merc. aside. Thou art a wicked Rogue, and wilt have thy
Bargain before hand: Therefore thou get'st not into the House
this Night; and thank me accordingly as I use thee.

Sosia. Now am I to give my Lady an Account of my Lord's
Victory; 'tis good to exercise my Parts before hand, and file my
Tongue into eloquent Expressions, to tickle her Ladyships
40 imagination.

Mer. aside. Good! and here's the God of Eloquence to judge
of thy Oration.

Sosia, setting down his Lanthorn. This Lanthorn, for once,
shall be my Lady: because she is the Lamp of all Beauty and
Perfection.

Mer. aside. No, Rogue, 'tis thy Lord is the Lanthorn by this
time, or *Jupiter* is turn'd fumbler.

Sos. Then thus I make my Addresses to her:———*(Bowes.)*
Madam, my Lord has chosen me out, as the most Faithful,
50 though the most unworthy of his followers; to bring your Ladi-
ship this following Account of our glorious Expedition.———
Then she:———O my poor *Sosia*, (*In a shrill Tone.*) how am I
overjoy'd to see thee!———She can say no less.———Madam,

25 Fellow] D; ~ , Q1–2, F.   27 *Sosia*] D; Sosia Q1–2, F.
43 *Sosia*] D; Sosia Q1–2, F.   48 her:———] ~ :ᴧ Q1–2, F, D.
48 *s.d. Bowes.*] D; ~ᴧ Q1–2, F.   51 Expedition.———] ~ .ᴧ Q1–2, F, D.
52 she:] ~ᴧ Q1–2, F, D.
52 *s.d. In . . . Tone.*] in . . . Toneᴧ Q1–2, F, D (*Tone.* D).
53 thee!———] ~ !ᴧ Q1–2, F, D.   53 less.] ~ : Q1–2, F, D.

you do me too much Honour, and the World will envy me this glory.————Well answer'd on my side.————And how does my Lord *Amphitryon?*————Madam, he always does like a Man of Courage, when he is call'd by Honour.————There I think I nick'd it.————But when will he return?————As soon as possibly he can: but not so soon as his impatient Heart cou'd
60 wish him with your Ladyship.

Merc. aside. When *Thebes* is an University, thou deservest to be their Orator.

Sosia. But what does he do, and what does he say? Prethee tell me something more of him.————He always says less than he does, Madam: and his Enemies have found it to their cost. ————Where the Devil did I learn these Elegancies and Gallantries?

Merc. So; he has all the natural Endowments of a Fop; and only wants the Education!

70 *Sosia, staring up to the Sky.* What, is the Devil in the Night! she's as long as two Nights: the seven Stars are just where they were seven Hours ago! high Day—high Night, I mean, by my favour. What, has *Phœbus* been playing the Good-fellow, and overslept himself, that he forgets his duty to us Mortals?

Merc. How familiarly the Raskal treats us Gods! but I shall make him alter his tone immediately.

[Mercury *comes nearer, and stands just before him.*

Sosia, seeing him, and starting back, aside. How now? what, do my Eyes dazle, or is my dark Lanthorn false to me! is not that a Giant before our Door? or a Ghost of some body slain in the
80 late Battel? if he be, 'tis unconscionably done, to fright an honest Man thus, who never drew Weapon wrathfully in all my life!————Whatever Wight he be, I am devilishly afraid, that's certain: but 'tis discretion to keep my own Counsel: I'll sing, that I may seem Valiant. [Sosia *sings; and as* Mercury *speaks, by little and little drops his Voice.*

Merc. What sawcy Companion is this, that deafens us with

55 glory.————Well] ~ :————well Q1–2, F, D (Well F, D).
70 *Sosia*] D; Sosia Q1–2, F.   70 What,] D; ~ᴧ Q1–2, F.
73 What,] ~ᴧ Q1–2, F.   77 *Sosia*] D; Sosia Q1–2, F.
77 what,] ~ᴧ Q1–2, F, D.

his hoarse Voice? what Midnight Ballad-singer have we here? I shall teach the Villain to leave off Catterwawling.

Sosia. I wou'd I had Courage, for his sake; that I might teach him to call my singing Catterwawling; an Illiterate Rogue; an 90 Enemy to the Muses and to Musick.

Merc. There is an ill savour that offends my Nostrils; and it wafteth this way.

Sosia. He has smelt me out: my fear has betray'd me into this savour.————I am a dead Man: the bloody Villain is at his *fee, fa, fum,* already.

Merc. Stand, who goes there?

Sosia. A Friend.

Merc. What Friend?

Sosia. Why a Friend to all the World that will give me leave 100 to live peaceably.

Merc. I defie Peace and all its Works; my Arms are out of exercise, they have maul'd no body these three days: I long for an honourable Occasion to pound a Man; and lay him asleep at the first Buffet.

Sosia aside. That wou'd almost do me a kindness; for I have been kept wakeing, without tipping one wink of sleep these three Nights.

Merc. Of what Quality are you, Fellow?

Sosia. Why I am a Man, Fellow.————Courage *Sosia.*————
110 *Merc.* What kind of Man?

Sosia. Why a Two-leg'd Man, What Man shou'd I be?————
(Aside.) I must bear up to him, he may prove as errant a Milksop as my self.

Merc. Thou art a Coward I warrant thee, do not I hear thy Teeth chatter in thy Head?

Sosia. Ay, ay, that's only a sign they wou'd be snapping at thy Nose.————*(Aside.)* Bless me, what an Arm and Fist he has,

89   Catterwawling;] ∼ , Q1–2, F, D.   92   way.] D; ∼ ? Q1–2, F.
94–95   *fee, fa, fum*] in romans in *Q1–2, F, D.*
103   asleep] Q2, F, D; a sleep Q1.
109   Fellow.] Q2, F; ∼ , Q1; ∼∧ D.   109   *Sosia.*] ∼∧ Q1–2, F, D.
112   s.d. *Aside.*] Q2, F, D; ∼∧ Q1.   112   I must]————I must Q1–2, F, D.
117   s.d. *Aside.*] D; ∼∧ Q1–2, F.   117   Bless]————Bless Q1–2, F, D.

with great Thumbs too: and Gols and Knuckle-bones of a very Butcher.

120   *Merc.* Sirrah, from whence come you, and whither go you? answer me directly, upon pain of Assassination.

    Sosia. I am coming from whence I came, and am going whither I go: that's directly home————though this is somewhat an uncivil manner of proceeding, at the first sight of a Man, let me tell you.

    Merc. Then to begin our better Acquaintance, let me first make you a small Present of this box o' the Ear.————

                                     (Strikes him.

    Sosia. If I were as cholerick a Fool as you now, here wou'd be fine work betwixt us two; but I am a little better bred, than 130 to disturb the sleeping Neighbourhood, and so good night Friend.————   *(Is going.*

    Merc. stopping him. Hold Sir; you and I must not part so easily; once more, whither are you going?

    Sosia. Why I am going as fast as I can, to get out of the reach of your Clutches: let me but only knock at that Door there.

    Merc. What business have you at that Door, Sirrah?

    Sosia. This is our House; and when I am got in, I'll tell you more.

    Merc. Whose House is this, Sawciness, that you are so familiar 140 with, to call it *ours?*

    Sosia. 'Tis mine, in the first place; and next, my Masters; for I lye in the Garret, and he lyes under me.

    Merc. Have your Master and you no Names, Sirrah?

    Sosia. His Name is *Amphitryon,* hear that and tremble.

    Merc. What, my Lord General?

    Sosia. O, has his Name mollify'd you! I have brought you down a Peg lower already, Friend.

    Merc. And your Name is————

    Sosia. Lord, Friend, you are so very troublesom————What 150 shou'd my Name be but *Sosia?*

127+   *s.d. Strikes*] Q2, F, D; *strikes* Q1.
132   *stopping*] Q2, F, D; *stoping* Q1.
140   *ours*] ours Q1-2, F, D.   142   Garret] Q2, F, D; Garrret Q1.

Merc. How, *Sosia,* say you? how long have you taken up that Name, Sirrah?

Sosia. Here's a fine question: why I never took it up Friend, it was born with me.

Merc. What, was your Name born, *Sosia?* take this Remembrance for that Lye.   (*Beats him.*

Sosia. Hold Friend, you are so very flippant with your Hands, you won't hear Reason: What offence has my Name done you, that you shou'd beat me for it? *S.O.S.I.A.* They are as civil,
160 honest, harmless Letters, as any are in the whole Alphabet.

Merc. I have no quarrel to the Name, but that 'tis e'en too good for you, and 'tis none of yours.

Sosia. What, am not I *Sosia,* say you?

Merc. No.

Sosia. I should think you are somewhat merrily dispos'd, if you had not beaten me, in such sober sadness. You wou'd perswade me out of my Heathen Name, wou'd you?

Merc. Say you are *Sosia* again at your Peril, Sirrah.

Sosia. I dare say nothing, but Thought is free; but whatever
170 I am call'd, I am *Amphitryon*'s Man, and the first Letter of my Name is *S.* too. You had best tell me that my Master did not send me home to my Lady, with news of his Victory?

Merc. I say he did not.

Sosia. Lord, Lord, Friend, one of us two is horribly giv'n to lying————but I do not say which of us, to avoid Contention.

Merc. I say, my Name is *Sosia,* and yours is not.

Sosia. I wou'd you cou'd make good your words, for then I shou'd not be beaten, and you shou'd.

Merc. I find you wou'd be *Sosia* if you durst————but if I
180 catch you thinking so————

Sosia. I hope I may think I was *Sosia;* and I can find no difference between my former self, and my present self; but that I was plain *Sosia* before; and now I am lac'd *Sosia.*

Merc. Take this, for being so impudent to think so.
                              (*Beats him.*

Sosia kneeling. Truce a little, I beseech thee! I wou'd be a
Stock or a Stone now by my good will, and wou'd not think at
all, for self preservation. But will you give me leave to argue the
Matter fairly with you? and promise me to depose that Cudgel,
if I can prove my self to be that Man that I was before I was
190 beaten?

Merc. Well, proceed in safety; I promise you I will not beat
you.

Sosia. In the first Place then, is not this Town call'd *Thebes?*

Merc. Undoubtedly.

Sosia. And is not this House *Amphitryon's?*

Merc. Who denyes it?

Sosia. I thought you wou'd have denyed that too; for all hangs
upon a String. Remember then, that those two preliminary
Articles are already granted. In the next place, did not the
200 foresaid *Amphitryon* beat the *Teleboans,* kill their King *Pterelas,* and send a certain Servant, meaning some Body, that for
sake-sake shall be nameless, to bring a Present to his Wife, with
news of his Victory, and of his Resolution to return to morrow?

Merc. This is all true, to a very tittle; but who is that certain
Servant? there's all the question.

Sosia. Is it Peace or War betwixt us?

Merc. Peace.

Sosia. I dare not wholly trust that abominable Cudgel; but
'tis a certain Friend of yours and mine; that had a certain Name
210 before he was beaten out of it; but if you are a Man that depend not altogether upon force and brutality, but somewhat
also upon Reason, now do you bring better Proofs that you are
that same certain Man; and in order to it, answer me to certain
Questions.

Merc. I say I am *Sosia, Amphitryon's* Man; what reason have
you to urge against it?

Sosia. What was your Fathers Name?

Merc. Davus; who was an honest Husbandman, whose Sisters

---

194   Undoubtedly] Q2, F, D; Uundoubtedly Q1.   197   too;] F, D; ~ ? Q1-2.
204   tittle] Q2, F, D; little Q1.
205   Servant? . . . question.] ~ , ... ~ ? Q1-2, F, D.

Name was *Harpagè,* that was married, and dyed in a foreign
220 Country.

Sosia. So far you are right, I must confess; and your Wife's
Name is————

Merc. Bromia, a devilish Shrew of her Tongue, and a Vixon
of her Hands; that leads me a miserable Life; keeps me to hard
duty a Bed; and beats me every Morning when I have risen
from her side, without having first————

Sosia. I understand you, by many a sorrowful Token; this
must be I.————   (*Aside.*

Merc. I was once taken upon suspicion of Burglary, and was
230 whipt through *Thebes,* and branded for my pains.

Sosia. Right me again; but if you are I, as I begin to suspect;
that whipping and branding might have been past over in
silence, for both our Credits.————(*Aside.*) And yet now I
think on't, if I am I, (as I am I) he cannot be I. All these Circumstances he might have heard; but I will now interrogate him
upon some private Passages.————What was the Present that
Amphitryon sent by you or me, no matter which of us, to his
Wife *Alcmena?*

Merc. A Buckle of Diamonds, consisting of five large Stones.
240 *Sosia.* And where are they now?

Merc. In a Case, seal'd with my Masters Coat of Arms.

Sosia. This is prodigious, I confess; but yet 'tis nothing now
I think on't, for some false Brother may have reveal'd it to him.
(*Aside.*)————But I have another Question to ask you, of somewhat that pass'd only betwixt my self and me; if you are *Sosia,*
what were you doing in the heat of Battel?

Merc. What a wise Man shou'd, that has a respect for his own
Person. I ran into our Tent, and hid my self amongst the
Baggage.

250 *Sosia aside.* Such another cutting Answer, and I must provide my self of another name.————(*To him.*) And how did
you pass your time in that same Tent? You need not answer to

222   is————] Q2, F, D; ~ .———— Q1.   227   you,] ~ ; Q1-2, F, D.
233   s.d. (*Aside.*) And] And Q1-2, F, D.   236   Passages.] ~∧ Q1-2, F, D.
244   s.d. *Aside.*] Q2, F, D; ~∧ Q1.   244   ————But] But Q1-2, F, D.
251   name.————] name. Q1-2, F, D.

every Circumstance so exactly now; you must lye a little, that I may think you the more me.

Merc. That cunning shall not serve your turn, to circumvent me out of my name: I am for plain naked Truth:—There stood a Hogshead of old Wine, which my Lord reserv'd for his own drinking———

Sosia aside. O the Devil! as sure as Death, he must have hid 260 himself in that Hogshead, or he cou'd never have known that!

Merc. And by that Hogshead, upon the ground, there lay the kind Inviter and Provoker of good drinking———

Sosia. Nay, now I have caught you; there was neither Inviter nor Provoker, for I was all alone.

Merc. A lusty Gammon of———

Sosia sighing. Bacon:———that word has quite made an end of me:———let me see,———this must be I, in spight of me. ———But let me view him nearer.

           (Walks about Mercury *with his dark Lanthorn.*

Merc. What are you walking about me for, with your dark 270 Lanthorn?

Sosia. No harm, Friend; I am only surveying a parcel of Earth here, that I find we two are about to Bargain for.——— *(Aside.)* He's damnable like me, that's certain. *Imprimis,* there's the Patch upon my Nose, with a Pox to him.———*Item,* a very foolish Face with a long Chin at end on't: *Item,* one Pair of shambling Legs, with two splay Feet belonging to them. And ———*summa totalis,* from Head to Foot all my Bodily Apparel.———*(To* Mercury.) Well, you are *Sosia;* there's no denying it; but what am I then? for my Mind gives me, I am some 280 body still, if I knew but who I were.

Merc. When I have a mind to be *Sosia* no more, then thou maist be *Sosia* again.

Sosia. I have but one request more to thee, that, though not

258 drinking] F, D; $\sim$. Q1–2.   266 Bacon:] $\sim_\wedge$ Q1–2, F, D.
268 But] but Q1–2, F, D.   271 harm,] Q2, F, D; $\sim_\wedge$ Q1.
272 for.] $\sim$: Q1–2, F, D.   273 *s.d. (Aside.)] omitted from Q1–2, F, D.*
273 certain.] Q2, F, D; $\sim_\wedge$ Q1.   274 him.] $\sim_\wedge$ Q1–2, F, D.
275 *Item,*] Q2, F, D; $\sim_\wedge$ Q1.   278 *s.d.* Mercury.] *Mercury*$_\wedge$ Q1–2, F, D.

as *Sosia,* yet as a stranger, I may go into that House, and carry a civil Message to my Lady.

Merc. No Sirrah, not being *Sosia,* you have no Message to deliver, nor no Lady in this House.

Sosia. Thou canst not be so barbarous, to let me lye in the Streets all night, after such a Journey, and such a beating———
290 and therefore I am resolv'd to knock at the Door in my own defence.

Merc. If you come near the Door, I recal my word, and break off the truce:———and then expect——— ˙
                             (Holds up his Cudgel.

Sosia. No; The Devil take me if I do expect: I have felt too well what sowr Fruit that Crab-tree bears: I'll rather beat it back upon the Hoof to my Lord *Amphitryon;* to see if he will acknowledg me for *Sosia;* if he does not, then I am no longer his Slave; there's my Freedom dearly purchas'd with a sore drubbing; if he does acknowledg me, then I am *Sosia* again; so
300 far 'tis tolerably well; but then I shall have a second drubbing, for an unfortunate Ambassador as I am; and that's intolerable.
                                     [*Exit* Sosia.

Mercury alone. I have fobb'd off his Excellency pretty well. Now let him return, and make the best of his Credentials. I think too I have given *Jupiter* sufficient time for his Consummation. Oh, he has taken his Cue; and here he comes as leisurely and as lank as if he had empty'd himself of the best part of his Almightyship.

SCENE II.

Enter Jupiter *leading* Alcmena, *followed by* Phædra:
Pages with Torches before them.

Jupiter to the Pages. Those Torches are offensive: stand aloof.

302   *Mercury alone.* I] *Mercury alone.* / I Q1-2, F, D.
SCENE] Q2, F, D; Scene Q1.   s.d. Phædra:] ∼ . Q1-2, F, D.
1   *them.* / *Jupiter to the Pages.* Those . . . aloof.] *them.* Jupiter *to the Pages.* /
Those . . . aloof: Q1-2, F (aloof∧ F); *them.* / *Jup.* Those . . . aloof: [*To the
Pages.* D.

For, though they bless me with thy heav'nly sight,   [*To her.*
They may disclose the Secret I would hide:
The *Thebans* must not know I have been here;
Detracting Crowds wou'd blame me that I robb'd
These happy Moments from my publick Charge,
To Consecrate to thy desir'd embrace:
And I cou'd wish no Witness but thy self;
For thou thy self art all I wish to please.
10 *Alcm.* So long an absence, and so short a stay!
What, but one Night! one Night of joy and love,
Cou'd only pay one Night of Cares and Fears;
And all the rest are an uncancell'd Sum!
Curse on this Honour and this publick Fame;
Wou'd you had less of both, and more of Love!
      Jup. Alcmena I must go.
      Alcm.   Not yet my Lord.
      Jup. Indeed I must.
      Alc.   Indeed you shall not go.
      Jup. Behold the ruddy Streaks o're yonder Hill,
Those are the Blushes of the breaking Morn,
20 That kindle Day-light to this neather World.
      Alcm. No matter for the Day, it was but made
To number out the Hours of busie Men.
Let 'em be busie still, and still be wretched;
And take their fill of anxious drudging day:
But you and I will draw our Curtains close,
Extinguish Day-light, and put out the Sun:
Come back, my Lord, in faith you shall retire.
You have not yet lay long enough in Bed,
To warm your widdow'd Side.
30 *Phædra, aside.* I find my Lord is an excellent Schoolmaster,
my Lady is so willing to repeat her Lesson.
      Merc. aside. That's a plaguy little Devil; what a roguish Eye
she has! I begin to like her strangely; she's the Perquisite of my
Place too; for my Ladies Waiting-Woman is the proper Fees of
my Lords Chief Gentleman. I have the Priviledg of a God too;

---

20 World.] Q2, F, D; ~ : Q1.   30 *aside.*] Q2, F, D; ~ , Q1.

I can view her naked through all her Clothes:————Let me see
————Let me see: I have discover'd something that pleases me
already.

  Jup. Let me not live but thou art all Enjoyment!
40 So charming and so sweet, that not a Night,
But whole Eternity, were well employ'd,
To love thy each Perfection as it ought.
  Alc. kissing him. I'll bribe you with this kiss to stay a while.
  Jup. kissing her. A Bribe indeed that soon will bring me back.
But, to be just, I must restore your Bribe.
How I cou'd dwell for ever on those Lips!
O I cou'd kiss 'em pale with eagerness!
So soft, by Heav'n, and such a juicy sweet,
That ripen'd Peaches have not half the flavour.
50   *Alcm.* Ye niggard Gods! you make our Lives too long:
You fill 'em with Diseases, Wants and Woes,
And only dash 'em with a little Love;
Sprinkled by Fits, and with a sparing Hand:
Count all our Joys, from Childhood ev'n to Age,
They wou'd but make a day of ev'ry year:
Take back your sev'nty years, (the stint of Life)
Or else be kind, and cram the Quintessence
Of Seav'nty years, into sweet Seav'nty days:
For all the rest is flat, insipid Being.
60   *Jup.* But yet one Scruple pains me at my parting;
I love so nicely, that I cannot bear
To owe the Sweets of Love which I have tasted,
To the submissive Duty of a Wife:
Tell me: and sooth my Passion e're I go,
That in the kindest Moments of the Night,
When you gave up your self to Love and me,
You thought not of a Husband, but a Lover.
  Alcm. But tell me first, why you wou'd raise a Blush

40–41 sweet, that . . . Night, / But . . . Eternity, were . . . employ'd,] sweet, /
That . . . Night, but . . . Eternity, / Were . . . employ'd, Q1–2, F, D (employ'd∧ D).

Upon my Cheeks, by asking such a Question.

70   *Jup.* I wou'd owe nothing to a Name so dull
As Husband is, but to a Lover all.

   Alcm. You shou'd have ask'd me then, when Love and Night,
And Privacy, had favour'd your demand.

   Jup. I ask it now, because my tenderness
Surpasses that of Husbands for their Wives.
O that you lov'd like me! then you wou'd find
A thousand, thousand Niceties in Love;
The Common love of Sex to Sex is brutal:
But love refin'd will fancy to it self

80 Millions of gentle Cares, and sweet Disquiets;
The being happy is not half the Joy;
The manner of the happiness is all!
In me (my charming Mistris) you behold
A Lover that disdains a Lawful Title;
Such as of Monarchs to successive Thrones:
The Generous Lover holds by force of Arms;
And claims his Crown by Conquest.

   Alcm. Methinks you shou'd be pleas'd, I give you all
A Vertuous and a Modest Wife can give.

90   *Jup.* No, no, that very name of Wife and Marriage,
Is Poyson to the dearest sweets of Love:
To please my niceness you must separate
The Lover from his Mortal Foe, the Husband.
Give to the yawning Husband your cold Vertue,
But all your vigorous Warmth, your melting Sighs,
Your amorous Murmurs, be your Lovers part.

   Alcm. I comprehend not what you mean, my Lord,
But only love me still, and love me thus,
And think me such as best may please your Thought.

100   *Jup.* There's Mystery of Love in all I say:
Farewel; and when you see your Husband next
Think of your Lover then.

68–69 *as in D; set as prose in Q1–2, F.*   69 Question.] ∼ ? Q1–2, F, D.
79 refin'd] Q2, F, D; refind Q1.

Exeunt Jupiter *and* Alcmena *severally:* Phædra *follows her.*
Merc. alone. Now I shou'd follow him; but Love has laid a
Lime-twig for me, and made a lame God of me. Yet why shou'd
I love this *Phædra?* She's Interessed, and a Jilt into the Bargain. Three thousand years hence, there will be a whole Nation
of such Women, in a certain Country that will be call'd *France;*
and there's a Neighbour Island too, where the Men of that
Country will be all Interest. Oh what a precious Generation
110 will that be, which the Men of the Island shall Propagate out of
the Women of the Continent!

Phædra *re-enters.*

And so much for Prophesie: for she's here again, and I must
love her in spight of me. And since I must, I have this Comfort,
that the greatest Wits are commonly the greatest Cullies; because neither of the Sexes can be wiser than some certain Parts
about 'em will give 'em leave.
   Phædra. Well *Sosia,* and how go Matters?
   Merc. Our Army is Victorious.
   Phædra. And my Servant Judge *Gripus?*
120   *Merc.* A Voluptuous Gourmand.
   Phædra. But has he gotten wherewithal to be Voluptuous, is
he Wealthy?
   Merc. He sells Justice as he uses, fleeces the Rich Rebells,
and hangs up the Poor.
   Phædra. Then while he has Money he may make love to me.
Has he sent me no Token?
   Merc. Yes, a Kiss; and by the same Token, I am to give it you,
as a Remembrance from him.
   Phæd. How now, Impudence! A beggarly Serving-man pre-
130 sume to kiss me?

111–112 Continent! / Phædra *re-enters.* / And] Continent? / (*Phædra re-*
*enters*ᴧ)————And Q1–2, F, D.
121   wherewithal] Q2, F, D; where withal Q1.
127   Yes,] D; ~ᴧ Q1–2, F.   129   now,] Q2, F, D; ~ᴧ Q1.

Merc. Suppose I were a God, and shou'd make Love to you?

Phæd. I wou'd first be satisfi'd, whether you were a poor God or a rich God.

Merc. Suppose I were *Mercury,* the God of Merchandise?

Phæd. What, the God of small Wares, and Fripperies, of Pedlars and Pilferers?

Merc. aside. How the Gipsie despises me!

Phædra. I had rather you were *Plutus* the God of Money, or *Jupiter* in a Golden Shower: there was a God for us Women!
140 he had the Art of making Love: Dost thou think that Kings, or Gods either, get Mistrisses by their good Faces? no, 'tis the Gold and the Presents they can make: there's the Prerogative they have over their fair Subjects.

Merc. All this notwithstanding, I must tell you pretty *Phæ-dra,* I am desperately in love with you.

Phæd. And I must tell thee, ugly *Sosia,* thou hast not where-withal to be in love.

Merc. Yes, a poor Man may be in love I hope?

Phæd. I grant a poor Rogue may be in love, but he can never
150 make love: Alas *Sosia,* thou hast neither Face to invite me, nor Youth to please me, nor Gold to bribe me: And Besides all this thou hast a Wife, poor miserable *Sosia!*————What ho *Bromia!*

Merc. O thou merciless Creature, why dost thou conjure up that spright of a Wife?

Phæd. To rid my self of that Devil of a poor Lover: since you are so lovingly dispos'd, I'll put you together, to exercise your Fury upon your own Wedlock.————What *Bromia,* I say, make hast; here's a Vessel of yours, full fraighted, that's going off, without paying Duties.

160 *Merc.* Since thou wilt not let me steal Custom, She shall have all the Cargo I have gotten in the Wars: but thou mightst have lent me a little Creek to smuggle in.

---

135 What,] D; ~_∧ Q1–2, F.   137 me!] ~ ? Q1–2, F, D.
146–147 wherewithal] Q2, F, D; where withal Q1.
152 ————What] What Q1–2, F, D.
157 Wedlock.————] ~ :_∧ Q1–2, F, D.
160 Custom,] D; ~ : Q1–2, F.

Phæd. Why, what have you gotten, good Gentleman Soldier, besides a Legion of———   (*Knaps her Fingers.*

Merc. When the Enemy was rowted, I had the plundering of a Tent.

Phæd. That's to say, a House of Canvas, with moveables of Straw.———Make haste *Bromia*———

Merc. But it was the Generals own Tent.

170 *Phæd.* You durst not fight I'm certain; and therefore came last in, when the rich Plunder was gone before hand.——— Will you come, *Bromia?*

Merc. Prithee do not call so lowd:———A great Goblet that holds a Gallon.

Phæd. Of what was that Goblet made? answer quickly, for I am just calling very loud.——— *Bro*———

Merc. Of beaten Gold. Now call aloud, if thou dost not like the Mettal.

Phæd. Bromia.   (*Very softly.*

180 *Merc.* That struts in this Fashion, with his Arms a kimbo, like a City Magistrate: and a great bouncing Belly, like an Hostess with Child of a Kilderkin of Wine. Now what say you to that Present, *Phædra?*

Phæd. Why I am considering———

Merc. What I prithee?

Phæd. Why, how to divide the Business equally; to take the Gift, and refuse the Giver, thou art so damnably ugly and so old.

Merc. aside. Now the Devil take *Jupiter,* for confining me to 190 this ungodly shape to day!———(*To her.*) But *Gripus* is as old and as ugly too.

Phæd. But *Gripus* is a Person of Quality, and my Ladies Uncle, and if he marries me I shall take place of my Lady.

---

164   s.d. *Knaps*] *knaps* Q1–2, F, D.
168   Straw.———Make] Straw; make Q1–2, F, D (Straw: D).
172   Will] Q2, F, D; will Q1.   176   loud.] ~⌃ Q1–2, F, D.
176   *Bro*———] D; *Bro.*———Q1–2, F.   177   aloud] Q2, F, D; a loud Q1.
179   *Bromia*] D; Bromia Q1–2, F.   187   Giver,] Q2, F, D; ~ . Q1.
190–191   day!———(*To her.*) But . . . too.] day! / But . . . too. (*To her.* Q1–2, F; Day! / But . . . too. D.

Hark, your Wife! she has sent her Tongue before her. I hear the Thunderclap already: there's a storm approaching.

Merc. Yes, of thy Brewing, I thank thee for it: O how I shou'd hate thee now if I cou'd leave loving thee!

Phæd. Not a word of the dear Golden Goblet, as you hope for—you know what, *Sosia.*

200 *Mer.* You give me Hope then———

Phæd. Not absolutely Hope neither: but Gold is a great Cordial, in love matters; and the more you apply of it, the better.———[*Aside.*] I am honest, that's certain; but when I weigh my honesty against the Goblet, I am not quite resolv'd on which side the Scale will turn.   [*Exit* Phædra.

Merc. aloud. Farewell *Phædra;* remember me to my Wife, and tell her———

Enter Bromia.

Brom. Tell her what, Traytor! that you are going away without seeing her?

210 *Merc.* That I am doing my Duty, and following my Master.

Brom. Umph———so brisk too! your Master did his Duty to my Lady before he parted: He cou'd leave his Army in the lurch, and come galloping home at Midnight, to have a lick at the Honey-pot; and steal to Bed as quietly as any Mouse, I warrant you: My Master knew what belong'd to a marri'd life; but you, Sirrah———You Trencher-carrying Raskal, you worse than Dunghill-Cock; that stood clapping your Wings and crowing without Doors, when you shou'd have been at roost, you Villain———

220 *Merc.* Hold your peace, Dame *Partlet,* and leave your Cackling: My Master charg'd me to stand Centry without Doors.

Bro. My Master! I dare swear thou bely'st him, My Masters

205 s.d. Phædra] F, D; Phœdra Q1–2.
206 aloud] D; a loud Q1; a-loud Q2, F.
208 her what,] ∼ , ∼ Q1–2, F; ∼∼ ? D.   209 her?] F; ∼ . Q1–2, D.
216 Sirrah] F, D; ∼ . Q1–2.   219 Villain] F; ∼ . Q1–2, D.
222 *My Master*] My Master Q1–2, F, D.

more a Gentleman than to lay such an unreasonable command
upon a poor distressed marri'd Couple, and after such an absence too. No, there's no comparison between my Master and
thee, thou Sneaksby.

Mer. No more than there is betwixt my Lady and you, *Bromia.* You and I have had our time in a civil way, Spouse, and
much good love has been betwixt us: but we have been married
230 fifteen Years, I take it: and that hoighty toighty business ought,
in Conscience, to be over.

Bro. Marry come up, My sawcy Companion! I am neither
old, nor ugly enough to have that said to me.

Merc. But will you hear reason, *Bromia?* My Lord and my
Lady are yet in a manner Bride and Bridegroom; they are in
Honey Moon still: do but think in decency what a Jest it
wou'd be to the Family, to see two Venerable old married
People, lying snug in a Bed together, and sighing out fine
tender things to one another!

240 *Bro.* How now, Traytor, dar'st thou maintain that I am past
the Age of having fine things said to me?

Merc. Not so, my Dear: but certainly I am past the Age of
saying 'em.

Bro. Thou deserv'st not to be yok'd with a Woman of
Honour, as I am, thou perjur'd Villain.

Merc. Ay, you are too much a Woman of Honour, to my
sorrow: many a poor Husband wou'd be glad to compound for
less Honour in his Wife, and more quiet. Prethee be but honest
and continent in thy Tongue, and do thy worst with every
250 thing else about thee.

Brom. Thou wou'dst have a Woman of the Town, wou'dst
thou! to be always speaking my Husband fair, to make him
digest his Cuckoldom more easily: wou'dst thou be a Wittol,
with a vengeance to thee? I am resolv'd I'll scoure thy Hide,
for that word.   [*Holds up her Ladle at him.*

Merc. Thou wilt not strike thy Lord, and Husband, wilt
thou?

Brom. Since thou wilt none of the Meat, 'tis but justice to
give thee the bastings of the Ladle.   [*She courses him about.*

260 *Mercury running about (aside).* Was ever poor Deity so Hen-
peck'd as I am! nay, then 'tis time to charm her asleep with my
enchanted Rod————before I am disgrac'd or ravish'd.————
                    [*Plucks out his* Caduceus *and strikes her upon
                        the Shoulder with it.*

Brom. What, art thou rebelling against thy annointed Wife?
I'll make thee————How now————What, has the Rogue be-
witch'd me! I grow dull and stupid on the sudden.————I can
neither stir Hand nor Foot.————I am just like him; I have
lost the use of all my—Members.————[*Yawning.*]————I
can't so much as wag my Tongue—neither, and that's the last
live—ing part about a—Woman.————   [*Falls down.*
270 *Mercury alone.* Lord what have I suffer'd, for being but a
counterfeit marri'd Man one day! If ever I come to this House,
as a Husband again————then————and yet that then, was a
lye too————For while I am in love with this young Gipsie,
Phædra, I must return.————But lie thou there, thou Type of
Juno: thou that want'st nothing of her Tongue, but the immortality. If *Jupiter* ever let thee set Foot in Heaven, *Juno* will
have a rattling Second of thee; and there will never be a fair
Day in Heaven or Earth after it.
        For two such Tongues, will break the Poles asunder;
280 And, hourly scolding, make perpetual Thunder.
                                        [*Exit* Mercury.

ACT III.   SCENE I.

Scene, *before* Amphitryon's *Pallace.*

Enter Amphitryon *and* Sosia.

---

260 *Mercury . . . about (aside).*] Mercury . . . *about. aside.* Q1-2, F, D
([*Aside.*] D).
262+ *s.d.* Caduceus] *Caduceus* Q1-2, F, D.   264 How] how Q1-2, F, D.
265-266 sudden.———— . . . Foot.] sudden∧———— . . . Foot∧ Q1-2, F, D.
267 Members.] ∼∧ Q1-2, F, D.   267 *s.d. Yawning*] D; *yawning* Q1-2, F.
269 Woman.] ∼∧ Q1-2, F, D.   269 *s.d. Falls*] D; *falls* Q1-2, F.
270 *Mercury alone.* Lord] Mercury *alone.* / Lord Q1-2, F, D.
274 *Phædra*] F, D; *Phœdra* Q1-2.   274 return.] ∼∧ Q1-2, F, D.
ACT III. SCENE I.] D; A.ct III. Q1; ACT. III. Q2, F.
s.d. Enter Amphitryon] Amphitryon Q1-2, F, D.   *s.d.* Sosia] Q2, F, D; *Sosia* Q1.

Amp. Now Sirrah, follow me into the House, thou shalt be convinc'd at thy own cost, Villain! What horrible lyes hast thou told me! such improbabilities, such stuff, such nonsense!—that the Monster with two long Horns, that frighted the great King, and the Devil at the Stone-cutters, are Truths to these!

Sos. I am but a Slave, and you are Master; and a poor Man is always to lye, when a rich Man is pleas'd to contradict him: but as sure as this is our House———

Am. So sure 'tis thy place of Execution. Thou art not made
10 for lying neither.

Sos. That's certain: for all my Neighbours say I have an honest Face; or else they wou'd never call me Cuckold, as they do.

Amp. I mean thou hast not wit enough to make a lye, that will hang together: thou hast set up a Trade, that thou hast not Stock enough to manage: O that I had but a Crab-tree Cudgel for thy sake!

Sos. How, a Cudgel, said you! the Devil take *Jupiter* for inventing that hard-hearted, merciless, knobby Wood.

20 *Amp.* The bitterness is yet to come: thou hast had but a half Dose of it.

Sos. I was never good at swallowing Physick: and my Stomach wambles at the very thought of it; but, if I must have a second beating, in conscience let me strip first, that I may show you the black and blue streaks upon my Sides and Shoulders. I am sure I suffer'd them in your service.

Amp. To what purpose wou'dst thou show them?

Sos. Why to the purpose that you may not strike me upon the sore places: and that as he beat me last Night cross-ways, so
30 you wou'd please to beat me long-ways, to make clean work on't, that at least my Skin may look like Checquer-work.

Amp. This request is too reasonable to be refus'd; but, that all things may be done in order, tell me over again the same story, with all the circumstances of thy Commission: that a blow may follow in due form for every lye. To Repetition, Rogue, to Repetition.

---

19   hard-hearted] Q2, F, D; heard-hearted Q1.
35   Repetition,] F, D; ~∧ Q1-2.

Sos. No, it shall be all a lye if you please, and I'll eat my
Words to save my Shoulders.

Amp. Ay, Sirrah, now you find you are to be disproved: but
40 'tis too late: to Repetition, Rogue, to Repetition.

Sos. With all my heart, to any Repetition but the Cudgel:
but, wou'd you be pleas'd to answer me one civil question? Am
I to use Complaisance to you, as to a great Person, that will
have all things said your own way; or am I to tell you the naked
Truth alone, without the Ceremony of a farther beating?

Amp. Nothing but the Truth, and the whole Truth, so help
thee Cudgel.———

Sos. That's a damn'd conclusion of a Sentence: but since it
must be so———Back and Sides, at your own peril.———I set
50 out from the Port in an unlucky Hour: the dusky Canopy of
Night inveloping the Hemisphere.———

Amph. strikes him. Imprimis for Fustian:———now proceed.

Sos. I stand corrected: in plain Prose then, I went darkling,
and whistling, to keep my self from being afraid; mumbling
Curses betwixt my Teeth, for being sent at such an unnatural
time of Night.

Amp. How Sirrah, Cursing and Swearing against your Lord
and Master! take———   [*Going to strike.*

Sos. Hold, Sir———pray consider, if this be not unreason-
60 able, to strike me for telling the whole Truth, when you commanded me: I'll fall into my old dog-trot of lying again, if this
must come of plain dealing.

Amp. To avoid impertinences, make an end of your journey;
and come to the House: what found you there a God's Name?

Sos. I came thither in no God's Name at all; but in the Devils
name, I found before the Door a swingeing Fellow, with all my
Shapes and Features; and accoutred also in my Habit.

Amp. Who was that Fellow?

Sos. Who shou'd it be, but another *Sosia!* a certain kind of
70 other me: who knew all my unfortunate Commission, precisely,

---

46 Truth, so] ~ : ~ Q1–2, F; ~∧~ D.   47 Cudgel.] ~∧ Q1–2, F, D.
49 peril.] ~∧ Q1–2, F, D.   52 *Amph.*] D; Amph. Q1–2, F.

to a word, as well as I *Sosia;* as being sent by your self from the Port, upon the same errand to *Alcmena.*

Amp. What gross Absurdities are these!

Sos. O Lord, O Lord, what Absurdities! as plain as any Pack-staff. That other me, had posted himself there before me, me. You won't give a Man leave to speak Poetically now; or else I wou'd say, That I was arriv'd at the Door, before I came thither.

Amp. This must either be a Dream, or Drunkenness, or Mad-ness in thee. Leave your Buffooning and Lying, I am not in 80 humour to bear it, Sirrah.

Sos. I wou'd you shou'd know I scorn a Lye, and am a Man of Honour in every thing, but just Fighting. I tell you once again in plain sincerity, and simplicity of Heart, that before last Night I never took my self but for one single individual *Sosia;* but, coming to our Door, I found my self, I know not how, divided, and as it were split into two *Sosia's.*

Amp. Leave Buffooning: I see you wou'd make me laugh, but you play the Fool scurvily.

Sos. That may be: but if I am a Fool, I am not the only Fool 90 in this company.

Amp. How now Impudence! I shall————

Sos. Be not in wrath Sir: I meant not you: I cannot possibly be the only Fool; for if I am one Fool, I must certainly be two Fools; because, as I told you, I am double.

Amp. That one shou'd be two, is very probable!

Sos. Have not you seen a Six-pence split into two halves, by some ingenious School-Boy; which bore on either side the Im-pression of the Monarchs Face? now as those moieties were two Three-pences, and yet in effect but one Six-pence————

100 *Amp.* No more of your villanous Tropes and Figures.

Sos. Nay, if an Orator must be disarm'd of his similitudes

———

Amp. A Man had need of patience, to endure this Gibberish: be brief, and come to a conclusion.

Sos. What wou'd you have Sir? I came thither, but the t' other

85–86 self, . . . how,] ~ᴧ . . . ~ᴧ Q1–2, F, D.   98 Face?] D; ~ : Q1–2, F.
99 Six-pence] ~ . Q1–2, F, D.   101 similitudes] Q2, F; ~ . Q1, D.

I was there before me: for that there was two I's, is as certain,
as that I have two Eyes in this Head of mine. This I, that am
here, was weary: the t' other I was fresh: this I was peaceable,
and t' other I was a hectoring Bully I.

110   *Amp.* And thou expect'st I shou'd believe thee?

Sos. No, I am not so unreasonable: for I cou'd never have
believ'd it my self, if I had not been well beaten into it: But a
Cudgel you know is a convincing Argument in a brawny Fist:
What shall I say, but that I was compell'd at last to acknowledge
my self! I found that he was very I, without fraud, cozen, or
deceit. Besides, I view'd my self, as in a Mirror, from Head to
Foot: He was Handsome, of a noble presence, a charming Air,
loose and free in all his Motions: And saw he was so much I,
that I shou'd have reason to be better satisfied with my own
120 Person, if his Hands had not been a little of the heaviest.

Amph. Once again to a Conclusion: Say you pass'd by him,
and entred into the House.

Sosia. I am a Friend to Truth, and say no such thing: He defended the door and I could not enter.

Amph. How, not enter!

Sosia. Why, how shou'd I enter, unless I were a Spright to
glide by him, and shoot my self through Locks, and Bolts, and
two-inch-boards?

Amph. O Coward! Didst thou not attempt to pass?

130   *Sosia.* Yes, and was repuls'd and beaten for my pains.

Amph. Who beat thee?

Sosia. I beat Me.

Amph. Didst thou beat thy self?

Sosia. I don't mean *I,* here: but the absent *Me,* beat me here
present.

Amph. There's no end of this intricate piece of Nonsense.

Sosia. 'Tis only Nonsense because I speak it who am a poor
fellow; but it wou'd be Sense, and substantial Sense, if a great
Man said it, that was back'd with a Title, and the Eloquence
140 of ten Thousand Pounds a year.

105–109   t' other . . . t' other . . . t' other] Q2, F, D; to'ther . . . to'ther . . .
to'ther Q1.
118   Motions:] ∼ . Q1–2, F, D.

Amph. No more; But let us enter: Hold; my *Alcmena* is coming out, and has prevented me! How strangely will she be surpriz'd to see me here, so unexpectedly!

Enter Alcmena *and* Phædra.

Alcm. to Phædra. Make haste after me to the Temple; that we may thank the Gods for this glorious Success, which *Amphitryon* has had against the Rebels.

  Oh Heavens!   [*Seeing him.*

Amph. Those Heav'ns, and all their blest Inhabitants,

              [*Saluting her.*

Grant, that the sweet rewarder of my pains

150 May still be kind, as on our Nuptial Night.

 Alcm. So soon return'd!

 Amph. So soon return'd! Is this my Welcome home?

             [*Stepping back.*

So soon return'd says I am come unwish'd.

This is no Language of desiring Love:

Love reckons Hours for Months, and Days for Years:

And every little Absence is an Age.

 Alcm. What says my Lord?

 Amph.   No, my *Alcmena,* no:

True Love, by its impatience measures Time,

And the dear Object never comes too soon.

160 *Alcm.* Nor ever came you so, nor ever shall:

But you your self are chang'd from what you were,

Pall'd in Desires, and surfeited of Bliss;

Not so I met you at your last return,

When, Yesternight, I flew into your Arms,

And melted in your warm Embrace.

 Amph.   How's this?

 Alcm. Did not my Soul ev'n sparkle at my Eyes,

And shoot it self into your much lov'd Bosome?

Did I not tremble with excess of Joy?

---

144 *to*] D; to Q1–2, F.   152 *So soon return'd*] So soon return'd Q1–2, F, D.
153 *So soon return'd*] So soon return'd, Q1–2, F, D.
161 But you] D; ∼ ∼ , Q1–2, F.   163 return,] ∼ ; Q1–2, F, D.

Nay agonize with pleasure at your sight,
170 With such inimitable Proofs of Passion,
As no false Love could feign!
    Amph.   What's this you tell me?
    Alcm. Far short of Truth, by Heav'n!
And you return'd those Proofs with Usury;
And left me, with a Sigh, at Break of Day.
Have you forgot?
    Amph.   Or have you dream't *Alcmena?*
Perhaps some kind, revealing Deity,
Has whisper'd in your Sleep, the pleasing News
Of my Return; and you believ'd it real!
Perhaps too, in your Dream, you us'd me kindly;
180 And my preventing Image, reap'd the Joys
You meant awake to me.
    Alcm. Some Melancholy Vapour, sure, has seiz'd
Your Brain, *Amphitryon,* and disturb'd your Sense:
Or Yesternight is not so long a time,
But you might yet remember; and not force
An honest Blush into my glowing Cheeks,
For that which lawful Marriage makes no Crime.
    Amph. I thank you for my Melancholy Vapour.
    Alc. 'Tis but a just requital for my Dream.
190   *Phædra.* I find my Master took too much of the Creature last
night, and now is Angling for a Quarrel, that no more may be
expected from him to Night, when he has no Assets.   [*Aside.*
    [*In the mean time* Amph. *and* Alcm. *walk by themselves,
       and frown at each other as they meet.*
    Amph. You dare not justifie it to my face.
    Alcm. Not what?
    Amph.   That I return'd before this hour.
    Alcm. You dare not, sure, deny you came last night,
And staid till Break of Day?
    Amph.   O Impudence!———

192+ *s.d.* Alcm.] Q2, F; Alch. Q1; Alc. D.   194 hour.] D; ~ ? Q1–2, F.
196–197 Impudence!——— / Why] Impudence!———Why Q1–2, F, D.

Why *Sosia!*

Sosia. Nay, I say nothing; for all things here, may go by Enchantment (as they did with me) for ought I know.

200   *Alcm.* Speak, *Phædra;* Was he here?

Phædra. You know, Madam, I am but a Chamber-maid; and
by my place, I am to forget all that was done over-night in Love-
Matters,————unless my Master please to rub up my Memory
with another Diamond.

Amph. Now in the name of all the Gods, *Alcmena*,
A little recollect your scatter'd Thoughts;
And weigh what you have said.

Alcm. I weigh'd it well, *Amphitryon*, e're I spoke:
And She, and *Bromia*, all the Slaves, and Servants,
210 Can witness they beheld you, when you came.
If other Proof were wanting, tell me how
I came to know your Fight, your Victory,
The Death of *Pterelas*, in single Combat?
And, farther, from whose hands I had a Jewel:
The Spoyls of him you slew.

Amph.   This is amazing!
Have I already given you those Diamonds,
The Present I reserv'd?

Alcm.   'Tis an odd Question:
You see I wear 'em; Look.

Amph.   Now answer, *Sosia.*

Sosia. Yes, now I can answer with a safe Conscience, as to that
220 point, all the rest may be Art Magick; but, as for the Diamonds,
here they are, under safe custody.

Alcm. Then what are these upon my Arm?   [*To* Sosia.

Sosia. Flints, or Pebbles, or some such Trumpery of enchanted
Stones.

Phædra. They say the proof of a true Diamond is to glitter
in the dark; I think my Master had best take my Lady into
some By-corner, and try whose Diamond will sparkle best.

Sosia. Yet now I think on't, Madam, did not a certain Friend
of mine present 'em to you?

---

219   safe] Q2, F, D; fafe Q1.

230   *Alcm.* What Friend?

    Sosia. Why another *Sosia;* one that made himself *Sosia* in my despight, and also unsociated me.

    Amph. Sirrah, leave your nauseous Nonsense: break open the Seal, and take out the Diamonds.

    Sosia. More words than one to a Bargain, Sir; I thank you: That's no part of prudence for me to commit Burglary upon the Seals: Do you look first upon the Signet, and tell me in your Conscience, whether the Seals be not as firm as when you clapt the Wax upon them.

240   *Amph.* The Signature is firm.   *[Looking.*

    Sosia. Then take the Signature into your own custody, and open it; for I will have nothing done at my proper peril.

                        [Giving him the Casket.

    Amph. O Heav'ns! Here's nothing, but an empty space; the Nest where they were laid.   *[Breaking open the Seal.*

    Sosia. Then if the Birds are flown, the Fault's not mine; here has been fine conjuring work; or else the Jewel, knowing to whom it shou'd be given, took occasion to steal out, by a natural instinct, and ty'd it self upon that pretty Arm.

    Amph. Can this be possible!

250   *Sosia.* Yes, very possible: You, my Lord *Amphitryon,* may have brought forth another You my Lord *Amphitryon,* as well as *I Sosia* have brought forth another *Me Sosia;* and our Diamonds may have procreated these Diamonds; and so we are all three double.

    Phædra. If this be true, I hope my Goblet has gigg'd another Golden Goblet: and then they may carry double upon all four.

                               [Aside.

    Alcm. My Lord, I have stood silent, out of wonder What you cou'd wonder at.

    Amph. A chilling Sweat, a damp of Jealousie,   *[Aside.*
260 Hangs on my Brows, and clams upon my Limbs.
I fear; and yet I must be satisfied:
And, to be satisfy'd, I must dissemble.

---

234 Diamonds.] Q2, F, D; ∼ʌ Q1.   252 *Sosia;*] Q2, F, D; ∼ . Q1.
254 double.] Q2, F, D; ∼ , Q1.

Alcm. Why muse you so, and murmur to your self?
If you repent your Bounty, take it back.

Amph. Not so: but, if you please, relate what past,
At our last Enterview.

Alcm. That Question wou'd infer you were not here.

Amph. I say not so;
I only wou'd refresh my memory;
270 And have my Reasons to desire the Story.

Phædra. So: This is as good sport for me as an Examination
of a great Belly before a Magistrate.

Alcm. The Story is not long: you know I met you,
Kiss'd you, and prest you close within my Arms,
With all the tenderness of Wively Love.

Amph. I cou'd have spar'd that Kindness.   [*Aside.*
And what did I?   [*To her.*

Alcm. You strain'd me with a Masculine Embrace;
As you wou'd squeeze my Soul out.

Amph.   Did I so?
280 *Alcm.* You did.

Amph.   Confound those Arms that were so kind.
———   [*Aside.*
Proceed, proceed.———   [*To her.*

Alcm. You wou'd not stay to sup; but, much complaining
Of your drowsiness, and want of natural Rest———

Amph. Made haste to Bed: Ha, was't not so? Go on———
And stab me with each Syllable thou speak'st.   [*Aside.*

Phædra. So, now 'tis coming, now 'tis coming.

Alcm. I have no more to say.

Amph.   Why, went we not to Bed?

Alcm. Why not?
Is it a Crime for Husband and for Wife
290 To go to Bed, My Lord?

Amph.   Perfidious Woman!

---

264 back.] D; ~ – Q1; ~ ———Q2, F.   280 kind.] ~∧ Q1–2, F, D.
282–283 complaining / Of . . . Rest———] complaining of . . . Rest———
Q1–2, F, D.
284–285 s.d. on——— / And . . . speak'st. [*Aside.*] on——— [*Aside.* / And . . .
speak'st. Q1–2, F; on——— / [*Aside.*] And . . . speak'st. D.

Alcm. Ungrateful Man!

Amph.   She justifies it too!

Alcm. I need not justifie: Of what am I accus'd?

Amph. Of all that prodigality of Kindness,
Giv'n to another, and usurp'd from me.
So bless me Heav'n, if since my first departure,
I ever set my foot upon this Threshold.
So am I innocent of all those Joys,
And dry of those Embraces.

Alcm.   Then I, it seems, am false?

Amph. As surely false, as what thou say'st is true.

300   *Alcm.* I have betray'd my Honour, and my Love?
And am a foul Adultress?

Amph.   What thou art,
Thou stand'st condemn'd to be, by thy Relation.

Alcm. Go, thou unworthy Man; for ever go:
No more my Husband; go thou base Impostour;
Who tak'st a vile pretence to taint my Fame;
And, not content to leave, wouldst ruine me.
Enjoy thy wish'd Divorce: I will not plead
My Innocence, of this pretended Crime:
I need not; spet thy Venom; do thy worst:

310 But know, the more thou wou'dst expose my Vertue,
Like purest Linen laid in open Air,
'Twill bleach the more, and whiten to the view.

Amph. 'Tis well thou art prepar'd for thy Divorce:
For, know thou too, that after this Affront,
This foul Indignity, done to my Honour,
Divorcement is but petty Reparation:
But, since thou hast, with Impudence affirm'd
My false Return, and brib'd my Slaves to vouch it,
The Truth shall, in the face of *Thebes* be clear'd;

320 Thy Unkle, the Companion of my Voyage,
And all the Crew of Sea-men, shall be brought,
Who were embark'd, and came with me to Land;
Nor parted, till I reach'd this cursed Door:
So shall this Vision of my late Return,

Stand a detected Lye; and woe to those
Who thus betray'd my Honour.

    Sosia. Sir, Shall I wait on you?

    Amph. No, I will go alone: Expect me here.

                                      [*Exit* Amphitryon.

    Phædra. Please you————that I————   [*To* Alcmena.

330   *Alcm.* Oh! Nothing now can please me:
Darkness, and Solitude, and Sighs, and Tears,
And all th' inseparable Train of Grief,
Attend my Steps for ever.————   [*Exit* Alcmena.

    Sosia. What if I shou'd lye now, and say we have been here
before? I never saw any good that came of telling truth. [*Aside.*

    Phædra. He makes no more Advances to me: I begin a little
to suspect, that my Gold Goblet will prove but Copper.   [*Aside.*

    Sosia. Yes, 'tis resolv'd, I will lye abominably, against the
Light of my own Conscience. For suppose the t' other *Sosia* has
340 been here: perhaps that strong Dog has not only beaten me,
but also has been predominant upon my Wife, and most car-
nally misus'd her! Now, by asking certain Questions of her,
with a Side-Wind, I may come to understand how Squares go;
and whether my Nuptial Bed be violated.   [*Aside.*

    Phædra. Most certainly he has learn'd Impudence of his
Master; and will deny his being here: but that shall not serve
his turn, to cheat me of my Present! [*Aside.*]————Why *Sosia!*
What, in a brown Study?

    Sosia. A little *cogitabund,* or so; concerning this dismal Revo-
350 lution in our Family!

    Phædra. But that shou'd not make you neglect your duty to
me, your Mistress.

    Sosia. Pretty Soul; I wou'd thou wert: upon condition that
old *Bromia* were six Foot under ground.

    Phædra. What! Is all your hot Courtship to me, dwindl'd
into a poor unprofitable Wish? You may remember, I did not
bid you absolutely despair.

    Sosia. No; for all things yet may be accommodated, in an

---

333 ever.] ~∧ Q1–2, F, D.   339 t' other] F; tother Q1–2; other D.
347 Present! [*Aside.*]————Why] Present!————[*Aside.* Why Q1–2, F, D.

amicable manner, betwixt my Master and my Lady.

360   *Phædra.* I mean, to the Business, betwixt you and me———

Sosia. Why, I hope we two never quarrell'd?

Phæd. Must I remember you of a certain Promise that you made me at our last parting?

Sosia. Oh, when I went to the Army: that I shou'd still be praising thy Beauty to Judge *Gripus,* and keep up his Affections to thee.

Phæd. No, I mean the Business betwixt you and me this Morning,———that you promis'd me———

Sosia. That I promis'd thee———I find it now: That strong

370 Dog, my Brother *Sosia,* has been here before me, and made Love to her.   [*Aside.*

Phæd. You are considering, whether or no, you should keep your Promise———

Sosia. That I shou'd keep my Promise.———The truth on't is, she's anotherghess Morsel than old *Bromia.*   [*Aside.*

Phæd. And I had rather you should break it, in a manner, and, as it were, and in some Sense———

Sosia. In a manner, and as it were, and in some Sense, thou say'st?———I find, the strong Dog has only tickl'd up her

380 Imagination, and not enjoy'd her: so that with my own Limbs, I may perform the sweetness of his Function with her. [*Aside.*]
———No, sweet Creature, the Promise shall not be broken; but what I have undertaken, I will perform like a Man of Honour.   [*To her.*

Phæd. Then, you remember the Preliminaries of the Present———

Sosia. Yes, yes, in gross I do remember, something; but this disturbance of the Family, has somewhat stupify'd my Memory: Some pretty *Quelque chose,* I warrant thee; some acceptable

390 Toy, of small value.

Phæd. You may call a Gold Goblet, a Toy: But I put a greater value upon your Presents.

---

368   Morning.———] Q2, F; ～ ———: Q1, D.
369   thee] Q2, F; ～ . Q1, D.   377   Sense] F; ～ . Q1–2, D.
381–382   her. [*Aside.*]———] her. [*Aside.* Q1–2, F, D.
389   *chose*] Q2, F, D; chose Q1.

Sosia. A Gold Goblet, say'st thou! Yes, now I think on't, it was a kind of a Gold Goblet; as a Gratuity after Consummation.

Phæd. No, no; I had rather make sure of one Bribe before hand, than be promis'd ten Gratuities.

Sosia. Yes, now I remember, it was, in some Sense, a Gold Goblet, by way of Earnest; and it contain'd————

Phæd. One large————

400 *Sosia.* How, one large————

Phæd. Gallon.

Sosia. No; that was somewhat too large, in Conscience: It was not a whole Gallon; but it may contain, reasonably speaking, one large————Thimble-full: But Gallons and Thimble-fulls are so like, that in speaking, I might easily mistake them.

Phæd. Is it come to this? Out Traytor!

Sosia. I had been a Traytor, indeed, to have betray'd thee to the swallowing of a Gallon: but a Thimblefull of Cordial-water, is easily sipt off: and then, this same Goblet, is so very
410 light too, that it will be no Burthen, to carry it about with thee, in thy Pocket.

Phæd. O Apostate to thy Love! O perjur'd Villain!

Enter Bromia.

What, are you here, *Bromia!* I was telling him his own: I was giving him a Rattle for his Treacheries to you, his Love: You see I can be a Friend, upon occasion.

Brom. Ay, Chicken, I never doubted of thy Kindness: but, for this Fugitive,————this Rebel,————this Miscreant————

Sosia. A kind Welcome, to an absent Lover, as I have been.

Brom. Ay; and a kind Greeting you gave me, at your Return;
420 when you us'd me so barbarously, this Morning.

Sosia. The t' other *Sosia* has been with her too: and has us'd her barbarously: barbarously, that is to say, uncivilly: and un-civilly; I am afraid that means, too civilly.   [*Aside.*

————

412+ *s.d. Enter*] D; [~ Q1–2, F (*s.d. at right margin on line 412*).
417 Miscreant] F; ~ . Q1–2, D.

Phæd. You had best deny you were here this Morning! And by the same Token————

Sosia. Nay, no more Tokens, for Heaven's sake, dear *Phædra.* ————Now must I ponder with my self a little, whether it be better for me, to have been here, or not to have been here, this Morning. [*Aside.*

Enter a Servant.

430 *Servant. Phædra,* My Lord's without; and will not enter till he has first spoken with you. [*Exit Servant.*

Phæd. Oh that I could stay to help worry thee for this Abuse: but the best on't is, I leave thee in good hands. [*To him in private.*]————Farewell Thimble.————To him, *Bromia.* [*Exit* Phædra.

Brom. No; you did not beat me, and put me into a Swound, and deprive me of the natural use of my Tongue for a long Half-hour: You did not beat me down, with your little Wand: But I shall teach you to use your Rod another time————I shall.

440 *Sosia.* Put her into a Swound, with my little Wand, and so forth: That's more than ever I cou'd do. These are terrible Circumstances that some *Sosia* or another, has been here: Now, if he has literally beaten her, Grammercy, Brother *Sosia;* he has but done, what I wou'd have done, if I had durst: But I am afraid it was only a damn'd Love-figure; and that the Wand that lay'd her asleep, might signifie the Peace-maker. [*Aside.*

Brom. Now you are snuffling upon a cold Scent, for some pitiful Excuse: I know you: twenty to one, but you will plead a Drunkenness: You are usd to be pot-valiant.

450 *Sosia.* I was pumping, and I thank her, she has invented for me.————Yes; *Bromia,* I must confess I was exalted: and, possibly, I might scoure upon thee, or perhaps be a little more familiar with thy person, by the way of Kindness, than if I had

426–427 *Phædra.*————] ~ .ʌ Q1–2, F, D.
433–434 hands. [*To . . . private.*]] hands————[*To . . . private.* Q1–2, F, D. (*private.*] D).

been sober; but, prithee, inform me what I did; that I may consider what satisfaction I am to make thee.

Bromia. Are you there, at your Dog-tricks! You wou'd be forgetting, wou'd you? like a drunken Bully that affronts over-night, and, when he is call'd to account, the next Morning, re-members nothing of the Quarrel; and asks pardon, to avoid
460 fighting.

Sosia. By *Bacchus,* I was overtaken; but I shou'd be loth that I committed any folly with thee.

Bromia. I am sure, I kept my self awake all night, that I did, in expectation of your coming.   [*Crying.*

Sosia. But what amends did I make thee, when I came?

Bromia. You know well enough, to my sorrow; but that you play the Hypocrite.

Sosia. I warrant, I was monstrous kind to thee.————

Brom. Yes, monstrous kind indeed: You never said a truer
470 word: for, when I came to kiss you, you pull'd away your Mouth, and turn'd your Cheek to me.

Sosia. Good.

Brom. How, Good! Here's fine Impudence: He justifies!
————.

Sosia. Yes, I do justifie, that I turn'd my Cheek, like a pru-dent person, that my Breath might not offend thee: for, now I remember, I had eaten Garlick.

Brom. Ay, you remember, and forget, just as it makes for you, or against you: but, to mend the matter, you never spoke
480 one civil word to me: but stood like a stock, without sense or motion.

Sosia. Yet better.   [*Aside.*

Brom. After which, I lovingly invited you to take your place in your Nuptial Bed, as the Laws of Matrimony oblige you: and you inhumanly refus'd me.

Sosia. Ay, there's the main point of the Business! Art thou morally certain, that I refus'd thee? Look me now in the face, and say I did not commit Matrimony with thee!

465   came?] ~ ! Q1-2, F, D.   487   thee?] D; ~ : Q1-2, F.

Brom. I wonder how thou canst look me in the face, after
490 that refusal!

Sosia. Say it once again, that I did not feloniously come to
Bed to thee!

Brom. No, thou cold Traytor, thou know'st thou didst not.

Sosia. Best of all; 'twas discreetly done of me to abstain.

Brom. What, do you insult upon me too!

Sosia. No, I do not insult upon you;————but————

Brom. But what? How was it discreetly done then? Ha!

Sosia. Because it is the receiv'd Opinion of Physicians, that
nothing but puling Chitts, and Booby-Fools, are procreated in
500 Drunkenness.

Brom. A receiv'd Opinion, Snivel-guts! I'll be judg'd by all
the marry'd Women of this Town, if any one of 'em has receiv'd it: The Devil take the Physicians, for medling in our
Matters: If a Husband will be rul'd by them, there are five
weeks of Abstinence in *Dog-days* too; for fear a Child that was
got in *August,* should be born just nine Months after, and be
blear-ey'd, like a *May*-Kitten.

Sosia. Let the Physicians alone; they are honest Men, whatever the World says of 'em. But, for a certain reason, that I best
510 know, I am glad that Matter ended so fairly and peaceably betwixt us.

Brom. Yes 'twas very fair and peaceable: to strike a Woman
down, and beat her most outrageously.

Sosia. Is it possible that I drubb'd thee!

Brom. I find your drift: You wou'd fain be provoking me to
a new Trial now: but, i' faith, you shall bring me to no more
handy-blows: I shall make bold to trust to my Tongue hereafter: You never durst have offer'd to hold up a finger against
me, till you went a Trooping.

520 *Sosia.* Then I am a Conqueror: and I laud my own Courage:
This Renown I have atchiev'd by Souldiership and Stratagem.
Know your Duty, Spouse, henceforward to your supream Com-
mander.   [*Strutting.*

Enter Jupiter *and* Phædra, *attended by Musicians and Dancers.*

---

495 What,] F, D; ~∧ Q1-2.

Phædra. Indeed I wondred at your quick return.

Jup. Ev'n so Almighty Love will have it, *Phædra;*
And the stern Goddess of sweet-bitter Cares,
Who bows our Necks beneath her brazen Yoke.
I wou'd have mann'd my heart, and held it out;
But, when I thought of what I had possest,
530 Those joys, that never end, but to begin,
O, I am all on fire to make my peace;
And die, *Jove* knows, as much as I can die,
Till I am reconcil'd.

Phæd. I fear 'twill be in vain.

Jup.   'Tis difficult:
But nothing is impossible to Love;
To Love like mine: for I have prov'd his force,
And my *Alcmena* too has felt his Dart.
If I submit, there's hope.

Phæd. 'Tis possible I may sollicit for you.

540 *Jup.* But wilt thou promise me to do thy best?

Phæd. Nay I promise nothing———unless you begin to
promise first.———   [*Curt'sying.*

Jup. I wou'not be ungrateful.

Phæd. Well; I'll try to bring her to the Window: You shall
have a fair shoot at her: if you can bring her down, you are a
good Markes-man.

Jup. That's all I ask:
And I will so reward thee, Gentle *Phædra*———

Phæd. What, with Cats-guts and Rosin! This *Sol-la* is but a
550 lamentable, empty sound.

Jup. Then there's a sound will please thee better.
                          [*Throwing her a Purse.*

Phæd. Ay, there's something of Melody in this sound. I cou'd
dance all day, to the Musick of *Chink, Chink.*   [*Exit* Phædra.

---

529 possest,] ∼ ; Q1–2, F, D.   531 peace;] ∼ : Q1–2, F, D.
535–536 Love; . . . mine:] D; ∼ : . . . ∼ ; Q1–2, F.
541–542 *set as verse in Q1–2, F, D* (begin / To).
548 *Phædra*] Q2, F, D; ∼ . Q1.   549 *Sol-la*] D; ∼ ; Q1–2, F.
550 empty] D; ∼ , Q1–2, F.
552–553 *set as verse in Q1–2, F, D* (sound. / I).

Jup. Go *Sosia* round our *Thebes*,
To *Polydas,* to *Tranio,* and to *Gripus,*
Companions of our War; invite 'em all,
To joyn their Pray'rs to smooth *Alcmena's* Brow;
And, with a solemn Feast, to crown the day.

    Sosia, taking Jupiter about the Knees. Let me embrace you,
560 Sir.———[Jupiter *pushes him away.*] Nay, you must give me
leave to express my Gratitude; I have not eaten, to say eating,
nor drunk, to say drinking, never since our villanous encamp-
ing so near the Enemy: 'Tis true, I scap'd the bloody-Flux, because I had so little in my Bowels to come out; and I durst let
nothing go, in Conscience, because I had nothing to swallow in
the room on't.

    Jup. You, *Bromia,* see that all things be prepar'd,
With that Magnificence, as if some God
Were Guest, or Master here.

570   *Sosia.* Or rather, as much, as if twenty Gods were to be
Guests, or Masters here.

    Brom. That you may eat for to day, and to morrow.

    Sosia. Or, rather again, for to day and yesterday; and as many
Months backwards, as I am indebted to my own Belly.

    Jup. Away both of you. [*Exeunt* Sosia *and* Bromia *severally.*

    Jup. Now I have pack'd him hence; thou, other *Sosia,*
(Who, tho' thou art not present, hear'st my voice,)
Be ready to attend me at my Call;
And to supply his place.

    Enter Mercury *to* Jupiter. Alcmena *and* Phædra
    appear above, Jupiter *seeing* Alcmena.

    Jup.   See, she appears:
580 This is my Bribe to *Phædra;* when I made

---

559 *Sosia, taking Jupiter . . . Knees.*] Sosia. (*Taking* Jupiter . . . *Knees.*) Q1–2,
F; *Sos.* [*Taking* Jupiter . . . *Knees.*] D.
560 s.d. *away.*]] D; ∼ ·ʌ Q1–2, F.
564 out;] Q2, F; ∼ , Q1, D.
579 s.d. *Enter . . . Jupiter.*] D; [∼ . . . ∼. Q1–2, F (*at right margin;*
(*Enter* F).
579 s.d. *above,*] ∼ . Q1–2, F, D.

This Gold, I made a greater God than *Jove,*
And gave my own Omnipotence away.

Jupiter *signs to the Musicians. Song and Dance: after which,*
Alcmena *withdraws, frowning.*

SONG.

I.

> Celia, *that I once was blest*
> *Is now the Torment of my Brest;*
> *Since to curse me, you bereave me*
> *Of the Pleasures I possest:*
> *Cruel Creature, to deceive me!*
> *First to love, and then to leave me!*

II.

> *Had you the Bliss refus'd to grant,*
> *Then I had never known the want:*
> *But possessing once the Blessing,*
> *Is the Cause of my Complaint:*
> *Once possessing is but tasting;*
> *'Tis no Bliss that is not lasting.*

III.

> Celia *now is mine no more;*
> *But I am hers; and must adore:*
> *Nor to leave her will endeavour;*
> *Charms, that captiv'd me before,*
> *No unkindness can dissever;*
> *Love that's true, is Love for ever.*

Jup. O stay.
Merc.   She's gone; and seem'd to frown at parting.

582+   SONG.] Q2, F, D; ∼ – Q1; First Song, in the third Act. f1; A New song
sung at the Theatre Royall, in the last new Play call'd Amphitrion————*The
words by Mr. Dryden, Sung by Mr. Bowman*ʌ q; A SONG. d; *omitted from* m1.

Jup. Follow, and thou shalt see her soon appeas'd:
For I, who made her, know her inward state;
No Woman, once well pleas'd, can throughly hate:
I gave 'em Beauty, to subdue the strong:
(A mighty Empire, but it lasts not long:)
I gave 'em Pride to make Mankind their Slave;
But, in exchange, to Men I Flattery gave:
Th' offending Lover, when he lowest lies,
610 Submits, to conquer; and but kneels, to rise.

[*Exeunt.*

The End of the Third Act.

ACT IV.   SCENE I.

Enter Jupiter *following* Alcmena; Mercury *and* Phædra.

Jupiter. O Stay, my dear *Alcmena,* hear me speak.
Alcm. No, I wou'd fly thee, to the ridge of earth,
And leap the Precipice, to scape thy sight.
Jup. For pity———
Alcm.   Leave me, thou ungrateful Man.
Jup. I cannot leave you: no; but like a Ghost
Whom your Unkindness murder'd, will I haunt you.
Alcm. Once more, be gone: I'm odious to my self
For having lov'd thee once.
Jup. Hate not the best and fairest of your kind:
10 Nor can you hate your Lover, tho' you wou'd:
Your Tears, that fall so gently, are but grief:
There may be Anger; but there must be Love.
The Dove, that murmurs at her Mate's neglect,
But counterfeits a coyness, to be courted.
Alcm. Courtship, from thee, and after such affronts!
Jup. Is this that everlasting Love you vow'd,

610+ s.d. [*Exeunt.*] *omitted from* Q1–2, F, D.
ACT IV. SCENE I.] D; The FOURTH ACT. Q1–2; ACT IV. F.
s.d. *Enter* Jupiter] Jupiter Q1–2, F, D.

Last Night, when I was circled in your arms?
Remember what you swore.———

Alcm. Think what thou wert, and who cou'd swear too much?
20 Think what thou art, and that unswears it all.

Jup. Can you forsake me, for so small a fault?
'Twas but a Jest, perhaps too far pursu'd:
'Twas but at most, a Trial of your Faith,
How you cou'd bear unkindness:
'Twas but to get a reconciling Kiss,
A wanton Stratagem of Love.

Alcm. See how he doubles, like a hunted Hare,
A Jest, and then a Trial, and a Bait;
All stuff, and dawbing!

Jup.   Think me jealous, then.
30 *Alcm.* O that I cou'd; for that's a noble Crime;
And which a Lover can, with ease, forgive:
'Tis the high pulse of Passion, in a Fever;
A sickly draught, but shews a burning Thirst:
Thine was a Surfeit, not a Jealousie:
And in that loathing of thy full gorg'd Love,
Thou saw'st the nauseous Object, with disdain.

Jup. O think not that: for you are ever new:
Your fruits of Love, are like eternal Spring
In happy Climes, where some are in the bud,
40 Some green, and ripening some, while others fall.

Alcm. Ay, now you tell me this,
When rous'd desires, and fresh recruits of force,
Enable languish'd Love to take the field.
But never hope to be receiv'd again:
You wou'd again deny you were receiv'd;
And brand my spotless Fame.

Jup. I will not dare to justifie my Crime,
But only point you where to lay the blame:
Impute it to the Husband, not the Lover.
50 *Alcm.* How vainly wou'd the Sophister divide,
And make the Husband and the Lover two!

---

29 then.] F, D; ~ : Q1-2.   51 Lover] ~ , Q1-2, F, D.

Jup. Yes 'tis the Husband is the guilty Wretch:
His Insolence forgot the Sweets of Love,
And, deeming them his due, despis'd the Feast.
Not so the famish'd Lover cou'd forget:
He knew he had been there, and had been blest,
With all that Hope can wish, or Sense can bear.

    Alcm. Husband, and Lover, both alike I hate.

    Jup. And I confess I have deserv'd that hate: [*Kneeling.*
60 Too charming fair, I kneel for your forgiveness:
I beg by those fair eyes,
Which gave me wounds that time can never cure;
Receive my Sorrows, and restore my Joys.

    Alcm. Unkind, and cruel! I can speak no more.

    Jup. O give it vent *Alcmena*, give it vent;
I merit your reproach, I wou'd be curs'd:
Let your Tongue curse me, while your Heart forgives.

    Alcm. Can I forget such Usage!

    Jup.   Can you hate me?

    Alcm. I'll do my best: for sure I ought to hate you.

70   *Jup.* That Word was only hatch'd upon your Tongue,
It came not from your Heart. But try again,
And if, once more, you can but say *I hate you*,
My Sword shall do you justice.

    Alcm.   Then, I hate you.————

    Jup. Then you pronounce the Sentence of my Death?

    Alcm. I hate you, much; but yet I love you more.

    Jup. To prove that Love, then say, that you forgive me:
For there remains but this Alternative:
Resolve to pardon, or to punish me.

    Alcm. Alas, what I resolve appears too plain:
80 In saying that I cannot hate, I pardon.

    Jup. But what's a Pardon worth, without a Seal?
Permit me, in this Transport of my Joy————

                           [*Kisses her Hand.*

---

62 wounds] F; ~ , Q1–2, D.   62 that] Q2, F, D; That Q1.
66 your] Q2, F, D; yonr Q1.   72 say *I hate you*] say, I hate you Q1–2, F, D.
77 Alternative] Q2, F, D; Alternetive Q1.

Alcm. Forbear; I am offended with my self,

> [*Putting him gently away with her Hand.*

That I have shewn this Weakness.———Let me go,

Where I may blush, alone.———[*Going; and looking back on
him.*] But come not you:

Lest I shou'd spoil you, with excess of Fondness,

And let you love again.———   [*Exit* Alcmena.

    Jup. Forbidding me to follow, she invites me: [*Aside.*

This is the Mould of which I made the Sex:

90 I gave 'em but one Tongue, to say us nay;

And two kind Eyes, to grant.———[*To* Mercury.] Be sure that
none

Approach, to interrupt our privacy. [*Exit* Jupiter *after* Alcmena.

Mercury *and* Phædra *remain.*

    Merc. Your Lady has made the Challenge of Reconciliation
to my Lord: Here's a fair Example for us two, *Phædra.*

    Phæd. No Example at all, *Sosia:* for my Lady had the Dia-
monds aforehand, and I have none of the Gold Goblet.

    Merc. The Goblet shall be forth-coming; if thou wilt give
me weight for weight.

    Phæd. Yes, and measure for measure too, *Sosia:* that is, For
100 a Thimbleful of Gold, a Thimbleful of Love.

    Merc. What think you now, *Phædra?* Here's a weighty Ar-
gument of Love for you.

> [*Pulling out the Goblet in a Case, from under his Cloak.*

    Phæd. Now *Jupiter,* of his Mercy, let me kiss thee, O thou
dear Metal!

> [*Taking it in both Hands.*

    Merc. And *Venus,* of her Mercy, let me kiss thee, dear, dear
Phædra.

    Phæd. Not so fast, *Sosia!* there's a damn'd Proverb in your

---

85   *s.d. him.*] But . . . you:] *him.* / But . . . you: Q1–2, F, D.

91   grant.———] ∼ ·ᴧ Q1–2, F, D.

91   *s.d.* [*To* Mercury.] Be . . . none] Be . . . none [*To* Mercury.ᴧ Q1–2, F, D.

92   privacy.] D; ∼ᴧ Q1–2, F.   92+   *s.d. remain*] Q2, F, D; remain Q1.

way: *Many things happen betwixt the Cup and the Lips,* you
know.

110   *Merc.* Why, thou wilt not cheat me of my Goblet?

    Phæd. Yes; as sure as you wou'd cheat me of my Maiden-
head: I am yet, but just even with you, for the last Trick you
play'd me. And, besides; this is but a bare Retaining Fee; you
must give me another, before the Cause is open'd.

    Merc. Shall I not come to your Bed side, to Night?

    Phæd. No, nor to Morrow-Night, neither: but this shall be
my Sweet-heart in your place: 'tis a better Bed-fellow, and will
keep me warmer, in cold Weather.   [*Exit* Phædra.

Mercury alone.

    Merc. Now, what's the God of Wit in a Woman's Hand? This
120 very Goblet I stole from *Gripus;* and he got it out of Bribes too.
But this is the common fate of ill gotten Goods, that as they
came in by Covetousness, they go out by Whoring.

Enter Amphitryon.

————Oh, here's *Amphitryon* again, but I'll manage him above,
in the Balcony.   [*Exit* Mercury.

    Amph. Not one of those I look'd for, to be found!
As some Enchantment hid 'em from my sight!
Perhaps, as *Sosia* says, 'tis Witchcraft all:
Seals may be open'd, Diamonds may be stol'n;
But how I came, in person, yesterday,
130 And gave that Present to *Alcmena*'s hands,
That which I never gave, nor ever came,
O there's the Rock, on which my Reason splits:
Wou'd that were all! I fear my Honour, too!
I'll try her once again: She may be mad:
A wretched Remedy; but all I have,

122-123 Whoring. / *Enter* Amphitryon. / ————Oh, . . . I'll manage] D;
Whoring.————Oh, . . . I'll [*Enter* Amphitryon. / manage Q1-2; Whoring.
————Oh, . . . I'll manage [*Enter* Amphitryon.] / F.

To keep me from despair.

Mercury. This is no very charitable Action of a God, to use
                              [*From the Balcony, aside.*
him ill, who has never offended me: but my Planet disposes me
to Malice: and when we great Persons do but a little Mischief,
140 the World has a good bargain of us.

Amph. How now! what means the locking up of my Doors,
at this time of day?   [*Knocks.*

Merc. Softly, Friend, softly: You knock as loud, and as sawc-
ily, as a Lord's Footman, that was sent before him, to warn the
Family of his Honour's Visit. Sure you think the Doors have
no feeling! What the Devil are you, that rap with such Authority?

Amph. Look out, and see: 'tis I.

Merc. You: What You?

150 *Amph.* No more, I say, but open.

Merc. I'll know to whom first.

Amph. I am one that can command the doors open.

Merc. Then you had best command 'em, and try whether they
will obey You.

Amph. Dost thou not know me!

Merc. Prithee, how shou'd I know thee? Dost thou take me
for a Conjurer?

Amph. What's this? Midsummer-Moon? Is all the World
gone a madding? Why *Sosia!*

160 *Merc.* That's my Name indeed: Didst thou think I had forgot it!

Amph. Dost thou see me?

Merc. Why, dost thou pretend to go invisible? If thou hast
any business here, dispatch it quickly; I have no leasure to
throw away upon such pratling Companions.

Amph. Thy Companion, Slave? How dar'st thou use this insolent Language to thy Master!

Merc. How! Thou my Master? By what Title? I never had
any other Master, but *Amphitryon.*

170   *Amph.* Well: and for whom dost thou take me?

    Merc. For some Rogue or other; but what Rogue I know not.

    Amph. Dost thou not know me for *Amphitryon*, Slave!

    Merc. How shou'd I know thee, when I see thou dost not know thy self! thou *Amphitryon?* In what Tavern hast thou been? And how many Bottles did thy business, to metamorphose thee into my Lord?

    Amph. I will so drub thee, for this insolence!

    Merc. How now, Impudence! are you threatning your Betters! I shou'd bring you to condign punishment, but that I have
180 a great respect for the good Wine, though I find it in a Fool's Noddle.

    Amph. What, none to let me in? Why *Phædra! Bromia!*

    Merc. Peace, Fellow; if my Wife hears thee, we are both undone. At a word, *Phædra* and *Bromia* are very busie; one in making a Cawdle for my Lady; and the other in heating Napkins, to rub down my Lord, when he rises from Bed.

    Amph. Amazement seizes me.

    Merc. At what art thou amaz'd? My Master and my Lady had a falling out, and are retir'd, without Seconds, to decide the
190 Quarrel. If thou wert not a meddlesome Fool, thou woud'st not be thrusting thy Nose into other Peoples Matters. Get thee about thy business, if thou hast any; for I'll hear no more of thee.   *[Exit* Mercury *from above.*

    Amph. Brav'd by my Slave, dishonour'd by my Wife,

To what a desp'rate plunge am I reduc'd,

If this be true the Villain says! But why

That feeble *If!* It must be true; She owns it.

Now, whether to conceal, or blaze th' Affront?

One way, I spread my infamy abroad;
200 And, t' other, hide a burning coal, within,

That preys upon my Vitals: I can fix

On nothing, but on Vengeance.

    Enter to him Sosia, Polydas, Gripus, Tranio.

---

177 insolence!] D; ~ . Q1–2, F.   183 Peace,] F; ~∧ Q1–2, D.
196 says!] ~ ? Q1–2, F, D.   197 feeble *If*] ~ , If Q1–2, F, D.
200 within,] D; ~ ; Q1–2, F.

Gripus. Yonder he is; walking hastily to and fro, before his door; like a Citizen, clapping his Sides before his Shop, in a frosty Morning: 'tis to catch a Stomach, I believe.

Sosia. I begin to be affraid, that he has more stomach to my Sides, and Shoulders, than to his own Victuals. How he shakes his head! and stamps, and what strides he fetches! He's in one of his damn'd Moods again; I don't like the Looks of him.

210 *Amph.* Oh, my mannerly, fair-spoken, obedient Slave, are you there! I can reach you now, without climbing: Now we shall try who's drunk, and who's sober.

Sosia. Why this is as it shou'd be: I was somewhat suspicious that you were in a pestilent humour; Yes, we will have a crash at the Bottle, when your Lordship pleases: I have summon'd 'em, you see; and they are notable Topers; especially Judge *Gripus.*

Grip. Yes, 'faith; I never refuse my Glass, in a good Quarrel.

Amph. Why, thou insolent Villain; I'll teach a Slave how to
220 use his Master thus.   [*To* Sosia.

Sosia. Here's a fine business towards! I am sure I ran as fast as ever my legs cou'd carry me, to call 'em: nay you may trust my diligence, in all affairs belonging to the belly.

Grip. He has been very faithfull to his Commission, I'll bear him witness.

Amph. How can you be witness, where you were not present?
———The Balcony! Sirrah, the Balcony!

Sosia. Why, to my best remembrance, you never invited the Balcony.

230 *Amph.* What nonsence dost thou plead for an Excuse, of thy foul language, and thy base replies!

Sosia. You fright a man out of his senses, first; and blame him, afterwards, for talking nonsence:—but 'tis better for me to talk nonsence, than for some to do nonsence: I will say that, what e'er comes on't. Pray Sir, let all things be done decently: what, I hope, when a man is to be hang'd, he is not truss'd

---

210 *Amph.*] Q2, F, D; *Amph*ᴀ Q1.   215 summon'd] Q2, F, D; summo'nd Q1.
220 thus] Q1 (*corrected form*), Q2, F, D; hus Q1 (*uncorrected form*).
220 s.d. Sosia] Q2, F; *Sosia* Q1, D.
226–227 present?———The] ∼ ? the Q1–2, F, D (The F).

upon the Gallows, like a dumb Dog, without telling him wherefore.

Amph. By your pardon, Gentlemen: I have no longer pa-
240 tience to forbear him.

Sosia. Justice, justice, my Lord *Gripus:* as you are a true Magistrate, protect me. Here's a process of Beating going forward, without sentence given.

Grip. My Lord *Amphitryon,* this must not be: Let me first understand the demerits of the Criminal.

Sosia. Hold you to that point, I beseech your Honour, as you commiserate the Case of a poor, innocent Malefactour.

Amph. To shut the door against me, in my very face, to deny me entrance, to brave me from the Balcony, to laugh at me,
250 to threaten me: what proofs of Innocence call you these? but if I punish not this Insolence————[*Is going to beat him and is held by* Polydas *and* Tranio.] I beg you let me go————

Sosia. I charge you in the King's name, hold him fast; for you see he's bloodily dispos'd.

Grip. Now, what hast thou to say for thy self, *Sosia?*

Sosia. I say, in the first place, be sure you hold him, Gentlemen; for I shall never plead worth one farthing, while I am bodily affraid.

Polyd. Speak boldly; I warrant thee.

260 *Sosia.* Then, if I may speak boldly, under my Lord's favour, I do not say he lyes neither: no, I am too well bred for that: but his Lordship fibbs most abominably.

Amph. Do you hear his Impudence? yet will you let me go?

Sosia. No Impudence at all, my Lord: for how cou'd I, naturally speaking, be in the Balcony, and affronting you; when at the same time I was in every Street of *Thebes,* inviting these Gentlemen to Dinner?

Grip. Hold a little: how long since was it that he spoke to you, from the said Balcony?

270 *Amph.* Just now; not a Minute before he brought you hither.

Sosia. Now speak, my Witnesses.

---

252   *s.d.* Tranio.]] ~ .∧ Q1-2, F, D.   271   speak,] ~∧ Q1-2, F, D.

Grip. I can answer for him, for this last half hour.

Polyd. And I.

Tran. And I.

Sosia. Now judge equitably, Gentlemen; whether I was not a civil well-bred person, to tell my Lord he fibbs onely.

Amph. Who gave you that order, to invite 'em?

Sosia. He that best might; your self: by the same token, you bid old *Bromia* provide and 'twere for a God; and I put in for
280 a brace, or a lease; no, now I think on't, it was for ten couple of Gods, to make sure of plenty.

Amph. When did I give thee this pretended Commission?

Sosia. Why you gave me this pretended Commission, when you were just ready to give my Lady the Fiddles and a Dance; in order, as I suppose, to your second bedding.

Amph. Where, in what place, did I give this order?

Sosia. Here, in this place; in the presence of this very door, and of that Balcony: and if they cou'd speak, they wou'd both justifie it.
290 *Amph.* O Heaven! these accidents are so surprizing, that the more I think of 'em, the more I am lost in my imagination.

Grip. Nay, he has told us some passages, as he came along, that seem to surpass the power of Nature.

Sosia. What think you now, my Lord, of a certain twin Brother of mine, call'd *Sosia?* 'tis a sly Youth: pray Heaven you have not just such another Relation, within doors, call'd *Amphitryon*. It may be it was he, that put upon me, in your likeness: and perhaps he may have put something upon your Lordship too, that may weigh heavy upon the forehead.
300 *Amph. to those who hold him.* Let me go:———*Sosia* may be innocent, and I will not hurt him:———Open the door; I'll resolve my doubts immediately.

Sosia. The door is peremptory, that it will not be open'd without Keys: and my Brother, on the inside, is in possession; and will not part with 'em.

Amph. Then 'tis manifest that I am affronted; break open the door there.

Grip. Stir not a man of you, to his assistance.

Amph. Dost thou take part with my Adultress too, because
310 she is thy Niece?

Grip. I take part with nothing, but the Law; and, to break
the doors open, is to break the Law.

Amph. Do thou command 'em, then.

Grip. I command nothing without my Warrant; and my
Clerk is not here to take his Fees for drawing it.

Amph. aside. The Devil take all Justice-brokers:————I
curse him too when I have been hunting him all over the
Town, to be my Witness!————But I'll bring Souldiers to
force open the doors, by my own Commission.

[*Exit* Amphitryon.

320 *Sosia.* Pox o' these forms of Law, to defeat a man of a Dinner,
when he's sharp set: 'tis against the priviledge of a free-born
Stomack; and is no less than subversion of Fundamentals.

Jupiter *above in the Balcony.*

Jupit. Oh, my Friends, I am sorry I have made you wait so
long: you are welcome; and the door shall be open'd to you,
immediately. [*Exit* Jupiter.

Grip. Was not that *Amphitryon?*

Sosia. Why, who shou'd it be else?

Grip. In all appearance it was he: but how got he thither?

Polyd. In such a trice too!

330 *Tran.* And after he had just left us?

Grip. And so much alter'd, for the better, in his humour?

Sosia. Here's such a company of foolish questions, when a
man's a hungry: You had best stay dinner till he has prov'd
himself to be *Amphitryon* in form of Law: But I'll make short
work of that business: for I'll take mine Oath 'tis he.

Grip. I shou'd be glad it were.

Sosia. How, glad it were? with your damn'd Interrogatories,
when you ought to be thankfull, that so it is.

316   *aside.*] (*aside*) Q1; (*aside.*) Q2, F; (*Aside*) D.
319+   *s.d. Exit*] Q2, F, D; ~ . Q1.
322+   *s.d.* Jupiter] [Jupiter Q1-2, F, D.
325   *s.d. Exit*] Q2, F, D; ~ . Q1.   337   How,] ~∧ Q1-2, F, D.

Grip. aside. That I may see my Mistress *Phædra,* and present
340 her with my great gold Gobblet.

Sosia. If this be not the true *Amphitryon,* I wish I may be
kept without doors, fasting, and biting my own Fingers, for
want of Victuals; and that's a dreadfull Imprecation! I am for
the inviting, and eating, and treating *Amphitryon:* I am sure
'tis he that is my lawfully begotten Lord: and if you had an
Ounce of true Justice in you, you ought to have laid hold on
t' other *Amphitryon,* and committed him for a Rogue, and an
Impostour, and a Vagabond.

> [*The Door is open'd:* Mercury *from within.*

Merc. Enter quickly, Masters: The Passage on the right-hand
350 leads to the Gallery, where my Lord expects you: ———for I
am call'd another way.

> [Gripus, Tranio, *and* Polydas *go into the House.*

Sosia. I shou'd know that Voice, by a secret Instinct: 'tis a
Tongue of my Family; and belongs to my Brother *Sosia:* it
must be so; for it carries a cudgelling kind of sound in it.
———But put the worst: let me weigh this matter wisely:
Here's a beating, and a belly-full: against no beating, and no
belly-full. The beating is bad; but the dinner is good: now, not
to be beaten, is but negatively good; but, not to fill my belly, is
positively bad. ———Upon the whole matter, my final resolu-
360 tion is, to take the good and the bad as they come together.

> *Is entring:* Mercury *meets him at the Door.*

Merc. Whither now, you kitchen-skumm? From whence this
Impudence, to enter here without permission?

Sosia. Most Illustrious Sir: my Ticket is my hunger: shew the
full Bowels of your Compassion, to the empty bowels of my
famine.

Merc. Were you not charg'd to return no more? I'll cut you
into quarters, and hang you upon the Shambles.

---

339 *aside.*] (*aside*) Q1–2, F (*aside.* F); [*Aside.*] D.
339 *Phædra*] Q2, D; *Phœdra* Q1, F.
341 *Sosia.*] Q2, F, D; ~ , Q1.   360+ *s.d. Is*] [*Is* Q1–2, F, D.
363 *Sosia.*] Q2, F, D; ~ , Q1.

Sosia. You'll get but little credit by me: Alas, Sir, I am but mere Carrion! Brave *Sosia,* compassionate Coward *Sosia:* and
370 beat not thy self, in beating me.

Merc. Who gave you that privilege, Sirrah, to assume my Name? have you not been sufficiently warn'd of it? and receiv'd part of punishment already?

Sosia. May it please you, Sir, the Name is big enough for both of us: and we may use it in common, like a Strumpet: witness heaven, that I wou'd have obey'd you, and quitted my Title to the name; but, where ever I come, the malicious world will call me *Sosia,* in spight of me: I am sensible there are two *Amphitryons;* and why may not there be two *Sosia's?* Let those
380 two cut one anothers throats at their own pleasure: but you and I will be wiser, by my consent, and hold good Intelligence together.

Merc. No, no: Two *Sosia's* wou'd but make two fools.

Sosia. Then let me be the fool; and be you the prudent person: and chuse for your self some wiser name: or you shall be the Elder Brother; and I'll be content to be the Younger; though I lose my Inheritance.

Mer. I tell thee, I am the onely Son of our Family.

Sosia. Then let me be your Bastard Brother, and the Son of a
390 Whore; I hope that's but reasonable.

Merc. No, Thou shalt not disgrace my Father: For there are few Bastards now-a-days worth owning.

Sosia. Ah! Poor *Sosia!* What will become of thee?

Merc. Yet again profanely using my proper name?

Sosia. I did not mean my self: I was thinking of another *Sosia,* a poor fellow, that was once of my acquaintance, unfortunately banish'd out of doors, when dinner was just coming upon the Table.

Enter Phædra.

Phæd. *Sosia,* you and I must————Bless me! What have we
400 here, a Couple of you, or do I see double?

398+　*s.d.* *Enter* Phædra] Q2, F, D; Enter *Phædra* Q1.

Sosia. I wou'd fain bring it about, that I might make one of 'em: But he's unreasonable and will needs incorporate me, and swallow me whole into himself. If he wou'd be content to be but one and a half, 'twou'd never grieve me.

Merc. 'Tis a perverse Rascal: I kick him, and cudgel him to no purpose: for still he's obstinate to stick to me: and I can never beat him out of my resemblance.

Phæd. Which of you two is *Sosia?* For t' other must be the Devil.

410 *Sosia.* You had best ask him that has play'd the Devil with my back and sides.

Merc. You had best ask him who gave you the gold Gobblet?

Phæd. No, that's already given: but he shall be my *Sosia,* that will give me such another.

Merc. I find you have been Interloping, Sirrah.

Sosia. No, indeed, Sir; I onely promised her a gold Thimble: which was as much as comes to my proportion of being *Sosia.*

Phæd. This is no *Sosia* for my money: beat him away t' other *Sosia:* he grows insufferable.

420 *Sosia, aside.* Wou'd I were valiant, that I might beat him away; and succeed him at the dinner; for a pragmatical Son of a Whore, as he is!———

Merc. What's that you are muttering betwixt your Teeth, of a Son of a Whore, Sirrah?

Sosia. I am sure I meant you no offence: for, if I am not *Sosia,* I am the Son of a Whore, for ought I know: and, if you are *Sosia,* you may be the Son of a Whore for ought you know.

Merc. What ever I am, I will be *Sosia,* as long as I please: and whenever you visit me, you shall be sure of the civility of

430 the Cudgel.

Sosia. If you will promise to beat me into the house, you may begin when you please with me: but, to be beaten out of the house, at dinner time, flesh and bloud can never bear it.

[Mercury *beats him about, and* Sosia *is still making towards*

---

420   *Sosia, aside.*] ~ . *(aside)* Q1; *Sos. (aside.)* Q2, F; *Sos. [Aside.]* D.
422   is!] ~∧ Q1–2, F, D.

the door: but Mercury *gets betwixt; and at length drives him off the Stage.*

Phæd. In the name of wonder, what are you, that are *Sosia,* and are not *Sosia?*

Merc. If thou would'st know more of me, my person is freely at thy disposing.

Phæd. Then I dispose of it to you again: for 'tis so ugly, 'tis not for my use.

440 *Merc.* I can be ugly or handsome, as I please: go to bed old, and rise young. I have so many Sutes of persons by me, that I can shift 'em when I will.

Phæd. You are a fool then, to put on your worst Cloaths, when you come a wooing.

Merc. Go to: Ask no more questions; I am for thy turn; for I know thy heart: and see all thou hast about thee.

Phæd. Then you can see my back-side too; there's a bargain for you.———

Merc. In thy right pocket:—let me see:—three Love Letters
450 from Judge *Gripus,* written to the bottom, on three sides; full of fustian passion, and hearty non-sence: as also in the same Pocket, a Letter of thine intended to him; consisting of nine lines and a half: scrawl'd and false spell'd, to show thou art a Woman; and full of fraudulence, and equivocations, and shoeing-horns of Love to him; to promise much, and mean nothing; to show, over and above, that thou art a mere Woman.

Phæd. Is the Devil in you, to see all this? Now, for Heavens sake, do not look into t' other Pocket.———

Merc. Nay, there's nothing there, but a little godly Prayer-
460 book, and———a bawdy Lampoon, and———

Phæd. giving a great frisk. Look no farther, I beseech you.

Merc. And a Silver Spoon———

Phæd. shreeking.———Ah!

Merc. Which you purloin'd last Night from *Bromia.*

Phæd. Keep my Counsel, or I am undone for ever.

---

461 *giving . . . frisk.*] (*Giving . . . frisk.*) Q1-2, F; [*Giving . . . Frisk.*] D.
464 *shreeking.*] (*Shreeking.*) Q1-2, F; [*Shrieking.*] D.

[Holding up her hands to him.

Merc. No: I'll mortifie thee, now I have a handle to thy Iniquity, if thou wilt not love me.————

Phæd. Well, if you'll promise me to be secret, I will love
470 you: because indeed I dare doe no other.

Merc. 'Tis a good Girl; I will be secret; and further, I will be assisting to thee in thy filching: for thou and I were born under the same Planet.

Phæd. And we shall come to the same end too, I'm afraid.

Merc. No; no; since thou hast wit enough already to couzin a Judge, thou need'st never fear hanging.

Phæd. And will you make your self a younger man; and be handsome too: and rich? for you that know hearts, must needs know, that I shall never be constant to such an ugly old *Sosia.*
480 *Merc.* Thou shalt know more of that another time: in the mean while, here's a cast of my Office for thee.

*He stamps upon the ground: some Dancers come from
underground: and others from the sides of the
Stage: A Song, and a fantastick Dance.*

Mercury's *S O N G* to Phædra.

I.

Fair Iris *I love, and hourly I dye,
But not for a Lip, nor a languishing Eye:
She's fickle and false, and there we agree;
For I am as false, and as fickle as she:
We neither believe what either can say;
And, neither believing, we neither betray.*

II.

*'Tis civil to swear, and say things of course;
We mean not the taking for better for worse.*
490 *When present, we love; when absent, agree;
I think not of* Iris, *nor* Iris *of me:*

The Legend of Love no Couple can find
So easie to part, or so equally join'd.

After, the Dance.

Phædra. This Power of yours makes me suspect you for little
better than a God; but if you are one, for more certainty, tell
me what I am just now thinking.

Merc. Why, thou art thinking, let me see; for thou art a
Woman, and your minds are so variable, that it's very hard
even for a God to know them. But, to satisfie thee, thou art
500 wishing, now, for the same Power I have exercis'd; that thou
mightest stamp, like me; and have more Singers come up for
another Song.

Phædra. Gad, I think the Devil's in you. Then I do stamp
in some body's Name, but I know not whose. (*Stamps.*) Come
up, Gentle-folks, from below; and sing me a Pastoral Dialogue,
where the Woman may have the better of the Man; as we always have in Love matters.

New Singers come up and sing a Song.

A Pastoral Dialogue betwixt *Thyrsis* and *Iris.*

I.

Thyrsis. *Fair* Iris *and her Swain*
          Were in a shady Bow'r;
510   *Where* Thyrsis *long in vain*
          Had sought the Shepherd's hour:
          At length his Hand advancing upon her snowy
               Breast;
          He said, O kiss me longer,

---

503   *Phædra.*] Q2, F, D; ∼ , Q1.
504   whose. (*Stamps*] ∼ ; (*stamps* Q1–2, F, D.
507–507+   s.d. matters. / *New* . . . . *Song.*] ∼ . [∼ . . . ∼ . Q1–2, F (*s.d. at right*
margin); ∼ . / [∼ . . . ∼ . D (*s.d. at right margin*).

And longer yet and longer,
      If you will make me Blest.

II.

Iris.   *An easie yielding Maid,*
    By trusting is undone;
    Our Sex is oft betray'd,
    By granting Love too soon.
520   *If you desire to gain me, your Suff'rings to redress;*
    Prepare to love me longer,
    And longer yet, and longer,
      Before you shall possess.

III.

Thyrsis. *The little Care you show,*
    Of all my Sorrows past;
    Makes Death appear too slow,
    And Life too long to last.
    Fair Iris *kiss me kindly, in pity of my Fate;*
    And kindly still, and kindly,
530   *Before it be too late.*

IV.

Iris.   *You fondly Court your Bliss,*
    And no Advances make;
    'Tis not for Maids to kiss,
    But 'tis for Men to take.
    So you may Kiss me kindly, and I will not rebell;
    And kindly still, and kindly,
      But Kiss me not and tell.

V.

A RONDEAU.

Chorus. *Thus at the height we love and live,*
    And fear not to be poor:

513–515 O . . . [*to*] . . . Blest] *in italics in* Q1–2, F, D, f1, m2.

540   *We give, and give, and give, and give,*
            Till we can give no more:
        But what to day will take away,
            To morrow will restore.
        Thus at the heighth we love and live,
            And fear not to be poor.

Phædra. Adieu, I leave you to pay the Musick: Hope well
Mr. Planett; there's a better Heav'n in store for you: I say no
more, but you can guess.

                                                          [*Exit.*

        Mercury, alone. Such Bargain-loves, as I with *Phædra* treat, ⎫
550 Are all the Leagues and Friendships of the Great: ⎪
    All seek their Ends; and each wou'd other cheat.   ⎬
    They onely seem to hate, and seem to love;   ⎭
    But Int'rest is the point on which they move.
    Their Friends are Foes; and Foes are Friends agen;
    And, in their turns, are Knaves, and Honest men.
    Our Iron Age is grown an Age of Gold:
    'Tis who bids most; for all Men wou'd be sold.   [*Exit* Mercury.

ACT V.   SCENE I.

Enter Gripus, Phædra. Gripus *has the Gobblet in his Hand.*

Phæd. You will not be so base to take it from me?

Grip. 'Tis my proper Chattel: and I'll seize my own, in whatever hands I find it.

Phæd. You know I onely show'd it you to provoke your
generosity, that you might out-bid your Rival with a better
Present.

Grip. My Rival is a Thief: and I'll indite you for a Receiver
of Stoln Goods.

Phæd. Thou Hide-bound Lover!

548+   *s.d.* [*Exit.*] *omitted from* Q1-2, F, D.
ACT V. SCENE I.] D; ACT. V. Q1; ACT V. Q2, F.
s.d. Enter Gripus, Phædra] D; *Gripus, Phædra* Q1-2, F.

10   *Grip.* Thou very mercenary Mistress!

    Phæd. Thou most mercenary Magistrate!

    Grip. Thou Seller of thy self!

    Phæd. Thou Seller of other People: thou Weather-cock of Government: that when the Wind blows for the Subject, point'st to Priviledge; and when it changes for the Soveraign, veers to Prerogative.

    Grip. Will you compound, and take it as my Present?

    Phæd. No: but I'll send thy Rival to force it from thee.

    Grip. When a Thief is Rival to his Judge, the Hangman will
20 soon decide the difference.   [*Exit* Phædra.

Enter Mercury, *with two Swords.*

    Merc. bowing. Save your good Lordship.

    Grip. From an Impertinent Coxcomb: I am out of humour, and am in hast: leave me.

    Merc. 'Tis my duty to attend on your Lordship, and to ease you of that undecent Burden.

    Grip. Gold was never any Burden, to one of my Profession.

    Merc. By your Lordship's permission, *Phædra* has sent me to take it from you.

    Grip. What, by Violence?

30   *Merc. still bowing.* No; but by your Honour's permission, I am to restore it to her, and perswade your Lordship, to renounce your Pretensions to her.

    Grip. Tell her flatly, I will neither do one, nor t' other.

    Merc. O my good Lord, I dare pass my word for your free consent to both.———Will your Honour be pleas'd to take your choice of one of these?

    Grip. Why these are Swords: what have I to do with them?

    Merc. Onely to take your choice of one of them; which your Lordship pleases; and leave the other to your most Obedient
40 Servant.

    Grip. What, one of these ungodly Weapons? take notice, I'll

20   *s.d. Exit*] Q2, F, D; ∼ . Q1.   21   *bowing.*] *Bowing.*] Q1–2, F; [*Bowing.*] D.
30   *bowing.*] *Bowing.*] Q1, D; ∼ .] Q2; ∼ .) F.

lay you by the heels, Sirrah: this has the appearance of an unlawfull bloody challenge.

Merc. You Magistrates are pleas'd to call it so, my Lord; but
with us Swordmen, 'tis an honourable Invitation to the cutting
of one anothers Throats.

Grip. Be answer'd; I have no Throat to cut. The Law shall
decide our Controversie.

Merc. By your permission, my Lord; it must be dispatch'd,
50 this way.

Grip. I'll see thee hang'd before I give thee any such permission, to dispatch me into another World.

Merc. At the least, my Lord, you have no occasion to complain of my want of respect to you: you will neither restore the
Gobblet, nor renounce *Phædra:* I offer you the Combat; you
refuse it: all this is done in the forms of honour: it follows, that
I am to affront, cudgel you, or kick you, at my own arbitre-
ment; and I suppose, you are too honourable not to approve of
my proceeding.

60   *Grip.* Here's a new sort of Process, that was never heard of in
any of our Courts.

Merc. This, my good Lord, is Law in Short-hand, without
your long Preambles, and tedious Repetitions, that signifie
nothing, but to squeeze the Subject: therefore, with your Lordship's favour, I begin.   [*Phillips him under the Chin.*

Grip. What's this for?

Merc. To give you an occasion of returning me a box o' th'
Ear: that so, all things may proceed methodically.

Grip. I put in no answer, but suffer a Non-suit.

70   *Merc.* No, my Lord; for the Costs and Charges are to be paid:
will you please to restore the Cup?

Grip. I have told thee, no.

Merc. Then from your Chin, I must ascend to your Lordship's Ears.

Grip. Oh, oh. Oh, oh.———Wilt thou never leave lugging
me by the Ears?

Merc. Not till your Lordship will be pleas'd to hear reason.
                                              [*Pulling again.*

Grip. Take the Cup; and the Devil give thee joy on't.

Merc. still holding him. And your Lordship will farther be
80 graciously pleas'd, to release all claims, titles, and actions whatsoever to *Phædra:* You must give me leave to add one small
memento, for that too.   [*Pulling him again.*

Grip. I renounce her, I release her.

Enter Phædra.

Merc. to her. Phædra; My Lord has been pleas'd to be very
gracious; without pushing matters to extremity.

Phæd. I over-heard it all: But give me Livery and Seisin of
the Gobblet, in the first place.

Merc. There's an Act of Oblivion shou'd be pass'd too.

Phæd. Let him begin to remember quarrels, when he dares;
90 now I have him under my Girdle, I'll cap Verses with him to
the end of the Chapter.

Enter Amphitryon *and Guards.*

Amph. to Gripus. At the last I have got possession without
your Lordship's Warrant. *Phædra,* tell *Alcmena* I am here.

Phæd. I'll carry no such lying Message: you are not here,
and you cannot be here: for, to my knowledge, you are above
with my Lady, in the Chamber!

Amph. All of a piece, and all Witchcraft! Answer me precisely; do'st thou not know me for *Amphitryon?*

Phæd. Answer me first: did you give me a Diamond, and a
100 Purse of Gold?

Amph. Thou know'st I did not.

Phæd. Then, by the same token, I know you are not the true
Amphitryon: if you are he, I am sure I left you in bed with your
own Wife: now you had best stretch out a leg; and feel about
for a fair Lady.

Amph. I'll undo this Enchantment with my Sword; and kill

79 *him.*] ~ .] Q1–2, D; ~ .) F.   84 *her.*] ~ .] Q1–2, D; ~ .) F.
92 *Amph. to Gripus.*] *Amph*∧ (*to Gripus.*) Q1–2 (*Amph.* Q2); *Amph. to Grip.*)
F; *Amph.* [*to Gripus.*] D.   93 Warrant.] ~ ; Q1–2, F; ~ , D.

the Sorcerer: Come up, Gentlemen, and follow me.

[*To the Guards.*

Phæd. I'll save you the labour; and call him down to confront you; if you dare attend him.   [*Exit* Phædra.

110   *Merc. aside.* Now the Spell is ended, and *Jupiter* can enchant no more; or else *Amphitryon* had not enter'd so easily.———— [Gripus *is stealing off.*] Whither now, *Gripus?* I have business for you: if you offer to stir, you know what follows.

Enter Jupiter, *follow'd by* Tranio *and* Polydas.

Jupit. Who dares to play the Master in my House?
What noise is this, that calls me from above,
Invades my soft recess, and privacy,
And, like a Tyde, breaks in upon my Love?
    Amph. O Heav'ns, what's this I see?
    Tran. What Prodigy!
    Polyd.   How, two *Amphitryons!*
120   *Grip.* I have beheld th' appearance of two Suns;
But still the false, was dimmer than the true;
Here, both shine out alike.
    Amph. This is a sight, that like the *Gorgon's* head,
Runs through my limbs, and stiffens me to Stone.
I need no more inquire into my fate:
For what I see, resolves my doubts too plain.
    Tran. Two drops of water, cannot be more like.
    Polyd. They are two very same's.
    Merc. aside. Our *Jupiter* is a great Comedian; he counterfeits
130 most admirably: sure his Priests have coppy'd their Hypocrisie from their Master.
    Amph. Now, I am gather'd back into my self,
My Heart beats high, and pushes out the Blood

107+   *s.d. Guards.*] F, D; ∼ .] Q1–2.
109   *s.d. Exit* Phædra] Q2, F, D; ∼ . Phœdra Q1.
110   *aside.*] (∼ʌ) Q1; (∼ .) Q2; ∼ .) F; [∼ .] D.
111–112   easily.————[Gripus . . . *off.*]] ∼ . [∼ . . . ∼ .]————Q1–2, F, D.
123   *Gorgon's*] D; Gorgon's Q1–2, F.   129   *aside.*] (∼ʌ) Q1–2; ∼ .) F; [∼ .] D.

[*Drawing his Sword.*
To give me just revenge on this Impostour.
If you are brave, assist me. [*To the Guards.*]————Not one stirs:
What, are all brib'd to take th' Enchanters part?
'Tis true, the work is mine; and thus————
　　[*Going to rush upon* Jupiter; *and is held by* Tranio *and*
　　　Polydas.
　　Polyd. It must not be.
　　Jupit. Give him his way: I dare the Madman's worst:
140 But still take notice, that it looks not like
The true *Amphitryon,* to fly out, at first
To brutal force: it shows he doubts his Cause,
Who dares not trust his reason to defend it.
　　Amph. struggling. Thou base Usurper of my Name, and Bed;
No less than thy Hearts-blood can wash away
Th' affronts I have sustain'd.
　　Tranio.　　　　　　　　We must not suffer
So strange a Duel as *Amphitryon*
To fight against himself.
　　Polyd. Nor think we wrong you, when we hold your hands:
150 We know our duty to our General:
We know the tyes of Friendship to our Friend:
But who that Friend, or who that Gen'ral is,
Without more certain proofs betwixt you two,
Is hard to be distinguish'd, by our reason:
Impossible by sight.
　　Amph. I know it; and have satisfy'd my self:
I am the true *Amphitryon.*
　　Jupit. See again.
He shuns the certain proofs; and dares not stand
160 Impartial Judgment, and award of right.

133+　*s.d. Sword.*] F, D; ~] Q1-2.
134-135　Impostour. / If . . . me. [*To the Guards.*]————Not . . . stirs:] Impostour. [*to the Guards.*] / If . . . me————not . . . stirs: Q1-2; Impostour.
(*To the Guards.* / If . . . me————Not . . . stirs: F; Impostor. / If . . . me
————not . . . stirs: [*To the Guards.* D.
136　What,] D; ~∧ Q1-2, F.　　　137　thus] F, D; ~ . Q1-2.
144　*struggling.*] Q2, F, D; ~∧ Q1.

But since *Alcmena's* honour is concern'd,
Whom, more than Heav'n, and all the World, I love,
This I propose, as equal to us both:
Tranio, and *Polydas,* be you Assistants,
The Guards be ready to secure th' Impostour,
When once so prov'd, for publick punishment;
And *Gripus,* be thou Umpire of the Cause.

 Amph. I am content: let him proceed to Examination.

 Grip. aside to Mercury. On whose side wou'd you please that
170 I shou'd give the Sentence?

 Merc. aside to him. Follow thy Conscience for once; but not
to make a Custom of it neither; nor to leave an evil precedent
of Uprightness to future Judges.————(*Aside.*) 'Tis a good
thing to have a Magistrate under Correction: Your old forni-
cating Judge, dare never give Sentence against him that knows
his haunts.

 Polyd. Your Lordship knows I was Master of *Amphitryon's*
Ship; and desire to know of him, what pass'd in private betwixt
us two, at his Landing, when he was just ready to engage the
180 Enemy?

 Grip. Let the true *Amphitryon* answer first.————

 Jupit. & Amph. together. My Lord I told him————

 Grip. Peace both of you.————'Tis a plain Case they are both
true; for they both speak together. But for more certainty, let
the false *Amphitryon* speak first.

 Merc. Now they are both silent.————

 Grip. Then it's as plain on t' other side, that they are both
false *Amphitryons.*

 Merc. Which *Amphitryon* shall speak first?

190 *Grip.* Let the Cholerick *Amphitryon* speak; and let the peaceable hold his peace.

 Amph. to Polydas. You may remember that I whisper'd you,

162, 163 love, . . . both:] ~ ; . . . ~ . Q1–2, F, D.
169 *aside . . . Mercury.*] (~ . . . ~∧) Q1–2; ~ . . . ~ .] F; [~ . . . *Merc.*] D.
171 *aside . . . him.*] (~ . . . ~∧) Q1–2; ~ . . . ~ .] F; [~ . . . ~ .] D.
173 ————(*Aside.*] D; ∧(~∧ Q1–2; ∧(~ . F.
182 *together.*] D; ~ .] Q1–2, F. 182 him] F, D; ~ . Q1–2.
183 you.] ~ : Q1–2, F, D. 184 together. But] ~ : but Q1–2, F, D (But F).
192 *Polydas.*] ~ .] Q1–2, F, D.

not to part from the Stern, one single Moment.

Polyd. You did so.

Grip. No more words then; I proceed to Sentence.

Jupit. 'Twas I that whisper'd him; and he may remember I gave him this reason for it; That if our Men were beaten, I might secure my own retreat.

Polyd. You did so.

200 *Grip.* Now again he's as true as t' other.

Tranio. You know I was Pay-master: What directions did you give me the night before the Battle?

Grip. To which of the You's art thou speaking?

Merc. aside. It shou'd be a double U: but they have no such letter in their Tongue.

Amph. I order'd you to take particular care of the great Bag.

Grip. Why this is demonstration.

Jupit. The Bag that I recommended to you, was of Tygers skin; and mark'd *Beta.*

210 *Grip.* In sadness I think they are both Jugglers: Here's nothing, and here's nothing: and then *hiccius doccius,* and they are both here again.

Tran. You peaceable *Amphitryon,* what Money was there in that Bag?

Jupit. The summ in gross, amounted just to fifty *Attick* Talents.

Tran. To a farthing!

Grip. Paugh: obvious, obvious.

Amph. Two thousand pieces of Gold were ty'd up in a Hand-
220 kerchief by themselves.

Tran. I remember it.

Grip. Then 'tis dubious again.

Jupit. But the rest was not all Silver; for there were just four thousand Brass half-pence.

Grip. Being but Brass, the proof is inconsiderable: if they had been Silver, it had gone on your side.

---

204 *aside.*] (~) Q1-2; ~ .] F; [~ .] D.
215 *Attick*] Attick Q1-2, F, D.
217 farthing!] ~ ? Q1-2, F; ~ . D.

Amph. to Jupit. Death and Hell, you will not perswade me,
that I did not kill *Pterelas?*

Jupit. Nor you me, that I did not enjoy *Alcmena?*

230   *Amph.* That last was poyson to me.(*Aside.*)————
Yet there's one proof thou canst not counterfeit:
In killing *Pterelas,* I had a Wound
Full in the brawny part of my right Arme;
Where still the Scar remains: now blush, Impostour;
For this thou canst not show.

  [*Bares his Arme; and shows the Scar, which they all look on.*
Omnes. This is the true *Amphitryon.*

Jupit. May your Lordship please————

Grip. No, Sirrah, it does not please me: hold your tongue, I
charge you; for the Case is manifest.

240   *Jupit.* By your favour then, this shall speak for me.

         [*Bares his Arme; and shows it.*
Tran. 'Tis just in the same Muscle.

Polyd. Of the same length and breadth; and the Scar of the
same blewish colour.

Grip. to Jupit. Did not I charge you not to speak? 'twas plain
enough before: and now you have puzzled it again.

Amph. Good Gods, how can this be!

Grip. For certain there was but one *Pterelas;* and he must
have been in the Plot against himself too: for he was kill'd first
by one of them; and then rose again out of respect to t' other
250   *Amphitryon,* to be kill'd twice over.

    Enter Alcmena, Phædra, *and* Bromia.

Alcm. turning to Phæd. and Brom. No more of this; it sounds
  impossible
That two shou'd be so like, no difference found.

Phæd. You'll find it true.

Alcm. Then where's *Alcmena's* honour and her fame?

---

227 *Jupit.*] ∼ .] Q1–2, F, D.
230 me. (*Aside.*)————] ∼ .————(∼ .) Q1–2; ∼ .————[∼ . F, D.
237 please] F, D; ∼ . Q1–2.   244 *Jupit.*] ∼ .] Q1–2, F, D.
249 rose] D; rise Q1–2, F.

Farewell my needless fear; it cannot be:
This is a Case too nice for vulgar sight:
But let me come; my Heart will guide my Eyes
To point, and tremble to its proper choice.

                    [*Seeing* Amphitryon, *goes to him.*

There neither was, nor is, but one *Amphitryon;*
260 And I am onely his.———   [*Goes to take him by the Hand.*

   Amph. pushing her away from him. Away, Adultress!

   Jupit. My gentle Love: my Treasure and my Joy;
Follow no more, that false and foolish Fire,
That wou'd mislead thy Fame to sure destruction!
Look on thy better Husband, and thy friend,
Who will not leave thee lyable to scorn,
But vindicate thy honour from that Wretch
Who wou'd by base aspersions blot thy vertue.

   Alcm. going to him, who embraces her. I was indeed mis-
taken; thou art he!
Thy Words, thy Thoughts, thy Soul is all *Amphitryon.*
270 Th' Impostour has thy Features, not thy Mind;
The Face might have deceiv'd me in my choice;
Thy kindness is a Guide that cannot err.

   Amph. What, in my presence to prefer the Villain!
O execrable cheat! I break the truce;
And will no more attend your vain decisions;
To this———and to the Gods I'll trust my Cause.

                    [*Is rushing upon* Jupiter, *and is held again.*

   Jupit. Poor Man; how I contemn those idle threats!
Were I dispos'd, thou might'st as safely meet
The Thunder lanch'd from the red arme of *Jove,*
280 (Nor *Jove* need blush to be *Alcmena's* Champion)
But in the face of *Thebes,* she shall be clear'd:
And what I am, and what thou art, be known.
Attend, and I will bring convincing proof.

   Amph. Thou wou'dst elude my Justice, and escape;
But I will follow thee, through Earth, and Seas;

258+ *s.d. him.*] F, D; ~ .] Q1–2 (*s.d. at left margin*).
273   What,] ~∧ Q1–2, F; ~ ! D.   279 *Jove,*] ~ :) Q1–2; ~ : F, D.

Nor Hell shall hide thee, from my just revenge.

    Jupit. I'll spare thy pains: it shall be quickly seen,
Betwixt us two, who seeks, and who avoids.——
Come in my Friends: and thou who seem'st *Amphitryon;*
290 That all who are in doubt, may know the true.

    Jupiter *re-enters the House: with him* Amphitryon,
        Alcmena, Polydas, Tranio, *and Guards.*

    Merc. to Grip. and Brom. who are following. Thou *Gripus,*
    and you *Bromia;* stay with *Phædra:*
Let their affairs alone, and mind we ours:
Amphitryon's Rival shall appear a God:
But know before-hand, I am *Mercury;*
Who want not Heav'n, while *Phædra* is on Earth.

    Brom. But, and't please your Lordship, is my fellow *Phædra*
to be exalted into the Heav'ns, and made a Star?

    Phæd. When that comes to pass, if you look up a-nights, I
shall remember old kindness, and vouchsafe to twinkle on you.

    Enter Sosia, *peeping about him: and seeing* Mercury,
               is starting back.

300   *Sosia.* Here he is again; and there's no passing by him into
the House, unless I were a Spright, to glide in through the Key-
hole.——I am to be a Vagabond I find.

    Merc. Sosia, come back.

    Sosia. No I thank you; you may whistle me long enough; a
beaten Dog has always the wit to avoid his Master.

    Merc. I permit thee to be *Sosia* again.

    Sosia. 'Tis an unfortunate Name, and I abandon it: he that
has an itch to be beaten, let him take it up for *Sosia;*——
What have I said now! I mean for me; for I neither am nor will
310 be *Sosia.*

    Merc. But thou may'st be so in safety: for I have acknowl-
edg'd my self to be God *Mercury.*

    Sosia. You may be a God, for ought I know; but the Devil
take me if ever I Worship you; for an unmercifull Deity, as
you are.

Merc. You ought to take it for an honour to be drubb'd by the hand of a Divinity.

Sosia. I am your most humble Servant, good Mr. God; but by the faith of a Mortal, I cou'd well have spar'd the honour
320 that you did me. But how shall I be sure that you will never assume my shape again?

Merc. Because I am weary of wearing so villanous an outside.

Sosia. Well, well; as villanous as it is, here's old *Bromia* will be contented with it.

Brom. Yes, now I am sure that I may chastise you safely: and that there's no God, lurking under your appearance.

Sosia. Ay; but you had best take heed how you attempt it: for as *Mercury* has turn'd himself into me, so I may take the toy into my head, to turn my self into *Mercury*, that I may
330 swinge you off, condignly.

Merc. In the mean time, be all my Witnesses, that I take *Phædra* for my Wife of the left hand; that is, in the nature of a lawfull Concubine.

Phæd. You shall pardon me for believing you, for all you are a God: for you have a terrible ill name below: and I am affraid you'll get a Footman, instead of a Priest, to Marry us.

Merc. But here's *Gripus* shall draw up Articles betwixt us.

Phæd. But he's damnably us'd to false Conveyancing:———
Well, be it so: for my Counsel shall over-look 'em before I Sign.
340 Come on, *Gripus;* that I may have him under black and white.
                    [*Here* Gripus *gets ready Pen, Ink, and Paper.*

Merc. With all my heart; that I may have thee under black and white hereafter.

Phæd. to Gripus. Begin, begin; Heads of Articles to be made, &c. betwixt *Mercury,* God of Thieves———

Merc. And *Phædra,* Queen of Gypsies.———*Imprimis,* I promise to buy and settle upon her an Estate, containing Nine thousand Acres of Land, in any part of *Bœotia,* to her own liking.

Phæd. Provided always, that no part of the said Nine thou-

338 us'd] Q2, F, D; u'sd Q1.   339 Well,] Q2, F; ~ₐ Q1, D.
339 Sign.] ~ : Q1-2, F, D.   343 *Gripus.*] ~ .] Q1-2, F, D (~ₐ] F; *Grip.* D).

350 sand Acres shall be upon, or adjoyning to Mount *Parnassus:*
for I will not be fobb'd off with a Poetical Estate.

Merc. *Memorandum,* that she be always constant to me; and
admit no other Lover.

Phæd. *Memorandum,* unless it be a Lover that offers more:
and that the Constancy shall not exceed the Settlement.

Merc. *Item,* that she shall keep no Male Servants in her
house: *Item,* no Rival Lap Dog for a Bedfellow: *Item,* that she
shall never pray to any of the Gods.

Phæd. What, wou'd you have me an Atheist?

360 *Merc.* No Devotion to any He-Deity, good *Phædra.*

Brom. Here's no provision made for Children yet.

Phæd. Well remember'd, *Bromia:* I bargain that my Eldest
Son shall be a Hero, and my Eldest Daughter a King's Mistress.

Merc. That is to say, a Blockhead, and a Harlot, *Phædra.*

Phæd. That's true; but who dares call 'em so? Then for the
Younger Children:————But now I think on't, we'll have no
more, but Mass and Miss; for the rest wou'd be but chargeable,
and a burden to the Nation.

Merc. Yes, yes; the Second shall be a False Prophet: he shall

370 have Wit enough to set up a New Religion: and too much Wit
to dye a Martyr for it.

Phæd. O what had I forgot? there's Pin-money, and Ali-
money, and Seperate maintenance, and a thousand things more
to be consider'd; that are all to be tack'd to this Act of Settlement.

Sosia. I am a fool, I must confess; but yet I can see as far
into a Mill-stone as the best of you. I have observ'd that you
Women-Wits are commonly so quick upon the scent, that you
often over-run it: Now I wou'd ask of Madam *Phædra,* that in

380 case Mr. Heaven there, shou'd be pleas'd to break these Articles, in what Court of Judicature she intends to sue him?

Phæd. The fool has hit upon't:————Gods, and great Men,
are never to be sued; for they can always plead priviledge of
Peerage: and therefore for once, Mounsieur, I'll take your word;
for as long as you love me you'll be sure to keep it: and in the

---

366 But] F; but Q1-2, D.   377 you.] ~ : Q1-2, F, D.

mean time I shall be gaining experience how to manage some
rich Cully; for no Woman ever made her Fortune by a Wit.

> *It Thunders; and the Company within doors,* Amphitryon,
> Alcmena, Polydas, *and* Tranio, *all come running
> out, and joyn with the rest, who were on
> the Theatre before.*

Amph. Sure 'tis some God: he vanish'd from our sight,
And told us we shou'd see him soon return.
390   *Alcm.* I know not what to hope, nor what to fear.
A simple Errour, is a real Crime;
And unconsenting Innocence is lost.

> *A second Peal of Thunder. After which,* Jupiter *appears
> in a Machine.*

Jupit. Look up, *Amphitryon,* and behold above,
Th' Impostour God, the Rival of thy Love:
In thy own shape, see *Jupiter* appear,
And let that sight, secure thy jealous fear.
Disgrace, and Infamy, are turn'd to boast:
No Fame, in *Jove's* Concurrence can be lost:
What he enjoys, he sanctifies from Vice;
400 And by partaking, stamps into a price.
'Tis I, who ought to murmur at my Fate;
Forc'd by my Love, my Godhead to translate;
When on no other terms I cou'd possess,
But by thy form, thy features, and thy dress;
To thee were giv'n, the Blessings that I sought,
Which else, not all the bribes of Heav'n had bought.
Then take into thy Armes thy envy'd Love;
And, in his own despight, triumph o'er *Jove.*
Merc. aside. Amphitryon and *Alcmena,* both stand mute, and
410 know not how to take it.
Sosia aside. Our Soveraign Lord *Jupiter* is a sly Companion;

387+ *s.d. doors,]* F, D; ~ : Q1–2.   389 told] Q2, F, D; ~, Q1.
409–411 *aside. . . . aside.]* (~ʌ) . . . (~ʌ) Q1; (~ .) ˏ ˏ ˏ (~ .) Q2; ~ .] . . .
~ .] F; [~ .] . . . [~ .] D.

he knows how to gild a bitter Pill.

Jupit. From this auspicious Night, shall rise an Heir,
Great, like his Sire, and like his Mother, fair:
Wrongs to redress, and Tyrants to disseize;
Born for a World, that wants a *Hercules.*
Monsters, and Monster-men he shall ingage,
And toil, and struggle, through an Impious Age.
Peace to his Labours, shall at length succeed; ⎫
420 And murm'ring Men, unwilling to be freed, ⎬
Shall be compell'd to Happiness, by need. ⎭

                           [Jupiter *is carry'd back to Heaven.*

Omnes. We all Congratulate *Amphitryon.*

Merc. Keep your Congratulations to your selves, Gentlemen: 'Tis a nice point, let me tell you that; and the less that is said of it, the better. Upon the whole matter, if *Amphitryon* takes the favour of *Jupiter* in patience, as from a God, he's a good Heathen.

Sosia. I must take a little extraordinary pains to night, that my Spouse may come even with her Lady, and produce a Squire
430 to attend on young *Hercules,* when he goes out to seek Adventures; that when his Master kills a Man, he may stand ready to pick his Pockets; and piously relieve his Aged Parents. Ah, *Bromia, Bromia;* if thou hadst been as handsome and as young as *Phædra;* I say no more, but some-body might have made his Fortunes as well as his Master, and never the worse Man neither.

For, let the wicked World say what they please,
The fair Wife makes her Husband live at ease:
The Lover keeps him too; and but receives,
440 Like *Jove,* the remnants that *Amphitryon* leaves:
'Tis true, the Lady has enough in store,
To satisfie those two, and eke, two more:
In fine, the Man, who weighs the matter fully,
Wou'd rather be the Cuckold, than the Cully.

                                        [*Exeunt.*

444+ s.d. [*Exeunt.*] *omitted from Q1–2, F, D.*

EPILOGUE.

Spoken by *Phædra*.   Mrs. *Mountfort*.

I'M *thinking, (and it almost makes me mad,)*
 How sweet a time, those Heathen Ladies had.
 Idolatry was ev'n their Gods own trade;
They Worshipt the fine Creatures they had made.
Cupid was chief of all the Deities;
And Love was all the fashion, in the Skies.
When the sweet Nymph, held up the Lilly hand,
Jove was her humble Servant, at Command.
The Treasury of Heav'n was ne're so bare,
But still there was a Pension for the Fair.
In all his Reign, Adultry was no Sin;
For Jove, the good Example did begin.
Mark, too, when he usurp'd the Husband's name,
How civilly he sav'd the Ladies fame.
The secret Joys of Love, he wisely hid;
But you, Sirs, boast of more, than e'er you did.
You teize your Cuckolds; to their face torment 'em;
But Jove gave his, new Honours to content 'em,
And, in the kind remembrance of the Fair,
On each exalted Son, bestow'd a Star.
For those good deeds, as by the date appears,
His Godship flourish'd full Two thousand Years.
At last, when He and all his Priests grew old,
The Ladies grew in their devotion cold;
And, that false Worship wou'd no longer hold.
 Severity of Life did next begin;
(And always does, when we no more can Sin.)

10

20

Caption: EPILOGUE.] F; ~ , Q1–2, D.
3 *Idolatry*] D; ~ , Q1–2, F. 5 Cupid] D; ~ , Q1–2, F.
8 Jove] Q2, F, D; ~ , Q1. 18 *'em,*] ~ . Q1–2, F, D.
22 *Godship*] D; ~ , Q1–2, F.

That Doctrine, too, so hard in Practice lyes,
That, the next Age may see another rise.
30 *Then, Pagan Gods may, once again, succeed;*
And Jove, *or* Mars, *be ready, at our need,*
To get young Godlings; and, so, mend our breed.

FINIS.

28 *hard . . . Practice*] ~ , . . . ~ , Q1–2, F, D.
30 *Gods*] D; ~ , Q1–2, F.

COMMENTARY

List of Abbreviated References

Dent: Edward J. Dent, *The Foundations of English Opera*, Cambridge, 1928

Evelyn, *Diary: The Diary of John Evelyn*, ed. E. S. de Beer, Oxford, 1955

JWCI: Journal of the Warburg and Courtauld Institutes

K.M.: Henry Cart de Lafontaine, *The King's Musick: A Transcript of Records Relating to Music and Musicians (1460–1700)*, 1909

Ker: *Essays of John Dryden*, ed. W. P. Ker, Oxford, 1900

Luttrell: Narcissus Luttrell, *A Brief Historical Relation of State Affairs from September 1678 to April 1714*, Oxford, 1857

Macdonald: Hugh Macdonald, *John Dryden: A Bibliography of Early Editions and of Drydeniana*, Oxford, 1939

Malone: *Critical and Miscellaneous Prose Works of John Dryden*, ed. Edmond Malone, 1800

MLR: Modern Language Review

Noyes: *Poetical Works of Dryden*, ed. George R. Noyes, rev. ed., Cambridge, Mass., 1950

OED: Oxford English Dictionary

Pidou de St. Olon: François Pidou de St. Olon, *The Present State of the Empire of Morocco*, 1695

PMLA: Publications of the Modern Language Association of America

Ranke: Leopold von Ranke, *A History of England, Principally in the Seventeenth Century*, trans. C. W. Boase *et al.*, Oxford, 1875

S-S: *The Works of John Dryden*, ed. Sir Walter Scott and George Saintsbury, 1882–1893

Summers: Dryden's *Dramatic Works*, ed. Montague Summers, 1931

Tilley: M. P. Tilley, *A Dictionary of the Proverbs in England in the Sixteenth and Seventeenth Centuries*, Ann Arbor, 1950

Van Lennep: *The London Stage, 1660–1800*, Part 1: 1600–1700, ed. William Van Lennep, with Critical Introduction by Emmett L. Avery and Arthur H. Scouten, Carbondale, Ill., 1965

Ward, *Letters: The Letters of John Dryden*, ed. Charles E. Ward, Durham, N.C., 1942

Watson: *John Dryden: Of Dramatic Poesy and Other Critical Essays*, ed. George Watson, 1962

Works: Dryden's works in the present edition

Albion and Albanius

As Dryden says in the preface, the opera was "Originally intended only for a Prologue to a Play, Of the Nature of the *Tempest*. . . . But some intervening accidents having hitherto deferr'd the performance of the main design, I propos'd to the Actors, to turn the intended Prologue into an Entertainment by it self, as you now see it, by adding two acts more to what I had already Written."[1] Operatic prologues were common enough in France, and the original version—the first act—probably would have excited much less discussion than the full version has done. In his postscript Dryden mentions that the opera had been performed before Charles II two or three times, "especially the first and third Acts."[2] When Charles died on 6 February 1685, the purpose of the opera was lost. Once more, however, Dryden conceived of a way of saving the efforts made by him and the great costs run by the company. With "the addition of twenty or thirty lines" to recognize the death of Charles and accession of James, the opera as we have it was at last publicly performed on 3 June 1685.[3] But the opera's problems were not done. The landing by Monmouth's invading forces in the west country closed the stage. Two days later publication was advertised in *The Observator,* and the first edition appeared in a larger than usual size, with at least one large copy version surviving.[4] About two years later, with the licensing date of 15 March 1687, a good-sized, well-printed edition of the music and libretto appeared for those who had subscribed in advance at a guinea a volume or for those who were willing to pay twenty-five shillings after publication. Tonson printed the libretto of the opera for the second time in 1691.

Contrary to its reputation, the opera seems to have been a reasonably successful venture. Interrupted only by an invasion and incipient civil war, it was printed three times in seven years. Everything of Dryden's composition holds interest of some kind, this opera included. But it can only be regretted that the importance of his libretto has more to do with his ideas about opera and language and with the development of English opera than it does with his literary art. Apart from a few things, *Albion and Albanius* probably qualifies for last place among the many kinds of writing Dryden composed for public performance. Perhaps it would seem turgid in any setting. In a volume including two such masterpieces as *Don Sebastian* and *Amphitryon,* it seems almost to be by another hand. Today, the preface and its postscript hold greater interest than the libretto. And as Dryden seemed to be aware himself, the libretto is most

---

[1] Preface, 10:25–11:3.   [2] Postscript, 12:22–23.
[3] Van Lennep, p. 337. Macdonald's date is 6 June 1685 (p. 127).
[4] Macdonald, p. 128.

interesting for what it led to in the way of elaborate staging and for the
musical setting by Louis Grabu. It is in such non-literary terms that Dryden's first opera still has claims on our interest.

The Libretto and Dryden's Comments on the Opera

Dryden's preface makes clear that the events depicted in *Albion and
Albanius* derive from the twenty-five years since Charles had been restored. As he said, the version of the opera in rehearsal just before the
death of Charles "plainly represents the double restoration of his Sacred
Majesty," that is, Charles's return in 1660 and his struggles in the Popish
Plot and over the succession, leading to the royalist triumph after the
Rye House Plot. For the production, Dryden added only the apotheosis
of Albion (III, i, 201–232). As he suggested, the allegory of the opera is
obvious to anyone acquainted with the main events of the Restoration.
In the preface to the full score of *Albion and Albanius* published in
1687, Grabu (with some English assistance from Dryden?) [5] made clear
that the political intent of the opera was quite central:

> The happy Invention of the Poet furnish'd me with
> that Occasion: The feigned Misfortune of two Perse-
> cuted Hero's, was too thin a veil for the Moral not to
> shine through the Fable; the pretended Plot, and the
> true Conspiracy, were no more disguis'd on the private
> Stage, than they were on the publick Theater of the
> World. Never were two Princes united more straightly
> together in common Sufferings for ungrateful and Re-
> bellious Subjects. The nearness of their Blood was not
> greater than the conformity of their Fortunes: But the
> Almighty has receiv'd the one to his Mercy in Heaven,
> and rewarded the Constancy and Obedience of the other
> here below: Vertue is at last Triumphant in both places.
> Immortality is actually possessed by one Monarch; and
> the other had the Earnest of it, in the Type of Earthly
> Glory.

Other historical characters and incidents enter in. For example, Archon
is clearly George Monck, Duke of Albemarle. In addition to representing
innocence, as the name implies, Acacia may also figure forth Catherine of
Braganza, Charles's queen. Specific glossings of such matters will be found
in the notes.

Dryden was aware that his idea for a historical plot was strange in
opera, and he promised to give "a more pleasing Fable" if English audiences took to the full-scale opera.[6] The day of the happier fable came
with *King Arthur* and collaboration with Henry Purcell. Much of Dryden's career involved relating poems to music, and it is true that such

---

[5] It will be recalled that Dryden later wrote for Henry Purcell the epistle dedicatory for the published score of *The Prophetess* (see *Works*, XVII, 324–326). If
not Dryden, then someone else assisted Grabu.

[6] Preface, 11:31.

poems require more than literary criteria for judgment. As a dramatist, Dryden had long since come to terms with music in songs that were but interludes in a play, songs often accompanied by, and being specifically written for, certain dance forms such as the zambra. In *Albion and Albanius* what Dryden calls "(for want of a proper *English* Word) . . . *The Songish Part*," [7] possesses greater attractiveness than does the recitative, as is always the case in operas. Without question, his two finest songs in the literary sense are that of Thamesis, "Old Father *Ocean*" (II, ii, 142–157), and that of the Nereids, "From the low Palace of old Father *Ocean*" (III, i, 35–42). Dryden's imagination was always inspired by "something of the sea," and as Saintsbury put it, the Nereids' song is "unusually cadenc'd" for a poem of its age: here is some small promise of the handling of sounds and rhythms for music in the two St. Cecilia Day odes.[8]

To people whose ideas of opera are formed by Verdi and Mozart, by Wagner and Richard Strauss, *Albion and Albanius* must seem scarcely an opera at all. It will not be immediately apparent, except to students of the history of the opera, why Dryden's definition, or description, of "an Opera" in the opening paragraph of his preface should be famous, or why his distinction of *"The Songish Part"* should be endlessly repeated in histories of opera. The notes deal with many such details, but it remains to set Dryden's short treatise on opera into perspective.[9] The first long paragraph of the preface gives a description and a history of opera, the latter in what is in effect one of Dryden's many progress pieces, or a *translatio studii* of a given art. In the postscript to the preface he shows that on reflection he has come to doubt his statement about the Italians having learned from the Spanish. His account accords with what is known, and his implicit sequence of Italy, France, and England is obviously correct. Because of the close relations between the English and the French courts in the reigns of Charles II and James II, Italian opera was largely unknown in England, except of course by virtue of its major part in what had become French opera. Italian opera had its impact on England in the eighteenth century, as readers of Pope will recall.[10] Dryden's account of opera, however brief, has priority in English in many respects, and not least for its detailed knowledge and its largeness of historical conception.

The second paragraph of the preface deals with the genius of various

---

[7] *Ibid.*, 4:4–5. [8] See "Grabu's Music," below.

[9] Information on early English opera is to be found in *Roger North on Music,* ed. John Wilson (1959) and in full detail in North, "The Musicall Grammarian or a practick Essay upon Harmony, plain and artificiall" (British Museum MS Add. 32533); Edward J. Dent, *Foundations of English Opera* (1928); and Alfred Loewenberg, *Annals of Opera, 1597–1940* (1943).

[10] A valuable example of early eighteenth-century attitudes will be found in the English translation of François Raguenet's *A Comparison Between the French and Italian Musick and Opera's,* to which is added *A Critical Discourse upon Opera's in England* (1709). The Cambridge University Library copy reprinted by Gregg International Publishers Limited (1968) includes very interesting and full annotation by an anonymous contemporary.

languages, according Italian the highest praise. The comparison of the vernaculars was long since traditional in English Renaissance criticism and had been given renewed interest by the learned if rather strange book by the learned and strange Isaac Vossius, *De Poematum Cantu et Viribus Rhythmi* (1673).[11] The rise of opera in England aroused in Dryden renewed interest in ancient *topoi* concerning the relation between music and poetry. Historians of such matters have found it strange that English poets and composers before him should have been so much less touched than he by "musical humanism." [12] Quite apart from the misunderstanding of the seventeenth century and of Dryden's place in it, such historians have failed to observe Dryden's distinct advantage in being a contemporary of the brothers Lawes, of Locke and Blow, and of the brothers Purcell. He numbered among his acquaintances such collectors and composers as Pepys, Evelyn, Grabu, Draghi, and Purcell, not to mention lesser figures. Moreover, his deep critical devotion to the understanding of his own art fostered his advantages and nourished his critical intelligence.

The remainder of Dryden's preface concerns *Albion and Albanius* in particular, adducing the claim that it "has attempted a discovery beyond any former Undertaker of our Nation" (7:31–32). Dryden implies that the attempt has not been fully realized. At least that inference suggests itself from talk of the difficulties encountered and of the claque aroused against Grabu because he had the ill judgment to be French. Dryden next discusses in practical terms the problems presented by the operatic form and by the necessity of adapting English to opera, so bringing to focus the general problems of language discussed earlier in theoretical terms. His strongest feelings burst out in his lament that as librettist he has been "a Slave to the composition, which I will never be again: 'Tis my part to Invent, and the Musicians to Humour that Invention." [13] Such a position hardly makes its advocate an ideal librettist. He concludes the preface

---

[11] For the comparison of European languages, see Sir Philip Sidney, *An Apology for Poetry*, in G. Gregory Smith, ed., *Elizabethan Critical Essays* (1904), I, 204–205. And in J. E. Spingarn's *Critical Essays of the Seventeenth Century* (1957), see George Chapman's "Preface to Homer" (I, 79). The feature of English that received most attention was its abundant monosyllables. For example, see George Puttenham (Smith, ed., *Essays*, II, 117, 121–122) and George Gascoigne (*ibid.*, I, 51), who somewhat unusually finds virtues in them. The European setting of Vossius' ideas and the place of Dryden's ideas in the musical tradition is well discussed by D. T. Mace, "Musical Humanism, the Doctrine of Rhythmus, and the Saint Cecilia Odes of Dryden," *JWCI*, XXVII (1964), 251–292. See also the commentary on *A Song for St. Cecilia's Day* in *Works*, III, 459–467.

[12] For Renaissance and seventeenth-century ideas of "speculative music," see John Hollander, *The Untuning of the Sky* (1961); see also Mace, "Musical Humanism," for a full review and valuable supplement as well as other citations.

[13] See 10:17–19. Dryden is the first author quoted here who uses "composition" in the modern sense relating to a musical composer.

with very warm praise for Thomas Betterton, the great actor and director with whom he had so often worked before, for his colleague Grabu, and with a moral for loyal Englishmen.

Dryden's text shows, in every respect, an unusual compound of the political and the lyric. The political element was of course present in the opera from the outset as one of its most prominent, because most unusual, features.[14] The main source for Dryden's plot was obviously Restoration history itself, but he also levied on Spenser and Jonson. The steps by which "Brutes Albyon," as Chaucer called England, developed from a nation into a person and then into the king are no doubt many, but for Dryden's and our purposes it is sufficient to begin with the eleventh canto of the fourth book of *The Faerie Queene*. In celebrating the marriage of the Thames and the Medway, Spenser envisioned a masque-like procession of personifications so rich that subsequent poets as late as Pope drew on it. Much of Dryden's alluvial and marine detail, and some of his pageantry, will be found already in Spenser, including that personification, "mightie Albion, father of the bold / And warlike people, which the Britaine Islands hold" (IV, xi, 15, 8–9). What then follows (st. xvi) is even closer to Dryden's historical vein:

> For Albion the sonne of Neptune was,
> Who for the proofe of his great puissance,
> Out of his Albion did on dry-foot pas
> Into old Gall, that now is cleeped France,
> To fight with Hercules, that did advance
> To vanquish all the world with matchlesse might,
> And there his mortall part by great mischance
> Was slaine: but that which is th' immortall spright
> Lives still: and to this feast with Neptunes seed was dight.

Jonson drew on Spenser and classical equivalents for his masque *Neptunes Triumph for the Returne of Albion*. The masque was to have been performed on Twelfth Night, 1624, to celebrate the return of Charles I (Albion), then still Prince of Wales, from Spain. James I (Neptune) apparently wished to welcome back his son in royal fashion, and most Englishmen were also glad to have their prince back, at least without the Spanish wife whom he had gone to seek. The performance was postponed by disputes between the French and Spanish ambassadors over precedence until the point was lost. Jonson returned to his text for performance on Twelfth Night the following year and celebration of the betrothal of Charles and Henrietta Maria. Again there was a delay, but only of three days, and the new version, *The Fortunate Isles and Their Union,* was performed. The title and part of the plot of the revision connect both backward to Spenser's canto and forward to *Albion and Albanius.* But *Neptunes Triumph for the Returne of Albion* had the advantage of celebrating return or restoration—one of Dryden's central concepts—and

---

[14] "No worse form than the operatic can possibly be imagined for political satire," wrote Saintsbury (S-S, VII, 227) with some justice, although ignoring the fact that Dryden's opera is more a panegyric in the masque tradition than a satire.

its use of marine detail simply made more sense than did that of Jonson's *Fortunate Isles*. The later masques of Jonson combine the loftiest symbolic and allegorical figures with the homely and realistic in ways more complex than in his earlier celebrations. This is not the place to discuss Jonson's masques, however, and it is enough to say that the combination of elements that modern critics find strained in *Albion and Albanius,* with gods and personifications representing historical reality, simply did not trouble the seventeenth century early or the seventeenth century late. Again, Jonson's final chorus celebrating James I might have been written by Dryden, at least as to political conception:

> And may thy Subjects hearts be all on flame:
> Whilst thou dost keepe the earth in firme estate,
> And, 'mongst the winds, dost suffer no debate.
> But both at sea, and land, our powers increase,
> With health, and all the golden gifts of peace.[15]

Both Spenser's "warlike people" ruled by Albion and Jonson's vision of "the golden gifts of peace" would have found response in Dryden. As he so presciently observed in *Annus Mirabilis,* England's imperial future lay in commercial activity, and for an island kingdom that meant trade. Such activity was possible, Dryden knew, only in peace; but he also understood that the *pax Britannica* would be possible only after eliminating England's great rival, the Netherlands, that Carthage to the new Rome. England's triumph was not to come until the next century but, as Dryden showed in *Annus Mirabilis,* and as he implies by his symbolism in the opera, Charles II and James II were great fosterers of the navy and of naval trade. To the end of his life Dryden was a navy man, which also meant —as the examples of Pepys and Captain Christopher Gunman [16] show— a "Yorkist," a supporter of James. Even writing to his Williamite cousin, John Driden, in the last year of his life, Dryden centers his hopes for England on peace, trade, and the defensive navy. He acknowledges William's triumph at Namur, insisting to be sure that it is a wholly English achievement, but the implications and the emphasis are clear:

> Our Foes, compell'd by Need, have Peace embrac'd:
> The Peace both Parties want, is like to last:
> Which, if secure, securely we may trade;
> Or, not secure, shou'd never have been made.
> Safe in our selves, while on our selves we stand,
> The Sea is ours, and that defends the Land.
> Be, then, the Naval Stores the Nations Care,
> New Ships to build, and batter'd to repair.[17]

---

[15] From *Neptunes Triumph,* ll. 550–554. The text has been taken from *Ben Jonson,* ed. C. H. Herford, Percy and Evelyn Simpson (1925–1952), VII, 700. The same chorus concludes *The Fortunate Isles.* For more recent general comment on Jonson's masques, see the introductory comments in *Ben Jonson: The Complete Masques,* ed. Stephen Orgel (1969).

[16] See I, i, 212+ *s.d.,* note.

[17] *To My Honour'd Kinsman,* ll. 142–149. William III, as a general, was in his element on land.

The nautical symbolism and detail of Dryden's opera create a system of values that had been anticipated by *Annus Mirabilis* and had been used to comparable thematic ends by Spenser and Jonson.

Given Dryden's allegiances and their practical political implications, it is no wonder that he allotted James a role even before Charles's death. One may guess that the role was not specified in the original title, which probably had the spirit of "Albion's Triumph" or "Albion's Restoration." The existing title skillfully associates Albanius-James with Albion-Charles in a nice alliteration. "Albanius" does not have the same rich lore that surrounds Albion, however. Dryden derives the name from a good enough fact: even before becoming king, James was Duke of York *and* Albany.[18] It is possible that to Dryden the name also held associations with earlier dukes of Albany, who were powerful, warlike Scots, or with a literary figure like the noble Duke of Albany in Shakespeare's *King Lear*. Whatever the overtones, the appearance of Albanius-James in Dryden's story inevitably made a political point, since James, Duke of York and of Albany, represented the principles, or dogmas, of Stuart royalism better than had the more flexible Charles II. With whatever fears and regrets he would look upon James, Dryden never wavered in his loyalty.[19]

It can be said of few operas, as it must be said of *Albion and Albanius*, that the very act of performance constituted a political event, and this is yet another tie between the Dryden-Grabu opera and the earlier English masque. What was true of the first run and the first printing of the opera was probably even truer of subsequent publications. The 1687 folio edition with music, and accompanied by Grabu's dedication to the king, was an offering of incense, of what we must presume to have been a popular piece, to James II at the pinnacle of his power. The publication in 1691 could only have been construed as a Jacobite gesture during those first five or six difficult years for William III. The 1691 edition certainly can-

---

[18] The title of Duke of Albany was an English one held by the Stewart family, beginning with Robert Stewart, first Duke of Albany (?1340–1420) and later by James I, Charles I, as well as by James II. Dryden had only to Latinize the name of the dukedom to relate in sound but distinguish in title of honor James from Charles II, who held the dukedom of Cornwall. Standard reference works are considerably at variance on the details of James's accession to the title, and the standard biography does not help. It appears that James was *declared* Duke of York and Duke of Albany shortly after birth; but that he was *created* Duke of York in 1643 and Duke of Albany in Edinburgh in 1660.

[19] See Dryden's letter to Sir George Etherege (February 1687), wishing that James would emulate his brother's "noble idleness," because, Dryden believes, he will "not much advance his affaires by Stirring" (Ward, *Letters*, p. 27). All the same, Dryden wrote to Chesterfield in 1697, saying that he had delayed publishing his *Virgil* "thus long in hopes of his return, for whom, and for my Conscience I have suffered, that I might have layd my Authour at his feet" (Ward, *Letters*, pp. 85–86). Perhaps the finest thing that can be said of James is that so many men of principle and intelligence felt such lasting loyalty to him and what he stood for, although they recognized his failings and often feared his policies.

not represent any stage revival.[20] But the situation was quite different in 1697 when George Powell and John Verbruggen had performed *A New Opera; Called, Brutus of Alba: Or, Augusta's Triumph.* Part of the score and libretto had been published earlier as *The Single Songs, With the Dialogue* (1696), the music attributed to Daniel Purcell. The evidence indicates that this *Brutus of Alba* was performed in October or November of 1696.[21] The "New Opera" represents a forced union of Nahum Tate's tragedy, *Brutus of Alba* and *Albion and Albanius,* so making a "Triumph" out of the revolutionary settlement. By 1696, domestic unrest had quieted and William was firmly in control, enjoying the support of the majority and the resignation of most Jacobites. The achievement deserved some celebration, and this "New Opera" sought to supply it with a hotch-potch of Dryden's opera and Tate's tragedy in a five-act play graced by songs, dance, and a few machines. In brief, the self-styled opera reverts to the "plays with music" formula long since passé.[22] The political import of *Albion and Albanius* had been acknowledged—and inverted—to celebrate the triumph of the Revolution.

Such tributes from adversaries cannot have cheered Dryden much, and his own preface shows that he chafed under the necessity of writing poetry to a composer's measure. For all that, his text is at least formally characteristic of much of his work. It combines a simplified version of his couplets, versions of his song styles, and something new, the irregular strophes of the "pindaric" ode. As far as can be told, at the very time that he was writing his creaky libretto, he composed his first pindaric ode, his splendid translation of Horace's twenty-ninth ode of the third book, which appeared in *Sylvæ*. The experimentation in an opera and a translation prepared the way for a succession of major odes in the pindaric form. *Threnodia Augustalis* and the Anne Killigrew ode soon followed. By then Dryden was prepared to write for musical setting those odes that were cantatas and which include his finest lyric poetry. His first great such triumph came in 1687 with *A Song for St. Cecilia's Day.* After an interval of some years, there followed, in 1696, a lesser piece, *An Ode, on the Death of Mr. Henry Purcell,* beautifully set (for the first two of the three stanzas at least) by Purcell's teacher, John Blow. The next year, and

---

[20] Van Lennep, p. 386, raises the possibility of performance in 1691 on the generally sound principle that re-publication of a play commonly followed a revival. But that was not possible for *Albion and Albanius* under William III. Quite apart from the subtitle repeated from the earlier editions, "Perform'd at the QUEENS Theatre, in *Dorset* Garden" (the name the theater held for a time on the accession of James II), the Lord Chamberlain could not have allowed on the stage a play so un-Williamite in the early unsettled years after the Revolution. Even if he had, the finances of the United Company would not have allowed performance, and even if the company had had the money, the resulting production would have aroused such commotion that the records of the time would have written it up for us as a notorious event.

[21] Van Lennep, p. 468. Dent's commentary, p. 178, is confused.

[22] The excellent phrase is Dent's, for his ch. vii. The cost of putting on "plays with music" was far less than producing operas like *Albion and Albanius* with so many "machines" and other spectacular effects.

again for St. Cecilia's Day, he wrote one of his most popular poems, *Alexander's Feast*. The problem of writing poetry for music had been so triumphantly solved that nearly half way between the two St. Cecilia's Day odes he could collaborate with Purcell on *King Arthur* (1691). That very English opera had indeed "a more pleasing Fable," [23] but it is doubtful that the success to be expected from combining the talents of two of England's great artists would have been realized without the experience of *Albion and Albanius*.

Whatever the popularity of his first venture into opera, the immediate effect was loss, something Dryden had not suffered in a first attempt for many years. The gains from unsatisfactory experience were to follow. *Amphitryon*, for example, shows how Dryden had gained control of a milieu intermixing gods and men to meaningful ends. But the chief benefit earned by the realization of what had gone wrong came in the accession of strength and seriousness to his lyric powers. If we join to *Albion and Albanius* the translation of Horace's *Ode 29. Book 3, Threnodia Augustalis,* and the Anne Killigrew ode, we can observe that in 1685 Dryden joined the other great poets of his century in that distinctive and varied lyric achievement which sets them off from the major poets of the next age. His poetic practice and numerous references show that Dryden loved music, although unlike Milton and Pepys he seems to have played no instrument, and he showed a preference for the human voice over instrumental music.[24] That preference for the human element is sufficiently characteristic of the poet and the man to be reflected in his choice of portraiture over landscape painting.[25] In *A Song for St. Cecilia's Day* (*Works*, III, 201–203), the *de rigeur* praise of the saint's traditional instrument, the organ, is qualified by a word-play, for its greatness came when she gave it "vocal Breath" (l. 52). The essential creation in human art, like the divine creation of the world, required a harmony made possible by "tuneful Voice" (l. 6). The apparent theatrical success and the evident literary frustration brought by *Albion and Albanius* was a disguised benefit that gave rise to a new dimension in Dryden's literary achievement.

The Staging

The basic features of English staging in 1685 remained those of the sixties, and for ordinary dramatic practice the reader is referred to the discussion in an earlier volume of this edition.[26] *Albion and Albanius* is, however, "an astonishing field for study," [27] and it seems worthwhile to discuss its remarkable exploitation of scenes and machines, especially because the information we possess is unusually detailed and authoritative.

---

[23] *Albion and Albanius*, preface, 11:31.

[24] See *Britannia Rediviva*, ll. 320–323 (*Works*, III, 220); *The Flower and the Leaf* (in *Fables*), ll. 146–152.

[25] See the Anne Killigrew ode, ll. 108–141 (*Works*, III, 112–113), where landscape painting is imaged as a pastoral France with ruins, and portraiture as royal England represented by a heroic James II and his beautiful Queen Mary.

[26] See *Works*, VIII, 307 ff.

[27] Richard Southern, *Changeable Scenery* (1952), p. 157. In spite of the devoted study by many historians of the theater, much remains conjectural.

The opera was performed at the Dorset Garden Theatre, which after its opening by the Duke's Company in November 1671 became the principal house for the performance of operas. The two companies were united in 1682. Dorset Garden presented the company with the maximum available flexibility and capacity for scenic effect. Dryden and the management seized the opportunities and provided theatergoers with one of the most lavish pieces thus far presented on the English public stage. It is small wonder that to regain their costs the company raised prices for admission.

The account that follows seeks to amplify the stage directions provided Dryden by Betterton (and perhaps revised by the poet for inclusion in the printed play). The references to line numbers are, therefore, to be taken as references to the stage directions at such lines. Where line numbers are not given, the stage direction will be found at the beginning of an act or scene.

With the rising of the curtain the audience discovered a "new Frontispiece . . . joyn'd to the great Pylasters, which are on each side of the Stage." The frontispiece was in the form of an arch, similar to that described at the beginning of the "operatic" *Tempest*, 1674.[28] Betterton describes in detail the figures and objects painted on the revealed frontispiece, beginning at the base (his *basis*) of each column and moving up across the arch. There are shields, scrolls, allegorical and symbolic figures, and prominently placed in "the Sweep of the Arch" are "two Imperial Figures; one representing his present Majesty; the other the Queen," over each of whom is a scroll with a verse from Virgil.

Act I

a. The curtain is again said to rise, but the statement refers to the same rising as that which revealed the Frontispiece, in order that description may now be given of what lies behind the Frontispiece. At either side there are replicas, apparently statues rather than painted versions, of *"the late King"* and *"his present Majesty"* on horseback. These statues are distinguished from the *"Scene,"* which depicts a *"Street of Palaces,"* leading to the Royal Exchange. A series of scenes sliding together in pairs was probably devised to give the perspective of the street, and one pair is partly cut out to reveal more behind.

b. A machine descends with Mercury in a chariot drawn by ravens. This is one of the machines that the audience would have observed hanging from the top of the theater when they entered.

Southern's excellent analysis and conjecture are based on fact where possible, and on intimate knowledge of the stage as a functioning mechanism. We are indebted to him in much of this discussion.

[28] The "operatic" *Tempest* was also produced at Dorset Garden. Southern (*Changeable Scenery*, p. 185) notes that the "same curious phrase" respecting the frontispiece and the great pilasters occurs in the opening stage directions of both operas. It may be noted, perhaps, that in *Albion and Albanius* this phrasing occurs in the description which prefaces the opera (and which concerns only the frontispiece proper); the opening stage direction describes the elaborate scene on the stage itself (see Act I. *a.* below).

c. Mercury, having descended, walks to Augusta and Thamesis, who have been revealed by the curtain's rising; they lie on couches *"at a distance from each other."* Mercury's words begin the opera's libretto.

d. 24–25. Alternate singing (*"by Reprises"*) by Augusta and Thamesis.

e. 76. Dance by the followers of Mercury, such action requiring the stage apron. (It is not said when the "followers" come on stage, but as with later similar incidents, they join him on stage to make up his train when he alights from his chariot.)

f. 114–115. Singing together by Augusta and Thamesis.

g. 148, 153, 166. Archon touches Democracy and Zelota asleep with Mercury's caduceus.

h. 170. Ascent of a double pedestal; Democracy and Zelota fall asleep on it and they sink with it. (Here and later there is evidence that the trapdoors and related machines below stage are of considerable size.)

i. 189. A dance of Watermen in the King's and Duke's liveries.

j. 189. Machine. The clouds divide. Juno appears in a machine drawn by peacocks. We must accept as most likely the explanation that the scenes for the Royal Exchange were painted on independent lower flats, or shutters, and that clouds were painted on independent upper flats.[29] Those clouds open as the upper slides are drawn, and Juno's machine *"moves gently forward"* to music; when it has reached the front of the stage, it descends, and as it does so a peacock's tail opens so widely *"that it almost fills the opening of the Stage between Scene and Scene,"* that is, those scenes painted and partly visible at either side of the stage.

k. 212. Machine. Iris *"appears"* on a very large machine whose decoration is modeled on a celestial display seen in Calais (see the note, and illustration on p. 28). It is not stated where the machine comes from, but from l. 238 *s.d.,* it is evident that her very large machine, capable of holding three people, has descended from the top of the theater.

l. 222. *Ritornello* (musical interlude).

m. 238. Machine. The machine that brought down Iris now ascends with Mercury and Juno as well as Iris.

n. 246. Scene change. Scenic flats depicting the Royal Exchange are withdrawn; as they disappear from sight, they reveal a scene depicting four triumphal arches.

o. Discovery. Because Albion, Albanius, and others are not said to enter but to appear, the disappearance of the forward scenes reveals them, while the Chorus remains on the stage apron.

p. 255. Dance. An "Entry" by the Four Parts of the World.

Act II, Scene i

a. There is an unusual "Total" change of scene. The frontispiece remains, but the *"Side Scenes"* have been replaced, as well as the *"Upper part of the House,"* probably meaning those independent cloud

---

[29] *Ibid.,* pp. 155–156.

flats above the lower Royal Exchange flats of Act I (see j). The new
scene is Hell. The characters present are Pluto, the Furies (including
Alecto), Democracy, and Zelota.

b. 123. Dances. First an "Entry" of a single Devil, then of twelve Devils.
Characters leave the stage.

Act II, Scene ii

a. The Scene changes. That is, sliding flat scenes are taken back reveal-
ing hitherto unseen flats showing a prospect of the Thames, with the
London-Westminster side in the foreground and the Southwark-
Lambeth area in the background. Augusta enters.

b. 18. Enter Democracy and Zelota partly disguised.

c. 54. Enter Albion, Albanius, and their train to the same scene.

d. 74. Machine descends with Mercury.

e. 88. Machine ascends with Mercury.

f. 128. *Ritornello.*

g. 128. Machine with Apollo and his horses gradually discovered. One
of the most complex spectacles, this involves the dividing of a *"farther
part"* of the flats used here to represent the sky. They are farther toward the back of the stage and lower, leaving the higher, front scenes
for the Heaven in place. Apollo's machine is first revealed far back,
as it descends *toward* the stage but not to it, his painted horses behind
and above him are revealed, and he sings his aria.

h. 141. Machine with Apollo now continues coming forward; but rising
upward toward the frontispiece, it disappears from the sight of the
audience.

i. 141. Ascent of Neptune as from the water, with a train of Rivers,
Tritons, and Sea Nymphs attending him by walking on stage as he
rises from beneath.

j. 157. *Chaconne*, or dance-music finale in moderately slow tempo, interspersed with singing by a Chorus of Nymphs and Tritons and by a
single Triton and two Nymphs.

k. 181. Descent of Neptune; other characters leave the stage.

Act III, Scene i

a. Scene changes: slides reveal a view of Dover from the seaside toward
the land. Enter Albion bareheaded (highly unusual for a stage king
or hero) and Acacia with him.

b. 34. Ascent of Nereids as from the sea to sing while Tritons, who
have walked onto the stage, dance.

c. 42. Unmarked descent (or exit) of Nereids and departure of Tritons
from the stage. Enter Tyranny and Democracy represented by men,
along with Asebia and Zelota, who are women.

d. 85. Dance by mute characters who walk or dance onto the stage to
play Boys in White, performing a "Fantastik Dance."

e. 96. Dance. Among the characters on stage or coming on stage are six Sectaries, termed Saints in earlier singing; they perform a stiff, affected dance and engage in a pantomime of conspiracy.

f. 125. Dance by White Boys and Saints; pantomime of a fight; the Saints or Sectaries drive out the White Boys.

g. 141. Ascent of the Cave of Proteus as if from the sea.

h. 141. An instrumental composition played ("Symphony").

i. 156. Descent of Proteus.

j. 156. Re-entry of Democracy, Zelota, and followers.

k. 167. Advance of the one-eyed Archer, who is stopped from harming Albion by an intervening burst of fire.

l. 167. *Ritornello.*

m. 178. *Ritornello.*

n. 178. After the music the faction seeks to retreat toward the front of the stage, but a fire arises behind them, and the whole group sinks beneath the stage.

o. 189. Ascent of another machine as if from the sea; it opens, revealing Venus (attended by Loves and Graces) and Albanius (attended by Heroes). It rises backstage, advances toward the audience during an instrumental composition, brings the characters to the forestage, and then sinks through a trapdoor in the forestage. As usual, the attendants of Venus and Albanius walk up to them, not being important enough, and being too numerous, for machines.

p. 194. Dance of an Entry by Graces and Loves.

q. 199. Dance by the Heroes.

r. 200. *Ritornello.*

s. 200. An instrumental composition accompanies the descent of a very large and splendid machine, oval in shape. Apollo sits on a throne of gold in its center and, on descending, leaves the machine and approaches Albion.

t. 232. Machine ascends, Albion mounting that used by Apollo and slowly being taken up.

u. 232. Full chorus singing the words of Acacia's last aria, followed by a piece by Venus and then the departure of the characters from the stage.

Act III, Scene ii

a. The scene changes: new flats are shown depicting the area of Windsor, emphasizing St. George's chapel and in the air a vision of Knights of the Garter in procession before the king.

b. Ascent of Fame in the middle of the stage, standing on a globe which is based on a pedestal with a scene.

c. 14. Full chorus with all voices and instruments interspersed with *ritornelli* by trumpets and oboes, the chorus repeating the phrases of Fame's song; meanwhile twenty-four dancers join in a Chorus, and their dancing concludes the opera. The curtain descends.

One understands from such a relation the force of Dryden's acknowledgment in the preface: "The descriptions of the Scenes, and other decorations of the Stage, I had from Mr. *Betterton,* who has spar'd neither for industry, nor cost, to make this Entertainment perfect, nor for Invention of the Ornaments to beautify it" (11:11–14). As usual, Dryden gives credit to others, and it must be confessed that the directions supplied by Betterton are useful to understanding the acting of Dryden's libretto as they are also valuable for the history of Restoration staging.

There is, however, in the preface, that other passage revealing something of Dryden's character (10:26–11:3). It

> allows us to catch sight of Dryden so concerned with the
> welfare of his actors that he commits himself to extra
> work so that they will not lose their small wages.[30]

No doubt he had as well the interests of the manager, the King, and himself in mind. He knew the theater well enough to appreciate the talents of those who performed his works, and well enough, too, to realize that the lavish staging of *Albion and Albanius* was sufficiently important for him to ask Betterton for detailed directions.

Louis Grabu in England

No sooner did Louis Grabu become "Composer-in-ordinary" to Charles II's court in 1665 [31] than other preferments came his way in rapid succession. In 1666 he was appointed Master of the English Chamber Musick [32] upon the death of Nicholas Laniere. (Incidentally, this appointment lent official recognition to a general preference for the latest French styles [33] which had been developing both at court and around and about London since the Restoration. Even the fact of Grabu's succession to Laniere's office symbolizes the trend, for the latter had figured as one of the most important composers in the transplanting of Italian second practice to England during the first quarter of the seventeenth century.) [34] Two years later, Grabu became Master of the King's Violins,[35] to the chagrin of the incumbent, John Bannister, who was unceremoniously forced to step down from office. It was at that point, no doubt, that Bannister began to think of launching his own venture in London as a free-lance concert entrepreneur—a venture of considerable historical importance, since from it developed one of the first public concert series in history.

Grabu had flourished also as a figure in London's musical life. Even before the preferments mentioned above he had performed for the public his setting of an English "Song on Peace," as reported by Samuel Pepys

---

[30] Charles E. Ward, "Challenges to Dryden's Biographer," in *John Dryden* (Clark Library Publication, 1967), p. 17.

[31] Henry Cart de Lafontaine, *The King's Musick* (1909), p. 177.

[32] *K.M.,* 193.

[33] Jack Allan Westrup, "Foreign Musicians in Stuart England," *The Musical Quarterly,* XXVII (1941), p. 75.

[34] Vincent Duckles, "English Song and the Challenge of Italian Monody" in *Words to Music* (Clark Library Publication, 1967), pp. 7–9, *et seq.*

[35] *K.M.,* 191.

on 1 October 1667.[36] And on Wednesday, 15 April 1668 Pepys had gone
by water to White Hall, 1s., and there [sic] to the Chapel,
expecting wind musick: and to the Harp-and-Ball. . . .
Back, and to the fiddling concert, and heard a practice
mighty good of Grebus.

To this it need only be added that Pepys's praise was not lightly given.
Perhaps Grabu had risen too rapidly. Certainly it seems clear, even
though few records are available, that he was thoroughly disliked by his
English colleagues. This we know from Pelham Humphrey's comments
cited by Pepys in his entry for 15 November 1667:

Thence I away home, calling at my mercer's and tailor's,
and there find, as I expected, Mr. Cæsar and little Pelham Humphreys, lately returned from France, and is an
absolute Monsieur, as full of form, and confidence, and
vanity, and disparages everything, and everybody's skill
but his own. The truth is, every body says he is very
able, but to hear how he laughs at all the King's musick
here, as Blagrave and others, that they cannot keep time
nor tune, nor understand anything; and that Grebus, the
Frenchman, the King's master of the musick, how he
understands nothing, nor can play on any instrument,
and so cannot compose: and that he will give him a lift
out of his place; and that he and the King are mighty
great! and that he hath already spoke to the King of
Grebus would make a man piss.

Some hint of inner opposition is also reflected in the royal order to John
Bannister that he

and the 24 violins appointed to practice with him and
all his Majesty's private musick doe, from tyme to tyme,
obey the directions of Louis Grabu.[37]

This seemingly casual directive was something more than a mere straw in
the wind, as Pepys intimated in reporting the latest tidbit of court
gossip on 20 February that same year:

Here they talk also how the King's viallin, Bannister,
is mad that the King hath a Frenchman come to be chief
of some part of the King's musique, at which the Duke
of York made great mirth.

Two points are worth considering here. It is interesting that Grabu had
managed to be put in charge of a small, select group of violins, for this
action closely parallels the machinations Lully used at the French court
to gain control of musical activities there. Pepys's mention of the Duke
of York's "great mirth" is also instructive, for it makes clear that Grabu's
promotion was regarded as a victory by the Francophile Catholic element
at court, of which the Duke was a leading political figure. By 14 March,
the French faction reigned supreme, and poor Bannister's disgrace was

---

[36] *The Diary of Samuel Pepys,* ed. Henry B. Wheatley (1899), VII, 130.
[37] *K.M.,* 191.

complete. On that date came down an order from the Lord Chamberlain establishing Grabu as the leader of the select "12 violins." [38]

By the end of 1667/68 the French vogue reached its zenith. Numerous favorable developments such as the above-mentioned had culminated in a splendid concert given at Whitehall on 1 October 1667. The indefatigable Pepys, however, was less pleased with the music on that occasion than with its manner of performance, which he found impressive:

> to White Hall, and there in the Boarded-gallery did hear the musick with which the King is presented this night by Monsieur Grebus, the master of his musick; both instrumentall—I think twenty-four violins—and vocall; an English song upon Peace. But, God forgive me! I never was so little pleased with a concert of musick in my life. The manner of setting of words and repeating them out of order, and that with a number of voices, makes me sick, the whole design of vocall musick being lost by it. Here was a great press of people; but I did not see many pleased with it, only the instrumental musick he had brought by practice to play very just.[39]

During the course of the next few years Grabu continued to flourish, as may be gathered from the regular entries in the Lord Chamberlain's records for payments of his annual stipends and liveries. Then, in September of 1673,[40] there arrived in London one Robert Cambert, who had left Paris a victim of the machinations by which Lully had taken over the royal privilege to perform operas in France. He was Grabu's former teacher and the two lost no time after his arrival in London in establishing a "Royall Academy of Musick in Bridges Street, Covent Garden." Cambert's opera *Ariane, ou Le Mariage de Bacchus* was produced there, opening on 30 March 1674, and running for thirty days.[41] There is some question as to whether this was the version Cambert had originally composed for Paris, or whether Grabu actually had had a hand in its composition for the London performance. But there is no doubt that the latter helped with the production and musical performance, for on 27 March there came down a warrant from the Lord Chamberlain which ordered that there be delivered

> to Monsieur Grabu, or to such as he shall appoynt, such of the scenes remayning in the theatre at Whitehall as shall be useful for the French opera at the theatre in Bridges Street, and the said Monsieur Grabu to return them again safely after 14 days' tyme, to the theatre in Whitehall.[42]

One success led naturally to hope for another, and on 4 July following,

---

[38] *K.M.*, 193.   [39] Pepys, *Diary*, VII, 130 (1 October 1667).

[40] *Grove's Dictionary of Music and Musicians*, ed. Eric Blom (1955), II, 25.

[41] *Die Musik in Geschichte und Gegenwart*, ed. Friedrich Blume (1952), II, col. 695.

[42] *K.M.*, 269.

the twelve violins were ordered to report to Cambert at Whitehall at seven o'clock the next Wednesday morning for the royal entertainment to be performed at Windsor on Saturday, 11 July.[43] The pieces performed included *Pomone,* the very same opera with which Cambert and Perrin had begun their ill-starred enterprise in Paris three years earlier, and a *Ballet et Musique pour le Divertissement du Roy de Grande Bretagne.* The libretto for the latter, probably by Sebastian Bremond, as set to music by Cambert and Favier,[44] was printed by "Thomas Nieucombe dans la Savoy" later that year.

As if to capitalize on these successes among lovers of music in the French style, in 1675 Thomas Shadwell brought forth his version of *Psyche,* an "opera" in English. It was produced at Dorset Garden on Saturday, 27 February, with music by G. B. Draghi and Matthew Locke.[45] The libretto rests directly on the *Psyche* of the *tragédie-ballet* of Lully and Racine, the choreography was under the care of Monsieur St. André, the scenes were painted by Stephenson, and the production, apparently, was under the joint guidance of the author and Thomas Betterton. Shadwell's professed intent was "to entertain the town with variety of music, curious dancing, splendid scenes and machines." It is clear that he intended to carry out this mixture of objectives on the French plan, even though he did not say so, and even though his colleagues in the venture included notable Englishmen and Italians as well as French masters. Shadwell carefully labeled the whole *The English Opera* (italics ours) as if it were the first of its kind, and Locke just as carefully defended himself against known enemies of innovation among the English public, calling attention to the "soft, easy and agreeable" nature of his compositions, and also—as if to defend these against any charge of narrow provinciality —referring to their formal variety:

> you have from Ballad to single Air, Counterpoint, Recitative, Fuge, Canon and Chromatic Musick; which variety (without vanity be it said) was never in Court or Theatre till now presented in this nation.[46]

On balance, the work still manifests mainly French influence, but the emphasis on other elements, both foreign and native, indicates a significant shift in English taste towards elaborate entertainment.

Whatever French influence upon London's musical life may have continued, no other major French musical spectacles were staged until May of 1677, when Madame de la Roche-Guilhen's *Rare en Tout* was performed at Whitehall, as we know from a letter written by John Verney to Edmund Verney on 31 May 1677:

> On Wednesday his Majesty's birth night was some gallantry at White Hall, where was acted a French opera, but most pitifully done, so ill that the King was aweary on't, and some say it was not well contrived to entertain

---

[43] *K.M.,* 273.   [44] Van Lennep, p. 213.   [45] *Ibid.,* pp. 229–230.
[46] Matthew Locke, *The English Opera; or The Vocal Musick in Psyche,* as cited by Percy M. Young, *A History of British Music* (1967), p. 237.

the English gentry, who came that night in honour to
their King, with a lamentable ill-acted French play, when
our English actors so much surpass; however, the dances
and the voices was [*sic*] pretty well performed.[47]

Again, the French company seems to have required official Royal support in order that rehearsals might run smoothly and according to the
wishes of author and producer. For the same date another entry in the
Lord Chamberlain's book records an

Order to Mr. Staggins, master of his Majesty's musick,
and in his absence to Mr. Lock who officiates for him:
That all His Majesty's musitians doe attend to practise
in the theatre at Whitehall at such tymes as Madame
Le Roch and Mr. Paisible shall appoint for the practis-
ing of such musick as is to be in the French comedy to be
acted before His Majesty on the 29 May instant.[48]

Clearly, a general disenchantment with French music on the part of
English audiences was in progress, establishing a trend which possibly may
be linked with Grabu's fall from favor. His low condition is reflected
not only in the absence of any reference to him in the above document,
but also, and more specifically, in the official memorandum of a matter
which must have been under serious consideration all during this period,
but which was entered into official records only on 5 June 1677:

Report———
In observance of Your Majesty's reference upon the
petition on Lewis Grabu by the Hon. Sir Joseph Wil-
liamson, one of Your Majesty's Secretaries of State, I do
humbly certifie that there is due in arrears to Lewis
Grabu, late Master of Your Majesty's music, the sum of
£450; out of the office of the Treasury Chamber,
£145.4s.6d; and out of the Great Wardrobe, £32.5s.
And I find his condition to be very poor and miserable,
all which I humbly submit to Your Majesty's wisdom.
(Signed) ARLINGTON [49]

Perhaps Grabu's falling-off was due not alone to musical misfortunes
but also to the fact that Charles II could no longer afford his services.
Moreover, it was difficult for the King openly to employ foreigners who
were known to be Catholics. As his impecuniousness placed him more
and more at the mercy of Protestant enemies he had to be increasingly
careful. In brief, the failure of the Royal Academy of Music and the fall
of Grabu may have been due as much to political adversity as to any
artistic shortcomings. Cambert, indeed, was doubly *persona non grata* to
most Whigs and Protestants who disliked him as much for the enormous
expenses his "Frenchyfied" productions entailed as for the fact that he
had been a close friend of the Papal Nuncio in Paris.[50] In the end, the

---

[47] *Great Britain, The Royal Commission on Historical Manuscripts, Seventh
Report* (1879), Appendix, p. 469.
[48] *K.M.,* 318.   [49] *K.M.,* 319.   [50] *Grove's Dictionary,* p. 25.

best that Charles II could do was to grant Grabu a passport for travel to France for himself, his wife and three children, issued 31 March 1679.

Grabu remained in France until late in 1683, his condition still unfortunate. Meanwhile, French musical interests at the court of Charles II continued to decline. The Italian musical element on the other hand was growing from strength to strength at court. Here is not the place to trace the growth of an Italian vogue, which was soon to supplant that for French music. Suffice it to say that from the time Nicolo Matteis arrived on the scene until the death of Charles II the Italian musicians, not the French, were getting most of the favor. After Charles II's death French musicians lost out altogether, as the new queen, Mary of Modena, became leading arbiter in courtly musical life.

Origins of the Opera

Charles, however, retained his interest in French music, and in August 1683 he sent Betterton to Paris, instructing him, as Lord Preston wrote to James in the following month, "to endeavour to carry over the [French] Opera" into England.[51] Failing in that attempt, Betterton instead negotiated with Grabu, "a poor servant of his Majesty's. . . . to go over with him to endeavour to represent something at least like an Opera in England for his Majesty's diversion. He . . . also assured him of a pension from the House, and [found] him very willing and ready to go over." [52] Once back in England, Grabu took the opportunity to publish, apparently at his own expense,[53] his *Pastoral in French*, which was advertised in the *London Gazette* for 14–17 July 1684 as "to be sold by Rowling Gilbert at the Duke's House."

The real point of Betterton's trip and Grabu's return soon became obvious, for Grabu had managed at last to get permission for a court production of his and Dryden's opera, which was eventually to be called *Albion and Albanius*.[54] Earliest notice of the work occurs in a letter from Edward Bedingfield to the Countess of Rutland, written on 1 January 1685:

> We are in expectation of an opera composed by Mr.
> Dryden and set by Grabuche, and so well performed at
> the repetition that has been made before His Majesty at
> the Duchess of Portsmouth's, pleaseth mightily, but the
> rates proposed will not take so well, for they have set
> the boxes at a guinea a place and the pit at half. They

---

[51] Preston's letter, dated 22 September 1683, is quoted by W. J. Lawrence in *The Elizabethan Playhouse and Other Studies* [First Series] (Stratford-upon-Avon, 1912), p. 149.

[52] *Ibid.*, p. 149.

[53] See Eleanore Boswell Murrie, "Notes on the Printers and Publishers of English Song-Books 1651–1702," *Edinburgh Bibliographical Society Transactions*, I (1935–1938), 257 and n.

[54] However, as we know from the title page of the published score, the opera actually was produced at Queen's Theatre, Dorset Garden.

advance £4,000 on the opera, and therefore must tax
high to reimburse themselves.[55]

Then Charles died suddenly, on 6 February 1685, and with him hope
for the production of Grabu's opera, which had to be hastily revised if
it was to survive at all. Five months passed before the new version, called
Albion and Albanius, was at last performed, not at Whitehall as had
been intended, but at the Queen's Theatre in Dorset Garden.[56] As mentioned earlier, the new production included additional portions which
Dryden and Grabu felt were necessary to fit the opera to both the departed and the reigning king. The general effect of these was to expand
further a work already too lengthy for the slender dramatic base upon
which the libretto had been originally planned, as a prologue to *King
Arthur.* Roger North's analysis of the fate of the opera was accurate, although curiously incomplete:

> The first full opera that was made and prepared for
> the stage, was the Albanio of Mr. Grabue, in English,
> but of a French Genius. It is printed in full score, but
> proved the ruin of the poor man, for the King's death
> supplanted all his hopes, and so it dyed.[57]

North was usually very careful in recording such events, but his use of
the curious short title *Albanio* diminishes the usefulness of this entry.
His note must therefore be supplemented by that of John Downes, who
recorded the later title in *Roscius Anglicanus:*

> In *Anno* 1685. The opera of *Albion* and *Albanius*
> was perform'd; wrote by Mr. Dryden, and compos'd by
> Monsieur Grabue: This being perform'd on a very Un-
> lucky Day, being the Day the Duke of Monmouth,
> Landed in the West: The Nation being in a great
> Consternation, it was perform'd but Six times, which
> not Answering half the Charge they were at, Involv'd
> the Company very much in Debt.[58]

The actual dates of the six performances are not known certainly al-
though the opening clearly occurred on Wednesday, 3 June. It seems
likely that there were later performances on Wednesday, 10 June and on
Saturday, 13 June, with the latter possibly being the final performance.[59]
However, since news of Monmouth's insurrection definitely arrived in
London during the day of the 13th,[60] it might be more reasonable to assume that the sixth and last performance took place on the evening of
Friday, 12 June. As to the dates of others, we cannot be certain. Nor can
we know the results of the advertisement of the publication of the full
score, which ran in the *London Gazette* for 11–15 June 1685:

> The Opera of Albion and Albanius, containing one
> Hundred and Three score sheets in Folio, is to be

---

[55] *Historical Manuscripts Commission, Rutland,* II (1889), 85.
[56] Allardyce Nicoll, *A History of English Drama 1660–1900* (1961), I, 158, 406.
[57] See *Roger North on Music,* p. 31, or B.M. Add. Ms. 32533, fol. 179.
[58] John Downes, *Roscius Anglicanus,* ed. Montague Summers (n.d.), p. 40.
[59] Van Lennep, p. 337.   [60] *Ibid.*

Printed, therefore the Author by the advice of his Friends
doth propose, That whoever will Subscribe for one Book
or more of the said Opera at a Guinea each Book, and
pay half of the whole in Hand towards the charge, shall
have the said Book or Books delivered to them as soon as
possible they can be Printed: That whoever doth not
subscribe shall not have a Book under the rate of
Twenty five Shillings for each Book. The subscribers
may if they please subscribe and Pay their half Guinea
or whole at Mr. Notts Bookseller in the Pall-Mall, or
Mr. Carr Bookseller by Temple-Bar, who will give them
a Receipt for what they shall receive.[61]

As we know from extant copies, the printing was carefully and elegantly done, a fact which only increases our regret that it should be both
the first and the only opera in English to be so published in the seventeenth century. It seems that the work was doomed to oblivion from the
start. Although one J. de Beaulieu did advertise in *The Post Man* for
24 June 1697, a performance of "Albion and Albianius [*sic*] . . . over
against St. Martin's Church, Charing Cross," the silence which settled
around the opera at the time of Monmouth's rebellion seems to have remained otherwise undisturbed up to the present day. Let us turn now to
the opera itself, to discover whether or not the limbo in which it has
existed for the better part of these three centuries be altogether justifiable.

Grabu's Music

As suggested above, Grabu's successes in England may have come too
quickly. Certainly, his rapid rise to royal favor aroused some very negative
reactions from Pelham Humphrey and John Bannister. Furthermore, Grabu
was treated none too kindly by public and court audiences in London, as
we may infer both from Samuel Pepys's criticisms and from Dryden's
elaborate defense of Grabu in his preface and postscript to *Albion and
Albanius*.[62] What with professional jealousies (which have always been
too common a part of musical life), and what with these being augmented
by a strongly xenophobic element among many people at court, one
senses that from the start Grabu would have had very little chance to
please his colleagues, Charles, and the general public all at once. On
these grounds, it is quite possible that this poor "prologue-grown-opera"
did not quite deserve all the censure then heaped upon it, nor all that it
has suffered during the course of the approximately three centuries that
have elapsed since its creation.

This is as much as to say that whatever its defects the opera deserves
objective appraisal of all its components—including libretto, stage decor,
machines, and choreography as well as lyrical and instrumental musical
portions—as these might be viewed in the light of the author's and composer's intentions. If careful consideration of all these factors only tended

---

[61] *London Gazette,* 11–15 June 1685.
[62] See above, pp. 337, 338; preface, 8:13–9:2 and postscript, 12:23–28.

to confirm modern scholarly evaluation of the work as mere royal flattery, perhaps it would be time now to dismiss *Albion and Albanius* once and for all. Before we could arrive fairly at such a conclusion, however, it would be necessary to see and hear the whole produced according to Dryden's, Grabu's, and Betterton's original intentions, as did those who, as Bedingfield reported, were so mightily pleased with the performance. Since this is most unlikely, we will have to do our best to imagine our way through the published full score, examining and analyzing both poetry and music on their own terms, relinquishing as many preconceptions as we possibly can as to what the opera should or should not have been, and at the same time, dismissing all reservations which might be based on earlier criticisms, however learned or eloquent their authors. In this connection it would be interesting, in view of the unanimity of received opinion, to know how many of the opera's most trenchant critics actually have taken the time and trouble required to play and sing through the whole of *Albion and Albanius*. Moreover, some of the criticisms involve assumptions which do not stand up under careful examination.

For instance, several authors have assumed that Grabu must necessarily have brought with him to England elements of Lullian operatic style, which had risen to a supreme position in the musical world by the time Grabu's opera was at last performed. Several considerations weaken such an assumption. First of all, Lully had not yet accomplished his brilliant rise to fame by the time Grabu left France, which was no later than 31 March 1665, possibly much earlier.[63] That is as much as to say that the Lullian style so frequently referred to had actually not yet been formulated. In fact, Lully was still very much opposed to Italianate opera in France until 1672, when he composed *Cadmus et Hermione,* his first opera, which appeared opportunely upon the heels of his joining forces with the operatic faction after successful machinations for the royal privilege for opera productions. Secondly, what we know of Grabu's French acquaintances indicates that he was a friend of Robert Cambert and Pierre Perrin, the very persons whom Lully had outwitted. It should not surprise us therefore to discover that Grabu's aesthetic differed both in small details and in grand design from that of the Lullian model.

Grabu's musical style as shown in *Albion and Albanius* reveals very few characteristics held in common with that of Lully in *Cadmus et Hermione.* His general manner of setting recitative resembles that of Lully so far as concerns the orchestral or basso continuo setting itself. But there is not a sign of the declamatory precision Lully was able to recreate—admittedly a much easier task in a French than in an English libretto. Nor in Grabu's setting can one speak of any "logogenic Principles" of organization. Few motives take rhythmic shape and pictorial quality from key words in the text. Descriptive nuances there are aplenty, but these are to be found mainly in arioso or aria-like passages. Like Lully, Grabu does use stylized dance rhythms in both lyric and choral

---

[63] *K.M.,* 177.

portions, and falls from time to time into what might be called "dance prosody" à la Vossius.[64] But these few instances of similarity are too general to indicate Lullian influence. Like other resemblances which might be pointed out, these indicate rather a common tradition which shaped the styles of both Grabu and Lully.

It would be equally unsound to contrast Grabu's "French Operatic Style" with contemporary Italian operatic manner, deploring, as some have done, its lack of contrast between fast-moving, staccato recitatives and lyrical arias. Obviously the very nature of this allegory, originally merely a prologue, and the fact that its text is in English would militate against close imitation of the aesthetic of either French or Italian models. Discussion of French and Italian influences of course will not be irrelevant, and certain technical and formal features of the opera clearly reflect these influences, as we shall later see. Basically, however, the central problems faced by Grabu and Dryden arose from the fact that their libretto was in English. Dryden clearly recognized the source of difficulties:

> The *English* has yet more natural disadvantages than the *French;* our original *Teutonique* consisting most in Monosyllables, and those incumber'd with Consonants, cannot possibly be freed from those Inconveniences. The rest of our Words, which are deriv'd from the *Latin* chiefly, and the *French,* with some small sprinklings of *Greek, Italian* and *Spanish,* are some relief in Poetry; and help us to soften our uncouth Numbers, which together with our *English* Genius, incomparably beyond the triffling of the *French,* in all the nobler Parts of Verse, will justly give us the Preheminence. But, on the other hand, the Effeminacy of our pronunciation, (a defect common to us, and to the *Danes*) and our scarcity of female Rhymes, have left the advantage of musical composition for Songs, though not for recitative, to our neighbors.
>
> Through these Difficulties, I have made a shift to struggle, in my part of the performance of this *Opera.*[65]

Thus far John Dryden on problems of setting English to music—problems which he clearly saw from a poet's point of view, and which he unwisely thought Grabu might be able to solve successfully. As for the essential elements and contours of English opera as these were to be embodied in *Albion and Albanius,* again we can do no better than to turn to Dryden's views, as expressed in the preface and postscript. There we discover that the formal components of the opera are to consist of the recitatives, the lyrical part (or arias), the choruses, the instrumental dances and *ritornelli* all compounded together as "a poetical Tale or Fiction, represented by Vocal and Instrumental Musick, adorn'd with Scenes,

---

[64] These samples are all drawn from *Cadmus et Hermione,* as published by Henri Prunières in the *Œuvres complètes de J.-B. Lully* (1930), I.

[65] 7:15–30.

Machines and Dancing." Recitative, according to Dryden, "requires a more masculine Beauty of expression and sound." The arias, or *"Songish Part,"* must "abound in the softness and variety of Numbers . . . to please the Hearing, rather than to gratify the understanding" (see 3:9–11; 4:3–7). Note that Dryden mentions neither *recitativo secco* nor the aria as a vehicle for effect. In turning to apply these to considerations of Grabu's setting, we must temper our view with the knowledge that the poet's requirements would not always be possible to meet, even at the hands of a master such as Purcell—witness the difficulties he had with Dryden over certain passages in *King Arthur*.[66] It is also important to recall that Dryden had then only recently begun to accept opera as a workable form, and could not yet have developed a seasoned understanding of what opera actually should be. It would be foolish to expect Grabu's setting to conform in every detail to Dryden's notions, but they will at least provide a safer general guide than supposed French or Italian models, particularly with regard to the conventional distinctions of *recitativo secco, recitativo accompagnato,* and *aria,* which distinctions were of later origin.

As for the nature and quality of the work itself, Grabu's music cannot be fairly criticized except in the context of Dryden's libretto. Technically speaking, this may have provided Grabu with better lyrical poetry than most librettos of that day could boast of. But the matter of the poem was such as to arouse very little deep inspiration, a fact which imposed severe limitations upon Grabu's creative faculties. We have no way of judging how well he might have risen to an inspiring occasion in setting texts, for the libretto provided none. The single fact may explain why it is that none of the choruses or arias rise to any heights, although a few of the instrument pieces really are quite good, as we shall see.

To do justice to the work, one must also view it in the political and religious context of the times. The opera has been called "a monument of stupidity" by a critic who nevertheless thought it worth considering as an example of the way in which attempts have always been made, and are still made occasionally, to achieve English opera at one blow.[67] He also objected to Dryden's attempt to expand the original prologue into a three-act opera, thus hitting upon the matter which seems responsible for the essential weakness of the opera. Finally, the aesthetic significance of the whole depends heavily on the spectacular staging and choreography which Dryden, Betterton, and Grabu had planned for the original production. (See "The Staging," above.) In short, the work cannot be appraised except in the light of what it was intended originally to be: a spectacular panegyric and satire, reflecting the royalist position in English political life under Charles II and James II.

With all these considerations in mind, we may turn now to examine the opera itself, viewing it as an artistic composite best understood within the context of the political situation in which it was designed to function. *Albion and Albanius* did not have the aesthetic strength to outlive the social and political events it reflected—as did Purcell's *Dido and Aeneas,*

---

[66] *The Purcell Society Edition* (1928), XXVI.
[67] Edward J. Dent, *Foundations of English Opera*, p. 165.

The Prophetess, and *King Arthur.* Whatever this tells us about the opera as a work of art on a comparative basis, it also provides an interesting frame of reference for Grabu's opera, while teaching us to examine more closely the historical situations similarly reflected in these undeniably greater works by Purcell.

The "Ayres Before the opera," i.e., *Prelude, Ritornel,* and *Ayre* with which the score begins—represent the conventional "First" and "Second" music, designed to be performed at half-hour intervals before the curtain. These are five-part settings for string orchestra in the French style, like those Charles II had learned to love in the period of his "travels" in France during the Interregnum. The first is a spirited C-major opening piece in the latest *stil brisé,*[68] the over-dotted manner similar to that which Lully was soon to popularize and perfect as Louis XIV's *surintendant de la musique.* The similarity is such as to caution us not to attribute this important development in the history of musical style wholly to Lully, as is so often done.

What Grabu's opening pieces may lack in lyric melodic quality is amply made up for by the graceful *tripla Ritornel* which follows—a delightful binary with *hemiola* cadences, shifting elegantly via sharp and flat cycles combined, to a minor in the second strain. The *Ayre,* also in binary form, ends the preliminary set with a quiet saraband-like movement in c-minor, its interesting harmonic structure all the more effective because of the lyric simplicity of the individual parts. Whatever the musical value of movements to follow, and whatever the view of contemporary and later detractors, Grabu's achievements in these opening movements clearly show him to be a master of orchestral resources, capable of turning out music well-attuned to the happy political victory which the work was designated to celebrate. (See MUSICAL EXAMPLE 1A, B, C.)

The over-dotted rhythmic style returns with the elegant four-movement overture in d-minor with which the curtain rises to reveal a "glorious Fabrick" done in marble and gold, before the Royal Exchange in London. The scene represents Mercury in a chariot drawn by ravens, descending to console Augusta (i.e., London) and Thamesis, both bereaved by disasters suffered during the Interregnum. Grabu's penchant for mixing "flat" and "sharp" harmonies here lends itself admirably to the melancholy effect required for this opening scene. (See MUSICAL EXAMPLE 2.)

The separate movements of the overture are sensitively attuned to the staging in a manner that could not have failed to be effective. At the main climactic dominant cadence, the scene would have come into view, with Grinling Gibbons' statue of James II serving as an impressive visual counterpart to the solid and expressive phrases of the opening *Grave.*[69]

---

[68] As Pepys noted, this style was reported to have been introduced into England even earlier (*Diary,* V, 313n), but surely this was in error. See also *Roger North on Music,* pp. 350–52. The crediting of this style wholly to Lully greatly oversimplifies its origin and genesis—processes which ought properly to be the subject of new and careful research and analysis.

[69] See discussion of both the genuine and the spurious Grinling Gibbons pieces, pp. 369–370.

The sprightly imitative *canzona* accompanying the appearance of Mercury in a raven-drawn chariot also is effective, particularly in view of the telling contrast with movements on either side of it. The tender and melancholy slow third movement draws attention to the dejected figures of Augusta and Thamesis, after which Mercury finishes his descent, approaching to address the two recumbent figures. (See MUSICAL EXAMPLE 3A, B.)

Grabu's setting of the opening recitative is worth examining in some detail, since this is the technique for which he has so frequently been damned for not conforming to the popular conception of what recitative should be. That is to say, he did not use purely declamatory recitative merely as a foil for the occasional affective aria. As a composer, Grabu belonged to an earlier tradition in which composers of recitative still adhered to the ideals of the Florentine humanist musicians—i.e., the *Camerata*—who had invented it. Grabu's recitative, like Monteverdi's, but unlike Lully's, was still in that early form wherein narrative statement in recitative and affective reflection in aria had not yet become, *de rigeur*, opposite though mutually functional formal types. In this earlier tradition, recitative served as the fabric of the entire opera, providing a melodic, rhythmic continuum that contrasted with choral, dance, and orchestral movements rather than with other solo passages.

As we see in the opening scene, Grabu did not use recitative merely as a narrative thread upon which to string set arias, choruses, and instrumental pieces. Instead of being damned for this, he might well have been praised. Thus he neatly avoided the shortcomings of the "numbers opera" and its attendant evils, the spectacular star system and the disregard for dramatic coherence which that system was to breed much to the detriment of the operatic tradition.

At any rate, Hermes sings his opening lines in this lyric kind of recitative, *quasi-arioso*, attuned rather to effect and mood than to natural declamation. Harmonically, Grabu's recitative is anything but static in the manner of *recitativo secco*, for it moves with simple *basso continuo* accompaniment in an expressive harmonic progression designed to underline affective intervals occurring at moments of particular emotive force in the recitative. The plaintive quality of Augusta's reply, after a quick modulation to B flat major, is enhanced by full orchestral accompaniment. The result is not true *recitativo accompagnato*, but the effect is similar, and the fact that Grabu reserved such recitative accompaniments for cardinal points in the unfolding drama indicates something of his awareness of the expressive potential of this form.

The entry of Thamesis is illustrated in a setting of flowing parallel tenths and sixths, quite appropriate to the nature of this allegorical figure representing the river Thames. (See MUSICAL EXAMPLE 4.) The musical simile is all the more effective in that it ceases immediately upon Augusta's joining in with the plaintive petition: "O *Hermes!* pity me!" Thereafter the two benighted allegorical figures proceed in duo-recitative until moved by Hermes' cross-questioning to confess their shortcomings in Grabu's affective *duo-arioso*, now brought into sharper rhythmic focus by Dryden's quadrisyllabic closed quatrain of trochaic couplets:

> Faction sway'd me,
> Zeal allur'd me,
> Both assur'd me,
> Both betray'd me!

After Thamesis' equally abject confession, and upon Hermes' (the *Mercury* of the *dramatis personae*) suggestion that he "wash away the stain," a *Chorus of Rivers* joins in with cooperative enthusiasm, to help him

> . . . wash away the stain
> That blots a noble Nation,
> And free this famous Town again
> From force of Usurpation.

It is unfortunate that just here the plot comes so near to being mere nonsense, for Grabu's music itself, particularly in the instrumental portions, is quite effective. (See MUSICAL EXAMPLE 5B.) Dryden's ubiquitous feminine endings are rather sensitively handled throughout, and with the choral climax Grabu did not rest content with a mere setting of the soloist passage it echoes, as Lully would have done, but rather constructed an independent choral-orchestral movement. To be sure, the flowing main descriptive choral motif is related to that sung by Hermes, but it is nevertheless a different subject. (See MUSICAL EXAMPLE 5A.) At any rate, the *tutti* choral setting with its double imitative polyphonic texture in flowing parallel tenths and thirds leads to a climactic orchestral *ritornello* in a *grand rondo* form, foretelling similar techniques Purcell was to employ so successfully in his semi-operas within a few years. A sprightly *tripla*-dance in the form of an "Ayre for Mercury's Followers" brings the scene to a close. This spirited binary is excellent dance music, and shows Grabu at his best.

Thereupon Democracy, Zelota and Archon enter to demand financial tribute from Augusta and Thamesis. Urged to resist by Hermes, then by the *Chorus of Rivers* in fine resistive accents (See MUSICAL EXAMPLE 6), city and river reply:

> A Commonwealth's a Load
> Our old Imperial Flood
> Shall never never never bear again.

Irked by this answer, and now bent upon rapine, Democracy and Zelota advance, the former urging his colleague to:

> Pull down her Gates, Expose her bare;
> I must enjoy the proud, disdainful fair.

But the two villains are foiled by their supposed ally, Archon, who turns on them, singing of his successful mission to save London and the Thames in a lovely d-minor aria with trio-sonata accompaniment. Here the style of the setting, the structure of the aria, the additive rhythms, and the climactic following chorus do remind us of Lully's aria settings. And the choral triumph, replete with bell-ringing motives, is very closely akin to those Purcell was just then employing in his welcome odes and birthday songs. Thus orchestra and chorus celebrate the envisioned political triumph, perhaps somewhat prematurely, to prophetic musical strains simulating bell sounds, crowd noises, and acclamations to peace and freedom, all building to a climax to commemorate the victory of anti-Commonwealth forces—all this even before the return of the monarchy.

This chorus exemplifies one feature of Grabu's compositional style which has been the source of severe criticism. At first glance, the passage seems to have been set to music so as to contradict all principles of natural declamation. Closer inspection reveals, however, that the fault lies rather with the critics' poor understanding of bar accents, than with Grabu's original conception. The entire passage is conceived in *hemiola* rhythms, which govern rhythmic propulsion and therefore word setting from the cadence of the previous movement onward. The continuous rhythmic and choreographic flow achieved by the application of the *hemiola* principle, and the attendant resolution of supposed barbarisms, may be clearly seen in the parallel passages shown. (See MUSICAL EXAMPLE 7.)

Meanwhile, Mercury, Archon, Augusta and Thamesis sing an exuberant call to arms. Then calm and security prevail as the military gets everything in hand. At that point Archon asks, rather meekly, it seems, in view of all that he has just accomplished, "What then remaines for me?" To this Mercury replies in an a-minor *accompagnato*, rather in the Italian style than in the Lullian, which effectively suggests the Orphic powers soon to be unleashed:

> Take my *Caduceus!* take this aweful Wand,
> With this th' Infernal Ghosts I can command,
> And strike a Terror thro the *Stygian* Land.
> Common-wealth will want pretences,
> Sleep will Creep on all his Senses;
> Zeal that lent him her assistance,
> Stand amaz'd without resistance.

He hands the wand to Archon, who immediately casts the spell, as the orchestra develops a suggestive descending slumber motif, to which Democracy and Zelota drowsily sing as they sink away, along with their accomplices, Hypocrisy and Phanaticism, Hell-bound on a disappearing pedestal. In the five-part accompaniment to this recitative, Grabu again reveals the touch of an orchestral master. The long, gradually ascending and descending lines, the ponderous but steady harmonic rhythm, and the ebb and flow of the expressive texture beautifully conjure up a mood most suitable to scene and action. (See MUSICAL EXAMPLE 8.)

A chorus acclaims Charles II "Godlike *Albion* . . . . Glorious as the Star of Morning." Here again Grabu has been severely criticized for frequent apparent barbarisms, all of which vanish when the underlying *hemiola* scheme is realized. (See MUSICAL EXAMPLE 8B.) Thamesis sings in praise of sailors. Rather arbitrarily this introduces a sailors' dance which, however, partakes of the form and style of a *gavotte*. Two short scenes follow as Juno, then Iris, in turn appear to explain the glorious arrival of Charles II at Dover. This furnishes the matter of the final scene, in which triumphant ensembles and choruses alternate with orchestral *ritornelli* and dances of various sorts, including a march in the style of a *branle,* and two "Ayres for the four parts of the World," which are closely

akin to the foregoing *Marche* in spirit and matter, as is the choral-orchestral *tutti* which ends the first act in a final repetition of the royal acclamation: "Hail, Royal *Albion*, Hail." (See MUSICAL EXAMPLE 9.)

The Hellish panorama described in the stage directions at the beginning of Act II finds no expressive parallel in the music of a blithe trio-
sonata prelude in F-major. Nor does Pluto's *arioso* "Infernal Offspring of
the Night" convey in musical terms any feeling of the evil, gloomy scene
so vividly caught in Dryden's lines. Even when Zelota and Democracy
arrive below, the momentary shift to d-minor is not sufficient to cloud the
somewhat merry atmosphere produced by the nimble rhythmic pace and
F-major tonality of the setting. By comparison with Purcell's sinister
music at the beginning of Act II of *Dido and Aeneas*, Grabu's attempt here
falls quite flat. However, skillful soloists may easily mend this passage, with
suitable histrionics, as in the trio dialogue between Democracy, Zelota
and Pluto, which follows, and in the latter's long accompanied binary
aria, "I wonder'd how of late our Acherontique shore / Grew thin . . . ."

Assured by Democracy and Zelota that reestablishment of the Commonwealth would reverse the current dwindling in the traffic of souls of
the slain, Pluto readily agrees to a wicked design which will soon surface
on the Earth as the Popish Plot. Meanwhile, Pluto sends Alecto to scatter
her snakes—that is, envy and discord—about London, and she departs
earthward, with the specific instruction from Democracy that she

> Spare some to fling
> Where they may sting
> The Breast of *Albion*'s King.

And Zelota adds:

> Let Jealousies so well be mixt,
> That great *Albanius* be unfixt!

The entire passage, indeed the whole of the first scene in Act II, depends
almost entirely on Dryden's poetic devices for illustration, effects, and
atmosphere. Only with the perfection of Oates's plot to undermine the
so-called Catholic succession of James II and Mary of Modena does Dryden's poem provide Grabu with the needed touch of inspiration to lift
his composition of vocal portions above the ordinary. When Pluto sings
with Hellish glee:

> Let us laugh, let us laugh, let us laugh at our Woes,
> The Wretch that is damn'd has nothing to lose.
> Yee Furies advance
> With the *Ghosts* in a Dance, *etc.*,

Grabu fashions a laughter aria, the effect of which is all the better in the
laughter chorus, which follows immediately after the Devil's Dance ending
Pluto's part of the scene. (See MUSICAL EXAMPLE 10A, B.) However, the
total effect falls considerably below that achieved by Purcell in the
Witches' choruses in *Dido and Aeneas*, by Lully in the chorus of the Great
Muphti in *Le Bourgeois Gentilhomme*, or by Handel in the chorus "Haste
thee, nymph" in *L'Allegro ed il Penseroso*. Still, properly performed,
Grabu's laughter chorus could be most realistic and entertaining, despite
the fact that it is still stuck in F-major, with a feeling of tonal monotony

unalleviated by the occasional brief sally into relative minor and other related key areas.

A second Devils' Dance, though still in F-major, furnishes a nicely-turned choreographic ending for the first scene. Then, as the scene shifts again to the upper world, a woebegone Augusta appears, snake in bosom, lamenting the fact that she and her citizens have been victimized by Alecto. Her *accompagnato* brings a welcome change of key to f-minor:

> O Jealousy! Thou raging ill,
> Why hast thou found a Room in Lovers Hearts,
> Afflicting what thou can'st not kill,
> And Poysoning Love himself, with his own Darts?

The whole develops as a rather moving recitative soliloquy, remaining in f-minor up to the next change of scene with the entry of Democracy and Zelota, who sing again, inevitably (it seems) in F-major.

Again, dramatic effect depends on Dryden's lines and on performers' excellence in the histrionic vein. The whole fifth scene, which explains why James, Duke of York, had to go into exile, makes better political history—as seen from the Royalist point of view—than opera. There are some rather good moments in Mercury's long *accompagnato* and in that of Albanius, which are devoted to explanation of the moral and political aspects of the Duke's self-imposed exile. However, the whole scene falls flat by comparison with the lively instrumental pieces which precede it, even though tonal variety is much improved.

In the sixth scene Apollo descends to applaud the "Royal Pair," promising better times for them in a c-minor *accompagnato* which remains dark and melancholy despite his happy prophecies. In the seventh scene, however, there is a change to C-major as Neptune offers his good offices in a merry embarkation tune. Again, the resemblance to Purcell's embarkation scene in *Dido and Aeneas* invokes damaging comparison, and again Grabu's instrumental piece, the "Ayre for the Gods of the Rivers" which follows, surpasses the vocal portion in assurance and excellence of effect. The dance which ends the scene is really quite good composition, and should furnish the basis for interesting choreographic development. Throughout this seventh scene, Neptune and his Tritons cavort as Thamesis celebrates his new office, and all at last join in a grand *Chacon,* which unites all forces—instrumental, terpsichorean and vocal—in a resounding, happy finale to Act II. The whole cannot be compared with Purcell's similar climactic *chaconnes* in *The Prophetess* and in *King Arthur,* but this finale definitely stands as one of the high points of the second act of *Albion and Albanius.* (See MUSICAL EXAMPLE 11.)

The first scene in Act III takes place at sea, just off Dover, where Albion and Acacia, along with other persecuted personages, commiserate with one another, lamenting in a melancholy d-minor dialogue duet the troubles assailing the King and his realm. The occasion, the arrival of Catherine of Braganza by sea, was recorded graphically and somewhat roguishly by an anonymous contemporary artist, and engraved by I. A. for *Complementum Fortunarum,* which appeared in print the year following her arrival, late in 1662.[70] For a change, Grabu's tonal variety is quite satisfactory, and the resulting musical interest is further enhanced by considerable improvement in the diction of both Albion and Acacia. These manage to recount their tales without barbarisms in sensitive *accompagnato* passages, as in turn the chorus, likewise free of barbarisms, and also touching on interesting tonal areas, extols their plan

> To rule by Love
> To shed no Blood . . .

But it then adds, cynically, that although such actions

> May be extol'd above;
> . . . here below,
> Let Princes know
> 'Tis fatal to be good.

A d-minor "Ayre for Tritons" (a stately *gavotte*), sets in motion another small dance suite in which the lovely first minuet is followed by a second, with vocal text, during which "Nereids *rise out of the Sea and Sing,* [as] Tritons *dance.*" (See MUSICAL EXAMPLE 12.)

For the sudden reappearance of Tyranny and Democracy, which follows immediately, Grabu modulated again to parallel major. In these villains' gleeful discussion of the imminent plot, in which they are to be assisted by Asebia and Zelota, there is no opportunity for "seriousness and gravity"—a lack recalling Purcell's oft-quoted remark in the *Sonatas of 1683* relating to the "levity and balladry" of the French. At any rate, these conspiring characters scheme together as villainy goes its merry way. At last, all join in a Masque in which:

> To fill the Dance,
> . . . the Property Boys come in.

These are dressed in white to lead a *"Fantastik Dance,"* in this case another *branle,* which is followed alternately by recitative or dialogue interspersed with dance movements, and ending with a spirited "Ayre for the Sectarys." By the time the villains enter again, the steady D-major setting has begun to pall, yet Grabu carries on in that key right through to the end of the scene, which ends with another dance-like "Ayre for the fighting White Boys and Sectaries." This is a quick moving *bourrée,* with bold, wide melodic intervals, interesting rhythmic patterns, and very welcome tonal digressions into sub-mediant, sub-dominant, second dominant, and dominant areas. (See MUSICAL EXAMPLE 13.) Albion and Acacia, returning to their now familiar d-minor, find Proteus sleeping in a cave. They capture him and bring him forward as, true to a dire prediction in the text, he turns himself into a lion, a crocodile, a dragon, and back into his own shape again, while a symphony is playing. Through change of time and tonality the orchestra mimics some of these transformations, both in the g-minor symphony and in the *accompagnato* which follows as Proteus prophesies Charles II's eventual victory over the villains. But again, Grabu's programmatic effects pale by comparison

---

[70] Zimmerman, *Henry Purcell,* Plate No. 4, opp. p. 31.

with a similar prophetic scene by Purcell in *The Indian Queen*.[71] The symphony continues in g-minor as Proteus descends.

Next, as if in immediate answer to the prophecy, come the villains Democracy and Zelota again, with a one-eyed archer hired to assassinate the king. But their plot is foiled by a sudden conflagration, referring to the providential Newmarket fire, which in actual history hastened Charles II and the Duke of York back to London. One senses that Grabu had at last become aware that his opera was growing a little too long, for his short sample of "Fire Music" is almost too brief to be effective, although the descriptive motif does return in both the vocal portion and the *ritornello*. Democracy and Zelota, accompanied by "Asebia and the Frustrated archer" sink away again. Scarcely has the blaze died down when *"a Machine rises out of the Sea"* and opens to discover "Venus, *and* Albanius *sitting in a great Scallop-shell . . . . drawn by Dolphins . . .* [accompanied by] *Fluts-Doux"* (i.e., recorders).

Again the passage is reminiscent of, though inferior to, a similar passage by Purcell—"Land him safely on our shore," from "Swifter, Isis, swifter flow," the welcome song for Charles II's return from Windsor at the end of August, 1681. (See MUSICAL EXAMPLE 14.) The orchestration itself is quite interesting.

An acclamation sung by Venus is echoed by full chorus and orchestra, followed by an "Ayre for the Graces and Loves," then another song and chorus in *gavotte* rhythm flattering the newly returned Duke in what for once is a rather elegant declamatory chorus, free from any violent barbarisms.

Anti-climactically on the heels of all this comes the apotheosis of Charles II, the portion which had to be inserted into the whole after his untimely death. On the whole, the style of the composition is rather better than earlier sections of the opera, but there is really little that is novel in an expressive sense; in fact, because Grabu elected to keep the new material in g-minor, the same tonality already used rather too long in the previous scene, the apotheosis soon palls. Not until the closing modulation to C-major is the listener released from the confines of g-minor.

In conclusion, Grabu's music for *Albion and Albanius* can be faulted in many ways, perhaps most seriously because of its prevailing lack of tonal variety. Compared with Purcell, Blow, Locke, or even Lully, Grabu is clearly an inferior composer in this regard. Similarly, his maladroit vocal style and his tendency to lose pace and clear diction in his choruses place him at great disadvantage especially in comparison with Purcell and other English contemporaries.

In orchestral passages, and particularly in dance pieces, however, Grabu emerges as one of the most talented and striking opera composers active in England during the early 1680's. Certainly no one was writing better orchestral dance music in England up to the time in question—the season of 1684–5—when Grabu was busy with *Albion and Albanius*. Purcell was

---

[71] *The Purcell Society Edition* (1912), XIX.

soon to surpass him in this genre, as in all others, but he had not as yet clearly done so.

In any case, most extant criticism of *Albion and Albanius* seems at best unbalanced, if only because the work has been approached as a "closet opera" and examined in accordance with criteria which did not figure in its original creation and production. Moreover, criteria which were a part of the original design have been ignored. In short, our body of received opinion on this work is unnecessarily prejudicial. It is patently a mistake that the work has been assessed, up to the present, almost wholly on the basis of very negative criticisms made by later critics who have never seen the work produced. Clearly, the existence of at least thirteen surviving printed scores in British libraries does not lend support to the negative view of *Albion and Albanius*. But perhaps the most telling testimonial in favor of the work is that of Thomas Augustine Arne, who borrowed the entire finale as the ending to his masque, *The Fairy Prince*, produced at Covent Garden 12 November 1771.[72] Moreover, eminent scholars of dramatic history [73] have found much that is commendable in *Albion and Albanius* as a product of the joint labors of Dryden and Grabu. While there are legitimate grounds for dispute in matters of taste, certainly the balanced view of this work allows for a more moderate and charitable general opinion of its aesthetic value than it has received. As performable opera, the work is probably irretrievable. But the case against it is not quite so dark as it has been painted. And some of the orchestral music is really quite elegant, representing the French style of the time altogether respectably.

---

[72] See Roger Fiske, *English Theatre Music in the Eighteenth Century* (1973), pp. 361–362. Fiske points out that "Grabu has been consistently denigrated by those anxious to do their best for Purcell, and it is usually said that *Albion and Albanius* was a total failure. The degree of failure has probably been exaggerated, for [the British Union-Catalogue of Early Music] lists as many as thirteen surviving scores, many more than can be found of any Purcell opera."

[73] See Allardyce Nicoll, *History of English Drama 1660–1900*, I, 158, and Montague Summers, *The Playhouse of Pepys* (1935), p. 59.

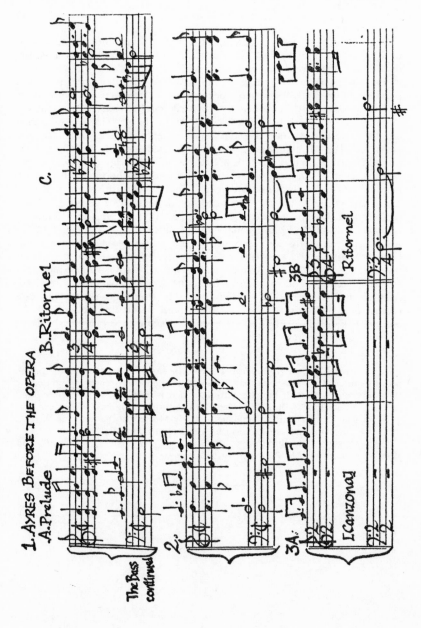

357

358

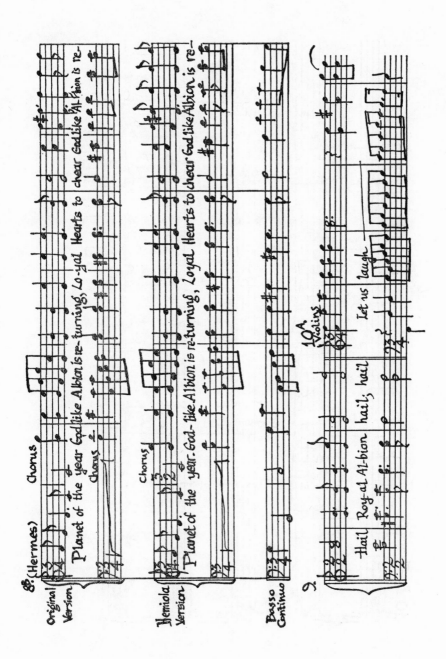

359

360

*In the notes throughout this volume, a reference to lines
is to lines within the part being annotated (scene, act,
preface, etc.) unless otherwise indicated, and therefore
no indication is made of "above" or "below."*

PREFACE

3:1 *If Wit has truly been defin'd* etc. As Malone recognized, Dryden
had so defined wit in *The Authors Apology for Heroique Poetry and
Poetique Licence,* prefixed to *The State of Innocence* [(1677), sig. C2v;
Watson, I, 207]. A similar, earlier characterization of wit, with much else,
was included in the "Account" prefixed to *Annus Mirabilis* (1667; *Works,*
I, 53). In the *Life of Lucian* (1711, written ca. 1696, p. 42; Watson, II,
210–211) Dryden recurs to his definition, adding that he then believed
Aristotle had anticipated him. Watson suggests that Dryden probably
had in mind Aristotle's discussion of decorum: *Rhetoric,* III; *Poetics,*
XXII.

3:4 *an Opera.* The *OED* definition may be given here: "A dramatic
performance in which music forms an essential part, consisting of recitatives, arias, and choruses, with orchestral accompaniment and scenery;
also, a dramatic or musical composition intended for such performance, a
libretto or score." The first use cited is by Evelyn in 1644; Dryden's
definition (see ll. 9–11) is also given.

3:6 *the cloathing of those thoughts.* Dryden's specific metaphor is one
of the first recorded uses (cf. Milton, *Paradise Regained,* II, 65), although
the "dress" of expression was common throughout the century, and the
conception of rhetorical ornament was, of course, widespread in the
Renaissance.

3:13 *Heroes.* The concept of heroes as demigods in a strict sense has
a long history. The name was "given (as in Homer) to men of super-
human strength, courage, or ability . . . ; at a later time [heroes were]
regarded as intermediate between gods and men, and immortal" (*OED,*
citing Dryden, *Georgics,* III, 56: "Resembling Heroes, whose Etherial
Root / Is *Jove* himself"). See also 5:34–6:13.

3:20–25 *The Gods are all* etc. Dryden here observes what Molière calls
the "decorum de la Divinité," as Dryden conspicuously does not in
Amphitryon; even here, however, the tone is ironic, as in 6:8–13.

4:2–3 *The recitative part of the Opera.* Evelyn and a few others had
used the word *recitative* from about 1645 (*OED*).

4:4–5 *for want of a proper English word . . . The Songish Part.* The
word that Dryden lacked was "aria," the first recorded usage of which
comes in 1742 (*OED*). Dryden's coinage was a hapax legomenon motivated
by the inadequacy of the ambiguous "air," which sometimes was used for
"aria," as in the "fifteen or sixteen Airs" that pleased in *Thomyris*
(François Raguenet, *A Comparison Between the French and Italian
Musick and Opera's* [1709; rptd. 1968], p. 71). Dryden opposes "Songs" to
"recitative" in 7:27–28 and 8:15.

4:8–9 *That Rhyme, on any consideration* etc. Dryden plays on the proverbial rhyme/reason distinction. Cf. Tilley, R98 ("Neither Rhyme nor reason") and R99 ("It may Rhyme but it accords not"). See also *OED*, s.v., *Rhyme*. Dryden's tone in the prologue shows his impatience with his role as librettist.

4:29 *Ethnique Worship*. Pagan religious observances.

5:6–7 *Zambra's*. A "Zambra" is "A Spanish or Moorish dance" (*OED*, citing a use in *The Conquest of Granada* [1670] as the first before 1832).

5:9 *Sortiia's*. A *Sortiia* is a running at the ring in jousting or similar activity; cf. Spanish, *Sortija*, "ring" (does not appear in *OED*).

5:10 *Moresque*. The *OED* defines the term to mean "Moorish," as might be expected, but shows no usage except in reference to "Painting, carving, architecture, etc."

5:12 *Carousels*. A *Carousel* is "A tournament in which knights, divided into companies (*quadrilles*) distinguished by their liveries and dresses, engaged in various plays and exercises; to this were often added chariot races, and other shows and entertainments" (*OED*).

5:29 *Pastor Fido*. This drama by Battista Guarini circulated in manuscript from ca. 1585 and was published in 1590. Its combination of tragedy, comedy, and pastoral occasioned one of the great literary quarrels of the Renaissance. See Bernard Weinberg, *A History of Literary Criticism in the Italian Renaissance* (1961), II, 1074–1105.

5:30–34 Dryden speaks very perceptively of the ways in which Italian opera was adapted to the French stage and probably had in mind plays like Corneille's *Andromède*, which begins with a prologue spoken by Melpomene in praise of Louis XIV. See 7:31–32n.

6:8–13 *and therefore Shepherds* etc. The dry wit resembles that in 3:20–25. The love plot in *Albion and Albanius* between Albion and Augusta does not endanger Thamesis with fire.

6:14–7:28 Dryden's comparison of the major European tongues presents a shortened and independent version of Isaac Vossius' long description of the virtues and faults of those languages in *De Poematum Cantu et Viribus Rhythmi* (Oxford, 1673), pp. 39–50.

6:29–31 *as Pyrrhus did the Roman Discipline* etc. See Plutarch, *Lives*, "Pyrrhus," XVI, 5; see also Samuel Daniel, *A Defence of Rhyme*, in *Elizabethan Critical Essays*, ed. G. Gregory Smith (1904), II, 367.

6:33 *the Gothick*. Dryden's usage is taken by the *OED* to involve the obsolete "extended sense, now expressed by Teutonic or Germanic." Since Dryden had remarked in 6:25–29 that Italian derived its vocabulary from Greek and Roman, the refinement of Italian *from the Gothick* probably means its purification of elements "Belonging to the 'dark ages'" (*OED*, another definition, comparing "les siècles gothiques"). This latter definition seems the more likely in context, and especially so since Dryden later took the word farther to mean "Barbarous, rude, uncouth, unpolished" (*OED*, first use cited being Dryden's in his translation of Dufresnoy's *De Arte Graphica* [1695], p. 93).

7:15–28 Cf. Vossius, *De Poematum Cantu*, p. 56: *Mollis & muliebris est omnino Anglorum lingua, cum litera A rarissime, ἦτα vero ubique fere utantur. Istam tamen mollitiem temperat multum syllabarum asperitas &*

consonantium frequentia literarum (The language of the English is altogether soft and feminine, especially since the letter *A* is used most rarely
and the η sound is used virtually always. Still that very sweetness is tem-
pered by the asperity of many syllables and the frequency of consonant
letters).

7:27 *Songs.* That is, arias; see 4:4–5n.

7:31–32 *it has attempted a discovery* etc. Dryden does not mean that no
previous self-styled "opera" had been produced; he would have thought at
once of Davenant's *Siege of Rhodes,* the operatic *Tempest,* and Shadwell's
Psyche. But he has in mind "opera" more closely defined along Italian and
French lines rather than "a Tragedy mix'd with *Opera,*" as he says in
10:27. Dryden's sense of the possibilities of opera and his pride in being
the first to attempt them can be understood by reference to France. Two
of the greatest French artists of the time, Molière and the composer Lully,
had been cooperating in a series of *comédies-ballets* that included *Le
Mariage forcé,* which Dryden knew well enough to draw upon for a
scene in *Amphitryon* (see commentary on that play, p. 492 below). But
England was to prove even more resistant to full Italian opera than had
France. Dryden's experiment shows his awareness of continental trends
and his willingness to develop new forms. His early interest in such matters is shown by a remark on Corneille's *Andromède* in *Of Dramatick
Poesie* (*Works,* XVII, 50). See also 10:25–35 for Dryden's distinctions between previously existing English "operas" and his new form; see also
the note to that passage for comment on his altered conception of his
opera.

8:1 *North-East Passage.* Dryden obviously disbelieves in the possibility
of sailing to Asia *via* Norway and Russia, but it is strange that he did not
use the more familiar Northwest Passage as a metaphor.

8:2–5 *as Ben. Johnson tells us* etc. Ker notes that Face says to Sir
Epicure Mammon (*The Alchemist,* IV, v, 91–93):

> There will be, perhaps,
> Something, about the scraping of the shardes,
> Will cure the itch.

8:7 *the Curiosity or Itch of Sight and Hearing.* Apparently Dryden
doubts that in its musical and staged aspects an opera could "gratify the
understanding." See 4:2–7.

8:15 *the Lyrical part.* See 4:4–5n.

8:23–9:2 Dryden's handsome tribute to Grabu has upset those who
think it should have been paid to Purcell. Dryden did praise Purcell, both
before and after the death of that gifted younger contemporary: see his
prefatory remarks to *Amphitryon* and his *Ode, on the Death of Mr. Henry
Purcell.* Dryden's willingness to praise is one of his handsomest characteristics, and this praise of Grabu is a welcome exception to his anti-
Gallicism.

9:3–5 *If I thought it convenient* etc. It is possible only to speculate
what Dryden's essay on operas, or operatic poetry, might have been like;
it remained one of his unwritten works, like the projected essay on English

non-dramatic poetry (see "To the Reader," *Of Dramatick Poesie* [*Works,* XVII, 7]).

9:12 *Fond.* "A source of supply, stock, store or stores" (*OED* giving this as first use).

9:17–18 *as great a certainty of quantity in our Syllables* etc. Setting aside problems of the actual nature of Latin and of Dryden's seeming distinction between *Syllables* and prosody, it is plain that he is reacting to Vossius, *De Poematum Cantu*, in which much is made of the special virtue of quantity, and therefore of the superiority of ancient to modern poetry. For example, Vossius remarked (p. 48) that in modern-day Greece herself, the Greeks have assumed, along with their customs, a barbarous language and music. He added that if you looked at their language, you saw nothing in it of concinnity and elegance, no observation of the true quantity of syllables (. . . *una cum moribus, linguam quoque & Musicam adsumsere barbaram. Linguam si spectes, nihil in ea concinnum & elegans, nulla observatio verae syllabarum quantitatis*). Dryden seems to be seeking in Vossius the *affectiveness* attributed by tradition to ancient music and to believe it could be found not in the lost musical modes but in the language of poetry and its disposition into rhythms. See also Vossius, p. 73; D. T. Mace, "Musical Humanism, the Doctrine of Rhythmus, and the Saint Cecilia Odes of Dryden," *JWCI*, XXVII (1964), 264–265; and 9:24–25n.

9:20–31 *When they have chaw'd awhile* etc. In "Musical Humanism," p. 260, Mace shows that Dryden's remarks depreciate the possibilities of significance for music and take too narrow a view of the relation between language and music. Dryden's later appreciation of music is discussed in *Works*, III, 459–467.

9:24 *The necessity of double Rhymes.* "The scarcity of feminine rhymes is a difficulty which is only too well known to anyone who has attempted to translate other languages for musical purposes; but the English librettist of the future will probably not feel as much bound to them as Dryden did. It was, however, a difficulty which Dryden and the other poets of his day felt themselves in duty bound to overcome; their lyrics are so rich in double rhymes that a foreigner might almost have supposed single rhymes to be as rare in English as in Italian" (Dent, p. 162). But that goes too far. On the first two pages of the 1685 edition (ll. 1–64), there are only four pairs of double rhymes.

9:24–25 *the Words and Numbers.* That is, diction and prosody. Dryden does not wholly associate or dissociate the two: see 9:17–18n, and *To the Memory of Mr. Oldham*, l. 14 (*Works*, II, 175): "the numbers of thy native Tongue."

9:30 *a Seventh in Musick.* The *OED* quotes from the dialogue in Thomas Morley, *A Plaine and Easie Introduction to Practicall Musicke* (1597): "Which distances make discord . . . ? [Answer] . . . a second, a fourth, a seventh."

9:34–37 *the choice of Words* etc. Cf. 3:1n, 9:17–18n.

9:37–10:4 *Perhaps a time may come* etc. The veneration of Homer and

Virgil as the sole poets to understand "the Art of Numbers," and the designation of that art as *"Rhythmus"* clearly show the influence of Vossius' *De Poematum Cantu* (Vossius' favor for the ancients will be found, e.g., pp. 75–79, but in attitude, *passim*). Nowhere else does Dryden seem so wholly committed to the Ancients. Although the preface as a whole possesses a different outlook, Vossius has certainly affected Dryden's usual views here.

10:4 *Rhythmus.* As Mace shows in "Musical Humanism," p. 261, the concept of *rhythmus* had been widely known on the continent for almost a century. For some reason Dryden appears to be the first English critic to make something explicit of this concept of "speculative music," and had Vossius not published *De Poematum Cantu* in England in 1673, the idea might never have found an English proponent.

10:11 *clogg'd with Consonants.* See the quotation in 7:15–28n.

10:13 *botch.* "To make good or repair (a defect, damage, damaged article); to patch, mend" (*OED*).

10:19–22 *I . . . will never part with the Power of the Militia.* To Dryden and his fellow royalists, the armed forces were responsible, as they still are formally in England, to the sovereign, and at crucial junctures both Charles II and James II struggled with Parliament for control of the militia. Charles fought for control during November, 1678, as the Popish Plot began to thicken (see David Ogg, *England in the Reign of Charles II* [1934], II, 574). James's failure to win agreement from Parliament on 9 November 1685 led him to prorogue it (see H. C. Foxcroft, *The Life and Letters of Sir George Savile, Bart.*, [1898], I, 458–459). Since Dryden says in the first sentence of the postscript that this preface had been wholly written before the death of Charles II, the metaphor here must involve allusion back to Charles's struggles and to the general royalist principle.

10:25–35 *It was Originally intended only for a Prologue* etc. Dent (p. 163) commented:

> In its original form, therefore, *Albion and Albanius* would have corresponded exactly to the conventional prologue of a French opera, the first act being sufficiently complete in itself for this purpose. A prologue of this kind was not at all in accordance with English custom, but if we are to grant the adoption of a French tradition, Dryden's effort will serve the purpose no worse than any of Quinault's. But to expand such a prologue into a three act opera was an absurdity which not even the court of Louis XIV could have tolerated.

10:28 *Machines.* The complex stage devices of the play were used to give audiences an air of "supernatural means, or Magick," as Dryden says in 10:33–34. See the discussion, "Staging," in the headnote.

11:6–10 *'Tis divided* etc. On the three acts, or *jornadas*, of Spanish plays, see Dryden's remarks in *Of Dramatick Poesie* (*Works*, XVII, 24).

11:12 *Mr. Betterton.* The great actor of his day and a manager of the company Dryden worked with so long, Thomas Betterton always won expressions of appreciation and admiration from Dryden. See, for example, the preface to *Don Sebastian*, 66:7–11 above.

11:19 *uninteress'd*. A common seventeenth-century form for "uninterested" in the sense of "disinterested," "lacking self-interest."

POSTSCRIPT

12:2–3 *quem semper acerbum* etc. As Ker recognized, Virgil, *Aeneid*, V, 49–51: "[And now, if I err not, the day is at hand] which I shall keep (such O gods, was your will) ever as a day of grief, ever as of honour" (Loeb trans.). For Dryden's response to the death of Charles, see *Threnodia Augustalis* (*Works*, III, 92–107). It will be observed that the poem and the opera share certain elements of subject matter, movement, and lyricism.

12:5 *After four Months*. Presumably referring to the period since the death of Charles II, who fell ill on 2 February and died on 6 February 1685.

12:11–12 *possibly the Italians went not so far as Spain* etc. See the preface, 5:4–13; these speculations are not indebted to Vossius.

12:17 *the Learned Monsieur Vossius*. In *De Poematum Cantu*, Vossius often touches on the superiority of the ancients and on such combinations of singing and instruments as that found in the Greek tragic chorus (e.g., p. 83). He has little to say about dancing (although see pp. 134–135 on various performers or *saltatores*).

12:25–26 *How nice an Ear he had in Musick*. The musical tastes of Charles II were affected by his experience in exile. During the 1640's and 1650's he witnessed the development of operatic forms in Paris. As Dent (p. 47) observed:

> During the whole of this period Henrietta Maria had been living in Paris with her son, the future Charles II, and their names are constantly mentioned in the records of the time as having been present at performances of these operas.

12:33–13:2 *the addition of twenty or thirty lines* etc. See the notes to III, i, 200+ *s.d.* and III, ii, 1–14; see also the notes to the Frontispiece, 17:27–18:14.

13:3 *invented*. Discovered, created, found.

13:4–8 Dryden observes a happy destiny or *fatality* in both changes: the ending of his opera and the succession of James II after Charles II. His writing about his opera takes on some of the allegory of the opera itself.

NAMES OF THE PERSONS REPRESENTED

As Dent (p. 163) observed: "it is curious to note that Dryden in printing the play anticipated the modern custom of naming [the characters] in the order of their first appearance on the stage."

FRONTISPIECE

17:1 *The Curtain rises* etc. Almost the same words will be found at the beginning of the scene description of the "operatic" *Tempest* (1674); see Southern, *Changeable Scenery*, p. 185. The *OED* defines "Frontispiece" as "the front scenery; also, the forepart of the stage"; it is a special front frame surrounding and masking the proscenium sides and top. See the headnote, "Staging."

17:2 *Pylasters.* A "pilaster" is "a square or rectangular column or pillar; *spec.*, such a pillar engaged in a wall" (*OED*).

17:3 *Basis.* "The base of a pillar" (*OED*).

17:7 *Saltyre.* A heraldic term for "An ordinary in the form of a St. Andrews cross" (*OED*). Dryden means that the quivers of arrows are so crossed.

17:14 *one presents Poetry.* In 17:8, the scene *represents* Peace. To "present" may mean very nearly the same thing (*OED*), *Present*, 4 and 7).

17:16–17 *Pallat.* A palette.

17:27–18:14 *two Imperial Figures* etc. Some or all of this necessarily was revised after the death of Charles II. See the postscript to the preface, 12:33–13:2n.

18:2–3 *by the King stands Pallas* etc. Dryden's symbolism fits with that of the century. Alexander Ross described Pallas Athene as "the President of War" and "the type of wisdome" (*Mystagogus Poeticus* [1647], p. 161 and sig. V1v). For such associations with James, see the Anne Killigrew ode, ll. 127–133 and *Threnodia Augustalis*, ll. 429–490.

18:12 *Discite justitiam* etc. Virgil, *Aeneid*, VI, 620–621 (Loeb trans.): "Be warned; learn ye to be just and not to slight the gods!" This motto also appears on the title page.

18:14 *Non ignara mali* etc. Virgil, *Aeneid*, I, 630 (Loeb trans.): "Not ignorant of ill do I learn to befriend the unhappy." Dryden's freer version is clearer: "I learn to pity Woes, so like my own" (*Aeneis*, I, 891).

PROLOGUE

The specific designations in the titles of both prologue and epilogue —*To the OPERA* and *By Mr. Dryden*—derive from the fact that the two pieces were separately printed and sold before being bound up with the opera.

1 *Full twenty years and more.* That is, since the Restoration, which is the subject of the opera. In spite of the depreciation of opera in this prologue, it quickly becomes clear that Dryden compares the difficulty he expects with English audiences over an opera to the king's difficulties with the nation. The more restrictedly political matters are set forth in an unusually sober tone in the epilogue. *lab'ring.* The exact meaning is unclear. The *OED* glosses somewhat similar uses by Dryden in differing ways: "to endeavour strenuously"; also "to be trammeled by or suffer from some disadvantage or defect." Dryden often seems to use it as a Latinism and in participial form: cf. Dryden's translation of Juvenal's

Satire VI, l. 572, and *Threnodia Augustalis,* l. 150; cf. also, *The Hind and the Panther,* II, 661.

3 *the John Ketches.* John (or Jack) Ketch became the generic name for the public hangman after a notorious executioner of that name (d. 1686). For a more famous comparison of the writer and the hangman, see the *Discourse of Satire* (*Works,* IV, 71 and n, 573).

4 *excoriation.* The "action or process of flaying (a man or beast)" (*OED*).

6 *bore like Hero's.* Endured like the brave. *brib'd like Oates.* Like Titus Oates, the notorious informer of the Popish Plot, who suffered during the Tory reaction; Oates was "said (falsely it would appear) to have prevailed on the hangman to be lenient in inflicting the frightful flogging which he suffered a few days before the play appeared" (Saintsbury).

8 *Like beating Nut-trees* etc. A version of the proverb, Tilley, W644, "A Woman, a spaniel (an ass), and a walnut tree (nut), the more they're beaten the better they be."

10 *what your Maker meant you.* Predestinated fools, it seems.

16 *Julep.* A sweet drink used for its comforting or mildly stimulating properties (*OED*). *Ptisan.* "A palatable decoction of nourishing and slightly medicinal quality" (*OED*).

17 *Give you strong Sense.* That is, were we to give you, etc.

22 *leading strings.* "Strings with which children used to be guided and supported when learning to walk" (*OED*).

24 *show.* In the wide sense of spectacle, display, entertainment (*OED*).

25 *Noble Pageant.* The tone is ironic, as the passage suggests. Cf. *Absalom and Achitophel,* ll. 751–752 (*Works,* II, 28):

> Thus, in a Pageant Show, a Plot is made;
> And Peace it self is War in Masquerade.

See also the *"crumbling Pageant"* of *A Song for St. Cecilia's Day,* l. 60 (*Works,* III, 203).

27 *Zeal.* Cf. the character Zelota in the opera. *chous'd.* Cheated, tricked, swindled (*OED,* citing Dryden's *Wild Gallant,* II, i).

31 *Change for the worse has ever us'd to please.* Dryden's conservatism emerges clearly.

39 *Le plus grand Roy* etc. A phrase used for Louis XIV. See l. 22 of the prologue to *Don Sebastian.*

43 *Citesses.* This is the sole usage given by the *OED* for a female cit, or town citizen, usually a shop-keeper.

45 *Charter.* On Charles's calling in of municipal and other charters in 1682–1683, see David Ogg, *England in the Reign of Charles II,* II, 634 ff. James's exercise of the prerogative took different forms and came later.

I, i

s.d. one of these Statues . . . at Windsor. Dryden's stage direction and the statues referred to involve Stuart iconography and politics. The statue of Charles II at Charing Cross had been a matter of political dispute and satire in 1675–1676; see George deF. Lord, ed., *Poems on Affairs of State,*

I (1963), pp. 266–283. The statue was meant to assert visibly the king's presence in the City of London. Executed by Joshua Marshall, it was long attributed (although obviously not by Dryden) to Grinling Gibbons, who perhaps designed it. Gibbons (1648–1720), protegé of John Evelyn and one of the world's great woodcarvers, executed at least one bronze statue of James II. The one standing presently at the Chelsea Hospital (Evelyn, *Diary*, IV, 317, n. 2) is presumably the statue to which Dryden refers and which was formerly said to be at Whitehall (DNB).

s.d. The Scene etc. As with the statues, so with the "scene," Dryden deliberately asserts the royal presence, now in the very heart of the City, at what he is careful to term the *Royal* Exchange. Application of the term "baroque" seems particularly appropriate here in the royalism, iconography, allegory, classicism, the immediate present, and the symbolically transcendent. The entire *Decorations* cover what the seventeenth century typified in terms of court, country, and city—the state in its principal guises of values and activities.

s.d. He comes to Augusta, and Thamesis. Dryden had popularized the old name for London and, implicitly, the Augustan analogy. See *Annus Mirabilis*, l. 1177 and Dryden's note; *Mac Flecknoe*, ll. 64–65. By long tradition, the Thames is a male river-god; the personification of rivers has a venerable tradition: Virgil, *Aeneid*, I, 124–127, etc.; Ausonius, *Mosella*, ll. 469–471; Silius Italicus, *Punica*, VII, 254–259; and, among all earlier English examples, preeminently Spenser, *The Faerie Queene*, IV, xi, sts. viii–liii.

s.d. On the side of Augusta's Couch etc. On the falling of towers as a symbol of disorder in Augusta's London, cf. *Mac Flecknoe*, ll. 64–69. The images following are emblems of City office: see *OED*, s.v. *Chain* 3; *Charter* 1c; *Gown* 4a; *Mace* 2; *Maintenance* 9; and see the examples quoted. Like the towers, these emblems are disordered.

s.d. Before Thamesis etc. Here follow similar emblematic details representing disorder, which is now seen in the country and its people, the so-called "country party." The symbols of the court are alone ordered and inviolate as the opera opens.

1 *Thou glorious Fabrick.* London in its architectural (fabricated) guise.

3 *The God of Traffique, and of Gain.* Mercury himself. *Traffique* is commerce, exchange.

8 *Busie Bargaines deafer sound.* The cryptic line appears to mean: the more deafening sounds of busy bargainings.

13 *I was* etc. For the relation between Charles II and the City of London, see *Annus Mirabilis* in detail and the commentary in *Works*, I.

20 *her Silver Margent.* The shores of the Thames in London. Cf. *Annus Mirabilis*, ll. 1189–1192.

24–25+ *s.d. sung by Reprises.* The *OED* designates this a rare usage but defines the phrase "alternately." Saintsbury is probably right in terming it "A Gallicism, 'à reprises.'" The music shows Augusta repeating the lines with change of pronouns.

32 *The Sedgy Honours of my Brow's disperst.* This is one of Dryden's rare ungrammatical lines. *Honours* seems to combine the sense of a

garland with the Virgilianism for hair; cf. *Aeneid*, I, 591 (*Aeneis*, I, 827).

48–50 *It seems the Gods* etc. Man's subjection to a larger fatal order becomes a commonplace in dramatic apostrophes like this: cf. *Pericles*, III, i, 22–26; *King Lear*, IV, i, 38–39; Webster, *The Duchess of Malfi*, V, iv, 63–64. Dryden's use of the commonplace outside tragedy or tragicomedy proves the surprising thing. What is incidental here, however, becomes central in *Don Sebastian* and *Amphitryon*. Cf., in the latter, Alcmena's speech, II, ii, 50–59; and see the headnotes to the two plays.

77–79 *Behold Democracy and Zeal.* Democracy's male sex is somewhat surprising—see III, i, 42+ *s.d.*—but is clear enough at ll. 117–120, when he seeks to ravish Augusta. Zelota is considered female as the feminine ending of the word indicated (see also l. 148). The *OED* citations for "Zealot" show that the word in its original meaning of a theocratic and extreme sect among the Jews was often applied to the Puritans.

82–84 *Nymph of the City* etc. The association of democracy or liberty with libertinism lasted on, giving Mozart's Don Giovanni a notable opportunity for celebration.

87 *Thou Horny Flood.* The phrase derives from classical set-pieces on river-gods raising their horned heads above the water: cf. Virgil's *corniger . . . fluvius regnator* (*Aeneid*, VIII, 77; *Aeneis*, VIII, 103, "King of horned Floods").

90–93 *Not all the Gold* etc. Dryden includes the whole world by his antipodes of northern and southern hemispheres, and of the Orient (*Levant*) and that New World whence Spain exacted treasure.

99 *Resistless Arms are in my hand.* Such a clash between *Arms* and *hand* is so un-Drydenian that it must be a symptom of his writing a libretto for sound rather than sense.

100 *Barrs.* A "bar" is "A bank of sand, silt, etc. across the mouth of a river or harbour, which obstructs navigation" or provides defense (*OED*).

101 *Thy Towry Head.* Zealota now addresses Augusta (see ll. 30–31).

119 *Haste, Archon.* Archon is identified as "the General" in the "Names of Persons" and is of course George Monck (1608–1670), created Duke of Albemarle after the Restoration. His march from Scotland (see l. 126) in 1660 was at first interpreted, as by Democracy here, as an effort to rescue the declining Protectorate. His support of the royal cause proved crucial to the Restoration.

140 *All other Isles excelling.* Cf. Venus' song in Act V of *King Arthur*, "Fairest Isle, all Isles Excelling."

149 *amaz'd.* In a maze, stupified.

153 *Till I wake again.* In l. 156, Zelota also threatens to wake up; they do so in Act II.

166 *And seem to have restor'd him.* The asyntactic relation of the clause to what precedes again gives evidence of Dryden's discomfiture in writing a libretto.

176–177 *Glorious as the Star of Morning* etc. William Lilly wrote in *Christian Astrology* (1659) of "the Planet Venus": "She is of a bright shining colour, and . . . common people call her the morning Starre, and the learned Lucifer, when she is seen long before the rising of the

Sunne" (p. 72). Lilly also explains (p. 720) that "Profections" enable one to know

> who is the Lord or Governour of the yeer; and he is no
> other then the Lord of that Signe who ascends; as if
> the beginning of a Signe ascend, then one Planet may
> be *Dominus Anni*, or Lord of that yeer; but if the mid-
> dle of a Signe ascend, then there will be two Lords,
> *viz.* that Planet who rules the first fifteen degrees ascend-
> ing, and he that rules the next fifteen degrees succeeding.

The Planet of the Year could be, then, any one or sequential two of the traditional seven: Saturn, Jupiter, Mars, Sun, Venus, Mercury, Moon. The scene suggests that after the reference to Venus, Mercury refers to himself, Lord of the next sign, as *Planet of the Year*.

189+ *s.d.* *Symphony*. "A passage for instruments alone . . . occurring in a vocal composition as an introduction, interlude, or close to an ac-companiment" and overlapping as a term with ritornello (*OED*). See 222 *s.d.* and the headnote, "Staging."

197 *his wandring Love*. For "his errant love."

208 *firm'd*. To "firm" is "To ratify formally; to confirm" (*OED*, citing this use).

212+ *s.d.* Captain Christopher Gunman had distinguished himself for naval valor from 1666. He rose steadily, becoming second captain of the *Prince* under James's command in 1672. He was accused in the *Gloucester* disaster off the Yorkshire coast in 1679, although he was later acquitted, and did not forfeit James's famous loyalty to those who served him. Evelyn attended his funeral on 26 March 1685 (*Diary*, IV, 432), speaking of "that excellent Pilot, & sea-man . . . taken away by the gangrene which happn'd in his cure, upon his unhappy fall from the peere of Calais." Scott (I, 300–301n) quotes the following "Extract from the Jour-nal of Captain Christopher Gunman, commander of his Royal Highness's yacht the Mary, lying in Calais pier, Tuesday, 18th March [1683–4]":

> March 18th. It was variable cloudy weather: this
> morning about seven o'clock saw in the firmament three
> suns, with two demi-rainbows; and all within one whole
> rainbow, in form and shape as here pourtrayed [*see the
> illustration on p. 28 above*]: The sun towards the left
> hand bore east, and that on the right hand bore south-
> east of me. I did sit and draw it as well as the time and
> place would permit me; for it was seen in its full form
> about the space of half an hour; but part of the rain-
> bow did see above two hours. It appeared first at three
> quarters past six, and was over-clouded at a quarter past
> seven. The wind north-by-west.

213 *Batavia*. The Netherlands. Charles II awaited in the Hague the party that was to return him to England.

222 *Etesian gales*. Summer winds from the northeast. Cf. line 6 of Dry-den's *Horace. Ode 3. Lib. I*, 6 (*Works*, III, 77): "Supplying soft *Etesian* Gales"; and *To the Dutchess of Ormond*, l. 46.

222 *s.d. Retornella.* A ritornello, "An instrumental refrain, interlude, or prelude in a vocal work" (*OED*, citing the last stage direction of this opera). See the headnote, "Staging."

232–238 *And send Astræa down* etc. For the Restoration lore of Astræa (justice, the golden age, and strong central government), see Dryden's *Astraea Redux* and the commentary in *Works*, I.

246+ *s.d. the 4 Triumphal Arches.* The arches are shown in engravings included by John Ogilby in the second edition of *The Relation of His Majestie's Entertainment* (1662), which well suggests the kind of iconography employed in *Albion and Albanius*. A reproduction of the most pertinent of the four to this opera, "The Return of Monarchy," will be found in Earl Miner, *Dryden's Poetry* (1967), p. 81.

255+ *s.d. Entry . . . the Four parts of the World.* An "Entry" is "A dance introduced between the parts of an entertainment; an interlude." The term is derived from *"entrée* (or *entrée de ballet)"* (*OED*). It is not clear whether the term was then a Gallicism, as Saintsbury thought, or whether it was already anglicized. The *Four parts* are presumably the four quarters, north, etc., as often depicted on old maps. As Dent remarked (p. 163), this dance and the events leading to it in Act I would have provided a complete operatic "prologue" of the French kind (see 10:25–35n). The term, *Entry*, however, is appropriate only to Dryden's three-act version.

II, i

s.d. a Poetical Hell. That is, a classical, mythological hell as opposed to that conceived of by Christians. A somewhat similar scene of diabolic plotting between Malicorne and the Spirit Melanax will be found in Act IV of *The Duke of Guise,* and in Act I a devil appears before the Duke of Guise.

s.d. Side Scenes. See headnote, "Staging," pp. 333–334.

s.d. There is the Figure of Prometheus etc. Cf. Dryden's nearly contemporaneous *Translation of the Latter Part of the Third Book of Lucretius,* ll. 183–211. Dryden adds to the names mentioned by Lucretius only the Belides, or the daughters of Danaüs. Forty-nine of the fifty daughters slew their husbands (fifty cousins) on their wedding night and were condemned in the underworld forever to pour water into a leaky vessel. Dryden obviously recalls Virgil's tonally more appropriate account of evildoers in the underworld of the *Aeneid* (VI, 548–625), since that passage includes the line (620) given as the motto for "the King" at the end of "The Frontispiece."

s.d. Alecto. Or Allecto, one of the Furies, stirred up at Juno's urging a war between the Trojans and the Latins in *Aeneid,* VII. Virgil introduces Allecto as one *cui tristia bella / iraeque insidiaeque et crimina noxia cordi* (ll. 325–326; Loeb trans.: "Allecto whose heart is set on gloomy wars, passions, plots, and baneful crimes"). Her association with war and plots well qualifies her for a place in Dryden's "Poetical Hell."

1–16 These lines contain numerous allusions to Milton, *Paradise Lost,* in the order of I, 84–124; IV, 105–113; and II, 681–814.

11–16 Democracy and Zeal apostrophize Pluto as a principle of chaos, whence things began and whither they tend at the end of the world. With such paganism may be contrasted Dryden's Christian eschatology as in the last stanza of the ode *To Mrs Anne Killigrew* and elsewhere.

13–16 See the Pythagorean doctrine of transmigration of souls explained by Anchises to Aeneas in *Aeneid*, VI, 703–751 (*Aeneis*, VI, 964–1020).

48–58 However hyperbolical, the background is Virgilian: see the opening *s.d.* of this scene.

62 *For He a Race of Rebels sends*. *He* is of course Democracy, who is addressed by Pluto in l. 70 as "Common-wealth," perhaps a more familiar English nickname than the Greek-originated "Democracy."

63 *And Zeal*. The enduring charge against the Puritans, hypocrisy, is of course implied.

65–72 Pluto and Zelota hatch the Popish Plot.

70 *Common-wealth*. Democracy; see l. 62n.

74 *And all thy Snakes*. The Furies were usually depicted as having snakes on their heads.

89 *his Brother and his Wife*. That is, James, then Duke of York, and Charles's queen, Catherine.

97–101 The story of Cain is told in Genesis, IV; that of Sodom in Genesis, XIX; and that of "two men, sons of Belial" who slandered Naboth in 1 Kings, XXI. The soul being sought is that which will become the archwitness, Titus Oates. The passage curiously resembles Donne's *Metempsychosis*, as the dance of devils (l. 123+ *s.d.*) and the murders of kings is reminiscent of *Macbeth*.

119 *With the Ghosts in a Dance*. The same imagery in a stanza of *Annus Mirabilis* (ll. 889–892) much admired by Dr. Johnson suggests that here, too, the *Ghosts* are "The Ghosts of Traitors." Cf. ll. 121–123.

120 *Jubilee*. "A season or occasion of joyful celebration or general rejoicing" (*OED*).

II, ii

s.d. Prospect. "A pictorial representation of a scene or the like; a view, picture" (*OED*). The *Prospect* includes both sides of the river, as also London and Westminster: the City and the Court. The view from the London-Westminster side of the river extends from York-Stairs near Charing Cross at the left to Whitehall and beyond on the right; and on the Southwark side a similar distance from the Saw-Mill on the left to Lambeth Palace on the right.

1–18 Cf. the "Song of Jealousie" in Dryden's last play, *Love Triumphant*, III, i.

8 *One writ in Sand* etc. Augusta's repentance is *writ in Sand*, Albion's love *in Marble*.

23 *publick good*. A recollection of Satan's self-justifying soliloquy, pleading that "public reason just . . . compels me now" (*Paradise Lost*, IV, 389–391). See also III, i, 21.

24 *Inflame*. "To heat, . . . to raise (the body or blood) to a feverish or morbid heat" (*OED*).

44 *A pleasing ill* etc. The mingling of the sexual and political recalls Achitophel's advice to Absalom: "Commit a pleasing Rape upon the Crown" (*Absalom and Achitophel*, l. 474; *Works*, II, 19).

55–74 Albion's aria reflects in its first stanza Dryden's sense of public madness expressed at the opening of *The Medall*. The details of the second and third stanzas recall the king's speech at the end of *Absalom and Achitophel*.

57 *fumes.* "Something which 'goes to the head' and clouds the faculties or the reason" (*OED*).

70 *Petitions.* Various kinds of *Petitions* sought royal agreement or curtailment of the royal prerogative (see *OED*), and the art of petition by those opposed to the king's measures became highly developed during the reign of Charles II. As a result, royalists distinguished between loyal "addresses" and *haughty* or "seditious" *Petitions*.

86–88 The royal blood is that of the Martyr King, Charles I. For the crying of blood, see Genesis, IV, 10.

89–91 A measure propounded by Shaftesbury and others, and steadfastly resisted by Charles, was to set aside legitimacy and succession by acknowledging Monmouth as his successor. It will be observed that Monmouth is passed over in this opera as if he did not exist.

110 *My Brother, and what's more, my Friend.* Cf. *Threnodia Augustalis*, ll. 248–279.

123 *The Rosy-finger'd Morn.* As in *Odyssey*, II, 1 and elsewhere.

128+ *s.d. discovers.* Discovery or revelation scenes were usually staged by having the paired flat or shutter scenes drawn to either side in their grooves, revealing characters before another set of flats indicating another location.

141 *equal to the God of Day.* Equal, that is, to Apollo himself.

142–157 Thamesis' song is the most often anthologized of the songs in the opera. It catches in cadence and atmosphere the character of the songs in *The Tempest*. "Welcome to the watry Plain" is a courtesy to James going into exile.

157+ *s.d. Chacon.* A *chaconne*, "An obsolete dance, or the music to which it was danced, moderately slow, and usually in 3-4 time" (*OED*, citing this as first use).

III, i

s.d. a view of Dover, taken from the Sea. It is the view *from the Sea* that is unusual.

s.d. Acacia or Innocence. Dryden derives the name naturally enough from Greek. Ἀκακία means "guilelessness"; ἄκακος means "unknowing of ill," "innocent" (Liddell and Scott).

1–3 The frontispiece to Dryden's translation of Maimbourg, *The History of the League* (1684), shows a triumphant version of the present scene of dejection (see *Works*, XVIII, frontispiece). The point of the Dover situation relates to Charles's having landed there on his return from the Netherlands in 1660. Also, although it is not certain that James left on his second exile by Dover for Brussels in March, 1679, it is certain that he returned in late August through Dover. In other words, Dryden identifies

Dover with major events in the lives of Charles and James, which also helps account for the Dover scene of the frontispiece to *The History of the League.*

9–14 Acacia expresses the commonplace, found among the Stoics and others, *Sibi imperare, imperium maximum* (To rule oneself is the greatest dominion); see *Synopsis Communium Locorum* (1700) cap. cxviii. Among the *loci classici* are Horace, *Odes,* II, ii, 9–10 and *Satires,* II, vii, 83–87; Seneca, *Thyestes,* ll. 345–368, 388–390, and 470; Martial, II, liii.

21 *fac'd with publick good.* That is, masked with pretense of the public good: cf. II, ii, 23–24.

37 *Sea-raceing Dolphins are train'd for our Motion.* See the textual notes for Dryden's revision, characteristically to greater precision and concreteness. *Motion* is "Change of abode." *(OED).*

42 *Vows.* Prayers, a common Latinism with Dryden.

42+ *s.d. Enter Tyranny, Democracy* etc. The two characters, "Tyranny" and "Democracy," are distinguished as being *"represented by Men,"* because the gender of both words in Latin and Greek is feminine. This kind of concern for niceties suggests that Dryden revised Betterton's notes. Following this logic, *"Attended by* Asebia, Zelota, *Women"* means attended by those characters represented by women, rather than by those characters and other women.

49–50 *A false Plot* etc. That is, the false Popish Plot was *invented* to *cover* the *true* plot against the king.

62 *his Heir.* James.

69–77 *But you forget the noblest part* etc. As Dryden said of *Albion and Albanius,* "The Subject of it is wholly Allegorical, and the Allegory it self so very obvious, that it will no sooner be read than understood" (see the preface, 11:3–5). Occasionally, however, as in this passage, Dryden touches on events not likely to be immediately understood. Asebia and Zelota are discussing Charles's state of mind and body during the height of the Popish Plot. As Arthur Bryant well shows in *King Charles II* (1955), pp. 225ff., Charles did indeed keep his nerve, even when his council lost theirs. The rumor of his illness and approaching death has reference to the fever Charles had contracted in Portsmouth in August, 1679. See Bryant, *ibid.,* p. 235.

83–85 As Scott noted (S-S, VII, 272):

> By the *White Boys* or *Property Boys* are meant the adherents of the Duke of Monmouth, who affected great zeal for liberty and property, and assumed white badges, as marks of the innocence of their intentions. When the Duke came to the famous Parliament held at Oxford, "he was met by about 100 Batchellors all in white, except black velvet caps, with white wands in their hands, who divided themselves, and marched as a Guard to his person." [*An Historical Account of the Heroick Life and Magnanimous Actions of the Most Illustrious Protestant Prince, James Duke of Monmouth* (1683)], p. 107. In the Duke's tour through the west of England,

he was met at Exeter by "a brave company of brisk
stout young men, all clothed in linen Waistcoats and
drawers, *white and harmless* [Scott's stress], having not
so much as a stick in their hands; they were in number
about 900 or 1000."————*Ibid.* p. 103. . . . The saints,
on the other hand, mean the ancient republican zealots
and fanatics, who, though they would willingly have
joined in the destruction of Charles, did not wish that
Monmouth should succeed him, but aimed at the restoration of the Commonwealth. Hence the following dispute
betwixt Tyranny and Democracy [and the pantomimic
dance of the fight between the White Boys and the
Saints].

Scott only needs correction concerning *Property Boys.* A "property boy"
is "a person who appears in a scene but takes no part in the action" (*OED*).
Dryden distinguishes this group of dancers from actors speaking lines,
although Scott is of course right about the importance of financial property to many of Monmouth's supporters.

87–89 *Saints have Wives* etc. The usual charges against dissenting
"Saints" included lasciviousness, greed, and hypocrisy. All three are in-
volved here, along with political agitation as part of the larger context.
In l. 89 *get* touches on money and begetting.

94–96 The passage refers to the Civil Wars, Commonwealth, and Protectorate much in the vein of *Absalom and Achitophel,* ll. 45–74, 753–754,
and *The Medall,* ll. 127–134.

96+ *s.d.* A libel is "A leaflet, bill, or pamphlet posted up or publicly
circulated," and usually abusive (*OED*).

102 *The Gods have put him in our hand.* This "atrocious and blasphemous sentiment . . . was actually used by the fanatics who murdered
Sharpe, the Archbishop of St. Andrews. When they unexpectedly met him,
during their search for another person, they exclaimed that 'the Lord had
delivered him into their hands' " (Scott).

107 *another Sun.* In the old system of correspondences, the king had
his correspondent in the sun, the royal planet, just as other corresponsive
elements for the king were gold, the lion, etc. See 200+ *s.d.* and n. See
also l. 112 and n; and the conflict of fire and water, ll. 156ff.

112 *a Common-wealth of Stars.* The sun, on the other hand, was considered a planet. See I, i, 176–177n and 107n.

115 *drug.* "A commodity which is no longer in demand" (*OED*).

116–117 *An empty Name* etc. A cynical application of the proverb
"Virtue is its own reward" (Tilley, V81).

122 *close.* "Shut up from observation; concealed" (*OED*).

123 *Fall on.* "To come with violence; to make an attack" (*OED*).

125+ *s.d. The White Boys dance about the Saints.* On the former,
see ll. 83–85 and n. The *Saints* are the *Six Sectaries* of l. 96+ *s.d.*

125+ *s.d. the Association.* See the commentary on the "Epistle to the
Whigs" prefixed to *The Medall* (*Works,* II, 292–293).

125+ *s.d. Protestant Flails.* A "weapon consisting of a short staff, loaded with lead, attached to the wrist by a strap; it is said to have been carried during the excitement of the 'Popish Plot' . . . by persons who professed to be in fear of murderous assaults by 'Papists' (*OED*, with three references). Scott commented on the action represented in this scene: "It is easy to believe that, whatever was the nature of the schemes nourished by Monmouth, Russell, and Essex, they could have no concern with the low and sanguinary cabal of Ramsay, Walcot, and Rumbold, who were all of them old republican officers and Commonwealth's men" (S-S, VII, 274). Scott felt with some justice that only Shaftesbury held together the strange alliance against Charles. For the best modern account of Shaftesbury and this period of plotting, see K. H. D. Haley, *The First Earl of Shaftesbury* (1968), pp. 713–725.

141 *For he can change his hew*. Scott suggested that "The reader may judge, whether some distant and obscure allusion to the trimming politics of Halifax . . . may not be here insinuated" (S-S, VII, 275). Dryden's favorable attitude toward the policies of Halifax (see *Absalom and Achitophel*, ll. 882–885 and n in *Works*, II, 31–32, 279–280) lasted as long as Halifax supported James. James excited lasting loyalty in many people, among them Dryden and Pepys, and one can often judge what may have been the opinions of the poet and the diarist about others by observing how the others acted in relation to James.

142–154 *Albion, lov'd of Gods and Men* etc. In its use of Davidic and Christological lore, this song echoes the symbolism Dryden had used in various fashions from *Astraea Redux* onward: in *Astraea*, see "Prince of Peace" (l. 139) and other details.

156 *Neptune's Foe*. Scott recognized that the reference is to the "Providential Fire" enabling Charles and James to escape the Rye House Plot, fire being that one of the four elements opposed to water, Neptune's element.

157–160 See ll. 83–85n.

164–167 *That Archer* etc. Richard Rumbold (see l. 125+ *s.d.* and n) had one eye blemished and was therefore a *Cyclop*. Rumbold held by rent a farm, Rye House, at Hoddesdon in Hertfordshire. Since Charles had to pass the farm on his return from his habitual April visit to Newmarket, it was decided to waylay and kill him with his party at that isolated place. When a fire broke out in Newmarket days before Charles planned to return, he at first moved with the Duke to another part of the city. A changing wind began to threaten that quarter, however, and so he returned early. The change in date frustrated the plans of Rumbold and his associates, who were subsequently betrayed. See Ogg, *England in the Reign of Charles II*, II, 647ff.; and Thomas Sprat, *A True Account and Declaration of the Horrid Conspiracy Against the Late King* (1685). Like others of his time, including Dryden, Sprat made much of divine dispositions and contrivances, terming the Newmarket episode "a Providential Fire."

167 *Cyclop*. This form for "Cyclops" was standard, and probably derivative from the "Cyclope" of French and Portuguese or the "Ciclope" of Italian and Spanish (*OED*).

168–169 *Heav'n and Earth* etc. Apparently a contrast is meant between them and the sea, as represented by Proteus. Their realm is associated with the fire to which the sea is opposed.

189+ *s.d. Venus.* As later, in *King Arthur* and in *The Secular Masque,* Dryden associates Venus with Charles and James. *Hero's.* Presumably their role was indicated by their wearing plumed helmets, as was usual for the heroes of heroic plays and tragedies.

200+ *s.d.* From this point to the end of the scene we have the material Dryden said he added after the death of Charles (see postscript to the preface, 12:30–13:2).

200+ *s.d. Apollo on a Throne of Gold.* Apollo as god of the sun and associated with gold carries emblems of royalty. See l. 107 and n.

209 *fill.* Dryden's usage substitutes for the more natural "occupy": cf. *The Hind and the Panther,* III, 733. He seems to wish to convey by the Anglo-Saxon verb the more vigorous senses of the Latin *occupo.*

211–212 *Orion. . . . tempestuous sign.* "This constellation ariseth in the winter at which time great stormes are raised and much rain falls" (Alexander Ross, *Mystagogus Poeticus* [1647], p. 194). Dryden seems to associate Orion with Aquarius; see l. 213n.

213 *Betwixt the Balance and the Maid.* Between Libra and Virgo in the zodiac, that is, between summer (which ends with Virgo) and autumn (beginning with Libra), in opposition to the winter of Orion-Aquarius (see ll. 211–212n). The *Balance* also may allude to the scales of justice, which are portrayed, for example, in the frontispiece to *The History of the League* (see *Works,* XVIII, frontispiece to volume).

214–216 Dryden associates justice, majesty, and peace with the position between Virgo and Libra. The association arises easily from Libra's scales and other such details. The three qualities also recall the attributes assigned to Augustus Caesar by name and in Ovid, *Metamorphoses,* XV, 832–833: *Pace data terris animum ad civilia vertet / iura suum legesque feret iustissimus auctor* (Loeb trans.: "When peace has been bestowed upon all lands he shall turn his mind to the rights of citizens, and as a most righteous jurist promote the laws"). The section on Augustus of course follows that on the stellification of Julius Caesar. Dryden had followed a similar movement from Charles to James in *Threnodia Augustalis* (especially in ll. 465–517 on James).

225 *The joy of men, and Jove's increase.* Describing Charles II as *The joy of men,* Dryden recalls the phrase in *Absalom and Achitophel,* l. 318, "Mankinds Delight" (*Works,* II, 15). Both echo Suetonius' opening sentence on the Emperor Titus: *amor ac deliciae generis humanae* (Loeb trans.: "the delight and darling of the human race"). *Jove's increase* is somewhat obscure, but it probably bears the sense of "enlarging the family of Jove."

III, ii

s.d. a Vision of the Honors of the Garter etc. Dryden's interest in this order is beautifully expressed again in *To the Dutchess of Ormond,* ll. 17–18, 168.

s.d. a Man with a long, lean, pale Face etc. This extraordinary tableau refers to Shaftesbury, Dryden's Achitophel. As Scott said (S-S, VII, 282–283):

> Shaftesbury having been overturned in a carriage, received some internal injury which required a constant discharge [through a silver tube effected by his physician, John Locke]. Hence he was ridiculed under the name of Tapski [also alluding to his pretensions to the Polish throne]. . . . There are various allusions to this circumstance in the lampoons of the time. A satire called "The Hypocrite," written by Caryl, concludes thus:
>
> His body thus and soul together vie,
> In vice's empire for the sovereignty;
> In ulcers shut this does abound in sin,
> Lazar without and Lucifer within.
> The silver pipe is not sufficient drain
> For the corruption of this little man;
> Who, though he ulcers have in every part,
> Is no where so corrupt as in his heart.

For a prophetic passage on such "swelling Poyson," see *The Medall*, ll. 287–317 (*Works*, II, 51–52). The feeding on venom from the parent of venom is traditional, as in Spenser's Error and Milton's Sin.

1–14 Because Fame's song does not mention Albanius, it seems likely that this scene concluded the original version of the three-act opera. The terrestrial image of l. 2 (*From Pole to Pole*) seems inconsistent with the celestial location specified in III, i, 208–217, suggesting that Dryden left a thread loose in the revision.

14+ *s.d. A full Chorus* etc. It is sometimes said that early operas often end their acts or conclude the whole rather lamely because of the necessity for characters to leave in full view of the audience. Since the same was true of plays, it is hard to appreciate the force of the excuse for weak endings. Dryden's first act ends in a masque-like triumph. The second and third end with displays, the drama of the acts having in effect concluded beforehand. The *chaconne* at the end of II, and the full chorus and dance at the end of III, possess considerable artistic life, the former of music, the latter of music and dance. If well-performed, these endings must have been very effective in the theater, although it cannot be claimed that they are especially dramatic in the usual sense. In fact, the very ending of the play was probably left to the composer and Betterton to work out.

14+ *s.d. Ho-Boys.* Haut boys, oboes.

EPILOGUE

1 *our Æsop's Fable.* That is, the opera's allegory of the double restoration of Charles II.

7–10 *When Heav'n made Man* etc. The traditional interpretation of God's creation of man in His image held that man was created with reason and therefore free. (Cf. the creation passage in *The Hind and the Panther*, I, 247–273.) Dryden shows in l. 10 that he alludes to the traditional idea; *Truth* in the largest sense is therefore fidelity to justice, the ethical expression of reason or divine wisdom: see ll. 16–22. More simply, *Truth* is honesty, holding to one's word: see ll. 33–34.

12 *touch*. The test by touchstone (*OED*), again employing the king-gold correspondence.

15–34 The passage recalls *Threnodia Augustalis*, ll. 481–490, as it anticipates *Britannia Rediviva*, ll. 349–361.

23–26 *The Saint* etc. The Apostle Peter: see Matthew, XIV, 22–33.

30 *Set Privilege against Prerogative*. As the *OED* quotations show, *Privilege* bore particular connotations of Parliamentary rights, whereas *Prerogative* referred to that never perfectly defined preeminence and special power of the throne. Cf. *To My Honour'd Kinsman*, ll. 171–179; *The Hind and the Panther*, I, 256–262.

33 *on a Word*. See ll. 7–10 and n. James was famous for keeping his word. Cf. the passages in *Threnodia Augustalis* and *Britannia Rediviva* cited in ll. 15–34n.

Don Sebastian

Don Sebastian was produced by the United Company and was performed sometime late in 1689, although the exact date of the first performance remains uncertain.[1] In his preface to the printed play Dryden acknowledges the civility and patience of the *"first days Audience,"* but points out that the reception *"sufficiently convinc'd me of my error . . . that the Poem was insupportably too long."* [2] Presumably it was immediately after

[1] Possibly on 4 December. Evidence of a performance on this date is given in the Lord Chamberlain's List, Public Record Office, L.C. 5/149, p. 368 (see also Van Lennep, p. 378):

> Dec.ʳ the 4th The Queen a Box, and a Box for the ⎫
> Maids of Honoʳ at Don Sabastian ⎬ 15:00:00
> King of portugal—— ⎭

Peter Vernier, who has supplied us the correct version of that entry, has also provided the following information from the *Entring Book* of Roger Morrice, 4 vols. folio, Morrice MSS., vol. R (Dr. Williams's Library, London), p. 41, among entries for the week ending 14 December 1689:

> *Saturday, December 14, 1689*
>
> *Tragoedia* This Weeke the Queene and the Prince of Denmarke were at the Playhouse to see Mʳ Dreydens new Play called *Sabastion* King of Poland, It was well liked, but very much Curtled before it was suffered to be Acted. The concourse was great at the Playhouse, as of late it Ordinarily useth to be. It's said the Poet hath sold his day for 120. Guinneas.

If the same performance is being referred to in the Lord Chamberlain's List as in Morrice's entry (considering that the latter might have mistaken the week ending 7 December for that ending 14 December), then the performance of 4 December would seem not to have been the first, since in his preface Dryden makes it clear that the uncut version of the play was given first (see his opening statement, 65:1–6 above). On the other hand, if Morrice had news of a second performance attended by Queen Mary in the company of George, Prince of Denmark (the latter not being included in the Lord Chamberlain's entry), then the performance of 4 December may well have been the first, with the "Curtled" version here recorded by Morrice taking over in the week following. It will be noted, in this connection, that the reception of the play as reported by Morrice would not seem in keeping with Dryden's own account of the *"first days Audience."* Although too much should not be made of Morrice's slips (i.e., *"Sabastion* King of Poland," and the statement that the play was cut *before* it was "suffered to be Acted"), it must nonetheless be said that his position as a dissenting minister probably made him remote from the facts.

[2] 65:5–6 above. It appears that Dryden may have considered and then rejected the idea of cutting the play even before the first performance. In the preface (see 70:32–71:3) he states—as a defense of the play against the *"Cavillers"*—that the Earl of Dorset (then the Lord Chamberlain) *"was pleas'd to read the Tragedy twice over before it was Acted; and did me the favour to send me word, that I had written beyond any of my former Plays; and that he was displeas'd any thing shou'd be cut away."*

the initial performance that Dryden sought the assistance of Thomas Betterton—who played the role of Dorax—who *"so judiciously lopt"* more
than twelve hundred lines from the play that the plot remained intact.[3]
Performances thereafter appear to have been well received.[4] In spite of
his gratitude to Betterton, however, and in consideration of the "vast
difference betwixt a publick entertainment on the Theatre, and a private
reading in the Closet," for the printed version which appeared in early
January, 1690,[5] Dryden chose to replace the cut lines throughout the play,
and so *"restor'd it, to that clearness of conception, and . . . lustre, and
masculine vigour, in which it was first written."* [6]

The play continued to enjoy popularity until the middle of the eighteenth century, although not the great popularity of *All for Love*, *The
Spanish Fryar*, and *Amphitryon*. Between March, 1705 and April, 1725,
for example, *Don Sebastian* was performed at least twenty-one times.[7] All
considered, in 1689 Dryden had reason to feel satisfaction as he returned
to dramaturgy after a lapse of several years. He himself knew that his
play was of high quality, and after the first night's difficulties were overcome, he had the gratification of an enthusiastic reception. *Don Sebastian*
has long been the rival of *All for Love* for the title of Dryden's greatest
tragedy, and not a few critics have given it a clear preference. Sir Walter
Scott's presentation of the case for the play is one of the earliest and best
(S-S, VII, 293):

> "Don Sebastian" has been weighed, with reference
> to its tragic merits, against "All for Love;" and one
> or other is universally allowed to be the first of Dry-
> den's dramatic performances. To the youth of both
> sexes the latter presents the most pleasing subject of
> emotion; but to those whom age has rendered incred-
> ulous upon the romantic effects of love, and who do not
> fear to look into the recesses of the human heart, when
> agitated by darker and more stubborn passions, "Don
> Sebastian" offers a far superior source of gratification.

For a century or more the tragic story of the death of Don Sebastian,
King of Portugal, excited Europe and filled pages with often heated prose

---

[3] See the preface, 66:7–11 above.

[4] Aside from the performance or performances reported in the Lord Chamberlain's List and by Morrice, none other is of record until that of 26 May 1697.
But if Morrice's report is accurate (see the quotation in footnote 1 above) it
would indicate that Dryden's play was confidently expected to take, given the
large fee which he is said to have received for his third-day rights, 120 guineas.
To this may be added the testimony of Gerard Langbaine—no friend of Dryden's—who wrote in his *Account of the English Dramatick Poets* (Oxford, 1691),
p. 161, that *Don Sebastian* "was I have heard acted with great Applause."

[5] See Ward, *Life*, p. 242.   [6] See the preface, 66:18–22 above.

[7] Taken from *The London Stage*. Montague Summers proffers two other per-

accounts, plays, poems, and romances. For no adequate reason, there grew the hope or the belief that the king had not really died. As Spain moved upon impoverished and undirected Portugal, several impostors pretending to be Sebastian rose up and were severally disposed of. Sebastian was believed by cultists to be a hidden king who, like Arthur, would one day return to his people. The historical aspects of the reign of Sebastian are now well established, but no study exists of the numerous literary treatments of it. What is plain enough is that although the central facts about the reign can be stated in few words, writers chose to embellish the short and simple annals.

The historical sources for *Don Sebastian* include many possible works and few certain ones. In the preface Dryden refers to certain historians as the *"Writers of those times,"* suggesting either that he had been reading historians that belonged to those times or others who had dealt with them.[8] Since he speaks of those historians comprehensively—they are "all" agreed on the bare facts—almost any historian writing before 1689 and in the languages Dryden read is a theoretical possibility, and indeed the wisdom of Dryden's speaking of *"Writers"* rather than historians soon becomes apparent. Quite apart from the chroniclers, numerous others wrote about the defeat of Don Sebastian at Alcazar.[9] The story, both of the battle and of those who thereafter claimed to be Sebastian, quickly spread over Europe, being rendered into several vernacular languages as well as into Latin. The story had a special popularity in England, no doubt because it was believed that Sebastian had been aided in battle by the English adventurer, Captain Thomas Stukeley.

A number of Elizabethan plays treating these matters appeared with surprising quickness after Sebastian's defeat in 1578. One of these was Peele's play, *The Battle of Alcazar,* which was probably performed in the spring of 1589.[10] The ultimate source for Peele's play was an anonymous account that Dryden might conceivably have seen, *Historia de Bello Africano* (Nüremberg, 1580), whether in this or in its Spanish or French versions. Among the Elizabethan plays based on the Alcazar story, a number are now grown very rare or have been altogether lost.[11] *Muly Molocco* was produced, and another play with the same title is mentioned by

---

formances, but these appear to be merely his mistakes, by one month, of performances recorded in *The London Stage.*

[8] Preface, 67:14.

[9] The quickness with which news spread about the defeat of Sebastian can be judged by a poem attributed to an unknown Englishman, "Magnifici Oratoris Angliae, in Effigem Sebastiani . . ." in the two-volume collected works of Resende, *L. Andreae Resendi Eborensis, Antiquitatum Lusitaniae* (Cologne, 1600), II, 83. The verses were perhaps written shortly after Sebastian's state funeral.

[10] See W. W. Greg, *Two Elizabethan Stage Abridgements,* Malone Society, Extra Volume (XLVII), 1922. Greg reviews much of the history of the battle and later events. He thought (p. 7) it very likely that other plays on the subject were performed.

[11] Our account follows Greg, *ibid.,* pp. 11–12.

Henslowe. A quarto edition of Peele's version, *The Battle of Alcazar,* was printed in 1594. English patriotism was fed by *The Life and Death of Captain Thomas Stukeley* (Stationers Register, 11 August 1600; printed 1605); and a lost play, perhaps related in subject, *Mahomet,* was acted in August, 1594. For 1596 and 1597 Henslowe records information about a new play, "stewtley," (presumably *Stukeley*). In April and May of 1601 Chettle and Dekker received full payment for a play entitled *King Sebastian of Portingale.* And there was also a play by Massinger, *Believe as You List,* first acted in 1631, but lost and only recovered in the last century.[12] Massinger transposes the story to classical times, Sebastian becoming the defeated Antiochus who seeks Carthaginian help, is betrayed, sent to the galleys, and at last imprisoned.

Similar romantic stories were given in prose accounts. As has been said, and as Dryden observes in his preface, there came to be some doubt that the king had actually been slain. From this circumstance, and from the absence of any direct successor to the throne of Portugal, there arose a considerable commotion over the impostors who presented themselves as Don Sebastian.[13] One of them could not even speak Portuguese. The best known of the pretenders in England was the fourth, one Marco Tullio Catizzone, whose cause was preferred by three translations of the "Texere" tracts and letters written by the Dominican José Teixeira. Scott's diligence or memory led him to *The True History of the . . . Adventures of Don Sebastian* (1602) and to *A Continuation of the . . . Adventures of Don Sebastian* (1603), both of which were printed, as he said, in the *Harleian Miscellany.*[14] Scott thought that these "may have furnished our author with some slight hints," especially the episode of the rings in Act V. The Teixeira *Continuation* involves, however, only one ring and that used under very different circumstances. Scott failed to observe that there had been a first Teixeira pamphlet, *The Strangest Adventure That Ever Happened,* translated (as apparently the other two were as well) by Anthony Munday, and published in 1601. This pamphlet dealt more fully with the history previous to the time when the impostors began appearing.[15]

---

[12] See *Philip Massinger,* ed. Arthur Symons (1887), II, 381ff.

[13] See Tomas Garcia Fugueras, *La Leyenda del Sebastianismo* (1944), with its excellent brief account of Sebastian and the rise of the cult of Sebastianism. For historical purposes, see *Testemunhos Historicos O Desejado,* ed. Antonio Sergio (1924), which reprints seven nearly contemporary accounts of Sebastian, including the very valuable if also "redundante e floreado" *Crónica del-Rei D. Sebastião* of Fr. Bernardo Da Cruz. The best total account in English of the story of Sebastian, of the so-called "Madrigal" pretender, Gabriel de Espinosa, and of the origin of Sebastianismo is that by Mary Elizabeth Brooks, *A King for Portugal: The Madrigal Conspiracy, 1594–95* (1964).

[14] *Harleian Miscellany* (1808–1811), II, 355–411.

[15] Whether because of its historical account, or because of his own self-confidence in such matters, Summers declared of *The Strangest Adventure* that "with this version, or with the original, Dryden was almost certainly acquainted."

Had there been any continuous interest in the story of Sebastian on the part of English writers, one might accept the hypotheses of Scott and Summers that these tracts were Dryden's source of information. Since, however, the story was forgotten, as it were, by English writers for about sixty years, the possibility that Dryden sat down with slim Elizabethan tracts, or that he learned somehow of what was in lost plays, must be thought very remote, if not impossible. Moreover, Dryden had all the information he needed, in histories, travel accounts, and the translation of the French romance that he explicitly acknowledges as his source.

The historical writings may be considered first. Although the English translation by Captain John Stevens appeared in 1698—too late for Dryden to have used the translation for his play—*The General History of Spain* by Juan de Mariana, has "Two supplements," in the first of which (on p. 24 of its separate numbering) there is a crisp summary of the fateful events of 1578.[16] Dryden may have seen the Spanish account, but it cannot be regarded as the sufficient source. Because he was writing for Spanish readers, and because the pretenders had been an inconvenience to Philip II's enterprise to take over Portugal, Mariana explicitly states that "The King of Portugal was killed in Battle." Dryden, however, makes it quite clear in his preface (67:21–31) that the fact was doubted and that there was a pretender (probably Marco Tullio Catizzone is meant) who was sent by the Spaniards to the galleys and at last executed in prison. Among the accounts Dryden may have found it easier to come by, John Dauncey's *Compendious Chronicle of the Kingdom of Portugal* (1661) contains the information found in Mariana and deals with the same pretender, neglecting (like Dryden) to give his name. In a work attributed to Pepys, *The Portugal History* (1677), which mostly concerns events in 1667 and 1668, the reader is given a résumé of the older history, including the story of Don Sebastian, "of one Stewkly, an English Man," of the king's escape and appearance at Venice, of his capture by the Spaniards and his execution. Another early Restoration account, *A Genealogical History of the Kings of Portugal,* translated from the "French by Scevole and Louis De Saincte-Marthe" by Francis Sandford (1662), more closely resembles Dryden's account than do the other historians mentioned (see pp. 75–80). Were any single historical work to be singled out, this work would hold the strongest claim for having provided Dryden with his facts.

However, when it has been acknowledged that Dryden could well have been acquainted with such purely historical accounts, it must be added that the romance version contained very nearly everything he needed for the serious plot of *Don Sebastian*. The anonymous French version, *Dom Sebastien Roy de Portugal: Nouvelle Historique,* was published in Paris in 1680. Three years later there appeared in London *Don Sebastian King of Portugal. An Historical Novel. In Four Parts. Done out of French*

---

[16] Our colleague in this edition, and a Hispanist as well as Anglicist, John Loftis, came upon this summary in a Spanish edition and is of the belief that it was Dryden's source. Dryden mentions the theological writings of Mariana in the preface to *Religio Laici,* and it is quite possible that he had read the Spanish original. But we cannot accept it as certain, nor if certain, as sufficient.

by Mr. Ferrand Spence.[17] The romance *Don Sebastian* (so to distinguish it henceforth from Dryden's play) contains much that is unrelated to the story of Don Sebastian but that is required by the involuted genre of the romance. One of the major contributions of the romance, for example, is the introduction of the Moorish princess Almeida, a non-historical daughter of Abdala, ruler of three North African kingdoms (Pt. I, p. 43). Don Sebastian, who has had a romance in Portugal, finds all other women driven from his mind by the sight of Almeida after his capture of Arsila. In what would seem appropriate in a heroic play, he pays court to her, "But she received his Compliments with so haughty an Air, and retired with so much Majesty" that he was preoccupied thereafter with thoughts of her (II, p. 107). After the defeat of her brother Mahumet by Moluc, Almeida accompanies her brother to Portugal and falls in love with Sebastian at his court. After reading about all this, one suddenly recalls that Dryden is remarkably silent about what has happened before the action of his play begins. He said with considerable justice of his story, *"I take it up where the History has laid it down."* [18] Part III of the romance deals with the battle and subsequent events in North Africa and Spain, especially as they touch on Almeida and "Pretenders to the Crown of Portugal" (III, p. 54). Part IV ends the other plots happily or sensationally (or both). It also takes the reappeared Sebastian to Almeida, to whom he relates—as had Aeneas to Dido—his many tribulations. He leaves her, hoping to regain his throne against the Spanish. They capture him, however, and put him into the galleys. When the Portuguese clamor for their king, the Spaniards remove him from the galleys, imprison, and poison him. As this summary indicates, and as the frequent references in the notes will show, Dryden was right in mentioning his indebtedness to the romance, and accurate in emphasizing his own departures from it.

Something must also be said of another romance, which antedates the one to which Dryden refers. This one is by Marie-Catherine Hortense Desjardins and appears in her *Les Annales Galantes* (1670), translated as *The Annals of Love* (1672), which Dryden had used for *The Assignation* (1673).[19] Her story anticipates the romance *Don Sebastian* by introducing a Moorish princess, Xerine, who has been in love with Dom Sebastien. After the battle, she hunts among the slain, finds what she mistakenly thinks to be his body, embraces it and revives the man. Quickwitted as he is, he yields to the situation and before long is her husband and a pretender to the Portuguese throne; others also mistake him for the dead king whom he so closely resembles. Later, they return to Portu-

---

[17] The translation is faithful at those points checked. The French version has three rather than four parts, but all that is involved is differing division. Both the English and French first parts end at the same place. The French second part ends at the English version (first pagination), p. 49, and its third part begins with the original of Spence's "The pleasure Cardinal Henry enjoy'd," etc. To conclude these minute details: the pagination of the English version is consecutive in two series, Parts I and II, Parts III and IV, and subsequent citations therefore cite both the part and the page within the series.

[18] Preface, 67:13.   [19] See *Works*, XI.

gal. By this time they have a son, and after various events, the pretender is put in jail and, it seems, is tortured or poisoned. At his dying moment he reveals to Xerine his true identity, charging her to return to Morocco with her son and so to free his country from further turmoil over the succession. She responds handsomely, and shortly "observed the last orders of her counterfeit *Sebastian,* with exceeding punctuality." [20] Dryden could well have read the Sebastian-Xerine romance in *The Annals of Love,* in *Annales Galantes,* or in either the French or English versions of Jean Baptiste de Rocoles, *Les Imposteurs Insignes,* both of which were published in 1683.[21] Most of its emphases, however, were wrong for his purposes; in particular, the radical assumption that the hero was a "faux Sebastien" was itself enough to make the tale of no use to him.

The major difference felt between Dryden's version of the story and that of the anonymous romance *Don Sebastian* is the force of Dryden's characterization. His Sebastian and Almeyda possess greater vitality, are more "real." Although Dryden takes up the story where history had left it off, as a man who had seen how a court behaves he was better able to give a convincing sense of what may be called political behavior. This is not to say that Dryden's hero possesses any greater historical accuracy than the hero of the romance. The historical king of Portugal disdained any interest in women and is thought to have been homosexual. He was vain, stupid, and bellicose. His qualities of courage could as readily be termed foolhardiness, and his religious dedication yet more easily bigotry. Disregarding all advice, he encompassed the destruction of his army and himself, the ruin of his nation, and the delivery of it to Spain. Of course it must be said that no contemporary account drew the picture of Don Sebastian that has been given by modern historians. It was, instead, a world of idealized heroism that Dryden transformed into tragedy, as is obvious from the opening sentences of the anonymous romance (I, pp. 1–2):

> This King had hardly attained his fifteenth year, but he made himself admired by all his People, and fear'd by all his Neighbours: The vivacity of his Wit, the elevation of his Soul, the dexterity he made appear in all his exercises, and the greatness of his Courage rendred him the most accomplished Prince of that Age. He was Handsome, well made, Valiant, and Liberal; He had a Majestick Port, Royal Inclinations, and it seemed as if Nature had taken leisure to form him with all the Qualities that can make a Prince recommendable to Mankind.

Such a description is of course wholly conventional and tells us no more

---

[20] *The Annals of Love,* p. 378.

[21] The French version was published with an Amsterdam imprint, and the Sebastian episode is on pp. 253–285. The anonymous, but very royalist, English version is *The History of Infamous Impostors,* and "The Counterfeit Don Sebastian" occupies pp. 113–137. The account begins with a brief and reasonable history (pp. 113–120) of actual events before retelling Desjardins' story of the Xerine/Almeyda figure and the false Sebastian.

about the Portuguese king than about Amadis of Gaul. Among the few virtues not attributed to Sebastian is piety, a virtue that Dryden himself stresses.[22] This virtue is also conventional enough not to exercise conjecture unduly, but if an explanation is required, the best would probably be the hypothesis that Dryden was indebted to another play about a Portuguese prince, Fernando, captured by the "Moors" and constant in his faith. That play is *El príncipe constante* by Calderón de la Barca.[23] Performed in 1628 or 1629, the play had been published several times, in Spanish, before 1689. This play, like most of the historical accounts mentioned, belongs to a class of works that Dryden might have read, but would not need to have read, before writing his *Don Sebastian*.

છ∾ળ

To this point, consideration of Dryden's possible sources has turned on the historical narrative and the serious plot of his play. There remain to be considered those works that could have provided him with a sense of, or details for, the milieu of his play. No one book contains the wealth of detail found in *Don Sebastian* concerning what was then referred to commonly as Barbary or the Moors. Many of the elements making up Dryden's Moorish milieu simply came from years of reading. But it is possible to give some sense of the kind of book to which Dryden had access, and which shaped his Moorish world. The first that must be mentioned, as a kind of formal source, is *The Alcoran of Mahomet, Translated out of the Arabique into French by the Sieur Du Ryer* (1649). The translation into English was done by Alexander Ross, who, after the brief "Life and Death of Mahomet," added a "needfull Caveat or Admonition" against Muhammed and his book.[24] In his *Africa* (1670), John Ogilby had given a long account of Barbary that was levelheaded, compendious, widely derivative, but not very well organized; Dryden may have remembered from this work details about coins and customs.[25] Another better organized book treating of life in Muslim countries was *The Travels of Monsieur de Thevenot into the Levant* (1686). Thévenot was a careful observer, although, like his fellow travel-writers, he took more

---

[22] See the preface, 68:23–25. It is not clear whether Dryden means that piety is a virtue he has added or whether he says that it was possessed by the original Sebastian, although the latter seems more likely.

[23] In "Dryden and Calderón: A New Spanish Source for 'The Indian Emperour,'" (*MLR*, LXI [1966], 369–383), N. D. Shergold and Peter Ure suggested that Calderón's hero was the original of Montezuma in *The Indian Emperour*. (See *Works*, IX, 306 for reasons why this is unlikely.) The parallel between Fernando and Sebastian is closer in many respects, but not close enough to make Calderón's play a certain source.

[24] The "Alcoran" is "some Monster brought out of Africa, for people to gaze, not dote upon." Cf. the play, I, i, 372 and n.

[25] One way of narrowing to some extent the possible range of books Dryden used is to work through the *OED* glossings of rare words used by Dryden. By examining the books cited for illustration, and by use of other evidence, it is possible to limit reference to books that he had likely read.

from other books than from observation. What he has to say, however, on
Turkish women, and on ideas about women and marriage (pp. 55–57),
provides perhaps the closest analogue to Dryden's details. But essentially
the same matter will be found repeated in numerous books.

The provenance of exotic names sometimes provides evidence of bor-
rowing, and as we note, Dryden makes an interesting slip in the first act
of the play by referring to his intriguing villain Benducar as "Bemboucar."
Bemmoucar, or Ben-Boucar, was the ruler of one of the principalities in
Morocco, and his efforts to expand his territories were related at some
length by Lancelot Addison in *West Barbary* (Oxford, 1671).[26] "Benbucar" is also mentioned in *The Present State of the Empire of Morocco*
by François Pidou de St. Olon. It may seem impertinent to mention
this work, considering the fact that neither its French original nor its
English translation had appeared before Dryden's play.[27] Yet this account
provides the best gloss of its kind on *Don Sebastian,* and it is evident that
a common source is involved. From what may be termed Pidou de St.
Olon's French tradition, came Dryden's Muley-Zeydan (pp. 95–96 and
119), important details of clothing (pp. 89–95) and of "the Mufty's powers" (pp. 104–105), and the model for Benducar, Mahomet Addo Ben
Ottar (pp. 118–119).[28] Although it is true that Pidou de St. Olon mentions Benbucar earlier, it is his description of Ben Ottar that perfectly
fits Dryden's intriguer:

> Mahomet Addo Ben Ottar . . . is to this Prince [Muley-
> Ishmael] as his Chief Minister, and has there the same
> Access and the same Trust as a Favorite; and indeed, of
> all them that approach him, he best knows how to flatter
> his Passions and humour him in whatever may please
> him. . . . he is about five and fifty Years of Age; he has
> a quick Eye and an ingenious Look; his Ways and Dis-

[26] *West Barbary*, pp. 25–34; he is introduced on p. 22. The slip on Benducar's
name in Act I is unlikely to be a printer's error, for the coincidence of coming
up inadvertently with a name actually used in other books would seem too
great. Possibly Dryden started by calling his villain Bemboucar, changed to
Benducar, and missed making the change in these particular places, which are
less prominent because they are not speech tags.

[27] Pidou de St. Olon was briefly in Morocco as ambassador to Dryden's
"Muley-Ishmael" in 1693. The English translation appeared in 1695. The brevity
of Pidou de St. Olon's stay shows that his remarkably rich account was largely
manufactured from one or more earlier studies that we have not discovered.
The only alternative hypothesis to that of a French tradition from the 1680's
is that which is touched on in the note concerning the "Prologue, Sent to the
Authour" (p. 421 below), namely that Dryden heard much more than that Muley-
Ishmael was a tyrant from those officers to whom he had talked (see the preface,
70:16–19). Some of the details are so particular or minute, however, that indebtedness to a book or books seems much more likely.

[28] To take a specific instance, the *OED* gives no usage earlier than Pidou de
St. Olon in translation for the "burnous," "bernous," or "barnus" (also other
spellings), a hood or veil used in Muslim countries. But Almeyda enters in
Act I (238+ s.d.), "*her face veil'd with a* Barnus."

course discover a great deal of Cunning; he is deceitful and wicked to the highest degree . . . at the same time he loves nothing but Money, and is pleas'd with nothing but Mischief; he is fear'd but not at all belov'd by the Moors, who universally hate his Ministry, and in private give him all the Curses imaginable; he is likewise very great with Muley Zeydan the King's Son, and the Partner of all his Pleasures." [29]

From travel-writers, and especially from what seems a French tradition represented by Pidou de St. Olon, Dryden was able to take, then, numerous details comprising the Moorish milieu and specific details of names and characters for his play.

⁅ ﹋ ⁆

It cannot often be the case that a work published after a play provides the best gloss on its details. But in considering the sources for Dryden's comic plot, we must return again to Pidou de St. Olon. The standard study of the sources for Dryden's comic plots sets forth, as the source for the comic plot of *Don Sebastian,* a romance, *Le Pelerin,* by Sebastian Bremond, which was translated into English as *The Pilgrim. A pleasant Piece of Gallantry . . . Translated . . . By P. Belon. Gent.*[30] and which had assisted Dryden in forming the comic plot for *The Spanish Fryar.* The romance unquestionably provided Dryden with the basis for his red-faced Father Dominic in *The Spanish Fryar,* and may have supplied some similar shading to the comic plot of *Don Sebastian.* But even the Mufti's red face follows Restoration stage practice in presenting comic priests, and *The Pilgrim* bears only the slightest resemblance to Dryden's comic plot in *Don Sebastian.*[31]

The comic plot employs a motif recurrent in travel stories, especially those in which Europeans recount their visits to exotic countries: the native women find European men sexually irresistible, and often they rescue their European lovers from positions of danger or slavery. In the romance

---

[29] Pidou de St. Olon, pp. 118–119. He (or his translator on his own) also mentions that Ben Ottar had been in England "Twelve Years since," *ca.* 1682, in time perhaps to savor the last part of the Popish Plot. With the description quoted, compare especially I, 1–44 and 57–64.

[30] Cf. Ned Bliss Allen, *The Sources of John Dryden's Comedies* (1935), pp. 145–149. *The Pilgrim* seems to have been published in parts: I in 1680–81 (2d ed. 1684); II in 1684. It was reprinted, or gathered, in the series, *Modern Novels* (1692), vol. X in the Clark Library series, vol. V in that of the British Museum.

[31] *The Pilgrim* details the geographically and artistically meandering pursuit by an Italian of a Spanish wife under her suspicious, irate husband's nose; the Pilgrim has the help of a friar and eventually gets the lady in marriage. It is strange of Allen to claim this as a source. Significantly, he admits that he was unable to find a copy of the romance *Don Sebastian* and so follows Summers, as one often does to one's peril, in saying "there is no indication that Dryden consulted this book" (i.e., the romance) more than any other (*Sources of Dryden's Comedies,* p. 145).

Don Sebastian (IV, pp. 110–147) Sebastian relates to Almeida in Venice how he survived the interval between the battle and his arrival in Venice. He had been rescued from the Moorish troops when he was purchased by Abdeliza, who maintained him as her prisoner-lover, much as Johayma has hopes of doing in Dryden's play, although Abdeliza's age and attractions more nearly resemble those of Morayma. There is a similar tale in *The Adventures of (Mr. T. S.) An English Merchant, Taken Prisoner by the Turks of Argiers* (1670). This time it is "One of the King's Wives" who has him bought and who keeps him "about two years" as her slave and lover (pp. 34–41).

When his royal mistress died, Mr. T. S. was sold to a gardener (p. 59). This seemingly small detail shows that the garden scenes of *Don Sebastian* deserve some attention. In fact, the gardens of the Muslim peoples from Tunis to Constantinople constitute one of the *de rigeur* motifs of description. Ogilby mentions the royal garden of Morocco (*Africa*, p. 166), Thévenot the gardens of Persia (*Travels*, II, 77–78, 82–83), Addison those of Barbary (*West Barbary*, p. 80), and so do other writers on other places. In view of the fact that in Dryden's play the Mufti's garden is tended by that amorous spark Antonio, none of the other descriptions of gardens has quite the interest of Pidou de St. Olon on "The King's Gardens":

> The Walks are very narrow; there are no Water-works,
> but some Rivulets glide through the Place and serve to
> Water it. A Spanish Slave whose Name is Antonio Lopes
> has the Care of it.[32]

And a few pages later we have an explanation for the Johaymas of that part of the world:

> The Reservedness and Restraint, in which the Moors
> keep their Wives, serve rather to quicken the Desire,
> which they have naturally to run astray, than to stifle it;
> . . . as those Women have more Wit and Vivacity
> than those of Europe, these Qualifications inable 'em
> to out-do 'em in all the Arts and Tricks by which they
> may gratifie their Inclinations.
>
> They are particularly fond of Christians because they
> are not Circumcis'd, and there are no Stratagems but
> what are us'd by some of 'em, to intice the Slaves that
> live with them, or who are allow'd to come where they
> dwell.[33]

In brief, the comic plot derives from the romance *Don Sebastian*, from lore about Muslim countries, and from Dryden's own provision of wit and comic tradition. In *An Evening's Love, The Assignation*, and *The Spanish Fryar* will be found "gay couples" related by comic blood to Morayma and Antonio. Moreover, there is something of a shared Mediterranean character, since the first and third of those comedies are set in Spain, and

---

[32] Pp. 76–77. A gardener named Antonio in a Moorish garden would ordinarily provide proof presumptive to claim a source, especially with the coincidence of other likenesses. But we emphasize again that Dryden's play predates Pidou de St. Olon's account.

[33] Pp. 82–83. Cf. *Don Sebastian*, II, ii, 8–15 and I, 132–133n.

the second in Rome. And in *An Evening's Love* the English blades seem
to have acquired Spanish by finding themselves in Spain as readily as
Antonio picks up, by location, whatever tongue (probably "Turkish")
was imagined to have been spoken in Barbary. In a wider dramatic context but still within the exotic range—this time offered by India—*Aureng-
Zebe* presents a character somewhat like Johayma. Queen Nourmahal is a
sexually designing older woman, who seems to be the more worth recalling
in this context because her intentions toward Aureng-Zebe involve incest.

The comic plot also shares with the tragic plot certain characters (the
Mufti, Mustapha, Antonio, and even Almeyda and Benducar) as well as
a certain political energy. To the extent that we can differentiate the
political aspects of the two plots, the rise of the *mobile* can be taken as
the distinctive feature of the comic plot, just as the intrigues and fortunes
of kingship distinguish the tragic plot.[34] The *mobile vulgus, mobile,* or
simply the mob is at one point (IV, iii, 31 ff.) divided partitively, with lines
assigned to those unprepossessing characters, First Rabble, Second Rabble,
and Third Rabble, as if three rabbles make a mob. Because the entire
Latin phrase was classical, it was current for centuries. As the *OED* shows,
"mob" was used as early as 1600, but full awareness of the *mobile* as a
political tool did not seem to rise in English minds until the time of the
Popish Plot. On 17 November 1679, Shaftesbury is said to have aroused a
crowd of 200,000 people for the excitement of a "Pope-Burning" and for
a demonstration of strength against the royalist party.[35] Although England
has never suffered a mass or mob revolution, the fear of that possibility
has often worried conservatives like Dryden, and has occasionally seemed
sufficient in itself to offer radicals like Shaftesbury a lever with which to
bring about political change. Certainly revolution seemed a distinct possibility during the second half of the short reign of James II and during
the first two years of the reign of William III. What distinguishes the
concerns of those years (and of the eighteenth century) from the concerns
of earlier decades is that the opposing sides were required to pay as close
attention to the London populace as to the high and mighty. That many-
headed Hydra, the *mobile,* could indeed cause disorder, even when no
agency was manipulating it politically, as accounts of chroniclers like
Narcissus Luttrell show (see, e.g., Luttrell, I, 99).

The *mobile* scene in Act IV must have provided the ladies, gentlemen,
and "Citts" of the audience with that thrill which accompanies a stage action depicting what is frightening in actual life. Considering, however, that
Dryden's conservatism was so deeply ingrained, two matters require observation.[36] First, we observe that the *mobile* is not just ridiculous, though
it is that, but also bumblingly good-hearted. If he had wished, Dryden

---

[34] In the preface, 72:11–16, Dryden singles out Antonio as the character most
crucial to the joining of the two plots.

[35] See K. H. D. Haley, *The First Earl of Shaftesbury* (1968), p. 557.

[36] For a similar account of Dryden's complex presentation of political elements
in this play, and one to which we are indebted, see Michael Alan Seidel, "Satiric
Theory and The Degeneration of State—The Tyrant and The Mob in Satiric
Literature of The Restoration and Early Eighteenth Century" (Diss. University
of California at Los Angeles, 1970, ch. vii).

might have commanded another tone and might have deployed his hostility very differently. Why he did not can only be explained by a second reflection: the *mobile* finally supports and aids the good characters. Even before Dorax arrives with his forces, the *mobile* has saved Almeyda and rejected Benducar. However stupid, avaricious, and fickle the *mobile* of the play may be, in the end both its heart and its politics are constitutionally sound. In the next century there were to be Tory as well as Whig mobs, but until then the mob normally meant anarchy and revolution. It is all the more striking that the mob plays the positive, if also comic, role that it does in *Don Sebastian*. If it is ridiculous, it is also much more likable and even normal than is the "Almighty Crowd" of *The Medall* (l. 91). Something in the energy of the *mobile* of *Don Sebastian* appealed to Dryden, and not only as a dramatic convenience. That energy, and its surprising appeal to Dryden, came from English experience rather than from lore about the Moors or the romance *Don Sebastian*. Any attempt to read a political allegory into the play must be vigorously resisted for reasons already given. But the mob-like actions in England during the first two years under William III must have seemed to Dryden as a part of the way in which God in His wisdom dealt with usurpers like the Prince of Orange or with would-be usurpers like Benducar. There are senses, then, in which Dryden could agree with the Mufti's disingenuous declaration that "The voice of the Mobile is the voice of Heaven" (IV, ii, 219–220).

⚬⚬⚬⚬⚬⚬

One further aspect of Dryden's story deserves separate discussion because of its importance to the play and its appearance in numerous other plays, stories, and tales: the incest motif. This motif has recurred so frequently in the literature of various cultures that it has elicited extensive study.[37] Dryden was obviously acquainted with numerous stories of incest —in the Bible, in Ovid's *Metamorphoses,* and elsewhere. He may have known of the treatment of incestuous love in such of Calderón's plays as *La Devoción de la Cruz* and *La Dama Duende*. Still staying with dramatic treatments, we may recall that in 1678, within the year after publication in France of Racine's *Phèdre,* Dryden himself had published some of his opinions about the play.[38] Also in 1678, he and Nathaniel Lee brought

---

[37] See Otto Rank, *Das Inzest-Motiv in Dichtung und Sage* (1912, enlarged 1926), which is encyclopedic but follows Freud too dogmatically to be of assistance. There is a very full examination of aspects of the subject in Paull Franklin Baum, "The Mediæval Legend of Judas Iscariot," *PMLA,* XXXI (1916), 481–632, especially pp. 593–624. For references to numerous incest stories, see Stith Thompson, *Motif-Index of Folk Literature* (1955–1958); and D. P. Rotunda, *Motif-Index of the Italian Novella* (1942). Further references will be found in all these works.

[38] *Phèdre* was first published in 1677. Dryden's comments came as quickly as the following year; see the preface to *All for Love* (1678, sig. b2 *r–v*; Watson, I, 224–225).

to the stage their version of the most famous of all plays using an incest motif, *Oedipus*. Shakespeare, John Fletcher, and John Ford also had provided brief or extensive treatments of the taboo.

Certainly literary treatment of incest was widespread in the period. But *Don Sebastian* does appear to be unique in the particular version of incest that it presents. What differentiates the incest in Dryden's play is a combination of the following four conditions: the relationship involves brother and sister (rather than mother and son, for example); the character of the relationship is unknown to the participants; the incestuous love is consummated; the revelation of their blood relationship is subsequently revealed.[39] Many writers treat brother-sister incest, but almost invariably in one of two ways: either the relationship is known and love is consummated, so that the emphasis on sensation and guilt may be heightened; or, the relationship is falsely assumed, so that a maximum amount of concern can be raised without prohibiting a happy ending when the assumed relationship is disproved. A familiar version of the former, or tragic and sensational, version of brother-sister incest is given by John Ford's *'Tis Pity She's a Whore,* and a good example of the latter, or tragicomic, version of brother-sister incest is Beaumont and Fletcher's play, *A King and No King.* There can be no doubt that Dryden knew this play very well. He had praised it in the preface to *Troilus and Cressida* (1679, sig. a3; Watson, I, 247). Beaumont and Fletcher's play was to become the major source for *Love Triumphant* and, in its focus upon the question whether incest renders a king unfit, it quite possibly had some bearing on *Don Sebastian* as well.

The implications of *Don Sebastian* differ entirely, however, from those of the kinds represented by Ford and Fletcher. The brother-sister relationship is revealed, but only after love has been consummated. To alter the title of Southerne's later play, Dryden's might have run, "The Fatal Marriage; Or, The Innocent Incest." Given certain standards of poetic justice, and given certain taboos, incest must be punished even if committed unknowingly. Moreover, as Sophocles had shown so persuasively, when the protagonist acts unaware of his incestuous relations, the dramatist gains the means to depict a powerful fatal force in human affairs. And it is fate that is a major theme of the play, a fate dramatized by the incest motif. It must be thought remarkable that in *Don Sebastian* and, a year later, in *Amphitryon*, Dryden found two such different dramatic fables to show the operation of fate in human affairs. The very word, *Fate,* enters as early as the eighteenth line of *Don Sebastian;* thereafter it frequently reappears in that form and in other forms such as that of the adjective, and even in such a substitution for it as seems remarkable in Dryden, that is, *Predestination.* The wooing scene leading to marriage and incest (II, i, 499–633) is marked by concern with fate, prediction, and

---

[39] In view of the many aids to locating stories of incest (see n. 37, above), it is strange that the closest analogue found for *Don Sebastian* is in the *Heptameron* by Marguerite of Navarre, III, Nouvelle xxx, a tale of double incest which does not involve disclosure to the brother and sister of their relation, and is hence crucially unlike *Don Sebastian.*

human destiny. In her last speech of the scene, Almeyda remarks (II, i, 628), with attention to old emblems, that she goes to her marriage "with Love and Fortune, two blind Guides." Moreover, Dryden explicitly says that the general moral of the play is to be found in its last four lines, which speak of *"Sebastian* and *Almeyda*'s Fate." Presumably, similar meanings are conveyed by *"another Moral couch'd under every one of the principal Parts and Characters."* [40]

Only the fact that the relationship between the hero and the heroine is unknown to them enables Dryden to develop a theme of fate. At the same time, and it is one of the most interesting aspects of the play, its theme of fate does not imply the absence of free will. The "Laws Divine, and Humane" that Sebastian speaks of (V, 629) may be followed or broken. Both the hero and heroine have had ample warning, dark hints, and flat injunction against their act. They fail to heed. Dryden's use of such devices as terrible intuitions and warnings in dreams enables him to communicate to the audience the nature of the relationship between his hero and heroine well in advance of their discovery of it. Similarly, he delays the revelation of that relationship by Alvarez until the tragic consequences are inevitable. Dryden's techniques are clear enough to any reader familiar with English drama. When, in the wooing scene, Almeyda reports that she seems to hear

> My Mothers Voice, that cries, Wed not, *Almeyda!*
> Forewarn'd, *Almeyda,* Marriage is thy Crime,

we are duly instructed (II, i, 572–573). When Sebastian replies that "Love is not Sin, but where 'tis sinful Love" (l. 575), the instruction is continued to the point of certainty. And on that clear instruction rests our recognition of the dramatic irony in Almeyda's next speech:

> Mine is a flame so holy, and so clear,
> That the white taper leaves no soot behind;
> No smoak of Lust; but chast as Sisters love,
> When coldly they return a Brothers kiss,
> Without the zeal that meets at lovers mouths.[41]

We are aware not only of the irony involved in the assumption that her love is normal, but also that she deceives herself in thinking that her love is without physical passion. The projection and heightening of such irony can be accomplished in a stage production by various means. At all events, from the second act forward, we know and the characters do not, until the end, that they head for disaster. Like Oedipus, they choose freely and foolishly and so enmesh themselves (with assistance from their parents' foolish or sinful acts) in the web of fate. It was unnecessary for Dryden to have written of Sebastian and Almeyda's *tragic* fate, for as he wrote William Walsh, criticizing a phrase in one of Walsh's poems, "fate without an epithet, is always taken in the ill sence. *Kind* added, changes

---

[40] See V, 724–727 and preface, 71:18–19.

[41] II, i, 576–580. The dramatic irony in *Don Sebastian* is observable to any reader, as is also the fact that it proceeds by hints rather than by use of a well-known story, the situation that so assists Sophocles to his more powerful irony in *Oedipus the King.*

that signification. (*Fati valet hora benigni*)." [42] Nor did Dryden think that the action, the fate, or the tragedy of Sebastian and Almeyda required death as poetic justice. Having acted in ignorance, however much they willingly contributed to that ignorance, a lesser punishment satisfied the code of moral causality.

༄༅

The handling of the incest motif in the plot reveals Dryden's mastery of dramatic form. At the beginning of Act III the problem raised by their act concerns not the possibility of divine retribution but rather the jealous fury of Muley-Moluch that Almeyda should have married Sebastian. Throughout the third and fourth acts the thickening problems never seem to turn on incest; and when tragedy seems nearest, at the end of Act IV, the duel of friends leaves Dorax exclaiming over his "extasy of joy" (IV, iii, 647). After all the many subordinate problems are solved and after the political issues have been seemingly decided, Dryden at last brings before his central characters and us a scene of recognition, reversal, and tragedy. What astounds Sebastian and Almeyda causes no surprise in the audience. On the other hand, the resolution of the catastrophe—the separation rather than the deaths of the principals—would come as a surprise, or at least as a fresh approach, to an audience familiar with the traditional punishments of incest in drama. By having the characters continue to live, but live apart, Dryden stresses their fate rather than—as in Sophocles' *Oedipus*—the horror of the revelation. But by having the characters *agree* on separation, Dryden allows once again for an element of free choice within the fatal scheme. Whether Dryden's handling of the incest motif is viewed from the standpoint of its conditions (brother-sister relation; relationship unknown; love consummated; and relationship revealed), or whether it is viewed from the standpoint of his dramaturgy, his treatment is distinctly unusual. But it is still altogether fitting that the final revelation of the blood relationship should, in this sophisticated play, borrow from the timeless store of folklore. Recognition by tokens is a common motif in folk tales (as well as in more sophisticated stories), and so is identification by a ring.[43] Dryden joins the two motifs, as had sometimes been done previously. He goes farther, multiplying the single ring token to two, and having the brother's and sister's rings, when fitted together in a union, reveal the sinful parents' names and their union. The token becomes in fact a symbol of illicit union, a theatrical revelation, and an indication of the solution: the rings, and their wearers, must part.

In considering the dramaturgy of this tragedy, both Dryden and later critics have aired the question of its unity. Dryden himself acknowledged:

> *I have not exactly kept to the three Mechanick rules*
> *of unity: I knew them and had them in my eye, but fol-*

---

[42] Ward, *Letters*, p. 35.

[43] See Thompson, *Motif-Index of Folk Literature*, H 80, H 86.3, and H 94ff. Aristotle on peripeteia and anagnorisis ("recognition") is also relevant; see *Poetics*, XI, 1–7.

> *low'd them only at a distance. . . . My Scenes are there-*
> *fore sometimes broken, because my Under-plot requir'd*
> *them so to be . . . and I have taken the time of two*
> *days, because the variety of accidents, which are here*
> *represented, cou'd not naturally be suppos'd to arrive*
> *in one: But to gain a greater Beauty, 'tis lawful for a*
> *Poet to supersede a less.*[44]

Dryden's experience in dramaturgy fully enabled him to give coherence in spite of his enlarging upon, or transgressing, the "Mechanick" rules of place and time. But a question remains to be answered. Is the action one, do the tragic and the comic plots contribute to a single end?

If, by definition, plays with double plots, serious and comic, lack unity, then *Don Sebastian* lacks unity, as do such plays by Shakespeare as the two parts of *Henry IV*. On the other hand, if a play with a double plot can possess unity, that unity must be demonstrable. Neither Dr. Johnson nor Scott explicitly addressed himself to the question; Dr. Johnson seems to have held a negative view and Scott was more willing to skirt than to confront the issue.[45] *All for Love* is more unified than *Antony and Cleopatra*, but it is not a greater play. But this much can be said: unity of action as a mark of a harmonious, energetic coherence is of significant importance in Dryden's art. Questions of tone and theme become necessarily entwined with those of form. Dryden himself seemed content to weigh the issue on purely formal grounds, no doubt having the uneasy sense that Thomas Rymer was looking over his shoulder. Consequently, he prided himself on the role of Antonio in this regard.[46] In what he terms *"the Uniformity of the design,"* the comic plot could hardly have been, he asserts, *"more of a piece, and more depending, on the serious part of the design."* [47] The judgment is almost legal in having been decided on relatively narrow and technical grounds. Ultimately, the judgment does not really settle the question, and we must open the question to wider view.

In most respects, it may be said that the double plot of *Don Sebastian* is confined to the second and third acts. In the first act Sebastian and Antonio are both described by Dorax, and both are depicted drawing black lots. Their varying reactions not only represent their differing characters but also determine their separate movements in the next two acts. Their common plight as prisoners of the Moors during the first three acts helps bring them together in Act IV when their captors have been overcome. Since Antonio contributes far more to the release of Sebastian than does Sebastian to Antonio's freedom, Dryden might have said that the serious design depends on the comic. Dryden's greatest risks are run with

---

[44] Preface, 69:35–70:10.

[45] In *Restoration Tragedy* (1967), Eric Rothstein first explored in clear detail certain formal parallels between the two plots and thematic elements relating them.

[46] See preface, 72:11–16. Dryden ought to have given the role of the Mufti at least equal credit.

[47] Preface, 72:1, 7–9.

the tone of the comic plot. Like all the principal English comic dramatists, he employs a considerable element of farce, even though he consistently deplored farcical comedy. Whether, ultimately, a serious play
can admit such a comic plot probably depends on one's assumptions about
art and one's ideas about life. Differing answers are of course possible, and
in what follows, the argument for unity is premised on one view of art
and life.

Although the comic plot has a farcical stratum in it, the characters involved are all of high social rank. Because Antonio is dressed as a slave,
he is able to join the *mobile* and lead it to the aid of Sebastian and the
Portuguese cause. When he resumes his own identity, clothes, and position, he prospers in a singular way as a courtier. Sebastian and Almeyda's
identities are concealed by the uncertainty of their origins. When they
come back, as it were, to themselves, the revelation of what they have
done and who they are dooms them. This contrary movement is reflected
in other aspects of the dramatic and scenic movement of the play. At the
opening, all share a common public atmosphere in a rather unlocalized
scene *"at* Alcazar, *representing a Market-Place under the Castle,"* as the
first stage direction tells us. In the course of the play, the arena of the
serious plot is increasingly restricted, and the stage direction at the beginning of the last act reads appropriately: *"The Scene is a Room of
State."* Fittingly enough for the incest motif, the serious plot con-
stantly occupies a public arena where literally nothing is allowed to be
hidden for long. Exposure is a central feature of that scene, as much for a
Benducar as for a Sebastian. If the tragic plot requires exposure, the comic
plot requires changing or hiding identities, from Antonio's capering like
a horse in the first act, to the crucial garden scenes of Acts II and III.
These scenes are private, and the second of them takes place under the
yet more intimate conditions of night. By virtue of the darkness and the
degree of disguise employed in this plot, Antonio reaches an impasse until he can get out of the garden and, by motivating the rabble in the
right way, assume his proper role, as he finally does in rejoining the public arena and daylight in Act V. Moreover, his union with Morayma in
Act V is accompanied by a version of the revelation that will follow for
Sebastian and Almeyda. The revelation must be public to be true, to be
moral; and it also has its token, not of rings that must join to part, but
of a box of jewels that constitutes Morayma's self-assigned dowry. Because
of the somewhat farcical version that the comic plot offers of the serious
issues and motifs of the tragic plot, Antonio and Morayma are unworthy
of a tragic role at the ending. Or, to put it another way, their marriage
is typical and comic, whereas that of Sebastian and Almeyda is atypical
and tragic.

In both plots, then, the ultimate question turns on certain fundamental
moral issues. Another problem is that of the dynamism of social order.
Simply put, there are three questions of rule: who will rule the kingdom,
who will rule the Mufti's garden, and who will rule himself?[48] The king-

---

[48] On Dryden's usage of the kingdom-garden analogy in his non-dramatic
works, see Alan Roper, *Dryden's Poetic Kingdoms* (1965), pp. 104–135.

dom and the garden have been got by immoral acts, and the same cloud darkens the play's two principals. Both the kingdom and the garden are threatened by betrayal from within, and very much the same may be said of Sebastian and Almeyda. The legitimacy of the regimes of both are threatened by prisoners claiming a superior mandate, and it is even true that that problem is at the center of the love of Sebastian and Almeyda. As was observed earlier, the *mobile* effects the changes in all three orders: what a tyrant had divided at the beginning of the play is united by the mob at the end. From the times of Plato and Aristotle, the mob and the tyrant had represented theoretical political extremes, and therefore parodies of the dynamic political and moral order sought. The true choice of that order is sought for in both plots by the means of love, and again the play turns upon something like parodies of true love. Obviously Muley-Moluch is wrong in wishing to marry or to ravish Almeyda, and Johayma is wrong in wishing to seduce Antonio. But as the love of Antonio and Morayma is at worst wanton, that of Sebastian and Almeyda is at best, and at worst, that of a brother and sister. The past of the tragic love and the future of the comic are alike dark in their respective generic colorings. The proper rule of self depends on Sebastian and Almeyda's staying apart and upon Antonio and Morayma's staying together.

The tragedy that comes with the revelation of incest would not provide the only possible fifth act of the play, had not Dryden seen to it that the reader or audience is apprised of the incest as early as the second act. Without such dramatic irony, there would be no reason whatever for preferring a tragic to a tragicomic ending. In a sense, the higher issue of the unity of *Don Sebastian* lies in the question whether the play is more truly a tragicomedy or a tragedy augmented by comedy. The first alternative had been taken, as we have seen, in the play *A King and No King* and would be taken by Dryden in *Love Triumphant*. In *Don Sebastian* the presence, or absence, of dramatic irony involving both plots provides the crucial test. That dramatic irony is involved is borne out by evidence from the end of the fourth act and the beginning of the fifth. At the conclusion of Act IV Sebastian is saved from captivity, married to Almeyda (herself a queen), and reconciled with his friend Dorax (or perhaps one should say, Alonzo). A speech by Sebastian concludes the act:

> Some Strange reverse of Fate must sure attend
> This vast profusion, this extravagance
> Of Heaven, to bless me thus. . . .
> Be kind, ye Powers, and take but half away:
> With ease the gifts of Fortune I resign;
> But, let my love, and Friend, be ever mine.[49]

Sebastian argues from the more or less superstitious principle that deprivation follows unusual abundance. We understand the same principle in the light of dramatic irony. He has forebodings, and we have foreknowledge. The "reverse of Fate" will not seem "Strange" to us.

Such points emerge even more clearly at the beginning of Act V from

---

[49] IV, iii, 663–665, 667–669.

comments exchanged by Dorax and Antonio (who is not yet reunited with Morayma). They agree on the happy state of things, Dorax saying,

> Joy is on every face, without a Cloud:
> As, in the Scene of opening a Paradice,
> The whole Creation danc'd at their new being:
> Pleas'd to be what they were, pleas'd with each other.[50]

That the Eden trope can include the kingdom and the garden is evident enough; and that the terrestrial "Paradice" does not survive a fall is equally well known. That such matters are implied can be understood by Antonio's summing up his life, his world, as he now speaks in verse:

> Pleasure has been the bus'ness of my life;
> And every change of Fortune easy to me,
> Because I still was easy to my self.
> The loss of her I lov'd would touch me nearest;
> Yet, if I found her, I might love too much;
> And that's uneasy Pleasure.[51]

Nothing in Antonio's previous (or, indeed, his subsequent) behavior indicates that, like Adam, he would fall in "Paradice" out of uxoriousness. Our recollection of his behavior provides an irony underscored by Dorax's reply in the mode of popular cynicism about marriage conventional to Restoration *comedy:*

> If she be fated
> To be your Wife, your fate will find her for you:
> Predestinated ills are never lost.[52]

Any knowledgeable playgoer knows that Morayma will shortly return to Antonio with her father's jewels. She is "fated" to that; it is her "fate"; it is among "Predestinated ills." The iteration of idea is remarkable, even for this play.

Dorax's cynical jest to Antonio relates to the "Paradice" he had so beautifully described, and especially to the last two lines of that speech:

> Such Joy have I, both in my self, and Friends:
> And double Joy, that I have made 'em happy.[53]

Dorax is as enmeshed in the dramatic irony as Sebastian or Almeyda, because the pride that had made him a renegade still prevents his taking an adequate view of his world. In respect to him as well, then, it may be said that he reveals how the play (with some looseness in the double-plotting of Acts II and III) moves harmoniously if not unanimously toward tragedy. The conductor of that movement is dramatic irony, and the fact that that irony affords parallels between the serious and the comic plots shows the integrity of the play. For example, just as Almeyda is mistaken about her paternity, so Morayma mistakes her father the Mufti for Antonio (IV, ii, 17–20), and so Antonio mistakenly thinks Johayma to be her stepdaughter (III, ii). By comparing the evil characters with the good,

---

[50] V, 1–4.   [51] V, 7–12.

[52] V, 12–14. It may be added that Dorax's comments on sex and on women, both here and early in the play, are sometimes more disturbing than the story of incest or Antonio's wantonness.

[53] V, 5–6.

we also obtain a kind of foreshadowing of the ends of Muley-Moluch
and the Mufti. In such instances, something as much like dramatic convention as dramatic irony functions to allow us to see through their
pretensions.[54]

Dryden is careful to develop formal devices that assist in giving the
play unity and whatever beauty may be thought to be derived from patterns in plays. Each act except the last begins with Benducar on stage. In
Acts I–III he is attendant on Muley-Zeydan or Muley-Moluch, who speak
first (Dryden usually observes such social decorum). Muley-Zeydan is the
first to speak and, in a sense, the first to disappear. Muley-Moluch opens
Acts II and III; his last appearance is in Act IV, where he is already a
diminished figure. (Like Maximin in *Tyrannick Love*, Muley-Moluch is
a love-smitten tyrant with a Christian princess in his power. In *Don
Sebastian*, however, the tyrant also confronts a heroic, although captive,
king who overshadows him.) At the beginning of Act IV Benducar appears alone to give the traditional villain's soliloquy, which in effect
points to his disappearance from the play. Benducar's opposite number
in the tragic plot, Dorax, opens and closes Act V. These two speeches in
Act V reveal Dryden's aim: a balancing, a voicing, and a realization of
tragic irony, as well as a statement of a moral order.

Another, perhaps even finer, aspect of dramaturgy involves the revelations in the play. No act is without at least one, and each has a different
function within the recurrent pattern and the movement of the play.
The most important revelation of course comes last, the disclosure of the
brother-sister relationship of Sebastian and Almeyda (Act V). But as early
as Act I we see them engaged in revelation, disclosing their identity to the
other characters. In his asides, Dorax reveals to the audience what the
Moors take time to learn, that one of the prisoners is Sebastian (I, 242–
285). Subsequently, Dorax provides the same service for Alvarez (I, 276–
285) and for Antonio (I, 293–296). How deliberate all this is can be
shown by Dryden's own words. Speaking of the comic episode involving
Antonio and Morayma, Dryden said that *"To prepare this Episode, you
see* Dorax *giving the Character of* Antonio, *in the beginning of the Play,
upon his first sight of him at the Lottery."* [55] It is only after Dorax has
prepared us for the character of Sebastian that Sebastian reveals himself
to the Moors (I, 338–341), and it is only after Sebastian's characterization
of the goodness of Alvarez and the wantonness of Antonio that their roles
demonstrate what has been said. But we know. The revelation of Almeyda is an exception. When she unveils (I, 439 *s.d.*) in the climactic
revelation of Act I, the news is as fresh to the audience as it is to the
Moors. In another sense to be sure, at the end of the play Almeyda takes
the veil again and so hides herself from the world. Similarly, Sebastian,
who in his first speech depicts himself reappearing from the clouds of
his disguise and his fate like "a setting Sun" (I, 339), will disappear at the

---

[54] For Muley-Moluch, see IV, i, 117–126 and n; also 131–142 and n. For the
Mufti, see II, ii.
[55] Preface, 72:11–16.

end into "a Cave" that lies "Under the ledge of *Atlas*" (V, 669), at the very base of the world. The first act ends with a countermovement, Antonio's becoming a slave rather than a courtier, a beast rather than a man (I, 511ff.).

Something like revelation, or self-presenting, takes place in the differing ways that Johayma (II, ii, 41–45) and Morayma (II, ii, 86–89) first offer themselves to Antonio. As with Almeyda, they reveal themselves with no help from a presenter like Dorax. A similar self-presenting, which does involve dramatic irony, is Johayma's revelation of herself to Antonio, who has mistaken her for Morayma in Act III (ii, 1–45+ *s.d.*). Yet another example occurs in the Mufti's self-revelation to Morayma (IV, ii, 1–20) and still another in his self-revelation to his servants (IV, ii, 188–209) who think him Antonio. But a more significant revelation follows in the serious plot (IV, iii, 381ff.) when Dorax reveals himself to be Alonzo and when Sebastian gradually reveals to Dorax—as if the king held up a mirror to his friend—his true character. With this revelation in the serious plot, and with the serious and the comic plots already rejoined, we are fully prepared for the climactic revelations of Act V. In brief, it may be said that although *Don Sebastian* fails to achieve the tight unity of *All for Love,* it acquires sufficient unity within a more various and more capacious scheme.

❧

The numerous revelations, with their different pacing of moments of understanding by the audience and the characters, do not simply constitute a theatrical motif giving pleasure when recognized and unity by patterning. More importantly, they relate to the fundamental concern of the play: man's attempt to discover his place in the scheme of things, amid countless uncertainties, by rising to a vision of a world possessed of moral order. This theme is also central to *Amphitryon* (see the headnote, below), and it will be found in other of Dryden's finest works of his later years.[56] In his last eleven years, faced by uncertainties himself, Dryden grappled with the problem of an individual's relationship to his world, reaching some very sobering, but in the end assured, answers to his questions. To illustrate very simply how such matters work in the play, one need only observe that the succession of revelations progressively reduces the uncertainties, until finally Sebastian and Almeyda confront themselves as they are, not merely king and queen, but also brother and sister, husband and wife.

Such major discovery comes only to those who traverse the largest number of uncertainties and whose capacity for understanding, as well as for suffering, is greatest. Some of the uncertainties are of course less central than others. For example, the uncertainty over who is Christian and who is Moor impinges on Dorax, Almeyda, and Morayma, and therefore pre-

---

[56] Among the most neglected of Dryden's important works, *Cleomenes* deserves mention. On the theme of the search for the good life in *Fables,* see Earl Miner, *Dryden's Poetry* (1967), ch. viii.

sents significant questions to the men in their lives. This uncertainty does not, however, possess the importance of another, a set of political uncertainties that may be typified most readily by the question of who is king.

For Dryden's purpose, the romance *Don Sebastian* had a great advantage over Desjardins' *Dom Sebastien* in that its hero was a king, not an impostor. This assumption, which was by no means the only possible one in view of the lore about Sebastian, is crucial to Dryden's play. As in so many of Dryden's plays, however, and especially as in other tragedies, the true king in *Don Sebastian* finds himself in an alien environment. Sebastian's state of captivity is perhaps somewhat extreme, but Montezuma, Antony, Cleomenes, and even Almanzor would recognize the problem. Again, the hero's finding himself under the sway of a tyrant, caught in the intrigue of rival claims to the throne, and involved in a revolutionary situation—all this is common in Dryden's serious plays. The political element in such serious plays is, then, very volatile and the changes that come often entail major revolutions in the state.

Don Sebastian shares with Dryden's other serious plays an uncertain and tragic (or heroic) polity. That must be stressed, because otherwise too much might be made of the fact that Sebastian is a king fighting outside his country, and that the nation is ruled by a tyrant. Certainly James II was out of England, fighting in Ireland from a base in France, when Dryden wrote this play; and William III was to Dryden a usurper and a tyrant. Readers must resist such comparisons, and not least because there are more important differences than there are resemblances between Dryden's plot and the history of the time. In a word, *Don Sebastian* does not allegorize events following the Revolution of 1688. What it does do is to present certain concerns that had interested Dryden for years, as can be seen in *The Indian Emperour, Aureng-Zebe,* and *All for Love.* These concerns turn on the serious polity of kingship, rule, government, and the life of the state; and Dryden's treatment of them shows a remarkable consistency on either side of 1688. Such consistency, like that observable in Shakespeare's history plays, argues not only a consistent view of man in the state but also a consistent possibility of revolution in seventeenth-century England. To speak of consistency is of course not to speak of sameness, and we can observe, for example, a major shift in one respect between *The Conquest of Granada* and *Don Sebastian.* For a conservative, Dryden surprises many readers by positing an element of volatile and decisive energy at variance with an established order. In the early two-part play, that force resides in the heroic dissident, Almanzor, whose force must be reconciled to society. In *Don Sebastian* it is, of all things, the *mobile* that rescues society with an energy restoring a proper order. Two such different sources of force have of course different political emphases, but they share certain elements. It is widely known that Dryden seems to be the first to have introduced (in *1 The Conquest of Granada,* I, i, 209) the phrase, "the noble Savage." Almanzor is not precisely a "noble Savage"; he merely claims to enjoy the freedom of that creature in a state of nature. But in Almanzor and in the *mobile* of *Don Sebastian* we observe Dryden's recognition of the inevitability—the necessity, perhaps even the desirability—of an energy almost primitive in origin if the polity is to function. The king's "Body Politic" must possess vitality, just as much as his "Body Natural."

Such considerations in no wise diminish the extent to which Dryden espoused a conservative royalism enhanced by ritual, symbol, and typology, governed by decorum, and concerned with order, legitimacy, and power.[57] But Dryden's royalism is dynamic, like the very principles of physics being discovered in his day. What distinguishes his serious plays is that in them defeat, suffering, deprivation, disaster, or at all events a central uncertainty marks them, and that resolution comes only with the reconciliation of energy and order or with a grasp of the nature of the individual's relation to his world. Uncertainties as to who is the king certainly do not mark Dryden's non-dramatic poetry. The plays therefore reveal a whole side of his understanding of man that is hardly to be guessed from the non-dramatic works alone.

Once such distinctions have been drawn and such continuities observed, it becomes possible to consider the contemporary significance for Dryden of the polity in *Don Sebastian*. The play offers no allegory. Obviously Dryden knew what was going on in England, Ireland, and Europe. He had only to read the gazettes, listen in the coffee house, talk with friends who had visited the court. Obviously he was concerned. And obviously he knew that his first play presented after the Revolution of 1688 would be carefully scrutinized. In arguing that his critics should be silenced when they learn that the Earl of Dorset has twice read the play and wished that nothing should be cut, he is, no doubt, taking pleasure in his long-time patron's discerning appreciation of the play's literary merits.[58] But he is also telling the world that Dorset, now counted among the moderates supporting William III, has found nothing objectionable from a political standpoint, even after reading the play a second time.

The important thing about the political implications of *Don Sebastian* is, to put it negatively, that Dryden had to take care that the play *not* be construed a parallel like *Absalom and Achitophel,* or a "fable" like *The Duke of Guise.* England seemed once again on the verge of revolution, and Dryden was in danger of losing his life. So strained was the atmosphere in 1689 and 1690, so deeply in trouble was William, that the king could not answer demands for his presence in Ireland or the Dutch states. One need only follow Narcissus Luttrell's *Brief Relation* of events during the two years following the flight of James II to discover at once the disorder of the country and, bred by fear, the strength of the anti-Catholic hysteria. Numerous people "suspected for popish preists" were jailed on charges of high treason (Luttrell, I, 524). Among the penal orders there was a proclamation recorded on 13 March 1689 forbidding London to Catholics within a ten-mile radius of the city (Luttrell, I, 533). As time went on, efforts increased to root out the Catholic danger. Both in Lon-

---

[57] As a simple illustration, one need only recall Dryden's remark in the preface about *"the rule of decency"* in making Dorax submit first because Sebastian is king (71:23–26).

[58] Preface, 70:32–71:3.

don and the provinces certain Catholics, usually of some eminence, were arrested and jailed. The physician Betts and Sir John Symonds were among those imprisoned and facing possible death by being hanged, drawn, and quartered. The terror did not end with 1689. On 31 January 1690, "sir Edward Hales and Mr. Obadiah Walker came to the court of the kings bench by habeas corpus from the Tower, being committed for high treason in being reconciled to the church of Rome" (Luttrell, II, 10–11). Everybody knew, and not least Dryden, that he was guilty "in being reconciled to the church of Rome."

It is small wonder, then, that Dryden asked Dorset to inspect his play carefully, or that he chose a noted Protestant to whom he might dedicate it. It was prudent at the least to take such precautions, and Dryden must have felt that he enjoyed protection from highly placed friends. But the general peril for a known Catholic makes the more remarkable his open stress on his religion in the prologue. The audience could only have responded strongly to this piece of daring, or of foolhardiness. Dryden was not out of danger. On 22 June 1690, the year in which the play was published, and about six months after it was first performed, Dryden's friend, Samuel Pepys, and several others were arrested on charges of high treason (Luttrell, II, 63–64). On 2 July, "Several suspected houses have been lately searched for disaffected persons" (Luttrell, II, 67). And on 4 July, "Several of the eminent and noted Roman catholicks are taken up and committed to prison" (Luttrell, II, 70).

Don Sebastian was obviously written, acted, and published at a time when it was impossible not to consider political matters. But the very dangers that required such consideration made it certain that Dryden could not possibly attack the government of a prince he considered a usurper nor express his allegiance to his true king. What he could do and what he did do were two things at once far smaller and far larger than the political state of the realm. The smaller was the personal gesture in the prologue—the open stress upon his Catholicism at a time when men were being arrested for high treason only on the suspicion of adhering to that religion. The larger was the exploration of the uncertainty attendant on man as a political creature, in terms of the polity of this play. There can be no question about the integrity or the strength of Dryden's religious and political convictions. If there were not so many examples it would be surprising—as it is certainly ungracious—that some critics living in no such time of terror for themselves have questioned Dryden's moral stature.

We can observe one of Dryden's subtlest revelations of himself within the political context of history and literature in his dedication to Leicester. As a man named Philip Sidney befriending a poet, Leicester is a patron of a latter-day Spenser. Yet more importantly, he is a friend, like Pomponius Atticus, to those in distress or in danger of their very lives. Two or three sentences from Dryden's closing quotation from Cicero's letters to Atticus may be noted. Leaving for banishment and half expecting to be purged—as indeed he later was—Cicero wrote to his good friend: "I am still the same. My enemies have robbed me of all I had; but they have not robbed me of myself. Take care of your health." [59] Here, in small compass, is Dryden's response to the dangers of his time. As in the play he had just written, so also in his dedication of it he suggests that man's role is clarified by seeing it in terms of similar experience at other times and in other places.

It is no wonder, then, that he should have treated in his dramatic fable, as he had often done before, the uncertainties of man immersed in the contingencies of politics. Who indeed is the true king? Sebastian is the best candidate (with whatever doubts may be thought to leak through from history), but Sebastian's father, the king before him, had undone Sebastian by the adultery that made possible, or almost inevitable, the incest of the play. The marriage of Sebastian and Almeyda, like marriages throughout serious English drama of the sixteenth and seventeenth centuries—or indeed among the royal families of Europe at that time—was potentially a way of uniting two kingdoms, in this case, Portugal and Morocco. Ironically, tragically, the marriage that might have established beyond doubt the identity of the king in both lands, turns out to be a marriage that brings division and dethronement, because Sebastian and Almeyda have been too closely allied from their births.

In such fashion, the political uncertainty of *Don Sebastian* reflects a larger uncertainty over human identity and human relations. With the major exception of Otway, not since the Jacobean dramatists had such uncertainties over human identity, and uncertainties over what loving might entail, been made so central to the vision of a great play. In his feverish treatment of love and all else he wrote about, Otway raised more intensely than Dryden many of the same questions, but in the end Otway found no answer except in the intensity of experience itself. Dryden's questions, or uncertainties, are more numerous and his answers cooler. In *Don Sebastian* (as, in the comic terms in *Amphitryon*) the most fundamental human identities and relationships are obscure. Not only is it uncertain who is king. More importantly, one cannot assume that one knows who is or is not wife or sister, husband or brother (Almeyda, Sebastian), who is mother or daughter (Johayma, Morayma), who is parent or lover (the Mufti, Antonio), slave or master (Antonio, Mufti), and who is friend or enemy (Muley-Zeydan, Benducar and, above all, Dorax). Such uncertainties require the extraordinary number of revelations Dryden employs in the play, in one way to instruct the audience, and in others to give understanding to the characters in their world. His characters must understand as well as confront an uncertain world.

In the preface Dryden argues that love and honor are *"the mistaken Topicks of Tragedy,"* and have in any case been *"worn out"* through constant use.[60] But it was an altogether different matter to create a play that explored the uncertainties attendant on love and evident human integrity (*honestas, honor*). In the comic plot, and to the end of the epilogue itself, there is little certainty that in this imperfect world such love really unites. Dryden seems to leave it open to question whether this

---

[59] Loeb translation. See also 64:9–12n.   [60] Preface, 65:29–30.

"wanton love" of Antonio and Morayma will lead to "nuptial love." But prior to the epilogue at least, the answer seems much more positive than negative. The love of Antonio and Morayma possesses, with whatever limitations, a dignity, a charm, and indeed a normality and a legality lacking in any other love relation of the play, Sebastian and Almeyda's especially included.[61] Still, it is the love of the hero and heroine that brings the greatest ecstasy and the greatest guilt. In itself a perfect unity of the best matched lovers, the unity of that love is doomed to cause division precisely because the lovers are too closely matched. The study of love in such terms is the study of human relations and of man's place in the world.

Don Sebastian presents a special version of possible gain in tragic experience and understanding. What has been said of the tragic effect of all Dryden's tragedies is true rather of a play like *All for Love* than of *Don Sebastian:* that finally the play leaves "a graciousness, a compensation for the hardness of existence." [62] In *Don Sebastian* understanding is more important than graciousness, and being right is the consolation for suffering. Dryden's late plays—preeminently *Don Sebastian* and *Amphitryon*—make clear how difficult it is to understand one's place in the world, one's relation to others, and one's own identity. Those plays also show, however, that the acquiring of such understanding is the source of human dignity.

TITLE PAGE

Epigraph. *Nec tarda Senectus / Debilitat vires* etc. From Virgil, *Aeneid,* IX, 610: "and sluggish age weakens not our hearts' strength nor changes our vigour" (Loeb trans., the Latin text reading *viris* instead of *vires*).

DEDICATION

P. 59 *To . . . Philip, Earl of Leycester.* Philip Sidney, third earl of Leicester (1619–1698), had led an active early life on embassies abroad, as representative for the borough of Yarmouth in the Isle of Wight in the Long Parliament, as military leader for two parliamentary expeditions into Ireland during the Interregnum, and as adviser to Cromwell. Being rather a consultant than an executor of Protectorate affairs, he incurred little danger at the Restoration, obtained a general pardon, and participated no further in public affairs after that time, although he is said to have been consulted in private on affairs of state by Charles II. During his father's lifetime he resided at Shene, near Richmond in Surrey, "where he entertained himself with some of the greatest Wits of the Age," and "set

---

[61] *Amphitryon* by itself suffices to show how serious a fully comic vision of love may be. And when Dryden writes, towards the beginning of the last poem in *Fables, Cymon and Iphigenia* (l. 20), that "Love's the Subject of the Comick Muse," it is the *comédie humaine* that he has in mind; see the discussion of *Fables* referred to in note 56, above.

[62] Bonamy Dobrée, *Restoration Tragedy 1660–1720* (1929), p. 97.

a-part one Day in the Week for Entertainment of Men of Letters" (see *Letters and Memorials of State . . . transcribed from the Originals at Penshurst Place in Kent,* 1726, I, 149). On becoming Earl of Leicester in 1677, he lived at Leicester House, London, so that his gardens adjoined the house in Gerrard Street in which Dryden was living in 1690. In the dedicatory epistle Dryden casts Leicester in the role of a "second Atticus."

59:15 *Atticus.* Titus Pomponius Atticus (109–32 B.C.) was a man of great inherited wealth and culture, friend and correspondent of Cicero, and considered to be one of the most noble and generous men of ancient Rome. He derived his name from his long residence in Athens (88–65 B.C.), where he stayed to escape the political distractions of his native land. After his return to Rome he devoted himself to study and the pleasures of friendship, refusing to take any part in political affairs, though he was not without influence since he lived on familiar terms with leading statesmen to whom he willingly gave his counsel. He survived the Civil Wars by remaining consistently neutral, and was a patron of the arts, his house on the Quirinal being a notable literary center (*Oxford Classical Dictionary,* 2d ed., p. 146). Although he was an author himself, his fame rests upon his friendship with Cicero and on his being the addressee of sixteen books of Cicero's letters. Dryden's source of information is clearly the life of Atticus written by Cornelius Nepos, Atticus' friend, in which certain details missing in Dryden are also missing, and where a most flattering portrait is drawn of him. Dryden has been criticized for drawing the Atticus-Leicester comparison, but there were clearly certain parallels in the lives and attitudes of the two men which must have seemed to him more than sufficient to justify a dedicatory compliment.

59:19–20 *I have . . . ventur'd into the Holy Grove.* The *Holy Grove* is a *lucus,* a wood or thicket of trees sacred to deity; Dryden's phrase as a whole suggests the violation of a sanctuary by one profane. See 62:33–34 and note on the contiguity of Dryden's house to Leicester's gardens; and, for a similar image, see the play, II, i, 2–4.

60:2 *Revolutions.* The primary sense of "revolution" here is "alteration, change, mutation" (*OED*), but Dryden also anticipates the astronomical figure later in this sentence (60:7–8).

60:7 *like the Moon in the Copernican Systeme.* Dryden did not commit himself to any one of the rival cosmologies of the century, but towards the end of his life he speaks more frequently of the "Copernican" view, with the sun (here, of course, Leicester) at its center; see, e.g., *Discourse Concerning Satire* (*Works,* IV, 79); *A Parallel betwixt Painting and Poetry* (1695, p. xli; Watson, II, 199); and *Of the Pythagorean Philosophy,* l. 94 (in *Fables,* 1700).

60:20 *there is but one Phœnix in an Age.* Dryden's stress on the uniqueness of an Atticus or a Leicester involves the Phoenix as an emblem of a special hero, as for Milton's Samson (*Samson Agonistes,* ll. 1699–1707). Dryden had used the emblem for Charles II in *Threnodia Augustalis* (ll. 364–369) in a general context of patronage for the arts (st. XIII) which seems also to be implied here.

60:20–22 *centring on himself, remains immovable* etc. The tradition of *integer vitae* drawn on in these phrases is best discussed by Maren-Sofie Røstvig, *The Happy Man* (rev. ed., 1962), ch. I. Dryden uses ideas and images drawn from commonplaces associated with Horace and Neo-Stoicism. His depiction of Leicester represents this "Atticus" as a Stoic sage unshakable in that *constantia* which was likened to the center of a circle, as a person tranquil amidst the turbulent waves (*mediis tranquillus in undis;* see Røstvig, p. 18; see also Horace, *Odes,* III, iii). The idea of reigning over oneself appears again in *To My Honour'd Kinsman,* l. 18, "Lord of your self"; it derives from often-cited sources such as Horace, *Satires,* II, 7, 83, on the wise man, who rules himself (*sapiens, sibi qui imperiosus*) and numerous commonplaces (e.g., *sibi imperare, imperium maximum;* for nine examples, see *Synopsis Communium Locorum,* 3d ed., 1719, ch. CXVIII). Virgil's description of Aeneas (*mens immota manet,* ["the mind remains unshaken"] *Aeneid,* IV, 449) also enters into this idealized version of Leicester.

60:33 *the Sanctuary.* Athens; see also 59:19–20n.

61:3 *prevented.* Anticipated.

61:4–5 *longo sed proximus intervallo.* Virgil, *Aeneid,* V, 320, "Next to him, but next by a long distance" (Loeb trans.).

61:6–7 *frons læta* etc. Virgil, *Aeneid,* VI, 862: "gloomy were his Eyes, dejected was his Face" (Dryden, *Aeneis,* VI, 1191).

61:7–8 *si qua fata* etc. *Aeneid,* VI, 882–883 (*Aeneis,* VI, 1220–1221):

> Ah, cou'dst thou break through Fates severe Decree,
> A new *Marcellus* shall arise in thee!

61:21 *when they were just.* Referring to *Countrymen,* not to the Attici.

61:34 *offices.* An "office" is "That which one ought, or has, to do in the way of service; that which is required or expected: a. *gen.* Duty towards others; a moral obligation" (*OED*). Cf. Cicero, *De Officiis.*

62:5–24 *The eldest of them* etc. The eldest is Atticus, who Dryden wishes to suppose "for his honour" was "of the Academick Sect," whose sceptical philosophy Dryden himself favored except in matters of faith. Dryden's phrasing shows his awareness that Atticus was in fact closer to the Epicureans, a "Sect" that he, like Cicero, regarded as "Dogmatist." For another characterization of the Epicureans as dogmatists, see Dryden's preface to *Sylvæ* in *Works,* III, 10:6ff. and especially 11:5ff. Dogmatism in matters of reason is a species of pride, and so Dryden also includes "the ruggedness of a Stoick" among the targets of criticism in pagan philosophy. Specifically, he criticizes the Stoic notion that a wise man can be god-like in indifference to pain, or can "debase" himself in the scale of nature to an inanimate and insensate object. Against such pretenses he sets the Christian position that to "find within our selves the Weaknesses and Imperfections of our Wretched Kind" leads to that compassion and charity towards others in which the "second *Atticus,*" Leicester, deserves "precedency" (62:25, 8) over the first.

62:8 *his younger Brother.* That is, Leicester.

62:8–9 *stiffness of Opinion.* Cf. the portrait of Zimri in *Absalom and Achitophel,* l. 547 (*Works,* II, 21): "Stiff in Opinions, always in the wrong."

62:16–17 *Homo sum* etc. Terence, *Heauton Timorumenos,* l. 77 (Loeb trans.: "I am a man, I hold that what affects another man affects me").

62:28–33 *The Praises which were given* etc. As Malone noted, Henrietta Maria, then Queen Mother, visited Charles II in 1660, coming again in 1662 and residing till 1665. In those years she refurbished Somerset House, which stood across the river from what were then, in Cowley's phrase, "the meaner Cabanes" on the other side. In applying them to Leicester, Dryden has slightly altered the lines he takes from *On the Queens Repairing Somerset-House* (Cowley, *The Works* [1688], p. 27):

> For the distrest and the afflicted lye
> Most in their Care, and always in their Eye.

62:33–34 *Neither has he so far forgotten* etc. Dryden, then living in a house in Gerrard Street which adjoined the gardens of Leicester House, is of course the *poor Inhabitant,* given the favor by Leicester that Henrietta Maria had bestowed upon the poor, according to Cowley.

63:3–4 *another Sidney . . . another Spencer.* Dryden here shifts temporarily from the Atticus-Cicero analogy, calling Leicester "another *Sidney*" (as in name and blood he was), while declining to think of himself as "another *Spencer*." In spite of the explicit denial, Dryden has suggested his relationship to Spenser.

63:25 *The Hero's Race* etc. Dryden gives the last line of Waller's brief poem, "These verses were Writ in the Tasso of her Royal Highness," substituting *transcends* for "excells." Thomas Rymer also quoted this apparently highly esteemed line in his *Short View of Tragedy* (see *The Critical Works of Thomas Rymer,* ed. Curt A. Zimansky [1956], p. 89).

63:27 *where Praise is undeserv'd* etc. Cf. Dryden's *Parallel betwixt Painting and Poetry* (1695, p. xlv; Watson, II, 202): "the better [likeness] is a *Panegyrick* if it be not false, and the worse is a *Libel.*"

64:9–12 *Me, O Pomponi* etc. Dryden brilliantly fuses (and somewhat alters) the endings of two of the letters Cicero sent as he was leaving for banishment in 58 B.C. From *Ad Atticum,* III, iv, he adapts *Me, mi Pomponi, valdè pœnitat vivere* (Loeb trans.: "I indeed, Pomponius, am heartily sick of life"). With some similar variants, Dryden then adds the conclusion of III, 5 (Loeb trans.: "One thing only I beg of you, since you have always loved me for myself, to preserve your affection for me. I am still the same. My enemies have robbed me of all I had; but they have not robbed me of myself. Take care of your health"). Cicero's letter III, 5, is dated: *Data IIII Idus April. Thurii.* Dryden uses the same formulation to date his: *Dabam Cal. / Jan. 1690.* (Given 1 January 1690). The praise of Leicester as a "second Atticus" ends by representing Dryden as a second Cicero, as has been implied throughout. Cicero's *Me . . . valdè pœnitat vivere* resembles Dryden's earlier description of himself in a "World, of which his Misfortunes have made him weary" (63:2–3). Adopting the role of Cicero about to be purged under a dictatorship, he suggests the dangers faced by a Catholic and Jacobite in the years following 1688. Amid such dangers, Dryden insists—with Cicero—that no one can take from him his most important possession, himself. In this insistence he appropriates for himself as well as Leicester the constancy of the

Stoic sage. With some self-dramatizing, then, Dryden ends his dedication movingly, and no less so because its Roman analogy presents his own role in post-Revolutionary England and his own concept of the moral stance to be taken with reference to issues raised in his tragedy.

PREFACE

65:1 *through a long disuse of Writing.* "Apart from the opera *Albion and Albanius* (1685), Dryden had not written a play to be performed since *The Duke of Guise* (1683), acted late in 1682" (Watson II, 44).

65:3 *crowding it, with Characters and Incidents.* The *dramatis personae* (see "Persons Represented") takes the unusual step of numbering twelve named characters. It includes four others without names, as well as the "Rabble." Dryden later takes up the question of the unity of a play crowded with *Incidents.*

65:6 *the Poem was insupportably too long.* The quarto first edition of *Don Sebastian* gives the play in 124 (misnumbered 132) pages. For *Cleomenes*, the length is 102 pages; for *All for Love* and *Oedipus*, seventy-eight pages. As he often does, Dryden refers to his play as a *Poem:* see 71:11 and the dedication of *Amphitryon*, 223:30.

65:10–11 *There is a nauseousness in a City feast.* For one description of a Lord Mayor's feast, see Thomas Jordan, *London in Luster* (1679). But as the *OED* citation (s.v. *City*) shows, the comparison was an old one. Cf. Shakespeare, *Timon of Athens*, III, vi, 75: "Make not a Citie Feast of it."

65:15 *explode.* "To clap and hoot (a player, play, etc.) off the stage; hence gen. . . . to cry down; to banish ignominiously" (*OED*).

65:16–18 *an Author, whose misfortunes have once more brought him . . . upon the Stage.* Dryden refers specifically to his loss of the offices of poet laureate and historiographer royal in 1688. Those losses merely represented the larger loss of a royal cause that had brought him numerous real and intangible benefits.

65:28–29 *that Love and Honour* etc. In the preface to the *Conquest of Granada* (1672) Dryden had declared that "Love and Valor ought to be the subject" of the heroic play.

66:9 *Mr. Betterton.* Thomas Betterton, the greatest Restoration actor (Dorax in this play), had adapted a number of earlier plays and so must have been a good judge of what would take before an audience.

66:15 *Mobile.* Or *mobile vulgus*, the inconstant crowd, the "Rabble" of the "Persons Represented." The full phrase appears in Statius, *Silvae*, II, ii, 123 and, according to the *OED*, dates in England from 1600. *Mobile* alone is first recorded in 1676, and *mob*, 1688.

66:19 *I have replac'd those lines.* Dryden's statement, and the great length of the play as printed, suggests that the extant version is complete.

66:35–67:11 *I dare boldly promise* etc. "Shakespeare laid aside, it will be perhaps difficult to point out a play containing more animatory incident, impassioned language, and beautiful description"—so Scott, beginning in his excellent critique the line of those critics who think *Don*

Sebastian rather than *All for Love* the finest tragedy after Shakespeare (See S-S, VII, 292).

66:36 *the roughness of the numbers and cadences.* Like Shakespeare's last plays, Dryden's immediately following *All for Love* show a progressive loosening of metrics (*numbers*), as well as a deliberate harshness of *cadences.* In *Don Sebastian* this is noticeable especially in the more disturbing speeches of Dorax, in many speeches by Muley-Moluch, and in some by Sebastian himself. The loosening of the blank verse continues in *Amphitryon* and is extended to almost Jacobean license in *Cleomenes.* Examples of various kinds of *numbers and cadences* are pointed to in the notes. Some general categories and examples may be given here. Often the departures from the more controlled blank verse of *All for Love,* for example, simply represent a loosened style. These include the marked increase in the use of heavy internal pauses, the increase in the number of lines with a supernumerary unstressed final syllable ("feminine" endings), and the frequency of fragmentary or hypometric lines. These last vary from a single verse foot to the more frequent use of two or three-foot lines, often with a "feminine" extra syllable, to at least one tetrameter—a most unusual deviation. There are also numerous lines with extra medial syllables, and many otherwise hypermetric lines, both those of "feminine" endings and alexandrines. Another technique provides less a loosening than a deliberate breaking of verse patterns. One of the most marked is the great increase (in terms of his earlier practice) in the number of lines broken between two or more speeches. This effect is very often heightened by ending one speech at an unstressed syllable so that the next speech may begin with a heavily stressed syllable or word, as in I, i, 111:

> *Bend.* You cou'd not meet him then?
> *Dorax.*   No, though I sought. . . .

Examples of a roughened although fully controlled cadence will be found throughout the play, as in II, i, 52: "Like some old Oak, rough with its armed Bark." As this example shows, what is *rough,* or seemingly loose, constitutes a metrical technique controlled to discernible ends. As has been said, Dorax's character, which is illuminated by speeches disturbing in other ways, is also heightened by means of a metrical roughness that may even skirt prose in its looseness, as in II, i, 139–140:

> *Dor.* Not very far; not farther than zeal goes
> Of course; a small days journey short of Treason.

Dryden had long since shown a comparable loose vigor in his dramatic prose, and that vigor is noticeably heightened here and in *Amphitryon* by earthy, racy, and comic touches more difficult to specify but illustrated so far as is possible by notes on proverbs or with glossings from the *OED,* which often show that Dryden's use is the first or last recorded. In prosody and language, then, Dryden's late plays reveal a new conception of the poetry possible to tragedy. It is difficult not to feel that this conception is inseparable from the tragic themes discussed in the headnote, because in his *Aeneis* and in his *Fables* Dryden fashioned two still different styles and prosodies expressive of other views of life.

67:8 *Salust.* The reputation of Sallust has varied widely. Dryden's favorable opinion could have been confirmed from Quintilian, *Institutes,* X, i, 101; from Tacitus, *Annals,* III, 30; or from Martial, *Epigrams,* XIV, cxci, 2: *primus Romana . . . in historia.* Sallust's use of archaisms was widely remarked and sometimes censured in antiquity: cf. Suetonius, *The Grammarians,* XV.

67:9–11 *Milton's Paradise . . . obscuring of his sense.* Dryden is kinder to Milton's archaisms and classicisms in the *Discourse of Satire* (*Works,* IV, 85).

67:12 *story.* In the sense of a "succession of incidents, 'plot' (or a novel, poem, or drama)," this usage antedates the first in the *OED* (1715).

67:13 *where the History has laid it down.* On the historical Don Sebastian and other matters touched on in this paragraph, see the headnote.

67:25–26 *the House of Braganza.* See 69:7–12 and n.

67:31 *Portugueses.* As late as the Restoration, natives or inhabitants of Portugal were still being called "Portugals" or "Portingals," but during the seventeenth century, "Portugueses" or "Portugez's" predominated and became the basis of the modern form (*OED,* supplemented by usage in Restoration histories of Spain and Portugal and usage in Restoration prose fiction).

68:2–3 *the usage which they had from their new Conquerors.* The plight of the Portuguese under the Spaniards was described by John Stevens in *The History of Portugal* (1698), p. 381:

> The Nobility . . . durst not appear in that Splendor which became their Quality, or claim all the Priviledges due to their Birth, for fear of raising the Jealousie in the Spanish Ministers, at a time when Riches, Birth, or Merit were thought sufficient to render a Man suspicious, and cause him to be persecuted. The Gentry were in a manner banished to their Country Houses, and the Commonalty groaned under the heavy Burthen of Taxes.

68:16 *as I have somewhere said.* The indefatigable Malone identified the reference to the dedication of *The Spanish Fryar* (1681, sig. A4; Watson, I, 279).

68:19 *the Laws of the Drama.* As the explicit reference in 68:35–69:1 shows, Dryden has in mind the *"Learned Mr.* Rymer," the leading exponent of common sense and the "rules." After paying Rymer such compliments, Dryden proceeds (69:35–70:10) to reject the need to abide by the rules.

68:23 *In the drawing of his character I forgot not piety.* It is agreed today that Sebastian was not so much pious as fanatic in his crusading zeal. In his *History of Portugal* Stevens concludes with Dryden, approvingly, that "King Sebastian . . . was Religious, Merciful, a Lover of Justice . . ." (p. 348).

68:33–34 *he may be a Saint* etc. Presuming that Sebastian died in battle, he was in some sense a martyr.

69:2 *Poetical justice.* Thomas Rymer is usually given credit as the first to use the phrase, in *The Tragedies of the Last Age,* ed. Zimansky, p. 26. Throughout that work Rymer is exercised over failures by English dramatists to observe due decorum for kings.

69:7–12 *For what relates to Almeyda* etc. The connection is drawn between Almeyda and Catherine of Braganza, widow of Charles II, daughter of Juan IV, Dryden's *"Don* John de Braganza" (r. 1640–1656), the first king of Portugal after the country regained independence from France. The connection also casts some oblique aspersion on William III, as the echo of 67:24–25 shows. Dryden's exact source of information about the historical Almeida family cannot be known, but his point was confirmed by John Stevens, *The History of Portugal,* p. 386: "The rest that made up this Assembly [working on behalf of independence and "Don John," later Juan IV], were D. Michael de Almeida, so great an Enemy to the Spaniards, that he could never be perswaded to appear at Court."

69:12 *The French Author* etc. The anonymous French version, *Dom Sebastien Roy de Portugal: Nouvelle Historique,* was published in Paris in 1680. It was translated by Ferrand Spence in 1683, copies of which edition were bound up in the series of *Modern Novels* published by Bentley.

69:20–21 *Augustus Cæsar wrote an Ajax* etc. Suetonius suggests (II, lxxxv, 2) that after beginning the play, Augustus dropped it out of disaffection for the style it assumed. All Augustus' writings are lost, and perhaps that circumstance led Dryden to believe that the play as well as the epigrams had once existed in complete form. In the dedication of *The Rival Ladies* (1664; *Works,* VIII, 96) he makes the same assumption.

69:23–24 *Corneille writ an Oedipus* etc. Corneille's *Oedipe* (1659) and the Dryden-Lee *Oedipus* were both popular successes, and like Seneca's play before theirs, distinctly carry the stamp of their nations and times.

69:26 *the new turn.* The "turn" is one of Dryden's most difficult critical terms to define strictly. For a discussion of the various nuances attached to the term in the period, see *Works,* IV, 580–581, 583–584.

69:29–34 *Thus in our Chronicles* etc. Dryden suggests the possible superiority, and additionally the originality, of one who comes last, as Samuel Daniel (1562–1619) came last with his *Collection of the History of England.* Daniel came after Matthew Paris (d. 1259), John Stow (?1525–1605), and Raphael Holinshed (d. ?1580), all three of them chroniclers and perhaps less attractive to Dryden than a fellow poet.

69:5–70:1 *have not exactly kept . . . the three Mechanick rules of unity.* Dryden's divagations from the rules of unity are not extravagant. They involve *"broken"* (see 70:5) scenes rather than strict *liaison des scènes* in the French manner and a temporal span of two days rather than one. He later (72:1–16) insists himself on the play's unity of action. Dryden seems very like Corneille as translated by Dryden for *Of Dramatick Poesie* (1668, 1684) in wishing for "more latitude to the Rules" rather than rejecting them out of hand (*Works,* XVII, 51).

70:2–4 *the Genius of the English* etc. Cf. *Of Dramatick Poesie* (*Works,* XVII, 45:25–54:15).

70:12 *the death of Muley-Moluch* etc. Dryden is accurate about Moluch's death. Later in the paragraph he credits certain returned English officers for giving him information. Just what he learned cannot be ascertained, and, in fact, the romance *Don Sebastian* well relates Moluch's cruelty, his ability as a general, and his fatal illness.

70:14–19 On the brutality of the then ruler of Morocco, see Francis Brooks, *Barbarian Cruelty. Being a True History of the Distressed Condition of the Christian Captives Under the Tyranny of Mully Ishmael Emperor of Morocco* (1693).

70:20 *I have been listning.* The phrase inclined Malone "to believe, that most of the criticisms which he has noticed, were made at his favourite haunt, Will's Coffee-House. He had been *listning* to learn what objections were made by those unacquainted with his person; who might there occasionally deliver their sentiments on theatrical subjects, and after they had smoked the second pipe, probably thought themselves at least as wise as any of the poets of the day, not excepting the Laureate himself." A pleasant fancy.

70:22–23 *play'd booty.* To "play booty" is defined by the *OED* as "to play or act falsely so as to gain a desired effect."

70:24–25 *ætatem habet de se loquatur.* Summers noted the quotation of John IX, 21 (reading *ipse de se,* Vulgate): "He is of age; ask him: he shall speak for himself" (Authorized Version).

70:26 *Ausonius his famous Epigram. Epigrams,* III, on the adulteress Eumpina, who gave her husband first one poison and then added a second, mercury, to speed his end: "If one keep these apart, separate they act as poison; who so shall drink them together, will take an antidote. Therefore while these baleful draughts strove with each other, the deadly force yielded to the wholesome" (ll. 5–8, Loeb trans.). See also the play, IV, iii, 322 and n.

70:28–32 Scott held a nearly unbounded admiration for Dorax and the climax of his *inconsistent* behavior in the quarrel scene with Don Sebastian (IV, iii): "the scene betwixt Dorax and the king, had it been the only one ever Dryden wrote, would have been sufficient to ensure his immortality. There is not,—no, perhaps, not even in Shakespeare,—an instance where the chord, which the poet designed should vibrate, is more happily struck" (S-S, VII, 292). The "duel of friends" as it has sometimes been called, had achieved notable expression in *Julius Caesar* and thereafter became highly popular in the drama. Among Dryden's earlier uses of it there is that between Antony and Ventidius in the first act of *All for Love.*

70:31–32 *that Chapter of the Wise Montaigne* etc. Montaigne, *Essays,* II, i, "De l'inconstance de nos actions." The excellent translation by Charles Cotton the Younger (1686) includes such a passage as this, which Dryden perhaps had in mind: "If I speak variously of my self, it is, because I consider my self variously. All contrarieties are there to be found, in one corner or another, or after one manner or another" (Cotton, II, 9).

70:35 *the Earl of Dorset.* Dryden had dedicated *Of Dramatick Poesie* to Charles Sackville (1638–1706), then Lord Buckhurst, who in 1675 was created Earl of Middlesex, and in 1677 succeeded his father as sixth earl of Dorset. Dryden particularly valued Dorset's patronage and protection. In 1693 he was to dedicate to Dorset the translations of Juvenal and Persius (*Works,* IV, 3ff.).

71:5–6 *concurrere bellum, atque virum.* Lucan, *Pharsalia,* VI, 191–192: "a man against an army" (Loeb trans.).

71:15–21 *This is not a Play* etc. Although the moral purpose of drama was a commonplace in England from Jonson to the eighteenth century, Dryden is unusual in claiming that each character embodies a moral. It is not easy today to penetrate the moral intended in each of the characters and parts. The moral of the four last lines of the play is, of course, clear enough:

> And let *Sebastian* and *Almeyda's* Fate,
> This dreadfull Sentence to the World relate,
> That unrepented Crimes of Parents dead,
> Are justly punish'd on their Childrens head.

72:26 *Tu, ne cede malis* etc. Virgil, *Aeneid,* VI, 95: "Yield not thou to ills, but go forth to face them more boldly" (Loeb trans.). Dryden is freer in *Aeneis,* VI, 143–144, but much more satisfactory: "But thou, secure of Soul, unbent with Woes, / The more thy Fortune frowns, the more oppose." The reassertion of self-sufficiency and return in allusion to *Aeneid,* VI, deserve remark.

PROLOGUE

1 *The Judge remov'd.* Dryden begins by referring specifically to the kind of event that was exercising the English as they tried to come to terms with their immediate past and present. Judges often lost office for having opinions at variance with the king's. Speaking of the something less than four years during which James II ruled, one authority reports that "in his short reign . . . there were twelve removals in addition to the same number who were discharged during the latter years of Charles II," adding that none of the ten judges remaining on the bench at the end of James's reign "continued in their seats at the revolution" or was "ever replaced on the bench" (Edward Foss, *The Judges of England* [1848–1864], VII, 201). During 1689 and continuing into 1690, the Convention Parliament was reviewing events of the previous two reigns, including judicial matters, partly to determine any exceptions to a forthcoming Act of Indemnity. A number of judges were called to the House of Lords, one at least as late as December, and some were taken into custody or sent to the Tower. (See *The History and Proceedings of the House of Commons* [ed. Richard Chandler?], [1742–1744], II, 328, 331ff., 338–340, 345; see also Foss, VII, 243–246.) These references and much in what follows on the prologue are owed to C. P. Vernier and Harold F. Brooks.

1 *he's no more My Lord.* Although a lawyer (here, a barrister) could be removed from his position as judge, which entitled him to be addressed, *My Lord,* he could still practice law. Cf. Roger North, in *Lives of the Right Hon. Francis North* [and others], ed. Henry Roscoe (1826), II, 40, referring to Sir Francis Pemberton, who was questioned by the Commons and taken into custody for a time: "After his removal, he returned to his practice and by that (as it seems the rule is) he lost his style of lordship, and became bare Mr. Serjeant again." The king's power to remove judges

was being debated during the first two or three years after the 1688 Revolution. See Stephen B. Baxter, *William III* (1966), p. 270.

2 *the Council-Board.* Perhaps the Privy Council in its judicial function over "admiralty matters, and in all matters civil and criminal arising in the king's lands beyond the seas" (F. W. Maitland, *The Constitutional History of England* [1908], p. 320).

3 *cast.* "Cashiered, dismissed from office" (*OED*); Dryden refers to his dismissal from the office of poet laureate and historiographer royal. As James Sutherland observed in "Prologues, Epilogues and Audience in the Restoration Theatre" (*Of Books and Humankind, Essays and Poems Presented to Bonamy Dobrée* [1964], p. 52), " 'cast Poets' plays obviously but wittily on the phrase 'cast mistress,' one of the recurring characters in Restoration comedy."

4 *loss of Pension.* Dryden had irregularly received the stipends set by Charles II and James II for their poet laureate and historiographer royal.

7–8 *The British Nation* etc. Dryden is talking about himself as one vanquished, but also about events in Ireland. It was to the credit both of James II and William III that they did their best to restrain the forces under their command. James saved Dublin from being razed, and within a short time William had disciplined his troops. But the Irish themselves and the continental troops fighting on both sides commonly exercised unrestrained ferocity. See Baxter, *William III*, ch. xix.

10 *And lay your Paws upon him, without roaring.* Dryden perhaps imagines the rampant *English lion* of the royal crest. He plays on *roaring*, an activity of lions no doubt, but also commonly used in such a phrase as "roaring boys"; a "roarer" was "A noisy, riotous bully or reveller" (*OED*).

12–14 *Yet now, the bus'ness of the Field is o'er* etc. By late 1689 William was consolidating his military position in the British Isles. Dryden is accurate in terming the strife as *Civil Wars*, even if not fought on English soil, because the dispute turned symbolically and materially on who was to rule the three kingdoms.

14 *Winter-quarters.* Warfare was thought possible for only about half the year. In 1690, the year after the play was performed, Luttrell (II, 109) reports on 26 September that English troops in Ireland were going into winter quarters.

15 *Jove was alike to Latian and to Phrygian.* Perhaps Dryden's kindest remark about Jove, this implies that the Thunderer treated equally the inhabitants of Latium favored by Juno and the Trojans (for whom Phrygian was a common Roman appellation) under Aeneas and favored by Venus. Dryden recalls the opening scene of the *Aeneid*, especially I, 107–113.

16 *And you well know, a Play's of no Religion.* Dryden gives a clever dodge to the actress speaking: if the moralists accused playwrights and plays of lacking religion, then there could be no danger in a play by a Catholic playwright.

21–23 *When, with full bowls* etc. The triplet concludes the first twenty-three lines of a forty-six line prologue, a part imagined to have been provided by the poet, as the actress delivering it is imagined to speak what follows from her own *Noddle* (l. 25). Dryden's touch is very sharp and sure in the triplet. England then had an embargo on goods from France, with wines named at the head of the list: see "An Act for Prohibiting all Trade and Commerce with France" (1 Gul. & Mar., cap. xxxiv). The embargo on wine seems to have been resented; the "Prologue, Sent to the Authour" also touches on the matter in ll. 28-30. The *Mighty Monarch* is of course Louis XIV, *le grand monarque* (see the prologue to *Albion and Albanius*, l. 39). And *most Christian*, or *rex christianissimus*, was a title held by French kings intermittently from the time of Pepin the Short and consistently from the time of the Hundred Years' War and the reign of Charles V or Charles VI. (See *The Catholic Encyclopedia* [1913], VI, 168-169.)

26-29 *You've seen young Ladies* etc. The principle, that the gods esteem the gift for the giver, is one Dryden uses with some frequency; for examples near in time to this play, see *The Hind and the Panther*, III, 63; and *Britannia Rediviva*, l. 178. Dryden has a particular event in mind. On 12 August 1689, Luttrell (I, 569) recorded that "Two or 3000 men and women of trade of silkweavers &c. went to Westminster to petition the lords against passing the bill for the woollen manufacture, that it would undoe them." Their reception was not as favorable as Dryden implies here.

32-37 *I heard him make advances* etc. The metaphor, of agreement on articles of peace, touches numerous activities in the kingdoms and on the continent. But the actress also offers a rapprochement between Dryden and his society that he certainly needed during these years just after the Revolution.

33 *his cutting Satyr.* Horace provides the *locus classicus* on the sharp style, *sermo acer* or *sermo acutus*, in *Satires*, II, i, 1: *Sunt quibus in satura videar nimis acer* (Loeb trans.: "There are some critics who think that I am too savage in my satire").

37 *As Times go now, he offers very fair.* Although the playwright's offer in itself may not seem so attractive, it must be thought a fair one in these bad times. Anthony à Wood complained in the last entry in his diary for December, 1689: "Money dead; no trading; all complaine for these three months last past;—occasioned by taxes, warrs, a lingering warr in Ireland" (*The Life and Times of Anthony Wood*, ed. Andrew Clark [Oxford, 1891-1900], III, 319).

39 *do not set your Teeth together.* To "set one's teeth" means "to press or clench one's teeth firmly together from indignation" or similar motive (*OED*, citing the epilogue to *Marriage A-la-Mode*, ll. 27-28: "You . . . set your teeth when each design fell short").

41-46 *Horses, by Papists are not to be ridden* etc. It would be difficult to exaggerate Dryden's daring in setting his Catholicism so clearly before his contemporaries here. His phrase, *Rate-Book* (l. 43), is the last usage recorded by *OED* for "A book of rates or prices," but Dryden has in mind specifically the penal laws recently enacted against Catholics. In the "Act for the better secureing the Government by disarming Papists and

reputed Papists" (1 Gul. & Mar., cap. 15, sect. vii), "noe Papist or reputed Papist" was allowed a horse "above the value of five pounds."
Luttrell (I, 590) reported for 7 October 1689 that "The justices of peace
of Middlesex" had given orders for papists' horses worth above five
pounds to be seized. It is difficult to know how strictly the penal laws
were enforced in London and the provinces, but they were applied to
more than office-holders alone, in spite of what is sometimes thought.
Luttrell records an incident for 6 November 1689 (I, 601):

> Wrote from Lewis in Sussex, that some justices of
> peace meeting there on affairs of the countrey, had in-
> formation of several persons that came into the town
> on horseback, suspected to be papists, whereon they
> caused them to be apprehended, and tendered them the
> oaths, which refusing, they paid down their 40s. in a
> bravado; upon which the justices ordered the seizing
> of their horses, pursuant to the late act of parliament;
> which was done accordingly.

45 *Fine him to daily Drudging and Inditing.* That is, the anti-Catholic
fines would require him to heavy labors in writing, whether in prose
("Drudging") or verse ("Inditing").

46 *pay his Taxes out.* As a Catholic, Dryden also became subject to
double taxation (2 Gul. & Mar., cap. 2, sect. xxxv). Since even without
double rates people were complaining, Dryden must have struck a respon-
sive chord in his audience. Anthony à Wood concluded his diary for 1689
with the heading "Taxes this yeare," which included the following paid on
17 July: "I paid 20s as a gentleman; 10[s] for 100 *li.;* 1s for my head
[the detested poll tax]:—taxed by the towne, the vice-chancellour angry at
it" (*Life and Times,* ed. Clark, III, 319).

PROLOGUE, SENT TO THE AUTHOUR

As Scott observed, "The humour of this intended Prologue turns upon
the unwillingness displayed to attend King William into Ireland by many
of the nobility and gentry, who had taken arms at the Revolution. The
truth is, that, though invited to go as volunteers, they could not but
consider themselves as hostages, of whom William did not choose to lose
sight, lest, while he was conquering Ireland, he might, perchance, lose
England, by means of the very men by whom he had won it" (S-S, VII,
318). Even "George of Denmark was taken along [to Ireland by William],
probably to insure the loyalty of his wife [the Princess Anne]" (Stephen B.
Baxter, *William III* [1966], p. 263). The three kingdoms were, then, once
again combustible in 1689–1690. In 1689, James II invaded Ireland with
French help. Englishmen remained divided among themselves, hateful of
William, and suspicious of James II (Ranke, IV, Bk. XIX, vi–ix). William
Penn the Quaker, who had long been friendly with James II, undertook
to sound out attitudes in various parts of England and reported that it
was thought that "the country was ruined, the nobility discontented, the
Church of England estranged by the treatment of the bishops, William III

suspected of aiming at absolute power, and a combination against his supposed aims was being formed by Scots and Englishmen" (quoted by Ranke, IV, 579). William himself was unable to go to campaign in Ireland until June, 1690, lest his much-needed presence there (and for that matter, in Holland) would lose him England. At last he went because he had to. On 30 June (Old Style), shortly after he left, the French fleet won a victory over the combined English and Dutch fleets off Beaches Head. There was danger that William would be blockaded in Ireland. So different were those charged days from later descriptions given by the Whig historians. As Scott pointed out, even Shadwell, now poet laureate, had satirized (in the epilogue to *Bury-Fair*) the disbanding of a royal regiment.

This "Prologue, Sent to the Authour" denounces critics for being as cowardly as the erstwhile supporters of William. It is the comparison, as Scott noted, that made the piece the offensively Jacobite attack which precluded its use in the theater. The "unknown hand" that sent it to Dryden was said by Summers to be Sir Henry Sheeres (d. 1710), on the evidence of a manuscript ascription in "a copy of the 1690 4to of *Don Sebastian,* which belonged to Messrs. Dobell." The identification is likely enough. Sir Henry Sheeres was a military engineer, author, Jacobite, and friend of Dryden's and Southerne's. He had served in the Mediterranean. He had been Surveyor of the Ordnance to James II and in the thick of the Revolution (see Baxter, *William III,* p. 245). He was the translator of Polybius (1693) for which Dryden wrote the *Character,* and one of the translators of the works of Lucian, for which Dryden provided the *Life.* In the latter, Dryden places Sheeres among the "finer Spirits of the Age." It may indeed be that Sir Henry (who was also a friend of Pepys until he interested Mrs. Pepys too much) was among those "English *Officers*" who had told Dryden about "*the present Emperor* Muley-Ishmael" (see the preface, 70:17–19).

By Mrs. Montford. "Susanna Percival, who was born in 1667, married William Mountfort at S. Giles-in-the-Fields on 2 July 1686. Her husband was then twenty-two years old. . . . She excelled in breeches parts, and Cibber in his *Apology,* Chapter V, after highly applauding her as 'mistress of more variety of humour than I ever knew in one woman actress,' says: 'Nor was her humour limited to her sex; for, while her shape permitted, she was a more adroit pretty fellow than is usually seen on the stage; her easy air, action, mien, and gesture, quite changed from the quoif, to the cocked hat and cavalier in fashion' " (Summers).

1 *Circle.* "One of the galleries or tiers of seats in a theatre" (*OED*); that is, the boxes, the most fashionable seats.

2 *grave Synod.* Characterizing the men in the pit in terms of the Presbyterian "body or assembly of ministers and other elders, constituting the ecclesiastical court next above the presbytery" (*OED*). These are the men less than eager to accept invitation by William III to go to Ireland.

3 *The Upper-tire of pop-gun wit.* The upper gallery—*tire* or tier— was the cheapest and commonly the rowdiest part of the house. But a *tire* is also "The simultaneous discharge of a battery of ordnance; a volley or broadside" (*OED,* citing *The Hind and the Panther,* III, 317).

12 *For he has kept the Pen* etc. Besides the obvious meaning, that Dryden continues to write though no longer poet laureate, the line plays on the writer's goose-quill pen and a feather of honor.

16–18 *Sure 'tis a Judgment* etc. Ostensibly, the *Dispensation* is the gift of wit (l. 15), which contemporary writers have abused by not devoting it to the ladies. But as is shown by the *OED* and Ranke (especially, IV, Bk. XIX, iv), throughout the reigns of Charles and James *Dispensation* referred to one thing: the use of royal prerogative to effect a religious toleration. William III also wished for such a toleration, excepting Catholics, and he too aroused the anger of the Establishment.

19 *buff.* "Military attire," for which *buff* or leather was used (*OED*).

23–24 *But one reply'd* etc. He protests that he can *bleed* or lose money fast enough gambling at court. The *Groom-Porter* was "An officer of the English Royal Household, abolished under George III; his principal functions, at least from the 16th c., were to regulate all matters connected with gaming within the precincts of the court" (*OED*).

25–27 *Another* etc. This man implies that his horses are unfit. According to the *OED*, "*body-cloaths*" are cloths or rugs "to cover horses or other animals."

28–30 *A third* etc. This man will refuse until Parliament raises the embargo on French wines: see Dryden's prologue, ll. 21–23 and n.

32 *I'd draw my Sword in Ireland, Sir, to chuse.* The expression *to chuse* here seems to mean "to take one's own way" (*OED*), and perhaps was contemporary slang.

42 *Iniskelling.* "Enniskellen is the county town of Co. Fermanagh, Ireland" (Summers). Fierce Protestant irregular troops from the place routed larger numbers of opponents by their furious attacks led by shouts of "No Popery!" Dryden also alludes to their actions in his prologue to *The History of Bacon in Virginia* (see l. 41 and n in *Works*, III, 253, 506).

43 *On Carrion tits those Sparks denounce their rage.* A "tit" is a "horse small of kind" (*OED*). Scott quotes at length from a contemporary account of the Enniskellen horse that joined with William's forces at Dundalk: "They were followed by multitudes of their women; they were uncouth in their appearance; they rode on small horses called Garrons"; and so on, concerning their guerrilla-like appearance and ways. Dryden's *Carrion* is not the "Garrons" of this account: none of the nine spellings in the *OED* begins with a "c" or ends as Dryden's word does. His is rather a usage meaning "poor, wretched, or worthless," said of a beast (*OED*, not citing any example so late). His *denounce* means "proclaim, announce, declare" (*OED*). Hence, he shows the *Bully Criticks* (l. 22) proclaiming their ire astride their worthless horses.

44 *In boot of wisp and Leinster freese ingage.* The image is not clear. The nearest possible definition of "wisp" in the *OED* is "a handful, bunch, or small bundle (of hay, straw, grass, etc.)." A "frieze" is "a kind of coarse woollen cloth, with a nap, usually on one side only," and Leinster in southeast Ireland was one area where such goods were produced.

46–48 *The Siege of Derry* etc. In 1689, forces under James II besieged

Londonderry in a particularly bitter campaign marked by starvation among the besieged until English ships brought succor. See Ranke, IV, 556–559.

56 *in your Service.* "Service" carries, of course, the military and amorous senses.

PERSONS REPRESENTED

A Servant to Benducar. In the play as printed, Benducar has not one but three servants, each of whom is specifically named at his entrance in Act IV (see note at IV, i, 12+ *s.d.*). It is possible that the list of *Persons Represented* was added belatedly to the first edition since it appears on the verso of the title page. The fact that the names of the actors and actresses who played the various roles are given would suggest that Betterton may have supplied the list, and that he included on it only the *dramatis personae* of the play as it was acted after the considerable cutting done by him (see the Headnote above).

I, i

s.d. The Scene of Alcazar etc. Cf. Pidou de St. Olon, p. 29:
> Alcasar is also become famous by the bloody Battle, which Sebastian King of Portugal lost near it, with his Life, in the Year 1578, in the Plain between that Town and the River Mukazem: It is little, thinly Peopled, and very ill built, but stands most pleasantly by that River, with fine Gardens all round it. Gayland [French overseer till defeated in 1666] most commonly chose to reside there in a large Palace, which is now altogether ruin'd.

1–14 In the preface (67:13) Dryden says truly of his plot that he takes *"it up where the History has laid it down."* These opening lines are wholly faithful to history as it was then known.

11 *Mucazer's Flood.* In the romance *Don Sebastian* (III, 20), the spelling is clearly "Mucasen" (see opening *s.d.*) for the River Ould-Molchazem. It cannot be ascertained whether Dryden chose to alter the name, whether he forgot, whether his handwriting was poor, or whether the printer erred.

13 *whelm'd over.* The *OED* cites but four such "poetic" usages, including this line and *Aeneis*, IX, 725.

15 *Thus, then, a doubtful Title is extinguish'd.* None of the king's sons had regal title. See Pidou de St. Olon (p. 113) speaking of "The Kingdom, which is neither Hereditary nor Elective," and of the rivalry among the king's sons (p. 99):
> As these Children grow in Years the King makes 'em Alcaydes, or Governors of several Parts of his Dominions: And, after the death of the Father, he who is the most in Favour, and has the strongest Party, overcomes and

> kills the rest, to secure the Empire to himself. . . .
> That Son who is with the King at his death, is gen-
> erally in a Capacity of enslaving the rest, because he is
> Master of the Arms, and sometimes of the Treasure when
> he can discover it.

Since this was true of most of the Muslim countries for centuries and a feature of accounts about them, Dryden could not have but known it. He is preparing for the "discovery" of Almeyda: see ll. 429–432, 451–459.

19 *The Heavens and all the Stars* etc. Planets and stars with their "in-telligences" or angels were traditionally regarded as acting as intermedi-aries between divine prescience and disposition on the one hand and the men on whom they exercised their influence on the other.

31–44 *So often try'd* etc. Benducar inherits his villainy from a long line of intriguing evil characters in plays, but every reader of Dryden will recall Achitophel working on Absalom to rebel.

45 *Alcalde.* Pidou de St. Olon (p. 114) distinguished "three sorts of Alcaydes, the chief are the Governours of Provinces, where they are ef-fectually like so many Vice-Roys; the other are either particular Gov-ernours of great Towns, or General Officers of his Armies."

61 *Stale.* From the literal meaning of "a decoy-bird," the term came to be used figuratively for "A person . . . made use of . . . as a cover for sinister designs" (*OED*).

64+ *s.d. Enter Dorax.* Muley-Zeydan and Benducar have seen Dorax from afar; but only now does he come into the "Market-Place" repre-sented by the stage.

65–72 *Now Dorax* etc. The scansion and even the lineation here are complex. Such variations from the iambic pentameter contribute to *"the roughness of the numbers and cadences"* for which Dryden was striving (see the preface, 66:36).

65 *Benducar.* The reading in the first edition, *Bemboucar,* might have been taken as a deliberately made mistake by the "sullen" Dorax if he had not got the name right a few lines later (l. 71). More than that, in *West Barbary* (1671) Lancelot Addison mentions Ben-Boucar (pp. 22–23) and describes the actions he took to enlarge his dominions (pp. 25–34). In Pidou de St. Olon there appears (pp. 4ff.) a Morabite ruler, Benbucar. It is possible that the printer erred early in the play and later corrected all but these two instances. But it seems much more probable that, having taken Addo Ben Ottar as his model for Benducar, Dryden derived "Bendu-car" from "Ben-Boucar" and here lapsed unintentionally into the original version. It will be observed that Benducar does not object to the wrong version of his name but to its being "Bare," i.e., without his title.

68 *Minion.* "A favourite of a sovereign . . . *esp.* opprobriously, one who owes everything to his patron's favour, and is ready to purchase its continuance by base compliances" (*OED*). As the next line shows, Dryden's usage suggests homosexuality. Cf. Marlowe's use of "minion" for Gaveston in *Edward II.* See also IV, iii, 459 and n.

74–75 *I have cause* etc. The implication is that although the general low state of human behavior is itself enough to merit satire, Dorax has his own particular reason for being "out of humor." It is this particular motivation, subsequently revealed, that distinguishes him from the line of malcontents in earlier drama, and that makes him a more human and credible—and therefore also a more disturbing—character.

79 *Emmets*. That is, ants.

91 *hoop'd in Iron*. In armor.

95 *run off from biass*. To turn from course or direction (*OED*); here, to speak irrelevantly.

97 *I kill'd not one that was his Makers Image*. Dorax the renegade maintains ideas from his Christianity; he means of course that he has killed no true man, and his comment here adds force to the iterated description of Sebastian, "he was a Man," in ll. 99, 101.

101–105 *he was a Man* etc. Such hyperbolic praise is common enough in plays and romances (see the headnote concerning the opening pages of the romance and its description of Sebastian). It will be observed that Dorax adds piety (l. 103) to Sebastian's other virtues, a quality Dryden emphasizes in the preface (68:23).

118 *Defac'd*. The *OED* gives no such late usage for "deface": "To destroy, . . . lay waste," but Dryden's figurative usage seems natural enough.

126 *Predestination*. It is significant of the role played by fate in the play that in spite of his opposition to Calvinism Dryden should introduce this word, which is used only once in his non-dramatic poems (*The Cock and the Fox*, l. 508).

130–131 *Whose fatal Beauty* etc. See Revelation, XII, 4: "And his [the dragon's] tail drew the third part of the stars of heaven, and did cast them to the earth." Milton, following long tradition, had applied the line to Satan's rebellion.

132–133 *I hope she dy'd* etc. Dorax is responsible for many of the extraordinarily strong sexual undertones in the play (and much else disturbing). Like Jews, Muslims practice circumcision; see II, ii, 8–12n.

143 *a black shirt-less train*. The *train* of pillagers is probably *black* as to Dorax's disgust rather than as to race. By the concluding part of the seventeenth century, Europeans were learning that the "Moors" were not black, although black slaves were kept by Moorish rulers and although some black peoples took up Mohammedanism.

144–147 *Each of 'em an Hoast* etc. This and Dorax's next speech illustrate his view that "all mankind is cause enough for Satyr" (l. 75).

150–153 *I wou'd use 'em / Like Dogs* etc. Domestic animals and birds were killed as a measure to fight the spread of the plague: see Daniel Defoe, *A Journal of the Plague Year*, ed. Louis A. Landa (1969), pp. 121 and 276. The English practice has special point in a Muslim context. Thomas Smith, *Remarks Upon the Manners, Religion and Government Of the Turks* (1678) held that the Mohammedans have "a peculiar love and kindness for Dogs" (p. 104). He adds a story to illustrate their affection (pp. 105–106):

> The Plague raging very hot, the Emperour and the
> Bassas at last seemed to make a mighty discovery, that
> it was necessary to destroy the Dogs in and about Con-

stantinople, to prevent the further spreading of the Infection: but the Mufti, who was consulted in this weighty
Affair, would by no means give way to so bloody and
cruel a sentence, maintaining . . . that Dogs had souls.

156+ *s.d. the Mufti.* That officer's role is well described by Pidou de St.
Olon (pp. 104–105):

[The King's] Authority which appears, and is indeed
so Despotic, has nevertheless one Superior to it, to which
it is subordinate, which is the Mufty's and his Officers,
whom the King has not the Power of Deposing, tho'
he has that of making 'em: He as well as others submits
to the Decrees of this Jurisdiction, and neither can dis-
claim it, nor withdraw himself from it, if the least of
his Subjects has a mind to cite him before it; but, at
the same time, it must be acknowledg'd, that a fatal Revenge, which surely wou'd follow, sufficiently restrains
'em from it; therefore generally that Jurisdiction does
not affect him unless when he consults it, or it thinks fit
to make him some Remonstrances necessary to his Service, and the Good of his Empire.

The next paragraph has a nice relation to the comic subplot of the play:
"This Mufty is the proper and supreme Judge of Adulterers, whom
commonly he sentences to death."

159 *Atabals.* "A kind of kettle-drum or tabour used by the Moors"
(*OED*, with but three usages, including one from *The Conquest of
Granada*).

161 *the Xeriff's blood.* Cf. the apposition in Pidou de St. Olon (p. 92):
"the Xeriffs, or Mahomet's Posterity."

174 *a Religious, ruddy Countenance.* Priests like Dryden's Dominic in
The Spanish Fryar were commonly made up in red for the stage.

185 *Renegade.* "An apostate" (*OED*).

186 *Relicks.* That is, "survivors" (*OED*).

186+ *s.d. Mustapha.* The comic Mustapha foreshadows Sosia in *Amphitryon.*

186+ *s.d. the Black Guard.* Cf. Pidou de St. Olon (p. 113): "Tho' this
Prince [the ruler of Morocco] has no regular Forces, he has nevertheless
a standing Guard of three or four Hundred Blacks."

189 *garbidge.* Or garbage, "The offal of an animal used for food; esp.
the entrails"; also "Refuse in general; filth" (*OED*). Dryden plays on the
two meanings.

235 *Sultanins.* "A former Turkish gold coin valued at about 8*s*" (*OED*,
citing this passage).

238 *a farewel.* "An after-taste, twang" (*OED*).

238+ *s.d. Barnus.* "A mantle or cloak with a hood, an upper garment
extensively worn by Arabs and Moors" (*OED*).

240 *This is the porcelain clay of human kind.* On porcelain as a metaphor for fineness, see *To the Dutchess of Ormond,* ll. 120–121.

243 *'Tis he.* Dorax recognizes Don Sebastian in spite of his "mean habit"; and he recognizes Alvarez and Antonio as well. Their failure to recognize him allows for a subsequent revelation.

262 *Our Law says plainly* etc. Accounts of the Muslim countries varied greatly on the religious role of women. Pidou de St. Olon reported (p. 52): "Their Women do not enter into the Mosques, because they esteem them incapable of being receiv'd into Heaven," although the beauties who delighted men in the Muslim paradise provided great scandal to Christians. Thévenot (*The Travels of Monsieur de Thevenot into the Levant* [1686], p. 56) said substantially the same thing as Pidou de St. Olon.

264–270 *Yet were Almeyda here* etc. In the romance *Don Sebastian* (II, 107–108), Sebastian inquires about "Almeida," and is told "that she was a Princess called Almeida, Sister of Mahumet; that this King having already lost two considerable Battels against Moluc his Uncle, had sent her to that City [Arsilla], where he believed her in more safety than in the midst of his Kingdom, which Moluc furiously ravaged."

270+ *s.d. Here an Urn is brought in* etc. In this lottery scene, the stage properties and action illustrate the play's theme of fate.

277–279 *Old venerable Alvarez* etc. The character is based on the "Duke d'Avero" in the romance *Don Sebastian* (see, e.g., I, 6).

290 *grubble.* "To feel or search with the hands" (*OED*), but "squeeze" or "hold closely" would seem better here.

293 *th' Amorous airy spark, Antonio.* An "Anthony" figures importantly in the love plot of the romance *Don Sebastian* after the death of Sebastian.

297 *I've a moist sweaty palm.* As Summers noted, this condition suggested an amorous, passionate nature. Cf. *Othello*, III, iv, 35–42.

300–302 *To wash this Ethiope white* etc. From Jeremiah XIII, 23 ("Can the Ethiopian change his skin, or the leopard his spots?") grew various proverbs about the vain effort "To wash an Ethiop (blackamoor, Moor) white" (Tilley, E186).

310–318 *Mark him* etc. Cf. these descriptions of Don Sebastian with Dorax's speech, ll. 96–110. Such descriptions prepare the audience for the hero's entrance, and Dryden heightens interest by keeping him silent until ll. 338ff. at a point more than halfway through the first act.

322 *Genius.* "With reference to classical pagan belief: The tutelary god or attendant spirit allotted to every person at his birth, to govern his fortunes and determine his character, and finally to conduct him out of the world" (*OED*).

323 *Demon.* "An attendant, ministering, or indwelling spirit; a genius" (*OED*).

338–346 *Then there's no more* etc. For the first speech by Don Sebastian, King of Portugal, Dryden introduces the old royal emblem, the sun.

340 *Glory.* "Any circle or ring of light; a halo, corona" (*OED*, citing Dryden, *Georgics*, I, 504).

347 *in this despicable now.* The unusual expression, founded on abnormal use of a part of speech (*now*) exemplifies the "*daring in the Figures*" of which Dryden speaks in the preface, 67:2.

351–367 *Here satiate* etc. This speech illustrates very well what Dryden has to say of the style and imagery of the play (preface, 66:35–67:11).

354 *verge.* A noun usage, this extends the *Shield* image (l. 353). The shield proper is *ample* enough for all that Don Sebastian has endured. For what may lie ahead, he has sufficient *verge:* "a . . . bounding belt or strip" (*OED*), a kind of rim to the shield of his *ample* soul.

372 *Affrick is stor'd with Monsters.* The Emperor (Muley-Moluch) has said that he will show Don Sebastian throughout Africa as a monster. The showing of "monsters" was highly popular in the Restoration, and playwrights like Dryden were irritated by the competition such foolish exhibitions presented. Dryden so complains of the Mamamouchi in the prologue to *The Assignation* (ll. 30–31); of a "Monster *Muscovite*" in *To Mr. Southern* (ll. 11–12; *Works*, III, 227); and of "some Foreign Monster" in *To Mr. Granville* (l. 22). Africa was thought prodigal of the strange, the new, the monstrous, producing something every day, according to one version of a common proverb, or *Africa semper aliquid apport noui* (*Late Newes out of Barbary* [1613], sig. A3). See Tilley, A56. What Sebastian's reply claims is that a true man is a prodigy in Africa.

376–377 *Till Dooms-day* etc. Cf. the fuller apocalyptic vision of III, i, 132–135.

382–383 *In what a ruine* etc. Such was the result of the historical Don Sebastian's African enterprise, as Dryden knew and as he has his hero partly acknowledge in his next two speeches. Muley-Moluch also seems to suggest a comparison to Satan. Both he and Benducar elicit from Sebastian one aspect of the *piety* that Dryden said he drew in the character (preface, 68:23).

402–404 *They plead* etc. The tears of Muley-Moluch seem out of character, or unprepared for. His change of mind proves important for the ensuing action, however, and he will be shown mercurial enough subsequently. His reprieve in ll. 405–407 accounts for l. 409 s.d., *A general shout.*

419 *Kings, who are Fathers, live but in their People.* Two royalist ideas are present here. The idea of the paternal king whose legitimacy is founded on analogy with God the Father, Adam, etc., will be found treated at length in Sir Robert Filmer's *Patriarcha* (1680). The concept of the king's two bodies, his body natural and his body politic, is very old, and it assumed a "privity" between the two such as that expressed here. On the king's two bodies, see the commentary on *Threnodia Augustalis* in *Works*, III, 301–303, 306, 316.

428–432 *Hear me* etc. Almeyda's revelation follows that of Don Sebastian. No one had recognized her. On the substance of her claim here, cf. ll. 15–18.

441 *She whom thy Mufti tax'd to have no Soul.* In l. 262.

463 *My Brother.* In the romance *Don Sebastian* (II, 20) his fate is set forth: "Mahumet seeing the Portugezes routed, and willing to avoid the Cruelty of his Enemies [led by "Muley-Moluch"], who would not have failed to have Sacrificed him to the repose of the State, endeavouring to escape, was drowned in the River of Mucasen." And on Almeida's affection for her brother (II, 23): "She had ever loved Mahumet very tenderly, and often shed Tears for his death."

464 *My wandring Mother.* The romance does not feature any itinerant mother or any father. Dryden here takes the first small step toward the revelation of the relation between the hero and heroine.

468 *Still . . . still, still.* Emphasizing the usual seventeenth-century meaning, on every occasion, always (*OED*).

470–473 *Something, I know not what* etc. The love-smitten tyrant is familiar in many earlier plays, especially in the heroic drama as practiced by Dryden and others.

480+ *s.d. The Masters and Slaves* etc. Among the numerous accounts of the sale of Europeans as slaves, perhaps the closest in detail to the episode that follows is found in *The Adventures of (Mr. T. S.)* (1670), attributed to one Thomas Smith. As remarked in the headnote, the book also describes a number of erotic intrigues with Arab women which could have assisted Dryden in framing Antonio's escapades.

489 *a thousand Marvedi's.* The marvedi, maredi, or maravedi was "a former Spanish copper coin and money of account, valued at about ⅙ of a penny sterling" (*OED*, citing this line).

498 *Handsel.* "A first installment of payment; earnest money; . . . anything given or taken as an omen, earnest, or pledge of what is to follow" (*OED*). Cf. *Sir Martin Mar-all*, V, ii, 12 (*Works*, IX, 285).

500–502 *But oh the King* etc. It is a sign of the pains Dryden took to integrate his plot and slowly to introduce a dramatic irony that *the fatal Secret* so important to the tragic plot should be first hinted at early in the comic plot.

514 *Geers.* "Gears" or "gear": "Accoutrements of a riding horse, or his rider" (*OED*, citing this use).

520 *Thrum-cap.* As an attributive adjective, *Thrum* means "Made . . . of thrums or waste threads of yarn (or something resembling it)" (*OED*, citing this use).

521–522 *I see the Doctrine of Non-Resistance* etc. Dryden's political belief included the doctrine of non-resistance to the sovereign and the belief that God alone punished tyrants and usurpers. It is impossible to say just what tone Dryden meant this line to possess in relation to himself.

527 *Yeap.* A variant of "Gee-up," from "Gee," "To go": "A word of command to a horse, variously . . . used to direct it to turn to the right, to go forward, or to move faster" (*OED*).

529 *well chin'd.* Apparently a Drydenian nonce expression from "chine" or "The spine, backbone" (*OED*), meaning strong-backed.

533 *Eye-sore.* "On a horse: A scar; also a flaw, defect" (*OED*, citing this use).

534 *Splint.* "A callous tumour developing into a bony excrescence," developing on the metatarsal bones of a horse's leg, usually occurring on the inside (*OED*, citing this use).

534 *Spavin.* "A hard bony tumour or excrescence formed at the union of the splint-bone and shank in a horse's leg" (*OED*).

534 *Wind-gall.* "A soft tumour on either side of a horse's leg just above the fetlock" (*OED*, citing this use).

543 *washy.* "Of a horse or cow: Poor in quality or condition; esp. liable to sweat or scour after slight exertion" (*OED*, with one use given before Dryden's).

546 *forehanded.* Meaning " 'formed in the foreparts'. . . . Usually with a defining *adj.* or *adv.* Said of horses" (*OED*).

547 *Gennet.* Or Jennet. "A small Spanish horse" (*OED*, citing *The Conquest of Granada*, Pt. I, I, i).

547 *Barb.* "A horse of the breed imported from Barbary and Morocco, noted for great speed and endurance" (*OED*).

549 *Xeriffs.* A xeriff, or sheriff was "A gold coin formerly current in the Levant of the value of 9s. 4d." (*OED*, citing this line as the first usage in Dryden's spelling).

559 *Sacrifice.* It is appropriate that Dryden, the first recorded user of *malapropo,* should find comic use for what later would be called malapropism.

578 *Heriot.* Dryden develops his figurative meaning out of a feudal service or custom of granting the lord a gift on the decease of a tenant (*OED*); thus, the phrase might be rendered, "as your lordship's due."

595 *Resumption.* "The action, on the part of the Crown or any other authority, of reassuming possession of lands, rights, etc., which have been bestowed on others" (*OED*). Mustapha's reference to what he will do "in the next rising of the Mobile" foreshadows in the comic plot that action which will rejoin it to the tragic.

606–608 *Both rich and poor* etc. In the preface (71:17–20) Dryden remarked that the *"judicious Critick will observe"* a *"Moral, couch'd under every one of the principal Parts and Characters."* Since this passage resembles the concluding lines of the play with their *"general Moral,"* the *"judicious Critick"* may perhaps discover here, with due allowances for comic irony, that moral *"couch'd under"* Mustapha.

II, i

1 Dryden uses both "Emperor" and "Muley-Moluch" as speech tags. The variation perhaps represented his usage in different stages of composition.

2–4 *The thoughts of Kings* etc. See the dedication, 59:19–20, for a similar image of the *lucus* or sacred grove.

3 *muffled.* As the larger conceit of the sacred grove shows, the sense of *muffled* is that of the hidden or concealed. But the *OED* records no fully appropriate meaning, and Dryden's usage illustrates the claim he made for the highly figurative language of the play.

6 *brown horrors.* Cf. "the brown horrour" of *The Hind and the Panther,* II, 659 (*Works*, III, 158, and see note, 406) and similar expressions in *Love Triumphant,* IV, i, and *Theodore and Honoria,* l. 92. Some have thought the phrase a Latinism, some a Miltonism, as in *Paradise Lost,* IV, 246; IX, 1088.

7 *secret path.* Probably a Latinism with perhaps something of the usual English meaning; cf. *secretus,* "hidden."

12 *the hurt Lion.* Although there is an Aesopian fable on the sick lion, Dryden's context suggests the usual emblematic implications for kingship.

14–15 *a Tax / Impos'd on all by Nature* etc. As part of his exploration of man's place in the world, Dryden intermittently concerns himself with versions of natural law, its boundaries, exactions, etc. For some very different examples, see I, 150–153 and V, 628–631.

27 *deaf.* "Of sounds: So dull as to be hardly or indistinctly heard; muffled" (*OED,* citing as last uses two in *Fables*).

35 *Storm of Fate.* Dryden's return to a concern with fate marks the last ten to twelve years of his career (see Miner, *Dryden's Poetry* [1967], pp. 310–313). His image here derives from Aeneas' ordeal and from a passage in Petronius, echoed by Waller, that Dryden had recalled in *Annus Mirabilis* (see ll. 125–140, especially 139–140, and notes in *Works,* I, 64–65, 285).

49–54 *Weak Princes* etc. The tyrannical power of rulers in the Mohammedan countries was a commonplace of travel-writers and historians. Pidou de St. Olon typically writes (p. 66) of "this Absolute and Personal Empire."

52 *some old Oak.* An emblem of royalty, like the lion of l. 12. Cf. *Mac Flecknoe,* l. 27, "Monarch Oakes."

56 *Death.* "A vehement exclamation or imprecation" (*OED,* citing *An Evening's Love,* IV, ii); more commonly " 'Sdeath."

62 *Say I shou'd wed her.* Polygamy fascinated as well as shocked Europeans (cf. the opening lines of *Absalom and Achitophel*), but the point is often made that a Mohammedan could have only four wives (with no religious limit to concubines and slaves). See, e.g., Thévenot, *Travels,* p. 55; Pidou de St. Olon, p. 51.

81–82 *You wou'd not put* etc. The touch of rant in this exchange shows that Dryden still enjoys the amusement of hyperbole that he had employed for his heroes as well as villains in the heroic plays.

87–91 *Suppose some one* etc. As noted, Dorax had played the role of a *Malcontent* in Act I by his railing or "Satyr." Benducar hints that besides that, he himself can play the role of double or triple agent.

114–124 *Be sure I'll tell him* etc. The passage is an example of the villain's soliloquy traditional to English drama from the time of the Vice in the Morality plays. The usual place for its appearance is at the beginning of an act or episode later in the play, and Benducar is in fact given another such piece at the opening of IV.

118 *gust.* Another Drydenian figurative usage, derived from "a burst, outbreak, or outburst," but otherwise so used with a following phrase like "of grief" (*OED*).

140 *Of course.* "Belonging to the ordinary procedure, . . . customary; natural, to be expected" (*OED*): the prepositional phrase from which the modern single expression has grown.

152 *excursions.* "An outburst (of feeling); . . . an overstepping of the bounds of propriety or custom, a freak" (*OED*).

154 *flourish'd.* To "flourish" is "To embellish (a narration, etc.) with flowers of speech; to ornament or set off with fine words or phrases" (*OED*).

164 *wag one finger in.* To "wag" is "To stir, move" (*OED*).

177 *we ask you but our own.* Our own sphere and claim, not our own souls.

185–196 *Poor droaning Truants* etc. The bee imagery that Dryden often drew from Virgil is present here in a characteristic Drydenian constellation of *Cells* (l. 185) and *College* (l. 195). For another example in this play, see IV, i, 44–49. See also *The Hind and the Panther*, III, 1286.

206 *this little hanging Ball.* Cf. Milton, *Paradise Lost*, II, 1052–1053— "This pendant world, in bigness as a Starr / Of smallest Magnitude"—and the Satanic context, which Dryden seems to recall as well.

207–208 *For give you but a foot* etc. Archimedes is reported to have said in effect (there are differing versions), "Give me a place to stand and with a lever I will move the whole world" (Diodorus Siculus, XXVI, 18 [Loeb trans.]). Dryden's *a foot of Conscience* therefore means "a foot-hold for conscience."

209–213 *We know your thoughts* etc. Dorax attributes to the Mufti a comparison of two types of human creatures radically different in quality. Such a distinction resembles his own in Act I between the herd of men and creatures like Don Sebastian. For other such comparisons, see *Threnodia Augustalis*, ll. 435–445; *The Hind and the Panther*, I, 251–265. Dryden often uses this contrast between two examples which are of the same kind and yet qualitatively so different as to seem to be of two kinds.

210 *Lag.* "Last, hindmost" (*OED*, citing the Dryden-Lee *Oedipus*, III, i); cf. "laggard."

218 *jugglings.* Meaning both "the practice of magic or of legerdemain" and "the practice of trickery or deception" (*OED*).

219 *startle.* "To cause to waver; to shake (a person, his resolution, faith, etc.)" (*OED*).

229 *Both are less Poison to my Eyes and Nature.* Only the Basilisk is poisonous to the sight, of course, but the dragon probably is imagined to have a poisonous sting. The poison Dorax introduces figuratively here becomes a literal danger in the last three acts.

237 *my foolish Faith.* Christianity.

265 *insults.* With accent on the second syllable as in Milton's "the great consult began" (*Paradise Lost*, I, 798).

271 *think not to divide their punishment.* To "devise" their punishment seems more natural, but *divide* here seems to mean "To distribute among a number; to deal out, dispense" (*OED*).

274 *'Tis out: there needs no Oedipus* etc. In the Dryden-Lee *Oedipus*, Act I, there are, of course, references to the riddle of the Sphinx and her "rage" against the Thebans until Oedipus answered the riddle. Scott quotes Addison's objection to Dryden's "frequent allusions to ancient poetry, and the old mythology of the heathens" (*Guardian*, No. 110), and

some critics decry the allowance to a Muslim of knowledge of the Greek classics. Although both Thebes and "Alcazar" lay in north Africa, the proper reply is that such fuss is pedantic. We pay no more note to such things in the theater than we do to Sebastian and Muley-Moluch arguing in English, a language that neither of them knew.

294 *vacates.* To "vacate" is "To deprive of force, efficacy, or value; to render inoperative, meaningless, or useless" (*OED*).

298 *whoop'd.* To "whoop" is "To shout at, hoot (a person)" (*OED* citing this as first use).

321 *denounc'd.* To "denounce" is "To . . . declare . . . an event about to take place: usually of a calamitous nature, as war or death" (*OED*).

325 *triumph.* As usual with Dryden's pronunciation, the accent falls on the second syllable.

336 *head.* "One of the chief points of a discourse" (*OED*); that is, "your reasons were too much to the point."

346 *bare.* "Poor in quality, paltry, worthless." *saving game.* To "make a saving game" is "to retrieve one's losses in the end" (*OED*).

353 *And gaining time gains all.* The recurrent aphoristic quality of the play is suggested elsewhere in these notes by the indication of received proverbs. The standard proverb dictionaries do not list this aphorism which, as a subtitle to James Howell's *Lexicon Tetraglotton* (1660) puts it, is one of the "New Sayings, which in tract of Time, may serve for Proverbs to Posterity."

355–356 *I keep my Lions* etc. We have found no historical evidence in the lore about Morocco or the "Turks" for such punishment by beasts. This is no doubt another instance of the emblematic cruelty of "Turkish" tyrants.

358 *observance.* "The observing of . . . respectful or courteous attention, dutiful service" (*OED*).

370–372 *Sure our two Souls* etc. The two kings share a heroic *hauteur*, but Muley-Moluch's remark prepares rather for the incest plot when Almeyda is introduced into the talk.

385 *Strong in her Passion, impotent of Reason.* Although truer of Sebastian himself than of Almeyda, the characterization applies to every character in the play. Scansion of this speech would reveal much about Dryden's prosody and style in the play.

390 *Pile.* "A lofty mass of buildings; a large building or edifice" (*OED*).

393 *Then onely hear her Eyes.* Cf. *To Sir Godfrey Kneller*, ll. 3–6, and especially l. 11: "At least thy Pictures look a Voice" (*Works*, IV, 461).

396–399 *All Females have* etc. Cf. ll. 416–417 for a distinction between the human and the brute; and cf. V, 628–631 for a similar comparison of man and beasts in a far more tragic tone.

401 *She's Mistress of unevitable Charms.* The *unevitable* of course means "inevitable," "not admitting of escape or evasion; unavoidable" (*OED*). But Dryden's meaning is a bit stronger, and the concept of fate is linked indirectly to the beauty of Dryden's heroine, very much as later in *To the Dutchess of Ormond* (*Fables*, 1700, sig. A2, ll. 30–31): "O true *Plantagenet*, O Race Divine, / (For Beauty still is fatal to the Line,)."

404 *obnoxious.* "Subject to the rule, power, or authority of another; . . . submissive, obsequious, deferential" *(OED).*

432 *Wild-fire.* "A composition of highly inflammable substances, readily ignited and very difficult to extinguish, used in warfare, etc." *(OED).* In some meanings the word has associations with lightning: cf. l. 421.

451–452 *Lay by the Lions Hide* etc. Ostensibly, the lion image recalls the Emperor's own in ll. 418–419. But it also refers to Hercules, who gave up the skin of the Nemean lion for other clothes when, out of love for Omphale, he disguised himself as a woman and did *Distaff* work. See e.g., Propertius, III, xi, 17–20; Statius, *Thebaid,* X, 646–649.

460–463 *No, were we joyn'd* etc. The *Prodigy of Thebes* refers, as Summers recognized, to the story of Polyneices and Eteocles. When the bodies of these two, brothers and yet enemies in life, were burnt at one pyre, the flames parted, burning separately. See, among other accounts, Statius, *Thebaid,* XII, 429–436.

466–467 *like the seed of Dragons Teeth* etc. On the sowing of the dragon's teeth by Cadmus, founder of Thebes, see Ovid, *Metamorphoses,* III, 101–110. The recurrence of Theban details in this scene may be remarked.

473 *I am a Christian.* The revelation comes as news to the audience as well as to the emperor. It is important to subsequent development both of the tragic and of the comic plots and provides a contrast to Dorax's change of religion.

485–486 *Unless you wholly can put on Divinity* etc. Dryden plays on the proverb, "To err is human, to repent [or forgive] divine, to persecute is diabolical" (Tilley, E179).

496 *gust.* "Keen relish, appreciation, or enjoyment" *(OED,* citing a similar usage in Dryden's Juvenal VI, 119).

497–498 *They must be watch'd* etc. The wary Benducar has observed signs of love between Sebastian and Almeyda.

505–510 *You turn my Prison* etc. In the romance *Don Sebastian* (II, 23–24) Almeida has a long monologue, elements of which Dryden has adapted into this speech.

507–510 *In all your Wars* etc. Neither the historical Don Sebastian nor the hero of the romance had fought so very many wars; but in the romance (II, 116ff.) the king is motivated by love for Almeida to enter into his disastrous Moroccan venture.

516 *luggage.* Apparently an Anglicism for *impedimenta,* the supplies that Roman armies might have to give up if forced to flee.

526–529 *Brutus and Cato* etc. James Russell Lowell, after Scott Dryden's most perceptive critic in the last century, commented on this speech: "Dryden seldom borrows, unless from Shakespeare, without improving, and he borrowed a great deal. Thus in 'Don Sebastian' (of suicide)"—and he quoted these four lines, adding—"The thought is Cicero, but how it is intensified by the 'starless nights!'" (*My Study Windows,* ed. Richard Garnett [London, n.d.], II, 297). Three passages in Cicero make Sebastian's point about suicide: *De Republica (Somnium Scipionis),* VI, xv, 15;

Tusculan Disputations, I, xxx, 74 (referring to the younger Cato and Socrates); and *De Senectute,* xx, 73, where we read that we must "stand like faithful sentries and not quit our post until God, our Captain, gives the word." It was probably this that Lowell recalled, and which Dryden may have had in mind. However, both this passage and that from the *Tusculan Disputations* derive from Plato (*Phaedo*) who is himself indebted to Pythagoras. To such a tangle of possibilities, we may add with Lowell the possibility that Dryden took the classical image for the topic from Montaigne: "For many are of Opinion, that we cannot quit this Garrison of the World, without the express command of him, who has plac'd us here" (*Essays,* trans. Charles Cotton, II, 34). But if Dryden required a non-classical intermediary, that would have been Spenser in *The Faerie Queene,* I, ix, 41, as noted by Scott:

> The terme of life is limited,
> Ne may a man prolong, nor shorten it;
> The souldier may not move from watchfull sted,
> Nor leave his stand, untill his Captaine bed.

In brief, Dryden here enunciates one of the great Western commonplaces, making it distinctly his own by its appropriateness to a play dealing with fate's operations and, as Lowell said, by adding to the commonplace those "starless Nights." Cf. V, 432–434 and 440+ *s.d.* and n.

527 *Furlo's.* "Furloughs" in the sense of "A passport; a license, or permit" (*OED*).

532–539 *Divines but peep* etc. Almeyda's lovely speech perhaps gives some color to Lowell's speculation that Dryden had been reading Montaigne on suicide (*Essays,* II, iii).

535 *Manners.* As the context shows, the word bears the usual seventeenth-century meaning of habitual moral conduct (*OED*).

540 *thou canst not dye unperjur'd.* Almeyda, it emerges, has taken an oath or *Vows* (l. 542) to marry Sebastian, the breaking of which would be a kind of perjury.

541 *unaccomplish'd.* Incomplete (*OED*); unconsummated.

543 *The tye of Minds are but imperfect Bonds.* The use of a plural verb because of a plural predicate nominative, and in spite of a single subject, is very exceptional in Dryden's writing.

564 *seizure.* Possession (*OED*).

566 *grant.* Consent (*OED*), continuing Sebastian's legal figure.

575–579 *Love is not Sin* etc. In the original quarto this passage has initial double quotation marks in the right margin at ll. 575, 577, and 579; there is also a set beside l. 560, as well as others later in the play. It seems possible that these are vestiges of marks used by Betterton in cutting the play, since such marks were often used for such purpose in the next century, and since the speeches could be omitted without damage to the plot. Alternatively, it may be that someone is indicating lines of an aphoristic nature or of special beauty.

581–589 *Laugh then at fond presages* etc. The passage affords an example of that expression of hubris that the unknowing tragic hero is usually given in tragedies of fate from Sophocles forward: from this point the relation between Sebastian and Almeyda is certain and the dramatic irony relentless.

582 *Fam'd Nostradamus.* Nostradamus represents the generic prophet (see "Prologue to *The Prophetess,*" l. 1; the prologue to *The Kind Keeper,* l. 23), but in fact the historical Michel de Nostredame lived from 1503 to 1566 and might have cast Sebastian's horoscope. The truth of prophecy was sometimes taken to mean that the future is in some sense fixed and, hence, that human agency is limited: the problem is an old theological and philosophical issue.

595 *You gave Almeyda for the word of Battel.* A *word of Battel* is the slogan to be shouted to inspire the troops as they enter the fight.

596 *fatal Moment.* "Fraught with destiny; fateful" (*OED* s.v. *fatal*); but as the context and the sense of a moment's being so implies, fate involves human agency.

612 *dastardize.* "To make a dastard of; to cow, terrify" (*OED,* citing this passage, among others).

612 *cruddles.* Curdles (*OED,* citing *Aeneis,* II, 766, again of blood).

628 *Love and Fortune, two blind Guides.* Cupid is, of course, blind. A similar tradition, less widely known, holds for Fortune. According to Ross, *Mystagogus Poeticus,* Fortune is "blinde, and carried in a chariot drawn by blind horses" (p. 92).

II, ii

s.d. *Suppos'd a Garden.* See the headnote, p. 392, on the importance of gardens in accounts of Mohammedan countries. Some of the details of this scene recall the dance scene toward the end of Act III of *An Evening's Love* (*Works,* X, 260–264), where Jacinta disguises herself as a Moorish girl to see whether Wildblood will pursue other pretty women, even if of another religion.

s.d. *Enter . . . Johayma the Mufti's Wife.* In theory the wife of so important a person as a Mufti would not be seen by anyone but her husband, other women, and perhaps eunuchs. But as the headnote shows, Johayma is a recognizable type from the accounts of travelers: a Moorish version of Potiphar's Wife.

8–12 *Why honey-bird* etc. The Mufti's question and Johayma's reply show that her interest in a Christian slave is sexual, in particular that it turns on his not being circumcised, like a Jew or Mohammedan. Cf. Pidou de St. Olon (p. 83): "The [Moorish women] are particularly fond of Christians because they are not Circumcis'd, and there are no Stratagems but what are us'd by some of 'em to intice the Slaves that live with them, or who are allow'd to come where they dwell."

8 *honey-bird.* Dryden's nonce-word is not recorded in the *OED,* which defines *honey* as a "term of endearment," and *bird* as a "maiden, a girl." The combination suggests the Mufti's doting, or fear of his wife's tongue.

27 s.d. *making legs.* Performing polite (here, significant) bows, accompanied by a curtsy-like leg movement. Antonio is probably Dryden's finest

coxcomb and would provide a splendid role for a certain kind of comic actor.

37 *malapert.* "Presumptuous, impudent, 'saucy' " (*OED*); i.e., pert.

41–42 *Charity ev'n to Birds and Beasts.* Moorish love of animals was often remarked, and Thévenot has a discussion of "the charity of the Turks toward Beasts" (*Travels*, p. 51).

55–56 *a Rose-tree and a Myrtle.* Both are associated with love. Ross said of Venus in *Mystagogus Poeticus* (sig. V6) that "her flower [is] the rose, her tree the myrtle" (see also p. 263).

61 *I will follow my Pastor.* The play on *Pastor* to mean both minister and shepherd is taken up by the Mufti in something like the latter sense.

63 *mind your pruning knife* etc. Antonio's reply shows he feels a threat of circumcision, or worse.

66 *Wedlock.* "A wife" (*OED*, citing this use).

74 *chuckle 'em together.* ". . . call (*together*) with a chuckle" (*OED*, first usage).

76+ *s.d. A Grate opens.* In the staging, the grate was a window over one of the doors at either side of the stage. The *Grate* is, as usual in comic scenes, imagined to be an upper window of a house represented by the door below it, through which people go in and out as if in and out of the house.

78–80 *this is the Mystery* etc. Antonio's motives are natural enough, but he dresses them in an *arcanum* such as that propounded by neo-Platonists or criticized in Catholics by Protestants. Certain travelers' accounts showed that the Koran was widely read and expounded and certainly was not concealed from infidels.

80 *his Holyday Devotion.* Antonio persists in thinking Morayma a wife or concubine of the Mufti.

94 *pot-hooks.* "A curved or hooked stroke made in writing" (*OED*, citing this use); Dryden refers to the cursive character of Arabic script.

96 *eye-shot.* "The range of the eye; seeing distance" (*OED*, citing this use).

101–102 *Here the warm Planet ripens* etc. The *warm Planet* is the sun, because it dominates, in alchemical theory (and common sense), the hotter, more nearly equatorial climates. (See William Lilly, *Christian Astrology* [1647], ch. xi.) The term *sublimes* is an alchemical metaphor (see *OED*, citing this use). Sublimation was accomplished by the application of heat, of which the purest available form was thought to be the sun's rays. See François Secret, "Le Soleil chez les Kabbalistes chrétiens de la Renaissance," and B. Kedrov, "Deux orientations de l'alchimie à l'époque de la Renaissance," in *Le Soleil à la Renaissance: Sciences et Mythes* (1965). Antonio's speech prepares the audience for a favorable response to Morayma as opposed to Johayma.

III, i

s.d. A Terrace-walk etc. At this juncture in the play Dryden seems not to desire more than three things in staging: a general Moorish mood, a degree of proximity of scenes, and a movement from without the castle to within.

4 *clear*. To "free from obscurity or ambiguity; . . . explain, elucidate" (*OED*).

6 *the stormy South*. The sirocco or strong, hot winds for which there are numerous names in northern Africa.

20 *resume*. "To take back to oneself (something previously given or granted)" (*OED*).

24 *Dispatch*. "To make haste" (*OED*).

46–47 *The Reverend Father* etc. Summers compared *Sigismonda and Guiscardo*, ll. 163–169 (*Fables*, 1700, sig. S):

> The holy Man amaz'd at what he saw,
> Made haste to sanctifie the Bliss by Law;
> And mutter'd fast the Matrimony o're,
> For fear committed Sin should get before.
> His Work perform'd, he left the Pair alone,
> Because he knew he could not go too soon;
> His Presence odious, when his Task was done.

60 *Druggerman*. This use is cited as the first for the figurative meaning of "An interpreter; strictly applied to a man who acts as a guide or interpreter in countries where Arabic, Turkish, or Persian is spoken" (*OED*, s.v. *dragoman*).

69–71 *Why, verily the Law* etc. Cf. Thévenot, *Travels*, p. 53; The Mufti "is always a knowing Man in their way, and much versed in the Alcoran; [for] it is he who is consulted about matters of conscience."

72–74 *Forge one* etc. Much Christian indignation was expressed over the Koran as a hodge-podge of heresy, a "Gallimaufry of Errors" and impostures as Alexander Ross put it in his "needfull Caveat" appended to his rendering of the French translation of the Koran: see *The Alcoran*, p. [406].

79 *a misbelieving Race*. Mohammedans were as strict as Jews or Christians about marriage to one not of their faith, although they were very ready to accept conversion.

83 *have I rais'd thee* etc. Cf. Thévenot, *Travels*, p. 53: the Mufti "is not Elected by an Assembly of their Ecclesiasticks, but the Grand Signior prefers whom he pleases."

88 *post*. With "haste or speed" (*OED*); unusual with *send*.

126 *projection*. A metaphor, evidently suggested by the chemical sense of "precipitates" in the preceding line, from the final stage of the alchemical process, at which "the casting of the powder of philosophers' stone upon a metal in fusion" effected its "transmutation into gold or silver" (*OED*).

127 *at unawares*. "Unexpectedly, suddenly" (*OED*).

132–135 *Not the last sounding* etc. Cf. Dryden's ode to Anne Killigrew, ll. 178–187, for such an apocalyptic vision. It is remarkable how these first speeches by Almeyda and Sebastian elevate the tone and enlarge the vision beyond that offered hitherto in this act. Cf. also I, 376–377.

153–154 *that Gorgon Face* etc. A look at the face of the most famous of the Gorgons, Medusa, would turn the observer into stone, even after

Perseus had cut off her head (*Metamorphoses,* IV, 655ff.). The allusion here is part of the imagery of the monstrous for Africa: see l. 174; also see II, i, 458–467.

156 *amaz'd.* "Struck with sudden terror; . . . alarmed" (*OED*).

158–159 *Kings, like Gods, / Are every where.* Joining an attribute of God, omnipresence, to royalist notions of kings as God's vicegerents who include in their body politic all their subjects.

175–177 *He was the envy* etc. Cf. the quotation from the opening of the romance *Don Sebastian* quoted in the headnote, p. 388.

180 *Were I to choose again, and knew my fate.* This line incorporates, with dramatic irony, Dryden's view of the combination of human choice and fate. Sebastian is not yet aware that his choice is fatal in a much larger scheme than he has glimpsed.

195–199 *How can we better dye* etc. Almeyda's speech employs the usual terms for *Liebestod,* and Dryden treats as literal that death she expects shortly. The conception of parting as the death of lovers is more common in the seventeenth century than is the other quibble on sexual dying. See for example Donne, *The Expiration;* Jonson (or Donne), an elegy, "Since you must goe, and I must bid farewell" (ll. 9–14); Charles Cotton, *Song* ("Bring back my Comfort, and return"), l. 4, *Taking Leave of Chloris,* ll. 1–2, and *Ode Valedictory,* ll. 1–4. This motif is well explained in *The Ephesian and Cimmerian Matrons* (1668), second pag., p. 65: "yet can I not deny, but [love] is a kind of Death. For, who is ignorant that Lovers die as often as they kiss, or bid adieu: exhaling their Souls upon each others lips." Dryden's passage freshens a commonplace by a striking yet natural conceit of a funeral knell announcing parting.

202–203 The first edition marks these lines with double quotation marks, probably again for the phrasing.

248 *pity tempts the pass.* The conceit builds on *the inlets of my Soul* in the preceding line, extending the geographical image to military overtones. To "tempt" is "to adventure oneself in or upon; to risk the perils of" (*OED,* citing Dryden's *Georgics,* III, 123, 581). The *pass* is "a passage viewed strategically as commanding the entrance into a country or place" (*OED*). The *OED* gives a similar figurative example from Tom Brown's *Satire Against Woman:* "Thus all the unguarded passes of his mind she'll try."

249 *metal.* Meaning both "mettle" and "metal," as common in Dryden and other early writers. Cf. *The Hind and the Panther,* III, 735 and n (*Works,* III, 183, 434).

253 *Love and that are Twins.* The idea that Love and Pity are twins recalls Eros and Anteros. See Plato, *Phaedrus,* 255d; Pausanias, I, 30, 1; and Ross, *Mystagogus Poeticus,* p. 262.

255–256 *Thus compass you* etc. Almeyda is probably to be imagined to kneel, clasping the Emperor's legs with her arms (*Cords*), and pulling on them till, like Samson, she brings the *proud Fabrick* of his body down. *Supplanting* is used in the rare sense of "To throw down, overturn" (*OED*) and is a Latinism: cf. *supplantare.*

285 *one day of respite.* For all the drive of thought in Dryden's writing, he often shows, as here, something closely akin to the fairy tale and ro-

mance. The allowance of one day prevents Dryden from adhering to the "*Mechanick*" unity of time, as he says in the preface, 70:1–9, and permits him to encompass "*the variety of accidents*," or incidents, of the play.

290 *That Curse be thine.* That is, to be yourself.

297 *overwatch'd.* "Wearied with too much watching" (*OED*).

312 *Farewel, my last Sebastian.* Compare Almeyda's final speech (V, i, 707–711): "the last farewell. . . . my last *Sebastian.*" A usage unrecorded by *OED*, but perhaps meaning "my last of you, Sebastian," or "my Sebastian, last of your kind." Cf. *Marriage A-la-mode*, III, i: "Farewell, my last *Leonidas*" (1673, p. 40; S-S, IV, 308).

319+ *s.d. Sebastian . . . speaks not all the while.* Nor has he spoken since l. 238: "my life's not worth another word."

320–331 *I find* etc. Essentially a soliloquy (especially ll. 330–331), Dorax's speech is technically an aside, because another character, Sebastian, is also on stage.

320 *half-strain'd.* Half blooded; hence *mungril-mischievous* in l. 321.

352 *Muza* is not named in the "Persons Represented."

359 *But I shall bring him back.* The *him* refers to the person with *That voice* (l. 356), Dorax himself, or perhaps rather that Don Alonso who has become Dorax.

361 *front.* "To . . . confront; *esp.* to face in defiance or hostility" (*OED*, citing the dedication of *Aeneis*).

365 *like Bacchus born in thunder.* Bacchus "was the son of Jupiter and Semele, who was saved out of his mothers ashes, after that Jupiter had burnt her with his thunder" (Ross, *Mystagogus Poeticus*, p. 36). For a fuller account of Semele and her rashness, see Ovid, *Metamorphoses*, III, 256ff.

384–388 *Sir, let me bluntly say* etc. The doctrine espoused by Dorax includes in its thoroughgoing royalism the regal supremacy over the church, such as was enjoyed by English kings since the Reformation and by Louis XIV. On the centuries-old rivalry between the *imperium* and the *sacerdotum*, see Ernst H. Kantorowicz, *The King's Two Bodies: A Study in Medieval Political Theology* (1957).

389–392 *Holy Men . . . fam'd in State Affairs* etc. The Mufti gives as examples three cardinals. *Ximenes.* Francisco Ximénes de Cisneros (1436–1517) had full scholarly training before entering the Franciscan order in 1482. He rose to favor with Isabella, succeeding to the archbishopric of Toledo in 1495. He became cardinal in 1507. In 1509 he financed and led a military expedition to Africa, and on the death of Ferdinand became sole regent of Castile in the absence of the young king Carlos. The next year the king returned and rudely dismissed the cardinal, who died within months. *Albornoz.* Gil Alvarez de Albornoz (d. 1367) was educated in law, and while still young was preferred to the king's council through family influence. He fought against the Africans at the battle of Tarifa in 1340 and invaded Africa in 1344. His soldierly and diplomatic achievements won him a cardinal's cap in 1350. Most of the last fifteen years or more of his life were spent outside Spain working to restore papal authority. *Woolsey.* Thomas Wolsey (c. 1473–1530) came from humble origins, rose at Oxford to become master of Magdalen College, and from 1506 was chaplain and diplomat for Henry VII. By 1511 he was a privy counsellor for Henry VIII, and cardinal by 1515. Although brilliant, he aspired to the papacy and control of the English nobility. Such overreaching, with problems at home and abroad, led to his fall. He died on his way to London to face charges of high treason. The three cardinals are chosen so as to be appropriate in historical time for Don Sebastian. Two fought against the Moors in Africa, and all three contributed to the centralizing of power.

396 *which of 'em were Saints.* None of the three cardinals was canonized by the seventeenth century, although some later efforts have been made for Ximénes.

400–401 *and Ages oft depend* etc. The general sense is that the fate of whole centuries often depends on lengthy sermons that sway their listeners.

405–418 *The genius of your Moors* etc. The general charge against the Moors resembles Dryden's description of the English, or "Jews," in *Absalom and Achitophel,* ll. 45–66. The similarity suggests no particular attack on the English of 1689; it reflects Dryden's estimate of the mass of people everywhere. The statement about mutiny affords preparation for events in the next act and grows from the advice given by the Mufti and Benducar to the Emperor. And, it must be added, it recalls Dorax's own refusal to obey the Emperor's orders for handling Don Sebastian.

410 *perjur'd to a Proverb.* That is, perjured to the point of becoming a proverbial example.

411–414 *They love Religion sweeten'd* etc. Christians professed great scandal over the sensuous nature of the Mohammedan paradise. Cf. *The Hind and the Panther,* I, 376–391 and n (*Works,* III, 134, 373).

417 *And whose the Subjects are.* That is, whether they do not in fact pay allegiance to the "Clergy" (l. 415).

437 *By Holy Alha.* Alexander Ross, trans. *The Alcoran,* gives a version of the famous Mohammedan affirmation: "*La ilha illa allha Mehemet rasoul allha,* that is, There is but one God, Mahomet is his Prophet and Apostle" (sig. A5). Pidou de St. Olon mentions invocations of God (pp. 43, 53).

446 *Your Troops far off, beleaguering Larache.* In 1689 the Moors had recently recaptured from the Spaniards Larache, i.e., El Araish or Laraish, a port in northern Morocco that harbored pirates. Pidou de St. Olon describes the port on pp. 129ff. and includes a map (the only one in the book).

476–478 *Not the Nonacrian fount* etc. The *Nonacrian fount* is the Styx, which was thought to originate in the mountains about Nonacris in northern Arcadia. Pliny (*Natural History,* II, cvi, 231) wrote: "To drink of the Styx near Nonacris in Arcady causes death on the spot" (Loeb trans.). The best known description of the powers of the Lethe is that of Virgil, *Aeneid,* VI, 703–751. In view of Dorax's next speech, it must be remarked that the Styx was believed to kill by cold.

485 *Within my little World.* That is, the microcosm.

492–499 *Ingratitude's the growth* etc. These eight lines, the last six of which are rhymed, probably embody the *"Moral"* that Dryden said was to be found *"under every one of the principal Parts"* of the play (see the preface, 71:18–19).

493 *remov'd.* Shifted, changed (*OED*).

496 *my honest Corps.* My body, which has possessed honor, *honestas.*

498 *My shameful Death* etc. In modern syntax, "My shameful death alone will be divulged."

III, ii

2 *and a Virgin.* Virginity was essential to a favorable female character in Restoration drama. See John Harrington Smith, *The Gay Couple in Restoration Comedy* (1948), pp. 76–78.

11–12 *No, 'tis the Son of a Mare that's broken loose* etc. There is no earthly reason why Antonio should be able to tell the sex of a colt in the dark, why he should express knowledge of the sex in such a phrase, or why he should know what the colt is eating. But such expressions are in Dryden's full comic vein and will find their supreme expression in his next play, *Amphitryon.*

19–20 *has three Wives and six Concubines besides me.* See Alexander Ross's added comments in *The Alcoran* (sig. A5): the "Turks" are "permitted to have four wives, married at the same time, and as many Concubines as they are able to maintain." Morayma's *besides me* does not imply that she is the Mufti's concubine but suggests that, as his daughter, she includes herself among the principal women of his household.

35 *luxury.* "Lasciviousness; lust"; habitual indulgence in the costly and rich (*OED*).

45+ *s.d. Throwing off her Barnus.* For the garment, see I, i, 238+ *s.d.* and n and see the illustration facing p. 143.

87–88 *a fine exchange of that Diamond for this Pebble.* Antonio unwittingly conflates the traditional first two Aesopian fables. "Of the Cock and Pretious Stone" (in which the cock bypasses a diamond for food) and "Of the Dog and the Shadow" (in which the greedy dog, seeing the meat he carries reflected in the water, bites at the reflection, losing the meat in his mouth and the image in the water). On Dryden's use of John Ogilby, *The Fables of Aesop Paraphras'd in Verse*, see *Works*, III.

104 *peeking.* The nearest *OED* definition is "prying"; but Dryden seems to mean "inquisitive; furtive."

115 *I'll teach thee, to thy cost.* Dryden's comic version of the story of Joseph and Potiphar's wife (Genesis, xxxix, 7–20) is redirected for further comedy with yet another twist of intrigue, in which the Mufti is introduced.

129 *ganch him, impale him.* Dryden appears to have recalled Thévenot, *Travels*, pp. 68–69:

> Now the Ganche, or throwing upon Hooks is performed
> in this manner: They have a very high Strappado, stuck
> full of very sharp-pointed Hooks of Iron, . . . and hav-
> ing hoisted the Malefactor up to the top of it, they let
> him fall [upon the hooks]. . . . Christians that do or say

any thing against the Law of Mahomet, are taken with a
Turkish Woman, or go into a Mosque, are Empaled.

The *OED* cites Dryden's passage in defining *ganch*. Both the ganch and impaling stakes are shown in an illustration to Settle's *Empress of Morocco*. See *The Empress of Morocco and Its Critics*, ed. Maximillian E. Novak (Augustan Reprint Society [1968]), p. 70.

179 *He cost you five hundred Crowns.* As the *OED* states, "from the 15th to the 18th c." the "crown" was "the common English name for the F. *écu*, as well as for other foreign coins of similar value." Pidou de St. Olon (as rendered by his translator) states that the only foreign money current in Morocco was "Pieces of Eight," but that resident Jews used "French Silver Crowns" (pp. 142–143). A quotation in the *OED* suggests that in the early eighteenth century a crown was judged to be worth about five shillings, and at that rate Antonio seems to have cost the Mufti about £125. See ll. 291–308n.

211–213 *I have no mind to warm a frozen Snake in my bosom* etc. As Summers recognized, the ultimate source of Morayma's remark may be the fable in the fourth book of Phaedrus' collection (sometimes entitled *Aesopica*, sometimes printed with Aesop), "Serpens. Misericordia Nociva." See for example, *Phaedri, Aug. Liberti, Fabularum Aesopiarum Libri V* (Leyden, 1598), IV, lxxv; and *Phaedri, Augusti Caesaris Liberti, Fabularum Aesopiarum Libri Quinque* (Amsterdam, 1667), IV, xviii. Dryden may, however, have drawn directly on a poem by Waller, "To a fair Lady, playing with a snake," or on Waller and Phaedrus. Having told how the snake crept up the young woman's sleeve, Waller concludes (*Poems*, 1664), ll. 13–18:

> Contented in that Nest of Snow
> He lyes, as he his bliss did know,
> And to the wood no more would go.

> Take heed (fair Eve) you do not make
> Another Tempter of this Snake,
> A marble one so warm'd would speak.

As Philip R. Wikelund, who is editing Waller, has noted, Dryden is closer to Phaedrus than is Waller.

219 *a fresh-water Soldier.* The term *fresh-water* means "Unpractised; unskilled; untrained; raw"; it is commonly used of a soldier (*OED*).

225–230 *we meet upon treaty now* etc. The conceit turns on negotiations at time of war. Morayma declares that they negotiate in declared truce (*upon treaty*, rather than *upon defiance*); Antonio is quick to grant her full powers (*Carte blanche*) to negotiate freely. But she accuses him of having already entered on stipulations with her enemy, Johayma, in previous negotiation. The traditional trope of love as war is developed with a glance at the war in Ireland. Cf. *An Evening's Love*, IV, i (*Works*, X, 292–293, 450–451).

227 *Carte blanche.* The earliest use given by the *OED* for "A blank paper given to any one on which to write his own conditions" is one from 1707.

239 *the blast.* The sounding of the trumpet traditionally blown by Fame.

246 *truck.* "To trade by exchange of commodities; to barter" (*OED*).

249 *Vizard.* Properly, "a mask" (*OED*). Here, figurative.

261 *a Butchers Pen'worth.* A "pennyworth" is "A good bargain; something . . . fully worth what is given for it" (*OED*, citing Dryden's prologue to *Oedipus*, l. 33).

285 *an ill Husband.* Obviously Morayma means both as a husbandman or manager and as a spouse; *fingring your Rents* in the preceding line must therefore also be equivocal.

291–308 *And so you shall* etc. This episode and one later (IV, ii) recall the elopement of Jessica and Lorenzo who carry off Shylock's wealth in a casket: cf. *The Merchant of Venice*, II, iv. Dryden makes more of the episode than does Shakespeare so that the comic subplot may join the tragic main plot in the next act. If Morayma brings as dowry the *value of twelve hundred thousand Crowns,* that would be equivalent in Dryden's time to the fortune of about £300,000.

311 *a willing Titt.* "Tit" was a common diminutive and was often used, in depreciation, for girl or young woman (*OED*). Cf. "Epilogue to the King and Queen," l. 39 (*Works*, II, 199).

319 *to stay your stomach.* To stay the stomach is "to appease its cravings" (*OED*).

320–325 *Thus Conquer'd Infidels* etc. It would be difficult to prove that the rhymed close provides any very profound moral. But the passage provides the capstone to the "gay couple" repartee between Morayma and Antonio, she emerging the victor. In *The Gay Couple* (1948), John Harrington Smith discussed the forces putting "the Gay Couple on the Defensive" (ch. vi) in the 1690's. They thrive in two of Dryden's last plays by special condition: the comic subplot of *Don Sebastian,* between a Christian and a "Moor"; and the Mercury-Phaedra subplot of *Amphitryon,* between a pagan god and a termagant. There is no question whatever but that Morayma and Antonio are the more attractive pair of the two, or that the comic subplot in the tragedy is more romantic than that in *Amphitryon.*

325+ *s.d. She runs off* etc. Morayma and Antonio have been in the normal acting area, the apron of the stage, or stage front. She runs back and to one of the doors at a side of the proscenium. Antonio follows after, but since she gets within before he arrives, and since the door represents the entrance to a seraglio, from which all men are barred, he cannot enter. He therefore runs off stage through a counterpart door across the stage.

IV, i

s.d. Benducar's Pallace in the Castle of Alcazar. This is the play's first scene properly within doors, although the comic plot had been played in an imagined enclosure. Henceforth, except for the rabble scene, the play takes place in reduced spaces.

1 *My future Fate, the colour of my life.* The use of *colour* to represent the quality or nature of something is very striking. What Dryden probably has in mind are the alternatives of white or black. He often uses "white" in the Latinate sense of auspicious or fortunate, and "black" (V, 374) in the sense of the foreboding or tragic. It will be observed that the imagery and various versification of this whole scene provide poetry richer than any hitherto allowed to characters other than Sebastian, Almeyda, and Dorax.

12+ s.d. *Enter Haly—First Servant.* A second servant, Hamet, enters at l. 38 and a third, Orchan, at l. 56. None of the three is named among the "Persons Represented," which gives only "A Servant to Benducar" (perhaps reflecting the cast of the version as cut by Betterton). It will be observed that Benducar greets each by name on entrance, and that their exits and entrances follow each other too quickly for one actor to have played all three roles.

15–24 *Two hours I warily have watch'd* etc. This is one of the passages singled out for praise by Scott.

35–36 *In the blind Labyrinths* etc. Seventeenth-century interest in anatomy led some poets to draw upon it for conceited imagery. Cf. Phineas Fletcher, *The Purple Island;* John Donne, *The Extasie,* ll. 61–64; and Andrew Marvell, *A Dialogue between the Soul and Body,* ll. 1–10.

38 *As if his stronger Stars had interpos'd.* Although *stronger* may entail comparison with the stars affecting the lives of others, it seems to mean that Dorax's stars are stronger than Benducar's efforts to poison him. The astral lore presents another version of the play's theme of fate. See ll. 197–200.

38+ s.d. *Enter Hamet.* The name appears in the romance *Don Sebastian,* I, 41ff.

41–49 *What you wish* etc. The description of a controlled night mob could scarcely be bettered. Scott chose this as one of the passages for his praise, saying that it illustrates "the diligence and success with which Dryden has laboured even the subordinate points of this tragedy." It will be observed that the whole state—rabble and nobles, the Emperor's court and the Mufti's household—is in a condition of revolution, for which *noon of Night* is the appropriate paradox.

44–49 *All crowd in heaps* etc. For similar bee imagery, see II, 185–196n.

46 *imboss.* To "emboss" is "To cause to bulge or swell out, . . . to cover with protuberances" (*OED*).

47 *Their busie Captain.* Mustapha.

53 *the Lieutenant.* Subsequent events do not clearly show who is meant. Antonio seems to play the part under Mustapha, but Benducar can hardly have appointed him.

63–70 *O the curst fate* etc. Dryden might have taken the motif of a check to plans of rebellion from Shakespeare, especially from *1 Henry IV,* IV, i.

64–65 *They move on many Springs* etc. It may be that the image is that of a clock, which had supplied poets with comparisons for over a century, and Hobbes with a description of man in the introduction to *Leviathan.* However, Dryden's image of the *Machine* of rebellion should be understood in terms of the very general, wide, and figurative usages of the word in the century (see *OED*). Only in the last decade of the century did a fully mechanist view and vocabulary become a commonplace. What remains striking about Dryden's figure, however, is that it substitutes an inanimate, moving image for the usual beast image for the mob.

65 *restiff*. A variant of "restive": "refusing to go forward; resisting control of any kind" (*OED*). Usually applied to animals (Dryden, *Georgics*, III, 324), it is also frequently used figuratively (see, e.g., *The Hind and the Panther*, III, 1026).

75 *Career*. "Full speed," from a horse's short gallop at top speed (*OED*).

86 *Consult*. "A meeting for consultation," or those so meeting; here, as often in the usage of the time "a secret meeting for purposes of sedition or intrigue" (*OED*).

92 *a friendly Sword*. There is peculiar wit in the sense in which *friendly* is the accurate word.

97–98 *For, like the Twins of Leda* etc. Apollo and Diana, god of the sun and goddess of the moon, were reciprocal in their rise and fall. The weak Muley-Zeydan characterizes himself by presuming his brother Muley-Moluch to be the Apollo-sun, himself the Diana-moon.

107 *Whose parting Soul* etc. The belief that the soul issued from the lips at death is common to many peoples, often involving an association of the soul with the breath, as for example in Genesis, II, 7: "And the Lord God formed man of the dust of the ground, and breathed into his nostrils the breath of life; and man became a living soul." Cf. also Donne, *A Valediction forbidding mourning*, ll. 1–4.

117–126 *I will; and yet* etc. Part of Scott's note is well worth repeating:

> These presages of misfortune may remind the reader of the ominous feelings of the Duke of Guise [in Dryden's play], in the scene preceding his murder. The superstitious belief, that dejection of spirits, without cause, announces an impending violent death, is simply but well expressed in an old ballad called the "Warning to all Murderers":
>
> And after this most bad pretence,
>   The gentleman each day
> Still felt his heart to throb and faint,
>   And sad he was alway.
>
> His sleep was full of deadful dreams,
>   In bed where he did lie;
> His heart was heavy in the day,
>   Yet knew no reason why.

119 *pitch*. A figurative use, from "The height to which a falcon or other bird of prey soars before swooping down on its prey" (*OED*).

120–122 *Like Fowl in air too damp* etc. From the story of Prometheus, who stole fire from the heavens to give a soul to man (Ovid, *Metamorphoses*, I, 82ff.; Horace, *Odes*, I, xvi, 13ff.; and Ross, *Mystagogus Poeticus*, pp. 225–226) and from analogous stories there came the belief that the soul was a *substance made of Fire*. In scholastic physics, it was the nature of fire and other light things to ascend (cf. Donne, *Juvenilia* [1633], Paradox I, sig. A4). Thus, Muley-Moluch, knowing his to be a soul of fire, feels its natural humour of rising heat cast over by the moisture of water, another of the four elements. As Dryden explained in the preface, 70:11–16, the Emperor died under other circumstances, and he here departs more from then known historical detail than elsewhere in the play.

120 *lugs.* To "lug" is "To move *about, along,* heavily and slowly; to drag" (*OED,* citing this use).

131–142 *It may be so* etc. "There is great art in rendering the interpretation of this ominous dream so ingeniously doubtful" (Scott). Summers compared a passage in the third act of *The Spanish Fryar:*

> Queen. At break of day, when Dreams, they say, are true,
> A drowzie slumber, rather then a sleep,
> Siez'd on my Senses.

And in his lengthy note on that passage Summers adduced parallels from many writers, e.g., Ovid, *Heroides,* XIX, 195–196; Horace, *Satires,* I, x, 32–33; etc. A simpler and clearer example is afforded by *The Cock and the Fox,* ll. 205–206.

144 *portends you.* The verb has its modern sense, but the *OED* gives no example with a person as its object.

154–157 *I'll head my People* etc. The romance *Don Sebastian* and most histories emphasized Muley-Moluch's valor and bellicosity.

162 *Skulk'd.* A typical Drydenian usage for a military or political situation (see *OED*).

163–164 *Headed a Rabble* etc. These two lines also are marked with quotation marks in the right-hand margin of the first edition.

177–184 *So when our Prophet* etc. The passage casts yet another aspersion on the Mohammedan paradise. Dryden probably has in mind chap. lv of the Koran:

> There be in these gardens [of paradise] women, who
> have eyes exceeding black, and bodies exceeding white,
> they are covered with pavillions, & none, either men or
> angels shall touch them before their husbands.

From *The Alcoran,* trans. Ross, p. 336.

188 *after Acts.* The *OED* shows the phrase to be a natural one in usage earlier than Dryden.

197–200 *Now sleep ye Stars* etc. As in l. 38, Benducar here expresses the play's theme of fate in astral terms. For the climactic usage of the image, see IV, iii, 379–380 and n.

IV, ii

30 *Did I think I had begotten such a Monster.* After a considerable interval the motif of monstrosity surfaces again. Although the Mufti uses it for Morayma's undutifulness, in the rest of the act the Mufti himself and the rabble emerge as the most monstrous.

32–56 *You have been raking together* etc. Morayma tongue-lashes her father in order to put him rather than herself on the defensive. Pidou de

St. Olon wrote (p. 105) of the Mufti's corruption, saying that his power
is so Absolute in what concerns all particular Differences
that come before him, that his Sentence admits of no
Appeal nor Delay . . . and woe to him that summons
a richer Man than himself to appear at his Tribunal,
or who is cited thither by such a one; for, the Cadies,
who are in the nature of Sub-Delegates to the Mufty in
all the Towns and Villages, always sell their Suffrages
to them who give most.

But an Englishman did not need to look so far as Morocco for evidence
of bribery and judicial corruption, nor did it require any special pains
for Dryden to be anticlerical yet again.

47 *I am finely documented* etc. To "document" is "To give a 'lesson'
to; to instruct or admonish in an authoritative or imperious manner"
(*OED*, citing this as first use).

57–61 *Prithee Child, reproach me no more* etc. Dryden allows a curious
tenderness to emerge from the Mufti's pious fraud, a symptom of the finest
form of dramatic characterization. See also ll. 84–91.

58–59 *pitch and spots of the World* etc. Cf. Ecclesiasticus, XIII, 1: "He
that toucheth pitch shall be defiled therewith; and he that hath fellowship
with a proud man shall be like unto him."

86 *dear Daddy.* Although supposedly a term of endearment (*OED*), in
Restoration drama *Daddy* usually bears a jocular or ironic cast. Cf. *Sir
Martin Mar-all*, IV, i, l. 268 (*Works*, IX, 257).

103 *Comerade.* A common spelling variant of "comrade" (*OED*).

110–111 *I laid a trap for a Bitch Fox* etc. The vixen is Johayma (see
ll. 4–16), the *worse Vermine* Antonio. "Vermin" means "those animals or
birds which prey upon preserved game," sheep, etc. (*OED*). The animal
imagery continues in the speech.

132+ *s.d. Pulls him . . . with his Sword at his reins.* Antonio moves
backward, pulling the Mufti backwards as well, with his sword in the
pit of the Mufti's back.

140–141 *my Pythagorean Father-in-Law.* "Pythagorean" means "Meta-
morphosed, transformed" (*OED*), although Dryden's usage is far stronger:
the Mufti is not only in disguise but in a sorry pickle.

154 *full in the teeth.* "Exactly, directly, straight" (*OED*).

168+ *s.d. Servants . . . behind the Scenes.* Cf. l. 172 s.d., "*Servants
within,*" etc. It will be observed how much movement about the stage is
necessary for this comic scene, and how sound is important to a supposed
night scene. At this point, Dryden uses players in the wings, offstage.
Elsewhere he uses the basic stage apron, the stage window, the depths of
the stage, indeed almost all that could be used apart from trapdoors and
machines.

173 *O here's a gate open.* Antonio exits through one of the proscenium
doors and into the world of the rabble. Within fifty or so lines the Mufti
and the comic plot generally have been wholly joined to the tragic plot.

175–176 *what, is the Devil up at Midnight.* This is apparently a version
of a proverb not found in the usual collections. Cf. Shakespeare, *1 Henry
IV*, II, iv, 325, "What doth gravity out of his bed at midnight?"

176 *herding.* To "herd" may mean "to become one of any faction or party; to associate as one of the 'common herd' or crowd" (*OED*, citing Dryden, *Aeneis*, XI, 1188).

192 *Cockatrice.* The basilisk, but "A name of reproach for a woman: prostitute, whore" (*OED*).

197 *hunt . . . dry-foot.* A figurative use of the meaning "to track game by the mere scent of the foot" (*OED*).

198 *handselling.* Although the verb properly means "To inaugurate with some ceremony or observance of an auspicious nature," it was often used ironically in such senses as "pummel," "assault" (*OED*).

219–220 *The voice of the Mobile is the voice of Heaven.* A parody of the proverb, "The voice of the people is the voice of God" (Tilley, V95, giving examples from 1450 to 1659). The earlier Latin version, *Vox populi, vox dei,* lay behind a number of books and pamphlets issued on political and religious matters before and after the Civil Wars, from the *Vox Populi* of 1641 to the *Vox Populi, Vox Dei* (by Lord Somers or Daniel Defoe) of 1709. At this point the play enters on its most intensely political episode, the rabble scene. The Mufti is obviously no populist, nor even a Moroccan Whig. But Dryden joins to the stupidity of the fickle mob the humbuggery and hypocrisy of magnates like Shaftesbury who sought to manipulate the mobile in its "street capacity." And yet, as was mentioned in the headnote, the Mufti's remark holds a truth that he himself neither recognizes nor believes in, as the mob helps save the day for the central characters of the tragic plot. Given Dryden's unquestioned royalism, the mob's role here as a providential agent may seem altogether strange. But his political views allowed for as much liberalism in the area of human agency as conservatism in the area of social institutions. See Earl Miner, *The Restoration Mode from Milton to Dryden* (1974), pp. 213, 351–356, 447–451.

IV, iii

s.d. Scene changes to the Castle-yard. For this discovery scene, the sliding shutters, or scenery panels, towards the stage front would be slid into the wings, leaving at the far rear of the stage a castle scene "discovering" or revealing before it Antonio, Mustapha, and the Rabble.

4–5 *the first Petition.* Petitions, as opposed to loyal addresses, were regarded by royalists as impertinent if not disloyal papers. See *Threnodia Augustalis,* l. 100 and n in *Works,* III, 95, 307.

6 *Abib.* "The first month of the Jewish ecclesiastical, the seventh of the civil year" (*OED*). It is also the eleventh month of the (Christian) Coptic calendar. Dryden appears to have used the first month-name with Near Eastern associations that came to his mind. Either as a renegade or as an unlettered fool, Mustapha was unlikely to know in what *year of the Hegyra* the play's action takes place. The era of the Hegira began 16 July 622. Don Sebastian fought the battle of Alcazar on 4 August 1578.

9 *resolv'd to date my Authority.* Presumably to date by the years of his reign, as for example in royal pronouncements and codes of statutes of the realm.

17 *Letters of mark.* Crown license to engage in piracy upon foreign vessels (*OED,* under *marque*). Mustapha's "license" to seize the Mufti's *prize* (l. 16) consists in his supporting mob.

20 *Ragga-muffins.* Ragged, dirty, disreputable men or boys (*OED*).

24–55 *That's dutifully done* etc. Although richly comic, Dryden's presentation of the "voice of the mobile" and of the leaders of the rabble is particularly sardonic.

31 *First Rabble.* The prominence of this character among the three "rabbles" perhaps indicates that he is "the Lieutenant" of Mustapha spoken of by Benducar in IV, i, 53. Dryden's partitive treatment of the rabble is common enough, but the use of *First Rabble, Second Rabble,* and *Third Rabble* goes very far and appears to be unique to this play. The joke is of course available only to the reader, not to the playgoer. *OED* gives "Rabbler" as "One who rabbles; one of a rabble," but gives no such meaning under "Rabble."

40–43 *If a poor Man may speak his mind* etc. This speech and this episode in the scene probably illustrate what Dryden meant by his biting line in *Absalom and Achitophel,* "Drawn to the dregs of a Democracy" (l. 227; *Works,* II, 12) which was repeated in *The Hind and the Panther,* I, 211 (*Works,* III, 129).

57 *bate.* Abate.

82–83 *you were born to be Turks* etc. *Turks* signifies both Mohammedans and tyrants. The wordplay is a device of the Mufti's oratory and is employed several times more, eliciting Antonio's comment on the Mufti's "Figures" in l. 140.

84–86 *We find that in our decay of Trade* etc. Second Rabble voices the experience of the century: religion, politics, and economics were inseparable to observers at the time and have proved no easier to distinguish in later times.

106 *the Majesty of the People.* To Dryden an absurdity, to the Mufti the phrase is an oratorical convenience.

109 *timous.* That is, "timeous," "well-timed, seasonable, opportune" (*OED*).

113+ *s.d. All cry, A Mufti . . . and are following him off the Stage.* Since Antonio seizes the Mufti onstage (see l. 178 s.d.), it is plain that as the rabble *are following* the Mufti offstage, they are called back by Mustapha (ll. 117–119) before they have actually left. It is also clear that the Mufti never really leaves the stage, and that he either rejoins the group or at least comes close enough to be easily seized.

117 *my liege People.* The *OED* shows that *liege* may be used either of the superior or the vassal in feudal and similar relations.

122 *upon a Stall.* Apparently a place of dignity, as supported by some *OED* citations.

137–138 *he only loo'd you, but 'twas I that led you.* The sense is that the Mufti urged on from a safe position behind, whereas Mustapha led them from the front. To "loo" is "To incite by shouting 'halloo'; to urge *on* by shouts" (*OED*). Dryden's usage is apparently very unusual in lacking *on* or some similar word to complete the form, but as Antonio recognizes (l. 140), Mustapha is straining to match the Mufti's "Figures" of rhetoric.

148 *spet.* Spit (*OED,* citing Dryden, *Georgics,* IV, 148).

156 *Snack.* "A share, portion, part" (first *OED* usage from 1683).

164–166 *I have a Pigeon at home* etc. Cf. Ross, trans., *The Alcoran,* "The Life and Death of Mahomet" (p. 404): "a Pigeon being by him taught to come and pick a pease out of his eare, he told them that it was the Holy Ghost that came to tell him what God would have him do." The pigeon story was a favorite Christian aspersion.

169–170 *when Kings and Queens* etc. The image from playing cards is an apt and royalist "Figure."

177 *squeaks.* The *OED* cites this as first use in the slang sense "To confess; to turn informer."

256 *Imbas'd.* Embased, degraded (*OED*).

277 *look to your hits.* The phrase means "look to your chances" (*OED,* s.v. *Hit,* citing no use before 1699).

279–281 *Our Prophet* etc. Cf. Ross, trans., *The Alcoran,* "The Life and Death of Mahomet," (p. 396):

> In the mean time, Abdemonople [Muhamed's master]
> dyed, his riches being augmented through the care and
> industry of Mahomet, who having before insinuated into
> the favour of his Mistress Aijssa, by presents of rare toyes,
> procured in his Travels, by them, or through Sorcery
> . . . so charmed her affection, that of her slave, he was
> advanced to be Lord both of her person and fortunes.

294–295 *Our Mufti's is a Green coat* etc. The central distinction is one between Moors and Christians. As both Pidou de St. Olon (p. 92, quoted below) and Thévenot (*Travels,* p. 30) reveal, the chief distinctions shown by clothes among the Moroccans was in the color of cloth for the turban, and green was reserved to "the Xeriffs, or Mahomet's Posterity." But as Thévenot (pp. 81–82) makes clear, the distinctions were broader in practice:

> generally all who are not Turks, whether Christians or
> Jews (subjects to the Grand Signior, or not) dare not
> wear Green on their Head, or any part of their Body.
> . . . The Papas, or Greek [Christian] priests, are always
> clad in Black.

309 *I thank thee Prophet.* Benducar seems to be an atheist.

312–314 *Lay down your armes* etc. Perhaps recalling Othello's speech at a lesser disturbance: "Keep up your bright swords, for the dew will rust them" (*Othello,* I, ii, 59).

322 *Sodder'd.* To "solder" may mean to make whole, heal (*OED*).

323 *ribs of Iron.* The sense is almost literal, although the phrase is common: cf. Shakespeare, *Much Ado About Nothing,* IV, i, 153; Jonson, induction to *Everyman Out of His Humour,* l. 20. See also IV, i, 98–99.

330 *Thus, when Heaven pleases* etc. Adapting Ausonius, *Epigrams,* III, 12: *et, cum fata volunt, bina venena iuvant* (Loeb trans.: "and, when the Fates will, two poisons work for good"). See the preface, 70:26 and n.

331–358 *I will not tax thee* etc. This passage suggests in tone the conventional ending of a tragicomedy, as justice appears to be restored and characters are reunited. Dorax's role in restoring order has, however, ironic possibilities that have been suggested from the first act by his role as renegade. The tension is resolved in the "duel of friends" shortly to follow. Sebastian's triumph there is ironic in view of what transpires in the last act. In other words, the false tragicomic ending prepares for the true tragic ending.

343–345 *The best that can come of me* etc. The Mufti confesses that he has proved the fool and can expect little. That is, he believes someone will beg that his life be spared and then will beg to have wardship of him as a declared idiot. A statute said to be of 17 Edward II gave to the king "the Custody of the Lands of natural Fools, taking the Profits of them without Waste or Destruction," and such profitable wardship could be dispensed as a royal favor to a subject. See *The Statutes of the Realm* (1810; repr. 1963), I, 226.

352 *sheds.* A poetic usage for huts, poor dwellings (*OED*, citing Dryden's *Baucis and Philemon*, l. 30).

355–358 *Ye mungrill work* etc. Dorax is bitterest in his contempt for the rabble; cf. the similar lines in I, 150–153.

359–360 *With gratitude as low* etc. No reader will have difficulty in understanding the metaphorical tenor of Almeyda's thanks: she now thanks Dorax with gratitude as profound as one pays to one's guardian angel, and hopes later to find time for more than words to express her gratitude. But the metaphorical vehicle, or the imagery by which the meaning is conveyed, is such as to give trouble. The *blest holy Fires* and *our Guardian Angells* are set in apposition. Dryden had reason from traditional angelology to treat angels as fires (see Robert H. West, *Milton and the Angels* [1955]). See also Psalms, CIV (Vulgate CIII), substantially repeated in Hebrews, 1, 7. The Psalmist, addressing God, says, "Thou who makest Thy angels spirits; Thy ministers a flaming fire" (*Qui facis angelos tuos spiritus et ministros tuos ignem urentem* [Hebrews: *ignem flammam*]). The interlinear gloss identifies the ministers or fires as seraphim in the Psalms passage, and the same gloss in Hebrews goes yet further: *Etiam flammam ignis, id est, seraphim qui sunt de ordine superioris facit ministros* (Also a flaming fire, that is, seraphim who are of a superior order [God] makes his ministers). See *Biblia Sacra cum Glossa Ordinaria* (Douai and Antwerp, 1617), III, cols. 1227–1228; and VI, cols. 801–802. Within the context of the theme of fate in the play, these guardian angels are treated as the tutelary spirits or "intelligences" of planets that purvey God's will to man through their astral influence.

361 *Receive these thanks; till Altars can be rais'd.* The raising of altars was thought of as a religious act of gratitude, and not only by Roman Catholics setting up altars for saints at which candles might be lit and prayers of gratitude for intercession made: see *Paradise Lost*, XI, 323–324, where Adam tells Michael that in memory of having beheld God in Eden, "So many grateful Altars I would rear / Of grassy Turf." And for a meta-

phorical use somewhat similar to Dryden's, one may compare Shakespeare, *Twelfth Night*, V, 111–114.

379–380 *But now the hand of Fate* etc. Fate is stage manager, the stage is the world, the play is life, the players men and women: the old motif is revived with wonderful ease.

394 *The long expected hour is come at length.* Cf. *To my Dear Friend Mr. Congreve*, l. 1 (*Works*, IV, 432): "Well then; the promis'd hour is come at last."

397–400 *I have not yet forgot* etc. The symmetry of the verse contrasts fundamentally with the loose prose of the rabble scene.

410 *windy.* Blustering (*OED*, citing a Dryden prose usage from 1695).

422 *That Robe of Infamy.* Apparently Dorax still has on a Moorish robe, although according to 380+ *s.d.* he has *"taken off his Turbant and put on a Peruque, Hat and Crevat."* The combination would make a strange sight, but the retaining of the robe was probably necessary to insure recognition when he re-entered.

437 *Circle.* An assembly before the king.

445 *carp'd.* Reprehended, taken exception to (*OED*).

459 *thy Man Mistress.* Minion, as Dorax says in I, 68 (and see n). In accusing the Portuguese king of homosexuality, Dorax was nearer the truth than Dryden realized.

468–475 *Why Love does all* etc. Dryden has picked up names and some sense of court intrigue from the opening pages of the romance *Don Sebastian* (see pp. 6 and 7, e.g., where "Violanta" and "Don Henry" [Dryden's "Enriquez"] will be found). The rather simple outlines of the Violante interest in the play derive, however, from the complicated sub-plot of the romance. This concerns Eugenia who is loved by Don Henry and Souza. She marries Don Henry when Souza is banished. Later, after the Battle of Alcazar and news of Don Henry's death, she marries Souza. The plot continues, but this is enough to show the nature of Dryden's borrowings and changes. The first line was singled out for praise by James Russell Lowell in his "Dryden."

470 *fraughted.* "Stored, . . . furnished, filled" (*OED*).

486–487 *Under the wing* etc. In the royal courts of Europe, England included, certain kinds of behavior, whether of talk or action, subjected the offender to punishment at the king's pleasure.

488–489 *Even in the face of Heaven* etc. Dorax seems to say that he would have struck Enriquez even at the altar.

507 *spurn.* To kick, often with an implication of contempt (*OED*), and often figurative, as here.

507–517 *Thou hast dar'd* etc. Dorax's problems have grown from what he well terms his *long Avarice of honour:* see also such other striking phrases as *honourable malice*, l. 538. Until this moment Dorax is the most disquieting person among the characters, but he is among the few to be restored to health in the play.

518 *this honour'd Order which I wear.* Sebastian wears the *Order*, that is "the badge or insignia" (*OED*) of one of the orders such as that of

the Knights Templar dedicated to defense of Christian interest in the Holy Land and enmity to the "Turk."

551–552 *The sprightly Bridegroom* etc. With the relationship of the two friends restored, we are reminded of the larger problem facing the unwary Don Sebastian.

575 *when he could no more.* The verb implied seems to be "fight": cf. ll. 570, 572.

581–583 *I knew you both* etc. Don Sebastian's blasphemous comparison of himself to God reintroduces the theme of fate in the particularly Drydenian terms of divine prescience. Dorax will shortly (ll. 588ff.) consider his *Stars*.

584–585 *Had he been tempted so* etc. Dryden here violates his usual rule of not ending two successive lines with verbs, probably for deliberate stress on *fall'n* and *stood.* He is echoing the climax of Milton's *Paradise Regained,* IV, 561–562ff.

648–649 *What, in one moment* etc. Dorax implies that he has returned to Christianity (*reconcil'd / To Heaven*).

663–669 *Some Strange reverse of Fate* etc. Sebastian's premonitions are of course traditional for a tragic hero enjoying good fortune near the end of a play, but they reinvoke the theme of fate, helping to bridge a fourth-act triumph and fifth-act catastrophe.

V, i

s.d. The Scene is a Room of State. The gradual indoor movement of the scenes is completed, forecasting a revelation of the fates of the tragic hero and heroine.

1–4 *Joy is on every face* etc. On the implications of such lore concerning the earthly paradise, see Alan Roper, "The Kingdom of Adam," in *Dryden's Poetic Kingdoms* (1965), pp. 104–135; and A. Bartlett Giamatti, *The Earthly Paradise and the Renaissance Epic* (1966).

7–12 *Pleasure has been* etc. Antonio's first verse speech has something of the quality of his prose in the trochaic character of its movement.

12–14 *If she be fated* etc. Even in this ironic jest, it is startling to discover *fated, fate,* and *Predestinated* within three lines.

20–22 *The double poisons* etc. The images of countervailing poisons and of *Civill War* leading to restored order will be found in other guises at the end of *Absalom and Achitophel,* ll. 1010–1017, and at the end of *The Medall,* ll. 287–320. Dryden here reverses the satiric trope in which cure of the body politic is likened to cure of an individual.

39 *event.* The "outcome, issue; . . . result" (*OED*).

42 *the King.* Sebastian.

54–55 *two of the four Elements.* Morayma lacks the two heavy elements, water and earth.

65–67 *Little Devill if you please* etc. Morayma represents herself as Mephistopheles come to claim the pledged soul and body of Faustus.

77 *Not a mouthfull a piece.* Morayma so small, the rabble so many, she could furnish them no better.

92–93 *thy inexorable windows.* *OED* gives no precedent for *inexorable* so used. It means incapable of being persuaded or moved by the entreaties of gallants (or so Antonio hopes); alternatively, he may be acknowledging her *inexorable* charms.

117+ *s.d. Re-enter* etc. The latter part of this stage direction shows the social ceremony and stage action completing the reconciliation of the tragic and comic plots.

122–123 *Yet one thing wants* etc. The tragic peripeteia begins with this speech fraught with dramatic irony.

128+ *s.d. Enter Alvarez* etc. It is difficult to see why Dryden wishes the servant to leave the stage as soon as he has escorted Alvarez on, apart from a sense of decorum that the revelations about to come must be confined to the principal characters: see ll. 251–261.

143–144 *Such is my hast* etc. The image of *Fate* as "A falling house" (l. 139) is all too appropriate for the king and kingdom of Portugal, and Alvarez' haste merely heightens the dramatic irony.

145–150 *The Tempest is ore-blown* etc. From early in his career Dryden uses nautical imagery, and particularly that of shipwreck, to imply human ruin by fate or fortune, or sometimes merely by one's own action. In *Annus Mirabilis,* ll. 137–140, he expands on Petronius. In his translation of Horace, *Ode 29. Book 3,* he expands on the Horatian imagery (st. x; *Works,* III, 84). And the imagery is recurrent in other plays as well; for example, in *All for Love.*

199 *Tallyes.* A "tally" is "Each of the two corresponding halves or parts of anything; . . . a counterpart" (*OED*).

209 *Calenture.* "A disease incident to sailors within the tropics, characterized by delerium in which the patient, it is said, fancies the sea to be green fields, and desires to leap into it" (*OED*).

217–218 *But now decay'd* etc. The image is that of a nearly expired candle.

241 *Come down from off thy Tripos* etc. Summers compared with this line Dryden's comment on Aeschylus in *The Grounds of Criticism in Tragedy* prefixed to *Troilus and Cressida* (1679, sig. bv; Watson, I, 254): "The Inspiration was still upon him, he was ever tearing it upon the Tripos."

255 *nice as Ermines* etc. The fastidiousness of ermines is well illustrated by the *OED* quotation of William Garnall, *The Christian in Compleat Armour* (1669), p. 322: "The Ermine . . . will dye before she will be got into the dirt to defile her beautiful skin." Alvarez' ermine emblem receives its counterpart in the swan emblem of Almeyda's reply (ll. 263–265).

263–265 *my honour like a rising Swan* etc. As Sebastian recognizes (l. 266), the swan was an emblem of the "pure simplicity of truth" (*Simplicitas veri sana*), of "clear faith and clear morals" (*Fides candida, candique mores*), etc. See Henry Green, *Shakespeare and the Emblem Writers* (1870), pp. 215–217. Dryden may also have recalled the opening lines of the most famous of the *Heroides,* Dido to Aeneas: *Sic ubi fata vocant, udis abjectus in herbis / ad vada Mæandri concinit albus olor* (Dryden trans. [*Works*, I, 132]: "So, on *Mæander*'s banks, when death is nigh, / The mournful *Swan* sings her own Elegie").

302 *I'le believe the Phœnix*. That is, I'll believe the Phoenix exists. The Phoenix is an emblem of the king (as this line shows somewhat paradoxically) because only one of the species exists at a time.

355 *his Soul wou'd want her Heav'n*. Because *anima* (soul) is feminine in Latin gender, Dryden uses feminine pronouns in referring to a man's soul. This is normal in the century: cf. Donne, *Of the Progress of the Soul (Second Anniversary)*, ll. 191 ff.

374 *The black Adult'ry*. See IV, i, 1n.

395 *a rattling peal to eithers Conscience*. Cf. *Alexander's Feast*, l. 127, "And rouze him, like a rattling Peal of Thunder." Thunder, peals, and bolts of lightning often stand for ecclesiastical remonstrances, excommunications, etc. The genitive form *eithers* has one example (1548) given by *OED*, s.v. *Either*. 4.

437–440 *Ye Cruell Powers* etc. Notwithstanding his passion, Don Sebastian raises the issue of human agency or freedom in a world of fate.

440+ *s.d. Antonio and Alv. lay hold on him* etc. See the illustration facing p. 207 from an edition of the play in 1735. A number of eighteenth-century editions of *Don Sebastian* have as frontispiece a picture of this scene designed by Hubert François Gravelot—illustrator of Shakespeare and Dryden's plays—and engraved by Michael Van der Gucht. It shows three men struggling to prevent the king's suicide, a scene clearly regarded as one of the most memorable in the play. Sebastian's attempted action must be understood in the ironic light of his Christian counsel to Almeyda against taking her life: see II, i, 526–529 and n.

454–455 *That yet must languish long, in frosts and fires* etc. This allusion to what Summers termed "the temporal punishments of purgatory" is the more remarkable after 1688 for the fact that the doctrine of purgatory was one that Dryden had avoided in *The Hind and the Panther*. Of course, as a Portuguese and a Catholic, Sebastian does not speak out of character or milieu.

464 *Writ of ease*. Although the phrase has various figurative or adapted usages, its basic sense is "a certificate of discharge from employment" (*OED*) Cf. *The Hind and the Panther*, III, 745.

468 *What, to destroy himself, O Parricide*. In English Common Law, parricide is not restricted to murder of one's father. A *Parricide* is "One who murders his father or either parent, or other near relative; also, the murderer of any one whose person is considered specially sacred as being the ruler of the country" (*OED*). The *OED* quotes Clarendon's *History of the Grand Rebellion*, XI, 244 on the execution of Charles I: "This unparalleled murder and parricide was committed on the 30th of January." Dryden stretches the matter a bit farther: because Sebastian's suicide would also be regicide of a kind, the act would make him a parricide.

522 *Scriv'ner*. Although the word "scrivener" originally meant "a scribe, copyist; a clerk," and later took on the sense of a "notary," during the seventeenth century it was more commonly used, as here, for "one who 'received money to place out at interest, and who supplied those who

wanted to raise money on security'" (*OED*). As a money-lender, the scrivener charged somewhat less interest than the *Usurer* Dryden next mentions. But the distinction was a fine one.

524 *by advance*. It is not clear whether the phrase is an alternative one for "in advance," or whether *advance* here means "A personal approach; . . . an overture" (*OED*, citing a passage in *All for Love* as the first such usage).

525 *And gives all gone before-hand*. Dryden means a politician treats everything as lost spiritually from the outset.

528 *irremeable*. "Admitting of no return; from, by, or through which there is no return" (*OED*, citing Dryden, *Aeneis*, VI, 575).

539 *palliate*. Dryden plays on two senses. One, the literal, relates to his image of *wound*: "To alleviate the symptoms"; the other relates to Dryden's figurative meaning: "To disguise or colour the real enormity of (an offense) by favourable representations or excuses; . . . to cause to appear less guilty or offensive by urging extenuating circumstances" (*OED*).

550–551 *Affrick has desarts* etc. The monsters-of-Africa motif (see above, I, i, 372 and II, i, 370–372 and notes) surprisingly but justly, in view of the incest taboo, comes to rest on Don Sebastian.

554–555 *A Scepter's but a play-thing* etc. The lines present a somewhat special version of the common idea that the games of children are mirrors of the serious business of adults.

559–561 *Old as he is* etc. The romance *Don Sebastian* related the confusion in Portugal following the battle of Alcazar: "the Council was at length constrained to appease the Murmurs of the People, to cause Cardinal Henry to come out of the Abby of Calcobassa, to which place he was retired, and to proclaim him Governour General of the Kingdom" (II, 30). Historical accounts available to Dryden give a different picture of "Cardinal Henry" as senile and not wholly sane: see *A Genealogical History of the Kings of Portugal*, trans. Francis Sandford (1662), p. 82.

573 *And needs no farther forge*. The less common sense of *forge* is meant: "A hearth or furnace for melting or refining metals" (*OED*). Muley-Zeydan, that is, is already pure and well cast.

603–607 *Ah why were we not born* etc. Throughout the seventeenth century writers were ill at ease in philosophical defense of love, unless it were Christian charity or the nuptial love necessary to the race. Robert Burton gives the fullest analysis of the passion of love in *The Anatomy of Melancholy*, Partition III. No such doubts existed on the subject of friendship, which had the sanction of Plato, Aristotle, and Cicero, although overtones of homosexuality (see IV, iii, 459n) were also possible. Dryden concisely expressed his and his century's views in *The Grounds of Criticism in Tragedy* prefixed to *Troilus and Cressida* (1679, sig. b3v; Watson, I, 260): "Friendship is both a virtue, and a Passion essentially; love is a passion only in its nature, and is not a virtue but by Accident: good nature makes Friendship; but effeminacy Love."

629–631 *And I shou'd break through Laws* etc. For another comparison of man with beasts, see II, i, 396–399. A number of passages in Beaumont and Fletcher's play, *A King and No King*, anticipate this passage. (Citations of *A King and No King* refer to *The Works of Beaumont and Fletcher,* ed. Henry Weber [Edinburgh, 1812], XII.) For example, speaking of his love for his presumed sister Anthea, Arbaces says (III, i; p. 190):

> Such an ungodly sickness I have got,
> That he, that undertakes my cure, must first
> O'rethrow divinity, all moral laws,
> And leave mankind as unconfin'd as beasts.

And Tigranes tells Arbaces (III, i; p. 192):

> Such incivilities
> As these no barbarous people ever knew:
> You break the laws of nature, and of nations.

Or, two further passages spoken by Arbaces (IV, [iv]; p. 233 and IV, [iv]; p. 235):

> Know, that I have lost,
> The only difference betwixt man and beast,
> My reason.

> Accursed man,
> Thou bought'st thy reason at too dear a rate;
> For thou hast all thy actions bounded in
> With curious rules, when every beast is free.

The headnote touches on Dryden's high estimate of this play and his likely indebtedness to it.

639 *denouncer.* "One who announces, proclaims, declares" (*OED,* citing this use).

646 *Your fate has gratify'd you all she can.* The line is clear enough in general meaning, but some details repay attention. The concept that means so much to the play, *fate,* is feminine for the Latin gender of *fata.* She has *gratify'd* Sebastian in the sense of to "oblige; . . . do a favour to" him (*OED*). And interestingly enough, his *fate* herself is limited in power.

663 *close.* As an intransitive verb, it means "to join, unite, combine" (*OED*).

674 *savage.* "Of a plant, tree, etc.: Wild, uncultivated" (*OED*).

675 *wholesome bev'rage, and unbloudy feasts.* In *Fables,* Dryden was to include the well-known passage from Ovid's *Metamorphoses,* XV, in which good King Numa preaches to his people the vegetarian doctrine of Pythagoras.

677 *conscious of.* "Knowing, or sharing the knowledge of anything, together with another; privy to anything with another" (*OED*).

685 *I have a Sister, Abbesse in Tercera.* "Terceira, an island of the Azores, was so called (*Terceira,* the third) as being the third island of that archipelago discovered by the Portuguese. . . . The former capital of Terceira was Angra . . . [which] is an ecclesiastical see, and the convent to which Almeyda retires is a Franciscan house either of Poor Clares or of Capuchin nuns" (Summers). It seems more likely that Dryden simply took a hint from the romance *Don Sebastian* [IV, 92–93], where we read that "four Deputies from the Isles of Terceras [Dryden's spelling], came to

Court [in Portugal] to Inform that Don Sebastian was newly Landed in their Island [after escaping the Moors], and was lodged in the Convent of the Cordeliers." In the romance, Sebastian later (IV, 145) mentions the island, the convent, and Angra in telling Almeida of his adventures.

691 *recess.* "The (*or* an) act of retirement from public life or into privacy; the fact of living retired or in a private manner; a period of retirement" (*OED*, citing *To the Dutchess of Ormond,* l. 163).

702 *And bless thy Violante.* See IV, iii, 468–475n.

707–711 *last farewell . . . my last Sebastian.* Cf. III, i, and n.

722 *Your Father.* Morayma's, the Mufti.

EPILOGUE

If the prologue had shown Dryden daring in the risks he ran by flaunting his Catholicism, the epilogue shows that he chose to leave his audience thinking thoughts no more dangerous than those held by the two wags, Antonio and Morayma, although there is a last glance and tip at the audience in the closing couplet (ll. 35–36).

5 *I trembled when the Old Mans hand was in.* The old man is of course Don Alvarez, who reveals the blood relationship between Sebastian and Almeyda. The expression *hand was in* is perhaps parallel to one given by the *OED*, "*To have one's hand in:* to be actively engaged, to be in habitual practice, to be at it," but a degree of interference or of unwelcomeness seems implied by Dryden's phrase.

Amphitryon

The date Dryden completed *Amphitryon* and the date it was first performed are alike unknown. The first known performance was on Tuesday, 21 October 1690, by the United Company at Drury Lane. It is thought, however, that it may have been performed earlier in the month, when the playhouse was opened.[1] A warrant in the Lord Chamberlain's department of the Public Record Office relating to plays acted includes a cancellation of two boxes ordered for Queen Mary, an enthusiastic theatergoer, and her Maids of Honor. The warrant was for a performance of this play on April 30th.[2] It is not clear why the performance was cancelled. Cibber reported that Dryden had read the play to the company—very lamely:

> When he brought his Play of *Amphitryon* to the Stage, I heard him give it his first Reading to the Actors, in which, though it is true he deliver'd the plain Sense of every Period, yet the whole was in so cold, so flat, and unaffecting a manner, that I am afraid of not being believ'd when I affirm it.[3]

For a less experienced playwright such a reading might have been necessary to secure acceptance, but it is more likely in Dryden's case that he was seeking to instruct the players in his conception of the play.[4] If the play was scheduled for performance in April, the reading must have been sometime before that; therefore it is likely that the play was completed early in 1690. It may even have been performed as early as the spring of 1690, since no evidence to the contrary exists, and since Queen Mary had had warrants drawn. But it was certainly performed in October, and the delay between spring and autumn (if there was a delay) may have been caused by difficulty in getting proper music for the play, or in getting a proper cast.[5]

---

[1] Van Lennep, p. 389.

[2] Allardyce Nicoll, *A History of English Drama* (1961), I, 352. Van Lennep (p. 381) suggests that John Crowne's *Sir Courtly Nice* may have replaced a scheduled *Amphitryon* on 30 April, and he cites the entry given by Nicoll as evidence. At all events, there is evidence that Dryden's play was being readied for the stage in the spring but that for some reason production was delayed.

[3] Cibber, *Apology*, ed. R. W. Lowe (1888), I, 113. In this well-known passage, Cibber goes on to praise Nathaniel Lee, as a much better reader though less of an author.

[4] Emmett L. Avery, ed., *The London Stage, 1660–1800*, Pt. 2: 1700–1729 (1960), I, cl.

[5] Dryden's remark in the dedication that in Purcell "we have at length found an *English-man*, equal with the best abroad" (225:17–18) no doubt implies, as Scott suggested, that Dryden was but recently converted to English music; but it may also imply some difficulty before Purcell was engaged, in getting satisfactory music for the play.

As Dryden intimates in the dedication, both the music and the play itself met with a very favorable reception. The printed version was advertised in the *London Gazette* for 30 October—3 November 1690,[6] and was published in a second issue dated 1691. A second edition appeared in 1694.[7] The play was in fact one of Dryden's greatest theatrical successes over the years. The favorable contemporary reaction is clear from a letter to Dryden's publisher, Tonson, from of all people, Luke Milbourne, giving unsolicited praise of the play and ordering certain of Dryden's works to be sent to him at Yarmouth in Norfolk. Dryden would not have felt unalloyed joy at reading the verses enclosed. Milbourne began by patting Dryden on the back: "Hail, Prince of Witts! thy fumbling Age is past, / Thy youth and witt and art's renew'd at last." [8] Later on, the provincial admirer comes to the reasons for Dryden's success:

> Not Phœbus could with gentler words pursue
> His flying Daphne, not the morning dew
> Falls softer then the words of amorous Jove,
> When melting, dying, for Alcmene's love.
> Yet briske and airy too, thou fill'st the stage,
> Unbroke by fortune, undecayed by age.
> French wordy witt by thine was long surpast;
> Now Rome's thy captive, and by thee wee taste
> Of their rich dayntyes; but so finely drest,
> Theirs was a country meal, thine a triumphant feast.

Milbourne was kind enough to think that Dryden might go on completely to "endenizen" Plautus, presumably by rendering the whole canon into English versions. We notice that in his own fumbling and ungrammatical way Milbourne presumes that Dryden has outdone the Roman and French competition.

Dryden must have taken more pleasure from the public reception of the play. There were obviously performances of it that have not been recorded. Only two are known in 1690—on 21 October and 1 November.[9] For the latter, performed at the Inner Temple, the company received the customary fee of £20.[10] Since in the dedication Dryden speaks of his author's third night, it seems obvious that so popular a play is likely to have been performed periodically in 1690 and 1691. It is also very possible that the publication of the edition of 1694 implies a revival of the play about that time.[11] And from the more abundant evidence in the next century one discovers a stage popularity that was more likely to have continued from the last decade of Dryden's life than to have begun suddenly after his death. The records are in fact very spotty. There are no records known of performance between November 1690 and May 1705. Between May 1705 and May 1717, however, nineteen performances are

---

[6] Publication so soon after the first known performance on 21 October suggests either a more unusually favorable reception than Dryden implies or, what is more likely, that the play was produced before that first known date.

[7] See Macdonald, pp. 146–148 for collections of editions of plays between 1691 and 1701.

[8] For the poem, see Malone, I, 315–317. [9] Van Lennep, pp. 389, 391.

[10] *Ibid.*, p. 391. [11] *Ibid.*, p. 426.

mentioned, all but four being at Drury Lane.[12] The record is blank between May 1717 and November 1729, but in the seven years thereafter
eighteen performances are recorded, again mostly at Drury Lane.[13] Summers reported discovering a playbill of Drury Lane for a performance on
28 April 1747, claiming that the play was "not acted 9 years," which implies a performance in 1738 that is now unknown. The performance of
April, 1747 would be a significant one, because it would be the last known
presentation before 15 December 1756, when Hawkesworth's emasculated
version appeared. It is not any clearer than usual what Summers' evidence
may be, but he stated that the play was performed eleven times in the
season of 1756. Throughout the rest of the eighteenth century and in
the nineteenth, the play suffered increasing indignity, being made into
a ballad opera by the elder Dibdin in 1781 and dwindling to a two-act
farce in 1826.[14] Summers himself directed *Amphitryon* for the Phœnix
Society on 28 and 30 May 1922 in what he believed to be the first complete performance of Dryden's text since 1747.

It can be seen that there were undoubtedly more performances than
those known with certainty today, and especially more during Dryden's
lifetime. Even from the partial evidence available, *Amphitryon,* of all
Dryden's plays, was second in popularity only to *The Spanish Fryar* in
the eighteenth century. It is ironic that a playwright who claimed his gift
was more for tragedy than for comedy should have kept his popularity
longest in the lighter genre. *Amphitryon* met the severe test of the change
in taste about the turn of the century, and that triumph was due in no
small part to the fact that Dryden had built his play, as he himself
acknowledged in the dedication, on the firm bases provided by Plautus
and Molière, "the two greatest Names of Ancient and Modern Comedy."

The extent of Dryden's debt, especially to Molière, has been disputed,
as have the relative merits of the various plays. One who is committed to
the study of Plautus may hold that Molière has cheapened the Roman
story into "an ordinary comedy of intrigue," and that both Molière and
Dryden morally cheapen the Roman play.[15] Some, including Sir Walter
Scott, have held that Dryden coarsened Molière, but that both of the
moderns were superior to Plautus. Perhaps the only critic to judge with
an intimate knowledge of all three literatures was George Saintsbury, who
qualified Scott's judgment:

> I do not think that Scott has quite fully stated the
> advantages which remain to Dryden after a perusal of
> the three *Amphitryons.* . . . The Roman poet is the

---

[12] Nineteen are recorded by Emmett L. Avery, ed., *The London Stage,* Pt. 2:
1700–1729 (1960), and two others by Summers.

[13] Arthur H. Scouten, ed., *The London Stage, 1660–1800,* Pt. 3:1729–1747 (1961).
Since seventeenth-century accounts usually record only one day in a run,
whereas eighteenth-century accounts are fuller, we should probably make allowance upward for relative popularity in Dryden's lifetime.

[14] Summers, VI, 146. His evidence is usually a playbill of unspecified
provenance.

[15] W. B. Sedgwick, ed., Plautus, *Amphitruo* (1960), pp. 8–9.

most humorous of the three, as Molière is the most decent in treating a situation where to be decent without being dull is a proof of consummate art. But in the life and bustle proper to comedy Dryden excels both his formidable predecessors.

As a brief judgment, that seems likeliest to hold, and it can be appreciated the more by examining the Amphitryon story on which all three versions are based. The legend of Zeus going to Alcmena predated the sixth century B.C., as surviving depictions testify,[16] and Amphitryon's expedition against the Teleboans was attested to by Herodotus. Sophocles wrote an *Amphitryo* and Euripides an *Alcmene,* and there was a Latin *Alcmena,* probably by Ennius, or possibly by Pacuvius. Plautus was probably indebted to yet other versions, although because it is so illogically handled, his story of the birth of Hercules is likely to be a hasty addition of his own.[17] In brief,

> the myth as we have it in Plautus started from Sophocles' [*Amphitryo*] and reached the New Comedy via Plato. [Plautus'] source was a play of the New Comedy, though he may have taken hints from Southern Italian farce. But he who made possible [Plautus'] play was the unknown poet who first added Sosia.[18]

No other classical comedy rivals the Amphitryon story in continuity. Although condemned by early church fathers, it was the only one of Plautus' plays to be current, though in modified form, in the Middle Ages. It was not only performed publicly in the Renaissance but also was the second to be translated into English.[19] During the sixteenth century it was given three Spanish versions, two Italian, and one Portuguese, by Camões himself. Molière's great version was heavily indebted to the very

---

[16] Our information about classical versions derives from Sedgwick and from the much more detailed account by L. R. Shero, "Alcmena and Amphitryon in Drama," *Transactions of the American Philological Association,* 87 (1956), 192–238. Shero identifies fifty-five versions (excluding translations and slight adaptations) from antiquity to 1950. Of these, Plautus' is fourteenth, Molière's thirty-first, and Dryden's thirty-fifth. A discussion of the major versions by C. D. N. Costa, "The Amphitryo Theme," will be found in *Roman Drama,* ed. T. A. Dorey and Donald R. Dudley (1965); see pp. 101–107 on Dryden. Most classicists bristle over Dryden's depiction of the pagan gods and his dismissal of the pagan outlook by demeaning it. The ensuing discussion of Dryden's differing characterization of his human and divine characters will bear out what one classicist has to say of Dryden's treatment of the pagan: see Norman Austin, as in note 29 below.

[17] Plautus confuses the question whether Jupiter visited Alcmena twice or several times, whether the first was seven months or one night before the birth of Hercules; and so it remains unclear whether Jupiter's fondness is for a woman pregnant with his own and Amphitryo's child or whether Jupiter's intimacy with Alcmena speeds gestation.

[18] Sedgwick, ed., *Amphitruo,* p. 6.

[19] See the anonymous version, *The Birthe of Hercules,* ed. R. Warwick Bond for the Malone Society (1911).

successful *Les Sosies* of Rotrou (1638) or, under its later title, *La Naissance d'Hercule* (1650). Molière's *Amphitryon* was first performed on 13 January 1668 at the Théâtre du Palais-Royal. Numerous continental versions followed Molière's, including a Christianized play by Burmeister, in which the scene is Nazareth and Alcmena is the Virgin Mary; an *Amphitryon* by Kleist; and, in our own day, Giraudoux' *Amphitryon 38*, his number implying which version he thought his to be.

The English tradition of the play dated back to an imitation of Plautus' *Amphitruo*, ll. 273ff. in the interlude, *Jacke Juggler* (*ca.* 1550), and took on a fuller though still partial shape in John Marston's *What You Will* (1607), which combines features of the Ulysses and Amphitryon stories.[20] But the first English play to incorporate Plautus' story as a central feature is *The Silver Age* by Thomas Heywood (1613). The rest of the title gives a fuller description: *The Love of Jupiter to Alcmena: The Birth of Hercules. And the Rape of Proserpine. Concluding, with the Arraignement of the Moone.* It is a farrago, including thirty-two named characters and such others as "The seven Planets." Only its middle section concerns Amphitryon, Alcmena, and Sosia. Heywood followed Plautus closely, even to the point of confusion over the length of time Jupiter had been making love to Alcmena and of having her carry a child of Amphitryon's to be born with Hercules. Both its rattling survey of so many other classical stories and its closeness to Plautus give some weight to Summers' comment that "Even if Dryden glanced at this old drama it would not have served even a hint for *Amphitryon*." Summers is likely to be right on other grounds: no Restoration performance of Heywood's play is known and it had not been republished after 1630. There are, however, episodes near the beginning and end of Dryden's play that resemble *The Silver Age*, rather than the plays of Plautus or Molière.[21] In Act I of Dryden's play there is a resemblance to Heywood's depiction of Jupiter arriving in the guise of Amphitryon, although the circumstances differ. More like, and more important, is Dryden's scene in Act V, where Alcmena chooses the wrong Amphitryon as her husband. The choice and what it implies makes her role more important than it is in Plautus or Molière, and it is just possible that Dryden had read Heywood, whom he refers to slightingly in *Mac Flecknoe*, l. 102.[22] The evidence is after all too slight to be conclusive. The very few verbal resemblances, which are given in the commentary, are like the resemblances in plot: possibilities that might have occurred to Dryden or any playwright in developing the story.

There can be no doubt, however, of Dryden's debt to Plautus and, more specially, to Molière. The debt is apt to seem very great when one reads any pair together, although what was said of Molière's debt to Plautus as opposed to Rotrou can be applied to Dryden's use of Plautus as opposed to Molière: "it would have been easier for him to dispense

---

[20] See Marston, *The Works*, ed. A. H. Bullen (1887), II, 319.

[21] See Margaret Kober Merzbach, "The Third Source of Dryden's *Amphitryon*," *Anglia*, LXXIII (1955), 213–214.

[22] Dryden's disparaging reference in *Mac Flecknoe* probably was aimed at the less serious works of Heywood, which were reprinted during the Restoration.

with the former than the latter." [23] In the dedication Dryden claimed that "more than half of it is mine," that is, not indebted to either the Roman or the French dramatist. It is possible to read the plays for indebtedness simply by examining differences. Charts comparing characters and plotting in the versions by Dryden, Molière, and Plautus appear in an appendix to this volume, pp. 553–556 below.

The chart of characters (p. 553 below) reveals that Molière's innovation consists of an induction with La Nuit—which Dryden mostly follows, though not in an induction-style prologue—and the introduction of the Theban captains, whose presence gives a heroic air lacking in Plautus and only suggested in Dryden. Dryden follows Plautus in the names of characters. And he introduces a whole new plot by bringing in Phædra, Mercury's "Queen of the Gypsies," and Gripus, her paramour judge. This novelty integrated the preexisting story beyond Molière's version, which had one love triangle, Jupiter-Amphitryon-Alcmena, and a parallel plot involving Sosie and Cléanthis. Dryden added two triangles to the first: Mercury-Gripus-Phædra and Mercury-Sosia-Bromia (with some glance at a third including Jupiter-Juno-Alcmena). Dryden's version is the only one of the three with a triple plot, and yet in spite of the greater activity of his play, its action remains as clear as Molière's. The chart comparing acts and scenes (pp. 554–556) reproduces Molière's divisions, but subdivides Dryden's play on the basis of new entrances and exits, and divides Plautus' play by line numbers. Although the chart shows resemblances between the three plays, paralleling of scenes does not necessarily imply verbal debt or identical action.

The only other objective comparison possible is that of phrasing and idea, and resemblances of this kind are given in the notes.[24] Yet it is the less specifiable that first strikes the reader or playgoer with a sense of the difference between versions. During Dryden's lifetime, these more subjective differences contributed to a belief that he had improved on Plautus and Molière, as we have already seen to some extent in Milbourne's remarks. Similarly, the translator of *Plautus's Comedies* (1694) said of Dryden that "he has not only much improved the Humor, Wit, and Design in many places, but likewise the Thoughts," giving as an in-

---

[23] Henry Carrington Lancaster, *A History of French Dramatic Literature in the Seventeenth Century* (1963), Pt. III, vol. ii, 513.

[24] Dryden's use of Molière, if not of Plautus, has received considerable attention. Two of the most useful and detailed studies are Carl Hartmann, *Einfluss Molière's auf Dryden's Komisch-Dramatische Dichtungen* (Leipzig, 1885), which juxtaposes quotations from Dryden and Molière; and Max Besing, *Molieres Einfluss auf das englische Lustspiel bis 1700* (Borna-Leipzig, 1913). Other studies include W. Moseley Kerby, *Molière and the Restoration Comedy in England* (1907); Dudley Howe Miles, *The Influence of Molière on Restoration Comedy* (1910); and John Wilcox, *The Relation of Molière to Restoration Comedy* (1938), the best of the three. Some things about Molière's sources of use to readers of Dryden's play will be found in Nathan Bock, *Molière's Amphitryon im Verhältnis zu seinen Vorgängern* (Marburg, 1887); but the student of Dryden can consult much more usefully Henri Van Laun, trans., *The Dramatic Works of Molière* (Edinburgh, 1875–1876), whose detailed introduction and translation appear in IV, 229–331.

stance Alcmena's speech, beginning "Ye niggard gods!" on Jupiter's parting from her at dawn.[25] The compliment is no doubt partisan and it
omits to consider Molière. On both grounds the comments by Gerard
Langbaine, no friend to Dryden, provide a remarkable tribute:

> This Play is founded on Plautus's *Amphytruo,* and
> Molliere's *Amphytryon,* as the Author himself acknowl-
> edges in his Epistle Dedicatory. The Reader that will
> take the pains to compare them, will find that Mr. Dry-
> den has more closely followed the French, than the Latin
> Poet: but however it must with Justice be allowed, that
> what he has borrowed, he has improv'd throughout;
> and Molliere is as much exceeded by Mr. Dryden, as
> Rotrou is outdone by Molliere.[26]

As Saintsbury suggested, however, there is in Molière a special form of
"decency" or dignity to be found neither in Plautus nor Dryden. He con-
centrates more than does Dryden upon Amphitryon and, while not sacri-
ficing the comic spirit either to dignity or mere wit, he accommodates a
great deal of both, as a remark by La Nuit in her third speech shows to
perfection: "mais il faut sans cesse / Garder le decorum de la Divinité."
The one serious fault in Molière's version, as judged by the standards of
the English theater, is his tendency to long and often high-flown speeches.
Sosie's first speech is acceptable, although more than a hundred lines long,
but no English audience could accept numerous lengthy and rarified
declamations.

By comparison, Dryden's version suffers from a want of "decency," to
use Saintsbury's word, but it is far more convincing because, again as
Saintsbury observed, it has so much more life. It is natural motivation
rather than mere poetry, and the bustle of English comedy rather than
sentiment that makes his play hum. Plautus manages to be comic and
mythic, Molière comic and dignified. Dryden is comic and human, and
for all three, much of their effect comes from their styles. The dignity of
Molière's style comes in considerable measure from a lovely language
directed by decorum, but his effects also depend upon the fact that the
play is entirely in verse, and verse of an especially varied kind. The lines
of twelve, ten, eight, and seven syllables are variously interwoven and
rhymed, giving an effect not unlike an enormously lengthened and theatrical English "pindarique." Plautus also uses only verse, and verse given
considerable variety by the breaking of lines in dialogue and the introduction of passages of shorter lines. Dryden's style does not resemble that
of either of his predecessors very closely, but if we regard the blank verse
portions—as we probably must—as a step toward the very broken and
free blank verse of his next play but one, *Cleomenes,* then it is more
likely that Plautus rather than Molière was an inspiration. But what most
sharply distinguishes Dryden's style from the others' is his generous use

---

[25] *Plautus's Comedies,* preface, sig. b3v. The author and translator was
Laurence Eachard; see John Barnard, ed., *Prefaces to Terence's Comedies and
Plautus's Comedies* (Augustan Reprint Society Publication, 1968).

[26] Langbaine, *English Dramatick Poets* (Oxford, 1691), Appendix, sig. Oo1v.

of prose. By giving Sosia verse, Plautus and Molière had, so to speak, raised him to the level of Amphitryon and the gods. Dryden's use of prose in comedy is of course very English, and that medium is especially fitted to give life to Sosia and the other lower characters. What prose cannot do, on the other hand, is to maintain the same dignity that Molière so consistently upholds. Dryden even gives Jupiter some prose dialogue. This and other emphases that will be considered have the effect of lowering the dignity of those characters that would most naturally seem to require it: Jupiter and his fellow Olympian deities.

The mingling of prose and verse of several levels afforded Dryden a greater variety of language and tone than is to be found in his great predecessors. Much of the vitality of his play originates in his eagerness to be earthy, to express fully in vigorous English prose what Molière hints at in elevated verse. There are numerous instances of Dryden's use of highly colloquial language ranging from cant to proverb and aphorism. The wit directing the language is often shaded by a comic disillusion. Sometimes there is the familiar Restoration chime (IV, i, 143–145):

> *Mercury.* Softly, Friend, softly: You knock as loud,
> and as sawcily, as a Lord's Footman, that was sent before
> him, to warn the Family of his Honour's Visit.

Sometimes the wit depends upon an originality of language, as when Sosia, having been beaten by Mercury, protests, "you are so very flippant with your Hands, you won't hear Reason" (II, i, 157–158). The wit may also depend upon ideas rather than words, as when Amphitryon, kept outside his own house by Mercury-Sosia, loftily declares (IV, i, 152–154):

> *Amph.* I am one that can command the doors open.
> *Merc.* Then you had best command 'em, and try
> whether they will obey You.

And there is often that mingling of the realistic and the imaginative that is in the best English tradition, as when Gripus describes Amphitryon barred from his own house (IV, i, 203–205):

> Yonder he is; walking hastily to and fro, before his
> door; like a Citizen [shopkeeper], clapping his Sides
> before his Shop, in a frosty Morning: 'tis to catch a
> Stomach, I believe.

Dryden had never lost this quality in his comedy, but after such early plays as *The Wild Gallant* and *Sir Martin Mar-all,* the earthiness had been gradually refined away by repartée. What those early plays did not have was the higher reaches of style conveyed in the blank verse and occasional rhymed verse of *Amphitryon.*

Dryden's success in combining such different stylistic gradations is due in considerable part to his maintaining gradations of decorum in style to match the situation, and partly to the fact that the concentration of speech in the witty prose is matched by another kind of concentration in the verse. Jupiter tells Alcmena at one point, "The being happy is not half the Joy; / The manner of the happiness is all" (II, ii, 81–82). Such point and aphorism is given to Jupiter and suits Jovian sententiousness. What is important is not so much the mere differentiation of character

as the significance of differentiation, as a contrast between Jupiter's point
or antithesis and Alcmena's simpler truth will easily show. He continues
from the lines just quoted (II, ii, 83–89):

> In me (my charming Mistris) you behold
> A Lover that disdains a Lawful Title;
> Such as of Monarchs to successive Thrones:
> The Generous Lover holds by force of Arms;
> And claims his Crown by Conquest.
> *Alcmena.* Methinks you shou'd be pleas'd, I give you all
> A Vertuous and a Modest Wife can give.

Dryden clearly gives Jupiter the Hobbism of some of his questionable
characters in the heroic plays and opposes to it normal human decency.
The fact that indecency in the play depreciates the gods shows that questions of style inevitably raise others of theme and tone.

Any modern writer treating the Amphitryon story is faced at once with
the problem of what to make of the gods and, in necessary connection,
of how to assess man's role in relation to them. Molière addresses a little
very well-mannered wit at the gods, but "le decorum de la Divinité" is
safe in his hands. His Mercure is a bully, but the cruelty is that of a
nobleman beating a peasant—and it is just this relation between the gods
and man that his play sets forth. Jupiter "is certainly a seventeenth-
century *grand seigneur* in search of *bonnes fortunes,*" and although most
critics reject the belief that the play portrays the seduction of Mme. de
Montespan by Louis XIV,[27] Jupiter behaves very much in the fashion of
that Most Christian Monarch. Molière has a hierarchy from Jupiter to
Mercure, to Amphitryon and Alcmène, to the Theban Captains, down at
last to Sosie and Cléanthis. It is a rigid class structure, like that of France
at the time. At the end, Amphitryon has learned to accept, as he must, his
place in that hierarchy; and Molière touches such pathos that he can
maintain his general comic effect only by keeping Alcmène offstage after
Act II and by closing with Sosie. Dryden's picture of the gods is devastat-
ingly hostile, and although the treatment he accords them is personal, it
is also part of a general shift in taste in northern Europe:

> At precisely the moment when, in Italian art, mythology
> is being relegated to the stage machinery of opera, Flan-
> ders, with Rubens, recalls it to primitive realities, to
> brute and elemental force. Sated with wine, gorged with
> meats and fruits, the gods are nourished to a point where
> their majesty, it is true, may be lost, but their animal
> vigor reappears. The naturalism of the North once more
> lends them its own flesh and blood.[28]

---

[27] See the summary of critical views by Lancaster, *History of French Dramatic
Literature,* III, ii, 515–519. More recently, Wolfgang Wittkowski in "The New
Prometheus: Molière's and Kleist's *Amphitryon,*" *Comparative Literature
Studies,* VIII (1971), 109–124, has argued for a degree of covert attack on
authority in the French and German plays; Dryden is not treated, but what is
covert in the other versions is central to his vision.

[28] Jean Seznec, *The Survival of the Pagan Gods* (1953), p. 322.

From Dryden's first scene, we discover his comedy degrading the gods. It deprives Jupiter of his "majesty" and turns Phœbus and Mercury into coarse Olympian footmen. The "decorum de la Divinité" is lost, not because Dryden could not, but because he would not, keep it.

Dryden's handling of the Olympian gods varies from place to place in his works, but usually he treats them as heathen, indulgent of their will and pleasure, and given (especially Jupiter) to dictatorial exercise of their power. In *Palamon and Arcite,* Dryden, even more than Chaucer, never lets the reader forget that the deities are pagan.[29] He has especially little taste for Jupiter, whose characteristics provide a simile in *The Hind and the Panther* (III, 1144–1145; *Works,* III, 195):

> Black-brow'd, and bluff, like *Homer's Jupiter:*
> Broad-back'd, and Brawny built for Loves delight.

With such kinds of indulgence Dryden associated the fearsome exercise of power.

Strictly speaking, Jupiter is to Dryden not true, because he is a pagan parody of the true God. But he represents fearsome tendencies of indulgence and power—and also a disturbing, gratuitous intervention in human affairs. Although he lacks dignity, he is a far greater threat in Dryden's play than in Molière's or Plautus', because he is the source of a casual, deterministic power that Dryden always rejected but often feared. What such a conception implies for the human condition is expressed in the admired speech by Alcmena (II, ii, 50–59):

> Ye niggard Gods! you make our Lives too long:
> You fill 'em with Diseases, Wants and Woes,
> And only dash 'em with a little Love;
> Sprinkled by Fits, and with a sparing Hand:
> Count all our Joys, from Childhood ev'n to Age,
> They wou'd but make a day of ev'ry year:
> Take back your sev'nty years, (the stint of Life)
> Or else be kind, and cram the Quintessence
> Of Seav'nty years, into sweet Seav'nty days:
> For all the rest is flat, insipid Being.

The point is heightened by the fact that this is said in front of the disguised Jupiter and concerns him. When Dryden deals with the Christian dispensation, the tone is very different and optimistic because concerned with providence, wisdom, and freedom rather than willful caprice and tyranny.[30]

As such passages imply, the necessary corollary to Jupiter's tyrannic power is the limitation of human scope and joy. In both Molière and

---

[29] See, e.g., details added by Dryden in *Palamon and Arcite,* III, 201, 369. See also "Translation as Baptism: Dryden's Lucretius," *Arion,* VII (Winter, 1968), 576–602, where Norman Austin shows how Dryden often heightens elements in Lucretius or introduces new material "to expose the destitution of pagan philosophies."

[30] See *The Hind and the Panther,* I, 247–275; and the much expanded section on determinism and free will in *The Cock and the Fox,* ll. 507–548, especially the conclusion.

Dryden, Jupiter's decision to woo Alcmena in her husband's guise is a gratuitous intrusion of exalted power into human life. To Molière what happens is, unfortunately, what is apt to happen when some beings are so superior to others. To Dryden, the gods represent forces worthy of fear but not of respect. The first scene sets the terms of our regard for the gods throughout the play. Mercury tells his father (I, i, 73–79):

> I was considering into what form your Almighty-ship
> would be pleas'd to transform your self to night. Whether
> you wou'd fornicate in the Shape of a Bull, or a Ram,
> or an Eagle, or a Swan: What Bird or Beast you wou'd
> please to honour, by transgressing your own Laws, in
> his likeness; or in short, whether you wou'd recreate your
> self in Feathers, or in Leather?

No doubt it was such passages that Scott found "coarse"; what must be understood is that they are deliberately degrading, and that such degradation is attributed only to the gods. Jupiter, Mercury, Amphitryon, and, after a fashion, Sosia and Gripus, are the lovers of the play. The two gods are indecent and coarse, the two men much puzzled husbands, and Amphitryon at least is normal, decent, and honorable. Comments by Sosia in his conversation with Amphitryon at the opening of Act III possess a social significance implying, within human society, a kind of tyranny of the great over the humble not unlike that of Jupiter over man. But it is significant that, for all his threats, Amphitryon does not actually beat Sosia as Mercury does; and although there is much to question in the human justice administered by a Gripus, man receives better treatment from his fellows than from the gods. In *Amphitryon* Jupiter is a tyrant, but a tyrant half-ridiculous. One need only compare the relations between Juno and Jupiter as they are described in the first scene with those between poor harried Amphitryon and Alcmena to see where Dryden felt dignity lay.

The dignity approaches the seriousness of tragedy for Amphitryon and Alcmena, but it is yet qualified and rendered comic by the lesser human characters, and in particular Sosia, in whom the dilemma of man's incapacity in this world extends to realms where only laughter can be the response. In his Prologue, Plautus plays at some length on the idea that his play is a tragicomedy, but what he seems chiefly to mean is that it must approach tragic dignity if the Father of the Gods is a principal character: at the least, Plautus also had a serious purpose. Molière creates a real dilemma for Amphitryon: if the gods are one's aristocratic superiors, what defenses does one have against their violations of one's life? Dryden renders Amphitryon somewhat less tragic, chiefly by qualifying his dignity with outbursts against Alcmena. Dryden's great achievement is to make Alcmena's problem assume the central importance and her the one who is harried—by her husband as well as by a god disguised as her husband. It has been thought that Molière decided against bringing Alcmène on stage after his second act, because "her presence after the truth is known would have diminished the comic effect of the play." [31]

---

[31] Lancaster, *History of French Dramatic Literature*, III, ii, 516.

Dryden does bring her back and, by forcing her to choose between the two claiming to be her husband, he does in fact diminish "the comic effect" and brings the play closer to tragedy.

The balance of tones can be represented by the three versions of scenes of tragic recognition in Act V. The first involves the attempt of Polydas, Tranio, and the foolish, corrupt judge Gripus to decide which is the true husband, the angry Amphitryon or the smooth-talking Jupiter. The second version follows immediately with Alcmena's entrance. Unlike the preceding, it is in verse. The danger of choosing the wrong Amphitryon leads her to fear for her "honour and her fame." But with full faith that "my Heart will guide my Eyes," she goes up to her true husband and takes his hand. So abused has Amphitryon been that he pushes her away, calling her, "Adultress!" After a few kind words from Jupiter she turns to him saying, with great irony: "Thy kindness is a Guide that cannot err." The tragic notes are clear and full, but the play is saved for comedy by the immediate resolving of the other two love plots, that of Mercury, Gripus, and Phædra along with that of Mercury, Sosia, and Bromia. Thereafter the stage is set for the third recognition scene, Jupiter's self-revelation. His last remarks, predicting the birth of Hercules, have a fine irony (V, i, 413–421):

> From this auspicious Night, shall rise an Heir,
> Great, like his Sire, and like his Mother, fair:
> Wrongs to redress, and Tyrants to disseize;
> . . . .
> Peace to his Labours, shall at last succeed;
> And murm'ring Men, unwilling to be freed,
> Shall be compell'd to Happiness, by need.

Freedom from tyranny yet involves compulsion. At the basis of much of Dryden's *Amphitryon* lies a concern with an external power, a determinism limiting man's capacity for freedom and joy. The extent to which the theme approaches tragedy can be represented by the fact that this comedy is preceded by *Don Sebastian* and followed (after the interval of an opera) by *Cleomenes*. Both are full tragedies, and both are concerned with discovering the forces that, from outside man's scope, bring him to ruin. It was clearly a concern that occupied Dryden at this stage in his career as it had not since *Annus Mirabilis*. Why he should have chosen in this instance to give a comic expression to this concern seems clear from John Crowne's dedication of *Darius King of Persia, A Tragedy* (1688). Crowne wonders why he has

> medled with Tragedy; for there is nothing more plain,
> than that the humour of the present Age runs quite to
> another extreme, too far. Nor do the present Company
> of Actors abound with Tragedians enow, to master that
> Humour. And they have no reason to contend with it,
> since they can please at a much cheaper rate, by Farce
> and Comedy.[32]

Among the twenty-eight major dramatic pieces known to have been pro-

---

[32] Crowne, *Darius*, sigs. a2v-A1.

duced between January 1688 and October 1690 (when *Amphitryon* was certainly acted), there were sixteen comedies, five tragicomedies, two operas, and but five tragedies, including Crowne's *Darius* and Dryden's *Don Sebastian*. It is possible that had Dryden not sought to please "the humour of the present Age," he would have written a tragedy or, possibly, a tragicomedy like his last play, *Love Triumphant*. But it is evident that he himself took delight in accommodating his serious concerns to a version of the Amphitryon story. For all its darker shades, *Amphitryon* is one of Dryden's most hilarious plays. Sosia had delighted Roman and French audiences over a long period, and he gains in comic strength in Dryden's version—even while asking the fundamental human question: Who, then, am I? From such a profound comic base to the universal absurdity of Dryden's jaded and selfish Olympian deities is a considerable range. At the center of all the bewildered human characters Dryden places Alcmena, whose abuse has been greatest, whose dilemma is most severe, and yet whose natural human dignity surpasses that of any of the other characters. Only those who know Dryden or Restoration drama thoroughly have hitherto understood that *Amphitryon* is one of the unrecognized masterpieces of English comedy, quite unlike anything else in its age, before, or since in England. With *All for Love* and *Don Sebastian,* it is at the peak of Dryden's achievement as a playwright. The three plays together show that it is humanity, and Dryden's questions about man, that provide the basis of his dramatic greatness.

DEDICATION

P. 223 *Sir William Levison Gower*. Leveson-Gower became fourth baronet of Sittenham, Yorkshire on the death of his nephew in 1689. He himself died in 1691, and his descendents rose steadily in the peerage. Sir William had prepared for the rise by marrying Lady Jane Grenville (d. 1696), the eldest daughter of John Grenville, first Earl of Bath, and later by marrying his daughter, Jane—the "young *Berenice*" referred to in the last paragraph of the dedication—to Henry, Lord Hyde, the eldest son of Laurence, Lord Rochester. As Dryden suggests in the second paragraph, he sought to put his writings under the protection of prominent Protestant or even Whig noblemen and gentlemen in order to protect them from attack. At the same time, he seems to have sought protection from those whom he had known before the Revolution, and he mentions Leveson-Gower's benefactions before as well as after 1688. Dryden later speaks of Sir William's hospitality at Trentham, his seat in Staffordshire. Since Dryden was preparing to publish his play during the summer or autumn of 1690, he had every reason to seek support from known Protestants. The nation was seized by panic and turmoil: "One might have thought, that long before this time, none could have had the Impudence to deny, or the weakness to doubt of the Reality of a Plot in England, to bring [back] King James by the Assistance of the French" (*Mercurius Reformatus*, 18 July 1690). Luttrell (I and II, *passim*) records a stream of arrests throughout 1689 and 1690, including many of the nobility; and, as we have seen in connection with *Don Sebastian*, on 22 June 1690, Pepys, among many others, was arrested on charges of high treason. On 21 July 1690, the Assizes were put off a month because of expected invasion; on 4 July 1690, "Several of the eminent and noted Roman catholicks are taken up and committed to prison"; on 12 September, Jacobites were executed at Tyburn (Luttrell, II, 70, 103). Only by the protection of well-established Protestants could Dryden insure the safety of himself and his family.

223:10 *difference of Opinions*. In 1683 Sir William had been one of Monmouth's sureties and in 1688 he was active in promoting the Revolution (Malone). The passage is reminiscent of *The Hind and the Panther*, I, 236ff.

223:21 *Tract*. The word was formerly used for "track" in the figurative sense of a "Course of action or conduct; method of proceeding" (*OED*).

223:22 *acted by*. Activated or motivated by.

223:24 *a word*. The word must be *Tenderness*, by virtue of its being *commonly Despis'd* (as effeminate) and by being opposed in the next sentence to *Ruggedness and Harshness*.

223:30 *this Poem*. Even plays including a good share of prose were often called poems by Dryden and others, and Dryden was sometimes referred to as a "play-poet" by his contemporaries. Cf. the preface to *Don Sebastian*, 71:10–11 above.

224:1 *the Earl of Leicester*. Philip Sidney, Third Earl of Leicester, to whom Dryden dedicated *Don Sebastian*.

224:6 *a lost Cause*. Dryden's letters and poems show that his Jacobite hopes continued till at least 1697.

224:8–9 *as a great Wit has told the World*. Probably an ironic reference to Tom Brown, who taunted Dryden on his loss of the laureateship and the post of historiographer royal after the Revolution. See the preface to his *The Late Converts Exposed: Or The Reasons of Mr. Bays's Changing his Religion* (1690) (Malone).

224:10–12 *Sancho Panca* etc. In John Philips' translation of *Don Quixote*, II, iii, 2, Merlin gives the condition for release of Dulcinea from enchantment:

> But to restore her to her Former State,
> And make her happy that's unfortunate.
> Six hunder'd Stripes upon his naked Bum,
> Thy Peerless Squire must first receive.

In II, iv, 19, Sancho lashes himself "Seven or Eight Stroaks," and smarting severely he gives the remaining lashes to the trees.

224:13–14 *like Ovid, with a Lamentable Epistle from Pontus*. Referring to Ovid's *Ex Ponto*, four books of verse epistles written from exile at Tomis in Pontus.

224:17–18 *The Merry Philosopher* etc. The merry one is Democritus, whom Robert Burton dilated upon in his lengthy epistle to the reader for *The Anatomy of Melancholy;* the melancholy one is Heraclitus. Summers recognized that they were paired by Juvenal in his Satire X. As Dryden translated the passage (ll. 41–44; *Works*, IV, 209):

> Will you not now, the pair of Sages praise,
> Who the same End pursu'd, by several Ways?

> One pity'd, one contemn'd the Woful Times:
> One laugh'd at Follies, one lamented Crimes.

224:28 *Trentham.* Trentham Hall is about a mile west of Trentham, Staffordshire (Summers). The only known visit by Dryden to the area was in August, 1680, to "Sir Charles Woolsley's" (James M. Osborn, *John Dryden: Some Biographical Facts and Problems* [rev. ed., 1965], p. 220). Dryden's was a northern family and it may be that his connections with such families as the Catholic Howards, or the Staffords, also involved visits to their country estates, but Osborn (*ibid.*) observes that "the only time we can trace Dryden in [Staffordshire] is in August, 1680."

225:16 *Mr. Purcell.* Henry Purcell (?1658–1695), with whom Dryden entered into close relations about this time. See the Epistle Dedicatory for *The Vocal and Instrumental Musick of the Prophetess* (*Works*, XVII, 324–326, 482–483); "Prologue to *The Prophetess*" (*Works*, III, 255–256); and the *Ode, on the Death of Mr. Henry Purcell* (*Works*, IV, 468–469, 752–753). As Scott suggested, Dryden implies that he was but recently converted to English music. Summers printed a valuable "Note on the Music" by W. Barclay Squire, who remarked that the unusual step of publishing the music for the songs of *Amphitryon* argued special popularity in the theater. Although the instrumental music was published in *Ayres for the Theatre* (1697) and republished by the Purcell Society in 1906, Squire had access to a contemporary manuscript giving a better version than the *Ayres*. The instrumental music was as follows:

> *First and Second Music.*
> 1 Hornpipe.
> 2 Air.
> *Before the Prologue.*
> 3 Minuet.
> *After the Prologue.*
> 3 Minuet (*repeated*).
> 4 Overture.
> *1st Act Tune (before Act II).*
> 5 Saraband.
> *2nd Act Tune (before Act III).*
> 6 Bourrée.
> *3rd Act Tune (before Act IV).*
> 7 Hornpipe.
> *Act IV.*
> 8 *Dance for Tinkers.*
> *4th Act Tune (before Act V).*
> 9 Scotch Tune.

225:19 *the late Opera.* That is, *The Prophetess* (1690). Scott surmised that Betterton had recovered from a distaste for operas occasioned by the interruption of *Albion and Albanius*, and that he thereafter produced, with enormous success, Beaumont and Fletcher's *Prophetess* as an opera, with music by Purcell and dances by Priest.

225:23 *on the Third Day.* The profits from the performance on the third day accrued to the playwright, and his friends therefore sought to make it a success. Summers quoted Shadwell's dedication of *The Squire of Alsatia* (1688): "I had the great Honour to find so many Friends, that the House was never so full since it was built, as upon the third day of this Play."

225:25 *that young Berenice.* As noted, she was Jane, Lady Hyde, daughter of Sir William Leveson-Gower, married to Henry, Lord Hyde (later Earl of Clarendon and Rochester). She is referred to as the "admirable Daughter-in-law . . . a more true and brighter *Berenice*" of Laurence, Earl of Rochester, in the dedication of *Cleomenes*, which Dryden read before Rochester, "Berenice," and other members of the family.

PROLOGUE

5 *What gain you, by not suffering him to teize ye.* Dryden probably alludes, as Summers suggested, to the bitingly political "Prologue to *The Prophetess.*" The present prologue, like the dedication, suggests that Dryden somewhat unwillingly drew back from political comment after that outburst.

17 *Julian's interloping Trade.* Beginning with Malone, Dryden's editors have had much to say about Julian. In Scott's words, "Julian, who styled himself secretary to the muses, made a dirty livelihood, by copying and dispersing lampoons at the Wits' coffee house." Details about some verse satirizing Julian (and Dryden), and one attributed to Dryden, will be found concisely set forth by Noyes, p. 929. As *A Familiar Epistle to Mr. Julian, Secretary to the Muses*, it will be found in S-S, XV. From the time of Scott, no editor has allowed the verses into the canon. A definition for "interlope" quoted by the *OED* from Johnson is suggestive: "To run between parties and intercept the advantage that one should gain from another"; in other words, to take or steal advantage of someone dealing fairly or normally. Dryden's usage is figurative, as in *The Medall*, ll. 40–41 (*Works*, II, 44):

> Whoring to Scandal gives too large a scope:
> Saints must not trade; but they may interlope.

See also IV, i, 415.

20–21 *The first produces still* etc. The couplet is somewhat difficult to gloss and gives evidence of that colloquial and figurative or glancing style that marks *Amphitryon* and *Don Sebastian.* Line 20 means something like, The first libel always (*still*) produces a second dance, a second round. To *whip . . . out* means to " 'come *out* with' " [such lampoons] suddenly, vigorously (*OED*). But as *gig* implies, the whole couplet is a complex conceit. The verb *gig* is an obscure one, probably denoting "the action of some kind of 'gig' or whipping-top, having inside it a smaller 'gig' of the same shape, which was thrown out by the effect of rapid rotation. Hence *to gig* (*out*) appears to be used [figuratively] with the sense 'to throw out or give rise to (a smaller repetition of itself)' " (*OED*, citing this usage). The *OED* also cites III, i, 252–258, on which it has this comment: "The [dictionaries], on the ground of the Dryden [quotation], have plausibly, but erroneously, explained the transitive [verb] as meaning 'to engender,' assigning to it a derivation from [Latin] *gignere.*" The whipping of a top is a fine image for the personal abuse in some of the satire of the time, and Dryden's conceit envisions one whipped top or satire producing another lesser one out of its gyrations, which is also the point of l. 23.

24 *And much good Malice* etc. Cf. *The Hind and the Panther*, III, 1.

36 *Peace, after War; and after Toil, Repose.* Dryden combines two of a number of related formulas or commonplaces extracted from classical writers and often reprinted in collections of adagia, emblem books, and formulary rhetorics. For convenient collections of the classical sources under two heads, see *Synopsis Communium Locorum* (1700, 1719): *Pax bello potior* (Cap. LVII) and *Forsan miseros meliora sequentur* (Cap. CXXIX). Cf. also Spenser, *The Faerie Queene*, I, ix, 40, 8: "Sleepe after toyle, port after stormie seas."

37 *Hence ye Prophane.* Cf. *Aeneid*, VI, 258 (Summers); and Dryden, *Aeneis*, VI, 368: "Far hence be Souls prophane."

I, i

12 *some Petticoat Affair.* "Of, belonging, or relating to a woman or women" (*OED*, citing this usage).

15–19 Mercury's mother was Maia, his father Jupiter; Phœbus' mother was Leto, his father also Jupiter. Since Juno was mother of neither, both are bastards, as Mercury admits.

23–25 *to sue him in the Spiritual Court* etc. "A court having jurisdiction in matters of religion or ecclesiastical affairs" (*OED*). The sense is of course that Juno wishes to bring Jupiter to account, but that as sovereign of the gods he resists, whereupon she tongue-lashes him, Phœbus, and Mercury. The amusing wording plays upon matrimonial offenses, or perhaps adulterous commissions, which would be tried by an ecclesiastical or *Spiritual* court. See Edmund Gibson, *Codex Juris Ecclesiastici Anglicani* (Oxford, 1761), II, Tit. XLVII, cap. v: "Temporal Courts shall not disturb the Spiritual, for punishing Fornication, Adultery, and the like." As king of the gods, Jupiter is able to plead *Prerogative*, "A prior, exclusive, or peculiar right or privilege," especially of a king, which was "a sovereign right (in theory) subject to no restriction or influence" (*OED*).

25 *hit him on the Teeth of.* The usual expression is "to hit in the teeth with," "To reproach, upbraid, or censure with" (*OED*).

25–26 *all his Bastards.* One of the motifs running through Ovid's *Metamorphoses* concerns Jupiter's infidelities; and another Juno's rage, including her efforts to punish Jupiter's mortal lovers and any offspring. See, for example, the story of Jupiter and Io (I, 601ff.), Callisto (II, 466ff.), Semele (III, 261ff.), etc. Ovid also recounts (IX, 21, 176, 284, 295ff.) what is probably on Dryden's mind here, with other *Bastards*, Juno's hatred of Hercules, whose birth she delayed because of her jealousy of Alcmena.

34 *Samos.* Where Juno was said to have been born and where the cult of her worship particularly flourished.

37 *Petitions.* As opposed to loyal addresses, petitions were regarded by royalists as noxious and suspect Whiggish entreaties to the throne.

54 *Sowse.* "With a direct and rapid course" (*OED*, citing this line).

65 *smack.* A figurative usage of "A taste or flavour" (*OED*, citing this line).

66 *savourly.* "With enjoyment; with relish" (*OED*, citing this line). See also the prologue to *King Arthur*, l. 2, "When silly Plays so savourly go down."

69–70 *he who trusts a Secret / Makes his own Man his Master.* A version of Tilley S192, "He that tells his secret is another's servant."

70–71 *Makes his own Man* etc. If the two hypometric lines were joined to make one hypermetric line, the clash of sounds would be intolerable.

75–76 *in the Shape of a Bull* etc. It was in the form of a bull that Jupiter enjoyed Europa, as an eagle Asterie, and as a swan Leda. As a ram Neptune enjoyed Theophane, but Jupiter's "matrimonial omissions" were the more famous. Juno, jealous of Semele, persuaded Jupiter to visit her as a god, so killing her, but he rescued their unborn son, Bacchus (cf. *Don Sebastian,* III, i, 365 and n).

78–79 *recreate your self in Feathers, or in Leather.* That is, sport yourself, take recreation, although "re-create," make your image, may also be meant.

147 *Grumbletonian.* "A contemptuous designation applied in the latter part of the 17th c. to the members of the so-called 'Country Party' in English politics, who were accused by the 'Court Party' of being actuated by dissatisfied personal ambition" (*OED*, citing this use).

203+ *s.d. Night appears* etc. Cf. Molière's prologue:

LA NUIT *dans un Char traîné par deux chevaux*
        MERCURE.
Tout beau, charmante Nuit; daignez vous arrêter.
Il est certain sécours, que de vous on desire:
        Et j'ai deux mots à vous dire,
        De la part de Jupiter.

(Comparisons with specific lines of Molière follow in general Carl Hartmann, *Einfluss Molière's auf Dryden's Komisch-Dramatische Dichtungen* [Leipzig, 1885], pp. 30–39, but the edition of *Amphitryon* used is *Les Oeuvres de Monsieur de Molière* [Paris, 1718], IV; and of *Le Mariage forcé, Oeuvres de Molière* [Paris, 1739], III).

214–215 *Clippers, and Coiners, and Conspirators.* Alliteration for satiric effect is common in Dryden. Here, the series is ascending, although all three felonies entailed heavy punishments.

234 *stickle.* "To be busy, stirring, or energetic; . . . to take an active part in" (*OED*, citing this usage).

243 *ready Money.* As Summers noted, Dryden puns interlingually on *peculiatus* in the Latin sense of having plenty of money and having a capacity for venery.

246 *swinging.* "Hugely, immensely" (*OED*, first usage).

250–257 Dryden gives a mock encomium on Night, adapting the school exercise of the encomium to witty dramatic purposes. For an example of such an exercise, see Milton's First Prolusion, *Whether Day or Night is the more excellent,* in *Milton: Private Correspondence and Academic Exer-*

cises, trans. Phyllis B. Tillyard, introd. E. M. W. Tillyard (1932). Donald Lemen Clark, *John Milton at St. Paul's School* (1964) gives the standard description of school exercises in the century; see especially Chap. VIII.

259 *holding a Candle.* That is, assisting (*OED*).

273 *the Seven Stars.* The Pleiades (*OED*). So again, II, i, 71.

I, ii

20–25 Dryden establishes, in a single passage, Phædra's greed and cross-grained character, but the logic given her in these speeches is, after its fashion, irresistible.

46 *But swear by Jupiter.* The first of many such plays on the idea and character of Jupiter to provide dramatic irony.

50 *swinge you off.* "To chastise, castigate; to pay out, serve out" (*OED*, citing this usage). Cf. V, i, 330.

58–59 *penny-worths.* "A good bargain; something obtained at a cheap rate" (*OED*, citing the prologue to *Oedipus,* l. 33, "You needs will have your pen'worths of the Play."). Cf. Heywood, *The Silver Age* (1613), II, i, "he that hath hired a wench to lie with him all this night, hath time enough I thinke to take his peny worths."

60–63 There is a curious resemblance between Jupiter's avowal and Jonson's *Song. To Celia:* "But might I of JOVE'S Nectar sup," etc.

69 *colling.* To "coll" is to "throw one's arms around the neck of; to embrace, hug" (*OED*).

89 *my Lord.* The appropriate vocative title for a judge (Gripus) in court. See the prologue to *Don Sebastian,* l. 1.

118 *pinking.* To pink is "To peep or peer with half-closed eyes; to blink or wink in a sleepy or sly manner; to look slyly" (*OED*).

134 *recruit.* "To increase or restore the vigour or health; . . . to refresh, reinvigorate" (*OED*, citing *Georgics,* III, 766).

144 *Hilding.* "A contemptible, worthless person of either sex" (*OED*, citing usage in Dryden's *Troilus and Cressida,* III, ii, and *Spanish Fryar,* II, iii).

146–147 *for Jupiter but laughs / At Lovers Perjuries.* Cf. Tibullus, III, vi, 49–50, *perjuria ridet amantum / Juppiter, et ventos irrita ferre jubet.* Cf. also Dryden's prologue to Lee's *Princess of Cleves,* ll. 17–19 (*Works,* II, 188):

> But men are dipt for Soul and Body too,
> And when found out excuse themselves, Pox cant 'em,
> With *Latin* stuff, *perjuria ridet Amantum.*

Also, as Summers noted, *Palamon and Arcite,* II, 149: "*Jove* but laughs at Lover's Perjury."

158 *meer Elder-Brother.* Some dull Esau rather than clever Jacob, though also with a more general meaning taken from English laws of inheritance based on primogeniture.

178 *This Love can make a Fool of Jupiter.* As this and the last line of the scene exemplify, there is much that is aphoristic in the play.

190–201 *Why now I am, indeed, the Lord of all* etc. The combination of soliloquy and high style establishes Jove as something more than the almighty lecher of the opening of the play. It also lays the basis for the near tragic outcome of the action. To Dryden, the voiding of Providence could only seem a terrible thing, the metaphysical counterpart as it were of the earlier lechery in showing the destitution of the pagan gods.

199 *Oraisons.* Saintsbury objected to the spelling as a Gallicism, but the *OED* merely terms it obsolete.

II, i

11–12 *the greatest Plague of a Serving-man* etc. The first of a number of speeches objecting to tyranny of lower social orders by higher.

17–18 *a foot Pimp; a Waiter without Doors.* As a *foot-pimp* is a degenerate form of a *foot-man*, so a *waiter without doors* is gone from his element.

37–38 *Now am I . . . my Parts before hand.* Cf. Molière, I, i:

Je dois aux yeux d'Alcmene un Portrait Militaire
Du grand Combat qui met nos Ennemis à bas . . .
  Pour joüer mon Rôle sans peine,
  Je le veux un peu repasser.

43–67 *setting down his Lanthorn. This Lanthorn, for once, shall be my Lady* etc. Cf. Molière, I, i:

Voici la chambre, où j'entre en Courrier que l'on meine,
  Et cette Lanterne est Alcmene,
  A qui je me dois adresser.
    Il pose sa Lanterne à terre, & lui addresse son compliment.
Madame, Amphitryon, mon Maître, & vôtre Epoux. . . .
Bon! beau début! l'esprit toûjours plein de vos charmes,
  M'a voulu choisir entre tous,
Pour vous donner avis de succès de ses armes . . .
  Ha! vraiment, mon pauvre Sosie,
  A te revoir, j'ai de la joye au coeur,
  Madame, ce m'est trop d'honneur,
  Et mon destin doit faire envie.
Bien répondu! *Comment se porte Amphitryon?*
  Madame, en Homme de courage,
Dans les occasions, où la gloire l'engage.
  Fort bien! belle conception!
  Quand viendra-t-il, par son retour charmant,
  Rendre mon ame satisfaite?
Le plûtôt qu'il pourra, Madame, assurément:
Mais bien plus tard que son coeur ne souhaite.
Ah! *Mais quel est l'état où la guerre l'a mis?*
Que-dit-il? que fait-il? contente un peu mon ame.
  Il dit moins qu'il ne fait, Madame,
  Et fait trembler les Ennemis.
Peste! où prend mon esprit toutes ces gentilesses?

46 *thy Lord is the Lanthorn.* Horns, of course, signified a cuckold, and this horn joke is no better than those tirelessly reiterated by Shakespeare and other earlier playwrights.

58 *I nick'd it.* To "nick" is "to hit the mark, to make a hit; to guess rightly" (*OED*).

61–62 *When Thebes is an University, thou deservest to be their Orator.* Saintsbury and others have been reminded of Dryden's reference to Cambridge as Thebes in the "Prologue to the University of Oxford [1676]" (*Works*, I, 155–156), ll. 35ff. Concerning the latter part of the line, Saintsbury asked, "Can this be a reflection on a given person?" *The Historical Register of the University of Cambridge,* ed. J. R. Tanner (1917), p. 49, shows that Henry Felton, D.D. was elected Public Orator in 1689. Although Felton was among those welcoming William III to Cambridge on 8 October 1689 and took part in other ceremonies that Dryden was unlikely to approve of, no evidence has been found to suggest that Dryden was reflecting on Felton. The Thebes/Cambridge joke is witty enough as it stands, and Dryden need not have intended any single particular meaning in it. See also *To the Dutchess of Ormond,* l. 37.

70–74 *What, is the Devil in the Night* etc. Cf. Thomas Heywood, *The Silver Age,* II, i:

> *Socia.* Heere's a night of nights, I thinke the Moone
> stands stil and all the Stars are a sleepe, he that driues
> Charles wayne is taking a nap in his cart, for they are
> all at a stand, this night hath bene as long as two nights
> already. . . .

71 *the seven Stars.* See I, i, 273.

72 *high Day.* A version of *hey-day* ("An exclamation denoting frolicsomeness, gaiety, surprise, wonder, etc." *OED*).

83–84 *I'll sing, that I may seem Valiant.* Cf. Shakespeare, *A Midsummer Night's Dream,* III, i, 126: "I will sing, that they shall hear I am not afraid"; Molière, I, ii: "Pour faire semblant d'assurance, / Je veux chanter un peu d'ici."

93–94 *my fear has betray'd me into this savour.* A *savour* is "A smell, perfume, aroma" (*OED,* citing Dryden, *Georgics,* IV, 88). Summers compared Plautus, l. 321:

> Mer. *Olet homo quidam malo suo.*
> **Sos.**   *Ei, numnam ego obolui?*

(Loeb trans.: *Mer.* Ha! I smell somebody, and woe to him! / *Sos.* Oh, dear! It can't be he's got a whiff of me?)

108–109 *Of what Quality are you* etc. Cf. Molière, I, ii:

> MERCURE.
> Quel est ton sort? dis-moi.
> SOSIE.
> D'être homme, & de parler.

111 *A Two-leg'd Man.* Recalling the absurd definition of man, attributed to Plato, *implumis bipes.* Cf. *Absalom and Achitophel,* l. 170.

118 *Gols.* Hands (*OED,* citing this as last usage).

120–127 *Sirrah, from whence come you* etc. Cf. Molière, I, ii:

> MERCURE.
> . . . .
> Je veux sçavoir de toi, traître,

Ce que tu fais, d'où tu viens avant jour;
   Où tu vas, à qui tu peux être.
SOSIE.

. . . .

Je viens de là, vais là . . .
MERCURE.

. . . .

Il me prend un desir, pour faire connoissance,
   De te donner un soufflet de ma main.

132–135 *Merc. stopping him. Hold Sir* etc. Cf. Molière, I, ii:
MERCURE.

   Où vas-tu?

. . . .

SOSIE.

. . . .

Me faire ouvrir cette porte:
   Pourquoi retiens-tu mes pas?

157 *flippant with your Hands.* "Flippant" means "nimble" (*OED*) but probably also with the more usual sense of showing unbecoming levity and perhaps with a play on "flip."

167 *my Heathen Name.* Cf. "Christian name."

183 *plain Sosia . . . lac'd Sosia.* The word *lac'd* derives from the practice of adding spirits or sugar to a beverage (*OED;* Eric Partridge, *A Dictionary of Slang and Unconventional English* [1961] gives "Sugared: *ca.* 1690–1750"). The distinction between plain and fancied up Sosia probably entails another meaning, since *to lace* also means "To lash, beat, or thrash" (*OED*), so recalling poor Sosia's recent humiliation.

200 *the Teleboans.* "The islands of the Teleboae . . . are in the Ionian Sea. . . . They are mentioned by Homer as the haunts of notorious sea-pirates, and in Greek myth were celebrated on account of the war carried on between [the Teleboae] and Electryon, king of Mycenae, the father of Alcmena" (Summers).

202 *sake-sake.* The *OED* gives several examples of this and kindred forms, with various meanings. The phrase here probably means "for its own sake."

217 *What was your Fathers Name* etc. Dryden is drawing upon both Plautus, ll. 362ff. and Molière, I, ii.

230 *branded for my pains.* Henri Van Laun (trans., *Dramatic Works of Molière* [Edinburgh, 1875–76], IV, 254), comments on Molière: "Among the ancients, marking with red-hot iron upon the shoulder was unknown as a public punishment." In Plautus, Sosia says that he was whipped. Dryden's version makes clear that he followed both predecessors.

239 *A Buckle of Diamonds* etc. Cf. Molière, I, ii: "Cinq fort gros Diamans, en noeud proprement mis." In Plautus, l. 760, Alcmena insists that Amphitryon (i.e., Jupiter) gave her a golden bowl (*auream pateram*) on his return. Dryden transfers the bowl to the Mercury-Phædra plot.

241 *my Masters Coat of Arms.* Dryden follows Molière, I, ii: "Dans un coffre, scellé des Armes de mon Maître." Van Laun comments (trans.,

Dramatic Works of Molière, IV, 255): "Arms were unknown to the ancients, for heraldry came in only with chivalry." The seal is Plautine,
however.

256–257 *There stood a Hogshead* etc. The cask comes from Plautus,
l. 429; the gammon of bacon is of course English.

266 *Bacon.* The comedy and the pathos depend on our recalling that
poor Sosia has apparently gone without food for days. In his hunger he
supplies the needed word and gives himself up as lost: *that word has quite
made an end of me.* Mercury has, as it were, starved Sosia to death, stealing his identity.

273–277 *Imprimis . . . summa totalis.* The Latin itemizing perhaps
suits a character, like Sosia, who was invented by Plautus. *Summa totalis*
is the "Sum-total" (*OED*).

278–282 *Well, you are Sosia* etc. Cf. Molière, I, ii:

> SOSIE.
>
> . . . .
> Je ne sçaurois nier, aux preuves qu'on m'expose,
> Que tu ne sois Sosie; & j'y donne ma voix.
> Mais si tu l'es, dy-moy qui tu veux que je sois:
> Car encor faut-il bien que je sois quelque chose.
> MERCURE.
> Quand je ne serai plus Sosie,
> Sois-le, j'en demeure d'accord.

279 *My Mind gives me.* The sense here is "misgives" (*OED*).

302–307 Mercury's speech is loosely modelled on Plautus, ll. 463–98,
and has no equivalent in Molière.

306 *lank.* "Loose from emptiness" (*OED*).

II, ii

1–9 *Those Torches* etc. Cf. Molière, I, iii:

> Défendez, chere Alcmene, aux flambeaux d'approcher.
> Ils m'offrent des plaisirs en m'offrant votre vûë:
> Mais ils pourroient ici découvrir ma venuë,
>   Qu'il est à propos de chacher.
> Mon amour . . .
> Où me tenoit lié la gloire de nos armes,
> Aux devoirs de ma Charge, a volé les instans
>   Qu'il vient de donner à vos charmes.
> Ce vol, qu'à vos beautez mon coeur a consacré,
> Pourroit être blâmé dans la bouche publique;
>   Et j'en veux pour témoin unique
>   Celle qui peut m'en sçavoir gré.

18–20 *Behold the ruddy Streaks o're yonder Hill* etc. Cf. *Hamlet*, I, i,
166–167:

> But look, the Morn, in russet mantle clad,
> Walks o're the dew of yon high eastern hill.

25 *draw our Curtains close.* The curtains are those about the bed.

28–29 *You have not yet lay long enough* etc. Cf. Plautus, l. 513: *prius abis quam lectus ubi cubuisti concaluit locus* (Loeb trans.: "Here you are leaving me before your place on the couch had time to get warm"). Also Cf. Heywood, *The Silver Age*, II, ii: "You rise before your bed be thoroughly warme."

50–55 On such apostrophes to the gods and their normal tragic character, see *Albion and Albanius*, I, i, 48–50n.

56 *stint.* "An allotted amount or measure" (*OED*, citing this usage).

77 *Niceties.* The exact meaning is not clear; perhaps such a "nicety" means "luxuriousness" (last *OED* usage 1650), or "delicacy of feeling, scrupulosity" (earliest *OED* usage 1693), or some related sense.

101–102 *Farewel* etc. Cf. Molière, I, iii:

JUPITER.

Adieu . . .
Mais, belle Alcmene, au moins quand vous verrez l'Epoux,
  Songez à l'Amant, je vous prie.

103–104 *Love has laid a Lime-twig* etc. As the *OED* shows, a *Lime-twig*, properly "A twig smeared with birdlime for catching birds," is often used figuratively for devices and stratagems meant to capture someone or something. As *a lame God*, Mercury would resemble Vulcan, an object of sport for having been deceived by a woman, his wife Venus.

105 *Interessed.* A common form for "interested," that is, self-interested.

114 *Cullies.* Dupes (*OED*).

120 *Gourmand.* In Dryden's usage, greedy for voluptuary experience, money, etc. Cf. *The Hind and the Panther*, III, 969–970.

131 *Suppose I were a God* etc. The speech suggests the extent to which the Mercury-Phædra plot introduced by Dryden is a parodic version of the Jupiter-Alcmena relationship portrayed in the earlier part of this scene.

135 *Fripperies.* "Old clothes; cast-off garments" (*OED*).

164 *s.d. Knaps her Fingers.* To *knap* is "to knack, knock, rap" (*OED*).

182 *Kilderkin.* "A cask" measuring "half a barrel" (*OED*). Cf. *Mac Flecknoe*, l. 196.

201–202 *Gold is a great Cordial, in love matters.* An old trope. Cf. Chaucer, *Canterbury Tales*, A 443: "For gold in phisik is a cordial."

208–212 *Tell her what, Traytor* etc. Cf. Molière, I, iv:

CLEANTHIS.
[Dryden's Bromia]
Quoi! c'est ainsi que l'on me quitte?
MERCURE.
Et comment donc? ne veux-tu pas,
Que de mon devoir je m'acquitte?
Et que d'Amphitryon j'aille suivre les pas?
CLEANTHIS.
Mais avec cette brusquerie,
  Traître, de moy te séparer!

211–212 *his Duty to my Lady.* Bromia's conception of a husband's duty resembles the Wife of Bath's idea of a husband's debt.

216–217 *you worse than Dunghill-Cock.* As Bromia's following remarks show, she uses the cock as the traditional type of libidinousness, and *Dame Partlet* in Mercury's address answers to her implied charge of Chanticleer. For the names and the libidinous type, see *The Hind and the Panther*, III, 1021–1025 and commentary in *Works*, III, 191, 444–445.

226 *Sneaksby*. "A mean-spirited person; a paltry fellow" (*OED*, citing this usage).

230 *hoighty toighty*. "Frolicsome, ramping, giddy" (*OED*, first usage cited).

236–247 *what a Jest it wou'd be* etc. Cf. Molière, I, iv:

> MERCURE.
>
> . . . .
>
> En nous, vieux mariez, auroit mauvaise grace.
> Il nous feroit beau voir attachez face à face,
> A pousser les beaux sentimens!
> CLEANTHIS.
> Quoi! suis-je hors d'état, perfide, d'esperer
> Qu'un coeur auprés de moy soûpire?
> MERCURE.
> Non, . . .
> Mais je suis trop barbon pour oser soûpirer. . . .
> CLEANTHIS.
> Merites-tu, pendart, cet insigne bonheur,
> De te voir pour épouse une Femme d'honneur?
> MERCURE.
> Mon Dieu! tu n'es que trop honnête.

253 *Wittol*. "A man who is aware of and complacent about the infidelity of his wife; a contented cuckold"; also, a "half-witted person; a fool" (*OED*).

259 *bastings*. Probably playing upon the moistening of roasting meat and beatings.

268–269 *my Tongue . . . the last live—ing part about a—Woman*. Cf. Tilley, W677.

III, i

4 *the Monster with two long Horns*. Summers, on whatever evidence, glossed the reference as a story "circulated among the more ignorant vulgar that a great devil had appeared to Louis XIV, and although the King was at first frightened he soon learned to join league with Satan."

5 *the Devil at the Stone-cutters*. Alluding to a story of the young and wealthy widow of a certain Dudsey and of the stone-cutter she called in to make a monument for her dead husband. The stone-cutter courted the widow, a relative intervened, and the widow said she could not marry him until he was a knight. A whimsical nobleman appeared and arranged with the king for the knighthood, and the stone-cutter won the widow, but as it was popularly thought, only by bargaining with the Devil. See "The Noble Statuary," *The Gentleman's Journal*, January 1691–1692, pp. 37–47 (Summers).

6–8 *I am but a Slave* etc. Sosia's statement of the need for a social inferior to acknowledge as truth a lie insisted on by a superior recalls Maskall's reply to Wildblood in *An Evening's Love*, III, i, 541–546 (*Works*, X, 266). A number of verbal and situational parallels exist between that play and this, but Sosia here is less designing and better illustrates the sad human lot.

11–12 *an honest Face.* In the sense of "Ingenuous" (*OED*), even simple, and therefore a cuckold.

16 *O that I had but a Crab-tree Cudgel.* The same as that with which Mercury did beat Sosia in II, i. It is noteworthy that the exasperated Amphitryon never does beat Sosia, and that if he really wished to here, he could use his hands or the flat of his sword.

23 *wambles.* "To be felt to roll about (in nausea)" (*OED,* citing this usage).

27–143 In this section Dryden is closely indebted to Molière, II, i, for situation, ideas, and very often for wording.

32–33 *but, that all things may be done in order* etc. Cf. Heywood, *The Silver Age,* II, i: "Tell ore thy tale againe, make it more plaine."

61 *dog-trot.* "A steady or habitual course of action; a habit" (*OED,* first usage cited).

66 *swingeing.* Great, or large; huge, immense (*OED,* citing Dryden's *The Kind Keeper,* V, i, "I dream'd . . . that a great swinging Thief came in, and whipt 'em out").

74–75 *Packstaff.* "A staff on which a pedlar supports his pack when standing to rest himself" (*OED,* citing this usage). *As plain as a packstaff* is a proverb (Tilley, P322) playing alternatively on *packsaddle* and *pikestaff.* Dryden's is the last usage cited by Tilley.

117–118 *He was Handsome* etc. Cf. II, i, 273–278.

123–124 *defended.* To "defend" is "To prohibit, forbid" (*OED*).

128 *two-inch-boards.* Summers, in a very long note, held that Dryden alluded to that "extraordinary piece of Protestant superstition, 'the Strange and Wonderful Groaning Board.'" The board made intelligible sounds of a prophetic and Protestant tendency that found some acceptance by Gilbert Burnet and excited a good deal of mirth among the wits. But Summers' note seems altogether irrelevant: the allusion in the passage, if there is any, is rather to John, xx, 26.

143+ *s.d. Enter Alcmena and Phædra.* From here to l. 221 where Amphitryon is astonished to find that Alcmena has the diamonds ("*Amph.* Now answer, Sosia"), Dryden follows Molière more closely than elsewhere in the play, although the speeches of Mercury, Phædra, and Sosia are entirely his own.

175 *Or have you dream't Alcmena.* The dream attributed to Alcmena comes from Plautus, ll. 726, 738.

176 *some kind, revealing Deity.* Through numerous touchings on the central situation of the play, Dryden develops a varying irony; and from this point the comedy takes on progressively serious implications.

186 *An honest Blush* etc. Cf. II, ii, 68–69. The verbal echo of the earlier scene suggests the parallelism between the scenes of Jupiter's departure and Amphitryon's arrival.

190 *the Creature. OED* cites the passage to illustrate the usage for "intoxicating liquor," but it may well be that physical love is meant.

216 *Have I already given you those Diamonds* etc. Cf. II, i, 236–242 and IV, i, 127–132.

232 *unsociated.* The word is Sosia's coinage and means un-Sosiated or de-Sosia-tized, making him no longer himself.

235 *More words than one to a Bargain.* A proverb, Tilley, W819, Dryden's expression being later than any given by Tilley.

237–239 *Do you look first upon the Signet* etc. Cf. Plautus, ll. 787ff.:

Sos. *Vide sis signi quid siet,*
ne posterius in me culpam conferas.
Amph. *Aperi modo.*

(Loeb trans.: *Sos.* You please take a look at the seal, sir, so that you won't blame me later. / *Amph.* Yes, yes, open up!)

250–254 *You, my Lord Amphitryon* etc. Cf. Plautus, ll. 785–786: *tu peperisti Amphitruonem, ego alium peperi Sosiam; / nunc si patera pateram peperit, omnes congeminavimus* (Loeb trans.: "You have spawned another Amphitryon; I have spawned another Sosia; now if the bowl has spawned another bowl, we've all doubled"). Molière's Sosia says only, II, ii: "Et de même que moy, Monsieur, vous êtes double." For the different meaning of *gigg'd* in Phædra's "my Goblet has gigg'd another Golden Goblet," see the prologue, ll. 20–21n.

260 *clams.* "Clammy, or moist and sticky" (*OED,* citing this usage).

265–270 *Not so: but, if you please* etc. Cf. Molière, II, ii:

AMPHITRYON.

Non; mais à ce retour, daignez, s'il est possible,
Me conter ce qui s'est passé.

ALCMENE.

Puisque vous demandez un récit de la chose,
Vous voulez dire donc que ce n'étoit pas vous.

AMPHITRYON.

Pardonnez-moi; mais j'ai certaine cause,
Qui me fait demander ce récit entre nous.

273–277 *The Story is not long* etc. Cf. Molière, II, ii:

ALCMENE.

L'histoire n'est pas longue. A vous je m'avançai,
Pleine d'une aimable surprise:
Tendrement je vous embrassai;
Et témoignai ma joye, à plus d'une reprise.

AMPHITRYON *en soy-même.*

Ah! d'une si doux accueil je me serois passé.

273–275 *you know I met you* etc. Cf. Plautus, ll. 714ff.:

Alc. *Ecastor equidem te certo heri advenientem ilico,*
et salutavi et valuissesne usque exquisivi simul,
mi vir, et manum prehendi et osculum tetuli tibi.

(Loeb trans.: "Why mercy me, when you came home yesterday I certainly did welcome you the moment you appeared, and asked you in the same breath if you had been well all the time, and seized your hand and gave you a kiss.")

282–283 *but, much complaining / Of your drowsiness.* Cf. Plautus, l. 807: *Te dormitare aibas* (Loeb trans.: "You said you were sleepy").

289–290 *Is it a Crime* etc. Cf. Plautus, l. 817: *Quid ego tibi deliqui, si, cui nupta sum, tecum fui?* (Loeb trans.: "Pray tell me what [wrong] I have done in being with you, the man I married?").

310–311 *my Vertue, / Like purest Linen.* There is much in this confronting of Amphitryon and Alcmena that rings like a distorted echo of *Othello,* IV, ii, 72–108.

316–326 *Divorcement is but petty Reparation* etc. Cf. Plautus, ll. 849ff., though the thoughts are in different order.

> Amph. . . . *quid si adduco tuom cognatum huc ab navi Naucratem* [Dryden's Gripus],
>> *qui mecum una vectust una navi, atque is si denegat*
>> *facta quae tu facta dicis, quid tibi aequom est fieri?*
>> *numquid causam dicis, quin te hoc multem matrimonio?*

(Loeb trans.: ". . . what if I bring your own relative, Naucrates, over from the ship? He made the voyage with me on the same vessel: now if he denies that I did as you say, what do you deserve? Have you any reason to give that I should not divorce you?") Divorce is not mentioned in Molière.

317–318 *But, since thou hast, with Impudence* etc. Cf. Plautus, l. 818: *Tun mecum fueris? quid illac impudente audacius?* (Loeb trans.: "You [were] with me? Of all brazen shamelessness!").

327 *Sir, Shall I wait on you.* Sosia keeps decorum, continuing to speak prose in a context of verse.

328 *Expect me.* Wait for me, await me (*OED*).

330 *Oh! Nothing* etc. It might be argued that this line hypermetrically completes one begun by Phædra. Because the decorum of Phædra's dialogue is prose, however, we regard this first line of Alcmena's speech as an independent hypometric line.

343 *a Side-Wind.* "An indirect means, method, or manner" (*OED*).

343 *how Squares go.* How "Affairs, events, matters, proceedings" go (*OED*).

348 *in a brown Study.* In Dryden's usage, the old phrase retains the now obsolete sense of "brown" as "gloomy" (*OED*); cf. *The Hind and the Panther,* II, 659 and n (*Works,* III, 158, 406).

349 *cogitabund.* The word (meaning "Musing, . . . deep in thought," *OED*) was apparently introduced in mid-century.

375 *anotherghess Morsel than old Bromia. Anotherguess* means "of another sort or kind" and is a corruption of *anothergates* (*OED*, citing this passage).

389 *Some pretty Quelque chose.* Although some joke may have been intended in having Sosia use a French phrase, it seems more likely that the French spelling here had the common English pronunciation represented by "Quickshaws" or "Kickshaws" derived from the then (and modern)

common French pronunciation omitting the "l" (*OED*). See the "quelque chose" of Molière's Sosie in the speech quoted in II, i, 278–282n.

408–409 *a Thimblefull of Cordial-water, is easily sipt off*. Cordial water means "spirit," liquor (*OED*), with suggestions of medicinal restoratives.

412 *O perjur'd Villain*. The verbal echo of II, ii, 245 confirms the parallelism of Mercury/Sosia's scene with Bromia and this scene between Sosia and Phædra. In both, Bromia enters upon Phædra talking to the two Sosias.

414 *Rattle*. "A sharp reproof" (*OED*).

450 *pumping*. To *pump* is "to ply with questions in an artful or persistent manner"; "to labor or strive" (*OED*).

452 *scoure*. To scour is "To beat, scourge. Hence, to punish, treat severely" (*OED*).

461 *overtaken*. To be drunk, intoxicated (*OED*).

470–473 *for, when I came to kiss you* etc. Cf. Molière, II, iii.

> CLEANTHIS.
>
> . . . .
>
>   Et lorsque je fus te baiser,
>   Tu détournas le nez, & me donnas l'oreille?
>
> SOSIE.
>
> Bon!
>
> CLEANTHIS.
>
>   Comment, bon?

483–485 *After which, I lovingly invited you* etc. Cf. Molière, II, iii:

> CLEANTHIS.
>
>   Enfin, ma flâme eut beau s'émanciper,
>   Sa chaste ardeur en toy ne trouva rien que glace;
>   Et dans un tel retour je te vis la tromper,
>   Jusqu'à faire refus de prendre au lit la place
>   Que les loix de l'Hymen t'obligent d'occuper.

Some of the next eleven speeches parallel what follows in Molière.

504–505 *there are five weeks of Abstinence* etc. It was long thought that sexual relations were ill-advised in hot weather. See Thomas Cogan, *The Haven of Health* (1589), pp. 219–220; Pepys, *Diary*, 9 July 1664; and Lawrence Stone, *The Crisis of the Aristocracy 1558–1641* (1965), p. 660, for Cogan, Pepys, and other citations.

524 *Indeed I wondered* etc. We regard this as a prose line (see 533–534n) but it obviously could scan as verse.

533–534 *Till I am reconcil'd* etc. Although Phædra's reply might be taken to complete the verse of l. 533, we believe that here and in ll. 543–547 Jupiter completes his own verse-line, speaking as it were around her intrusive prose.

563 *the bloody-Flux*. Dysentery.

576 *thou, other Sosia*. Jupiter's mental summons of the absent Mercury/Sosia originates with Plautus, ll. 976ff.

583–600 *SONG*. There is no need to provide a scansion of the verse of this song, but the extra initial syllable in the first line of the second stanza may be pointed to, and more importantly the dominant trochaic rhythm in spite of the final stressed syllable of many lines. As Summers noted, it was sung by John Bowman, who played Phœbus.

IV, i

2–3 *to the ridge of earth* etc. Dryden consistently imagines the end of the earth's land mass as a cliff or height from which one may depart to the extremity of this sphere or beyond into space. Cf. *Annus Mirabilis,* ll. 653–656; and see Earl Miner, "Dryden's 'Ocean leaning on the sky,'" *Explicator,* XXIV (May, 1966), entry no. 75.

17 *circled in your arms.* Summers compared a line in a prologue intended for Rochester's *Valentinian,* printed in 1685: "And languish'd in the circle of his arms." There are, however, numerous earlier precedents for the usage. Dryden's image differs most importantly from the usual ones by showing Alcmena's wifely passion in taking Jupiter into her arms.

24–26 *How you cou'd bear* etc. Lines 24 and 26 are hypometric, giving further evidence of the great variety and freedom of versification Dryden allowed himself in this play.

37–40 *you are ever new* etc. Cf. *All for Love,* III, i (1677, p. 31; S-S, V, 378):

> There's no satiety of Love, in thee;
> Enjoy'd, thou still art new; perpetual Spring
> Is in thy armes; the ripen'd fruit but falls,
> And blossoms rise to fill its empty place.

47–57 *I will not dare* etc. Cf. Jupiter's words in Molière, II, vi:
JUPITER.

. . . .

> Cette action, sans doute, est un crime odieux:
>   Je ne prétens plus le défendre;
> Mais souffrez que mon coeur s'en défende à vos yeux,
>   Et donne au vôtre à qui se prendre
>   De ce transport injurieux. . . .
> C'est l'Epoux qu'il vous faut regarder en coupable.
> L'Amant n'a point de part à ce transport brutal.

49 *Impute it to the Husband, not the Lover.* The distinction, like much else, is taken from Molière, II, vi, whose lengthy, high-flown speeches Dryden has pruned.

58 *Husband, and Lover, both alike I hate.* Cf. Molière, II, vi: "Tous deux sont criminels; tous deux m'ont offensée: / Et tous deux me sont odieux."

70 *only hatch'd upon your Tongue.* A curious image, apparently meaning "brought forth, engendered" in a loose sense.

83 *Forbear; I am offended with my self.* Cf. Molière, II, vi: "Laissez. Je me veux mal de mon trop de foiblesse."

108 *Many things happen betwixt the Cup and the Lips.* According to Tilley, T191, this is the standard version of the proverb.

125 *Not one of those I look'd for* etc. Cf. Plautus, l. 1009: *Naucratem quem convenire volui, in navi non erat* (Loeb trans.: "Naucrates, whom I wanted to get hold of wasn't on the ship").

137–202 In this section Dryden closely parallels Molière, III, ii.

158 *Midsummer-Moon.* Madness. The midsummer month was thought conducive to lunacy. Proverbial: see Tilley, M1117 (citing this usage).

179 *condign punishment.* Beating, as threatened by Amphitryon; but Mercury/Sosia pretends to fear harm to the wine bottled, he says, in Amphitryon's head.

186 *Napkins.* Small towels (*OED*).

202+ *s.d. Enter to him Sosia* etc. Plautus, l. 1035, has one witness, the pilot of Amphitryon's ship. Molière (III, v) has two, and later (III, viii) two more.

203–205 *Yonder he is* etc. Summers well compared Dominic's speech concerning Gomez in *The Spanish Fryar*, IV, i: "Yonder I see him keeping Centry at his door: ———have you never seen a Citizen, in a cold morning, clapping his sides, and walking forward and backward a mighty pace before his shop?"

208–209 *He's in one of his damn'd Moods.* For *Moods* in the sense of "Fits of variable or unaccountable temper; esp. melancholy, gloomy, or bad-tempered fits," the *OED* cites no use before 1859.

214–215 *a crash at the Bottle.* A *crash* is "A bout of revelry . . . etc.; a short spell, spurt" (*OED*).

236 *what, I hope, when a man is to be hang'd.* Cf. Molière, III, iv: "Lorsque l'on pend quelqu'un, on lui dit pourquoi c'est."

248–250 *To shut the door* etc. Cf. Molière, III, iv:

> AMPHITRYON.
> Comment! il vient d'avoir l'audace,
> De me fermer la porte au nez,
> Et de joindre encore la menace
> A mille propos effrenez!
> Ah! Coquin.

277–285 *Who gave you that order* etc. Closely paralleling Molière, III, iv:

> AMPHITRYON.
> Qui t'a donné cet ordre?
> SOSIE.
> Vous.
> AMPHITRYON.
> Et quand?
> SOSIE.
> Aprés vostre paix faite.
> Au milieu des transports d'une ame satisfaite.
> D'avoir d'Alcmene appaisé le courroux.

280 *a brace, or a lease.* A *brace* is "a pair, a couple"; and a *lease* (or *leash*) is a "set of three" (*OED*, citing this usage).

292–293 *Nay, he has told us* etc. Cf. Molière, III, iv: "Tout ce que de chez vous il vient de nous conter, / Surpasse si fort la nature."

296–299 *another Relation, within doors, call'd Amphitryon* etc. Here, and in the earlier passage of procreating (III, i, 250–254), Sosia is given an insight into the true state of affairs that escapes the others until Jupiter's concluding speeches.

322 *subversion of Fundamentals.* Dryden plays on *fundamentals* as primary principles, the groundwork of the system and the *fundament* or buttocks (*OED*).

343–367 Poor Sosia is made to suffer from his "dreadfull Imprecation."

360+ *s.d. Is entring: Mercury meets him* etc. The encounter of Mercury and Sosia, to the entrance of Phædra, parallels Molière, III, vi.

381–382 *hold good Intelligence together.* The word "Intelligence" is here used in the sense of "A relation or footing of intercourse between persons or parties; a good understanding" (*OED*).

402 *incorporate.* "[Unite] in one body" (*OED*).

415 *Interloping.* See the prologue, l. 17 and n.

421 *pragmatical.* The *OED* shows that the word held a variety of meanings, including "brisk, energetic"; "officious, meddlesome, interfering, intrusive"; and, what seems closest to the present use, "conceited, self-important" (quoting Addison, "Lacqueys were never so saucy and pragmatical . . .").

421–422 *Son of a Whore.* Mercury had admitted as much of himself: see I, i, 15–19 and n.

447 *bargain.* Cf. *Mac Flecknoe,* l. 181: "Where sold he Bargains, whip-stitch, kiss my Arse" (see *Works,* II, 59, 325); and "Prologue to *The Prophetess,*" l. 47 (*Works,* III, 256). Bargaining in this sense implied inducing someone to ask an innocent question in order to return a coarse reply. Shadwell in *The Virtuoso* seems to have introduced the bargain into literature, and, as Summers noted, Fielding's Squire Western continued it.

455 *shoeing-horns.* "An appetizer for food or drink," hence a provocative (*OED*).

481 *cast of my Office.* To give a taste of one's office. See Tilley, C117.

481+ *s.d. He stamps.* As Summers noted, stamping was the common English theatrical signal for starting action involving trapdoors. He gave numerous examples, dating from Dekker's play, *The Whore of Babylon* (1607) to Orrery's *Guzman* (1669) and Ravenscroft's *Dame Dobson* (1683).

481+ *Mercury's SONG to Phædra.* The Thorn-Drury copy of this play in the Bodleian Library (Thorn-Drury d. 62) has the following manuscript note on the Song: "The Indifferent Lover, Or, The Roving Batchelor, To a Pleasant new Tune, Sung in the last new Comedy, called *Amphitryon,* Or, *Fond Boy.* [For Iris I sigh and hourly Dye,] Printed for Ch. Bates at the White Hart in West-Smithfield. Single leaf. . . ." Although the song is designated "Mercury's," it was sung (according to Summers) less appropriately by an actress, Charlotte Butler, who played Night; and, as the version with the music shows, was revised by Dryden or Purcell for the setting.

507+ *s.d. New Singers come up and sing a Song.* See l. 481+ *s.d.* Phædra repeats Mercury's miracle, stamping conventionally to signal a rise from below. The present song pairs stanzas I and II, and again III and IV, as part of the "Pastoral Dialogue." The "Dialogue" proper does not begin until l. 513, "O kiss me longer" etc. The preceding lines are narrative not spoken by Thyrsis *in propria persona,* and therefore his speech tag might be dropped to l. 513. We leave it where it appears in the printed text, believing it causes no real confusion and doubting that Dryden felt compulsion to distinguish "point of view" in lyrical relation.

538–545 The question to be asked is in what sense these lines can be called *A RONDEAU.* The *OED* mysteriously cites this heading as the first modern use to mean "A short poem, consisting of ten, or in stricter sense of thirteen, lines, having only two rimes throughout and with the opening words used twice as a refrain"—not a single condition of which is observed by Dryden's stanza. The meaning he intends is musical, a new musical movement reflected by his change to a new stanza form and from alternating parts in the *Dialogue* to duet (*Chorus*). The score by Purcell shows how closely the poet and the musician worked together. The fifth line of the *Rondeau* rhymes only internally.

538 *at the height.* Meaning "at the highest point or degree" (*OED*), and with Dryden, often having special humorous implications: cf. the epilogue to *An Evening's Love,* ll. 40–41, and the fourth song from the same play, st. 5 (*Works,* X, 314, 311).

546 *to pay the Musick.* A "music" is "a company of musicians" (*OED*).

546–547 *Hope well Mr. Planett; there's a better Heav'n in store for you.* Phædra's drollery depends on the old notion of Mercury as one of the seven planets in astrology, on the efficaciousness of planets in directing men's affairs, and on her prediction of his having as a lover a better "heaven" than he does as a planet.

552 *They onely seem to hate, and seem to love.* On the cynicism of the Great (l. 550), cf. *Absalom and Achitophel,* l. 223: "For Politicians neither love nor hate" (*Works,* II, 12).

V, i

9 *Hide-bound.* "Close-fisted, stingy, niggardly" (*OED*).

14–16 *that when the Wind blows for the Subject* etc. "The infamous Scroggs, and several of Charles the Second's judges, had huffed, and roared, and ranted, and domineered over the unfortunate victims who suffered for the Popish Plot; and had been equally partial to prerogative, when the king's party attained a decided ascendancy" (Scott). But Dryden may also have in mind the political changes of dramatists like Elkanah Settle and John Crowne.

17 *compound.* "To come to terms" (*OED*).

20+ *s.d. Enter Mercury, with two Swords* etc. Carl Hartmann, *Einfluss Molière's auf Dryden's komisch-dramatische Dichtungen* (p. 38) saw the resemblance of this episode to Molière's *Le Mariage forcé* (first acted 1668), scene xvi (ed. of 1739), in which Alcidas challenges Sganarelle. Dryden's attention may have been drawn to the scene by the illustration in such editions as that in *Les Oeuvres* (Paris, 1682), III, showing the presentation of swords. Subsequent notes observe the parallels.

35–36 *Will your Honour be pleas'd* etc. Cf. Molière, *Le Mariage forcé*, ix: "Monsieur, prenez la peine de choisir, de ces deux épées, laquelle vous voulez."

44–47 *but with us Swordsmen* etc. Cf. Molière, *Le Mariage forcé*, xvi: "& je viens vous dire civilement qu'il faut, si vous le trouvez bon, que nous nous coupions la gorge ensemble." Sganarelle's next speech but one may have suggested Gripus' rejoinder: ". . . je n'ai point de gorge à me couper."

65 *s.d. Phillips him under the Chin* etc. To "fillip" is "To strike smartly" (*OED*). The farcical action resolving the episode parallels that in Molière, *Le Mariage forcé*, xvi.

69 *a Non-suit*. Meaning "the cessation of a suit resulting from the voluntary withdrawal of the plaintiff" (*OED*).

86 *Livery and Seisin*. Properly, "Livery of seisin," "the delivery of property into the corporal possession of a person" (*OED*).

88 *an Act of Oblivion*. Referring to the Act of 1660 in which Charles II pardoned all rebels but those singled out by Parliament, and the comparable act by William III in 1690, the time of the play. The idea is that Gripus is to forget all affronts to him.

90 *under my Girdle*. Meaning "under one's control" (*OED*).

90–91 *cap Verses with him to the end of the Chapter*. To cap a verse is usually "to reply to one previously quoted with another, that begins with the final or initial letter of the first," etc. (*OED*), but Dryden here seems to mean replying to verses of the Bible in succession to the end of a given chapter.

114 *Who dares to play the Master* etc. From this point to Tranio's speech beginning "We must not suffer / So strange a Duel" etc. about thirty-five lines later, Dryden parallels Molière, returning from *Le Mariage forcé* to *Amphitryon* (III, v), where, however, Mercury is not present.

123 *the Gorgon's head*. Classical writers give varying accounts of the Gorgon (e.g., Hesiod, *Theogony*, ll. 270–283). But from classical to modern times it was common to refer to one of the three Gorgons, the snaky-haired Medusa, as *the* Gorgon. Dryden perhaps was recalling Ovid's account of Perseus (*Metamorphoses*, IV, 604ff.), who slew Medusa with great effort and who found that even after that her head could produce the effects Amphitryon describes here.

168 *I am content* etc. Amphitryon rarely speaks, as he does here, in prose.

204–205 *a double U: but they have no such letter in their Tongue*. The word-play is no better than many Elizabethan puns. The language is Greek, from what Jupiter next says.

211 *hiccius doccius*. "A formula used by jugglers in performing their feats; hence, 'a cant word for juggler; one that plays fast and loose.'" It is thought to be a corruption of *hicce est doctus*, "this or here is the learned man" (*OED*, citing this use). Summers well compared Wycherley's *The Country Wife*, III: "Burlesque is a Hocus-Pocus trick they taught, which by the virtue of *Hictius doctius, topsey turvey*, they made a wise and witty Man in the World, a Fool upon the Stage you know not how."

215–226 Dryden mixes Greek and English money so far that it is useless to attempt, as Summers did, to say what sum is involved here.

228 *Pterelas.* "Pterelas did not live in the time of Amphitryon, but was the son of Taphius, a son of a niece of Alcadus, the father of Amphitryon. Plautus and Molière have made the same mistake" (Van Laun, trans., *The Dramatic Works of Molière,* IV, 247).

254 *where's Alcmena's honour* etc. In what follows, the suffering in the human condition comes to be seen from Alcmena's as well as from Amphitryon's viewpoint.

279 *lanch'd.* A spelling variant for "launched," from the verb meaning "To hurl" (*OED*).

284–286 *Thou wou'dst elude my Justice* etc. Cf. Molière, III, v:

> AMPHITRYON.
> Fourbe, tu crois par là, peut-être, t'évader:
> Mais rien ne te sçauroit sauver de ma vengeance. . . .
> Le Ciel même, le Ciel, ne t'y sçauroit soustraire;
> Et jusques aux Enfers, j'irai suivre tes pas.

316–320 *You ought to take it for an honour* etc. Cf. Molière, III, ix:

> MERCURE.
> Et les coups de bâton d'un Dieu,
> Font honneur à qui les endure.
> SOSIE.
> Ma foi, Monsieur le Dieu, je suis vôtre Valet.
> Je me serois passé de vôtre courtoisie.

329 *toy.* "A foolish or idle fancy; a fantastic notion, odd conceit; a whim" (*OED*).

330 *swinge you off, condignly.* To *swinge* means "To beat, flog, whip, thrash"; *condignly* means "deservedly; suitably" as in the sense of "condign punishment" (*OED*). See also I, ii, 50n.

332 *Wife of the left hand.* The usual usage suggested morganatic marriage (*OED*), but it might also imply an irregular marriage, without benefit of the parson.

345 *Gypsies.* "A contemptuous term for a woman, as being cunning, deceitful, fickle, or the like; a 'baggage' " (*OED*).

367 *Mass and Miss.* Master and Miss, especially the eldest children of each sex. Phædra will have but one of each.

393–412 Jupiter's first speech and Sosia's reaction parallel Molière, III, x:

> JUPITER.
> Regarde, Amphitryon, quel est ton imposteur,
> Et sous tes propres traits, voi Jupiter paroître.
> A ces marques tu peux aisément le connoître;
> Et c'est assez, je croi, pour remettre ton coeur
>   Dans l'état auquel it doit être . . .
>   Un partage avec Jupiter,
>   N'a rien du tout qui des-honore;
> Et sans doute, il ne peut être que glorieux,
> De se voir le Rival du Souverain des Dieux.

Je n'y vois pour ta flâme aucun lieu de murmure;
  Et c'est moi, dans cette avanture,
Qui tout Dieu que je suis, dois être le jaloux.
Alcmene est toute à toi, quelque soin qu'on employe;
Et ce doit à tes feux être un objet bien doux,
De voir, que pour lui plaire, il n'est point d'autre voye,
  Que de paroître son époux;
Que Jupiter orné de sa gloire immortelle.
Par lui-même n'a pû triompher de sa foi . . . .
                    SOSIE.
Le Seigneur Jupiter sçait dorer la pilule.

398 *Concurrence.* "Pursuit of the same object; rivalry, competition" (*OED*).

400 *stamps into a price. To stamp into* is "to convert by authorization into" (*OED*). *OED* gives no example of Dryden's whole phrase, or of a meaning of *price* that is altogether appropriate. His phrase seems to mean "converts by his authorization into something current and valuable."

415 *disseize.* "To oust, expel" (*OED*, citing but two prior usages, of 1127 and 1675).

416 *Hercules.* Plautus opens the play with Alcmena near the end of her pregnancy—a strange double pregnancy by Amphitryon and Jupiter—and in V reports her delivery of the "twins." Only Hercules is described in detail—his quelling of serpents in his cradle being one of the things related. Molière and Dryden appear to have thought that Jove's fondness for Alcmena would likely have been stronger near the time of Hercules' conception than at his birth and so content themselves with a prediction.

417 *Monsters, and Monster-men.* See *Don Sebastian,* I, 372n.

429–432 *produce a Squire* etc. The roguish servant is of course patterned after Sancho Panza, introduced into *Don Quixote* in Bk. I, ch. vii. Like some other editions, John Philips' *The History of the most Renowned Don Quixote* (1687) includes among other waggish poems, an address, "Gandalin, Squire to Amadis de Gaul to Sancho Pancha, Squire to Don Quixote," which Dryden might have recalled.

437–444 Sosia's passage of verse alters his usual prose decorum. In advancing to the front of the stage to speak this disquieting speech, he offers a kind of pre-epilogue.

EPILOGUE

1–15 The passage offers an amusing feminine version of *Absalom and Achitophel,* ll. 1–10.

12 *For Jove, the good Example did begin.* This line, and its context, led John Loftis to suggest that Dryden may here be glancing back at the court of Charles II: see "Dryden's Comedies" in *John Dryden* (*Writers and Their Background* series), ed. Earl Miner (1972), p. 54.

TEXTUAL NOTES

Introduction

CHOICE OF THE COPY TEXT

The copy text is normally the first printing, on the theory that its accidentals are likely to be closest to the author's practice; but a manuscript or a subsequent printing may be chosen where there is reasonable evidence either that it represents more accurately the original manuscript as finally revised by the author or that the author revised the accidentals.

REPRODUCTION OF THE COPY TEXT

The copy text is normally reprinted *literatim,* but there are certain classes of exceptions. In the first place, apparently authoritative variants found in other texts are introduced as they occur, except that their purely accidental features are made to conform to the style of the copy text. These substitutions, but not their minor adjustments in accidentals, are recorded in footnotes as they occur. In the second place, the editors have introduced nonauthoritative emendations, whether found in earlier texts or not, where the sense seems to demand them. These emendations are also listed in the footnotes. In the third place, accidentals, speech headings, stage directions, scene headings, and so forth, are altered or introduced where it seems helpful to the reader. All such changes also are recorded in footnotes as they occur. In the fourth place, turned b, q, d, p, n, and u are accepted as q, b, p, d, u, and n, respectively, and if they result in spelling errors are corrected in the text and listed in the footnotes. The textual footnotes show the agreements among the texts only with respect to the precise variation of the present edition from the copy text; for example, in *Albion and Albanius* at I, i, 21, the footnote "state,] F2; ∼ : F1, Q, F3, D" has reference to the substitution of a comma for a colon; F2 actually reads "State,".

Certain purely mechanical details have been normalized without special mention. Long "s" has been changed to round "s," "VV" to "W"; swash italics have been represented by plain italics; head titles and any accompanying rules, act and scene headings, and display initials and any accompanying capitalization, have been made uniform with the style of the present edition; speeches beginning in the middle of verse lines have been appropriately indented; the position of speech headings and stage directions and their line division have been freely altered (braces in the speech tags have been omitted; those in the stage directions have where possible been replaced by brackets; erratic uses of capitals in stage directions have been normalized); wrong font and turned letters other than q, b, p, d, u, and n have been adjusted; medial apostrophes that failed to print have been restored; italicized plurals in -'s have been distinguished (by italic final "s") from possessives (roman final "s"); spacing between words and before and after punctuation has been normalized when no change in meaning results; the common contractions have been counted as single words, but otherwise words abbreviated by elision have been separated from those before and after if the apostrophe is present (for example, "bind 'em both"); if the elided syllable is written out as well as marked by an apostrophe, the words have been run together (*"speak'it"*).

TEXTUAL NOTES

The textual notes list the relevant printings and manuscripts, assign them sigla, and give references to the bibliographies where they are more fully described. Normally only the seventeenth-century printings and manuscripts, the folio edition of the plays (1701), and Congreve's edition (1717) are cited, since there is little likelihood that authoritative readings will be found in any later manuscripts or editions. The textual notes also outline the descent of the text through its various manuscripts and printings, indicate which are the authorized texts, and explain how the copy text was selected in each instance. A list of copies collated follows. If the differences between variant copies of an edition are sufficient to warrant a tabular view of them, it will follow the list of copies collated.

The sigla indicate the format of printed books (F = folio, Q = quarto, O = octavo, etc.) and of parts of printed books (f = folio, q = quarto, o = octavo, etc.) and the order of printing, if this is determinable, within the format group (F may have been printed after Q1 and before Q2; f may have been printed after q1 and before q2). If order of printing is in doubt, the numbers are arbitrary, and they are normally arbitrary for the manuscripts (represented by M or m).

Finally the variants in the texts collated are given. The list is not exhaustive, but it records what seemed material, viz.:

All variants of the present edition from the copy text except in the mechanical details listed above.

All other substantive variants and variants in accidentals markedly affecting the sense. The insertion or removal of a period before a dash has sometimes been accepted as affecting the sense; other punctuational variants before dashes have been ignored. Failure of letters to print, in texts other than the copy text, has been noted only when the remaining letters form a different word or words, or when a word has disappeared entirely.

All errors of any kind repeated from one edition to another, except the use of -'s instead of -s for a plural.

Spelling variants where the new reading makes a new word (e.g., *then* and *than* being in Dryden's day alternate spellings of the conjunction, a change from *than* to *then* would be recorded, since the spelling *then* is now confined to the adverb, but a change from *then* to *than* would be ignored as a simple modernization).

In passages of verse, variants in elision of syllables normally pronounced (except that purely mechanical details, as *had'st, hadst,* are ignored). Thus *heaven, heav'n* is recorded, but not *denied, deny'd.*

Relining, except when passages printed as prose are reprinted as prose.

When texts generally agree in a fairly lengthy variation, but one or two differ from the rest in a detail that would be cumbrous to represent in the usual way, the subvariations are indicated in parentheses in the list of sigla. For example:

Merc. to Arch.] *Merc. to Arch.* F1, Q, F3, D (*Archon* F3); *Hermes.* F2. This means that F3 agrees with F1, Q, and D in reading *"Merc. to"*, but that while the rest of the speech tag reads *"Arch."* in F1, Q, and D, *"Arch."* has been expanded to *"Archon."* in F3; in F2, the speech tag is *"Hermes."*.

When variants in punctuation alone are recorded, the wavy dash is used in place of the identifying word before (and sometimes after) the variant punctuation. A caret indicates absence of punctuation.

As in the previous volumes, no reference is made to modern editions where the editor is satisfied that reasonable care on his part would have resulted in the same emendations, even if he collated these editions before beginning to emend.

Albion and Albanius

The first edition of *Albion and Albanius* was published in 1685 (F1; Macd 88a). The leaf containing the prologue and the epilogue seems to have been issued a few days later than the other leaves of the first edition. As Osborn notes (p. 91), the title page of the Yale copy, which originally belonged to Narcissus Luttrell, is marked "1^s 3 June"; but in that same copy the leaf containing the prologue and epilogue is marked "1^d 6 June, 1685."[1] The copies of F1 collated for this edition disclosed press variants in outer [(a)] and (b), inner (b), outer C, inner C and D, and outer E. The second edition (F2; Macd 88b) was published in 1687 by Lewis Grabu. It contained Grabu's music for the opera and replaced Dryden's preface (and postscript) with a dedication to King James. In addition to numerous other less important changes, this edition omitted the "Names of the Persons Represented," the description of "THE FRONTISPIECE," the description of the "Decorations of the Stage in the First Act," the prologue, and the epilogue. The third edition was published in 1691 (Q; Macd 88c); the fourth, in 1701 in Dryden's *Comedies, Tragedies, and Operas*, II, 305–326 (F3; Macd 107ai–ii [two issues, the differences not affecting this opera]), and the fifth, in 1717 in Congreve's edition of Dryden's *Dramatick Works*, V, 363–408 (D; Macd 109ai–ii [two issues, the differences not affecting this opera]).

F1 and F2 were printed from different manuscripts. Q was printed

---

[1] Cf. Macdonald (p. 128): "Good copies, including the Ashley Library copy on L. P., are often found without it. The stabbing of a copy in Emmanuel College Library shows that the leaf must have been issued with this particular copy."

from a copy of F1 with corrected outer [(a)] and (b), inner (b), outer C, inner C and D, and outer E; F3 from a copy of Q; and, finally, D from a copy of Q. Since Dryden seems not to have revised the text after the publication of F1, a Clark copy of F1 containing the prologue and the epilogue (*fPR3417.A1.1685) has been chosen as the copy text.

The following copies of the various editions have also been examined: F1: Clark (*fPR3417.A1 [without the prologue and epilogue]; *fPR3417. A1.1685a), Texas (Wj.D848.685aa), Yale (Ij.D848.t685); F2: Clark (*fPR3417. A1.1687), Harvard (*EC65.D8474.685ab); Q: Clark (*PR3410.C93; *PR3412.1687; *PR3417.A1.1691); F3: Clark (*fPR3412.1701 [2 cop.], *fPR3412.1701a); D: Clark (*PR3412.1717 [2 cop.], *PR3412.1717a).

Press Variants by Form

F1

Sheet [(a)] (outer form)

Uncorrected: Clark (*fPR3417.A1), Yale

Corrected: Clark (2 copies), Texas

Sig. [(a)]1

Title Page Quotation *justitiam, moniti*] $\sim_\wedge \sim$,

Sheet (b) (outer form)

Uncorrected: Clark (*fPR3417.A1), Yale

Corrected: Clark (2 copies), Texas

Sig. (b)1

Running Title *Preface,*] $\sim$.

Sig. (b)2*v*

12:1 *Written,*] $\sim_\wedge$

2–3 honoratum$_\wedge$ . . . Dii,] $\sim$, . . . $\sim_\wedge$

Catchword *catchword omitted*] Names

Sheet (b) (inner form)

Uncorrected: Yale

Corrected: Clark (3 copies), Texas

Sig. (b)2

10:35 sung$_\wedge$] $\sim$.

36 defferr'd] deferr'd

Sheet C (outer form)

Uncorrected: Clark (*fPR3417.A1.1685a), Yale

Corrected: Clark (2 copies), Texas

Sig. C2*v*

I, i, 212+ *s.d.* Gunman;] $\sim$,

Sheet C (inner form)

Uncorrected: Clark (*fPR3417.A1.1685), Yale

Corrected: Clark (2 copies), Texas

Sig. C2

I, i, 189+ *s.d. Sympohny*] *Symphony*

Sheet D (inner form)

Uncorrected: Clark (3 copies), Texas

Corrected: Yale

Sig. D2
  II, i, 23 You] Yon
                    Sheet E (outer form)
  Uncorrected: Clark (*fPR3417.A1.1685)
  Corrected: Clark (2 copies), Texas, Yale
Sig. E2*v*
  II, ii, 75 thyate] thy State

Preface: THE PREFACE.] F1, Q, F3, D; TO THE KING, SIR,
F2.   3:1–11:34   IF Wit . . . [*to*] . . . Majesty.] F1, Q, F3, D; A*Fter*
the Shipwrack of all my fairest Hopes and Expectations, in the Death of
the late King my Master, Your Royal Brother of ever Blessed Memory,
the only Consolation I have left, is that the Labour I have bestowed in
this Musical Representation, *has partly been employ'd in paying my most*
humble Duty to the Person of Your most Sacred Majesty. The happy In-
vention of the Poet furnish'd me with that Occasion: The feigned Mis-
fortune of two Persecuted Hero's, *was too thin a Veil for the Moral not*
to shine through the Fable; the pretended Plot, and the true Conspiracy,
were no more disguis'd on the private Stage, than they were on the
publick Theater of the World. Never were two Princes united more
straightly together in common Sufferings from ungrateful and Rebellious
Subjects. The nearness of their Blood was not greater than the conformity
of their Fortunes: But the Almighty has receiv'd the one to his Mercy in
Heaven, and rewarded the Constancy and Obedience of the other here
below: Vertue is at last Triumphant in both places. Immortality is actually
possess'd by one Monarch; and the other has the Earnest of it, in the
Type of Earthly Glory. My late gracious Master was pleas'd to encourage
this my humble Undertaking, and did me the Honour to make some
Esteem of this my Part in the Performance of it: Having more than once
condescended to be present at the Repetition, before it came into the
publick View. Your Majesty *has been also pleased to do me the same*
Honour, when it appear'd at Your Theater in greater Splendour, and
with more advantages of Ornament: And I may be justly proud to own,
that You gave it the particular Grace of Your Royal Protection. As the
Subject of it is naturally Magnificent, it could not but excite my Genius,
and raise it to a greater height, in the Composition, even to surpass it
self: At least, a vertuous Emulation of doing well, can never be so faulty,
but it may be excus'd by the Zeal of the Undertaker, who laid his whole
Strength to the pleasing of a Master and a Soveraign. The only Displeasure
which remains with me, is, that I neither was nor could possibly be fur-
nish'd with variety of excellent Voices, to present it to Your Majesty in
its full perfection. Notwithstanding which, You have been pleas'd to par-
don this Defect, as not proceeding from any fault of mine, but only from
the scarcity of Singers in this Island. So that I have nothing more at this
time to beg, than the continuation of that Patronage, which your Princely
Goodness hath so graciously allow'd me: As having no other Ambition in
the World, than that of pleasing You, and the desire of shewing my self

on all possible occasions, and with the most profound Respect, to be / Your MAJESTY's / Most humble, most obliged, and / Most obedient Servant, / *LEWIS GRABU.* F2 (*Grabu's dedication replaced Dryden's preface*).   3:13   *Heroes*] Heroes F1, Q, F3, D; *omitted from F2.*   3:26 Characters.] Q, F3, D; ∼ₐ F1; *omitted from F2.*   4:4   other,] Q, F3, D; ∼ₐ F1; *omitted from F2.*   4:4   *English*] English F1, Q, F3, D; *omitted from F2.*   4:5   call] Q, F3, D; ∼ , F1; *omitted from F2.*   4:6   Numbers] F1 (*some copies*), Q, F3, D; Numb rs F1 (*some copies*); *omitted from F2.*   4:8   indeed] Q, F3, D; ∼ , F1; *omitted from F2.*   4:9   consideration,] D; ∼ₐ F1, Q, F3; *omitted from F2.*   4:13   after Undertakers] F1; after-undertakers Q, F3, D (After-Undertakers D); *omitted from F2.*   4:22   Author] F1 (*some copies*), Q, F3, D; Au hor F1 (*some copies*); *omitted from F2.*   4:29   Worship] Q, F3, D; Worsh p F1; *omitted from F2.*   5:6   *Moores*] Q, F3, D (*Moors*); Moores F1; *omitted from F2.*   5:6–7   *Zambra's*] Q, F3, D (*Zambra's* F3); Zambra's F1; *omitted from F2.*   5:9   *Sortiia's*] F1, Q, D; Sortia's F3; *omitted from F2.*   5:10   *Moresque*] Moresque F1, Q, F3, D; *omitted from F2.*   5:18–19   Treasury:] F1; ∼ , Q, F3, D; *omitted from F2.*   5:32   Goddess] F3; Goddesses F1, Q, D; *omitted from F2.*   6:1   generally] Q, F3, D; ∼ , F1; *omitted from F2.*   6:2   *Heroes*] Heroes F1, Q, F3, D; *omitted from F2.*   6:5   *Golden Age*] F1, Q, D; Golden-Age F3; *omitted from F2.*   6:24   *Dutch*] Q, F3, D; ∼ , F1; *omitted from F2.*   6:26   *Greek . . . Latin*] Q, F3, D; Greek . . . Latin F1; *omitted from F2.*   7:9–12   allow (as . . . Poet),] ∼ : ∼ . . . ∼ , F1; ∼ ; ∼ ⫶ . . ∼ ; Q, F3, D; *omitted from F2.*   7:15   *English*] Q, F3, D; English F1; *omitted from F2.*   7:15   disadvantages] Q, F3, D (Disadvantages); disadvantage F1; *omitted from F2.*   7:16   *Teutonique*] Q, F3, D (*Teutonick*); Teutonique F1; *omitted from F2.*   7:17   Consonants,] Q, F3, D; ∼ₐ F1; *omitted from F2.*   8:3   *Alchymist*] Q, F3, D; Alchymist F1; *omitted from F2.*   8:5   far be] F1; be Q, F3, D; *omitted from F2.*   8:13   *Grabu*] Grabut F1, Q, F3, D; *omitted from F2.*   8:31   have] F1, D; having Q, F3; *omitted from F2.*   8:34   glad,] Q, F3, D; ∼ₐ F1; *omitted from F2.*   9:4   the Writing] F1; writing Q, F3, D (Writing F3); *omitted from F2.*   9:13   there] F1, F3, D; their Q; *omitted from F2.*   9:20   awhile] F1, D; a while Q, F3; *omitted from F2.*   10:16   this] F1 (*some copies*), Q, F3, D; th s F1 (*some copies*); *omitted from F2.*   10:26   *Tempest*] Q, F3, D; Tempest F1; *omitted from F2.*   10:35–36   sung. . . . deferr'd] F1 (*corrected form*), Q, F3, D; ∼ₐ . . . defferr'd F1 (*uncorrected form*); *omitted from F2.*   11:28   *Tempest*] Q, F3, D; Tempest F1; *omitted from F2.*

Postscript: POSTSCRIPT.] F1, D; *POST-SCRIPT.* Q; POSTSCRIPT. F3; *omitted from F2.*   12:1–13:8   *This Preface . . . [to] . . . Happiness.*] *omitted from F2.*   12:1–3   *Written*ₐ . . . honoratum, . . . Dii_ₐ] F1 (*corrected form*), Q, F3, D (*written* D); ∼ , . . . ∼ₐ . . . ∼ , F1 (*uncorrected form*); *omitted from F2.*   12:13   *Shipwrecks*] F1, Q, F3; Shipwrecks D; *omitted from F2.*   13:3   luckily] F1, Q, D; luckly F3; *omitted from F2.*

Prologue: PROLOGUE / *To the*] F1 (*some copies*), Q, F3 (To the Q,

F3); PROLOGUE D; *omitted from some copies of F1 and from all copies of F2.* OPERA] OPERA. *By Mr.* Dryden F1 (*some copies*), Q, F3; *omitted from some copies of F1 and from all copies of F2, D.* 1–46 FULL . . . [*to*] . . . *roaring.*] *omitted from some copies of F1 and from all copies of F2.* 1–6 *twenty* . . . [*to*] . . . *like*] *italics and romans reversed in F1; omitted from F2.* 6–26 *or* . . . [*to*] . . . *last*] *italics and romans reversed in F1; omitted from F2.* 6 Hero's] F1; *Hero's* Q, F3, D; *omitted from F2.* 9 *Faith,*] ~‸ F1, Q, F3, D (Faith F1; *'Faith* D); *omitted from F2.* 16 *Julep dance*] F1, Q, F3 (Julep dance F1; *Dance* F3); *Julep-dance* D; *omitted from F2.* 18 *already.*] F1, F3, D (already F1); ~‸ Q; *omitted from F2.* 22 *leading strings*] F1 (leading strings); *Leading-strings* Q, F3, D; *omitted from F2.* 23 *Friends*] F1 (Friends); *Friend* Q, F3, D; *omitted from F2.* 27 Freedom . . . Zeal] F1; *Freedom . . . Zeal* Q, F3, D; *omitted from F2.* 27–42 *and* . . . *have* . . . [*to*] . . . *You*] *italics and romans reversed in F1; omitted from F2.* 28 *Pray*] D; *'Pray'* F1, Q ('Pray' F1); *'Pray* F3; *omitted from F2.* 29 *before.*] F1 (before); ~ ; Q, F3, D; *omitted from F2.* 35 *Sees*] F1, D (Sees F1); See Q, F3; *omitted from F2.* 39 Monde] ~ , F1, Q, F3, D (*Monde* F1). 42–46 *may* . . . [*italics*] . . . *roaring*] *in romans in F1; omitted from F2.*

Persons Represented: Names . . . [*to*] . . . *Graces.*] *omitted from F2.* Persons Represented;] F1; ~ , ~‸ Q, F3, D (PERSONS F3; represented D); *omitted from F2.* Stage] D; STAGE F1, Q; STAGE F3; *omitted from F2.* *Loves* and] *Loves and* F1, Q, F3, D (*Loves,* Q, D); *omitted from F2.* *Neptune.*] F1, Q, F3; *omitted from F2, D.*

Frontispiece: THE] F3; The F1, Q, D; *omitted from F2.* FRONTISPIECE . . . [*to*] . . . disco.]F1, Q, F3, D (FRONTISPICE D); *omitted from F2.* 17:1 *Frontispiece*] F1, Q, F3; *Frontispice* D; *omitted from F2.* 17:8 Peace] D; *Peace* F1, Q, F3; *omitted from F2.* 17:8–9 *Olive Branch*] F1; *Olive-Branch* Q, F3, D; *omitted from F2.* 17:9 Plenty] D; *Plenty* F1, Q, F3; *omitted from F2.* 17:14 Poetry] Q, F3, D; *Poetry* F1; *omitted from F2.* 17:15 *Hand,*] Q, F3, D; ~‸ F1; *omitted from F2.* 17:16 *other,* Painting,] Q, F3, D; *other painting* F1; *omitted from F2.* 17:18 Muses] *Muses* F1, Q, F3, D; *omitted from F2.* 17:18 *Base Vo*[illegible]] F1, Q; *Base-Voyal* F3, D (*Base-Viol* D); *omitted from F2.* 17:1[illegible] Muses] *Muses* F1, Q, F3, D; *omitted from F2.* 17:27 *shakl'd,*] Q, [illegible], D (*shackl'd*); *shakle'd*‸ F1; *omitted from F2.* 18:1 *Majesty; the*[illegible]1; ~ ; *and the* Q, F3, D; *omitted from F2.* 18:6 Harpyes] Q, F[illegible] (Harpies); *Harpyes* F1; *omitted from F2.* 18:7 *three*] F1; Thr[illegible], F3, D; *omitted from F2.* 18:7, 10 Graces] Q, F3, D; *Graces* F1; [illegible]*itted from F2.* 18:10 *his*] F1; *their* Q, F3, D; *omitted from F2.* 18:14 succurrere] Q, F3, D; succurere F1; *omitted from F2.*

Decoratio[illegible]*s of the stage:* Decorations . . . [*to*] . . . *Reverst.*] *omitted from F2.* *Frontispiece*] F1, Q, F3; *Frontispice* D; *omitted from F2.* Royal E[illegible]ange] F1, Q, F3; Royal-Exchange D; *omitted from F2.* *could*] Q, F3[illegible]D; ~ , F1; *omitted from F2.* Mercury] *Mercury* F1, Q, F3;

MERCURY D; *omitted from* F2.   descends . . . [*to*] . . . *Ravens*] *in romans in* F1, Q, F3, D; *omitted from* F2.   *painted*] *Painted* F1, Q, F3, D; *omitted from* F2.   Thamesis *are*] Q, F3, D; ~ , ~ F1; *omitted from* F2.

I, i

ACT I. SCENE I.] ACT I. F1–2, D; ACT. I. Q; ACT. V. F3.   s.d. *descends*] F3; *Descends* F1, Q, D; *s.d. omitted from* F2.   1 *Merc.*] F1, Q, F3; *Hermes.* F2; MERCURY. D.   1 Fabrick! stand for ever, stand:] F1, Q, F3, D; ~ , ~ ! ~ ~∧ ~ ! F2.   3 Gain!] F1; *Gain*, F2; ~ , Q, F3, D.   5 Main.] F1, Q, D; ~ : F2; ~ , F3.   6 meeting?] F1, Q, F3, D; ~ , F2.   7 Friends repeating,] F1, Q, F3, D; ~ , ~∧ F2.   8 Bargaines] F1; Bargain's F2; Bargains Q, F3, D.   8 sound?] ~ ! F1, Q, F3, D; ~ , F2.   9 every] F1, Q, F3, D; ev'ry F2.   9 Nation?] F1, Q, F3, D; ~ , F2.   12 *Hermes!*] Q, F3, D; Hermes! F1; ~ , F2.   13 while] F1, Q, F3, D; when F2.   15–16 *Europes . . . Albions*] F2–3, Q, D (*Europe's . . . Albion's*); Europes . . . Albions F1.   16 Bride;] F1, Q, F3, D; ~ ! F2.   17 gone . . . Lord!] F1, Q, F3, D; ~ , . . . ~ , F2.   21 Heav'n] F1–3, Q; Heaven D.   21 state,] F2 (State); ~ : F1, Q, F3, D (State F3, D).   22 revolving] F1, Q, F3, D; resolving F2.   24–25 *s.d. sung*] Q, F3, D; *Sung* F1; *s.d. omitted from* F2.   24–25 *s.d.* Thamesis] F3; Thamisis F1; Tham. Q, D; *s.d. omitted from* F2.   25 She!] F1, Q, F3, D; she; F2.   26–27 *Hermes! . . . Hermes!*] F1, Q, F3, D; ~ , . . . ~ , F2.   26–27 *s.d. omitted from* F2.   30 Turrets] F1; Turret's F2–3, Q, D.   32 disperst!] F1, Q, F3, D (dispers'd Q, F3, D); ~ , F2.   33 reverst!] F1, Q, F3, D (revers'd Q, F3, D); ~ . F2.   34 *Merc.*] F1, Q, F3, D; *Her.* F2.   36 *Augusta!*] F1, Q, F3, D; ~ , F2.   36 so!] F1, Q, D; ~ , F2; ~ ; F3.   40 Rise,] F2–3, Q, D; ~∧ F1.   40 *Augusta*, rise.] F1, Q, F3, D; ~ , ~ ! F2.   41 rise!] F1, Q, F3, D; ~ , F2.   44 returning!] F1, Q, D; ~ ; F2; ~ , F3.   45 Never,] F2–3, Q, D (never F2); ~∧ F1.   46 *Merc.*] F1, Q, F3, D; *Her.* F2.   46 Thee, Wretch,] F1, Q, F3, D (thee F3); the∧ ~∧ F2.   50 even] F1, Q, F3, D; ev'n F2.   50 know!] F1, Q, F3, D; ~ . F2.   51 *Merc.*] F1, Q, F3, D; *Her.* F2.   52 Town!] F1, Q, F3, D; ~ , F2.   55 true! too] F1, Q, F3, D; ~ , ~ F2.   56 I, . . . City,] F1, Q, F3, D; ~∧ . . . ~∧ F2.   60 me!] F1, Q, F3, D; ~ . F2.   61 *Merc.*] F1, Q, F3, D; *Her.* F2.   63 repent?] F1, Q, F3, D; ~ ! F2.   64 deplore!] F1, Q, F3, D; ~ . F2.   65 I] F1–3, D; ~ . Q.   67 *Merc.*] F1, Q, F3, D; *Her.* F2.   68 long lost] F1, Q, F3, D; long-lost F2.   70 Nation!] F1, Q, D; ~ , F2; ~ ; F3.   72 Usurpation!] F1; ~ . F2–3, Q, D.   73 *Chor. of all*] F1, Q, F3, D (*Chorus* F3); CHORUS F2.   73–76 We'll . . . [*to*] . . . Usurpation.] *in italics in* F2.   74 Nation,] F1–2, D (*Nation* F2); ~ . Q; ~ ; F3.   76 *s.d.* [*Dance . . . Mercury*] F1, Q, F3, D; AYRE for *Mercury's* Followers F2.   77 Behold] F1, Q, F3, D; BEHOLD! F2.   77 appear,] F1; ~ ! F2; ~ ; Q, F3, D.   80 *Merc.*] F1, Q, F3, D; *Her.* F2.   80 fear!] F1, Q, D; ~ . F2–3.   81 *Chor. of all.*] D; ~ . ~ ~ .] F1; CHORUS. F2; *Chorus* ~ ~ .] Q, F3.   81 Resist . . . [*to*] . . . fear!] *romans in* F1, Q, F3, D (fear. F3); *italics in* F2.   81–81+ *s.d.* fear! / Enter] F3, D (fear. F3); ~ ! [~ F1, Q (*s.d. at right margin*);

fear. F2 (*s.d. omitted*). 82 City!] F1, Q, D; ~ , F2–3. 83–84 **Bring** . . . **more** / **To** . . . **Pleasures**] F1, Q, D; bring . . . ~ to . . . Pleasures F2; ~ . . . ~ to . . . ~ F3. 85–86 **Thou** . . . **Store,** / **And** . . . **more**] F1, Q, D; ~ . . . ~ , and . . . ~ F2–3. 87 Flood,] F2–3, Q, D; ~∧ F1. 88 thy] F1, Q, F3, D; the F2. 93 Saint!] F1, Q, F3, D; ~ . F2. 94 Vanquisht,] F1; vanquish'd! F2; Vanquish'd, Q, F3, D. 94 woe!] F1–2, Q, D (Woe D); ~∧ F3. 95–96 **Slave** . . . **art,** / **Thy** . . . **impart**] F1, Q, D; ~ . . . ~ , thy . . . ~ F2–3 (Thy F3). 97 know!] F1, Q, F3, D; ~ . F2. 102 *line indented in F1, Q, D.* 102 Vanquish'd,] F1, Q, F3, D; ~ ! F2. 107 fear.] F1–3, Q (Fear F2); Fear, D. 111 Commonwealth's] F1–2, D; Common-wealth's Q, F3. 111 Load] F1, Q, D; ~ , F2–3. 113 Shall never,] F2–3 (shall F2); ~ ~∧ F1, Q, D. 114 Commonwealth's] F1–2, D; Common-wealth's Q, F3. 114 Load] F1, Q, D; ~ , F2–3. 116 never, never, never] F3; ~∧ ~∧ ~ F1, Q, D; ~ , ~ F2. 117 Gates,] F2–3, Q, D; ~∧ F1. 120 waste!] F1, Q, F3, D; wast. F2. 121–122 **I'll** . . . **fast** / **To** . . . **embrac'd!**] F1, Q, D; I'le . . . ~ to . . . ~ . F2–3 (I'll F3; embrac'd! F3). 125 Thousand . . . mee!] F1, Q, F3, D (me Q, F3, D); thousand, . . . me. F2. 126 *Archon to Aug.*] *Archon to Aug.* F1, Q, F3, D; *Archon.* F2. 126 *Caledonian*] F2–3, Q, D; *Caledonion* F1. 127 thee,] F1–3, Q; ~ . D. 128 thee,] F1–2, Q, D; ~ ! F3. 130 ring,] F1–2, D; ~ . Q, F3. 132 *Chor.*] F2, D (CHORUS F2; *Chorus* D); ~ .] F1, Q, F3. 132 ring,] F2–3, Q, D; ~ . F1. 134 Armes! to] F1–2, Q, D (Arms F2, Q, D); Arms, ~ F3. 135 I lead] F1–2, Q, D; *I lead* F3. 135 way!] F1, Q, F3, D; ~ . F2. 136 *Merc.*] F1, Q, F3, D; *Hermes.* F2. 136 Alarmes!] F1, Q, F3, D (Alarms Q, F3, D); Alarms, F2. 138 Decree!] F1, Q, F3, D; ~ , F2. 141 be!] F1, Q, F3, D; ~ . F2. 143 *Merc.*] F1, Q, F3, D; *Hermes.* F2. 143 Take . . . *Caduceus!*] F1, Q, F3, D; ~ , . . . *Cadaceus,* F2. 146 Common-wealth] F1, Q, F3; Common-wealth F2, D. 146 pretences,] F2–3, Q, D (Pretences Q, F3, D); ~∧ F1. 148 assistance] F1; Assistants F2; Assistance Q, F3, D. 148+ *s.d. omitted from F2.* 150 down!] F1, Q, F3, D; ~ , F2. 151 *Albion!*] F1, Q, D; ~ , F2–3. 151 Crown!] F1, Q, F3, D; ~ ; F2. 152–153 **Happy** . . . **reign,** / **Till** . . . **again!**] F1, Q, D (again. D); happy . . . Reign, 'till . . . ~ . F2; ~ . . . Reign, ~ . . . ~ . F3. 153 wake] F1, Q, F3, D; awake F2. 153 *s.d. Falls*] F3, D; *falls* F1, Q; *s.d. omitted from F2.* 154–155 vain / I] F3, D; ~ , / ~ F1, Q; ~ ~ F2. 155 Powers] F1, Q, F3, D; Pow'rs F2. 158–159 **Ev'n** . . . **slumber** / **I** . . . **him**] ~ . . . ~ ~ . . . ~ F1–3, Q, D (ev'n F2; Slumber F2–3, Q, D). 163 Soveraign power] F1, Q, F3, D (Sovereign Q, F3, D; Power Q, F3, D); Sov'reign Pow'r F2. 164–165 **Wee'll** . . . **gains** / **Of** . . . **paines**] F1, Q, D (We'll Q, D; Gains Q, D; Pains Q, D); We'll . . . Gains of . . . Pains F2–3 (we'l F2). 166 him!] F1, Q, D; ~ . F2–3. 166 *s.d. omitted from F2.* 167 *Aug. and*] *Aug. and* F1, Q, F3, D; *Augusta.* F2. 167 *Tham.*] F1, Q, F3; *Thamesis.* F2; *Tham,* D. 169 madness,] F1; Madness, F2–3; Madness. Q, D. 170+ *s.d. A* . . . [*to*] . . . *them.*] F1, Q, F3, D; *omitted from F2.* 170+ *s.d. Stone colour*] F1; *Stone-Colour* Q, F3, D; *s.d. omitted from F2.* 170+ *s.d. double-fac'd*] Q,

F3, D; *double Fac'd* F1; *s.d. omitted from F2.*   170+   *s.d.* Hypocricy]
F1 (*errata*); Hypocracy F1; Hypocrisie Q, F3, D; *s.d. omitted from F2.*
170+   *s.d.* Phanaticism. *When*] F3; ~ ; *when* F1, Q, D; *s.d. omitted from*
F2.   170+   *s.d. asleep*] Q, F3, D; *a sleep* F1; *s.d. omitted from F2.*
171 *Merc.*] F1, Q, F3, D; *Hermes.* F2.   171 Cease, *Augusta!*] F1, Q,
F3, D (CEASE F1); Cease∧ ~ , F2.   173 Godlike] F1; God-like F2-3,
Q, D.   174 Cheere!] F1, Q, F3, D (Chear Q, F3; chear D); chear: F2.
175 Every] F1, Q, F3, D; Ev'ry F2.   178 Godlike] F1; God-like F2-3,
Q, D (God-like F2).   179 *Merc. to Arch.*] *Merc. to Arch.* F1, Q, F3, D
(*Archon* F3); *Hermes.* F2.   181 Lord!] F1, Q, F3, D; ~ ; F2.   181
s.d. omitted from F2.   185 *line indented in* Q, D.   185 ashore;]
F1, Q, F3, D; ~ . F2.   186 Sea Men] F1; Sea-men F2-3, Q (Sea-Men
Q, F3); Seamen D.   189+   *s.d. A . . . [to] . . . Liveries.*] F1, Q, F3, D;
AYRE for the Mariners. F2.   189+   *s.d. Watermen*] F1, D; *Water-men*
Q, F3 (*Water-Men* F3); *omitted from F2.*   189+   *s.d. The . . . [to]*
. . . Scene.] F1, Q, F3, D; RITORNEL. F2.   189+   *s.d. Symphony*] F1
(*corrected form*), Q, F3, D; *Sympohny* F1 (*uncorrected form*); *s.d. omitted*
from F2.   190 *Merc.*] F1, Q, F3, D; *Hermes.* F2.   192 *Jove,*] F1;
~ ! F2-3, Q, D.   193 Hee!] F1, Q, F3, D (He Q, F3, D); he. F2.   194
Hermes] F2, D; Hermes F1; *Herme* Q, F3.   198 gathering] F1, Q, F3,
D; Gath'ring F2.   198 Clouds,] F2, D; ~ ; F1, Q, F3.   199 Floods,]
F1, Q, D; ~ ; F2-3.   200 See,] F2-3 (see F2); ~ ; F1, Q, D.   201
Thee!] F1, Q, F3, D; thee. F2.   204 Delights,] F1; ~ ; F2-3; ~∧ Q;
~ . D.   205 See,] F2-3 (see F2); ~ ; F1, Q, D.   205 Thee,] F2-3,
Q, D (thee F2); ~∧ F1.   206 Thee!] F1, Q, F3, D; thee. F2.   207
every] F1, Q, F3, D; ev'ry F2.   208 firm'd] F1, Q, F3, D; 'firm'd F2.
210 Fair,] F1, Q, F3, D; ~ ! F2.   212+   *s.d.* Iris . . . *[to]* . . . sits.]
F1, Q, F3, D; RITORNEL. F2.   212+   *s.d.* Gunman,] F1 (*corrected form*),
Q, F3, D; ~ ; F1 (*uncorrected form*); *omitted from F2.*   213 Newes!]
F1, Q, F3, D (News Q, F3, D); News, F2.   216 dares] F1-3, Q; dare D.
219 spread] F1-3, Q; spreads D.   222 *Etesian*] F1, Q, F3, D; *Elesian*
F2.   222 *s.d. Retornella.*] F2-3, Q, D (RITORNEL F2); ~∧ F1.
223-228 Archon . . . *[to]* . . . resound.] F1, Q, F3, D; *omitted from F2.*
226 *Welcome*] Welcome F1, Q, F3, D (Welcome, F3); *omitted from F2.*
227 *Welcome*] Welcome, F1, Q, F3, D; *omitted from F2.*   228 *Wel-*
come] Welcome, F1, Q, F3, D; *omitted from F2.*   236 down.] F1, Q,
D; ~ ; F2; ~ , F3.   237 *Mer. Ju. Ir.*] F1, Q, F3, D (*Me.* Q; *Jun.* F3;
Iris. F3); *Iris* and *Juno. Hermes.* F2.   238 *s.d. omitted from F2.*
239 *Aug. and Tham.*] *Aug.* and *Tham.* F1, Q, F3, D; *Augusta. Thamesis.*
F2.   240 Tryumphal] F1, Q, F3, D (Triumphal Q, F3, D); Triumphant
F2.   245 Triumphal] F1, Q, F3, D; Triumphant F2.   246 *Albanius*]
F1, Q, F3, D; *Albanius.* / MARCHE F2.   246+   *s.d.* Part . . . *[to]*
. . . &c.] F1, Q, F3, D; *omitted from F2.*   247 *Full Chor.*] F1, Q, F3,
D (*Chorus,* D); CHORUS. F2.   247 Hail.] F1, Q, F3, D; hail. / RITOR-
NEL. F2.   248 Hail,] D; ~∧ F1-3, Q.   248 *Albion,*] F1-2, D; ~ .
Q, F3.   249 expectation!] ~ : F1, Q, F3, D (Expectation Q, F3, D);
Expectation; F2.   250 free] Q, F3, D; ~ . F1; ~ , F2.   253 Nation!]
F1, Q, F3, D; ~ . F2.   254-255 *sung by both Augusta and Thamesis*

in F2.   254 Behold] F1, Q, F3, D; ~ ! F2.   254 differing] F1, Q,
F3, D; diff'ring F2.   254 agree,] F2–3, Q, D; ~ . F1.   255 thy] F1
(*errata*), F2–3, Q, D; the F1.   255 Restauration.] F1–3, Q; ~ , D.
255+ *s.d.* Entry; . . . [*to*] . . . Albion.] F1, Q, F3, D (Entry. Q, F3, D);
AYRE for the four Parts of the World. / Second AYRE. / CHORUS. HAIL
Royal *Albion*, hail; hail Royal *Albion*, hail; hail Royal *Albion*, hail; hail
Royal *Albion*, hail to thee, thy longing People's Expectation; sent from the
Gods to set us free, sent from the Gods to set us free, sent from the Gods
to set us free, from Bondage, from Bondage, and from Usurpation; sent
from the Gods to set us free, from Bondage, and from Usurpation, to set
us free, from Bondage, and from Usurpation. F2.   255+ *s.d.* [*Exeunt.*]
omitted from F1–3, Q, D.

<h2 style="text-align:center">II, i</h2>

ACT II. SCENE I.] F2; ACT II. F1, Q, D; ACT. II. F3.   *The Scene* . . .
[*to*] . . . Zelota.] F1, Q, F3, D; PRELUDE. F2.   *The Change is Total, the*]
The Change is Total. *The* F1, Q, F3, D; *omitted from F2.   Side Scenes*]
F1, Q, F3; *Side-Scenes* D; *omitted from F2.   Liver;*] ~ . F1, Q, F3, D; *omitted from F2.   &c.*] F3; *&c.* F1, Q, D; *omitted from F2.   Beyond*] D;
beyond F1, Q, F3; *omitted from F2.   Behind this,*] ~ ~∧ F1, Q, F3, D;
omitted from F2.   s.d. Enter Pluto] Pluto F1, Q, F3, D; *omitted from F2.*
1 Offspring] F1, Q, F3; Off-spring F2, D.   2 Heav'n] F1, Q, F3, D; ~ , F2.
3 Light,] F1, Q, F3, D; ~ ; F2.   9 disunite] F1–3, Q; dis-unite D.
11 *Democ. and Zelot. together.*] *Democ. and Zelot. together.* F1, Q, F3
(& Q, F3; *together* F3); *Zelota. Democracy.* F2; *Dem. and Zel.* D.   17
Pray'r.] F1, Q, F3, D; ~ ! F2.   18 you] F1, Q, F3, D; ye F2.   19
fell.] ~ ? F1–3, Q, D.   20 first begotten] F1, Q, F3; First begotten F2
(?); first-begotten D.   23 Yon] F1 (*errata and corrected form*), F2–3, Q,
D (yon F2; Yon' D); You F1 (*uncorrected form*).   24 Soveraign] F1, Q,
F3, D (Sovereign Q, F3, D); Sov'reign F2.   26 Degree:] F2; ~ , F1, Q,
F3, D.   33–34 But . . . Fame / And . . . Name] F1, Q, D (Fame, Q,
D; Name, Q; Name; D); But . . . Fame, and . . . Name, F2–3 (F2 *not
lined*).   33 loosing] F1, Q, F3; losing F2, D.   35 *Cause*] F1, Q, F3,
D; *Canse* F2.   37 lot?] F1, Q, F3, D (Lot Q, F3, D); Lot. F2.   38
and] and F1, Q, F3, D (& Q); *omitted from F2.*   39 stoopt] F1; stoop'd
F2–3, Q, D.   39 Tow'rs!] Q; Towr's! F1, D; ~ : F2; ~ . F3.   44
and] and F1, Q, F3, D (& Q); *omitted from F2.*   46 turn] F1, Q, F3,
D (Turn Q, F3, D); time F2.   47 Heaven controuling, sent . . . down.]
F2 (Heav'n; F2 *not lined*); ~ ~ , / Sent . . . ~ . F1, Q, F3, D (Heav'n
F3).   47 rowling, rowling,] F1, Q, F3; rouling, rouling∧ F2; ~ , ~∧ D.
48 wonder'd] F1, Q, F3, D; wonder F2.   48 *Acherontique*] F2
(*Acherontick*); Acherontique F1, Q, F3, D (Acherontick Q, F3, D).   49
unpeopl'd] Q, F3, D; unpeople'd F1; unpeopled F2.   49 Store;] F1,
Q, F3, D; ~ ! F2.   50 Oar.] F1, Q, D; ~ : F2; ~ , F3.   53 see] F1,
Q, F3, D; ~ , F2.   54 vengeful] F1, Q, F3; 'vengeful F2, D.   55–58
'Tis . . . [*to*] . . . World.] *lines indented in F1, Q, F3, D.*   55 too,
too] ~∧ ~ F1, Q, F3, D; too much, too F2.   57 By] F1, Q, D; by F2;
But F3.   61 *line indented in F1, Q.*   66 hath] F1, Q, F3, D; has

F2.   69 return;] F1, Q, D; ~ , F2; ~ : F3.   73 *Alecto*,] F1, Q, F3,
D; ~ ! F2.   73 go,] F1, Q, F3, D; go! go, F2.   79 unfixt!] F1; unfix'd. F2; unfix'd! Q, F3, D.   80 forbear;] F1, Q, F3, D; ~ ! F2.   83
them] F1–2, Q, D; then F3.   84 Y' have] F1–2, Q, D; Y've F3.   88
Clamours] F1, Q, F3, D; Clamour F2.   88 loud] F1, Q, F3; ~ , F2, D.
90 of] F1–2, Q, D; off F3.   91 *Stygian*] F2, D; Stygian F1, Q, F3.
95 every] F1, Q, F3, D; ev'ry F2.   99 ev'n] F1, Q, F3, D; e'ne F2.
100 every] F1, Q, F3, D; ev'ry F2.   109–110 For He / Can be] F1, Q,
D; For he can be F2–3 (for F2; F2 *not lined*).   111–112 ease. /
One] F1, Q, F3, D (Ease D); ease. / *Alecto*. Take him, make him what you
please, for he can be a Rogue with ease. / *Pluto*. One F2.   112 Mis-
chief] F1, Q, F3, D; Mischiefs F2.   113 Forsworn.] F1, Q, F3, D (forsworn D); forsworn: Take him, make him what you please, for he can be a
Rogue with ease: F2.   114 *and . . . take him*] and . . . take him F1,
Q, F3 (Take F3); & . . . D; *omitted from* F2.   115 ease.] F1, Q, F3,
D (Ease D); ease. / PRELUDE. F2.   119 Dance,] F1–3, Q; ~ . D.
120 here when] F1–2; when Q, F3, D.   120 trouble:] F1; ~ . F2–3,
Q, D (Trouble Q, F3, D).   123 double.] F2; ~ : F1, Q, F3, D.   123+
s.d. *A . . . [to] . . . Devils*] F1, Q, F3, D; AYRE for the Devils F2.
124 let us laugh,] F1, Q, F3, D; let us laugh at our Woes, F2.   125
hath] F1, Q, F3, D; has F2.   125 lose.] F1, Q, F3, D; lose; ye Furies
advance, with the Ghosts in a Dance, 'tis a *Jubilee* here when the World
is in trouble; 'tis a *Jubilee* here, 'tis a *Jubilee* here, when the World is
in trouble, when the World is in trouble. / 'tis a *Jubilee* here when the
World is in trouble; 'tis a *Jubilee* here when the World is in trouble:
When People rebel, we frolick in Hell; but when the King falls, the
Pleasure is double; but when the King falls, the Pleasure is double; but
when the King falls, but when the King falls, but when the King falls, the
Pleasure is double, the Pleasure is double. / Second AYRE for Devils. F2.
125+ s.d. *[Exeunt.] omitted from F1–3, Q, D.*

II, ii

SCENE II.] PRELUDE. F2; *omitted from F1, Q, F3, D*.   The . . .
[to] . . . Day.] omitted from F2.   Thames] Q, F3, D; *Thames* F1;
omitted from F2.   &c.] F3; *&c.* F1, Q, D; *omitted from* F2.   to the]
F1, Q, F3; to D; *omitted from* F2.   s.d. Enter . . . *[to] . . . down.]*
omitted from F2.   1 Jealousy,] F1, Q, F3, D (Jealousie Q, F3, D);
Jealousie! F2.   1 ill,] F1, Q, F3, D (Ill Q, F3, D); Ill! F2.   4 Poy-
soning] F1, Q, F3, D (poysoning Q; poisoning F3, D); poys'ning F2.   5
gone,] F1, Q, F3, D; ~ ! F2.   9 rave, . . . rave,] F1, Q, F3, D; ~ !
. . . ~ ! F2.   10 pouring] F2–3, Q, D; pou'ring F1.   12–13 burns.
. . . Love,] F1, Q, F3, D; ~ , . . . ~ ; F2.   18+ s.d. Enter . . . *[to]*
. . . Religion] F1, Q, F3, D; PRELUDE F2.   18+ s.d. Zelota: . . .
Patriot;] ~ ; . . . ~ , F1, Q, F3, D; *omitted from* F2.   18+ s.d. other,]
D; ~∧ F1, Q, F3; *omitted from* F2.   26 Gold;] F1, Q, F3, D; ~∧ F2.
37 oppression] F1, Q, F3, D (Oppression Q, F3, D); Oppressions F2.
37 'em.] F1; ~ : F2; them∧ Q; them. F3, D.   44 ill!] F2 (Ill); ~ ?
F1, Q, F3, D (Ill Q, F3, D).   51 Isle:] F1, Q, F3, D; ~ , F2.   54+

s.d. *The* . . . [*to*] . . . *continues*] F1, Q, F3, D; PRELUDE F2.   54+
s.d. *Enter* . . . *Train.* / *Albion.* Then] D (*Alb.*); *Enter* . . . *Train.* Then
F1, Q (THen; s.d. *set as speech tag*); *Albion.* Then F2; *Enter* . . .
Train. / Then F3.   61 sleeping] F1, Q, F3, D; sleepy F2.   62 Lord?]
F1, Q, F3, D; ~ ! F2.   63 Gods,] F1, Q, F3, D; ~ ! F2.   65 wrong]
F1, Q, F3, D (Wrong Q, F3, D); Wrongs F2.   66 Mad-mens] F1-2, D
(Mad-men's F2; Mad-Mens D); mad Men's Q, F3.   74+ s.d. *omitted from*
F2.   75 *Merc.*] F1, Q, F3, D (*Mer.* D); *Hermes.* F2.   75 Pity] F1
(*errata*), F2, D; pity F1, Q, F3.   75 thy State] F1 (*corrected form*),
F2-3, Q, D; thyate F1 (*uncorrected form*).   79 late! . . . late!] F1, Q,
F3, D; ~ , . . . ~ . F2.   81 *Merc.*] F1, Q, F3, D (*Mer.* D); *Hermes.* F2.
84 must] F1, Q, F3, D; shall F2.   87 Of] Q, F3, D; of F1-2.   88
Vengeance, Vengeance] Vengeance, Vengeance F1, Q, F3, D; Vengeance,
cries Vengeance F2.   88+ s.d. *omitted from F2.*   89 t' asswage]
F1, Q, F3, D; to 'swage F2.   91 destroy;] F1, Q, F3, D; ~ ? F2.   95
God's] F1, Q, F3, D (Gods Q, F3, D); Gods! F2.   99 Well] D; ~ , F1,
Q, F3; ~ ! F2.   99 Thee.] F1, Q, F3, D (thee D); thee! F2.   102 re-
warded;] F1, Q, F3, D; ~ , F2.   103 sufferings] F1, Q, F3, D (Sufferings
D); Suff'rings F2.   105 Go:] F1, Q, F3, D; ~ ! F2.   105 Thee?) go,]
F1, Q, F3; thee∧) ~ ! F2; ~ ?∧ ~ , D.   106 Fate:] F1, Q, F3, D; ~ , F2.
107 Go,] F1, Q, F3, D; go! F2.   107 State,] F1, Q, F3, D; ~ ! F2.   110
more,] D; ~∧ F1-3, Q.   110 Friend!] F1, Q, F3, D; ~ ; F2.   115
Whatever] F1, Q, F3, D; What ever F2.   116 Shall] Q, F3, D; shall F1-2.
116 Exile,] F1, Q, F3, D; ~∧ F2.   118 so e're,] F1, Q, F3 (e'er Q, F3);
soe're, F2; so e'er. D.   120 Isle;] F1, Q, F3, D; ~ ! F2.   123 *Albion*
and Alban.] *Albion.* and *Alban.* F1, Q, F3 (*Albion*∧ F3); *Albanius. Albion.*
F2; *Albi.* & *Alba.* D.   123 Rosy-finger'd] D (rosie-finger'd); Rosy finger'd
F1-3, Q (Rosie Q, F3; Finger'd F2).   124 from her] F1 (*errata*), F2-3,
Q, D; from andher F1.   125 Day:] F1, Q, F3, D; ~ , F2.   128+
s.d. *The* . . . [*to*] . . . Apollo.] *omitted from F2.*   129 Hail] F1, Q,
F3, D; hail! F2.   129 pair!] F1, Q, F3, D (Pair F3, D); Pair, F2.   130
Gods] F2-3, D; God's F1, Q.   141 Lustre] F1, Q, F3, D; Lusters F2.
141+ s.d. Apollo . . . [*to*] . . . sight.] *omitted from F2.*   141+ s.d.
Neptune . . . [*to*] . . . him] F1, Q, F3, D; PRELUDE F2.   141+ s.d.
Sea Nymphs] F1; *Sea-Nymphs* Q, F3, D (*Sea-* / *Nymphs* F3); *omitted from*
F2.   142 *Thames.*] F2, Q, F3, D (*Neptune* F2; *Tham* D); ~ , F1.
142 *Ocean*] F2; Ocean F1, Q, F3, D.   147 chide] F1, Q, F3, D; Chide,
F2.   150 *Come* . . . [*to*] . . . *away.*] *in romans in F1-3, Q, D.*   151
See] F1, Q, F3, D; An AYRE for the Gods of the Rivers. / *Thamesis.* See!
F2.   151 God . . . attends] F1, Q, F3, D; Gods . . . attend F2.   152
a] F1, Q, F3, D; and F2.   155-156 Every . . . Every] F1, Q, F3, D;
Ev'ry . . . ev'ry F2.   157+ s.d. *Two* . . . [*to*] . . . *Sing.*] *omitted*
from F2 (but lines 158-163 sung by three voices).   158 Nymphs,] F1,
Q, F3, D; Nymph! F2.   163+ s.d. *The* Chacon *continues*] F1, Q, F3,
D; *FLUTES* F2.   163+ s.d. *The* . . . [*to*] . . . *Verses.*] *omitted from*
F2 (but lines repeated by four voices).   163+ s.d. *The* Chacon *con-*
tinues] F1, Q, F3, D; *VIOLINS* F2.   163+ s.d. *Two Nymphs and*
Triton Sing.] *Two Nymphs and* Tritons. F1, Q, F3, D; *omitted from F2*

(but lines 164–174 sung by three voices). 164 Sports and Pleasures]
F1, Q, F3, D; Pleasure, Pleasure, F2.   164 you] F1, Q, D; ~ , F2; ~ .
F3.   171 Nor Billow] F1, Q, F3, D; no Billows F2.   174 you again]
F1, Q, F3, D; y'again F2.   174+ *s.d. The* Chacon *continues*] F1, Q,
F3, D; *FLUTES and GITTARS* F2.   174+ *s.d. The . . . [to] . . .
&c.] omitted from F2 (but lines repeated by four voices).*   174+ *s.d.*
Pleasure,] Q, F3, D; ~ . F1; *s.d. omitted from F2.*   174+ *s.d. The*
Chacon *continues.] omitted from F2 (but violins and Flutes play alter-
nately).*   174+ *s.d. The . . . [to] . . . Sing.*] F1, Q, F3, D *(sing D);
omitted from F2 (but lines 175–181 sung by three voices).*   175 See]
F1, Q, F3, D; ~ ! F2.   179 Flowers] F1, Q, F3, D; Flow'rs F2.   179
adorning,] F1; ~∧ F2–3, Q, D.   180 Pleasure] F1, Q, F3, D; Pleasures
F2.   181+ *s.d. The* Chacon *continues*] F1, Q, F3, D; *VIOLINS* F2.
181+ *s.d. The . . . [to] . . . &c.] omitted from F2 (but lines repeated by
four voices).*   181+ *s.d.* Tritons] Triton F1, Q, F3, D; *s.d. omitted
from F2 (but lines repeated by four voices).*   181+ *s.d. The* Chacon
continues] F1, Q, F3, D; *VIOLINS* F2.   181+ *s.d. Then . . . [to]
. . . &c.] omitted from F2 (but lines repeated by four voices).*   181+
s.d. repeat,] F1, F3, D; ~ . Q; *s.d. omitted from F2.*   181+ *s.d. And
. . . [to] . . . Act*] F1, Q, F3, D; *Finis Actus Secundus* F2.   181+ *s.d.*
[Exeunt.] omitted from F1–3, Q, D.

III, i

ACT III. SCENE I.] F2; ACT. III. F1, Q; ACT III. F3, D.   *The
. . . [to] . . . view*] F1, Q, F3, D *(View* F3, D); *PRELUDE* F2.   Devils-
Drop] D (Devil's-Drop); Devils drop F1, Q, F3; *omitted from F2.   s.d.
Enter . . . [to] . . . him.] omitted from F2.   s.d.* bareheaded] F1; bare-
headed Q, F3, D; *omitted from F2.*   1 Behold] F1, Q, F3, D (B*e*hold);
~ , F2.   1 Pow'rs] F1–2; Powers Q, F3, D.   3 uncrown'd] F1–3,
Q; un-crown'd D.   4 Offspring] F1–2, Q; Off-spring F3, D.   9
Acacia. Empire] F2–3, D *(Ac.* D); ~ . / ~ F1, Q.   12 despising,] F1–
3, Q; ~∧ D.   15 Unhelpt] F1; Unhelp'd F2–3, Q, D.   17 hope]
F1, Q, F3, D (Hope D); Hopes F2.   17 bereft.] F2, D; ~ : F1, Q, F3.
19 avail,] F1–2, D; ~ . Q; ~∧ F3.   20 Rebellion] F1, Q, F3, D; Religion F2.   21 good?] F1–2, Q, D (Good F2, Q, D); Good! D.   22
Monarch's,] ~∧ F1, Q, F3, D (Monarchs Q, F3, D); Monarchs! F2.   23
me!] F1, Q, F3, D; ~ , F2.   30 *Chorus of both*] F1, Q, F3, D; C*horus*
F2 *(sung by four voices).*   30 Love,] F2–3, Q, D; ~∧ F1.   31 Albion. . . . [to] . . . these?] F1–2 (these! F2); *omitted from Q, F3, D.*
31 see!] F1; ~ , F2; *omitted from Q, F3, D.*   34+ *s.d.* Nereids . . .
[to] . . . dance] F1, Q, F3, D *(Dance* F3); AYRE for the Tritons F2.
35–38 *in italics in F2.*   35 old] F1, Q, F3, D; our F2.   35 *Ocean*]
F2 (Ocean *[but fonts reversed in F2]*); Ocean F1, Q, F3, D.   36 Come]
F3, D; come F1–2, Q *(come* F2).   37 Sea-raceing] F1 (errata), Q, F3,
D (Sea-racing Q, F3, D); Sea-spouting F1; *Sea-sporting* F2.   37 train'd]
F1 (errata), Q, F3, D; tam'd F1–2 (tam'd F2).   37 Motion] F1 (errata),
Q, F3, D; motion F1–2 *(motion* F2).   38 a-shore.] F2–3, Q, D (ashore
F2); ~ , F1.   39–42 Ev'ry . . . *[to] . . .* vain.] *omitted from F2.*   40

off] Q, F3, D; of F1; *omitted from F2.* 41 unattending] F1 (*errata*), Q, F3, D; unattended F1; *omitted from F2.* 42+ *s.d.* Enter . . . [*to*] . . . *Women.*] *omitted from F2.* 42+ *s.d.* Asebia,] F1, Q, F3, D; Asebia *and* D; *omitted from F2.* 43 Ha, ha,] F1, Q, F3, D (HA F1, Q); ~ ! ~ ! F2. 45 wrought] F1, Q, F3, D; brought F2. 47 fomented, ——] ~ ,∧ F1–3, Q, D. 48 new!] F1, Q, F3, D; ~ ; F2. 49 invented,——] ~ ,∧ F1–3, Q, D. 51 flatter'd,——] ~ ,∧ F1, Q, F3, D; ~ ;∧ F2. 52 scatter'd.] F1, Q, D; ~ : F2; ~ , F3. 54 cause; ——] ~ ;∧ F1–3, Q (Cause F2–3, Q); Cause.∧ D. 55 Business] F1, Q, F3, D; Bus'ness F2. 56 applause:——] ~ :∧ F1–3; Q, D (Applause F2, D). 58 Law's] F1; Laws F2, Q, D; Law F3. 59 Chor.] F1, Q, F3, D (Chorus F3); *omitted from F2* (*but lines repeated by four voices*). 60 Prey;——] ~ ;∧ F1–3, Q, D. 61 sway,——] ~ ,∧ F1–3, Q, D (Sway; F2; Sway Q, F3, D). 64 poor.] ~ : F1, Q, F3, D; ~ ; F2. 69 the] F1, Q, F3, D; your F2. 70 Masterpiece] F1–2; Master-piece Q, F3, D. 73 th'] F1–2, Q, D; the F3. 73 grief,] F2 (Grief); ~ ; F1, Q, F3, D (Grief Q, F3, D). 77 'twas] F2–3, Q, D; t'was F1. 78 heigh] F1–3, Q; hey D. 83 Saints] F2; *Saints* F1, Q, F3, D. 85 come] F1–2; comes Q, F3, D. 85+ *s.d.* The . . . [*to*] . . . *Dance*] F1, Q, F3, D; AYRE for the Boys in white F2. 86 Chor.] F1, Q, D; *Asebia. Zelota. Democracy. Tiranny.* F2; *Chorus.* F3. 89 own.] ~ ; F1, Q, F3, D; ~ : F2. 90 Chor.] F1, Q, D; *Asebia. Zelota. Democracy. Tiranny.* F2; *Chorus.* F3. 91 *Asebia*] F1–3, Q; *Asel.* D. 93 Sovereign] F1, Q, F3 (Soverign Q); Sov'reign F2, D. 93 soar.] F1, Q, F3, D; ~ ; F2. 95 'em] F1–2; them Q, F3, D. 96+ *s.d.* Six . . . [*to*] . . . *receive*] F1, Q, F3, D; AYRE for the *Sectaries.* PRELUDE F2. 96+ *s.d. to* 'em] F1; *to them* Q, F3, D; *omitted from F2.* 101 done?] F1, Q, F3, D; ~ . F2. 103 slain!] F1, Q, F3, D; ~ . F2. 125+ *s.d.* The . . . [*to*] . . . *Flails*] F1, Q, F3, D; AYRE for the fighting white Boys and Sectaries F2. 125+ *s.d. White*] white F1, Q, F3, D; *omitted from F2.* 125+ *s.d. 'em*] F1; them Q, F3, D; *omitted from F2.* 125+ *s.d. White . . . White*] white . . . white F1, Q, F3, D; *omitted from F2.* 127 past!] F1, Q, F3, D; ~ . F2. 131 steep] F1, Q, F3, D (Steep Q, F3, D); Step F2. 139 true!] F1, Q, F3, D; ~ ; F2. 141+ *s.d.* The . . . [*to*] . . . *Sings.*] F1, Q, F3, D (sings, D); *omitted from F2.* 141+ *s.d. Rock work*] F1; *Rock-work* Q, F3, D (Rock-Work D); *omitted from F2.* 141+ *s.d.* Dover Peer] F3; Dover Peer F1; Dover-Peer Q; Dover-Peer D; *omitted from F2.* 141+ *s.d. asleep*] Q, F3, D; *a sleep* F1; *omitted from F2.* 141+ *s.d. like*] F3, D; Like F1, Q; *omitted from F2.* 141+ *s.d.* Symphony] F1, Q, F3, D; PRELUDE F2. 143 Reigning,] F1–2, D (reigning F2, D); ~∧ Q; ~ . F3. 144 sorrow] F1, Q, F3, D (Sorrow Q, F3, D); Sorrows F2. 156 more!] F1, Q, F3, D; ~ , F2. 156+ *s.d.* Proteus *descends*] F3; *Proteus* descends F1, Q, D; PRELUDE F2. 156+ *s.d.* Democracy . . . [*to*] . . . *Faction*] F1, Q, F3, D; PRELUDE F2. 159 disperst] F1; dispers'd F2–3, Q, D. 160 We . . . Souls remain.] F1, Q, F3, D; we, . . . ~ ! ~ : F2. 165 t' other] F1, Q, F3, D; th'other F2. 166 do't.] F1, Q, F3, D; do't: Shoot, shoot, holy *Cyclops*, shoot. F2. 167 *Omnes.*]

F1, Q, F3, D; *Asebia. Zelota. Democracy. Tiranny.* F2.   167 Shoot,]
F2 (Shoot, shoot,); ~∧ F1, Q, F3, D.   167 *Cyclop*] F1, Q, F3, D;
Cyclops F2.   167+ *s.d. The . . . [to] . . . Albion.*] F1, Q, F3, D;
omitted from F2.   167+ *s.d. one-Ey'd*] D; one Ey'd F1, Q, F3; *omitted
from F2.*   168 combine,] F1–3, Q; ~ . D.   175 Crimes?]'F3; ~ . F1,
Q, D; ~ , F2.   178 *Chor.*] F1, Q, F3, D (*Chorus.* F3); *Asebia. Zelota.
Democracy. Tiranny.* F2.   178 th' avenging] F2, D; the avenging F1,
Q, F3.   178+ *s.d. As . . . [to] . . . together.] omitted from F2.*   180
vaulted Arch] F1, Q, F3, D; Vaults F2.   182 'em.] F2; ~ : F1, Q, F3,
D.   187 main.] F1, Q, F3, D (Main Q, F3, D); Main! F2.   189
Loves . . . Graces] loves . . . graces F1; Loves . . . Graces F2–3, Q, D.
189+ *s.d. A . . . [to] . . . sinks*] F1, Q, F3, D; Concert of *Venus* F2.
189+ *s.d.* Venus *and*] Q, F3, D; ~ , ~ F1; *omitted from F2.*   189+
s.d. Loves . . . Graces] *Loves . . . Graces* F1, Q, F3, D; *omitted from F2.*
189+ *s.d. playing,*] F3; ~∧ F1, Q, D; *omitted from F2.*   189+ *s.d.*
Venus *Sings*] F3, D (VENUS D); *Venus* Sings F1, Q; *Venus* F2.   190
Hail;] F1, Q, F3, D; hail! F2.   192 Pleasures,] F1, Q, F3, D; Pleasures,
Peace and Plenty F2.   194 measures] F1, Q, F3, D (Measures Q, F3,
D); Measures. / CHORUS. Peace and Pleasures, Peace and Plenty to content
thee, dancing their Eternal Measures F2.   194+ *s.d.* Graces *and*
Loves *Dance an Entry*] Graces and Loves, Dance an Entry F1, Q, F3, D
(*Loves*∧ F3, D); AYRE for the Graces and Loves F2.   195 blessing,]
F2 (Blessing); ~ ; F1, Q, F3, D (Blessing Q, F3, D).   196 Brother;] D;
~ , F1–3, Q.   199–200 possessing. / [*Here . . . [to] . . . perform'd. /
Chor. of all.* But . . . [to] . . . *&c.* [*Ritor.*] F1, Q, F3, D (*performed* Q,
F3; *perform'd*∧ D; *Chorus* F3); possessing. / CHORUS. But . . . [to] . . .
possessing. / Entry of Hero's. / RITORNEL. F2.   199+ *s.d.* Heros]
Hero's F1–2 (*entire s.d. in romans in F2*); Heroes Q, F3, D.   200+ *s.d.*
Whilst . . . [to] . . . Albion.] omitted from F2.   210 Sea Gods] F1,
Q, F3, D (God's Q, F3, D); Sea-God's F2.   212–213 sign: . . . Maid,]
F1, Q, F3, D (Sign Q, F3, D); Sign, . . . Maid; F2.   217 Heav'n] F1,
Q, F3, D; Heaven F2.   218 obey'd.] F2; ~ : F1, Q, F3, D.   223
less:] F1, Q, F3, D; ~ , F2.   226 Thou! . . . mount'st . . . Throne,]
F1, Q, F3, D; thou∧ . . . mounts . . . ~ ! F2.   227 own.] ~ ; F1, Q,
F3, D; ~ , F2.   228 come,] F1, Q, F3, D; ~ ; F2.   229 of the] F1,
Q, F3, D; o'th' F2.   231–232 *in romans in F1–3, Q, D* (room, for F2;
Room for Q, F3, D; New Q, F3, D).   232 *Deity.*] F1, Q, F3, D (Deity);
Deity. / CHORUS. O thou who mounts th' Etherial Throne! O thou who
mounts th' Etherial Throne! O thou who mounts th' Etherial Throne! Be
kind and happy to thy own, be kind and happy to thy own. F2.   232+
s.d. Here . . . [to] . . . slowly] F1, Q, F3, D; VIOLINS F2.   232+ *s.d.*
A full . . . [to] . . . sung.] F1, Q, F3, D; *lines 228–232 repeated in F2.*
236 are they] F1–2; they are Q, F3, D.   236 fixt] F1; fix'd F2–3, Q, D.
237 ripening] F1, Q, F3, D; rip'ning F2.   237+ *s.d. [Exeunt.] omitted from F1–3, Q, D.*

III, ii

SCENE II.] PRELUDE. F2; *omitted from F1, Q, F3, D.*   The . . .
[*to*] . . . *Side.] omitted from F2.*   Castle-hill] F1, Q (Castle- / hill F1);

Castle-Hill F3, D; *omitted from F2.* Garter,] ∼; F1, Q, F3, D;
omitted from F2. incompast] F1; *incompass'd* Q, F3; *encompass'd* D;
omitted from F2. 1 *Fame*] F1, Q, F3, D; *The Renown* F2. 1 *Re-*
nown] F2; Renown F1, Q, F3, D (RƐnown). 1 Trumpet!] F1, Q, F3,
D; ∼∧ F2. 2 to Pole] F1, Q, F3, D; ∼ ∼, F2. 2 resounding] F2;
∼: F1, Q, F3, D. 5 Fame, shall] F1, Q, F3, D; Fame. / Chorus.
Renown, assume thy Trumpet from Pole to Pole, resounding great *Al-*
bion's Name, great *Albion's* Name, shall be the Theme of Fame. / *Fame.*
The Theme of Fame shall F2. 6 Name.] F1, Q, F3, D; Name; / *All.*
the Theme of Fame shall be great *Albion's* Name, great *Albion's* Name,
great *Albion's* Name. The theme of Fame shall be great *Albion's* Name,
great *Albion's* Name. The theme of Fame shall be great *Albion's* Name;
the theme of Fame shall be great *Albion's* Name, great *Albion's* Name;
the theme of Fame shall be great *Albion's* Name, great *Albion's* Name.
7 Record] F1, Q, F3, D; *Fame.* Record F2. 7–9 glory: / A Badge
for *Hero's,* and for Kings to bear: / For Kings to bear!] F1, Q, F3, D
(Glory Q, F3, D; Hero's F1; Heroes Q, F3, D); Glory, record the Garter's
Glory, F2. 13–14 hear; / For Gods to hear.] F1, Q, F3, D; hear. F2.
14+ *s.d. A . . . [to] . . .* Opera.] F1, Q, F3, D; Chorus. *Renown,* &c.
F2. 14+ *s.d. joyn*] F1; *are* Q, F3, D; *omitted from F2.* 14+
s.d. Opera.] F3, D; Opera. / FINIS. F1, Q (FINIS Q); *FINIS.* F2. 14+
s.d. [Exeunt.] omitted from F1–3, Q, D.

Epilogue: EPILOGUE / *To the*] F1 *(some copies),* Q, F3 (To the Q,
F3); EPILOGUE D; *omitted from some copies of F1 and from all copies*
of F2. OPERA] OPERA. *By Mr.* Dryden F1 *(some copies),* Q, F3;
omitted from some copies of F1 and from all copies of F2, D. 1–34
omitted from some copies of F1 and from all copies of F2. 1–2 *our*
. . . [to] . . . Play.] italics and romans reversed in *F1; omitted from F2.*
3 Feign'd Zeal,] F1; *Feign'd Zeal,* Q, F3, D; *omitted from F2.* 3–15
you . . . [to] . . . of] italics and romans reversed in *F1; omitted from F2.*
7 *Heav'n*] F1, Q, D (Heav'n F1); *Heaven* F3; *omitted from F2.* 8
stampt] F1 (stampt); *stamp'd* Q, F3, D; *omitted from F2.* 14 *true!*]
∼? F1, Q, F3, D (true F1); *omitted from F2.* 15 Great,] F1; *Great,*
Q, F3, D; *omitted from F2.* 15–34 *let . . . [to] . . . made]* italics
and romans reversed in *F1; omitted from F2.* 32 *Trust.]* F1 (Trust);
trust, Q, F3, D; *omitted from F2.* 34 *it self]* F1, Q, F3 (it self F1);
itself D; *omitted from F2.* 34+ *FINIS.]* F1 *(some copies),* Q (FINIS
Q); *omitted from some copies of F1 and from all copies of F2–3,* D.

Don Sebastian

The first edition of *Don Sebastian* was published in 1690 (Q1; Macd 89a).
Collation of multiple copies of this edition yielded insignificant press
variants in both inner and outer A. The sloppily printed second edition
(Q2; Macd 89b) appeared in 1692. *Don Sebastian* was later published
(without the second "PROLOGUE, *Sent to the Authour by an un-*
known hand") in Dryden's *Comedies, Tragedies, and Operas* (1701), II,
327–398 (F; Macd 107ai–ii [two issues, the differences not affecting this

play]), and (with the second "PROLOGUE") in Congreve's edition of Dryden's *Dramatick Works* (1717), VI, [5]–142 (D; Macd 109ai–ii [two issues, the differences not affecting this play]).

Q2 was printed from a copy of Q1, F from a copy of Q2, and D mainly from a copy of Q2 (with perhaps occasional references to Q1). Since Dryden seems not to have revised the text after the publication of Q1, the Clark copy of Q1 (*PR3417. I1) has been chosen as the copy text.

The following copies of the various editions have also been examined: Q1: Harvard (*EC65.D8474.690d), Huntington (122919), Texas (Wj.D848. 690D), Yale (Ij.D848.690D)); Q2: Clark (*PR3417.I1.1692; *PR3410.C94; *PR3412.1683); F: Clark (*fPR3412.1701 [2 cop.], *fPR3412.1701a); D: Clark (*PR3412.1717 [2 cop.], *PR3412.1717a).

Press Variants by Form

Q1

Sheet A (outer form)

Uncorrected: Yale
Corrected: Clark, Harvard, Huntington, Texas
Sig. A3
    Signature A3] *signature omitted*

Sheet A (inner form)

Uncorrected: Yale
Corrected: Clark, Harvard, Huntington, Texas
Sig. A2
    Signature a2] A2
Sig. A3*v*
    Catchwords *catchwords omitted*] I may
Sig. A4
    Catchword *catchword omitted*] THE

Epistle Dedicatory: Caption: Philip,] D (*PHILIP*); ~∧ Q1–2, F (*PHILIP* Q2; PHILIP F). 59:14 performances] Q1, F, D (Performances F, D); preformances Q2. 59:16 overmatch'd] Q1–2, D; over-match'd F. 59:18 whatever] Q1–2, D; whatsoever F. 59:22 Lordship,] ~ ; Q1–2, F, D. 60:7 *Copernican*] D; Copernican Q1–2, F. 60:9 Fellow creatures] Q1–2, F (Creatures F); Fellow-Creatures D. 60:15 and taking] Q1–2, F; taking D. 60:18 from] Q1, F, D; form Q2. 60:22 him.] Q1–2, F; ~ ? D. 60:30 *Rome;*] Q1–2; ~ , F; ~ ! D. 61:1 *Englishman*] Englishman Q1–2, F; *English* Man D. 61:2 *Roman?*] Q1; ~∧ Q2; ~ . F, D. 61:4 naming?] ~ . Q1–2, F, D. 61:5 *intervallo;*] F; ~ , Q1–2, D. 61:11 years:] ~ . Q1–2, F (Years D). 61:14 equal:] F; ~ . Q1, D (Equal D); ~ , Q2. 61:19 Party.] Q1–2, D; ~ : F. 61:25 them] Q1; 'em Q2, F, D. 61:27 composition:] ~ , Q1–2, F, D (Composition F, D). 62:3 *Cassius;*] F; ~ . Q1–2, D. 62:4 party,] D (Party); ~∧ Q1–2, F (Party F). 62:5 good will] Q1–2, F (Good Will F); Good-will D. 62:14 not] F; ~ ,

Q1–2, D. 62:15 True] D; ~ , Q1–2, F. 62:17 *puto.*] Q1–2, D;
~ : F. 62:24 fellow Creatures] Q1–2, F (Fellow F); Fellow-Creatures
D. 62:33 forgotten] Q1; forgot Q2, F, D. 62:34 *Leicester-House*]
Q1–2; *Leicester House* F, D. 63:18–19 *this . . . [to] . . . shades*] ex-
cept for "Atticus," in romans in Q1–2, F, D (Shades D). 63:20 greater]
Q1; greatest Q2, F, D. 63:24 it,] ~ ; Q1–2; ~ : F; ~ . D. 63:30
Atticus] Q2, F, D; *Aiticus* Q1. 64:3 Unworthiness,] F, D; ~ . Q1–2.
64:13 *Dabam Cal.] omitted from F.*

Preface: 65:1–72:26 *it . . . ito*] *romans and italics reversed in D.*
65:4 *lengthning*] D (lengthning); *lenghthning* Q1–2; *lengthening* F.
65:7 *than*] Q1, F, D (than D); *then* Q2. 65:8 *bear*] Q1; *hear* Q2, F,
D (hear D). 65:9 *our selves*] Q1–2, F; *ourselves* D (ourselves). 65:11
City feast] Q1–2, F (Feast F); *City-Feast* D (City- / Feast). 65:12 *place,*]
Q1–2, F; ~∧ D (place). 65:14 *good nature*] Q1–2, F; *Good-nature* D
(Good-nature). 65:22 *pityed,*] ~ ; Q1–2, F, D (pitied D). 65:28
please,] ~ ; Q1–2, F, D (please D). 66:37 *somewhat*] Q1, F, D (some-
what D); *some what* Q2. 67:5 Latin] D (*Latin*); *Latin* Q1–2, F.
67:8 Salust] D (*Salust*); *Salust* Q1–2, F. 67:8 Roman] F, D (*Roman*
D); *Roman* Q1–2. 67:9 Paradise] *Paradise* Q1–2, F, D (Paradise D).
67:14 Sebastian,] F; ~∧ Q1–2, D (*Sebastian* D). 67:18 *him,*] D (him);
~∧ Q1–2, F. 67:18 Muley-Moluch,] Muley-Moluch∧ Q1–2, F, D
(*Muley-Moluch* D). 67:22 *Don*] Don Q1–2, F, D (*Don* D). 67:23
slain:] ~ ; Q1–2, F, D (slain D). 67:26 *Don*] Don Q1–2, F, D (*Don*
D). 67:29 *Country-men*] Q1, F, D (Country-men D); *Country men*
Q2. 68:6 *ground-work*] F, D (*Ground-work* F; Ground-work D);
ground work Q1–2. 68:27 *self-murther*] F, D (*Self-murder* F; Self-
Murther D); *self murther* Q1–2. 68:29 *hind'ring*] Q1, F (*hindring*
F); *hindering* Q2, D (hindering D). 68:35 *him;*] Q1; ~ ? Q2, F; ~ :
D (him). 69:8 *fictitious*] Q1, D (fictitious D); *fictious* Q2, F. 69:9
surname] Q1–2, F (Surname F); *Sirname* D (Sirname). 69:10 *Don*]
Don Q1–2, D (*Don* D); *omitted from F.* 69:11 *Princess,*] F; ~∧ Q1–2,
D (Princess D). 69:25–26 French-man] Q2, F, D (French- / man F;
French-man D); French man Q1. 69:31 *him;*] F; ~ , Q1–2, D (him
D). 70:17 Muley-Ishmael] Q2, F, D (*Muley-Ishmael* D); Muley Ishmael
Q1. 70:25 *loquatur:*] ~ . Q1–2, F, D (*loquatur* D). 70:33 *those*]
Q1–2, D (those D); *these* F. 71:12 *too*] Q1, F, D (too D); *to* Q2.
71:14 *than*] Q1, F, D (than D); *then* Q2. 71:18 *there*] Q1, F, D
(there D); *their* Q2. 71:31 *Souls*] ~ ; Q1–2, F; ~ , D (Souls). 71:36
Poets,] F; ~∧ Q1–2, D (Poets D). 72:3 *underparts*] Q1–2, F (under- /
parts F); *Under-Parts* D (Under-Parts). 72:9 *design:*] F (*Design*); ~ .
Q1–2, D (Design D). 72:9 *for*] For Q1–2, F, D (For D).

Prologue: PROLOGUE TO] Q1–2, F (PROLOGUE. F); PROLOGUE.
D. *Don Sebastian, King of*] F (SEBASTIAN∧); DON SEBASTIAN∧
King of Q1–2 (SEBASTIAN∧ Q2); *omitted from D.* Portugal.] Q1–2;
Portugal. F; *omitted from D.* 8 foe.] D (Foe); ~ , Q1–2; ~ ; F. 13
Civil Wars] Q1–2, F; *Civil-Wars* D. 14 gone.] Q1, F, D; ~ , Q2.
22 Monarch] Q2, F, D; Monarch Q1. 24 *line not indented in Q2.*
25 Noddle.] Q1; ~ , Q2, F, D. 26 Senate door] Q1–2, F; *Senate-*

Door D.　　28　*However*] Q2, F, D; *How ever* Q1.　　28　*were,*] F, D;
~ . Q1-2.　　29　*fair.*] F, D (*Fair* D); ~ , Q1-2.　　31　*thing.*] Q1, F;
~ , Q2, D.　　38　*too*] Q1, F, D; *to* Q2.　　38　*neither;*] ~ , Q1-2, F,
D.　　42　*Muses*] Q2, F, D; *Muses* Q1.　　42　*forbidden:*] ~ . Q1-2, F,
D (*f rbidden.* Q2).　　44　*Five-pound*] Q1-2, F; *Five Pound* D.

Prologue: Entire prologue omitted from F.　　*Caption:* PROLOGUE,]
D; ~ . Q1-2.　　*Caption:* Montfort] Monford Q1; Montford Q2, D (*Montford* D).　　3　*pop-gun wit,*] Q1-2 (*wit.*); *Popgun-Wit,* D.　　4　*may:*]
D; ~∧ Q1-2.　　6　*Execution day*] Q1-2; *Execution-Day* D.　　7　*presume,*] D; ~∧ Q1-2.　　8　*doom,*] D (*Doom*); ~ : Q1-2.　　9　*room;*]
D (*Room*); ~ . Q1-2.　　13　*Honour, Ladies,*] D; ~∧ ~∧ Q1-2.　　13
avow,] Q1, D; ~ . Q2.　　14　*you:*] D; ~ , Q1-2.　　15　*who ever*] D;
whoever Q1-2.　　16　*Nation*] Q1; ~ . Q2; ~ , D.　　21　*enough?*] Q1,
D; ~ . Q2.　　22　*Bully Criticks*] Q1-2; *Bully-Criticks* D.　　23-24　thank
. . . [*romans*] . . . at] thank . . . [*italics*] . . . at Q1-2, D (*Thank* D).
24　Groom-Porters, Sir,] *Groom-Porters*∧ *Sir*∧ Q1-2; *Groom-Porter's, Sir,*
D.　　24　can safer bleed] *can safer bleed* Q1-2, D.　　28　Dam my
bloud, I'd] *Dammy bloud, I'de* Q1; *Dam my bloud, I'd* Q2, D (*Blood* D).
28-30　be . . . [*romans*] . . . Banishment] be . . . [*italics*] . . . *Banishment* Q1-2, D.　　31　*excuse,*] D (*Excuse*); ~∧ Q1-2.　　32　I'd . . .
[*romans*] . . . in] *I'de* . . . [*italics*] . . . *in* Q1-2, D (*I'd* D).　　32　Ireland,] D; ~∧ Q1-2.　　32-33　Sir, . . . [*romans*] . . . shoes.] *Sir*∧ . . .
[*italics*] . . . *shoes?* Q1-2, D (*Sir,* D; *Shoes:* Q2; *Shoes.* D).　　34　*march,
. . . I,*] D; ~∧ . . . ~∧ Q1-2.　　35　*blades,*] ~∧ Q1-2, D (*Blades* D).
35　*budge;*] D; ~ , Q1-2.　　38　*bought;*] D; ~ , Q1-2.　　39　*bloud,*]
~∧ Q1-2, D (*Blood* D).　　40　*whither*] D; *whether* Q1-2.　　41　*reveal?*] D; ~ , Q1-2.　　43　*Carrion tits*] Q1-2; *Carrion-Tits* D.　　43
rage,] D (*Rage*); ~∧ Q1-2.　　44　Leinster] D; *Leinster* Q1-2.　　44　*ingage:*] D (*engage*); ~ , Q1-2.　　49　*Wit, . . . honour, . . . fighting,*]
D (*Wit*∧; *Honour*); ~∧ . . . ~∧ . . . ~∧ Q1-2 (*Honour* Q2; *Fighting*
Q2).　　50　*writing!*] ~ , Q1-2, D (*Writing* D).　　53　*aright?*] D; ~ ,
Q1-2.

Persons Represented: Don Sebastian, King of Portugal. / A Tragedy.]
Q1-2 (*Sebastian*∧ Q1; *SEBASTIAN*∧ Q2); omitted from F, D.　　Persons
Represented.] Q1-2; Dramatis Personæ. F, D (*Personæ. / MEN.* D).
Sebastian,] D; Sebastian∧ Q1-2, F (Sebastian Q2).　　*Portugal*] D; Portu-
gal Q1-2, F.　　By] Q1-2, F; omitted from D.　　*Muley-Moluch,*] D;
Muley-Moluch∧ Q1-2; Muley-Moluch, F.　　*Barbary*] D; Barbary Q1-2,
F.　　*Dorax*] D; Dorax Q1-2, F.　　*Portuguese,*] D; Portuguese∧ Q1-2;
Portuguese, F.　　*Alonzo de Sylvera,*] D; Alonzo de Sylvera∧ Q1-2, F.
Alcalde] Q1-2, F; Alcade D.　　*Alcazar*] D; Alcazar Q1-2, F.　　*Bendu-
car*] D; Benducar Q1-2, F.　　*Mufti,*] Mufti∧ Q1-2, F, D.　　*Abdalla*] D;
Abdalla Q1-2, F.　　*Muley-Zeydan,*] D; Muley-Zeydan∧ Q1-2; Muley-
Zeydan, F.　　*Antonio*] D; Antonio Q1-2, F.　　young, noble,] D; Young∧
Noble∧ Q1-2, F.　　*Portuguese*] D; Portuguese Q1-2, F.　　*Montfort*]
Betterton Q1; Montford Q2, F, D.　　*Alvarez*] D; Alvarez Q1-2, F.
Sebastian] D; Sebastian Q1-2, F (Sebastian Q2).　　*Mustapha,*] D; Mus-
tapha∧ Q1-2; Mustapha, F.　　Rabble,] Q2, F (Rabble Q2); ~ . Q1,

D.   *Leigh.*] Q1–2, F (*Liegh* F); *Leigh.* / WOMEN. D.   *Almeyda,*] D;
Almeyda∧ Q1–2; Almeyda, F.   *Barbary*] D; Barbary Q1–2, F.   *Mo-*
rayma] D; Morayma Q1–2, F.   *Mufti*] D; Mufti Q1–2, F.   *Johayma*]
D; Johayma Q1–2, F.   *Mufti*] D; Mufti Q1–2, F.   *Benducar*] D;
Benducar Q1–2, F.   *Mufti*] D; Mufti Q1–2, F (Mufti Q2, F).   *Al-*
cazar] D; Alcazar Q1–2, F.

I, i

PORTUGAL.] Q1–2, D (Portugal); Portugal. / A TRAGEDY. F.
ACT I. SCENE I.] Q2, F, D (ACT. Q2; SCENE. Q2); ACT I. SCENE I. Q1.
s.d. Enter Muley-Zeydan, Benducar] D (*and* Benducar); *Muley-Zeydan,*
Benducar Q1–2, F.   1 end,] D (End); ~ ; Q1–2, F.   2 Blood,]
Q1–2, F; ~ ; D.   5 hear] Q1, F, D; here Q2.   6 *Moors*] D; Moors
Q1–2, F.   11 *Mucazer's*] Q1–2, F; *Mucazar's* D.   16 Fate,] Q1, D;
~ . Q2, F.   17 Throne;] ~ . Q1–2, F; ~ : D.   18 him:] Q1; ~ ;
Q2, F, D.   19 Servants,] D; ~ . Q1–2, F.   20 *Muley-Zeydan*] Q1,
D; *Muley-Zeyden* Q2; *Muley Zeyden* F.   22 soothing] Q1–2, D; smooth-
ing F.   40 King!] Q1; ~ ? Q2, F; ~ , D.   40 *Muley-Zeydan*] Q1–2,
D; *Muley Zeydan* F.   45 Alcalde] Alcald Q1; Alcade Q2, F, D.   50
Mul. Zeyd.] D; *Mul.* Q1–2, F.   51–52 *Bend.* I . . . far, by . . . stride /
And . . . port: retire . . . Lord.] *Bend.* I . . . far, / By . . . stride and
. . . port: / Retire . . . Lord. Q1–2, F, D (afar F, D; stride, F; Stride D;
Port D; Retire, F).   64+ *s.d. Enter* Dorax] D; Enter *Dorax* Q1–2, F
(*s.d. at right margin*).   65 *Dorax.*] F, D (*Dor.* D); ~ , Q1–2.   65
Well,] ~∧ Q1–2, F, D.   65 *Benducar . . . Benducar*] *Bemboucar . . .*
Bemboucar Q1–2, F, D.   66 wouldst] Q1–2, D (would'st D); wouldest
F.   66 'em] Q1–2, D; 'um F.   68 *Dorax.*] F, D (*Dor.* D); ~ , Q1–2.
69 too] Q1, F, D; to Q2.   72 than] Q1, F, D; then Q2.   74 *Dorax.*]
Q2, F, D (*Dor.*); ~ , Q1.   76 mankind;] ~ , Q1–2, F, D (Mankind D).
77 say] Q1–2, D; ~ , F.   79 *Dorax.*] Q2, F, D (*Dor.*); ~ , Q1.   86
Dorax.] Q2, F, D (*Dor.*); ~ , Q1.   86 title,] Q1–2, F; Title? D.   88
a King] Q1; King Q2, F, D.   95 say,] F; ~∧ Q1–2, D.   96 *Dorax.*]
Q2, F, D (*Dor.*); ~ , Q1.   99 Man:] Q1–2, D; ~ , F.   102 ev'n]
Q1–2, D; even F.   109 diffus'd] Q1, D; disus'd Q2; difus'd F.   111
Dorax.] Q2, F, D (*Dor.*); ~ , Q1.   115 still] Q2, F, D; st ll Q1.   115
too] Q1, F, D; to Q2.   116 Lightning] Q2, F, D; Lightning Q1.
116 Slaughters.] D; ~ , Q1–2, F.   117 across] Q1; a cross Q2; a-cross
F, D.   126 drag'd] Q1–2, F; drag D.   127 *Affrick's Affric's* Q1;
Affrica's Q2; *Africa's* F, D.   130 Brother] Q1–2, D; ~ , F.   136 below,] F, D; ~∧ Q1–2.   140 hear] Q1, D; here Q2, F.   145 ev'ry]
Q1–2, D; every F.   148 Friend,] Q2, F, D; ~∧ Q1.   152 brain'd,]
F; ~ ; Q1; ~ : Q2, D.   156+ *s.d. Attendants,*] ~ . Q1–2, F, D.
156+ *s.d. the*] *The* Q1–2, F, D.   156+ *s.d. Mufti*] F, D; Mufty Q1–2.
165 us'd] Q1–2, D; used F.   166 *Mufti*] *Mufty* Q1–2; *Muf.* F, D.
170 abolish'd] Q1–2, D; abolished F.   172 *Mufti*] F; *Mufty* Q1–2, D.
174 Countenance] Q2, F, D; Countenancc Q1.   181 that's] Q2, F, D;
thar's Q1.   183 a] Q1–2, D; an F.   183–184 Great. / *Dorax aside.*
This] Great. [Dorax *aside.* / This Q1–2, F (*aside*∧ Q2; *line 184 indented*);

Great. / Dor. [*aside.*] This D.   184–185 *set as verse in Q1–2, F, D*
(. . . / Renegade).   186+ *s.d.* Mustapha, . . . *Rabble,*] ~∧ . . . ~∧
Q1–2, F, D (*Rabble,* F, D).   186+ *s.d. Black Guard*] Q1–2 (*Gaurd*
Q2); *Black-Guard* F, D.   186+ *s.d.* Moors] D; *Moors* Q1–2, F.   186+
s.d. Slaves,] D; ~∧ Q1–2, F.   190 Offrings] Q1–2, D; Offerings F.
191 giv'n] Q1; given Q2, F, D.   193 who] Q1; that Q2, F, D.   194
All,] ~∧ Q1–2, F, D.   202 as] Q1; as if Q2, F, D.   205 Man,] F,
D; ~∧ Q1–2.   206 too,] Q1–2, F; ~∧ D.   207 scape] Q1–2; 'scape
F; escape D.   209 *Mufti winking . . . him.* Then] Mufti *winking . . .*
him. / Then Q1–2, F (*Mufty* Q2); *Mufty.* [*winking . . . him.*] Then D.
210 Paradise.] Q2, F; ~∧ Q1; *Paradise,* D.   216 *Mufti*] F, D; *Mufty*
Q1–2.   216 concern'd.] F, D; ~ : Q1–2.   219 troth] Q1–2, F;
Truth D.   219 is,] F, D; ~∧ Q1–2.   229 than] Q1, F, D; then Q2.
230 Greatness] Q1–2; ~ , F, D.   232 there] Q1, F, D; their Q2.
232 *Virgin*] Virgin Q1–2, F, D.   233 too] Q1, F, D; to Q2.
234 down for her] Q1–2, F; down D.   242 *Dorax . . . Benducar.* By]
Dorax . . . Benducar. / By Q1–2, F, D ("By" indented).   247 *Bend.*
to Dor. aside. The] [*Bend. to Dor. aside.* / The Q1–2, F (∧Bend. F;
speech tag at right margin; "The" *indented*); Benducar *to* Dorax
aside. The D.   249 no,] D; ~ . Q1–2, F.   250–251 *s.d.* 'em.
[*Aside.* / Shall . . . renounc'd,] 'em. / Shall . . . renounc'd, [*Aside.*
Q1–2, F, D (*aside* Q2, F).   260 *Mufti,*] D; ~ . Q1–2 (*Mufty* Q2);
~ ! F.   262 Souls.] F, D; ~ : Q1–2.   266 Rival House] Q1–2,
F; Rival-House D.   267 Alcoran] *Alcoran* Q1–2, F, D.   269 bet-
ter] ~ , Q1–2, F, D.   270+ *s.d. an Urn is*] Q1–2, F (*Urne* Q2);
is an Urn D.   270+ *s.d.* among] Q1; amongst Q2, F, D.   271
Creatures,] D; ~∧ Q1–2, F.   275 bear] Q1; bare Q2; dare F, D.
279 Minister, . . . Trade,] ~ ; . . . ~∧ Q1–2, F, D.   283–284 *my*
. . . [to] . . . swarthy] in romans in Q1–2, F, D.   284 there] Q1, F,
D; their Q2.   286 *Anton. . . . hand.* Here] D (*Hand*∧]); Anton. . . .
hand. / Here Q1–2, F (*speech tag in middle of page;* "Here" *indented*).
287 too] Q1, F, D; to Q2.   293 th'] Q1; the Q2, F, D.   296 b']
Q1; be Q2, F, D.   299 hope] Q1–2, F; hopes D.   300 *Ethiope*] D
(*Æthiope*); Ethiope Q1–2, F.   300 *s.d. Looks.*] Looks∧ Q1–2, F, D.
302 Devil's] F, D; Devils Q1–2.   310 *to*] to Q1–2, F, D.   312–313
thou . . . [to] . . . Creation] in romans in Q1–2, F, D.   320 chance!]
Q1–2, F; ~ . D.   325 Sword?] D; ~ ; Q1–2; ~ : F.   326 dye not] Q1;
not dye Q2, F, D (die F, D).   330 Rev'rence] Q1; Reverence Q2, F, D.
336 paw:] ~ , Q1–2, F, D (Paw F, D).   343 suff'ring] Q1; suffering
Q2, F, D.   348 *Affrick*] F, D (*Africk*); Affrick Q1–2.   350 *to*] to
Q1–2, F, D.   350 ev'n] Q1; even Q2, F, D (Even F).   362 burial,] D
(Burial); ~∧ Q1–2, F (Burial F).   364–365 air, . . . dust] ~ : . . .
~ , Q1–2, F, D (Air; F; Air D; Dust F, D).   370, 372 *Affrick*] F, D
(*Africk*); Affrick Q1–2.   377 call.] F, D (Call D); ~ , Q1–2.   378
Soldier.] F, D (Souldier F); ~ , Q1–2.   380 *Moors*] D; Moors Q1–2, F.
383 People.] Q1–2; ~ ? F; ~ ! D.   384 thou?] D; ~ , Q1, F; ~∧ Q2.
385 have] F; has Q1–2, D.   386 *Affrick*] Affric Q1; Affrick Q2; *Africk*
F, D.   395 shou'd] Q1, F, D; shon'd Q2.   398 Nor] Q1, D; Not

Q2, F.   399 dangers] Q1–2, F; Danger D.   400 own.] ~ : Q1–2,
F, D.   404 this] Q1; his Q2, F, D.   404 showr] Q1–2, D (Show'r D);
shower F.   409 *Mufti.*] Q2, F, D (*Mufty.* Q2, D; *Muft.* F); ~ , Q1.
412 reddens] F, D; *reddens* Q1–2.   418 giv'n] Q1–2, D; given F.
420 grateful,] Q1, F, D (Grateful F); ~∧ Q2.   425 *Almeyda.*] Q2, F,
D; ~ , Q1.   426 Title.] ~ : Q1–2, F, D.   428 *Almeyda.*] Q2, F, D;
~ , Q1.   429 *Affrick*] *Affric* Q1–2; *Africk* F, D.   433 *Almeyda.*]
Q2, F, D; ~ , Q1.   439 dar'st,] D; ~∧ Q1–2, F.   440 *s.d. Aside*] F,
D; *aside* Q1–2.   441 *Almeyda.*] Q2, F, D; ~ , Q1.   442 *Affrick*]
Affric Q1–2; *Africk* F, D.   445 scruple,] F, D (Scruple D); ~∧ Q1–2.
448 dare] Q1–2, D; dar'st F.   449 pow'r] Q1; Power Q2, F, D.   459
declar'd] Q1–2, D; declared F.   462 vent:] F, D (Vent D); ~ . Q1; ~∧
Q2.   465 died:] ~ . Q1–2, F, D.   474 Strange;] Q1–2, F; ~ ! D.
480 Slaves.] F, D; ~∧ Q1–2.   481 *Mustapha.*] F, D (*Must.* F); ~ ,
Q1–2.   483 comes] Q1–2, D; come F.   484 *First . . . Mustapha.
What*] *First . . . Mustapha. / What* Q1–2, F (Mustapha, Q2); *1st . . .
[. . . Must.]* What D.   485 at?] [*Pointing . . . Alvarez.*] He's] ~ ?
[~ . . . ~ . / ~ Q1–2, F, D (at? / [*Pointing* D).   489 *1st.*] 1st. Q1–2,
D (1st∧ D); *First* F.   489 *Marvedi's*] Marvedi's Q1–2, F, D.   492
1st.] 1st. Q1–2, D; *First* F.   493 Sir!] Q1–2, D; ~ ? F.   493 a] D;
ah Q1–2, F.   494 rich;] D; ~ , Q1–2, F.   496 *1st.*] D (1st∧); 1st.
Q1–2; *First* F.   497 rate:] Q1–2, D; ~ . F.   500 Secret!] Q1, F, D;
~l Q2.   502 pow'r] Q1; Power Q2, F, D.   504 Pimp I] Q1–2, F;
Pimp I'll D.   505–506 Merchandize.] F (Merchandise); ~ , Q1–2, D.
506 Sirrah!] ~∧ Q1–2; ~ . F, D.   506 *s.d. To*] F, D; *to* Q1–2.   507
have?] D; ~ ! Q1–2, F.   509 come,] Q1, F (Come F); ~∧ Q2, D.
513–514 Sawcyness. [*Lashes . . . Whip.*] Be] ~ . / [~ . . . ~ . / ~
Q1–2, F, D (Sawciness Q2, D; Sawciness. [~ F).   519+ *s.d.*–520 *Holds
. . . Whip. / Antonio . . . down.* Hold,] D (*Ant.; down*]; Hold∧);
~ . . . ~ . / Antonio . . . ~ . / ~∧ Q1–2 (*Whip*∧ Q2; *speech tag centered;* "Hold" *indented*); ~ . . . ~ , Antonio . . . ~ . / ~∧ F (*speech
tag flush, right;* "Hold" *not indented*).   523 *2d.*] 2d. Q1–2, D (2d∧ D);
Second F.   525 *Mustapha . . . Antonio.* Now] D (*Must.;* Ant.);
Mustapha . . . Antonio. / Now Q1–2, F (*speech tag centered;* "Now" *in-
dented*).   526 paces,] F, D (Paces D); ~∧ Q1–2.   529 *2d.*] 2d. Q1–
2, D (2d∧ D); *Second* F.   530 half.————] ~ .∧ Q1–2, F, D.   532
Man's flesh] Q1–2, D (Flesh D); Man's-flesh F.   533 Eye-sore] Q1–2, F;
Eye sore D.   535–536 *Merchant . . . side.* Out] Merchant . . . *side. /
Out* Q1–2, F, D ("Out" *indented*).   535 *s.d. to*] Q1–2, F; *on* D.   537
broken-winded] Q1, F; broken winded Q2, D.   538 Thick-breath'd] F;
Thick breath'd Q1–2, D.   539 ————but] Q1; ∧~ Q2, F, D.   543
2d.] 2d. Q1–2, D; *Second* F.   545 him?] D; ~ ; Q1–2, F.   549 *Xeriffs*]
Xeriffs Q1–2, F, D.   550 *Mufti.*] Q2, F, D; ~ , Q1.   553 Chattel]
Q1; Chattle Q2, F; Cattel D.   554, 560 *Mufti.*] Q2, F, D; ~ , Q1.
565 *Mufti.*] F, D; ~ , Q1; ~∧ Q2.   567 him?] D; ~ . Q1–2, F.   569
Mufti.] Q2, F, D; ~ , Q1.   573 thereupon,] Q1; ~∧ Q2, F, D.   573
about,] D; ~ ; Q1–2, F.   573 I took] Q1; took Q2, F, D.   574 re-
store] Q2, F, D; restote Q1.   576, 584 *Mufti.*] Q2, F, D; ~ , Q1.

589 hold fast] Q1-2, D; hold-fast F.   591 *Mufti to Antonio.* Follow]
F, D (Mufti F; Antonio F; *Muft.* D; Ant. D); Mufti *to* Antonio. / Follow
Q1-2 (Antonio∧ Q2; *speech tag centered in Q1-2;* "Follow" *indented in
Q1-2*).   591 Sirrah.———— [*To*] ~ :∧ [*to* Q1-2, F, D (*To* F).   602
easily?] D; ~. Q1-2, F.   606 interest] Q1-2, D (Interest D); Int'rest
F.   607 Fortunes] Q1-2, F (Fortuns Q2); Fortune D.

II, i

ACT II. SCENE I. / *Suppos'd*] Q2, F, D (ACT. Q2; SCENE. Q2);
Act II. / Scene 1. *Suppos'd* Q1.   s.d. *Enter Emperor,*] Emperor. Q1-2
(Emperour Q2); *Enter* Emperor, F, D (Emperor *and* D).   1 think'st
... discover'd] Q2, F, D (thinkst Q2, D); thinkest ... discovered Q1.
9 Labarynth] Q1-2; Labyrinth F, D.   17-18 winds ... sweep] Q1-
2, F (Winds Q2, F; Sweeps Q2; sweeps F); Wind ... sweeps D.   20
barren:] Q1-2, F; ~. D.   23 past] D; ~, Q1-2, F.   24 eyes,] ~ :
Q1-2, F (Eyes F); Eyes; D.   27 ev'n] Q1; even Q2, F, D.   28
Heav'n] Q1-2, F; Heaven D.   32 Conqueror,] Q1-2, F; ~. D.   38
th'] Q1; the Q2, F, D.   41 *ever, ever*] ever, ever Q1-2, F, D.   42
(I ... double,)]∧ ~ ... ~ ,∧ Q1-2, F, D.   43 Right,] F, D; ~∧
Q1-2.   45 must, be] D; ~∧ ~ Q1-2, F.   46 pow'r] Q1; power Q2,
F, D (Power D).   49 pow'r] Q1; power Q2, F, D (Power D).   50
bend,] Q1-2, D; ~ : F.   65 whom?] Q1, D; ~. Q2, F.   68 *Bend.
in disorder.* To] F, D ([*in disorder*]); [Bend. *in disorder.* / To Q1-2 (*dis-
ordar* Q2; "To" *indented*).   71 life.] Q1; ~, Q2, F, D (Life F, D).
74 rebel?] D; ~. Q1-2, F (Rebel F).   75 *Bend. aside.* This] F, D
([*Aside.*] F; [*aside*] D); [Bend. *aside.* / This Q1-2 (*aside*∧ Q2; "This"
indented in Q1).   75 wish.] ~ : Q1-2, F, D.   75 *s.d. To*] F; *to*
Q1-2, D.   75 *s.d. th'*] Q1-2, D; *the* F.   75 possible.] Q1, D; ~,
Q2, F.   93 there,] Q1, F, D; ~. Q2.   97 honest,] Q1; ~∧ Q2, F,
D.   102 difficulty;] ~, Q1-2, F, D (Difficulty D).   114 *to the Emp.*]
(to the *Emp.*) Q1-2, F; [*to the Emp.*] D.   114 him] ~. Q1-2, F, D.
116 Command.] D; ~, Q1-2, F.   125 *Dorax;*] ~, Q1-2, F; ~. D.
127 cov'tous] Q1; covetous Q2, F, D.   128 prepar'd] Q1-2, D; pre-
pared F.   137 *to*] to Q1-2, F, D.   143 Death, ... Heav'n;] ~ ;
... ~, Q1-2, F, D.   144 *s.d. Scornfully*] D; *scornfully* Q1-2, F.
148 *Mufti.*] F, D (*Muf.*); ~, Q1-2.   150 *Dorax.*] Q2, F, D (*Dor.* F,
D); ~, Q1.   150-151 began; ... heart,] Q1-2, F (Heart F); ~∧ ...
Heart; D.   157 *Mufti.*] F, D (*Muf.*); ~, Q1-2.   158 Property?]
~, Q1-2, F, D.   165 covet;] ~. Q1-2, F, D.   166 *Phaethons*] D
(*Phaetons*); Phaethons Q1-2, F (Phaetons F).   168 *Mufti.*] F, D (*Muf.*);
~, Q1-2.   170 *Dorax.*] F, D (*Dor.*); ~, Q1-2.   174 not] Q2, F,
D; nor Q1.   175 apart] Q1-2, D; a-part F.   182 neglect.] Q1, D
(Neglect D); ~, Q2, F.   182 *to the*] to the Q1-2, F, D.   183
Dorax.] Q2, F, D (*Dor.* F, D); ~, Q1.   201 *Dorax.*] Q2, F, D (*Dor.*);
~, Q1.   209 us,] F; ~∧ Q1-2, D.   209 are] Q1-2, F; ~, D.   213
Mufti.] Q1, D (*Muf.* D); *Must.* Q2, F.   214 thee,] D; ~∧ Q1-2, F.   216
Dorax.] Q2, F, D (*Dor.*); ~, Q1.   217 share.] ~ : Q1-2, F, D (Share
D).   220 Religions] Q1-2, D; Religion's F.   222 *s.d. To* Dorax.]

D (*Dorax*); to *Dorax*∧ Q1–2, F.　　222 Let] D; let Q1–2, F.　　227
Dorax.] Q2, F, D (*Dor.*); ∼ , Q1.　　232 brest.] Q1, D (Breast D); ∼ ,
Q2, F (Breast F).　　237, 241, 243, 246 *Dorax.*] Q2, F, D (*Dor.*); ∼ , Q1.
249　full,] D; ∼∧ Q1–2, F.　　251, 255 *Dorax.*] Q2, F, D (*Dor.*); ∼ ,
Q1.　　255 *Affrick*] Q2; *Africk* Q1, F, D.　　262 Alcalde] Q1–2, F;
Alcade D.　　262 *Dorax.*] Q2, F, D (*Dor.*); ∼ , Q1.　　263 Command;]
Q1; ∼∧ Q2; ∼ , F, D.　　265 insults.] Q2, F, D (Insults D); ∼.. Q1.
273 *Dorax.*] Q2, F, D (*Dor.*); ∼ , Q1.　　275 and] Q2, F, D; aud Q1.
281 own:] F, D; ∼ ? Q1–2.　　281 Brother,] D; ∼∧ Q1–2, F.　　282
Muley-Zeydan;] F, D (*Muley-Zeydan.* F; *Muley-Zeydan?* D); *Muley Zeydan;*
Q1–2 (*Zeyden:* Q2).　　282 *Dorax.*] Q2, F, D (*Dor.*); ∼ , Q1.　　285
Kingdom] Q1–2, D; Kingdam F.　　286, 288 *Dorax.*] Q2, F, D (*Dor.*);
∼ , Q1.　　294 more,] ∼∧ Q1–2, F, D.　　296 'twere] Q1, D; 'were
Q2; were F.　　297 betray,] Q1–2, F; ∼ ; D.　　300 *Dorax.*] Q2, F, D
(*Dor.*); ∼ , Q1.　　300 woud'st] Q1; wou'd Q2; would'st F; wou'd'st D.
302, 315 *Dorax.*] Q2, F, D (*Dor.*); ∼ , Q1.　　317 Crime.] Q1; ∼ , Q2,
F, D.　　320–322 worst. . . . denounc'd. . . . *Alonzo*] Q1–2, D; ∼ , . . .
∼ , . . . *Alonza* F.　　323 *Moors:*] Q1; ∼∧ Q2, F; ∼ , D.　　326, 328
Dorax.] Q2, F, D (*Dor.*); ∼ , Q1.　　332 our] Q2, F, D; onr Q1.　　335
Dorax.] Q2, F, D (*Dor.*); ∼ , Q1.　　336 driv'n] Q1; driven Q2, F, D.
338+ *s.d. Emp.*] Emp. Q1–2, F, D (Emperor D).　　339 thee,] F, D;
∼∧ Q1–2.　　341 firm.] Q2, F, D; ∼ , Q1.　　342 *Dorax.*] Q2, F, D
(*Dor.*); ∼ , Q1.　　343 serv'd? . . . him;] ∼ ! . . . ∼ , Q1–2, F, D.
345 *s.d. Exit* Dorax] Q1–2, F; *Exit* D.　　352 it] Q2, F, D; ∼ , Q1.
353+ *s.d. Emperour.*] Emperour.) Q1–2, F, D (Emperor.∧ D).　　353+
s.d. The] D; (∼ Q1–2, F.　　353+ *s.d. Emperour,*] F, D (Emperour F;
Emperor D); ∼ ; Q1–2 (Emperour Q2).　　353+ *s.d. Stage:*] D; ∼ .)
Q1–2, F.　　354 *to*] to Q1–2, F, D.　　361 Alcalde] *Alcayde* Q1; *Al-
cade* Q2, F, D.　　364 not] Q1–2, F; no D.　　370 acquainted] D; ∼ :
Q1–2; ∼ , F.　　372 *Affrick*] Q2; *Africk* Q1, F, D.　　373 deliverance.
———] ∼ :∧ Q1–2, D (Deliverance D); ∼ ;∧ F.　　373 *s.d. Turning to*
Alm.] turning to *Alm:* Q1–2, F (*Alm.* Q2, F); turning to *Almeyda.* D.
373 Here's] D; here's Q1–2, F.　　376 *Almeyda.*] Q2, F, D (*Alm.* F, D);
∼ , Q1.　　378 thou, Viper,] ∼∧ ∼∧ Q1–2, F, D (Viper Q2, F, D).　　380
gnaw'd] Q1, F, D; knaw'd Q2.　　381 again:———] Q1; ∼ :∧ Q2, F,
D (∼ ; F).　　389 there] Q1, F, D; their Q2.　　397 ev'n] Q1; even
Q2, F, D.　　398 And] Q1; All Q2, F, D.　　405 not.] Q1–2, F; ∼ , D.
409 me?] Q1; ∼ ! Q2, F, D.　　409 Sir,———] Q1; ∼ .——— Q2, D;
∼∧——— F.　　412 *Almeyda.*] Q2, F, D (*Alm.*); ∼ , Q1.　　420 Mark,]
F; ∼∧ Q1–2, D.　　422 kills,] D; ∼∧ Q1–2, F.　　424 you:] D; ∼ ,
Q1–2, F.　　425 love,] F, D (Love); ∼ ; Q1–2.　　435 Bed———] ∼ .
——— Q1–2, D; ∼ .∧ F.　　436 *Almeyda.*] Q2, F, D (*Alm.*); ∼ , Q1.
440 pow'r] Q1; power Q2, F, D (Power D).　　447 enjoy'd,] D; ∼∧
Q1–2, F.　　453 viewest] Q1–2, F; view'st D.　　455 Spring-tide,] Q1,
F (Spring-Tide∧ F); Spring tide, Q2, D (Tide D).　　455 in,] Q1, F, D;
∼∧ Q2.　　457 self,] Q1, D; ∼∧ Q2, F.　　458 what?] Q1, F; ∼∧ Q2;
∼ , D.　　458 *Affrick*] Q2; *Affric* Q1; *Africk* F; *Africa* D.　　458 with
new] Q1; with Q2, F, D.　　460 ev'n] F, D; e'vn Q1; e'ven Q2.　　468

again;] Q1; ∼∧ Q2, F; ∼ , D.　　469　show'rs] Q1; showers Q2, F, D
(Showers D).　　471　return] ∼ , Q1–2, F, D.　　473　deceiv'd,] Q1–2,
F; ∼ . D.　　474　true,] Q1, F, D; ∼∧ Q2.　　482　adjur'd,] Q1, F, D;
∼ . Q2.　　483　ill tim'd] Q1–2; ill-tim'd F, D.　　488　thee,] F, D; ∼∧
Q1–2.　　491　attempt———] ∼ .——— Q1, D; ∼ . Q2, F.　　494
wou'dst] Q1; wou'st Q2; wou'd'st F, D.　　497　*s.d. Aside*] F, D; *aside*
Q1–2.　　498+　*s.d. Exeunt*] Q1; *Exit* Q2, F, D.　　498+　*s.d. Em-
perour*] Emperour Q1–2, F, D (Emp. Q2, F, D).　　500　King] Q2, F, D;
∼ , Q1.　　501　Heavens] Q1–2, F; Heavn's D.　　508　Wheel,] ∼ ; Q1–
2, F, D.　　514　wou'd] Q2, F, D; ∼ , Q1.　　516　behind,] Q1, F; ∼∧
Q2, D.　　520　strength,] Q1, D (Strength); ∼ . Q2; ∼ : F.　　527　give
'em] Q1; give Q2, F; give them D.　　529　the 'pointed] the pointed
Q1–2, F; th' appointed D.　　530　good, then Death is good] Q1; good
Q2, F, D (Good D).　　533　Landshape] Q1–2, F; Landscape D.　　545–
546　give, . . . Love?] ∼ ? . . . ∼ . Q1–2, F, D.　　549　dropping] Q1–
2, F; drooping D.　　561　dang'rous] Q1; dangerous Q2, F, D.　　563
o'er] Q2, F, D (o're Q2); oer Q1.　　567　fright] Q1–2, D; 'fright F.
572　*Wed not,*] Wed not Q1–2, F, D (not, D).　　573　*Forewarn'd,*] Forewarn'd∧ Q1–2, F, D.　　573　*Marriage . . . [to] . . . Crime*] *in romans*
in Q1–2, F, D.　　578　Sisters] Q2, F, D; Sister's Q1.　　590　*s.d. Sighing*]
D; sighing Q1–2, F.　　593　Father.] F, D; ∼ : Q1–2.　　594　when,] ∼∧
Q1–2, F, D.　　599　Yet] Q2, F, D; ∼ , Q1.　　608　dy'd] Q1, D; dyed
Q2, F (died F).　　616　Christian;] Q1–2, D; ∼ , F.　　618　too] Q1, F,
D; to Q2.　　621　Bed;] Q1–2, D (bed Q2); ∼ , F.

II, ii

SCENE II. / *Suppos'd*] Q2, F (SCENE. Q2); Scene 2. *Suppos'd* Q1;
SCENE II. *Suppos'd* D.　　1　him?] ∼ , Q1–2, F, D.　　5　Garden-
plat:] Garden-plat. Q1–2, F, D (Garden plat Q2; Garden-/Plat F;
Garden-Plat D).　　8　honey-bird,] D (Honeybird); ∼∧ Q1–2, F (Honey-
bird F).　　8　a] Q1–2, F; on D.　　10　Ah] Q1; Ay Q2, F, D.　　14
self,] F, D; ∼∧ Q1–2.　　14–15　Husband. Speak] Husband: speak Q1–2,
F, D (Speak F, D).　　19　yond] Q1–2, F; yond' D.　　19　pruning knife]
Q1–2, F (Knife F); Pruning-Knife D.　　22　sallating] Q1–2, F (Sallating
F); Salladding D.　　27　*Antonio making legs.* Why] D (*Ant.* [*making*
Legs.]); [Antonio *making legs.* / Why Q1–2, F (∧Antonio F; *Legs* Q2, F;
"Why" *indented*).　　30　hot:] Q1; ∼∧ Q2; ∼ ; F, D.　　31　or by] Q1–
2, D; or F.　　34　fine,] Q1, F, D; ∼∧ Q2.　　39　has] Q2, F, D; ha's Q1.
42　Beasts. Here] ∼ : here Q1–2, F, D (Beasts; F).　　43　*s.d. Gives*] F,
D; *gives* Q1–2.　　43　*s.d. money.*] Q2, F, D (*Money* F, D); ∼∧ Q1.
45+　*s.d. Enter*] Q2, F, D; (∼ Q1.　　46　*Serv.* Sir] F, D; Sir Q1–2 ("Sir"
indented).　　47　Palace Gate] Q1–2; Palace-Gate F, D.　　48　*Muf.*]
Q1, F, D; *Mufti* Q2.　　50　Look how] Q1; how Q2; How F, D.　　51
World.] ∼ : Q1–2, F, D.　　52　This] F; this Q1–2, D.　　53+　*s.d.*
Turning] F, D; *turning* Q1–2.　　56　Myrtle] Q1–2, F; Myrtle-tree D.
57　another.] F; ∼ : Q1–2, D.　　62　sheeps eye] Q1–2, D (Sheeps D);
sheeps-eye F.　　63　pruning knife] Q1–2, F (Knife F); Pruning-knife D.
64+　*s.d. Johayma*] Q2, F, D; *Johayma* Q1.　　66　with] Q1; for Q2, F,

D.   74   *s.d. Pulls*] F; *pulls* Q1–2, D (*puls* Q2).   74   *s.d. Flute.*] F;
~∧ Q1–2, D.   75   *Moors* flesh] Moors ~ Q1–2, D (Flesh D); Moors-
flesh F (Moors- / flesh).   83   thee] Q1–2, F; hee D.   86   over-heard]
Q1–2; over heard F; overheard D.   88   you.] ~∧ Q1–2, F, D.   88–89
s.d. Throws down a handkerchief] F, D (*throws; Handkerchief* F); throws
down a handkerchief Q1–2.   90   hither?] F, D; ~ , Q1–2.   92   for]
Q1–2, F; upon D.   92   Treasure trove] Q1–2, D; Treasure-trove D.
93–94   *Arabick*] F; Arabick Q1–2, D.   99   Tobaccopipe-clay] Q1–2;
Tobacco-pipe-clay F; Tobacco-pipe Clay D.   102–104   *not indented in*
Q1.   102   well-bak'd] F, D; well bak'd Q1–2.   103   *Cupid's*] D; Cupid's Q1–2, F.   104   *Affrick*] F, D (*Africk*); Affrick Q1–2.   104+   *s.d.*
Exit Antonio] Q1–2, F; *Exit* D.

III, i

ACT III. SCENE I. / *A*] Q2, F, D (ACT. Q2; SCENE. Q2); Aᴄᴛ. III. /
Scene 1. *A* Q1.   *s.d. Enter Emperor* Muley-Moluch; Benducar] F, D
(Muley-Moluch, F, D; *and* Benducar D); *Emperor Muley-Moluch; Bendu-*
car Q1–2.   15   by] Q1, D; but Q2, F.   15   presumption.] Q1–2, D
(Presumption D); Presumption—— F.   20   Conquests] Q1; ~ . Q2,
F, D.   25   is,] Q1, F; ~∧ Q2, D.   25   considering] Q1–2, F; ~ , D.
25   earnestness] D; ~ , Q1–2, F.   30   Lover] Q1, D; Love Q2, F.
30   ill disguis'd] Q1–2, D (Ill Q2); ill-disguised F.   46   Father,] Q1–
2, F; ~∧ D.   52   ris'n] Q1; risen Q2, F, D.   53   Bride] D; ~ , Q1–
2, F.   54   *s.d. disorderly.*] F, D; ~∧ Q1–2.   58–58+   *s.d.* The . . .
enjoy; / [*Coming* . . . Mufti (*aside*).] Coming . . . Mufti *aside.* / The
. . . enjoy; Q1–2, F (Mufti. (*Aside.*) F; enjoy: F; *s.d. centered;* "The" *in-*
dented in Q1–2); [*Coming* . . . Mufti *aside.* / The . . . enjoy; D ("The"
indented).   60   *Emperor, seeing him.*] ~∧ ~ ~ . Q1–2 (*Emperour* Q2);
Emp. (seeing him.) F; [*Emp. seeing him.*] D.   60   You,] Q1–2, F; ~∧
D.   64   quick,] Q1; ~ . Q2, F, D.   65   *Mahomet*] F, D; Mahomet
Q1–2.   69   *Mufti.*] Q2, F, D (*Muf.*); ~ , Q1.   74   *Mufti.*] Q2, F, D
(*Muf.* F, D); ~ , Q1.   78   th'] Q1; the Q2, F, D.   87   thee] Q2, F,
D; the Q1.   91   *Mufti.*] Q2, F, D (*Muft.* F; *Muf.* D); ~ , Q1.   92, 94
Mufti.] Q2, F, D (*Muf.* F, D); ~ , Q1.   94   true,] Q1, D; ~∧ Q2, F.
100   promis'd] Q1–2, D; promised F.   103   *Mufti.*] Q2, F, D (*Muf.* F,
D); ~ , Q1.   106   Laws!] D; ~ . Q1–2, F.   119   *Emperor to the*
Mufti. Go] Emperor *to the* Mufti. / Go Q1–2 (Emperour Q2; *speech tag*
centered; "Go" *indented*); *Emp. (to the Muf.)* Go F; *Emp. [to the* Mufti.]
Go D.   127   *Almeyda.*] Q2, F, D (*Alm.* F); ~ , Q1.   127   breaks,]
Q1; ~∧ Q2, F, D.   127   unawares,] Q1–2, F (unawars Q2); ~∧ D.
130   comes] Q1, F, D; come: Q2.   130   answer,] Q1, D; ~ . Q2, F.
135   their] Q1, F, D; there Q2.   138   cannot!] Q1–2, F; ~ : D.   141
not] Q1–2, F; no D.   144   *Emp.*] Q1, F, D; *Em'* Q2.   149   God?] Q1;
~∧ Q2; ~ , F, D.   153   *Gorgon* Face] Q1, F, D; *Gorgan Face* Q2.
158   Kings,] Q1, D; ~∧ Q2, F.   164   Say,] Q1; ~∧ Q2, F, D.   166
thee?] Q1–2, F; ~ ! D.   170   Heav'n] Q1–2, F; Heaven D.   170
thee] Q1; ~ , Q2, F, D.   171   Usurpation;] Q1; ~∧ Q2; ~ , F, D.
174   *Almeyda.*] Q2, F, D (*Alm.* F); ~ , Q1.   185   bless'd] Q1; blest

Q2, F, D.   185   brings] Q2, F, D; bring's Q1.   203   detain,] D; ∼ .
Q1–2, F.   211   Sebast.] Now . . . rage;] ∼ . / ∼ . . . ∼ , Q1–2, F, D
(Sebastian Q2, F, D).   220   *Almeyda . . . Emperor.* Expect] D (*Alm.
. . . Emp.*]); Almeyda . . . ∼ . / ∼ Q1–2, F (Emperour Q2; Emperor F;
speech tag centered; "Expect" indented).   225   pleasure;] Q1; ∼ ? Q2,
F; Pleasure: D.   229   death.] F (Death); ∼ , Q1–2, D (Death).   239
too!] ∼ : Q1–2, F, D.   247   Soul,] Q1; ∼ ! Q2, F, D.   259   Tyrant,]
Q1, F, D; ∼∧ Q2.   260   pale;] ∼ , Q1–2, F, D.   263   approach.]
∼ : Q1–2, F, D.   265   of] Q1, F, D; on of Q2.   279   dear,] ∼∧ Q1–
2, F, D.   281   after-reck'nings] D (After-reck'nings); after reck-nings Q1–
2, F.   292   Life.] ∼ : Q1–2, F, D.   294   Heav'n?] D; ∼ , Q1–2, F.
295   roul.] ∼ : Q1–2, F, D (rowl F).   299   Tortoise pace] Q1–2;
Tortoise-pace F, D.   303   hearing;] ∼ , Q1–2, F, D.   303   send,] ∼∧
Q1–2, F, D.   309   lips,] F (Lips); ∼ ; Q1–2, D (Lips D).   313   now.]
∼ ; Q1–2, F, D.   319+   *s.d. Emperour*] Emperour Q1–2, F, D (Emperor F; Emp. D).   325–326+   *s.d.* first; / . . . righted. / [*Walks a
turn.*] Q1; first; [*Walks a turn.* / . . . righted. Q2, F, D.   327   disarm'd,] Q1; ∼ ; Q2, F, D.   329   self.] ∼ ? Q1; ∼ ; Q2, F, D.   329
s.d. Walks] F, D; *walks* Q1–2.   331   necessity.] ∼ : Q1–2, F, D (Necessity D).   337   work,] Q1, F, D (Work F, D); ∼∧ Q2.   340   reck'ning]
Q1–2, D; reckoning F.   342+   *s.d. Gives . . . Sword.*] F, D; *gives . . .*
∼∧ Q1–2 (*Sword. Q2*).   352   *Dorax to . . . Guards. Muza*] D (*Dor.
[to . . . Guards∧*]); (Dorax *to . . . Guards.*) / *Muza* Q1, F (*speech tag
centered; "Muza" indented*); [Dorax *to . . . Guards.*] / *Muza* Q2 (*speech
tag centered; "Muza" indented*).   355   And] *as in Q2, F, D; indented
in Q1*.   359   back,] F, D; ∼∧ Q1–2.   359   Man!] ∼ , Q1–2, F, D.
362   What,] ∼∧ Q1–2, F, D.   363+   *s.d. Emperor*] Emperor Q1–2,
F, D (Emperour Q2).   365   *Bacchus*] F, D; Bacchus Q1–2.   369
stands:] Q1; ∼ . Q2, F, D.   371   twines] Q1, F, D; twins Q2.   381
tumult,] D (Tumult); ∼∧ Q1–2, F (Tumult F).   384   far,] F, D; ∼∧
Q1–2.   385   State Affairs] Q1–2, F; State-Affairs D.   386   Heavenly]
Q1–2, F; heav'nly D.   391   *Spain,*] F, D; ∼∧ Q1–2.   392   *England,*]
F; ∼∧ Q1–2, D.   394   Church-men:] Q1–2, F (Churchmen F); Church-
men! D.   395   call'st] Q2, F, D; call st Q1.   398   pow'r] Q1, D
(Pow'r D); power Q2, F (Power F).   402   pay.] Q1; ∼ , Q2, F, D (Pay
D).   405   *Moors*] D; Moors Q1–2, F.   408   Blustring] Q1; Blustering
Q2, F, D.   408–409   opprest; . . . World;] D; ∼ . . . . ∼ . Q1–2, F.
411   sweeten'd] F; sweetn'd Q1–2, D.   413   pair,] Q1–2, D (Pair D);
Pair!) F.   416   too] Q1, F, D; to Q2.   419   what ere] Q1–2; whate'er
F, D.   419   by] Q1; my Q2, F, D.   425   will?] D (Will); ∼ ; Q1; ∼ .
Q2, F.   426   loath.] F; ∼ , Q1–2, D.   427   do't] Q1–2, F; ∼ . D.
428   time!] ∼ ? Q1–2, F, D (Time D).   431   *Or*] Or Q1–2, F, D.
438+   *s.d. Emperor*] Emperor Q1–2, F, D (Emperour Q2).   447   Chris-
tians] Q1–2, F; Christian D.   448   shall;] Q1; ∼∧ Q2, D; ∼ , F.   450
Hell-fire] Q2, F; Hell fire Q1, D (Fire D).   454   To] Q2, F, D; to Q1.
456   What,] F, D; ∼∧ Q1–2.   456   fortunes?] D (Fortunes); ∼ , Q1–2,
F (Fortunes F).   457+   *s.d. Emperor and*] Emperor and Q1–2, F, D
(Emperour Q2; Emp. D; *and* Q2, F, D).   459   unheard,] Q1, F; ∼ .

Q2; ~ : D.   463+   *s.d. Emperor*] Emperor Q1-2, F, D (Emperour Q2;
Emp. F, D).   464 *Benducar,*] D; ~∧ Q1-2, F.   465 round,] F, D;
~∧ Q1-2.   466 *Benducar,*] ~ . Q1-2, F, D.   471 it,] D; ~∧ Q1-2,
F.   476 *Nonacrian . . . Lethe's*] F, D; Nonacrian . . . Lethe's Q1-2.
480+   *s.d. Emperor*] Emperor Q1-2, F, D (Emperour Q2; Emp. D).   485
medley War] Q1-2, F (medly F); Medley-War D.   492 ev'ry] Q1-2,
F; every D.   493 *Affrick . . . Portugal*] F, D (*Africk*); Affrick . . .
Portugal Q1-2.   494 Court-service] Q1-2, F (Court-Service F); Court
Service D.   495 done,] Q1, F, D; ~∧ Q2.

III, ii

SCENE II. / *A*] Scene 2. *Is a* Q1-2, F (SCENE II. Q2, F); SCENE II.
A D.   *s.d. Night Scene*] Q1-2, F; *Night-Scene* D.   3 Why,] ~∧ Q1-
2, F, D.   10 Orange Trees] D (Orange-trees); *Orange* Trees Q1-2, F.
10 pit-a-pat] F; pit a pat Q1-2, D (Pit a Pat D).   15+   *s.d.* Moorish]
D; *Moorish* Q1-2, F.   18 self?] ~ ! Q1-2, F, D.   22 *Antonio . . .
looking.* At] Antonio . . . looking. / At Q1-2, F (*speech tag centered;*
"At" *indented*); Ant. . . . looking.] At D.   26 handsome] ~ . Q1-2,
F, D.   27 enough,] F; ~∧ Q1-2, D.   38-39 *Anton. aside. . . .
Affrick.――― [He . . . her.]* I] Anton. . . . Affrick. [*Aside. / He . . .
her.* / I Q1-2, F, D (*Ant.* Q2, F, D; *Affick* Q2; *Africk* F, D; *aside* Q2;
[*He . . . her.* D [*flush right*]).   40 *Morayma:*] Q1; ~∧ Q2; ~ , F, D.
45 Why,] F, D; ~∧ Q1-2.   45 not,] F, D; ~∧ Q1-2.   45+   *s.d.*
Throwing] F, D; *throwing* Q1-2.   47 all] Q1, F, D; alls Q2.   48
What,] F, D; ~∧ Q1-2.   49 hear] Q1, F, D; here Q2.   50 why,]
D; ~∧ Q1-2, F (Why F).   54 favours.] Q1-2, D (Favours D); Favours?
F.   56 Daughter.] Q1, D; ~ ? Q2, F.   60 *Johayma.*] Q2, F, D (*Joh.*);
~ , Q1.   62 fellow Slaves] Q1-2, F (Fellow F); Fellow-Slaves D.   78
you] ~ . Q1-2, F, D.   89 fall'n] Q1; fallen Q2, F, D.   99 in it] Q1;
in't Q2, F, D.   101 Daughter:] Q1; ~ ? Q2, F; ~ ; D.   106 *Af-
fricans*] F, D (*Africans*); Affricans Q1-2.   117 Love.] ~ : Q1-2, F; ~∧
D.   117 there!] ~ ; Q1-2, F, D.   117 no body] Q1-2, F (Body F);
no-body D.   119 Madam?] D; ~ , Q1-2, F.   122 pity.] F; ~ : Q1-2,
D (Pity D).   123-124 ravish'd! . . . me! . . . Creature!] ~ : . . . ~.
. . . ~. Q1-2, F, D (ravish'd; F).   126 what e'er] Q1-2 (e're Q2);
whate'er F, D.   127 *Mufti.*] F, D (*Muf.*); ~ , Q1-2.   128 What,]
D; ~∧ Q1-2, F.   130 after,] Q1, F, D; ~ . Q2.   133 *Mufti.*] Q2;
F, D (*Muf.*); ~ , Q1.   140 so,] Q1, F, D; ~ . Q2.   147 him.] ~ :
Q1-2, F, D.   149 *Mufti.*] Q2, F, D (*Muf.*); ~ , Q1.   150 Honor?]
Q1, D (Honour D); Honour. Q2, F.   169 fury] ~ . Q1-2, F, D (Fury
D).   171 fellow Slaves] Q1-2, F (Fellow F); Fellow-Slaves D (Fellow- /
Slaves).   173 as soon] Q1-2, D; assoon F.   178 What,] Q1, F, D;
~∧ Q2.   180 it.―――] Q1; ~ .∧ Q2, F, D.   198-199 winter quar-
ters] Q1-2, F (Winter Quarters F); Winter-Quarters D.   201 *Morayma.*]
F, D (*Mor.*); ~ , Q1-2.   202 alas, . . . say,] ~∧ . . . ~∧ Q1-2, F, D.
203 *Antonio.*] F, D (*Ant.*); ~ , Q1-2.   205 *Morayma.*] Q2, F, D
(*Mor.*); ~ , Q1.   207 cam'st] Q1; camest Q2, F, D.   213 my] Q1-2,
D; thy F.   215 night,] Q1-2, F (Night F); Night! D.   218 back

walk] Q1-2, F (Walk F); Back-Walk D (Back- / Walk).   230–231 *Any*
. . . *[to] . . . drudgery:] in romans in Q1-2, F, D* (Drudgery D).   231
those,] F, D; ~∧ Q1-2.   233 self preservation] Q1-2; Self-preservation
F; Self-Preservation D.   234 too.] Q2, F, D; ~∧ Q1.   240 worse
natur'd] Q1-2, F; worse-natur'd D.   246 truck.] Q1, F; ~∧ Q2; ~ : D
(Truck).   247 better:] D; ~ , Q1-2; ~ ; F.   255–256 Predecessors,
. . . memory,] ~∧ . . . ~∧ Q1-2, F, D (Memory D).   256–257 three-
pil'd] F; three pil'd Q1-2, D.   262 into] Q1-2, D; in to F.   264
come-off] F; come off Q1-2, D.   264 *s.d. Taking it.*] F, D; taking it:
Q1-2.   267 thee, thou] F, D; ~∧ ~ Q1-2.   271 you to;] Q1-2, D;
to, F.   271 doubt it,] Q1; doubt, Q2, F; doubt; D.   281 Moppet]
F; ~ , Q1-2, D.   284 fingring] Q1-2; fingering F, D.   286 it;] ~ ,
Q1-2, F, D.   289 intention,] Q1, F; ~' Q2; ~∧ D (Intention).   293
to morrow night] Q1-2, D (Night D); to morrow-night F.   295 How,]
Q1, D; ~ . Q2; ~ ! F.   296 mean,] ~∧ Q1-2, F, D.   298 carry.]
Q1; ~ ! Q2, F, D.   301 him.] Q1, F, D; ~ , Q2.   302 Postern gate]
Q1-2; Postern-gate F; Postern-Gate D.   304 me.———If] ~ ,———if
Q1-2, F, D (me∧——— D).   304 Courage] D; ~ . Q1-2, F.   305
love . . . abundance,] D (Love); ~ , . . . ~∧ Q1-2, F (Love F; abun-
dance, F).   309 burden,] F, D; ~∧ Q1-2.   313 Charity] Q1-2, D;
~ . F.

IV, i

ACT IV. SCENE I. / Benducar's] Q2, F, D (ACT. Q2; SCENE. Q2);
ACT IV. / Scene 1. Benducar's Q1.   *s.d. Enter Benducar.] omitted from
Q1-2, F, D.*   8 most,] F; ~ ; Q1-2, D.   10 Night,] Q2, F, D; ~ .
Q1.   12+ *s.d.* Haly] F, D; *Haly* Q1-2.   15 *Haly*.] Q2, F, D; ~ ,
Q1.   23 enquire,] ~ : Q1-2, F, D.   27 Council.] F, D; ~ , Q1-2.
29 I . . . prevent, by . . . Action.] D; ~ . . . ~ , / By . . . ~ . Q1-2,
F.   30 *Muley-Zeydan*] Q2, F, D; *Muley Zeydan* Q1.   31 importance,] D (Importance); ~∧ Q1-2, F.   40 *Mustapha*] Q2, F, D; *Mustafa*
Q1.   40 *Hamet.*] Q2, F, D (*Ham.* D); ~ , Q1.   41 Night,] D; ~ :
Q1-2, F.   43 awake;] ~ , Q1-2, F, D.   44 *as in Q2, F, D; line
indented in Q1.*   44 Alarm;] ~∧ Q1-2, F, D (alarm D).   48–49
and, . . . silence, . . . cease,] ~∧ . . . ~∧ . . . ~ ; Q1-2, F, D (Silence D).   51, 54 *Hamet.*] Q2, F, D (*Ham.* D); ~ , Q1.   56 *Musta-
pha*]Q2, F, D; *Mustafa* Q1.   56+ *s.d.* Orchan—] F; ~∧ Q1-2; ~ , D.
59 *Orchan.*] D (*Orc.*); ~ , Q1-2, F.   70 *s.d. Walks.*] Q2, F, D; ~ ,
Q1 (?).   70+ *s.d. Muley-Zeydan*] Q2, F, D; *Muley Zeydan* Q1.   71
Muley-Zeyd.] F, D; *Muley Zeyd.* Q1-2.   76 How e'er] Q1-2; Howe'er
F, D.   78 thick beating] Q1-2, D; thick-beating F.   82 *Mustapha*]
F, D; *Mustafa* Q1-2.   84 Pass] Q1, F, D; Pase Q2.   87 driv'n] Q1;
driven Q2, F, D.   91 false:] ~ , Q1-2, F, D.   92 home-thrust] Q1,
F; home thrust Q2, D.   95 in.] Q1-2, F; ~∧ D.   98 Skies.] Q1-2,
F; ~∧ D.   98 *s.d. Muley-Zeyd.*] F, D; *Muley Zeyd.* Q1-2.   103+
s.d. Muley-Moluch] D; *Muley Moluch* Q1-2, F.   104 Affairs, . . .
Dorax?] Q1, D; ~ , . . . ~ . Q2; ~ ? . . . ~ ? F.   105 more?] Q1, F,
D; ~∧ Q2.   107 lab'ring] Q1; labouring Q2, F, D.   110 glitt'ring]

Q1; glitering Q2, F, D (glittering D).   119   pitch,] ~ ; Q1-2, F, D (Pitch D).   125   Spirit] Q1-2, F; Spright D.   130   too] Q1, F, D; two Q2.   134   exhal'd,] Q1-2, F; ~ . D.   135   o'er-pow'ring] Q1; orepowering Q2; o'erpowering F, D.   143   Sir;] D; ~ , Q1-2, F.   143   Heaven] Q1; Heav'n Q2, F, D.   144   you,—— [*Aside*.] Which . . . death.——] you. / Which . . . death.—— [*Aside*. Q1-2, F, D (Death F; Death∧—— D).   150   Pray'rs] Q1; Prayers Q2, F, D.   152   forget] F, D; ~ , Q1-2.   157   Soul's] Q1, F, D; Souls Q2.   160   enjoy.] Q1, D; ~ , Q2, F.   161   What,] D; ~∧ Q1-2, F.   162   in] Q1-2, F; is D.   171   Crowd.] ~ ; Q1-2, F, D.   171   *s.d. To*] F, D; *to* Q1-2.   180   *Arabian*] F, D; Arabian Q1-2.   188   after Acts] Q1-2, F (acts Q2); After-acts D.   188   pow'r] Q1; power Q2, F, D (Power F, D).   191   Person;] ~ : Q1-2, F, D.   199-200   *lines not indented in Q1-2, F, D.*

IV, ii

SCENE II.] *omitted from Q1-2, F, D.*   1   *Mufti.*] Q2, F, D (*Muft.* Q2, D; *Muf.* F); ~ , Q1.   6-7   Gardiner] Q1-2, F (Gardener Q2, F); Gard'ner D.   8   all but] Q1, D; but all Q2, F.   10   Seraglio, if] Q1-2, F (If Q2); ~ : If D.   10   *Johayma*] Q1, F, D; *Johamay* Q2.   12   her:] ~ ; Q1-2, F, D.   21   mean?] Q1-2, D; ~ ! F.   22   *back.*] Q2, F; ~ , Q1; ~∧ D.   22   What] F; ——What Q1-2, D.   38   *Muftiship*] Muftiship Q1-2, F, D.   46   it, . . . best,] F, D; ~∧ . . . ~∧ Q1-2.   48   *Mor.* And] Q1, F, D; *Mor*∧ and Q2.   56   your] Q1; the Q2, F, D.   57   Child,] ~∧ Q1-2, F, D.   62   Sir,] F, D; ~∧ Q1-2.   63   tho,] F (tho',); ~∧ Q1-2, D (tho' D).   82   Heaven] Q1; Heav'n Q2, F, D.   84   *wiping*] *Wiping* Q1-2, F, D.   92   'em;] Q1, F, D; ~∧ Q2.   98   well,] D; ~∧ Q1-2, F.   102-103   ——(*To the* Mufti.)] (to the *Mufti*∧) Q1-2; (*To the* Mufti∧) F; [*To the* Mufti.] D.   104   flight;] D (Flight); ~ ? Q1-2, F.   104   postern gate] Q1-2, D (Postern Gate D); Postern-Gate F.   105   *Antonio,*] Q1, D; ~ . Q2; ~ ! F.   105   disguise!] Q1-2, F; ~ ? D.   110   Bitch Fox] Q1-2, D; Bitch-Fox F.   115   *Antonio, . . . throat.* No] F, D (*Ant.; Throat.*) F; *Throat.*] D); [Antonio, . . . throat. / No Q1-2 (*speech tag flush right;* "No" *indented*).   116   giv'n] Q1; given Q2, F, D.   126   Interjection.] ~ : Q1-2, F, D.   126   away,] F; ~∧ Q1-2, D.   127   Dialogues;] D; ~ , Q1-2, F.   130-131   tongue. [*He struggles.*] Nay] F, D (Tongue; *struggles.*∧ F); tongue. / [*He struggles. /* Nay Q1-2.   132+   *s.d. Stage,*] ~ ; Q1; ~∧ Q2, F, D.   140   *Pythagorean*] F; Pythagorean Q1-2, D.   142   at the Balcony] F, D (*At*); At the Balcony Q1-2.   142   A] F;——A Q1-2, D.   143   fly. What] ~ ; what Q1-2, F, D (What F).   146   silence.] ~ : Q1-2, F, D.   147   within?] ~ , Q1, F, D; ~∧ Q2.   147   Servants?] F, D (Servant D); ~ , Q1-2.   150   *Antonio . . . back.* O] F, D (*Ant.; back.*) F; *back.*] D); [Antonio . . . back. / O Q1-2 (*speech tag flush right;* "O" *indented*).   150   Schriech Owl] Q1-2, D (Schreich Q2; Screich D); Skriech-Owl F.   152   *Morayma . . . Casket.* 'Tis] F, D (*Mor.; Casket.*) F; *Casket.*] D); (Morayma . . . Casket.) / 'Tis Q1-2 ([Morayma . . . Casket.] Q2; *speech tag centered;* " 'Tis" *indented*).   156   then,] F, D; ~∧ Q1-2.   159 you!] Q₁-₂, F; ∼? D.   168+   s.d. This way, this way] *this way, this way* Q₁-₂, F, D (*This way, this* D).   170   Farewel] F, D (Farewell D); farewel Q₁-₂.   171   belly.] ∼∧ Q₁-₂, F, D (Belly F, D).   171   fortune?] ∼. Q₁-₂, D (Fortune D); Fortune∧ F.   172   Follow . . . [*romans*] . . . Villains] F; *Follow . . . [italics] . . . Villains* Q₁-₂, D (*Villrins* Q₂).   174+   s.d. *A shout behind the Scenes where* Antonio *is going out.*] F, D (*Shout* D; *Scenes,* F; *s.d. centered in* F); A shout behind the Scenes where *Antonio* is going out∧ Q₁-₂ (*s.d. flush left in Q₁, centered in* Q₂).   175   what,] ∼∧ Q₁-₂, F, D (What F).   176+   s.d. out. Mufti . . . Casket.] ∼. / (∼ . . . ∼.) Q₁; ∼. / ∼ . . . ∼.] Q₂; ∼. / ∼ . . . ∼. F; ∼. / [∼ . . . ∼. D.   182   none;] Q₁; ∼∧ Q₂; ∼, F, D.   184   your self] Q₁-₂, F; yourself D.   184+   s.d. *Enter*] F, D; [∼ Q₁-₂ (*at right*).   185   *from above*] Q₂, F, D (*From* Q₂, F); From above Q₁.   187   *Omar,*] D; ∼∧ Q₁-₂, F.   189   what,] Q₁, F; ∼∧ Q₂; ∼! D.   194-195   had, Madam,] F, D; ∼∧ ∼∧ Q₁-₂.   205   beating.] Q₂, F, D; ∼, Q₁.   207   Sir,] Q₁-₂; ∼. F, D.   207+   s.d. *Beats*] Q₁-₂, D; *Beat* F.   208   Rascal.] ∼; Q₁-₂, F, D.   209   your selves] Q₁-₂, F; yourselves D.   212   Sir;] ∼, Q₁-₂, F, D.

IV, iii

SCENE III.] *omitted from Q₁-₂, F, D.*   s.d. *The Scene*] Q₂, F, D (SCENE D); *Scene* Q₁.   s.d. *Castle-yard*] Q₁, F, D (*Castle-Yard* F, D); *Castle Yard* Q₂.   s.d. Antonio,] F, D; ∼∧ Q₁-₂.   s.d. Mustapha] Q₂, F, D; Mustafa Q₁.   s.d. shouting:] D; ∼, Q₁-₂, F (shoutiug Q₂).   1   escap'd] Q₁; scap'd Q₂, D; 'scap'd F.   4   it,] Q₁, F, D; ∼∧ Q₂.   7   Hegyra;——] D; ∼;∧ Q₁-₂, F.   16   'em:] D; ∼, Q₁-₂, F.   19   s.d. him.]] ∼·∧ Q₁-₂, F, D.   20   Your] F; your Q₁-₂, D.   22   us. These] ∼; these Q₁-₂, F, D.   23-24   deserving. Bear] ∼, bear Q₁-₂; ∼; bear F, D.   24   say. [*They . . . Circle.*] That's] ∼. / [∼ . . . ∼·∧ / ∼ Q₁-₂, F, D (say∧ Q₂; say. [They F, D).   25   done;] Q₁-₂, F; ∼! D.   26   that,] Q₁, F, D; ∼∧ Q₂.   30   that,] F; ∼∧ Q₁-₂, D.   31   please,] F, D; ∼∧ Q₁-₂.   32   there] Q₁, F, D; their Q₂.   41   Reign;] ∼, Q₁-₂, F, D.   43   *Mustapha, A Mustapha!*] F, D (*A Mustapha.* F); *Mustafa, A Mustafa.*] Q₁-₂.   44   All cry.] (*All Cry*∧) Q₁-₂; (*All Cry,* F; [*All cry,* D.   44   *A Mustapha, A Mustapha!*] *A Mustafa, A Mustafa.* Q₁-₂ (*Mustafa*∧ *A* Q₂); *A Mustapha, A Mustapha.* F; *A Mustapha, A Mustapha!* D.   46   be:] Q₁-₂, F; ∼! D.   50   *Muley-Zeydan!*] D; *Muley Zeydan.* Q₁-₂, F (*Muley-Zeydan* Q₂, F).   51   All cry.] (*All Cry*∧) Q₁-₂; *All Cry,* F; [*All cry,* D.   51   *A Muley-Zeydan, A Muley-Zeydan!*] *A Muley-Zeydan, A Muley-Zeydan.* Q₁-₂, F; *A Muley-Zeydan, A Muley-Zeydan!* D.   52   see,] F, D; ∼∧ Q₁-₂.   58   destin'd] Q₁; design'd Q₂, F, D.   62   *Mufti, . . . Mobile.* Good] F, D (*Muf.; Mobile.*) F; *Mobile*∧] D); (Mufti, . . . *Mobile.*) / Good Q₁-₂ (*speech tag centered;* "Good" *indented*).   68   Holy-day] Q₁; Holy day Q₂; Holyday F, D (Holiday D).   74   of] Q₁-₂, F; or D.   75   *aside*] *Aside* Q₁-₂, F, D.   75   upon!] D; ∼, Q₁-₂; ∼. F.   75-76   s.d.——[*To him.*] But . . . Jewels.] [*To him.* But . . . Jewels. Q₁-₂; (*To him.*) But . . . Jewels. F; But . . . Jewels. [*To him.* D.   88   your] Q₁-₂, D; our F.   97   Al-

coran] D; *Alcoran* Q1–2, F.　101　remember] ~ . Q1–2, F, D.　104
Mufti.] Q2, F, D (*Muf.* F, D); ~ , Q1.　109　assistance;— . . .
say,] ~ ;∧ . . . ~∧ Q1–2, F, D (Assistance D).　111　P's,] D; ~∧ Q1–2,
F.　113　Leader,] F; ~∧ Q1–2, D.　113+　s.d. A . . . A] *A . . . A*
Q1–2, F, D.　116　What,] F, D; ~∧ Q1–2.　116　Subjects?] Q1–2, D;
~ ! F.　118　Name,] F; ~∧ Q1–2, D (name Q2).　119　*1st.*] 1st. Q1–
2, D (1st∧ Q2, D); *First* F.　119　*Rabble.*] Q2, F, D; ~ , Q1.　119
What,] F, D; ~∧ Q1–2.　121　*2d.*] 2d. Q1–2, D (2d∧ D); *Second* F.
121　*Rabble.*] Q2, F, D; ~ , Q1.　123　*Omnes.*] Q2, F, D; ~ , Q1.
123　Speak,] D; ~∧ Q1–2, F.　133　*Omnes.*] Q2, F, D; ~ , Q1.　137
loo'd] F, D; lood Q1–2.　139　*Omnes.*] Q2, F, D; ~ , Q1.　144–145
A . . . No Mufti] a . . . no Mufti Q1–2, F, D (*Mufti* Q2, F, D).　146
Omnes.] Q2, F; ~ , Q1; ~∧ D.　146　no *Mufti!*] ~~. Q1–2, F, D.
149　Plundering] Q1, F; Plundring Q2; Plund'ring D.　150　Heaven]
Q1–2, F; Heav'n D.　154　*3d.*] 3d. Q1–2, D (3d∧ D); *Third* F.　154
Rabble.] F, D; ~ , Q1; ~∧ Q2.　157　*1st.*] 1st. Q1–2, D (1st∧ D);
First F.　157　*Rabble.*] Q2, F, D; ~ , Q1.　162　*Omnes.*] F, D;
~ , Q1–2.　162　Religion!] ~ . Q1–2, F, D.　166　'till] Q1–2, D
(till Q2, D); tell F.　168　*Mufti*] Q2, F, D; Mufti Q1.　171　*Omnes.*]
Q2, F, D; ~ , Q1.　171　depos'd!] ~ . Q1–2, F, D.　174　first fruits]
Q1–2, F (First Fruits F); First-Fruits D.　175　Boy?] ~ , Q1–2, F, D.
177　squeaks,] ~∧ Q1–2, F, D (squeeks Q2, D).　180　*Mufti.*] Q2, F,
D (*Muf.* F, D); ~ , Q1.　180　me;] D; ~ , Q1–2, F.　184　our selves]
Q1–2, F; ourselves D.　186　*1st.*] 1st. Q1–2, D (1st∧ Q2, D); *First* F.
186　*Rabble.*] Q2, F, D; ~ , Q1.　187　Mob] D; *Mob* Q1–2, F.　188+
s.d. Muley-Moluch's] F, D; Muly-Moluch's Q1–2 (Muly-Moluch's Q2).
189　*Must. Not*] Q2, F, D; Not Q1 (but c.w. are "Must. Not").　191
Here's] Q1, F, D; Here Q2.　192　s.d. Bowing.] ~∧ Q1–2, F, D.　195
Benducar to Almeyda] [*Benducar to /* Almeyda Q1–2; *Bend.* (to *Alm.* F;
Bend. [*to* Almeyda D.　197　That] Q2, F, D; that Q1.　198　*Almeyda
to him.*] [Almeyda *to /* [*him.* Q1–2; *Alm.* (to him.) F; *Alm.* [to him.] D.
199　*Bend.*] F, D; Bend. Q1–2 (Bend Q2).　208　Mustapha] *Mustafa*
Q1–2; *Must.* F, D.　210　Person. Be] D; ~ , be Q1–2, F.　212　and]
Q1–2, D (aud Q2); an't F.　213　speak,] F; ~∧ Q1–2.　219　s.d.
Aside.] F, D; aside∧ Q1; aside. Q1–2.　225　s.d. Aside] F, D; aside Q1–2.
226　Madam] Q1, F, D; Madan Q2.　226　s.d. To] F, D; to Q1–2.
230　My] Q2, F, D; my Q1.　231　Deliv'rance] Q1; Deliverance Q2, F,
D.　233　*Mustapha.*] *Mustafa.* Q1; *Mustafa,* Q2; *Must.* F, D.　235
silence,] F, D (Silence D); ~∧ Q1–2.　239–240　fall, / His . . . ours:]
D (ours.); fall, his . . . ours: Q1–2, F (ours. Q2, F).　246　reward?] Q1;
~ ! Q2, F, D (Reward D).　248　Christian] F, D; *Christian* Q1–2.
249　s.d. *Going*] F, D; going Q1–2.　250　*Almeyda . . . a*] F, D (*Alm.*);
[Almyda . . . / [a Q1–2 (Almeyda Q2).　250　me. Now *Affricans,*]
me; / Now *Affricans,* Q1–2, F, D (Now Q1; *Africans* F, D).　260　Chris-
tian] F, D; *Christian* Q1–2.　260　true,] F; ~∧ Q1–2, D.　261　Chris-
tians] F, D; *Christians* Q1–2.　267　*Almeyda . . . People*] F, D (*Alm.*);
[Almeyda . . . / [*People* Q1–2.　270–271　Men, . . . men,] D (. . .
Men); ~∧ . . . ~∧ Q1–2, F (. . . Men F).　272　*Antonio aside.*] F

(*Ant. (Aside.*)); [Antonio *aside*∧ Q1–2; *Ant.* D.   272 her.———] ∼ .∧
Q1–2, F, D.   273 *s.d.* [*To* Mustapha.]] [*To* Mustafa. Q1; *to* Mustafa∧
Q2; (*To* Must.) F; [*aside to* Must.] D.   275 *Mustapha.*] *Mustafa.* Q1–
2 (*Mustafa*, Q2); *Must.* F, D.   277 her.] ∼ ; D; ∼ , Q1–2, F.   278
Mustapha] *Mustafa* Q1–2; *Must.* F, D.   281 resolved] Q1; resolv'd Q2,
F, D.   283 Master?] Q1, D; ∼ . Q2, F.   284 *Mustapha*] F, D;
Mustafa Q1–2.   285 *Mustapha*] *Mustafa* Q1–2; *Must.* F, D.   286
too. What] ∼ : what Q1–2, F, D (What F, D).   290 *Mufti*] Q1; ∼ .
Q2; *Muf.* F; ∼ , D.   291 *Mustapha.*] *Mustafa.* Q1–2; *Must.* F, D.
294 *Mufti's*] D; *Mufti* Q1–2, F.   295 Green coat] Q1–2; Green-coat
F; green Coat D.   295 Christian's] D; *Christians* Q1–2; Christian F.
295 black coat] Q1–2, D (Coat D); Black-coat F.   299 *Muley-Zeydan*]
D; ∼∧ ∼ , Q1; ∼–∼ , Q2, F.   301 *Mustapha.*] *Mustafa.* Q1–2
(*Mustaafa*, Q2); *Must.* F, D.   302 *Muley-Zeydan*] F, D; *Muley Zeydan*
Q1–2.   305 you.] F, D; ∼ , Q1–2.   305+ *s.d.* hand.] F, D (*Hand*
D); ∼∧ Q1–2.   305+ *s.d.* Portugueses] F, D; *Portugueses* Q1–2.
305+ *s.d.* Almeyda] D; (∼ Q1–2, F.   306 and] and Q1–2, F, D.
309 *Moors*] Moors Q1–2, F, D.   310 *Muley-Zeydan*] F, D; *Muley
Zeydan* Q1–2 (*Zeyden* Q2).   316 here] Q1, F, D; hear Q2.   316
present.] D; ∼ ? Q1–2, F.   319 here,] Q1–2, F; ∼∧ D.   321 *Benducar to Dorax.*] D (*Bend.* [*to Dor.*]); [Benducar / *to* Dorax.] Q1; [*Benducar / to* Dorax.] Q2; *Bend.* (*to* Dorax∧) F.   332 hast] Q1, D; has Q2,
F.   336 fate,] D (Fate); ∼ . Q1–2 (Fate Q2); Fate; F.   338 poys'-
ning] Q1; Poysoning Q2, F, D (Poisoning F, poysoning D).   339 double
dilligence] Q1–2, D (Diligence D); double-diligence F.   340 fall'n]
Q1, F (fal'n F); fallen Q2, D.   341 *Morayma's*] Q2, F, D (*Morayma's*
Q2); Morayma's Q1.   346 *Dorax to Mustapha.*] [Dorax *to* / Mustafa.]
Q1; (Dorax *to* / Mustapha.) Q2; *Dor.* (*to* Must.) F; *Dor.* [*to* Must.] D.
350 bus'ness] Q1; business Q2, F, D (Business D).   355 Heaven] Q1–
2, D; Heav'n F.   358+ *s.d.* Mustapha] F, D; Mustafa Q1–2.   358+
s.d. Rabble] D; Rabble Q1–2, F.   359 *Almeyda kneeling . . . him.*
With . . . pay] [Almeyda *kneeling . . . him. /* With . . . pay Q1–2, F
((Almeyda Q2, F; "With" indented in *Q1–2*); *Alm.* With . . . pay /
[*Kneeling . . . him.* D.   360 blest] Q1–2, D; best F.   362 *Dorax
raising . . . up.* Arise . . . thanks,] [Dorax *raising . . . up*∧ / Arise . . .
thanks, Q1–2, F ((Dorax Q2, F; *up.* F; "Arise" indented in *Q1–2*); *Dor.*
Arise . . . Thanks, / [*Raising . . . up.* D.   365 *Portugal*] Q2, F, D;
Portugall Q1.   365 *Affrica*] Affrique Q1; *Affrique* Q2; *Afrique* F;
Africa D.   367 Universall] Q1, F, D (Universal F, D); Universail Q2.
373 me,] D; ∼ . Q1–2, F.   374 *to*] D; to Q1–2, F.   374 *Sebastian.*]
D (*Seb.*); ∼ : Q1–2, F.   375 *s.d.* Almeyda.]] D (*Alm.*); ∼ .∧ Q1–2 (*line
indented in Q1*); ∼ .) F.   375+ *s.d.* Portugueses] D; *Portugueses* Q1–
2, F (*Portugeses* Q2).   376 *to*] F; *To* Q1–2, D.   376 *Guard.* With]
D (*Guard.*]); ∼ . / ∼ Q1–2, F.   377 solus] D; Solus Q1–2, F.   378
of a] Q1; of Q2, F, D.   378 bounty:] ∼ . Q1–2, F, D (Bounty D).
380 *s.d.* Peruque,] F, D (*Peruke* D); ∼∧ Q1–2.   385 *Dorax.*] Q2, F,
D (*Dor.*); Dorax∧ Q1.   393 brought.] Q1, D; ∼ , Q2, F.   404 both.]
Q1, D; ∼ , Q2, F.   407 thee thus] Q1, D; thus Q2, F.   412

Prince!] ~ ? Q1-2, F, D.   417 Tyrant:] ~ , Q1-2, F, D (*Tyrant* Q1).
417 it] (~ Q1-2, F, D.   417 me,] ~∧ Q1-2, F, D.   417 Prince;]
~ .) Q1-2, D; ~ ,) F.   419 is,] D; ~∧ Q1-2, F.   420 How,] D; ~∧
Q1-2, F.   420 *Dorax*.] Q2, F, D (*Dor.*); ~∧ Q1.   420 Tyrant.] Q1-
2, F; ~ ! D.   421 Traytour!] ~ ? Q1; ~ ; Q2, F, D (Traytor F, D).
423 Ill] Q1, D; I'll Q2, F.   425 than] Q1, F, D; then Q2.   426
think,] Q2, F, D; ~∧ Q1.   427 treason,] D (Treason); ~ . Q1-2, F.
429 hurryed] Q1; hurry'd Q2, F, D.   436 thee;] Q1; ~∧ Q2, F; ~ ,
D.   439 Courts;] ~ : Q1-2, F, D.   441 face,] ~ ; Q1-2, F, D
(Face D).   444 of] Q1; or Q2, F, D.   451 *Enriquez*] Q1-2, D;
Henriquez F.   451 lye] ~ , Q1-2, F, D (Lie D).   453 *Enriquez*]
Q1-2, D; *Henriquez* F.   453 now, . . . Heaven,] ~∧ . . . ~∧ Q1-2,
F, D.   475 *Enriquez*] Q1-2, D; *Henriquez* F.   476 worth.] F, D
(Worth D); ~ : Q1-2.   479 rapacious] Q1, F, D; rapitious Q2.   479
stript] Q1; strip'd Q2, F, D (stripp'd F, D).   480 love.] F, D (Love
D); ~ , Q1-2.   481 should'st] Q1, F, D; should'd Q2.   485 Ev'n]
D; E'ven Q1-2; Even F.   488 Even] Q1, F; E'ven Q2; Ev'n D.   488
Heaven] Q1-2, F; Heav'n D.   489 who,] D; ~∧ Q1-2, F.   493
refus'd] Q2 (?), F, D; resus'd Q1 (?).   495 more,] D; ~∧ Q1-2, F.
497 To] Q2, F, D; o Q1.   498 interpose,] ~ ; Q1-2, F, D.   499
Swords.] F, D; ~ , Q1-2.   503 say,] D; ~∧ Q1-2, F.   503 *the . . .
[to] . . . intended*] in romans in *Q1-2, F, D* (Blow D).   505 power:]
Q1; ~ - Q2; ~ , F; Power ——— D.   517 it.] Q1-2, F; ~∧ D.   519
it:] Q1; ~ :——— Q2; ~ .——— F; ~∧ ——— D.   525 me? speak!]
~ ; ~ ? Q1-2, F, D.   533, 535 Isthmus] *Isthmus* Q1-2, F, D (*Istmus*
Q2).   541 Heaven] Q1-2, F; Heav'n D.   546 fair] Q1, D; fare Q2,
F.   548 *Sebas. drawing. Now . . . thank'd*:] [*Sebas. drawing*:] Now
. . . thank'd: Q1-2, F (Sebast. Q2; *Seb.* F); *Seb.* Now . . . thank'd: /
[*Drawing.* D.   554 Go] Q2, F, D; Go Q1.   554 *Enriquez*] *Henriquez* Q1-2, F, D.   560 there's] Q2, F, D; their's Q1.   565 promise;] Q1; ~ : Q2, F, D (Promise D).   565 preserv'd,] D; ~ : Q1-2, F.
568 thee,] D; ~∧ Q1-2, F.   581 Heaven] Q1-2, F; Heav'n D.   585
so,] Q1-2, D; ~∧ F.   586 been, . . . is,] D; ~∧ . . . ~∧ Q1-2, F.
590 Hell!] Q1, F, D; ~ ? Q2.   590 lost,] Q1-2, D; ~ ? F.   591
death!] Q1-2, D (Death D); ~ ? F.   592 fallen] Q1, D; fall'n Q2, F.
593 Bulwark] Q1, F, D; Bulwork Q2.   596–597 his . . . dy'd:] Q1-2,
D; ~ : . . . ~ , F.   604 whither] F, D; whether Q1-2.   606 *Enriquez*] *Henriquez* Q1-2, F, D.   611 Soul:] Q1, D; ~ ' Q2; ~ , F.   612-
613 name: / [*More calmly.* / Thou . . . King:] name: / [*more calmly.*]
Thou . . . King: Q1-2, F; name: / Thou . . . King: [*More calmly.* D.
613 meant'st] Q1; mean'st Q2, F, D.   614 Speak,] F, D; ~∧ Q1-2.
616, 620, 622 *Dorax*] Q2, F, D; *Dorax* Q1.   629 too] Q1, F, D; to
Q2.   631 first,] Q1; ~∧ Q2, F, D.   633–634 To . . . feet. [*Falls at
his feet.* / Now*] D (Feet. / [*Falls*); [*Falls at his* To . . . feet. / *feet*∧]
Now Q1-2, F (feet. Q2, F).   637 *s.d.* But . . . noble. [*Taking him
up.*] D (Noble. / [*Taking*); [*taking him up.* But . . . noble. Q1-2, F (*up,*
Q2; *up.*] F; noble, Q2, F).   649 Heaven] Q1; Heav'n Q2, F, D.   651
Enriquez] *Henriquez* Q1-2, F, D.   654–655 Here . . . arms: [*Em-*

bracing him. / And] D (Arms); *Embrac-* Here . . . arms: / *ing him.* And
Q1–2, F ([*Embrac-* F; *him.*] F).   657 *Enriquez*] Q1–2; *Henriquez* F, D.
658 *my . . . my*] my . . . my Q1–2, F, D.   662 Thou . . . [*to*] . . .
silent.] *omitted from D.*   663 must] F, D; ~ , Q1–2.   665 Heaven]
Q1–2, F; Heav'n D.   666–669 *lines not indented in Q1–2, F, D.*
669+ *s.d. Exeunt.*] Q2, F, D; ~∧ Q1.

V, i

ACT V. SCENE I. / *The*] D; ACT V. *The* Q1–2, F (ACT. Q2, F).
7 *Antonio.*] Q2, F, D (*Ant.*); ~ , Q1.   23 Guard] Q1, D (guard D);
Gaurd Q2, F.   26 came;] Q1; ~∧ Q2, F, D.   26 defence,] Q1, F,
D (Defence D); ~ . Q2.   30 Drawn-up] Q1–2, D; Drawn up F.   31
Christian] *Christian* Q1–2, F, D.   33 Int'rest] Q1; Interest Q2, F, D.
45 mine;] ~ : Q1–2, F, D.   46 fall'n] Q1; fallen Q2, F, D.   50+
s.d. Antonio.] Q2, F, D; ~ , Q1.   57 Servant.] Q2; *Servaut.* Q1; *Serv.*
F, D.   62 *Antonio . . . her.* Look] D (*Ant.; her.*]); [*Antonio . . .
her. / Look* Q1–2, F (*her.*] F; "Look" *indented*).   63 already:] Q1–2,
F; ~ ! D.   66 you] Q1–2; your F, D.   72 Rabble;] ~ : Q1–2, F,
D.   77 odds,] ~∧ Q1–2, F, D.   79 So,] ~∧ Q1–2, F, D.   82
Well,] D; ~∧ Q1–2, F.   90 into] Q2, F, D; iuto Q1.   96 leisure-
minuts] Q1 (leisure- / minuts); leasure-minuts Q2; leasure minutes F, D
(Minutes D).   97 few:] ~ , Q1–2, F, D.   100 she-Saint] Q1; she
Saint Q2, F, D.   100 there] Q1, D; their Q2, F.   102 enterviews]
Q1, D (Enterviews D); enter-views Q2, F.   103 an't] Q1; ar'not Q2;
are not F, D.   104 Meeting-houses] Q1, D; Meeting houses Q2, F.
105 Therefore] Q2, F, D; therefore Q1.   108 I] Q1–2, D; that I F.
110 Lover,] Q1, F, D; ~ - Q2.   117+ *s.d.* Re-enter] F, D; *Reenter*
Q1–2.   118 *Muley-Zeydan*] D; *Muley Zeydan* Q1–2, F.   123 hap-
piness;] D (Happiness); ~∧ Q1–2, F (happyness Q2).   126 ransome] F
(Ransome); ~ : Q1; Ransome. Q2; Ransom; D.   129 *Alvarez falling
. . . knees.* Now . . . hairs,] [~ ~ . . . ~ .] / ~ . . . ~ , Q1–2, F
(*Alvarez* F); *Alv.* Now . . . Hairs, / [*Falling . . . Knees.* D.   132
Sebastian, raising him. Thou . . . Man!] *Sebastian, raising him*∧] / Thou
. . . Man! Q1–2, F (*Sebastian*∧ Q2; *Sebastine*∧ F); him. Q2, F); *Seb.* Thou
. . . Man! [*Raising him.* D.   134 *Alv.*] Q1, F, D; *Aln.* Q2.   137
lost,] D; ~∧ Q1–2, F.   143 hast, . . . joy,] F; ~∧ . . . ~∧ Q1–2, D
(Haste, D; Joy D).   144 underneath] Q1, F, D; under neath Q2.
150 *s.d.* Aside] D; *aside* Q1–2, F.   155 a one] Q2, F, D; an one Q1.
156 Pow'rs] Q2, F, D; Power's Q1.   158 Heav'n] Q1, D; Heaven
Q2, F.   160 deliv'rance.] ~ , Q1–2, F, D (deliverance Q2, F; Deliver-
ance D).   172 giv'n] Q1; given Q2, F, D.   184 O!] Q1; ~∧ Q2,
F, D.   187 too] Q1, F, D; to Q2.   189, 190 Heav'n] Q2, F, D;
Hea'vn Q1.   190 grant;] ~ . Q1–2, F, D.   197 him:] ~ . Q1–2, F,
D.   204 past] Q1, F, D; paste Q2.   208 Shipbord,] Q2, F, D (Ship-
board F, D); ~ ,, Q1.   214 Age,] ~ ; Q1–2, F, D.   216 wise,] ~ ;
Q1–2, F, D.   222 impair'd.] D; ~ , Q1–2, F.   226–227 liv'd / And
. . . change, he . . . Same.] liv'd and . . . change, / He . . . Same. Q1–
2, F, D (Change D; same F, D).   233 Heav'n] F, D; Hea'vn Q1–2.

237 Believe,] Q2, F, D (Beleive Q2); ∼∧ Q1.   238 will:] ∼. Q1-2,
F, D (Will Q2, F, D).   240 Oracle,] D; ∼. Q1-2, F.   241 off] Q1,
D; of Q2, F.   243 'Tis] Q2, F, D; 'Tis Q1.   246 cost,] Q1-2, D;
∼. F.   250, 251 Heav'n] F, D; Hea'vn Q1-2.   254 more, . . .
honour,] ∼∧ . . . ∼∧ Q1-2, F, D (more, D; Honour D).   258 stay!]
∼. Q1-2, F, D.   260 Heav'n] F, D; Hea'vn Q1-2.   277 Heaven]
Q1-2, F; Heav'n D.   278 near,] ∼. Q1-2, F, D.   280 And . . .
heard, [*To* Almeyda.] D; [*To* Almeyda∧] And . . . heard, Q1-2, F (*to* Q2, F).
289-290 *Sebast. to Alme.* Thou . . . War: / My] *Sebast.* Thou . . . War:
/ *to* Alme.] My Q1-2 (Alm. Q2); *Seb.*] Thou . . . War: / *to Alm.*] My F;
Sebast. Thou . . . War: / [*To* Alm.] My D.   298 worth;] Q1-2, D
(Worth D); ∼? F.   305 Fathers] Q2, F, D (Father's D); Fashers Q1.
306 so,] D; ∼; Q1-2, F.   312 Fiend] Q1; Friend Q2, F, D.   313
Was't] D; Wa'st Q1-2, F.   315 Infamous, O] D (o); Infamous∧ Q1-2, F.
315 repair:] F; ∼. Q1-2, D (Repair D).   316 ill-concerted] D; ill con-
certed Q1-2, F.   321 she is] Q1-2, F; she's D.   323 shalt] Q2, F, D;
shallt Q1.   323 unheard;] ∼. Q1-2, F, D.   324 thy] Q1-2, D; the F.
326 head:] F; ∼, Q1-2; Head. D.   327 thinks] Q1; thinke Q2; think
F, D.   327 Jest.] Q1, D; ∼, Q2, F.   331 fame.] F; ∼; Q1-2;
Fame: D.   332 Int'rest] Q1-2, F; Interest D.   334 prov'd,] D;
∼∧ Q1-2, F.   334 me;] ∼, Q1-2, F, D.   334 unprov'd,] D; ∼∧
Q1-2, F.   334 Condemn.] D (condemn); ∼? Q1-2, F.   338 love.]
F, D (Love); ∼: Q1-2.   339 Impostor] Q1, D; Imposture Q2, F.
351 say.] F, D; ∼: Q1-2.   352 remains, . . . hand,] ∼; . . . ∼:
Q1-2, F, D (Hand D).   355 Heav'n] F, D; Hea'vn Q1-2.   355 a
while] Q1, F; awhile Q2, D.   357 *Alvar. to Dorax.*] [*Alvar. to Dorax*∧]
Q1-2, F (*Alv.* Q2, F); *Alv.* [*to* Dorax∧] D.   359 himself] D; ∼, Q1-2,
F.   362 *Dorax . . . King.* Untouch'd, . . . me,] Dorax . . . ∼. / ∼,
. . . ∼, Q1-2, F (*speech tag centered*); *Dor.* Untouch'd, . . . me, / [*giving
. . . King.* D.   365 *Sebast. . . . Seals.* Draw . . . concern'd;] Sebast.
. . . ∼. / ∼ . . . ∼. Q1-2, F (Sebastian∧ Q2, F; *speech tag centered*);
Seb∧ Draw . . . concern'd: / [*tearing . . . Seals.* D.   368 hand,] F,
D (Hand D); ∼∧ Q1-2.   376 not,] F; ∼∧ Q1-2, D.   377 Heav'n]
Q2, F; Hea'vn Q1; Heaven D.   385 thee,] Q1; ∼∧ Q2, F, D.   386
fair fame] Q1; fame Q2, F, D (Fame D).   386 wou'd I] Q1; mov'd
I'd Q2, F, D.   386 thus:——] Q2, D; ∼——: Q1; ∼∧—— F.
386+ *s.d.* (*Tearing . . . Paper.*] [(∼ . . . ∼∧ Q1; [∼ . . . ∼: Q2, F, D
(*Paper.* F, D).   388 forging] Q1-2, D; foregoing F.   388+ *s.d.*
Paper.] F, D; ∼∧ Q1-2.   389 hopes:] ∼. Q1-2, F, D.   393 with]
Q1; to Q2, F, D.   395 Conscience.] D; ∼: Q1-2, F.   401 present.]
∼: Q1-2, F, D.   402 come] Q1-2, F; came D.   402 yours.] D;
∼? Q1-2, F.   404 *Portugal,*] D; *Portugall*∧ Q1-2, F (*Portugal* F).
411-412 Those . . . Your] Q2, F, D; Yhose . . . Tour Q1.   413 'em,]
∼: Q1-2, F, D.   416 *Zayda:*] ∼. Q1-2, F, D.   417 (You] Q2, F,
D;) ∼ Q1.   418 plac'd.] Q1, D; ∼, Q2, F.   419 Rings,] Q1; ∼∧
Q2, F, D (rings Q2).   421 part.] F, D; ∼, Q1-2.   421+ *s.d.* [Seb.
. . . *other.*] D (Sebastian); *set in position of speech tag for lines 422 and
423 in Q1-2, F (other.*]*).   421+ *s.d. Ring,*] D; ∼. Q1; ∼∧ Q2, F.

422 *Seb.*] Q2, F, D; ∼ , Q1.　　422 ours.———] ∼ .ʌ Q1-2, F, D.　423 I'm] D; *Alm.* I'm Q1-2, F.　423 ever.] Q1-2, D; ∼ʌ F.　423 s.d. [*Swoons. The* . . . Morayma . . . *off.* Seb. . . . *upward.*] (*swoons*ʌ) / (*The* . . . Morayma, . . . *off.*) / [Seb. . . . *upward.*] Q1-2, F (Morayma∧ Q2; *off.*ʌ F); [*Swoons.* / [*The* . . . Morayma . . . *off.* / [Sebastian . . . *upward.* D.　432 *Seb.*] D; [Seb. Q1-2, F.　434 being:] ∼ . Q1-2, F, D (Being D).　437 Powers,] F; ∼ʌ Q1-2, D.　439 fate,] D (Fate); ∼ʌ Q1-2, F.　441 Heav'ns] Q1-2; Heave'ns F; Heav'n's D.　443 self?] Q1; ∼ʌ Q2, F, D.　443, 444 fault . . . Heav'n,] D (Fault); ∼ , . . . ∼ʌ Q1-2, F.　448 Heaven] Q1; Heav'n Q2, F, D.　448 y're] Q1; your Q2; you're F, D.　448 hands.] Q2, F, D (Hands D); ∼ , Q1.　455 Crime.] ∼ : Q1-2, F, D.　456-457 s.d. Stand . . . death; [*Struggling again.* / For] [*struggling* Stand . . . death; / *again.*] For Q1-2, F (*struling* F; death: Q2, F); [*Struggling again.* / Stand . . . Death: / For D.　459 What,] F, D; ∼ʌ Q1-2.　459 giving] Q2, F, D; given Q1.　459 comfort!] Q1-2, D (Comfort Q2, D); Comfort? F.　464 lingring Heaven] Q1; lingering Heav'n Q2, F, D.　466 *Dorax to Alv. and Anto.*] [*Dorax to Alv. and Anto.*] Q1-2, F; *Dor.* [*to Alv. and Ant.*] D.　467 obey'd.] D; ∼ : Q1-2; ∼ , F.　468 What,] D; ∼ʌ Q1-2, F.　468 himself,] Q1, F; ∼ʌ Q2; ∼ ? D.　473 *Anto.* . . . *hold.*] [*Anto.* . . . *hold.*] Q1-2, F; *Ant.* [. . . *Hold.*] D.　474+ *s.d.* Alvarez.] Q2, F, D (∼ .] F; Alv. D); ∼ʌ Q1.　475 *Dorax.*] D (*Dor.*); Dorax. Q1-2, F.　475 Fiend, is . . . part?] ∼ , / Is . . . ∼ ? Q1-2, F, D (Part D; "Is" *indented in Q1-2*).　477 dye,] F (die); ∼ . Q1-2, D (die D).　483 th'] Q1, D; the Q2, F.　484 Crime] F, D; ∼ . Q1-2.　489 Guilt] Q2, F, D; Guilt Q1.　491 was] Q2, F, D; 'was Q1.　492 *Dor.*] Q2, F, D; *Dor,* Q1.　492 know:] ∼ . Q1-2, F, D.　495 Damnation!] Q1-2, D; ∼ ? F.　503 death?] Q1-2, D (Death D); Death! F.　504 Death?] Q1-2, D; ∼ ! F.　507 Crime] ∼ , Q1, F, D; ∼ . Q2.　513 arms?] D (Arms); ∼ . Q1-2, F.　515 *Dor.*] Q2, F, D; *Dor:* Q1.　517 sure,] Q1; ∼ʌ Q2, F, D.　518 Why,] F, D; ∼ʌ Q1-2.　520 Damnation] D; ∼ ? Q1-2; ∼ , F.　521 this!] F, D; ∼ , Q1-2.　521 trade;] F (Trade); ∼ . Q1; ∼ , Q2, D (Trade D).　522 Scriv'ner] Q1; Scrivener Q2, F, D.　526 giv'n] Q1; given Q2, F, D.　528 irremeable] Q1-2, D; irremeciable F.　529 th'] Q1, D; the Q2, F.　529 Abyss,] D; *Abyss;* Q1-2; *Abyss,* F.　533 leisure;] F; ∼ . Q1; ∼ , Q2, D (leasure Q2; Leisure D).　534 think] Q1, F, D; thing Q2.　536 *Portugal*] F, D; *Portugall* Q1-2.　544, 545 Heav'n] Q2, F, D; Hea'vn Q1.　550 *Affrick*] Affrique Q1-2; *Africk* F, D.　551 am,] Q1-2, D; ∼ʌ F.　554 play-thing] F, D (Play-thing); play thing Q1-2.　558 Heav'n:] Hea'vn. Q1; Heav'n. Q2, F, D.　559 is,] D; ∼ʌ Q1-2, F.　559 Cardinall] D (Cardinal); ∼ , Q1-2, F (Cardinal F).　562 *Seb.*] Q2, F, D; *Seb,* Q1.　567 yon] Q1-2, F; yon' D.　575 Heav'n,] D; Hea'vn∧ Q1; ∼ʌ Q2, F.　579 Death?] ∼ , Q1-2, F, D.　580 all,] ∼ . Q1-2, F, D.　585 Heav'n] Q2, F, D; Hea'vn Q1.　586 Souls] D; ∼ ; Q1-2, F.　588 Heav'n] Q2, F, D; Hea'vn Q1.　588 thine!] ∼ . Q1-2, F, D.　589 Souls,] ∼ . Q1-2, F, D.　594 other,] ∼ . Q1-2, F, D.　596 athwart] Q2, F, D; a thwart Q1.

600 love.] F, D; ~ ; Q1-2. 601 *Alm.*] Q2, F, D; *Alm,* Q1. 602
lov'd. You] ~ ? you Q1-2, F, D (You F). 606 Parents guilt] Q1, D
(Guilt D); Parents Q2, F. 615 glorious,] F, D; ~ ; Q1-2. 616
Heav'n] Q2, F, D; Hea'vn Q1. 621 *Sebastian.*] ~ , Q1-2, F, D.
630 man] Q1-2, D (Man D); Men F. 632 world] Q2, F, D (World
F, D); ~ , Q1. 634 cold.] Q1, D; ~ , Q2, F. 638+ *s.d. Re-enter*]
Q2, F, D; *Reenter* Q1. 642 *Sebastian to Dorax.*] [Sebastian *to* Dorax.
Q1-2 (Dorax.] Q2); [*Sebast.* to *Dor.*] F; *Seb.* [*to* Dor.] D. 643 listen,]
~ . Q1-2, F; ~ ; D. 648 *Muley-Zeydan*] Q2, F, D; *Muley Zeydan* Q1.
655 one] F; ~ . Q1-2, D. 658 Ev'n] D; E'vn Q1; E'ven Q2; E'en F.
658 redemption;] ~ . Q1-2, F, D (Redemption D). 662 half-way]
Q1-2, D; half way F. 662 pilgrimage,] D (Pilgrimage); ~∧ Q1-2, F
(Pilgrimage F). 671 Hermites,] ~ . Q1-2, F, D (Hermits D). 673
Moors] D; Moors Q1-2, F. 677 life,] D (Life); ~∧ Q1-2, F. 678
Exile,] D; ~ : Q1-2; ~ ; F. 685 *Tercera*] S-S (Terceira); *Tercera's*
Q1-2, F, D (*Tercera's* F). 686 day.] Q1-2, D (Day D); ~∧ F. 697
death,] D (Death); ~ : Q1-2, F. 699 both.] ~ : Q1; ~ ; Q2, F, D.
706 *Ant.*] Q2, F, D; *Ant,* Q1. 710 thousand.] ~ ; Q1-2, F, D. 714
Death,] D; ~∧ Q1-2, F. 715+ *s.d. up.*] D; ~∧ Q1-2, F (*np* Q2).
716 flower,] ~ : Q1-2, F, D (Flower D). 717 This] Q2, F, D; 'This
Q1. 717 storm:] ~ . Q1-2, F, D (Storm D). 720 Soul] Q2, F, D;
Souls Q1. 720+ *s.d. Stage;*] ~ . Q1-2, D; ~∧ F. 720+ *s.d. other:*
Dorax] *other.* / Dorax, Q1-2, F, D (Dorax∧ Q2, F; Dor. D). 724-727
lines not indented in Q1-2, F, D. 727+ *s.d. Exeunt.*] *omitted from*
Q1-2, F, D. 727+ *Q1 and F append* "FINIS."; *Q2 appends* "FINIS.".
 Epilogue: Caption: EPILOGUE] ~ . Q1-2, F, D. *Caption:* TO]
Q1-2, F; *omitted from* D. *Caption: Don Sebastian, King of Portugal.*]
Don Sebastian, King of Portugall. Q1-2; *Don* SEBASTIAN *King of*
Portugal. F; *omitted from* D. 1 quak'd] D; Quak'd Q1-2, F. 9
Turk] D; *Turk* Q1-2, F. 11 Mufti-*Father*] Q1-2; Mufti *Father* F, D.
19 *are,*] D; ~∧ Q1-2, F. 20 *Example.*] D; ~∧ Q1-2; ~ : F. 22
Friends.] Q1-2, D; ~∧ F. 23 *Confusions,*] F, D; ~∧ Q1-2. 25
Example,] D; ~∧ Q1-2, F. 36 *thundring*] Q1-2, F; *thundering* D.
36+ *FINIS.*] *omitted from Q1-2, F, D.*

Amphitryon

The first edition (Q1) of *Amphitryon* was published either late in 1690 or,
more likely, early in 1691; issues with both dates are extant (Macd 90ai-ii).
Collation of multiple copies of the first edition revealed press variants in
both outer (among which, the variant dates) and inner A, in outer F,
and in inner I. The second edition was published in 1694 (Q2; Macd 90b),
with press variants in outer F and inner H. Later the play was published
in Dryden's *Comedies, Tragedies, and Operas* (1701), II, 399-440 (F; Macd
107ai-ii [two issues, the differences not affecting this play]), and in Congreve's edition of Dryden's *Dramatick Works* (1717), VI, 143-231 (D; Macd
109ai-ii [two issues, the differences not affecting this play]).

Q2 was printed from a copy of Q1 with corrected outer A and uncorrected [first state] inner A; F from a copy of Q2 with corrected outer F; and D from a copy of Q1 with corrected outer A and inner A. Since Dryden seems not to have revised the text after the publication of Q1, a Clark copy of Q1 (*PR3417.D1.1691.Cop.1) has been chosen as the copy text.

The following seventeenth-century and early eighteenth-century collections of songs have been examined: *The Songs in Amphitryon, with the Musick* (1690, bound with Q1 [f1; Macd 90ai–ii and D&M 104, 107]), pages 1–2 for "Celia, that I once was blest" (III, i, 583–600), pages 3–4 for "Fair Iris I love, and hourly I dye" (IV, i, 482–493), pages 5–13 for "Fair Iris and her Swain" (IV, I, 508–545); *Joyful Cuckoldom, or the Love of Gentlemen, and Gentlewomen* (1671 on the title page, actually published *c.* 1695 [q; D&M 133]), leaves 17 and 18 for "Celia, that I once was blest" and "Fair Iris I love, and hourly I dye"; and *Wit and Mirth: or, Pills to Purge Melancholy*, II (1700 [d; D&M 188]), pages 303–304 and 305 for "Celia, that I once was blest" and "Fair Iris I love, and hourly I dye." The sources of these versions are unclear, but it is possible that q ultimately derived from f1 and probable that d derived from q.

Six stanzas were added to "Fair Iris I love, and hourly I dye" in a broadside probably published in late 1690 or early 1691 (*The Indifferent Lover, or The Roving Batchelor* [f2]). The source of this version is unknown.

The British Museum has a manuscript (*c.* 1704) of the words and music (Addit. MS 22099 [m1]) of the first stanza of "Celia, that I once was blest" and a late seventeenth-century manuscript of the words and music (Egerton MS 2960, fols. 58*v*–59*v* [m2]) of "Fair Iris and her Swain." The texts of both seem to have derived from f1.

In addition to the Clark copy of Q1 chosen as the copy text, the following copies of various editions have also been examined: Q1: Clark (*PR3417.D1; *PR3417.D1.1691.Cop.2; *PR3417.D1.1691.Cop.3; *PR3410. C93); Q2: Clark (*PR3417.D1.1694; *PR3410.C94; *PR3410.C95a); F: Clark (*fPR3412.1701 [2 cop.], *fPR3412.1701a); D: Clark (*PR3412.1717 [2 cop.], *PR3412.1717a); f1: Clark (*PR3417.D1; *PR3417.D1. 1691 [3 cop.], *PR3410. C93); f2: British Museum (C.39.K.6[48]); q: British Museum (C.180.a); d: British Museum (C.117.a.19).

Press Variants by Form

Q1

Sheet A (outer form)

Uncorrected: Clark (*PR3417.D1)
Corrected: Clark (4 copies)
Sig. A1
  Title Page Socia's] Sosia's
  Title Page 1690] 1691
Sig. A3
  224:32 'Tris] 'Tis

Sheet A (inner form)

Uncorrected (*first state*): Clark (*PR3417.D1)
Corrected (*second state*): Clark (4 copies)
Sig. A4
  Prologue Caption Socia's] Sosia's
  Corrected (*third state, the above correction and the following*):
    Clark (*PR3410.C93; *PR3417.D1.1691.Cop.1; *PR3417.D1.1691. Cop.
    2; *PR3417.D1.1691.Cop.3)
Sig. A3v
  225:27 loosing] losing
      34 Undestandings] Understandings
Sig. A4
  Prologue Caption Mr.] Mrs.
                        Sheet F (outer form)
Uncorrected: Clark (*PR3417.D1; *PR3417.D1.1691.Cop. 1)
Corrected: Clark (3 copies)
Sig. F4v
  IV, i, 220 hus] thus
                        Sheet I (inner form)
Uncorrected: Clark (*PR3417.D1)
Corrected: Clark (4 copies)
Sig. I1v
  Epilogue 2 Hos weet] How sweet
                        Q2
                        Sheet F (outer form)
Uncorrected: Clark (*PR3410.C95a)
Corrected: Clark (2 copies)
Sig. F3
  IV, i, 52 Husband,] ~∧
      57 Withall] With all
                        Sheet H (inner form)
Uncorrected: Clark (*PR3410.C95a)
Corrected: Clark (2 copies)
Sig. H2
  Catchword THI m-] Th'Im-

Dedication: 223:4 Countrymen] Q1-2, D; Country-men F.   223:23
in a] Q1-2, D; in an F.   224:29 ago] Q2, F, D; a go Q1.   224:32
'Tis] Q1 (*corrected form*), Q2, F, D; 'Tris Q1 (*uncorrected form*).
225:17 *English-man*] Q1-2; *English* Man F; *Englishman* D.   225:19
judicious] Q2, F, D; judicious Q1.   225:27 losing] Q1 (*corrected form*
[*third state*]), Q2, F, D; loosing Q1 (*uncorrected form* [*first and second
states*]).   225:32 enough,] Q1-2, F; ~∧ D.   225:34 Understandings]
Q1 (*corrected form* [*third state*]), Q2, F, D; Undestandings Q1 (*uncorrected form* [*first and second states*]).
  Prologue: PROLOGUE / TO / *Amphitryon; or, The Two*] Q1-2, F
(PROLOGUE. F; Or, The TWO F); PROLOGUE D.   *Sosia's*] Socia's
Q1 (*uncorrected form* [*first state*]); Sosia's Q1 (*corrected form* [*second and

third states]); Socia's Q2; *Sosia's* F; *omitted from* D.   Mrs.] Q1 *(corrected form [third state]),* F, D; Mr. Q1 *(uncorrected form [first and second states]),* Q2.   23 one] F, D; ~ , Q1–2.   34 behind.] Q1–2, D;
~_∧ F.   37 Prophane,] F *(prophane);* ~ ; Q1–2, D *(prophane* D).   43
you,] F; ~ ; Q1–2, D.

Dramatis Personæ: PERSONÆ.] Q1–2, F; *Personæ.* / MEN. D.
PHŒBUS] F, D (Phœbus); PHOEBUS Q1–2.   AMPHITRYON] Q2,
F, D (Amphitryon F, D); AMPITRYON Q1.   Bowen.] Q1–2, F; *Bowen.*
/ WOMEN. D.   Mountfort] *Mountford* Q1–2, F, D.   Butler.] Q1–2,
F; *Butler.* / SCENE *THEBES.* D.

I, i

Title: OR,] Q2, F, D (Or Q2, F); Or_∧ Q1.   *Title:* SOSIA'S] F, D
(Sosia's D); SOCIA'S Q1–2.   The Scene *THEBES*] Q1–2, F; SCENE
THEBES D *(printed at end of "Dramatis Personæ").*   ACT I. SCENE
I.] D; *omitted from Q1–2,* F.   s.d. Phœbus] Q1, F, D; Phæbus Q2.   12
Petticoat Affair] Q1–2, D; Petticoat-Affair F.   12 guess.] F, D; ~ ,
Q1–2.   25 on] Q1–2, F; in D.   28 at the] Q1–2, F; at D.   29
to have thrown] Q1, D; to throw Q2, F.   36 way,] D; ~_∧ Q1–2, F.
46 worse,] Q1, D; ~_∧ Q2, F.   56+ s.d. Jupiter] *[Jupiter* Q1; [Jupiter
Q2, F, D (Jup. D).   61 Cadmus] F; *Cadmu's* Q1–2; *Cadmus'* D.   66
snuffs] Q1, F, D; suffs Q2.   82–83 secret, . . . Sanctity,] F; ~ ; . . .
~ ; Q1–2, D.   85 bound,] ~_∧ Q1–2, F, D.   86 Reverence sake]
Q1–2, D; Reverence-sake F.   121 be] Q2, F, D; ~ . Q1.   124
Human-kind] Q1–2, F; human Kind D.   134 knock-down] Q1–2, F;
knock down D.   139 Phœbus] Q2, F, D; *Pœbus* Q1.   143 Animal]
Q1–2, D; Animals F.   147 Merc. to Phœb.] *Merc. to Phœb.* Q1–2, F;
Merc. [to Phœbus.] D.   147 Morals,] Q2, F, D; ~_∧ Q1.   150 Gen-
eral,] Q1, D; ~_∧ Q2, F.   157 morrows] Q1–2, F (Morrow's Q2, F);
Morrow D.   162 Evening?] D; ~ ; Q1–2, F.   165 to morrow.] Q2,
F; ~ ~ ; Q1; to-Morrow. D.   168 day] D (Day); ~ , Q1–2, F.   168
well be] Q1–2, F; be well D.   185 Jup. to Merc.] To *Merc.* Q1–2, F;
[To Merc.] D.   185 form,] Q1, D (Form D); ~ . Q2, F.   203+
s.d. Night] D *(Night);* [Night Q1–2, F *(Night* F).   209 Merc. to Night.]
Merc. to Night. Q1–2, F; *Merc. [to Night.]* D.   212 make] Q1, D; makes
Q2, F.   214 broken] Q1–2, D; broke F.   215–216 assistance?] D
(Assistance); ~ . Q1–2, F.   217 Faith,] ~_∧ Q1–2, F, D.   218 kind
of Jack] Q1–2, F; Jack D.   235 Popular,] ~_∧ Q1–2, F, D (popular D).
249 What,] D (what); ~_∧ Q1–2, F.   260 double] Q1–2, F; doubly D.
263 waking] Q1–2, F; walking D.   272–273 Chariot Wheels] Q1–2,
F; Chariot-wheels D.   274 Serving-man] Q1, D; Serving man Q2, F
(Man F).   275 Amphitryon] Q1–2, D; *Alphitryon* F.   276+ s.d.
Exit] F, D; ~ . Q1–2.

I, ii

SCENE] Q2, F, D; Scene Q1.   6 foes,] ~ : Q1–2, F, D (Foes Q2, F,
D).   8 avert] Q2, F, D; aver. Q1.   33 safety;] ~ : Q1–2, F, D
(Safety D).   42 bedfellow] Q1–2, D (Bedfellow D); bed-fellow F.

47 *Jupiter?*] Q1–2, D; ~ . F.   59+   *s.d. He* . . . Alcmena.] F, D
([*He* F); [~ . . . ~ .] Q1–2.   63 *Amphitryon.*] F, D; *Amphitryn.* Q1;
~ , Q2.   68 Bedfellow] Q1–2, D (Bed- / fellow D); Bed-fellow F.   69
Sosia?] D; ~ : Q1–2, F.   75 Bribes?] Q2, F; ~ : Q1, D.   82 danger.]
D (Danger); ~ ? Q1–2, F.   84 think, . . . Conscience,] ~∧ . . . ~∧
Q1–2, F, D.   86 *Bromia pulling* . . . *side.*] Bromia *pulling* . . . *side.*
Q1–2, F; *Brom.* [*Pulling* . . . *Side.*] D.   87 me,] Q2, F, D; ~∧ Q1.
87 Lord.] Q1–2, F; ~ , D.   88 *Phædra pulling* . . . *side.*] Phædra
pulling . . . *side.* Q1–2, F; *Phæd.* [*Pulling* . . . *Side.*] D.   88 *t'other*]
Q2, F, D; *to'ther* Q1.   92–93 haste.——— / Was . . . Love, [*Aside.*]
haste.——— [*Aside.* / Was . . . Love, Q1–2, F, D (haste∧——— F; Haste
D).   93 worri'd!] Q1–2, F (worry'd Q2, F); worry'd: D.   99 Women]
Q1–2, F; Woman D.   112 *Brom. to Phædra.*] *Brom. to Phædra.* Q1–2,
F; *Brom.* [*to Phædra.*] D.   113 makes] Q1–2, D; make F.   137 *Alc.
to Jupiter.*] *Alc. to Jupiter.* Q1–2, F; *Alc.* [*To Jupiter.*] D.   139
Phædra, almost crying.] Phædra, ~ ~ . Q1; Phædra∧ ~ ~ . Q2, F; *Phæd.*
[*Almost crying.*] D.   141 Bedfellow] Q1–2, D; Bed-fellow F.   155
leave. You] ~ : you Q1–2, F, D (Leave D; You F).   156 *may*] Q1; may
Q2, F, D.   157 self.] ~ : Q1–2, F, D.   158 Elder-Brother] Q1–2,
D (Elder- / Brother D); Elder Brother F.   163 Heav'n,] ~∧ Q1–2, F,
D.   168 me———] Q2, F; me.——— Q1, D.   170 it.———] Q1–2,
D; it——— F.   171 say *any thing, any thing*] say, any thing, any thing
Q1–2, F, D.   175 Heav'n] Q1, D; Heaven Q2, F.   182 *Jupiter,
taking* . . . *it.*] Jupiter, *taking* . . . *it.* Q1–2, F; *Jup.* [*Taking* . . . *it.*]
D.   182 it; this . . . Woman:] it; / This . . . Woman: Q1–2, F, D.
185 What,] ~∧ Q1–2, F, D.   190 *Jupiter solus.* Why . . . all:] *Jupiter solus.* / Why . . . all: Q1–2, F (*Solus* F); *Jup.* Why . . . all: [*Solus.*
D.   192 human-kind] Q1–2; humane kind F, D (Human Kind D).
201 *s.d.* heard. [*Exit.*] heard. Q1–2, F, D.

II, i

ACT II. SCENE I.] D; Act II. Q1; ACT II. Q2, F.   *s.d. Night-Scene*]
Q1–2, F; *A Night-Scene* D.   *s.d. Enter* Sosia] Sosia Q1–2, F, D.   8
Ague fit] Q1–2, F; Ague-Fit D.   16 but I] Q2, F, D; bur I Q1.   17
foot Pimp] Q1–2, F; Foot-Pimp D (Foot- / Pimp).   19 say *Upon my
Honour*] say, Upon my Honour Q1–2, F, D.   25 Fellow] D; ~ , Q1–2,
F.   27 *Sosia looking* . . . *him.*] Sosia *looking* . . . *him.* Q1–2, F; *Sos.*
[*Looking* . . . *him.*] D.   43 *Sosia, setting* . . . *Lanthorn.*] Sosia, *setting* . . . *Lanthorn.* Q1–2, F; *Sos.* [*Setting* . . . *Lanthorn.*] D.   48
her:———] ~ :∧ Q1–2, F, D.   48 *s.d. Bowes.*] D (Bows); ~∧ Q1–2,
F (*Bows* F).   51 Expedition.———] ~ .∧ Q1–2, F, D.   52 she:] ~∧
Q1–2, F, D.   52 *s.d. In* . . . *Tone.*] in . . . *Tone*∧ Q1–2, F, D (*tone*
F; *Tone.* D).   53 thee!———] ~ !∧ Q1–2, F, D.   53 less.] ~ : Q1–
2, F, D.   55 glory.——— Well] ~ :——— well Q1–2, F, D (Glory
D; Well F, D).   55 side.] Q1, D (Side D); ~∧ Q2, F.   57 Honour.]
Q1–2, D; ~∧ F.   64 him.] Q1–2, F; ~∧ D.   65 cost.] Q1–2, F;
~∧ D.   70 *Sosia, staring* . . . *Sky.*] Sosia, *staring* . . . *Sky.* Q1–2, F;
Sos. [*Staring* . . . *Sky.*] D.   70 What,] D; ~∧ Q1–2, F.   73 What,]

D; ~∧ Q1–2, F. 77 *Sosia, seeing . . . aside.*] Sosia, seeing . . . aside.
Q1–2, F; *Sos. [Seeing . . . aside.*] D. 77 what,] ~∧ Q1–2, F, D (What
F). 79 Door?] Q1–2, D; ~ , F. 82 life!] Q1–2, F (Life Q2, F);
Life ∧ D. 89 Catterwawling;] ~ , Q1–2, F, D. 92 way.] D; ~ ?
Q1–2, F. 78 savour.] Q1–2, F; Savour∧ D. 94–95 *fee, fa, fum*] *in
romans in Q1–2, F, D.* 103 asleep] Q2, F, D; a sleep Q1. 109
Fellow.] Q2, F; ~ , Q1; ~∧ D. 109 *Sosia.*] ~∧ Q1–2, F, D. 112
s.d. Aside.] Q2, F, D; ~∧ Q1. 112 I must]————I must Q1–2, F, D.
117 Nose.] Q1–2; ~∧ F, D. 117 *s.d. Aside.*] D; ~∧ Q1–2, F. 117
Bless]————Bless Q1–2, F, D. 127 Ear.] Q1–2; ~∧ F, D. 127+
s.d. Strikes] Q2, F, D; *strikes* Q1. 129 two] Q1–2, D; too F. 130
Friend.] Q1–2; ~∧ F, D. 132 *stopping*] Q2, F, D (*Stopping* D); *stoping*
Q1. 140 *ours*] ours Q1–2, F, D. 142 Garret] Q2, F, D; Garrret
Q1. 150 *Sosia?*] Q1–2, D; ~ . F. 151 have you] Q1–2, F; have
D. 155 What,] ~∧ Q1–2, F, D. 163 What,] ~∧ Q1–2, F, D.
167 Name,] Q1–2, D; ~∧ F. 169 nothing] Q2, F, D; nothiug Q1.
174 *Sosia.*] Q1–2, D (*Sos.* D); ~ , F. 174 Friend,] Q1, D; ~∧ Q2, F.
187 self preservation] Q1–2, F; Self-Preservation D. 190 beaten?]
Q1–2, D; ~ . F. 194 Undoubtedly] Q2, F, D; Uundoubtedly Q1.
195 *Amphitryon's?*] Q1–2, D; ~ . F. 197 too;] F, D; ~ ? Q1–2.
200 foresaid] Q1–2, F; aforesaid D. 204 tittle] Q2, F, D; little Q1.
205 Servant? . . . question.] ~ , . . . ~ ? Q1–2, F, D (Question D).
222 is————] Q2, F, D; ~ .———— Q1. 227 you,] ~ ; Q1–2, F, D.
227 Token;] Q1–2, F; ~ . D. 228 I.] Q1; ~∧ Q2, F, D. 233
Credits.] Q1; ~∧ Q2, F, D. 233 *s.d. (Aside.)* And] And Q1–2, F, D.
236 Passages.] ~∧ Q1–2, F, D. 241 Case,] Q1, D; ~∧ Q2, F. 244
s.d. Aside.] Q2, F, D; ~∧ Q1. 244 ————But] But Q1–2, F, D. 247
has a] Q1, D; has Q2, F. 251 name.————] name. Q1–2, F, D (Name
D). 252 Tent?] Q1, D; ~ ; Q2, F. 258 drinking] F, D (Drinking
D); ~ . Q1–2. 266 Bacon:] ~∧ Q1–2, F, D. 267 me:] Q1–2, F;
~∧ D. 267 me.] Q1–2; ~∧ F, D. 268 But] but Q1–2, F, D.
271 harm,] Q2, F, D; ~∧ Q1. 272 for.] ~ : Q1–2, F, D. 273
s.d. (Aside.)] *omitted from Q1–2, F, D.* 273 certain.] Q2, F, D; ~∧
Q1. 274 him.] ~∧ Q1–2, F, D. 275 *Item*] Q2, F, D; ~∧ Q1.
277–278 Apparel.] Q1–2; ~∧ F, D. 278 *s.d.* Mercury.] *Mercury*∧
Q1–2, F, D. 287 nor no] Q1–2, F; nor D. 302 *Mercury alone.* I]
Mercury alone. / I Q1–2, F, D (Mercury Q2, F, D).

II, ii

SCENE] Q2, F, D; Scene Q1. *s.d.* Phædra:] ~ . Q1–2, F, D (Phœdra
Q2). 1 *them. / Jupiter to the Pages.* Those . . . aloof.] *them.* Jupiter
to the Pages. / Those . . . aloof: Q1–2, F (THose; aloof∧ F); *them. /
Jup.* Those . . . aloof: [*To the Pages.* D. 2 heav'nly] Q1, D; heavenly
Q2, F. 18 Hill,] Q1–2, D; ~ . F. 20 World.] Q2, F, D; ~ : Q1.
30 *aside.*] Q2, F, D (*Aside* D); ~ , Q1. 30 Schoolmaster] Q1–2, D
(School- / master D); School-Master F. 40–41 sweet, that . . . Night, /
But . . . Eternity, were . . . employ'd,] sweet, / That . . . Night, but
. . . Eternity, / Were . . . employ'd, Q1–2, F, D (employ'd∧ D). 68–

69 *as in D; set as prose in Q1–2, F.* 69 Question.] ∼ ? Q1–2, F, D.
79 refin'd] Q2, F, D; refind Q1. 89 and a] Q1–2, F; and D. 111–
112 Continent! / Phædra *re-enters.* / And] Continent? / (*Phædra re-*
enters∧)———And Q1–2, F, D ([Phædra *re-enters*] D). 121 where-
withal] Q2, F, D; where withal Q1. 127 Yes,] D; ∼∧ Q1–2, F. 129
now,] Q2, F, D; ∼∧ Q1. 135 What,] D; ∼∧ Q1–2, F. 137 me!]
∼ ? Q1–2, F, D. 146–147 wherewithal] Q2, F, D; where withal Q1.
151 please me,] Q1, D; ∼ ∼ : Q2; ∼ ∼ ; F. 152 ———What] What
Q1–2, F, D. 152 ho *Bromia!*] Q1–2, D; ha *Bromia?* F. 157 Wedlock.———] ∼ :∧ Q1–2, F, D. 160 Custom,] D; ∼ : Q1–2, F. 161
mightst] Q1–2, D; mightest F. 164 *s.d.* Knaps] *knaps* Q1–2, F, D.
168 Straw.——— Make] Straw; make Q1–2, F, D (Straw: D). 172
Will] Q2, F, D; will Q1. 176 loud.] ∼∧ Q1–2, F, D. 176
Bro———] D; Bro.——— Q1–2, F. 177 aloud] Q2, F, D; a loud Q1.
179 *Bromia*] D; Bromia Q1–2, F. 182 with Child] Q1–2, D; with-
Child F. 187 Giver,] Q2, F, D; ∼ . Q1. 190–191 day!——— (*To*
her.) But . . . too.] day! / But . . . too. (*To her.* Q1–2, F ([*To her* F);
Day! / But . . . too. D. 195 Thunderclap] Q1, D; Thunder-clap Q2,
F. 203 better.] Q1, D; ∼∧ Q2, F. 205 *s.d.* Phædra] F, D; Phœdra
Q1–2. 206 aloud] D (*Aloud*); a loud Q1; a-loud Q2, F. 208 her
what,] ∼ , ∼ Q1–2, F; ∼ ∼ ? D. 209 her?] F; ∼ . Q1–2, D. 213
Midnight] Q1–2, D (midnight Q2); mid-night F. 216 Sirrah] F, D;
∼ . Q1–2. 219 Villain] F; ∼ . Q1–2, D. 222 *My Master*] My
Master Q1–2, F, D. 260 *Mercury . . . about* (*aside*).] Mercury . . .
about. aside. Q1–2, F, D ([*Aside.*] D). 262+ *s.d.* Caduceus] *Caduceus*
Q1–2, F, D. 264 How] how Q1–2, F, D. 265–266 sudden.———
. . . Foot.] sudden∧——— . . . Foot∧ Q1–2, F, D. 267 Members.] ∼∧
Q1–2, F, D. 267 *s.d.* Yawning] D; *yawning* Q1–2, F. 269 Woman.]
∼∧ Q1–2, F, D. 269 *s.d.* Falls] D; *falls* Q1–2, F. 270 *Mercury*
alone. Lord] Mercury *alone.* / Lord Q1–2, F, D. 274 *Phædra*] F, D;
Phœdra Q1–2. 274 return.] ∼∧ Q1–2, F, D.

III, i

ACT III. SCENE I.] D; A.ct III. Q1; ACT. III. Q2, F. *s.d. Enter*
Amphitryon] Amphitryon Q1–2, F, D. *s.d.* Sosia] Q2, F, D; *Sosia* Q1.
5 these!] Q1–2, F; ∼ . D. 19 hard-hearted] Q2, F, D (hard- / hearted
F); heard-hearted Q1. 22 Physick:] Q1–2; ∼ ; F, D. 23 it;] Q1–2,
F; ∼ : D. 32–33 that all] Q1–2, F; all D. 35 Repetition,] F, D;
∼∧ Q1–2. 46 Truth, so] ∼ : ∼ Q1–2, F; ∼∧ ∼ D. 47 Cudgel.]
∼∧ Q1–2, F, D. 49 peril.] ∼∧ Q1–2, F, D (Peril D). 51 Hemi-
sphere.] Q1, D; ∼∧ Q2, F. 52 *Amph.*] D; Amph. Q1–2, F. 66
name,] Q1–2, D (Name D); ∼ . F. 73 these!] Q1–2, D; ∼ ? F. 77
before] Q1–2, F; just before D. 85–86 self, . . . how,] ∼∧ . . . ∼∧
Q1–2, F, D. 96 not you] Q1–2, F; you not D. 98 Face?] D; ∼ :
Q1–2, F. 99 Six-pence] ∼ . Q1–2, F, D (Six- / pence Q1–2; Sixpence
F). 101 similitudes] Q2, F; ∼ . Q1, D (Similitudes D). 105–109
t 'other . . . t' other . . . t' other] Q2, F, D; to'ther . . . to'ther . . .
to'ther Q1. 118 Motions:] ∼ . Q1–2, F, D. 120 heaviest] Q1–2,

D; haviest F.   124 enter.] Q₁–2, D; ~ ! F.   126 enter,] Q₁–2, F;
~ ? D.   128 two-inch-boards] Q₁–2, F; two Inch-Boards D.   132
I] Q₁, D; *I* Q₂, F.   134 *I*] Q₁–2, D; I F.   144 *to Phædra.*] D ([*To
Phæd.*]); to *Phædra* Q₁–2, F.   152 *So soon return'd*] So soon return'd
Q₁–2, F, D.   153 *So soon return'd*] So soon return'd, Q₁–2, F, D.
154 desiring Love] Q₁–2, D; desiring-Love F.   161 But you] D; ~
~ , Q₁–2, F.   163 return,] ~ ; Q₁–2, F, D (Return D).   192+ *s.d.*
Alcm.] Q₂, F; Alch. Q₁; Alc. D.   194 hour.] D (Hour); ~ ? Q₁–2, F.
196 Day?] Q₁–2, F; ~ . D.   196–197 Impudence!——— / Why] Im-
pudence!——— Why Q₁–2, F, D.   202 over-night] Q₁–2, F; over Night
D.   219 safe] Q₂, F, D; fafe Q₁.   234 Diamonds.] Q₂, F, D; ~∧
Q₁.   248 upon] Q₁–2, F; to D.   252 *I*] Q₁–2; I F, D.   252
Sosia;] Q₂, F, D; ~ . Q₁.   254 double.] Q₂, F, D; ~ , Q₁.   264
back.] D; ~ - Q₁; ~ ——— Q₂, F.   274 prest] Q₁–2, F; press'd D.
280 kind.] ~∧ Q₁–2, F, D.   280+ *s.d. Aside.*] Q₁–2, F; ~ , D.   281
proceed.] Q₁; ~∧ Q₂, F, D.   282–283 complaining / Of . . . Rest
———] complaining of . . . Rest——— Q₁–2, F, D.   284–285 *s.d.*
on——— / And . . . speak'st. [*Aside.*] on——— [*Aside.* / And . . .
speak'st. Q₁–2, F; on——— / [*Aside.*] And . . . speak'st. D.   296
Threshold.] Q₁–2, D; ~ , F.   303 unworthy Man;] Q₁, D; ~ ; ~ Q₂,
F.   333 ever.] ~∧ Q₁–2, F, D.   339 t' other] F; tother Q₁–2; other
D.   347 Present! [*Aside.*]———Why] Present!——— [*Aside.* Why Q₁–
2, F, D.   358 yet may] Q₁–2, D; may yet F.   368 Morning,———]
Q₂, F; ~ ———: Q₁, D.   369 thee] Q₂, F; ~ . Q₁, D.   377 Sense]
F; ~ . Q₁–2, D.   381–382 her. [*Aside.*]———] her. [*Aside.* Q₁–2, F,
D.   389 *chose*] Q₂, F, D; chose Q₁.   391 I] Q₁–2, D; *I* F.   403
reasonably] Q₁, F, D; reasonaly Q₂.   408 Thimblefull] Q₁–2; Thimble-
full F, D.   412+ *s.d. Enter*] D; [~ Q₁–2, F (*s.d. at right margin on
line 412*).   417 Miscreant] F; ~ . Q₁–2, D.   422–423 uncivily: . . .
uncivilly;] Q₁–2, F; ~ ; . . . ~ : D.   426–427 *Phædra.*———] ~ .∧
Q₁–2, F, D.   432–434 Oh . . . Abuse: . . . hands. [*To . . . private.*]]
Oh . . . Abuse:——— hands———[*To . . . private.* Q₁–2 (*brace rather
than bracket actually precedes s.d.*); Oh . . . Abuse: (*To . . . private.*
. . . hands——— F; (*To . . . private.*] Oh, . . . Abuse: . . . Hands
——— D.   434 Thimble.] Q₁–2, D; ~∧ F.   437 Half-hour] Q₁–2,
F; half Hour D.   456 Dog-tricks] Q₁, D; Dog tricks Q₂, F.   457–
458 over-night] Q₁–2, F; over Night D.   465 came?] ~ ! Q₁–2, F, D.
468 thee.] Q₁, D; ~∧ Q₂, F.   473 Here's] Q₁–2, F (*corrected form*),
D; ~ , F (*uncorrected form*).   487 thee?] D; ~ : Q₁–2, F.   495
What,] F, D; ~∧ Q₁–2.   497 what?] Q₁, D; ~ ; Q₂, F.   507 blear-
ey'd] Q₁–2, F; blear'd-ey'd D.   529 possest,] ~ ; Q₁–2, F, D.   531
peace;] ~ : Q₁–2, F, D (Peace F, D).   535–536 Love; . . . mine:] D;
~ : . . . ~ ; Q₁–2, F.   541–542 *set as verse in Q1–2, F, D* (begin /
To).   542 first.] Q₁–2; ~∧ F, D.   546 Markes-man] Q₁–2, F (Marks-
man F); Mark's Man D.   548 *Phædra*] Q₂, F, D; ~ . Q₁.   549 *Sol-
la*] D;~ ; Q₁–2, F.   550 empty] D; ~ , Q₁–2, F.   552–553 *set as
verse in Q1–2, F, D* (sound. / I Q₁–2, F; Sound. / I D).   556 all,]
Q₁–2; ~ . F; ~∧ D.   559–560 *Sosia, taking Jupiter . . . Knees.* Let . . .

Sir.———[Jupiter . . . *away.*] Nay] *Sosia. (Taking* Jupiter . . . *Knees.*) /
Let . . . Sir.———[Jupiter . . . *away.* / Nay Q1-2, F (*Sos.* Q2, F; Sir
——— Q2, F); *Sos.* [*Taking* Jupiter . . . *Knees.*] Let . . . Sir———
[Jupiter . . . *away.*] Nay D.   563   bloody-Flux] Q1-2, F; bloody Flux
D.   564   out;] Q2, F; ∼, Q1, D.   576   *Jup.*] Q1-2, D; *omitted from*
F.   579   *s.d.* place. / *Enter* . . . Jupiter. Alcmena . . . *above,* Jupi-
ter . . . Alcmena. / *Jup.* . . . appears:] place. [*Enter* . . . Jupiter. /
Alcmena . . . *above.* Jupiter . . . Alcmena. / *Jup.* . . . appears: Q1-2,
F ((*Enter* F; (Alcmena F; *above.*) F); Place. / *Enter* . . . Jupiter. Alcmena
. . . *above.* / *Jup.* . . . appears: [*Seeing* Alcmena. D.   581   *Jove,*]
Q1-2, D; ∼. F.   582+   *s.d. signs*] Q1, D; sings Q2, F.   582+
SONG.] Q2, F, D; ∼- Q1; First Song, in the third Act. f1; A New song
sung at the Theatre Royall, in the last new Play call'd Amphitrion———
The words by Mr. Dryden, Sung by Mr. Bowman∧ q; *A SONG.* d; *omit-*
ted from m1.   *583-600   italics and romans reversed in f1 and d, but*
normalized in the following textual notes.   585   *curse*] Q1-2, F, D, f1,
m1; Cure q, d (*cure* d).   585   *me, you*] Q1-2, F, D, f1, q, m1 (*me*∧ f1,
q, m1); me, You d.   586   *Pleasures*] Q1-2, F, D; *pleasure* f1, q, d, m1
(*Pleasure* q, d).   586   *possest:*] Q1-2, F, D; *possess't;* f1; *possest,* q;
possess, d; *possess*∧ m1.   587   *me!*] Q1-2, F, D; ∼; f1; ∼, q, d; ∼∧
m1.   588   *me!*] Q1-2, F, D; ∼; f1; ∼∧ q, m1; ∼. d.   590   *Then I*]
Q1-2, F, D; *I then* f1, q, d.   591   *possessing once*] Q1-2, F, D, q (*posses-*
ing q); *possessing, / Once* f1, d.   593   *tasting;*] Q1-2, D; ∼. F; ∼, f1,
q, d.   594   *no*] Q1-2, F, D, f1, d; *not* q.   596   *I am*] Q1-2, F, D,
f1; *I'm* q, d.   597   *her will*] Q1-2, F, D, q; *her, / Will* f1, d (*VVill* f1).
604   well pleas'd] Q1-2, F; well-pleas'd D.   610+   *s.d.* [*Exeunt.*] omitted from Q1-2, F, D.   610+   *The* . . . [*to*] . . . *Act.*] omitted from
F, D.

IV, i

ACT IV. SCENE I.] D; The FOURTH ACT. Q1-2; ACT IV. F.
s.d. Enter Jupiter] Jupiter Q1-2, F, D.   14   coyness] Q1-2, F (Coyness Q2, F); Coiness D.   18   swore.] Q1; ∼∧ Q2, F, D.   24   unkindness:] Q1-2, F; Unkindness, D.   29   then.] F, D; ∼ : Q1-2.   35   thy]
Q1, D; a Q2, F.   43   field.] Q1-2, D (Field D); ∼, F.   51   Lover]
∼, Q1-2, F, D.   51   two!] Q1-2, F; ∼∧ D.   52   Husband] Q1, Q2
(*corrected form*), F, D; ∼, Q2 (*uncorrected form*).   57   With all] Q1,
Q2 (*corrected form*), F, D; Withall Q2 (*uncorrected form*).   59, 61   *s.d.*
hate: [*Kneeling.* / . . . eyes,] Q1-2, F (Eyes Q2, F); hate: / . . . Eyes,
[*Kneeling.* D.   62   wounds] F; ∼, Q1-2, D (Wounds D).   62   that]
Q2, F, D; That Q1.   66   your] Q2, F, D; yonr Q1.   70   Tongue,]
Q1-2, D; ∼. F.   72   say *I hate you*] say, I hate you Q1-2, F, D.
73   you.] Q1-2, F; ∼∧ D.   77   Alternative] Q2, F, D; Alternetive Q1.
84   Weakness.] Q1-2, F; ∼∧ D.   85   alone.] Q1-2, F; ∼∧ D.   85
s.d. him.] But . . . you:] *him.* / But . . . you: Q1-2, F, D.   87   again.]
Q1-2, F; ∼∧ D.   91   grant.———] ∼ ·∧ Q1-2, F, D.   91   *s.d.* [*To* Mercury.] Be . . . none] Be . . . none [*To* Mercury.∧ Q1-2, F, D.   92
privacy.] D (Privacy); ∼∧ Q1-2, F.   92+   *s.d. remain*] Q2, F, D;

remain Q1.   96 aforehand] Q1–2, F; afore-hand D.   100 Thimbleful . . . Thimbleful] Q1–2, F; Thimble-full . . . Thimble-full D.   108
Lips] Q1–2, D; *Lip* F.   115 Bed side] Q1; Bed-side Q2, F, D.   115
Night?] Q1, D; ~ . Q2, F.   121 ill gotten] Q1–2, F; ill-gotten D (ill- /
gotten).   122–123 Whoring. / *Enter* Amphitryon. / ⸺⸺Oh, . . .
I'll manage] D; Whoring.⸺⸺ Oh, . . . I'll [*Enter* Amphitryon. /
manage Q1–2; Whoring.⸺⸺ Oh, . . . I'll manage [*Enter* Amphitryon.] / F.   126 As] Q1, D; Has Q2, F.   137+ *s.d. aside*] F,
D; *Aside* Q1–2.   149 You:] Q1–2, F; ~ ? D.   151 first.] D; ~ ?
Q1–2, F.   158 this?] ~∧ Q1–2, F; ~ , D.   167 Master!] Q1–2,
D; ~ . F.   177 insolence!] D (Insolence); ~ . Q1–2, F.   183
Peace,] F; ~∧ Q1–2, D.   185 Lady;] Q1, D; ~ ? Q2, F.   196
says!] ~ ? Q1–2, F, D.   197 feeble If] ~ , If Q1–2, F, D.   200
within,] D; ~ ; Q1–2, F.   202+ *s.d.* Gripus,] Q1–2, F; Gripus
and D.   210 *Amph.*] Q2, F, D (*Amp.* F); *Amph*∧ Q1.   215 sum-
mon'd] Q2, F, D; summo'nd Q1.   220 thus] Q1 (*corrected form*),
Q2, F, D; hus Q1 (*uncorrected form*).   220 *s.d.* Sosia] Q2, F; *Sosia* Q1,
D (*Sos.* D).   226–227 present?⸺⸺The] ~ ?∧ the Q1–2, F, D (The
F).   235 what e'er] Q1–2, F (e're Q2); whate'er D.   241 justice,]
Q1–2, F; ~ : D.   251–252 Insolence⸺⸺[*Is* . . . *Tranio.*] I . . . go
⸺⸺] Insolence⸺⸺[*Is* . . . *Tranio.* / I . . . go⸺⸺ Q1–2 (*s.d. flush
right on two lines*); Insolence⸺⸺ I . . . go⸺⸺ *Is* . . . *Tranio.* F;
Insolence⸺⸺ / [*Is* . . . *Tranio.* / I . . . go⸺⸺ D.   248 let] Q1,
D; not let Q2, F.   271 speak,] ~∧ Q1–2, F, D.   276 well-bred] Q1–2,
F, D (well- / bred Q1).   276 onely.] Q1–2, F (only Q2, F); only? D.
290 that the] Q1–2, F; the D.   307 door] Q1–2, D (Door D); doors F.
313 'em,] Q1–2, F; ~∧ D.   316 aside.] (*aside*) Q1; (*aside.*) Q2, F;
(*Aside*) D.   319+ *s.d. Exit*] Q2, F, D; ~ . Q1.   321 against] Q1–2,
D; again F.   322+ *s.d.* Jupiter] [Jupiter Q1–2, F, D.   325 *s.d.*
Exit] Q2, F, D; ~ . Q1.   333 a hungry] Q1–2, D; hungry F.   334
Amphitryon] Q1, F, D; *Amphitryon* Q2.   337 How,] ~∧ Q1–2, F, D.
339 aside.] (*aside*) Q1–2, F (*aside.* F); [*Aside.*] D.   339 may] Q1–2,
D; must F.   339 *Phædra*] Q2, D; *Phœdra* Q1, F.   341 *Sosia.*] Q2,
F, D (*Sos.*); ~ , Q1.   345 that is] Q1, D; is Q2, F.   354 it.] Q1–2,
F; ~∧ D.   356 belly-full] Q1–2, F; Belly-fully D.   359 bad.] Q1–2,
F; Bad∧ D.   360+ *s.d. Is*] [*Is* Q1–2, F, D.   363 *Sosia.*] Q2, F, D
(*Sos.*); ~ , Q1.   376 wou'd] Q1–2; wov'd F; would D.   377 where
ever] Q1–2, F; where-ever D (where- / ever).   378 *Sosia,*] Q1–2, D;
~ : F.   378 of me] Q1, D; me Q2, F.   379 those] Q1–2, D; these
F.   389 Then] Q1–2, F; Ah! Then D.   398+ *s.d. Enter* Phædra]
Q2, F, D; Enter *Phædra* Q1.   420 *Sosia, aside.*] ~ . (*aside*) Q1; Sos.
(*aside.*) Q2, F; Sos. [*Aside.*] D.   422 is!] ~∧ Q1–2, F, D.   423 your]
Q1–2, D; you F.   428 What ever] Q1–2, F; Whatever D.   433 din-
ner time] Q1–2, F; Dinner-time D.   448 you.] Q1, D; ~∧ Q2, F.
449 Love Letters] Q1–2, F; Love-Letters D.   458 into] Q1–2, F; in
D.   461 *giving . . . frisk.*] (*Giving . . . frisk.*) Q1–2, F; [*Giving . . .*
Frisk.] D.   463 Spoon] Q1–2, F; ~ . D.   464 *shreeking.*] (*Shreek-*
ing.) Q1–2, F (*Shrieking* Q2, F); [*Shrieking.*] D.   474 to] Q1, D; both

to Q2, F.   481+   Mercury's *SONG to* Phædra] Q1-2, F, D; The second Song, in the fourth Act f1; The Indifferent LOVER, OR, The Roving Batchelor. To a Pleasant new Tune, Sung in the last new Comedy, called *Amphitryon, Or, Fond Boy* f2; A Song in the last new Comedy call'd———— AMPHITRYON. Written by Mr. *DRYDEN* SET by Mr. *Henry Purcel.* Sung by Mrs. *Butler* q; *A SONG* d.   482-493   *italics and romans of text of song reversed in f1, f2, and d, but normalized in the following textual notes.*   482   Fair] Q1-2, F, D (FAir); For f1-2, q, d (For f2, d).   482 *love*] Q1-2, F, D; *sigh* f1-2, q, d.   482   *hourly I*] Q1-2, F, D; *hourely* f1-2, q, d (*hourly* f2, d).   485   For I am as false, and as fickle as she] Q1-2, F, D (false∧ F; false. D); O these are the Virtues that Captivate me f1-2, q, d (Oh! f2, d; Vertues f2; captivate f2).   490   present, . . . absent,] Q1-2, F, D; ∼∧ . . . ∼∧ f1-2, q, d.   493   or] Q1-2, F, D; and f1-2, q, d.   493   equally] Q1-2, F, D; easily f1-2, q, d.   493 join'd.] Q1-2, F, D, f1, q, d (joyn'd f1, q, d); joyn'd. / (3) / I like not that Lover who'll whimpering stand, / And wait a whole day to kiss Celias fair hand, / No Beauty i'th' Town, tho' ten times as fair, / Can ever, can ever with Celia Compare: / How happy am I, who hourly find, / Those fair as his Celia, as Iris kind. / (4) / I am still in the Fashion, or Mode-a-la-France, / I think not upon her, unless by a chance, / Iris when present I fancy the best, / When absent I praise her no more then the rest: / Iris and Phillis to me are all one; / So soon I can love, and as soon can have done. / (5) / I can love for an hour, fair Celia and then, / I am Cloy'd of the Bliss, and Love Iris agen, / Till tyered of Happiness I do depart, / Go the next way and give Phillis my Heart: / Till Cleo appears, whose delicate Eye, / For an hour or two makes me languishing lye. / (6) / I love all I see when just in the fit, / Yet can in a Moment my Mistriss forget, / Now Languish, now Love, now sigh and complain / Now love her, now hate her, and love her again. / I admire the Charms in Celias fair face, / Till Phillis appears to take up her place. / (7) / But of all the Beauties were ever admir'd, / Whose Company many fond Fops have desir'd, / Whose every Charm in their Faces so takes, / That several Coxcombs have dy'd for their sakes; / I never see any whose faces could Charm, / So much by their Smiles or Frowns for to harm. / (8) / If Iris Loves me, then I can Love her, / If she loves me not, then I can prefer, / Another before her; Or her 'fore another, / For I can Love one as well as the other; / My passion to all alike I'll discover, / And always remain an indifferent Lover. f2 (fonts of the text—but not the stanza indicators—reversed).   503   Phædra.] Q2, F, D (Phæd. D); ∼ , Q1.   504   some body's] Q1-2, F; somebody's D.   504   whose. (Stamps] ∼ ; (stamps Q1-2, F, D ([stamps D).   507- 507+   s.d. Love matters. / New . . . Song.] ∼ ∼ . [∼ . . . ∼ . Q1-2, F (s.d. at right margin); Love-Matters. / [∼ . . . ∼ . D (s.d. at right margin).   507+   A Pastoral Dialogue] Q1-2, F, D; Last Song. A Dialogue f1; A Dialogue Mr. Dryden m2.   508-537   *italics and romans reversed in f1, but normalized in the textual footnotes and the following textual notes.*   508   Thyrsis.] Q1-2, F, D, m2 (Thyrs. F; ∼∧ m2); *omitted from f1.*   511 Shepherd's Q1-2, F, D; happy f1, m2.   513-515   O . . . [to] . . . Blest] *in italics in Q1-2, F, D, f1, m2* (blest D, f1, m2).   516   Iris] Q1-2, F,

D, f1 (*corrected form*), m2; *omitted from f1* (*uncorrected form*). 518
oft] Q1-2, F, D, f1 (*corrected form*), m2; *of't* f1 (*uncorrected form*).
529 *kindly,*] Q1-2, F, D; *kindly still*, f1, m2 (*still*∧ m2). 533 *kiss*]
Q1-2, F, D; *give* f1, m2. 535 *and*] Q1-2, F, D; *and kindly still and
kindly, and* f1; *& kindly still & kindly, &* m2. 536 *And kindly still,
and kindly*] Q1-2, F, D; *but doe not kiss and tell, but doe not kiss and tell*
f1, m2 (*do* m2; *kis* m2; *& tell*∧ m2). 537 *But Kiss me
not*] Q1-2, F, D (*kiss* F, D); *no, never kiss* f1, m2. 537+ A RON-
DEAU.] *omitted from f1, m2*. 538–545 *italics and romans reversed
in f1, but normalized in the following textual notes.* 540 *We give,
and give, and give, and give,*] Q1-2, F, D; *We give, and we give, we give
and we give, we give and we give* f1, m2 (*& m2; & m2; give*∧; *&* m2).
542 *to day*] Q1-2, F, f1, m2; *to-day* D. 543 *To morrow*] Q1-2, F,
D (*Morrow* D); *to morrow, to morrow* f1, m2. 544 *love and live*] Q1-
2, D, f1, m2 (*Love* f1, m2); *live and love* F. 548+ *s.d.* [Exit.] *omitted
from Q1-2, F, D*. 557 *s.d.* [*Exit* Mercury.] Q1-2, F; [*Exit*. D.

V, i

ACT V. SCENE I.] D; ACT. V. Q1; ACT V. Q2, F. *s.d. Enter*
Gripus, Phædra] D (Gripus *and*); Gripus, Phædra Q1-2, F. 16 *veers*]
Q1-2, F; *veerst* D. 20 *s.d.* Exit] Q2, F, D; ∼. Q1. 21 *bowing.*]
Bowing.] Q1-2, F; [*Bowing.*] D. 30 *bowing.*] Bowing.] Q1, D; ∼.]
Q2; ∼.) F. 35 both.] Q1-2, D; ∼∧ F. 66 this] Q1, D; *that* Q2,
F. 75 oh. . . . oh.] Q1-2, D; ∼, . . . ∼∧ F. 79 *him.*] ∼.] Q1-2,
D; ∼.) F. 84 her.] ∼.] Q1-2, D; ∼.) F. 86 over-heard] Q1, Q2
(*some copies*), D; over heard Q2 (*some copies*), F. 92 *Amph. to
Gripus.*] Amph∧ (to Gripus.) Q1-2 (Amph. Q2); Amph. to Grip.) F;
Amph. [to Gripus.] D. 93 Warrant.] ∼; Q1-2, F; ∼, D. 100
Gold?] Q1, D; ∼! Q2, F. 107+ *s.d.* Guards.] F, D; ∼.] Q1-2. 109
s.d. Exit Phædra] Q2, F, D; ∼. Phædra Q1. 110 *aside.*] (∼∧) Q1;
(∼.) Q2; ∼.) F; [*Aside.*] D. 111–112 easily.———[Gripus . . . *off.*]]
easily. [Gripus . . . *off.*]——— Q1-2, F, D ((Gripus . . . *off.*) F). 113
you:] Q1-2, D; ∼, F. 123 *Gorgon's*] D; Gorgon's Q1-2, F. 129
aside.] (∼∧) Q1-2; ∼.) F; [*Aside.*] D. 133+ *s.d.* Sword.] F, D; ∼]
Q1-2. 134–135 Impostour. / If . . . me. [*To the Guards.*]———Not
. . . stirs:] Impostour. [*to the Guards.*] / If . . . me———not . . . stirs:
Q1-2; Impostour. (*To the Guards.* / If . . . me———Not . . . stirs: F;
Impostor. / If . . . me———not . . . stirs: [*To the Guards.* D. 136
What,] D; ∼∧ Q1-2, F. 137 thus] F, D; ∼. Q1-2. 144 *struggling.*]
Q2, F, D; ∼∧ Q1. 162, 163 love, . . . both:] ∼; . . . ∼. Q1-2, F,
D. 167 Cause.] Q1, F, D; ∼∧ Q2. 169 *aside . . . Mercury.*] (∼
. . . ∼∧) Q1-2; ∼ . . . ∼.] F; [*Aside . . . Merc.*] D. 171 *aside . . .
him.*] (∼ . . . ∼∧) Q1-2; ∼ . . . ∼.] F; [*Aside . . . ∼.*] D. 173
———(*Aside.*)] ∧ (∼∧) Q1-2; ∧ (∼.) F;———[∼.] D. 181 first.] Q1-
2, D; ∼∧ F. 182 *together.*] D; ∼.] Q1-2, F. 182 him] F, D; ∼.
Q1-2. 183 you.] ∼: Q1-2, F, D. 184 together. But] ∼: but
Q1-2, F, D (But F). 187 it's] Q1-2, F; 'tis D. 192 *Polydas.*] ∼.]
Q1-2, F, D (*Polyd.* D). 204 *aside.*] (∼) Q1-2; ∼.] F; [*Aside.*] D.

215 *Attick*] Attick Q1-2, F, D.   217 farthing!] ~? Q1-2, F; Farthing.
D.   227 *Jupit.*] ~.] Q1-2, F, D (*Jup.* F).   230 me. (*Aside.*)————]
~.———— (~.) Q1-2; ~.————[~. F, D.   237 please] F, D; ~. Q1-
2.   244 *Jupit.*] ~.] Q1-2, F, D.   249 rose] D; rise Q1-2, F.
258+ *s.d. him.*] F, D; ~.] Q1-2 (*s.d. at left margin*).   260 his.] Q1,
D; ~∧ Q2, F.   261 *Amph. . . . him.* Away, Adultress!] Q1-2, D (*him.*]
D); Away Adultress! [*Amp. . . . him.* F.   264 mislead] Q1-2, F;
mis-lead D.   269 *Alcm. . . . her.* I . . . he!] Q1-2, D (*her.*] / I D);
I . . . he! [*Alcm. . . . her.* F.   271 choice;] Q1, D (Choice D); ~∧
Q2, F.   273 What,] ~∧ Q1-2, F; ~! D.   273 Villain!] Q1-2, F;
~? D.   279 *Jove,*] ~:) Q1-2; ~: F, D.   295 on] Q1-2, D; no F.
338 us'd] Q2, F, D; u'sd Q1.   339 Well,] Q2, F; ~∧ Q1, D.   339
Sign.] ~: Q1-2, F, D.   343 *Gripus.*] ~.] Q1-2, F, D.   346 an]
Q1-2, D; and F.   357 Lap Dog] Q1; Lap-Dog Q2, F, D.   366 But]
F; but Q1-2, D.   372 Pin-money] Q1-2, F; Pin Mony D.   374 be
tack'd] Q1-2, D; bet ack'd F.   377 you.] ~: Q1-2, F, D.   387+
s.d. doors,] F, D (Doors D); ~: Q1-2.   389 told] Q2, F, D; ~, Q1.
409-411 *aside. . . . aside.*] (~∧) . . . (~∧) Q1; (~.) . . . (~.) Q2; ~.]
. . . ~.] F; [~.] . . . [~.] D.   434 some-body] Q1-2, D; some Body
F.   444+ *s.d.* [*Exeunt.*] *omitted from Q1-2, F, D.*

Epilogue: EPILOGUE.] F; ~, Q1-2, D.   2 *How sweet*] Q1 (*cor-
rected form*), Q2, F, D; *Hos weet* Q1 (*uncorrected form*).   3 *Idolatry*]
D; ~, Q1-2, F.   3 *ev'n*] Q1, D; *even* Q2, F.   4 *Worshipt*] Q1-2,
D (*worshipt* D); *Worship'd* F.   5 Cupid] D; ~, Q1-2, F.   8 *Jove*]
Q2, F, D; ~, Q1.   10 *Fair.*] Q1, D; ~, Q2, F.   11 *Adultry*] Q1-2,
D (*Adult'ry* D); *Adultery* F.   17 *'em;*] Q1, D; ~. Q2, F.   18 *'em,*]
~. Q1-2, F, D (*him* D).   19 *remembrance*] Q1-2, F; *Remembrace* D.
21 *those*] Q1-2, F; *these* D.   22 *Godship*] D; ~, Q1-2, F.   28
hard . . . Practice] ~, . . . ~, Q1-2, F, D.   29 *That*] Q1-2, D;
Then F.   30 *Gods*] D; ~, Q1-2, F.   32+ *FINIS.*] Q1-2; *omitted
from F, D.*

APPENDIX

Comparative Charts *for* Amphitryon

CHARACTERS AND EQUIVALENTS

Dryden	*Molière*	*Plautus*
Mercury	Mercure	Mercurius
Phœbus	———	———
Night	La Nuit	———
Jupiter	Jupiter	Jupiter
Amphitryon	Amphitryon	Amphitruo
Alcmena	Alcmene	Alcmena
Sosia	Sosie	Sosia
Bromia (slave of Alcmena; Sosia's wife.)	Cléanthis (maid of Alcmene; Sosie's wife.)	Bromia (maid of Alcmena.)
		Thessala (slave)
———	———	———
Phædra		
Gripus (Alcmena's uncle; Phædra's lover)	Naucratès	———
Polidas and Tranio (Theban officers)	Argatiphontidas, Naucratès, Polidas, and Posiclès (Theban captains)	Blepharo (A pilot)

ACTS AND SCENES COMPARISON

Dryden	*Molière*	*Plautus*
Prologue	———	———
I, i Mercury, Phœbus, Jupiter, Night	Prologue (induction) Mercure and Nuit	Prologue (monologue) Mercurius
ii (1) Alcmena, Phædra	———	———
(2) Jupiter, Bromia, Alcmena	———	———
II, i (1) Sosia and Mercury	I, i and ii Sosie and Mercure	153–462 Sosia and Mercurius
(2) Mercury: last speech in scene	———	463–498 Mercurius *solus*
ii (1) Mercury, Jupiter, Alcmena, Phædra	iii Jupiter, Alcmene, Mercure, Cléanthis	499–550 Jupiter, Alcmena
(2) Mercury, Phædra	———	———
(3) Mercury, Bromia	iv Mercure, Cléanthis	———
(4) Mercury *solus*	———	———
III, i (1) Amphitryon, Sosia	II, i Amphitryon, Sosie	551–632 Amphitruo, Sosia
(2) as in (1) and Alcmena, Phædra	ii as in i and Alcmene and Cléanthis	633–860, as above and Thessala
(3) Sosia, Bromia	iii Sosie, Cléanthis	———
(4) as in (3) and Jupiter, Phædra, etc.	———	———
———	iv Jupiter, Cléanthis, Sosie	———
———	v Sosie, Cléanthis	———
———	———	861–881 Jupiter *solus*
IV, i (1) Jupiter, Alcmena, Mercury, Phædra	vi Jupiter, Alcmene, Sosie, Cléanthis	882–955 Jupiter, Alcmena
———	vii Cléanthis, Sosie	———
(2) Mercury, Phædra	———	———
———	———	984–1008 Mercurius *solus*

Dryden	*Molière*	*Plautus*
(3) Amphitryon *solus*	III, i Amphitryon *solus*	1009–20 Amphitruo *solus*
(4) Amphitryon, Mercury	ii Amphitryon, Mercure	1021–1034 Amphitruo, Mercurius, Blepharo
(5) Amphitryon *solus*	iii Amphitryon *solus*	————
(6) Amphitryon, Sosia, Polidas, Gripus, Tranio	iv Amphitryon, Sosie, Naucratès Polidas	1035–40 Amphitruo, Mercurius, Blepharo
————	————	1041–52 Amphitruo *solus*
(7) as in (6) and Mercury, Jupiter	v as in iv and Jupiter	————
(8) Mercury, Sosia	vi Mercure, Sosie	————
(9) Mercury, Sosia, Phædra	————	————
(10) Mercury, Phædra, dancers, etc.	————	————
V, i (1) Gripus, Phædra	————	
(2) Gripus, Mercury	Molière's *Le Mariage forcé*, sc. ix	————
(3) as in (2) and Phædra		————
(4) as in (3) and Amphitryon, guards	vii Amphitryon, Argatiphon-tidas, Sosie, Policlès	————
————	viii as in vii and Cléanthis, Poli-das, Naucratès, Posiclès	————
————	ix as in viii and Mercure	
————	————	1053–1075 Bromia *solus*
————	————	1076–1130 Bromia, Amphitruo
(5) as in (4) and Jupiter, Tranio, Polidas	————	————
(6) as in (5) and Alcmena, Bromia	————	————

Acts and Scenes Comparison (cont'd)

Dryden	Molière	Plautus
(7) Mercury, Phædra	——	——
(8) as in (7) and Sosia	——	——
(9a) as in (8) and Amphitryon, Alcmena, Polidas, Tranio, Jupiter	xa as in ix and Jupiter	1131–1143 Amphitruo, Jupiter
(9b) as in (9a), without Jupiter: Sosia's closing remarks	xb as xa, without Jupiter: Sosie's closing remarks	1144–1146 Amphitruo: closing remarks
Epilogue	——	——

INDEX TO THE COMMENTARY